MW00826110

A History *of* Tennessee Arts

ARTS ALLOW US TO SEE THE WORLD THROUGH NEW EYES, BRINGING UNIQUE PERSPECTIVES TO THE HUMAN CONDITION. THE HISTORY AND BEAUTY OF TENNESSEE ARTS—THE STORIES, MUSIC, CRAFTS, PAINTINGS, SCULPTURE, textiles, basket weaving—are living testimony to the boundless creativity of humankind and are a powerful expression of who we are.

A History of Tennessee Arts: Creating Traditions, Expanding Horizons chronicles the colorful and ongoing evolution of the arts in Tennessee. The indigenous arts of Tennessee, as well as the influence of the larger art world on Tennessee artists, are expressed in this important encyclopedic work. I commend the Tennessee Arts Commission and the Tennessee Historical Society for supporting and nurturing this impressive work.

Andrea Conte
First Lady of Tennessee

A HISTORY *of* TENNESSEE ARTS

CREATING TRADITIONS, EXPANDING HORIZONS

CARROLL VAN WEST
Editor-in-Chief

MARGARET DUNCAN BINNICKER
Associate Editor

Sponsored by the
TENNESSEE ARTS COMMISSION AND THE TENNESSEE HISTORICAL SOCIETY
THE UNIVERSITY OF TENNESSEE PRESS / KNOXVILLE

First Edition.

Derita Coleman Williams, "Early Furniture Makers and Cabinetmakers," previously appeared in the *Tennessee Encyclopedia of History and Culture* and is reprinted here with permission of the Tennessee Historical Society.

This book is printed on acid-free paper.

LIBRARY OF CONGRESS CATALOGING-IN-PUBLICATION DATA

A history of Tennessee arts: creating traditions, expanding horizons/Carroll Van West, editor-in-chief; Margaret Duncan Binnicker, associate editor.— 1st ed.
p. cm.
Includes bibliographical references and index.
ISBN 1-57233-239-5 (cl.: alk. paper)
1. Arts, American—Tennessee.
I.West, Carroll Van, 1955–
II.Binnicker, Margaret Duncan.

NX510.T2 H58 2004
700'.9768—dc21 2003012373

Contents

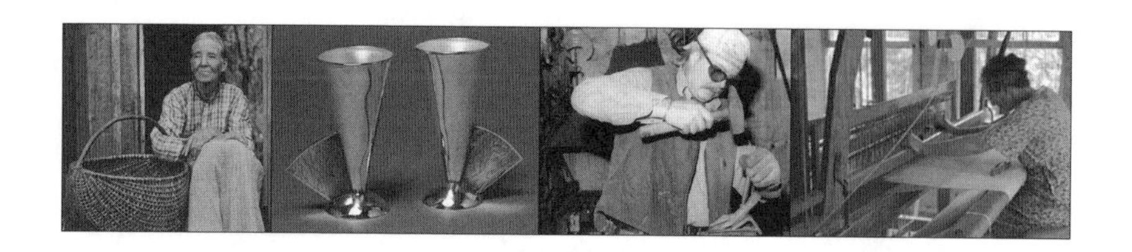

Part Two

The Craft Arts

Part Three

The Literary Arts

Part Four

THE PERFORMANCE ARTS
Speech, Theater, Dance, and Film

Part Five

THE PERFORMANCE ARTS
Music

Sidebars

FOREWORD

In 1965 the Tennessee General Assembly passed legislation to create the Tennessee Commission on the Performing Arts, funded by a $25,000 Study Grant from the National Endowment for the Arts. This commission surveyed the cultural activities and facilities of Tennessee by holding meetings throughout the state with artists, cultural organizations, and individuals interested in the arts. Questionnaires and personal contact provided information that would guide the commission in establishing the programs and activities of a new state arts agency. The results of their work were reported to the governor and Tennessee State Legislature, along with their recommendations, which resulted in the establishment of the Tennessee Arts Commission by the General Assembly in 1967.

From an initial budget of $131,383 in its first year of operation, the Tennessee Arts Commission has established an impressive thirty-five-year history as a grants-making agency, providing financial support, technical assistance, and encouragement to thousands of Tennessee artists and arts organizations. Since that first year, millions of grant dollars distributed by the commission have funded projects and programs in communities, small and large, rural and urban, throughout Tennessee.

As the commission approached its celebration of thirty-five years of operation, the staff began to research the work of the agency and record its contributions to the cultural life of Tennessee. Suddenly, it became obvious that a serious void existed. There was no recorded history of the arts in Tennessee. A state celebrated for its rich musical heritage, recognized for its legendary performing artists, well-known for its traditional craft artists, and distinguished by its great literary artists could not claim a general recorded history of its cultural heritage.

At the recommendation of former Executive Director Bennett Tarleton, the commission embarked on a four-year project that has resulted in the publication of this extraordinary work, *A History of Tennessee Arts: Creating Traditions, Expanding Horizons.* The Tennessee Arts Commission is grateful to the many talented individuals who contributed to this book—especially to Carroll Van West, who guided us through every phase of the project and produced an impressive literary work. He accepted our challenge by enlisting a distinguished group of scholars, writers, artists, essayists, and critics to contribute their knowledge and share their historical perspective of what the arts have meant to this state. The commission thankfully recognizes the cooperation and support from Ann Toplovich and the Tennessee Historical Society throughout this project. It is also important to acknowledge the involvement and contributions of the commission staff toward the development and publication of this book.

A History of Tennessee Arts is a celebration of our cultural heritage and a recognition of the creative individuals who proudly call themselves Tennessee artists, past and present. It is also a record of who we are as a people and how the arts have been, and continue to be, such an important part of our lives. The completion of this project documents the commission's gratitude to the thousands of Tennessee artists who have created our cultural heritage and our commitment to the artists of today, who are imagining, creating, producing, and writing their own history. It further demonstrates the Tennessee Arts Commission's mission to ensure that the citizens of this state have access to and the opportunity to participate in the arts.

Rich Boyd, Executive Director
Tennessee Arts Commission

Introduction

Creating Traditions, Expanding Horizons in Tennessee's Arts

Carroll Van West

Middle Tennessee State University

The harmonies of the Fisk Jubilee Singers, the measured brush strokes of painter Lloyd Branson, the intricate basket weaving of Maggie Murphy, the modernist compositions of composer-director Michael Ching, the soulful sounds of Tina Turner, and the theater barnstorming of actor-manager Sol Smith—such are the sounds, images, and expressions of Tennessee's arts legacy.

Through its interlocking themes of creating traditions and expanding horizons, this book traces the history of the arts in Tennessee from its formal, more academic side to its vernacular expressions of culture, self, and community. Both the formal and the vernacular are important to understanding what the arts have meant to Tennesseans and, in turn, what Tennesseans have contributed to the culture of the state, the region, and the nation. A history of the arts in the Volunteer State becomes then an evolving barometer of not only where we have been as a culture, but also a measure of how we have matured as a society.

The roots of the state's arts legacy lie with the prehistoric inhabitants of the land we now call Tennessee. Beautiful, compelling artifacts from ancient times—sculpture, cave paintings, remnants of basketry and cloth, intricately carved tools, and architectural monuments—remain to document past Native American cultures. Yet the deeper meaning and significance of these objects remain to be captured and understood.

Lion, limestone sculpture, by William Edmondson. Courtesy of Tennessee State Museum.

We often assume that function, not aesthetics, drove the first artists in Tennessee but we cannot be certain of that. We may more accurately assume that the artificial distinction we often make between objects of art and objects of life was unknown to these early artists, just as that same distinction meant little to much later generations of craft artists.

When twentieth-century collectors and scholars acknowledged craft traditions as art, they extended high culture legitimacy to creative works that their makers conceived as everyday utilitarian objects, creating a chasm in perception between collectors and creators that shaped relationships and the art itself. Basketmakers in Cannon County, for instance, still wonder to their neighbors and friends about how their work can command hundreds of dollars from art museums and galleries when the baskets were worth mere single digits—if that—when they were younger. Although appreciative of the attention and better income, most remain somewhat bemused by the sponsored trips to the American Folklife Festival in Washington, D.C., the glare of the documentary movie lens, and the general applause from festival-goers. They see themselves as merely following the traditions and lifeways of their parents, grandparents, and great-grandparents: in other words, making baskets is just what their family does. What is true for rural basketmakers is also the case for many traditional chairmakers, woodcrafters, quiltmakers, and weavers across the state.

Woman working at loom. Emma Bell Miles Collection. Courtesy of TSM.

The recognition of crafts and design arts as legitimate, serious artistic expression is one of the crucial cultural patterns shaping Tennessee arts in the twentieth century, but it is far from the only significant historical trend. Also important is how the broader boundaries of what constitutes art have, in turn, enlarged the boundaries of who may contribute to art. A history of Tennessee arts one hundred years ago would have honored formal art in the European tradition—painting, sculpture, classical architecture, decorative arts, and classical music—and would have championed white artists, most often from privileged backgrounds, who studied overseas or in major urban cultural centers. Pretensions toward "high" art produced by a specifically trained or educated elite defined almost precisely the artists and arts exhibited in the recreation of the Parthenon during the Tennessee Centennial Exposition of 1897. Within twenty years, however, those limited definitions of Tennessee arts and Tennessee artists began to evolve to the point that by 1940 only cultural snobs still limited their definitions of "true art" to that which merely mimicked European high culture.

Consider what happened in the state from the Jazz Age to the end of the Depression decade. In the visual arts, African American painters Beauford Delaney and Aaron Douglas were recognized as important interpreters of their culture and time. The Museum of Modern Art featured the spirit-filled sculpture of William Edmondson in his first major exhibition. James Agee was placing the finishing touches on his magical *Let Us Now Praise Famous Men* while filmmakers Ralph Steiner and Elia Kazan released the classic two-reeler *People of the Cumberland.* At the same time, nationally recognized documentary photographers Lewis Hine, Ben Shahn, and Dorothea Lange were recording the people and places of the Depression. In the literary arts, Tennesseans were influential writers, editors, and scholars. The Fugitives and the Agrarians had taken their stand for a more vibrant, yet rooted in the past, southern literature as they also created the body of ideas that would take shape as the New Criticism.

The craft and design arts by 1940 also enjoyed a new prominence as exemplars of Tennessee and southern culture. The influential Arrowmont shop and Pi Beta Phi settlement school at Gatlinburg made the various products of the handicraft revival available to collectors and interested tourists. Writer Allen Eaton published his path-setting study of southern Appalachian crafts, giving scholarly legitimacy to basketmaking, log buildings, quilts, and other everyday items of rural life. Blue Ridge pottery made in Erwin developed a national following at the same time that Phillip Kerrigan executed his individualistic vision of ornamental metal at Nashville's Cheekwood estate. New federal programs during the New Deal both enhanced and expanded formal and vernacular arts. Folk artist Bessie Harvey's mother received sewing training; sculpture and murals from some of the country's best-regarded artists soon adorned New Deal post offices and courthouses across the state. The Tennessee Valley Authority erected huge engineered landscapes, combining modern aesthetics and rural domestic environments, while at the same time they established schools and markets to conserve threatened Appalachian craft traditions.

The performance arts of 1940 were of different scope, quality, and quantity than those of a generation earlier. The New Deal's Cumberland Homesteads sponsored community theater while the "WPA" orchestra gave concerts of popular music, light classics, and "serious" orchestral music at the WPA-constructed Overton Park Shell in Memphis. But far more important than the government programs were the efforts of local citizens, artists, and patrons to give their audiences and communities new opportunities in the performing arts. By 1930, for example, the Chattanooga Little Theatre and the Knoxville Symphony were giving regularly scheduled performances, and modern dance pioneers Ruth St. Denis and Ted Shawn were teaching the Denishawn principles of dance in Nashville. Bessie Smith enthralled audiences with the blues, extending the state's earlier fame from the instrumental recordings of W. C. Handy into the vocal arena of popular music. The powerful radio signal from WSM brought national audiences both the sweet strains of ballroom music from Francis Craig and the hillbilly twang of the Grand Ole Opry. The "big bang" of country music occurred in Bristol in 1927 with the recording of the famous Bristol sessions while gospel music reached new heights of popularity and musical sophistication through enriched quartet singing and the modern compositions of Herbert Brewster.

By 1950, few doubted the state's contributions to American popular music, crafts, modern art, and literature. The development of professional arts schools and organizations—such as the Memphis Academy (later College) of Art, the Tennessee chapters of the American Institute of Architects, the Blair School of Music, the Joe L. Evins Center for Appalachian Crafts, and many university programs, departments, and degrees—opened up new horizons for artists trained in classroom settings across the state. Perhaps most clearly felt in painting, sculpture, classical music, theater dance, woodcraft, metal working, theater, and textiles, the creation of a cultural and educational infrastructure for the arts established a broad foundation from which Tennesseans expanded artistic expressions in new and exciting ways. Then in 1967, the creation of the Tennessee Arts Commission further extended encouragement and support for the arts and nurtured relationships between artists and their audiences.

A true flowering of the arts in Tennessee took place in the final decades of the twentieth century. By the end of the century, the state's arts, although affected by tradition and history, had shed their provincial trappings to join the mainstream of American culture. Several individual artists—Red Grooms, Robert Ryman, William Eggleston, Patricia Neal, Cormac McCarthy, Nikki Giovanni, Peter Taylor, Arlyn Ende, Barry Scott, Bobby Jones, and Elvis Presley, among them—were acknowledged as among the foremost voices of their generation.

There was a price to be paid, however, for the improved style, technique, and context of the professional art world of the late twentieth century, especially in the craft arts. As the classroom replaced the home and workshop, and instruction from a professional expert replaced the older tradition of self-taught artists who prepared and trained the next generation, a human bond between generations of artists was fractured, and, in some unfortunate situations lost altogether. Craft production once was very much a family affair, and interrelated networks of artisans dominated certain crafts. A degree of that still exists in the related families of basketmakers in Cannon County or the chairmakers of the Cumberland Plateau. But the role of family as the conservator and translator of traditional art was diminished, no matter the good intentions and dedication of key craft centers like Arrowmont, the Evins Center for Appalachian Crafts, and the National Museum of Ornamental Metal.

The professional art world also diminished the role of women in Tennessee art for a good part of the twentieth century. The big names in Tennessee culture one hundred years ago were dominated by women: artist Willie Betty Newman, who operated what was the most important studio in turn-of-the-century Tennessee; writers Mary Noailles Murfree and Will Allen Dromgoole; arts advocate and museum director Florence McIntyre; and actress-singer Kitty Cheatham. The academic world did not prove so hospitable to the aspirations and abilities of women, who found themselves increasingly on the outside looking in, or pigeonholed into the crafts of quiltmaking, basketmaking, and other so-called lesser arts.

But by the end of the century, women, African Americans, and many other once-excluded Tennesseans found new opportunities in the professional art world. As the academic world of the late twentieth century opened its doors to a broader spectrum of people, it also eventually led to much greater opportunities for almost any artistically inclined Tennessean. Here again, the influence of the Tennessee Arts Commission, and local art groups statewide, has been to provide opportunities for artists and arts enthusiasts of all stripes. Calls for diversity in the arts, rather than perceived as a bothersome hindrance, have proven to be a real inducement to artistic ingenuity and achievement.

This book uses four major categories—visual arts and architecture, craft arts, literary arts, and performance arts—to explore the themes and achievements of the arts in Tennessee history. Within each section are long essays tracing the development of a particular art form from its beginning through its period of greatest significance; most essays close with an overview of contemporary trends, although in some fields such an assessment proved difficult if not impossible. Within almost every essay, brief sketches highlight significant artists, events, and influences. The result is a multilayered book suitable for careful scholarly perusal or a quick flip of the page to locate favorite artists, objects, or styles.

With seventy-six contributing authors, the book also presents a multilayered perspective on the state's arts history. The authors, like their subjects, reflect different backgrounds, experiences, disciplines, and training. Several are artists, actively participating in their fields. Others are scholars, who have studied and analyzed the key people, places, patterns, and events. Still others are advocates, who have contributed to the arts through their enthusiasm, support, and encouragement. Finally there are those, like myself, who are the audience of the arts—those who enjoy and gain emotional nourishment from the arts, even if (as is my case) they cannot play or sing a note in tune, turn a potter's wheel, weave a basket, carve a wood block, dance a lick, or mix colors effectively. We all gain substantially, in ways both direct and indirect, from the state's vibrant arts scene. Even if we are just the audience, we can be an interactive part of the art experience and we have the responsibility to patronize and encourage those who bring so much to our lives through their performances, works, and expressions.

The book begins with architecture and visual arts—sculpture, painting, and photography—from the infancy of Tennessee arts in prehistoric times to the modernist media of the twentieth century. Anthropology professor Kevin E. Smith, editor of the *Tennessee Anthropologist,* reminds readers that the earliest Tennessee artisans were prehistoric peoples whose artistic vision in sculpture, painting, crafts, and architecture is startling to those who routinely ignore or denigrate the cultural accomplishments of Native Americans. Next come two essays on architecture from two scholars from the Center for Historic Pres-

Tennessee State Capitol, lithograph by P. S. Duval. Photograph by June Dorman. Tennessee Historical Society Collection, Tennessee State Library and Archives. Courtesy of TSM Photographic Archives.

ervation at Middle Tennessee State University. The first on the state's vernacular architectural traditions, by carpenter-scholar Michael T. Gavin of Summertown, looks at how settlers manipulated readily available materials, such as the state's abundant forests, seemingly endless supplies of rock outcroppings, and clay perfect for brickmaking, into an architectural vocabulary that defined the commonplace landscape until the twentieth century. The second article, by historic preservationist Leslie N. Sharp, who holds a Ph.D. in history from the Georgia Institute of Technology, presents a chronology of academic styles in Tennessee's community landmark architecture, emphasizing the twentieth-century rise of notable Tennessee architects and architectural firms.

Arts advocate and scholar Susan W. Knowles overviews sculpture, one of the oldest, and most dynamic, art forms in the state's history. Painting is such a huge topic that it has been divided into chronological halves. Marilyn Masler of the Memphis Brooks Museum of Art addresses nineteenth-century painting, from the dominance of portrait painting to the rapidly maturing professional, academic art world of the late 1890s. The famous art exhibition of the Tennessee Centennial serves as a bridge between her essay and that of Vanderbilt University's Celia Walker on twentieth-century painting. Walker, former curator at the Cheekwood Museum of Art, reviews the explosion of new subjects, techniques, and audiences for modern painting, giving equal weight to the creation of permanent institutions and museums and the rise of prominent, professionally trained painters. In her study of Tennessee photography, Beverly Brannan of the Library of Congress explores the relationship between the technology of the photographic process and the evolving subject of photography as a cultural expression.

The second section of the book has a wide-ranging discussion of the craft arts of Tennessee. Even at that, several deserving topics are either too briefly treated, or in some cases like foodways, left out entirely. (Pause for a moment and consider the international reputation, in addition to the just plain good taste, of Tennessee sour mash whiskey.) The authors explore both categories of and key individual examples of craft arts. Lisa Norwood Oakley of the East Tennessee Historical Society emphasizes the primary place of woodcrafters, be they chairmakers, cabinetmakers, coopers, basketmakers, or carpenters, in any discussion of Tennessee crafts. She found that while most modern crafters have incorporated machine-driven tools and modern materials in their work, their parents and grandparents still would recognize and find useful the chairs, tables, baskets, barrels, and boats that they make. Oakley's overview then leads to Derita C. Williams's summary of early Tennessee cabinetmakers and the remarkable furniture, from tall case clocks to corner cabinets to blanket chests, produced in the decades before indus- trialization and mass production diminished the prominence of individual craftsmen. White oak baskets are the focus of the editor's chapter on Tennessee basketmaking, which identifies areas in both East Tennessee and the Highland Rim that have remained cultural centers for this ancient craft.

Metalworking, ceramics, and textiles are three additional significant traditions in Tennessee crafts where a new generation has expanded artistic boundaries. Jack Hurley of the University of Memphis looks at the twentieth-century practice of ornamental blacksmithing, concentrating on such notables as Phillip Kerrigan, Robert Coogan, and Jim Wallace. Collector and scholar Benjamin H. Caldwell Jr., on the other hand, traces the mostly nineteenth-century history of Tennessee silver, ending with an assessment of the modern revival of silversmiths in the classrooms and craft centers of the state. Stephen T. Rogers of the Tennessee Historical Commission staff updates and expands his twenty-year-old survey of Tennessee's plain potters and their utilitarian vessels made at select locations in East, Middle, and West Tennessee. Contemporary artist Christi Teasley of Monteagle presents a thorough review of the broader contexts of Tennessee textiles, giving proper deference to the traditional practices of the nineteenth and twentieth centuries while at the same time introducing more recent trends of using textiles as an expressive art medium. Quiltmaking is so central to the textile history of Tennessee it deserves the separate treatment accorded here by acknowledged quilt scholars Bets Ramsey, who discusses the modern phenomenon of the Tennessee quilt as a work of art, and her frequent collaborator, Marikay Waldvogel, who points out the national significance of Anne Orr's designs and writings in the first half of the century.

Large white oak basket by Mildred Youngblood. Photograph by Carroll Van West. Courtesy of Sharon K. Tomes.

For decades scholars and the reading public have recognized the significant place of Tennessee writers in southern literature. The state's literary reputation did not come overnight, as Allison Ensor of the University of Tennessee emphasizes in his overview of Tennessee literature to 1920. Tennesseans made their mark, whether in the guise of southern backwood humorists (the legendary Davy Crockett and the fictional Sut Lovingood) or southern "color" writers and their romantic, often wrong, stereotypes of Appalachian peoples (novelist Mary Noailles Murfree). The Vanderbilt Fugitives and Agrarians remain acknowledged giants in modern American literature. George Core, editor of the *Sewanee Review,* presents a different, challenging view of the legacy of Allen Tate, Donald Davidson, John Crowe Ransom, and Robert Penn Warren, reminding readers of the profound importance of Tennessee poetry—an art form too often ignored today—during the southern renaissance. Appropriately, the dean of Tennessee's writers, Walter Sullivan of Vanderbilt University,

Acclaimed actor-director-producer Clint Eastwood prepares for a scene in his film *Honkytonk Man* in front of the world-famous Ryman Auditorium in Nashville. 1982, Warner Bros./The Malpaso Co. Courtesy of the Tennessee Film, Entertainment & Music Commission.

concludes the literary section with a cogent analysis of modern Tennessee fiction. Sullivan, whose own work was earned a place in the canon of southern literature, finds such illuminati as Andrew Nelson Lytle, Cormac McCarthy, and Peter Taylor as expanding the region's and nation's literary horizons.

An unusually large number of Tennesseans are widely acknowledged as significant in American performing arts history, especially in vernacular and popular music where such names as Elvis Presley, Tina Turner, Booker T. and the MGs, Bobby Jones, Roy Acuff, Dolly Parton, W. C. Handy, Amy Grant, Chet Atkins, and Bessie Smith are internationally renowned. Their achievements are justly celebrated in the book's final section, but just as deliberately, the authors have documented that Tennessee does have a history, and an interesting one at that, in theater dance, ragtime, theater, opera, and symphonic music, areas of the performance arts that are rarely associated with the state.

Folklorist Bob Fulcher of Norris starts off with the provocative premise that "plain talk" is one of the state's most shared performance arts, from the tall tales and bragging of Davy Crockett to the fractured fairy tales of radio and television personality Archie Campbell. Historian Antoinette G. van Zelm follows with the fascinating history of Tennessee theater, balancing the legacy of the nineteenth-century traveling troupes with the establishment of permanent institutions like the influential and regionally recognized Tennessee Repertory Theater in the past generation. Taking on the topic Tennessee and film, Leslie Richardson of the University of the South finds a contradiction between Hollywood's preference for Tennessee-associated stories with a decided disinterest in using the diverse Tennessee landscape of Appalachian Mountains and Mississippi Delta to depict either the state or the southern region for movie audiences. Karen Wilson of Chattanooga next addresses one of the most recent performance arts—theater dance (ballet and modern dance)—and its explosive growth in small-town studios and big-city theaters statewide.

Last but certainly not least in terms of notoriety and accomplishment comes Tennessee music. Arts patron, advocate, and writer Perre Magness of Memphis begins the book's five chapters on music by documenting the performance history of classical and opera music in the Volunteer State along with tracing the creation of permanent orchestras and opera companies across urban Tennessee in the twentieth century. Of all of the state's music traditions, that of classical music has garnered the least attention, and there remains work to be done on Tennessee-associated composers in addition to the performance history of chamber music in Tennessee. Turning to popular music, the editor reviews Tennessee sacred music, the oldest musical tradition and, in many ways, the foundation for the state's later intimate associations with country music and rock 'n' soul music. While other states can either lay claim to, or have equal star power, in rock and country music, no southern state can match the uncontested significance of the Fisk Jubilee Singers, James D. Vaughan, Herbert Brewster, Amy Grant, and Bobby Jones to American gospel music. Yet most Tennesseans are like the average American music fan: when Tennessee is mentioned, the immediate sounds that come to mind are of Elvis, Tina, and the Grand Ole Opry, never the pounding rhythms of a southern gospel quartet or the inspirational improvisations of a black gospel choir.

Most music-loving Tennesseans extend that same cultural amnesia to blues and jazz, yet both forms, as ethnomusicologist Paul F. Wells of the Center for Popular Music at Middle Tennessee State University demonstrates, have important Tennessee associations, from "father of the blues" W. C. Handy to blues master Bessie Smith to Fisk University–trained jazz pianist Lil Hardin. The surprise of Wells's essay is the prominent role of Tennessee artists and composers in ragtime music, that turn-of-the-century phenomenon that influenced all of the better-known forms of twentieth-century popular music.

Cultural historian Michael Bertrand of Tennessee State University accepted the daunting task of treating the state's dual significance in rock and soul music in a single essay. Bertrand reminds readers that the sounds coming from Memphis from the mid-1950s to the mid-1960s cannot be fully appreciated unless one understands the youth culture and civil rights era they were part of. Sun Records and Stax Records, two independent Memphis labels, are still viewed—now two generations removed from their time of greatest significance—as among the most important label names in the history of American rock and soul music.

The performing art most commonly associated with Tennessee—country music—is the subject of the book's final essay, by historian John W. Rumble of the Country Music Hall of Fame. Although its roots run deep into the vernacular musics of the South, country music, according to Rumble, cannot be adequately understood unless the music and performers are placed in the context of the country music industry—and while one could debate whether Tennesseans are at the center of country music, there is no doubt that Tennessee is the center of the country music industry. This is where Tennesseans have done more than the residents of any other state to make country music the mainstay of American popular culture it is today.

When the Tennessee Arts Commission graciously approached me in early 1999 to compile and edit a history of the arts in Tennessee, they asked for a book that would meet two goals. First, the book should celebrate the achievements of Tennessee artists, past and present, in honor of the Tennessee Arts Commission's thirty-fifth anniversary, which occurred in 2002. Second, the volume should serve as the first comprehensive history of Tennessee arts, useful for scholars but suitable for the broader audience who support and participate in the arts of the Volunteer State. Those dual goals, in turn, shaped the composition of the authors (scholars, curators, and artists from all three of the state's Grand Divisions) and of the book (the combination of chapters and shorter essays). Those who collaborated on this book understood the need to recognize the famous names, but they also felt an obligation to identify the not so famous and their neglected achievements and contributions. Creating the book has been a humbling experience for everyone since it became apparent that there was enough of a story, and a significant enough history, for every individual chapter to be its own book. Thus, the project ends with our awareness that we have not conveyed the whole story; we hope that our work will lead others to venture down paths we merely identified, and to explore arts expressions that we left out, either out of ignorance or plain frustration with where to begin. The words and illustrations gathered within these pages document an arts tradition in which all Tennesseans may take pride. They also suggest the dynamic face of Tennessee arts will be quite different when the next group of scholars, artists, and advocates gather to record the state's art history and to assess its achievements and contributions to American culture. ■

Part One

THE VISUAL ARTS AND ARCHITECTURE

One

Prehistoric Art and Artisans of Tennessee

Kevin E. Smith
Middle Tennessee State University

For two centuries, objects created by the prehistoric native peoples who inhabited what is now Tennessee have been collected for exhibition in museums both large and small. As early as 1800, Thomas Jefferson acquired two prehistoric stone statues from Tennessee to display in his museum, the entry hall of Monticello known as "Indian Hall." By the mid-nineteenth century, local elites had amassed tremendous collections of ancient "Indian relics" and, soon thereafter, emerging major archaeological museums began sponsoring dozens of expeditions to the river valleys of the state in a race to stockpile the largest and most impressive collections. Unfortunately, the literally hundreds of thousands of objects thus acquired and preserved have largely been relegated to the status of "artifacts" of lost cultures rather than objects illustrating a rich and vibrant symbolic tradition spanning more than a dozen millennia.

The neglect of the prehistoric art traditions of Tennessee is undoubtedly a byproduct of the legacy that cast Native Americans as "primitives" and "savages" during the period of European colonization and conquest of North America. Long since cast as "artifacts," these objects fell largely into the realm of archaeological museums and have yet to achieve the broader appreciation they merit as "art." We are somewhat conditioned to think of art in certain stereotyped categories: paintings, sculptures, drawings, and prints produced by colorful individuals who create according to personal inspiration. While "art for art's sake" is a widely accepted motto of our times, the objects created by indigenous peoples rarely fit this preconceived mold.

Generations of anthropologists working with traditional peoples in all parts of the world have found that few non-Western societies have a term for "art." The concept of "art" is characteristic of cultures of the so-called Western tradition and brings connotations that are often difficult to apply to non-Western cultures. From this perspective, while the artifacts depicted and discussed in this chapter were selected, from literally hundreds of thousands of possibilities, for their outstanding workmanship and beauty, they are all handmade things that were once useful. They include tools and ornaments used in daily life, things that were sometimes decorated with special symbols that made statements about economics, politics, religion, and society. Despite popular misconceptions that ancient peoples had little free time, the prehistoric peoples of Tennessee had more leisure to devote to matters of the mind—art, ceremony, music, dance, and myth—than did all but a few Western artists until recent times. Everyone possessed the skills to create objects needed in daily life; some took the opportunity to make them exceptionally well. As such, none of these objects are truly art for art's sake; the symbolism reflected on these objects was woven throughout the fabric of indigenous life. Through objects, music, storytelling, and dance, the traditions of the people were expressed and enacted. Artifacts become art not necessarily because their creators and users called them such but because of how we perceive them today. While the tangible physical properties of the objects remain unchanged, the meanings and values given to them change because art and artifact are not quite the same.

In order to appreciate fully the creations of the prehistoric indigenous peoples of Tennessee, it helps to understand something of their culture, patterns of thought, and the ways they may have viewed the world. While many of these objects can simply be contemplated as artistic, this approach overlooks the deeper and richer meanings to be derived by placing them within the context of an ancient and vibrant symbolic tradition. What did they mean to the people who created, used, and viewed them? The prehistoric nature of these objects complicates interpretation, but through cautious and careful examination of Native American symbolism and oral tradition, many clues are provided. Indigenous religious practices and beliefs undoubtedly underwent a great deal of change over more than twelve thousand years. Nonetheless, the raw materials of symbolic thought—the basic world view and system of visual metaphors used to describe the cosmos—seem to have remained surprisingly consistent over the last several thousand years. While scholars have long noted very real similarities between the art of Mexican civilizations and southeastern cultures, these similarities are not the result of migration or diffusion of watered-down Mexican symbols to Tennessee. Instead, they represent a deep, basic level of shared cultural symbols. As the cultures in each of these areas achieved complex social and political organization, old and widely shared ideological concepts assumed a similar cast. Ancient stories passed down in many parts of the New World from ancestral cultures were expressed in similar forms.

Among the indigenous cultures of the southeastern United States, the broad and central themes that may shed some clues on ancient beliefs and symbols are (1) their understanding, or world view, of the cosmos; (2) the importance of ritual and ceremony in maintaining harmony and mediating conflict; (3) the perception of transformation from one stage to another as a central focus of both secular and spiritual life; and (4) the veneration of family and community.

CONCEPTS AND ORIGINS OF THE UNIVERSE

Based on oral tradition, many southeastern Native American cultures perceived the universe as divided into three populated worlds: This World, Upper World, and the Under World. This World existed as a great, flat island (often conceived as a turtle) resting rather precariously on a great body of water, suspended from the vault of the sky by four cords attached at each of the cardinal directions. This island was circular in shape and was crosscut by the four cardinal directions. Most southeastern societies probably thought of themselves as occupying the center of the circle. Above This World, the Upper World generally represented stability and order. Between This World and the waters below was the Under World, which epitomized change and disorder. This World stood in balance somewhere between perfect order and complete chaos.

A key symbol found on many prehistoric objects was a representation of This World and the harmonic balance and linkages with the rest of the cosmos. The "cross-in-circle" epitomizing the earth and the four cardinal directions is incorporated as a symbol on many objects from throughout Tennessee, including most commonly the curved faces of marine-shell gorgets and ceramic vessels. As a complex and multivocal symbol, however, the cross-in-circle also expressed the linkages between This World and the others. The sacred fire, an "eternal flame" kept burning in sanctified public buildings (often atop earthen platform mounds in prehistoric times), was the earthly representation of the sun and provided links with the Upper World. Some southeastern cultures built their sacred fire by resting four logs together in the shape of a cross, so that the sacred fire burned in the center. Among several southeastern societies, the fires of each individual household were annually extinguished and relit from the sacred fire as part of a sacred ceremony celebrating community and world renewal. Hence, the cross-in-circle not only represented the physical structure and eternal nature of the cosmos but also linked the annual cycles of winter/spring and death/rebirth with those of the community. Other southeastern indigenous societies arranged the fuel of the sacred fire in a circle or spiral. In both ceramics and gorgets, the spiral-in-circle is a common symbol alternating with the cross-in-circle.

The linkages between the cross- or spiral-in-circle, the sun, and the sacred fire are readily seen in prehistoric art. In all cases, the circle element can often be found surrounded with arched triangles representing the rays of the sun. Once again reflecting the many voices of these symbols, the triangular rays at the same time may represent the natural decorations found on the shells of many southeastern tortoises and turtles, and hence also represent the Under World. As such, a single shell gorget may symbolically link the entire cosmos by representing the sun of the Upper World, the four cords suspending the earth in the cross, the sacred fire constructed in either cross, circle, or spiral in This World, and the Under World in the form of the turtle.

On shell gorgets from East Tennessee, the central cross-in-circle motif is often replaced by, or combined with, the water spider, which is another symbol supporting the interpretation of these objects as representative of the sacred fire, world renewal, and balancing the cosmos. In Cherokee mythology, the water spider brought the first fire to humans. After all other creatures had tried and failed, the spider wove a silk bowl, placed it on her back, and swam to an island where the Thunder Boys (inhabitants of the Upper World) had placed fire in the hollow of a sycamore tree. There she obtained a coal, placed it in her bowl, and returned with the gift of fire. Once again, the stories illustrate the harmony of the symbols: the sacred fire came from the Thunder Boys, who lived in the Upper World, but could only be acquired by a creature whose affiliations were with the waters of the Under World.

Transformation and Crossing Boundaries

In southeastern mythology, visitors from both the Upper World and Under World often frequented This World and interacted with humans. Interaction with any of these visitors was fraught with danger yet potentially bountiful. From the perspective of understanding prehistoric art, perhaps the most critical element is an understanding that indigenous societies perceived crossing boundaries of any kind as critical points that could affect the balance and harmony of the family, the community, and even the cosmos itself. As a result, indigenous societies emphasized the rituals and ceremonies that accompanied these events, and they appear dramatically in the symbolism.

Middle Mississippian shell gorget from Castalian Springs, Sumner County, with two perforations and incised decoration representing a human figure kneeling, holding a human head in one hand and a club in the other. A.D. 1250–1300. Photograph by David Heald. Courtesy of National Museum of the American Indian, Smithsonian Institution (15/0853).

Many of the animals commonly depicted in late prehistoric ceramic art can be interpreted as "liminal creatures" in the sense that they possess the ability to cross boundaries. Many cultures throughout the world share a perception of the natural world as divided into realms of earth, water, and sky. Some animals, of course, do not readily fit these categories and are often viewed as sacred or special creatures. Ducks are birds that cross the boundary of water and sky. Beavers are four-footed mammals that spend most of their time in the water. Most fish depicted in late prehistoric art are bottom-feeders, fish whose behavior can be described as walking on the land below the rivers, lakes, and streams. Dogs, as represented in some of the most exquisite art of the era, may also have been viewed as particularly unusual creatures. Unlike Old World societies that possessed a wealth of domesticated animals, New World societies had few domesticated animals; in the southeastern United States, only the dog has been firmly established as fully domesticated. As such, the dog was a singular creature with very special ties to human society. As described above, the turtle also featured prominently—not only in linking the four-legged world with the watery underworld but also in bearing the weight of the earth itself. Frogs hold a special and central place, exhibiting as they do the strong ability of transformation as they move from tadpole to adult. This interest in transformations appears to have been established in Tennessee by the Middle Woodland period, as evidenced by an effigy of a moth case recovered in 1973 from the floor surface of an Owl Hollow phase double-oven winter lodge (A.D. 395–455) in Normandy Reservoir. Each of these creatures provided linkages, doors, and gateways between this world and others. Their unique characteristics offered both opportunities for protection from, and communication with, the powers of the supernatural.

In addition, powerful supernatural creatures that emerged from rivers, lakes, waterfalls, and mountain caves, all entrances to the Under World, sometimes frequented This World. Born from an egg, the serpent is an enigmatic and Under World creature in both its natural and its supernatural states, but also one that can be encountered in many realms, whether swimming in the water, crawling on land, wrapped around a tree limb. Nonetheless, the Under World was ambiguous. As a world of monsters and a source of danger, it was also the source of water, fertility, and the power to cope with evil. Cherokee stories of the *uktena,* a great snake, provide our best understanding of many representations of serpentlike images with wings and horns in prehistoric art.

Middle Mississippian gorget from Castalian Springs, Sumner County, with two perforations near the edge and four in the center. Incised decoration representing woodpeckers and scroll work; the center is the world, the rays are the sun, and the woodpeckers, symbols of war. A.D. 1250–1300. Photograph by David Heald. Courtesy of National Museum of the American Indian, Smithsonian Institution (15/0855).

VENERATION OF ANCESTORS AND FERTILITY

Veneration and respect for ancestors, elders, women, and the family in general is woven throughout southeastern mythology and culture and reflects another consistent theme in the artistic tradition. The linkages between peoples, cultures, and the three worlds are equally reflected in these objects.

Tennessee's First Artists

FOR MOST PEOPLE, PREHISTORIC CAVE ART MEANS VIVID DEPICTIONS OF REINDEER AND BISON, IMAGINATIVELY painted on the walls of French and Spanish caves by very ancient artists whose skills rival modern masters. Beginning at least three thousand years ago, however, Native Americans in Tennessee decorated the walls, ceilings, and floors of certain caves, sometimes traveling several kilometers into the "dark zone" beyond the reach of natural light to do so. Today we know of more than thirty-five cave art sites in the Southeast; more than twenty of these are in Tennessee, and we have begun to outline parameters of a southeastern prehistoric cave art tradition, one with a long history and varied content.

The earliest known cave art is in northern Tennessee's Third Unnamed Cave, where prehistoric flint miners traveled nearly two kilometers underground seeking quality raw materials for their tools; while digging for flint, they decorated the ceiling of their mining chamber: simple geometric signs, meandering lines, and enigmatic scratches. More than twenty radiocarbon dates from torch remnants and fireplaces on the chamber floor place this activity at three thousand to thirty-five hundred years ago during the Archaic period (8000–1000 B.C.). In the Woodland period (1000 B.C.–A.D. 900), cave art became more common and elaborate, with representational images of humans and animals complementing the abstract designs of the Archaic period. Some Woodland cave art is associated with human burial sites; other caves contain a rich and varied array of images similar to designs found on Woodland pottery. Tennessee's cave art was most common and widespread during the late prehistoric Mississippian period (A.D. 900–1600). Nearly two-thirds of the known southeastern art caves have associated Mississippian artifacts or radiocarbon ages, and the imagery from these sites is clearly related to the Southeastern Ceremonial Complex iconography that was a

[Continued on next page]

Petroglyphs from a Middle Tennessee cave show three components. *Left:* a large, humanlike image with a rectangular body containing concentric circles; *right:* a more conventional human shape whose outreached arm touches the first image; below the box: a humanlike infant being born of the box image. The latter almost certainly depicts a mythological "birthing" event and dates to the Early Mississippian period (c. A.D. 900). Courtesy of Jan F. Simek.

central element in Mississippian cosmology and religion. Winged humans, game players, serpents with antlers or wings, and small nonfood animals all relate Mississippian dark zone cave images to wider religious practices. There is also evidence that Mississippians may have organized their imagery within a cave, resulting in a composition larger than individual glyphs or panels.

Tennessee's prehistoric cave artists used four different production techniques: mud glyphs, petroglyphs, pictographs, and stone sculptures. While only one technique was typically used in a cave, there are caves that contain two and even three different methods of production. The first technique identified by archaeologists (at Mud Glyph Cave in 1979) was mud glyphs, images traced into wet mud using fingers or tools. Mud glyphs are extremely fragile, as their production and preservation over time depends on a suite of special conditions that create and maintain damp clay surfaces on cave walls, ceilings, and/or floors. They are the most common type of prehistoric art so far found in Tennessee caves, and they have the widest chronological range with examples spanning the Late Archaic, Woodland, and Mississippian periods. Petroglyphs are images engraved directly into bare limestone walls and ceilings using sharp incising tools. Petroglyphs are nearly as common in prehistoric art caves as mud glyphs and similarly span the Archaic-Mississippian sequence. Pictographs are drawings on cave walls made with mineral pigments (charcoal, clay, or ochre). So far, relatively few pictographs are known from prehistoric cave sites, and these tend to occur in small numbers. In all cases, dated pictograph sites are quite late, corresponding to the late Woodland or Mississippian periods. Finally, early archaeologists in Tennessee reported finding stone sculptures in several East and Middle Tennessee caves. The context of these remains unclear, as most were discovered in the nineteenth century, but it is possible that prehistoric people occasionally left art in caves.

The most difficult aspect of prehistoric southeastern cave art is its interpretation. During the Mississippian period, cave art clearly represents one part of a wider religious, iconographic tradition that involved ceremonial activity on mounds, plazas, and public buildings by large groups of people, and in isolated areas by small groups or individuals. Mississippian cave art, therefore, was integrated into religion. Earlier in time, meaning is less clear. There seems to be a partial relationship between cave art and burial of certain individuals during the Woodland period, but this is not always apparent. Cave art may have had several functions at this time. Only two Archaic art caves are known; in one case petroglyphs are associated with mining activity, perhaps to protect or sanctify the space, but in the other site, mud glyphs (of simple geometric shapes) were produced on a cave floor without evidence for other activities. Interpretation of the origins of southeastern cave art must, therefore, await more examples.

Jan F. Simek, University of Tennessee

Suggested Readings

Faulkner, Charles H., ed. *The Prehistoric Native American Art of Mud Glyph Cave.* Knoxville: Univ. of Tennessee Press, 1986.

Simek, Jan F. "The Sacred Darkness: Prehistoric Cave Art in Tennessee." *Tennessee Conservationist* 63 (Mar./Apr. 1997): 27–32.

Simek, Jan F., Jay D. Franklin, and Sarah C. Sherwood. "The Context of Early Southeastern Prehistoric Cave Art: A Report on the Archaeology of 3rd Unnamed Cave." *American Antiquity* 63 (1998): 663–77.

Native Views of Exhibitions

In most Native American societies, reverence and respect for the dead is an important spiritual principle. In general and simplified terms, many Native people believe the spirits of the dead have embarked on a journey. Utilitarian and ceremonial objects are placed in graves for use on this journey. Disturbance of a burial site disrupts the journey, causing disastrous consequences for the spirit and the living.

In North and South America, countless Native American graves have been disturbed and destroyed by looting, scientific research, and construction projects. Thousands of human skeletons and burial objects from these graves are now in public and private collections. Until recently, when the practice became illegal, many exhibits featured Native American human remains displayed along with the burial offerings found in their graves. Today, most exhibitions of Native American artifacts contain some burial objects.

The display of burial goods is an extremely sensitive subject for Native people. While we do appreciate them for their artistic, scientific, and educational value, when we see a burial object on display it also reminds us of the thousands of individuals whose spiritual beliefs have been, and continue to be, violated. An injustice that has been perpetrated for hundreds of years and continues today, it arouses intense emotions in most Native people. Many refuse to view displays containing burial objects. Some, having seen such a display once, vow to never see another.

The majority view among Native Americans is that burial objects should be reinterred with the owner's remains whenever possible. To non-Natives, this may seem like an irrational act of destruction, especially since these pieces are unique and irreplaceable. But these objects were never intended to be put on display; they were meant to remain in the earth with their owner. Their greatest value lies in the spiritual function they were meant to perform. Retaining them in collections circumvents this function and corrupts the true value of the object.

The issue is more complicated if reburial with the owner is impossible. Often the owner's remains have been destroyed or lost. In such cases, many Native people believe the objects should be reburied anyway. Others maintain that reburial of an object alone is pointless because it will not accompany the owner to the spirit world. The latter group is divided further into those who believe the objects should be displayed for educational purposes and those who believe they should be kept from public view as a matter of respect.

When burial goods are displayed, the exhibition should be planned with Native consultation to ensure sensitive and accurate interpretation. From a Native perspective, a true appreciation of the significance of these objects cannot be gained by simply considering them as pieces of art or valuable relics: one needs to have some knowledge of the history and beliefs of those the ancestors who created these sacred objects long ago, and of their descendants who feel responsible for the protection of their cultural patrimony today.

Toye E. Heape, Nashville

Among the objects created by native Tennesseans are ceramic bottles depicting females (and occasionally males) showing spinal deformities or "hunched" backs. While often described as evidence of nutritional deficiencies and hard labor, these bottles may well have represented something else entirely for their creators. Grandmother stories abound in the Southeast and suggest the likelihood that the hunchbacked bottles represent such a mythological figure: an honored elderly woman. In the context of

Sandstone statues from Sellars Farm site, Wilson County. Courtesy of The Frank H. McClung Museum, University of Tennessee.

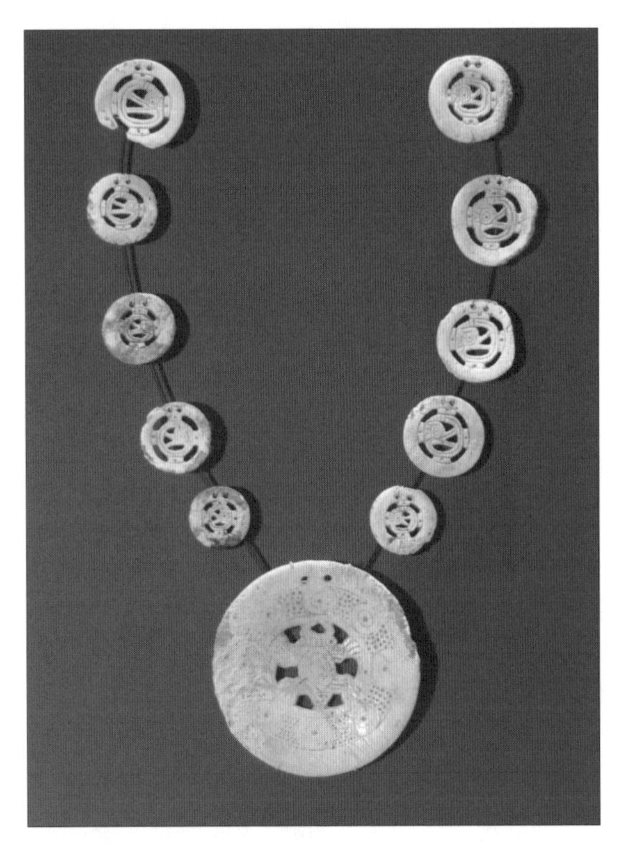

Gorget from Toqua site, Monroe County. Mississippian-period shell necklace with cut-out and engraved spider, sun disk, and rattlesnake motifs. Courtesy of The Frank H. McClung Museum, University of Tennessee.

southeastern societies, what we perceive as deformities may instead have been associated with the honored status of elder. Linkages with the agricultural world can also be found. Cherokee stories sometimes refer to corn as "Old Woman," while others tell of corn stalks transforming into beautiful young women at night.

Among the most interesting objects of Tennessee prehistoric art are the statuary and figurines of wood, stone, and ceramics in human form. While created at a few places outside the state, the majority of the known large stone statuary created north of Mexico were sculpted in Middle Tennessee at the sites of Sellars, Castalian Springs, and Dixon Creek in Wilson, Sumner, and Smith Counties, respectively. Often found in male-female pairs, these statues represent the real or perhaps semimythical "founding couple" for these Mississippian towns. Many of their faces exhibit the wrinkles and lines of elders. The Natchez of Louisiana told French explorers that their founding family turned themselves to stone so that they would not corrupt in the earth. While the French never viewed those two elders, more than fifty examples have been discovered over the past two centuries.

SYMBOLS OF WAR, PEACE, AND POWER

The native peoples of Tennessee also developed long traditions of respect for gifted hunters, warriors, and peacemakers. Among the earliest objects we might perceive as art are those that reflect one or all of these elements. While some spear points made some ten thousand years ago in Tennessee are incredibly skillfully crafted, the earliest examples usually recognized as art are the banner stones created between about 6000 and 500 B.C. Used as weights for spearthrowers, the weapon of the day, many of these objects show exquisite craftsmanship far beyond that necessary for a functional hunting weapon.

By about A.D. 200, one of the most famous kinds of Woodland period artifact is the platform

Iconography and Warfare

From the work of archaeologists, we know that a widespread set of images became a central feature for Mississippian warfare rituals beginning about A.D. 1200. Evidence for warfare is based on numerous examples of fortified towns, skeletal trauma, and iconography. Warfare iconography is now understood to be but one component of a set of warfare rituals, which included dancing, smoking tobacco, drinking purifying medicines, singing sacred songs, delivering oral mythic charters, striking the war pole, and exchanging prestigious gifts.

Symbolic motifs, widespread throughout prehistoric Tennessee, may be grouped into three basic categories based on their context. Perhaps the best known are the ritual warfare implements, such as stone and copper swords, clubs, and axes, used and manipulated as sacred icons. These include a panoply of artifacts worn or exhibited on ritual occasions and illustrated on copper plates and marine-shell gorgets. The ruling elite highly desired copper because its metallic and lustrous qualities made explicit their connection to the sun.

Another important element in Mississippian rituals includes the shell, wood, gourd, and pottery containers used in warfare rituals. They held the sacred war drinks, which purified mind and body. Surviving artifacts include elaborately carved conch-shell dippers and decorated pottery vessels, both of which exhibit a wide variety of motifs and symbols reflecting the relationship of humans with the animal and spirit world.

Pottery vessels were painted, incised, engraved, and 'appliquéd' with abstract ritual symbols including swastikas, scrolls, geometric patterns, and anthropometric designs. These vessels served to transform mundane liquids created by humans into potent sacred medicines that purified and consecrated warriors who then could attack their enemies with impunity.

A third context of Tennessee warfare images is the rock art found throughout the southern Appalachians and the Cumberland Plateau. These high landscape settings afforded the viewer a panoramic view of the world and suggest their association with the Upper World and the use of rituals for connecting humans with the power of the upper region. Rock art often includes petroglyphs and pictographs of animals, weapons, and geometric and abstract motifs. In East Tennessee, mud glyphs have been found in dark, private passages of caves where human, animal, and geometric images, as well as warfare themes, have been recorded.

Mississippian iconography reflects a vital and entrenched preoccupation with warfare. Linked with mythology, imagery was a crucial element in warfare rituals. Images and symbols, derived from weaponry, war trophies, and puissant animals, encapsulated powerful metaphors. Iconography, whether worn on costumes, used as ritual containers, placed in sanctified shrines, or carried in sacred bundles, provided access to supernatural powers sought by warrior chiefs, nobles, and commoners alike through ritual.

One iconographic theme focuses on images of aggressive and fierce elite warriors brandishing weapons and war trophies. These dancing warrior images, hammered on copper repousse plates and engraved on marine-shell gorgets, portray the use of weapons and war trophies in warfare rituals. Weaponry, especially war clubs, and weapon-derived motifs figure prominently in Mississippian iconography from prehistoric Tennessee. Icons show high-status warriors with war clubs raised above their heads mimicking combat. The functional counterparts of these status-identifying ritual maces or war clubs were the premier instruments of war for Mississippian warriors who fought in hand-to-hand combat for war honors and trophies.

[Continued on next page]

The depiction of war trophies centered on human heads, hands, forearm bones, and skulls. They were appliquéd, engraved, and painted on pottery vessels across much of the Mississippian world. These ceramic vessels and shell cups apparently held potent medicines used by warriors in warfare rituals. The container's surfaces invoked visible martial messages to be seen as participants used them: representations of powerful animals, including falcons, woodpeckers, turkeys, mountain lions, and rattlesnakes, conjured cosmological powers of Upper and Under World supernaturals. These animals possessed qualities esteemed and sought by priests and warriors. These and other supernatural animals could endow warriors with attributes such as stealth, courage, fidelity, and striking power for spiritual aid and military success in battle; they also provided access into the other world for priests.

David H. Dye, University of Memphis

Owl effigy water bottle, Toqua site, Monroe County. Courtesy of The Frank H. McClung Museum, University of Tennessee.

pipe, often ornamented with mammals, birds, or reptiles. Pipe rituals were a critical aspect of ceremonial life. Throughout historic times in the eastern United States, native peoples observed the custom of smoking a sacred pipe (the calumet) made in the form of a ritual arrow. Robert Hall suggested that these distinctive platform pipes symbolically represented an atlatl (the most common Woodland weapon prior to the bow and arrow was the spear-thrower), decorated with an effigy spur. Thus, ancient weapons of hunting and warfare became symbols of peace and alliance by Woodland times. These metaphors of war and peace that began in prehistoric Tennessee have also entered into our modern culture. We still speak of "smoking the pipe of peace" and "burying the hatchet." A tradition that emerged several thousand years ago in Native American cultures remains alive and well today.

As powerful and complex societies emerged throughout Tennessee in the late prehistoric era, symbols of leadership and power became more common. While initially associated with agricultural fertility and ancestors, symbols that equated leadership and power with warfare and peacemaking rapidly emerged. Some of the most spectacular stone artifacts created by the prehistoric peoples of Tennessee are ceremonial representations of weapons of war that were used primarily as symbols of office for chiefs. Spectacular caches of ceremonial swords, talon knives, maces, and other weapons have been discovered at many sites throughout the Southeast. Many were manufactured from Dover chert or flint, a type of stone found only in Middle Tennessee, and were traded to elites as far away as Oklahoma and Florida.

Other objects related to both peace and war include artifacts of the chungke game played by

Architecture of the Mississippian Period

THE MISSISSIPPIAN PERIOD REFERS TO BOTH A SPAN OF TIME IN NATIVE AMERICAN PREHISTORY AND a set of cultural characteristics. In Tennessee, the period is divided into Early Mississippian (c. A.D. 900–1300) and Late Mississippian (c. A.D. 1300–1600). Architecture is one of the salient characteristics that helps define each of these divisions.

Reconstruction of a Late Mississippian structure. Thomas R. Whyte, artist. Courtesy of The Frank H. McClung Museum, University of Tennessee.

Our knowledge of Mississippian architecture is incomplete in that most of what we know is based upon archaeologically defined structures and patterns. Chroniclers for early Spanish and French incursions into the interior Southeast provide limited data, but they hint at perishable elements, such as painted effigies and colors, that are missing from the archaeological record. The archaeological remains consist of earthworks, postholes, charred construction elements, impressions in clay, and fired clay floors, hearths, benches, and partitions.

Over seven hundred years there were changes in construction techniques and variations in building styles from site to site, but the distinctive architectural pattern of a Mississippian town remains the mound and plaza. Mounds were constructed as platforms on which to place public buildings and residences of elite individuals or village chiefs—their elevation making them a symbol of social, political, and religious power and the focal point of the town. Periodically, the platform structures were removed and a new level added, raising the mound higher above the plaza area. The principal mound at Mound Bottom in Cheatham County, for example, reached a height of over thirty-six feet; numerous other sites had mounds higher than twenty feet. Mound summits were accessed by either stairs or a ramp. The plaza was the public space used for various religious and secular activities—its modern counterpart being the plazas in many European cities. Around the plaza were individual dwellings and storage structures, and in most cases a palisade or protective embankment enclosed the whole settlement.

Early Mississippian houses involved a flexed construction of poles, anchored in either individual holes or wall trenches and bent to form a wall and roof frame. Late Mississippian houses employed a rigid construction of single-set wall posts and interior posts to support the roof

[Continued on next page]

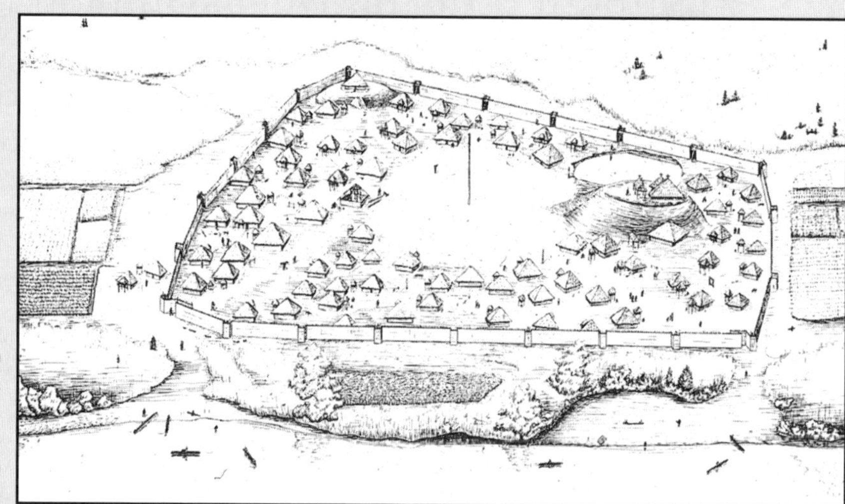

Reconstruction of a Late Mississippian town. Thomas R. Whyte, artist. Courtesy of The Frank H. McClung Museum, University of Tennessee.

superstructure. Roofs were of cane thatch or bark, and the walls were either thatch or waddle and daub. The public area and hearth formed the central portion of the house; along the walls clay partitions separated sleeping benches. Partition fragments indicate they were decorated with incised, punctate, or painted designs. Some Late Mississippian houses were constructed in a shallow pit, perhaps enhancing the insulating effects of the soil. Entrances to Early Mississippian houses were often in the corner; later, short passageway entrances were placed in one wall. In general, houses had about four hundred square feet of living area. Completing the minimal residential unit was a portico or shed where in warm weather most cooking and other activities took place. Raised corn storage cribs were also common.

As with much of Mississippian culture, architecture was linked to religion and world view. The placement of mounds, plazas, and other public structures was probably ritually prescribed. Many towns are placed on landforms that enhance a special sense of place. A great deal has been written about directional orientation in Mississippian site construction suggesting observation of equinoxes and solstices or use of other cosmological knowledge and principles. Placement, space, and size of structures were all closely linked to individual and group rank, status, and kinship. There was also a hierarchy of settlement patterns that ranged from single farmsteads to the great mound centers of the Southeast, such as those at Cahokia (southern Illinois), Moundville (Alabama), and Etowah (Georgia).

Jefferson Chapman, Frank H. McClung Museum, University of Tennessee

Suggested Readings

Lewis, R. Barry, and Charles Stout, eds. *Mississippian Towns and Sacred Spaces: Searching for an Architectural Grammar.* Tuscaloosa: Univ. of Alabama Press, 1998.

Morgan, William N. *Precolumbian Architecture in Eastern North America.* Gainesville: Univ. Press of Florida, 1999.

Nabokov, Peter, and Robert Easton. *Native American Architecture.* New York: Oxford Univ. Press, 1989.

Chucalissa site, c. fifteenth century. This restored Mississippian-era village features reconstructed buildings and a museum. Photograph by Carroll Van West.

many southeastern societies. Known as the "little brother of war," these games were sometimes used to settle disputes between tribes. While some of the stones used in these games are simple and unadorned, others are spectacular examples of stoneworking.

We have only begun to scratch the surface in our appreciation and understanding of the rich symbolic heritage of the indigenous peoples of Tennessee. Hampered by long traditions of conscious and unconscious perceptions of "primitive" art, we have failed to appreciate mythological and symbolic traditions spanning millennia. While we could simply appreciate the elegant beauty of a well-crafted frog bowl or negative painted bottle, our understanding and appreciation of the richness of prehistoric symbolism and world view is expanded tremendously as we begin to develop a clearer image of what these symbols meant to the peoples who created them. The prehistoric artisans of Tennessee were amazingly skilled in recreating their world view in the subtle, ingenious, and sophisticated patterns of their art. To fully appreciate these artifacts as art, we should not simply reinterpret them within our own modern contexts but also strive to deepen our heritage as Tennesseans by incorporating the richness of their symbolism.

Suggested Readings

Brose, David S., James A. Brown, and David W. Penney. *Ancient Art of the American Woodland Indians.* New York: Harry N. Abrams, 1985.

Chapman, Jefferson. *Tellico Archaeology: 12,000 Years of Native American History.* Rev. ed. Knoxville: Univ. of Tennessee Press, 1994.

Cox, Stephen D., ed. *Art and Artisans of Prehistoric Middle Tennessee.* Nashville: Tennessee State Museum, 1985.

Dickens, Roy S., Jr., ed. *Of Sky and Earth: Art of the Early Southeastern Indians.* Atlanta: Georgia Department of Archives and History, 1982.

Fundarburk, Emma Lila, and Mary D. F. Foreman. *Sun Circles and Human Hands.* Luverne, Ala.: Privately published, 1957.

Galloway, Patricia, ed. *The Southeastern Ceremonial Complex: Artifacts and Analysis.* Lincoln: Univ. of Nebraska Press, 1989.

Hall, Robert L. *An Archaeology of the Soul: North American Indian Belief and Ritual.* Urbana: Univ. of Illinois Press, 1997.

Hudson, Charles. *The Southeastern Indians.* Knoxville: Univ. of Tennessee Press, 1976.

McNutt, Charles H., ed. *Prehistory of the Central Mississippi Valley.* Tuscaloosa: Univ. of Alabama Press, 1996.

Thruston, Gates P. *The Antiquities of Tennessee and the Adjacent States.* Cincinnati: Robert C. Clarke, 1890.

Two

Building with Wood, Brick, and Stone
Vernacular Architecture in Tennessee, 1770–1900

Michael T. Gavin
Middle Tennessee State University

Vernacular architecture has been one of the more vital expressions of the collective spirit of the people of Tennessee. This spirit has taken its physical form from the natural materials found within the state and reflects the cultural coherence and basic conservatism of its residents. The approach most Tennesseans have taken to sheltering themselves has been an intuitive response to both their own needs and the nature of available materials serving those needs.

Years of struggling, first with Native Americans for possession of the land, then with the soil and the elements in order to grow crops, has bred strong-minded and highly individualistic citizens. Somewhat paradoxically, though insisting on substantial levels of personal freedom, Tennesseans have long sustained themselves by loyalty and mutual aid. Throughout the state, many of the inhabitants remain rural and egalitarian.

The domicile of the common man represents the character of a people, and the dwellings in the Volunteer State have been more firmly grounded in practicality and custom than in any abiding concerns for fashion or pretense. Despite the fact that most individual houses have relatively short lives and

Earnest Fort House, Greene County (c. 1780). This German-influenced two-story log house is part of the oldest Century Farm in Tennessee. Photograph by Carroll Van West.

Landon Carter House, Carter County (c. 1780), an outstanding example of a frame three-room-plan house. Photograph by Carroll Van West.

their rate of replacement is high, vernacular buildings tend to retain the same general characteristics locally over long periods of time. At times, several competing impulses have surfaced that have resulted in interesting mixtures of homespun and sophistication, such as when a richly paneled and decorative painted interior is found within a hewn-log house. These interpretations of high style architectural fashion within an overall vernacular context are not uncommon in Tennessee vernacular design.

Architecture should not be separated from its economic and geographical background, nor can we ignore the environmental and social conditions that help to articulate the forms of vernacular buildings. Ordinary house types continued to be perpetuated by conformity and anonymity until well into the twentieth century. Because ordinary citizens have practiced folk architecture collectively over the years, the need for specialists, such as architects or master builders, was slow in developing. Instead, the common people of Tennessee have relied on native genius and competent, hardworking craftsmen for most of their housing needs.

Although the early settlers constructed their houses from a variety of materials, primarily wood, brick, and stone, in many ways the story of early vernacular architecture in Tennessee is the story of log architecture. No other durable building method was so uniquely adapted to an untamed wooded environment. Historic log architecture shows a great variety that ranges from a primitive and expedient way of building based on defense and protection to a more sophisticated structural system that continued to underpin whatever later fashionable facade would be draped over it. The large numbers of domestic log buildings were solid, functional dwellings that amply served the needs of farmers and townspeople for generations.

Some scholars have suggested poverty and isolation as the causes for the persistence of log construction within Tennessee, but other, positive reasons make more sense. For example, the log house was frequently the product of work exchange within the community and represented its values and economy. By working together to raise cabins quickly, all the members of a rural neighborhood could be adequately housed with little or no cash exchange. This cooperative spirit also served to promote a conservative architectural tradition that tended to value conformity and reject signs of pretentiousness.

A log house usually represented the most economical housing choice. Each homesteader could produce most of the necessary construction materials from the trees on the farm. The family could complete many of the preliminary tasks in the winter months, when agricultural demands were low. In addition, properly built log structures are extremely durable and capable of many years of service. If

Single-pen log cabin. Photograph by Michael Thomas Gavin.

maintained regularly and kept in good condition, a hewn-log house represented a tangible asset that could be inherited and improved by succeeding generations. Finally, the solid walls of a log house provided a considerable measure of security, both physical and psychological, for folks living in the isolated countryside.

At the time of the movement westward, the pioneers used two different kinds of log structures for long-term shelter: the semipermanent cabin and the hewn-log house. The cabin primarily belonged to the transient pioneers who initially transformed forest land into a settlement landscape; the log house sheltered the farmers who succeeded them. These two building types had different origins and functions and need to be considered separately.

The Log Cabin, Blockhouse, and Stockade

The first Euro-colonial log structures appeared at opposite ends of Tennessee in the late seventeenth century. The squatters' cabins outside the French forts on the bluffs of the Mississippi and the log storehouses of the South Carolina deerskin traders were the earliest buildings in the state to feature horizontal log construction. Both utilized solid timber as a safeguard to provide protection from all types of predators. This new technology had a tremendous impact on the Native Americans. As historian Patricia Cooper has demonstrated, the Cherokees and other native peoples replaced their traditional wattle-and-daub dwellings with those of logs after observing the cabins that the early traders had built to store their deerskins.[1] The original part of Davies Manor, the oldest extant house in Shelby County, consists of a two-story log structure that was reputedly built by a Chickasaw man in 1807.

Soon after the pioneers became the first Euro-Americans to occupy the territory on the western side of the Appalachian Mountains in the late 1760s, they built hundreds of log cabins in small clearings throughout the backcountry. These backwoodsmen exploited the raw products of the forest for their building needs in lieu of other choices. Cultivation of the land was impossible unless the trees were removed.

In the early days of settlement even the iron needed to make simple hardware was largely unavailable, so most applications using metal were severely limited. Wood and wood alone served for most of the necessities of life at that time. After locating a favorable site, the typical homesteader built a log cabin and planted a corn crop to buttress his claim. Since the question of ultimate ownership was often decided by violence, the most important characteristics of frontier architecture were security, defensibility, and practicality.

Thus, the primary frontier structures were the cabin, the blockhouse, and the stockade.[2] Each one could be easily and quickly built from rough logs, and each served as a useful adjunct to the others in providing shelter and protection to its inhabitants. Although crude and simplistic, these solid structures possessed the degree of permanence and protection that the exposed frontier situation required during those perilous times.

A log cabin consisted of a solitary room without windows, possibly with a partial loft. One entered through a low door. Often the hearth was on the dirt floor with the smoke escaping through a hole at the ridge, although some cabins had puncheon floors, and many had a stick-and-dirt chimney lined with clay. A couple of people using only axes could raise a log cabin quickly, and its simplicity and ironless construction fit perfectly in a forested environment. In 1769, William and Lydia Bean built what is believed to be the first settler's cabin within the future state of Tennessee.[3]

Unbarked, saddle-notched logs and a low-pitched roof defined the pioneer's modest habitation. These unassuming characteristics reflect the minimal skill and time it took to erect a cabin. Either a simple shed roof or the more complex ridgepole-and-purlin type bore the long shingles that covered the small dwelling.

A log cabin provided shelter in a basic way, and its thick wooden walls offered sufficient protection from most dangers except fire or Indian raids. The Native Americans often destroyed isolated cabins and unprotected homesteads, but the temporary nature and relatively easy replacement of these primitive structures helped to sustain a unique sense of detachment within the pioneers about the loss of their homes.

The timber blockhouse had been known throughout Europe since the years of Roman occupation, but this part fort, part dwelling developed its fullest potential along the mobile American western frontier. During the frontier years, quite often civilians, rather than the military, erected blockhouses for temporary defensive use. The distinguishing feature of this two-story hewn-log structure was the massive second story that overhung the first floor by several feet on all sides. The pioneers cut loopholes in the puncheon floors so they could fire downward at the attackers at the base of the walls.

The thick, well-crafted wooden walls of the blockhouse itself were almost impervious to small-arms fire, and the carefully notched corners resisted demolition. The blockhouse could stand on its own as a strong house, where those inside would be able to take advantage of a 360-degree field of fire. However, when the settlers used a blockhouse as part of a fort, they usually positioned it on one of the corners, where the inhabitants could direct an enfilading fire along either of the two adjacent walls. Even if the enemy should breach the stockade walls, the defenders could still retire to safety of the blockhouse.

In the spring of 1794, Hanging Maw, an influential Cherokee leader, asked Territorial Governor William Blount to establish a fort at the confluence of the Tellico and Little Tennessee Rivers to protect him and his fellow Cherokees from aggressive white settlers. The governor had the Tellico Blockhouse built and stationed a small garrison of Federal troops there. The blockhouse proved to be a major force in maintaining the fragile peace in the Tennessee borderlands, and authorities of the United States negotiated several important treaties with the southeastern tribes during the fort's thirteen-year history.

The stockade, or palisade, has existed since time immemorial and undoubtedly can be traced back to the Stone Age. In its simplest form, the stockade was a tall fence made of whole trees set closely together with one end embedded in the ground. It was known throughout all of Europe, and was used by Native Americans in the New World long before they ever saw a white man. The palisade formed an integral element of the native village plan, which had developed early during the Mississippian period.

The simple stockade fulfilled a unique defensive requirement of the vulnerable homesteaders. Its bulk and height proved to be a formidable obstacle to an attacking force. Although the wooden palisades tended to decay from moisture and insects relatively quickly, they remained sound long enough to accomplish their immediate purpose. In East Tennessee, Eaton's Fort stood strong against the Native Americans during Lord Dunmore's War, yet the deteriorated stockade had to be hastily replaced only two years later for service against the Cherokees.

King's Mill Fort, located beside the North Fork of Reedy Creek in Sullivan County, was actually a gristmill fortified with palisades and a nail-studded gate. In addition to grinding grain, the building served as a storage place for flour and ammunition for settlers on the Clinch and Holston Rivers. After the Shawnees began depredations in the autumn of 1774, large numbers of the neighbors gathered within the shelter of the fort until the hard frost came.

When coupled with a stockade, or joined with other cabins and a blockhouse or two to form a forted station, a log cabin with a minimum number of occupants could repel the most determined foes. The stations were very effective defenses and were rarely taken, except by surprise attack. Although few other structures have played so important a part in our history as the rough stockade fort of the backwoods, this architectural feature disappeared from the cultural landscape when the Indian Wars had ended. The settlers quickly moved or dismantled the blockhouses and abandoned the crude log cabins, leaving them to mark the region's initial land claims.

The Hewn-Log House

When the pickets and the forts came down, most settlers moved to farms and soon built their second dwelling, the more architecturally distinctive and comfortable hewn-log house, which rested on rock foundations and was heated by stone fireplaces. Initially, builders favored the white oaks as the timber for their houses, a practice that hearkened back to the British Isles. But oak was heavy and hard to work, and not as stable in the extremes of temperature common to the southern states. The newcomers quickly learned to utilize more suitable trees, such as yellow poplar, red cedar, or hemlock.

Many of these early dwellings still demonstrated a late medieval quality in their architectural characteristics, of which the one-room plan, the use of oak timbers, roof overhangs at the eaves, exposed and beaded ceiling joists, a steep boxed corner stairway, a chamber room above, half-lapped and pegged rafters, shaped overhangs, and board-and-batten doors were the most obvious.

For the most part, the hewn-log house of Tennessee was a product of the meshing of Germanic and Ulster-Scot cultures that occurred in the Delaware Valley in the early eighteenth century. Pushed to the frontier by the Quaker majority, these two groups appropriated the log-building technology of the Swedes and Finns as their own. A spirit of self-reliance and the necessity of making do with limited materials often led builders into creative personal solutions; however, after generations of experimentation, it appears that the American hewn-log house evolved in the New World from a combination of the Northern European concept of horizontal log construction, ancient British floor plans, and traditional Germanic construction methods.

As the backwoodsmen progressed in a southwestward direction, most identifiable ethnic elements of the Scandinavian and Germanic log houses did not survive, but the one-and-a-half story form and a number of important construction techniques

Log Outbuildings and Cribs

ALTHOUGH THE STURDY LOG HOUSE PROVIDED ADEQUATE SHELTER AND SECURITY FOR THE SETTLERS and their families, they needed additional buildings to protect their animals and food supplies. Barns, smokehouses, dairies, corncribs, springhouses, and haymows represent some of the specialized building types usually found on farmsteads in both village and countryside. Constructed out of whole timbers in a manner similar to that of the "big house" and varying considerably in size, each of these dependencies had a primary function as well as the latent capacity to adapt to other needs upon demand.

Architecturally, the most important point of reference for the rural outbuildings of Tennessee is the prototypical Pennsylvania-German barn. This utilitarian structure, first appearing in the Delaware Valley in the late 1680s, consisted of either single or multiple log units built under one roof. These individual modules are commonly referred to as "cribs" in order to distinguish them from the "pens" of log houses. Southwestwardly moving pioneers brought with them as part of their culture this highly adaptable means of building.

Resembling the familiar dogtrot house, the typical log barn had a heavily planked threshing floor running between two cribs. This simple barn was the model for barns in the areas of later settlement. In the warmer climates, the cribs became smaller and a dirt runway replaced the planked threshing floor. Farmers used their barns less frequently for livestock shelter and more frequently for crop storage, particularly corn. Horses and mules could be sheltered under the shed additions that often flanked the outer walls of the log cribs.

Most farmers relied on a small building known as a smoke- or meathouse in which to cure and then protect their precious meat supply. Carpenters took great care in fitting the logs closely together in order to exclude vermin and other pests. Like most log outbuildings, the only door was centered on a gable end. Many smokehouses featured a hoodlike projection of the roof over the door for additional protection from the weather.

A classic four-crib barn with rear shed addition, Lewis County. The cedar logs are half-dovetail notched at the corners. Photograph by Michael Thomas Gavin.

Although the corncrib was the most common farm building, it has received relatively little attention, perhaps because of its singular function. The solid log walls provided security from most predators, while the open spaces between them allowed for essential ventilation. Unlike other dependencies, the floor was often raised several feet off the ground in order to discourage rodents. The spare and practical architecture of these outbuildings reflects the essence of utility.

The growth of agriculture is reflected in the buildings on the farmstead. Modern methods of husbandry and storage have changed so much that they bear little resemblance to those of even sixty years ago. The laborious days of planting, cultivating, and harvesting by hand or animals are long past, and food storage in traditional wooden buildings is only a distant memory. The momentous changes that occurred in the production and storage of crops spelled the end of the traditional vernacular building forms associated with them, and only a few fading shadows remain upon most of the modern landscape.

Michael T. Gavin, Middle Tennessee State University

remained. Some of the most important of these include carefully hewn, tightly notched, and neatly daubed logs, well-constructed doors that swung on newly manufactured hinges, and mass-produced wooden roofing shingles. The boxy, squarish log dwellings so common in the Delaware Valley and the Valley of Virginia gradually became narrower and longer as settlement moved south, and exterior stone chimneys appeared more and more often.

Single hewn-log pens were by far the most common structures, serving as houses, barns, outbuildings, mills, churches, schools, courthouses, stores; in short, settlers could adapt these stand-alone units to any number of uses. Most important, a single pen module served as the basic building block from which larger dwellings evolved. Many of the original one-room houses are now integrated into considerably expanded dwellings.

Multiroom houses constructed from separate log pens are very common.[4] The idea of using a group of linked units built as an additive series appears to be descended from the medieval concept of multiple "houses." Some of the earliest complex pioneer dwellings consisted of several separate pens. Andrew Jackson's first Hermitage in Donelson was not the present commodious country house that dates from 1819 but a much earlier group of log houses in close proximity to one another. John Sevier's "mansion" on the Watauga originally consisted of a "half dozen single cabins, tacked one upon the other, and covering space enough to serve for the foundation of a cathedral."[5]

As these examples demonstrate, log pens either could be left to stand independently or be connected to each other by means of covered porches or passages. The complex plans constructed in this manner not only had natural appeal, but the ease of construction and enlargement enhanced their adaptive value.

The arrangement and orientation of these units and the position of the fireplaces serving them could be quite random during the early years. As time passed, changing social conditions led to an evolution of building styles, and successive owners often modified or rebuilt the older houses in accordance with the prevailing customs of domestic architecture. Throughout much of the Southeast during the nineteenth century, this meant either the central hall arrangement or the two-story symmetrical three- to five-bay "I-house." The earlier individualistic and unorthodox room placements became more rare as time progressed. The forms that the familiar house types present can represent the final distillations of years of experimentation.

By the mid-nineteenth century, the grandchildren of the pioneers elevated the craft of log architecture to its highest level, where the old log house could become almost palatial in plan and appearance, inside and out, by the addition of milled boards, plaster, and a classical portico. Although aspiring to better things, such as style and grandeur, many of the new generation paid due respect to the past by continuing to build with hewn timbers as a structural frame. Domestic log architecture reached its zenith in Tennessee by 1840 through increased size, attention to detail, and quality of execution.[6]

In Maury County, master builder Nathan Vaught built at least fifteen log dwellings during his career as a contractor in southern Middle Tennessee. Seven of these residences have similar characteristics: a two-story double cedar log house, with two rooms and a hall below and the same above. Until the mid-1850s, Vaught continued to erect large log buildings for clients who were substantial men in the local community, such as Bank of Tennessee cashier J. C. Rye or wagon maker W. B. Chaffin.[7]

The log cabin appeared when circumstances demanded it, first as temporary shelter and later as refuge for the landless poor. The hewn-log house endured because it served Tennesseans faithfully and well. Later generations retained the old pioneer house not only as a symbol of the past but also as a solidly constructed framework on which to express their hope for the present and their dreams for the future.

Stone Houses

Stone, or rock, houses have been built in Tennessee since the earliest days of white settlement. Rarely more than roughly dressed, these sturdy dwellings exhibit a hard-won character and represent a transitional element in frontier architecture between the hastily erected structures of the initial pioneers and the more permanent buildings of the settlement era. Although the preeminent building material available in many parts of Tennessee, stone never enjoyed sustained popular success due to the relatively high cost of both labor and materials. At no time were these magnificent buildings common in any western settlement, but the handsome late-eighteenth- and early-nineteenth-century houses built by immigrants from Virginia, Maryland, or the Carolinas are true stylistic descendants of their Pennsylvania ancestors of the hundred years previous.

Significant amounts of loose rock lay on the ground, and outcroppings of layered limestone could be found throughout most of the state. Although easily broken into slabs, quarrying and cutting stone required long hours of labor and specialized tools. The production of suitable stone for building took considerably more time than the effort of actually laying it. Transportation of the heavy material proved to be a significant factor, so the builders commonly employed teams of oxen to haul the stone to the building site.

By 1783, the first domestic buildings made of stone stood in several East Tennessee counties. The George Gillespie house at Limestone in Washington County, built by Seth Smith in 1792, could be the oldest stone house in the state, but sadly it is now abandoned and deteriorating. Early surveyor and later politician Daniel Smith began construction on Rock Castle in Middle Tennessee in 1787, although Indian troubles delayed completion for another seven years or so. Smith and other well-to-do landowners undoubtedly viewed the completion of their majestic stone residences as symbolic of the fulfillment of the promise held by the frontier.

By far the most impressive and durable elements of the settlement landscape, stone houses required considerably more labor than any other kind in the gathering of material, as well as putting it in place. Although building with stone was a slow process, its qualities of permanence and resistance to fire made it an attractive option for those who were committed to a stable and long-lasting tenure on the land. The imposing two-story late Georgian

Hugh Rogan's house, "Rogana." Photograph by Michael Thomas Gavin.

and Federal style houses required the services of highly skilled masons who were always in short supply on the western frontier.

Stone houses were not for everyone. Many people believed that because of the dampness, masonry houses were more unhealthy than wood to live in. However, the use of hydraulic lime mortar when building the foundation walls would keep moisture from the ground from penetrating. As long as the faces of the interior walls were furred off, leaving an air space between solid wall and plaster, dampness could be avoided.

A related disadvantage of masonry construction was the necessity of lime for mortar. On the frontier, lime was not particularly scarce since it could be produced by burning limestone in a kiln, but because the process was time-consuming, the finished lime was somewhat expensive and varied greatly in quality. Ordinary clay could serve as a substitute, but since clay dissolves when exposed to rainwater, this practice resulted in the frequent repointing of the mortar joints.

Easy access to rock and lime made stone houses available to others besides the elite. Some Irish immigrants, such as legendary Indian fighter Hugh Rogan, built small houses of either roughly dressed ashlar or lightly worked rubble similar to the cottages they had known in Ireland. The roof of Rogan's two-room, central-chimney, dressed-limestone house near Bledsoe's Creek in Sumner County may have originally been thatched.[8]

Few stone houses were built after 1820; the appearance, convenience, and economy of brick effectively put an end to its use in domestic architecture, except for foundations and fireplaces. Interestingly though, a brief revival of the vernacular use of stone occurred at the Cumberland Homesteads, near Crossville, in the 1930s. Workers there used the indigenous Crab Orchard sandstone to construct the distinctive houses of this rural resettlement community in a restrained Tudor Revival style.

The few venerable eighteenth- and nineteenth-century stone houses that still remain on the landscape bear silent witness to a self-reliant people who worked hard to subdue an unfamiliar and demanding wilderness, yet simultaneously sought respectability and reassurance in familiar and acceptable models.

Brick Houses

Brick quickly became the material of choice for permanent structures in Tennessee, although it did not come into general use in domestic construction as

Trinity Episcopal Church, Mason. Brick craftsmanship presented in Gothic revival style highlights this historic (c. 1870) rural church. Photograph by Carroll Van West.

early as wood or stone. Brick making was delicate and time-consuming, but the only materials needed were clay, sand, wood for the kiln, and a few molds. Large numbers of suitable clay deposits meant that the bricks could often be produced near the home site, eliminating most transportation difficulties. An abundance of the appropriate raw materials close by kept the cost of a brick house comparatively low.

Builders have preferred brick for centuries because of its classic beauty and resistance to fire. Properly burnt brick resisted water better than limestone or sandstone, and even the improperly burnt ones could be used within the walls. Bricks also tended to be handier than stone, since they were nearly identical and therefore easier to lay. Considerable labor and material were saved because walls made of brick could be laid much thinner than those of stone, which were usually three to four feet thick. As with stone walls, proper ventilation for the brick partitions was essential to avoid dampness. All things considered, the brick's availability, small size, and standardized production made it the most important masonry material for domestic buildings.

The Campbell-Bowen House, built by Capt. William Bowen on Mansker's Creek in Sumner County in 1787, is the oldest known brick building surviving in the state. The original brick kiln was uncovered just fifty feet east of the house. Considering the state of the relations between white settlers and the Native Americans at that time, the very construction of this dwelling was a great leap of faith. But conflicts with Native Americans soon subsided, and impressive brick buildings emerged in almost every settlement. The brick house became the harbinger of permanent settlement, and the early residents took special notice of the first one in their neighborhood. At Cross Bridges, in Maury County, Revolutionary War veteran Jonathan Webster completed the first brick house west of the Duck River in 1810.

Several factors led to the increased use of brick in domestic architecture. The cessation of warfare between the settlers and Native Americans finally made complex building projects possible. The increased population density in the urban areas quickly created a public safety problem, and buildings of masonry became mandatory in cities like Nashville by 1812 because of the fire hazard posed by wooden houses crowded into city blocks. Practical brick and stone houses ceased to be curiosities after that.

The traditional one- and two-room dwellings of the eighteenth century soon yielded in favor of the more modern eastern styles. The Georgian-Federal building manner that came to Tennessee via Philadelphia, Baltimore, or Charleston in the 1820s and

1830s was not quite at home in the rugged southwestern landscape, but its belated appearance represented the ultimate social and aesthetic aspirations of the wealthier second generation pioneers at that time.

Settlement in West Tennessee was delayed until the Chickasaw Cession in 1818, and rapidly commenced after that date. The log cabins around the forts and the board shanties surrounding the flatboat landings under the Bluffs quickly gave way to more sophisticated architecture. As the Delta region steadily developed, the urbane merchants and bankers of the Memphis area continued to be influenced by the time-honored French building traditions found along the Mississippi River from New Orleans to St. Louis. During this same period, however, many rural inhabitants of the surrounding counties embraced the more restrained Greek Revival mode commonly found throughout most of the interior South for their building needs.

FRAME HOUSES

According to nineteenth-century Tennessee historian James Phelan, frame houses began to appear within the state about 1796.[9] Although his assertion is not entirely accurate, there is little doubt that thin, clapboard-covered braced-frame walls would have offered scant protection from predators, and the previously unsettled conditions had made any significant production of lumber impossible.

The pioneers produced their first sawn lumber by hand using long whipsaws. Through the efforts of a two-man team, a top sawyer and a pitman, each log produced much more usable material than when left intact. Whipsawing proved to be very laborious; an efficient pair of men could produce barely two hundred board feet per day. Increasingly, up-and-down sash type sawmills appeared as adjuncts to the gristmills and eventually became independent operations.

Carter Mansion, Elizabethton

THE JOHN AND LANDON CARTER MANSION (C. 1780) REPRESENTS A VARIANT OF THE HALL AND PARLOR plan. In a typical hall and parlor construction, the two rooms of the house are divided into the hall, usually living quarters, and parlor, a smaller room frequently used as a bedroom. The Penn plan variant, of which the Carter Mansion is an example, has the parlor divided into two rooms.

From the exterior, the two-story timber frame house is a well-proportioned example of an unpretentious frontier house in East Tennessee. The interior of the Carter Mansion is embellished with wood paneling and carpentry not seen elsewhere in the state. An ogee curve overmantel with dentil trim and fluted pilasters dominates the main hall in the mansion. Wood paneling is found throughout the first floor of the house. One downstairs room contains a corner fireplace with fluted pilasters and a curvilinear pattern overmantel capped with a scroll. Dentil work graces the cove molding, and there is a pastoral painting with three men over another mantel. Exceptional woodwork is continued in the stair and the second floor. A highlight of the second floor is the hunt scene painted on an overmantel. Pine wainscoting with faux finishes appears throughout the second floor. Overall, the second floor is not so elaborate as the first floor, lacking some of the intricate wood details.

Though the exact date of construction of the Carter Mansion in Elizabethton is unknown, the architectural character of the building suggests it could be as early as the 1780s. John Carter and his son Landon played important roles in the settlement of this region, and the Carter Mansion befits their prominence.

Claudette Stager, Tennessee Historical Commission

W. C. Crawford Store, Williston. False-front frame country stores like this Fayette County landmark were once common in Tennessee. Photograph by Carroll Van West.

These water-powered mills provided the boards and scantling that furnished the floors and siding of the houses. Even so, the difficulty of hauling logs and lumber long distances would often offset the economic advantages of the sawmills.

House carpenters would fit the lumber produced by a sawmill into a complex frame that would become the skeleton of the completed house. This process required precisely aligning a number of mortises and tenons between the slender posts and the heavier beams. These structural members were then strengthened with diagonal braces, and all of the joints pegged securely. Only a master carpenter and his crew could accomplish this demanding task satisfactorily.

The traditional braced wooden frame system was the most technologically complex among the four common building methods in use in the early nineteenth century. After cutting, hewing, planing, and mortising, the individual members were further removed from their natural state than any other material. More so than log, stone, or brick houses, heavy wood-framed dwellings required careful craftsmanship and specialized tools, as well as accurate measuring and fitting, in order to produce a satisfactory result. Not all settlers could take up the craft easily, and the province of skilled carpenters remained rare in the state until the mid-nineteenth century.

John Carter's house from the 1780s in Elizabethton is probably the oldest surviving frame residence in the state, although most of his neighbors continued to live in hewn-log houses for their entire lives. For a number of years the use of the costly timber frame system was restricted to the homes of the wealthy, such as Carter. Like others of his class, this successful planter further embellished his home with a richly carved and paneled interior, complete with two overmantel paintings, which were among the earliest known examples of plain painting in the state.

Fine frame houses, both elaborate and simple, were built throughout the length and breadth of the Volunteer State. Seven Hills Plantation, at Woodstock, is the oldest farm in Shelby County and has been in the possession of the same family since 1821. The house has a two-story central section with flanking single-story wings, and was built entirely of lumber cut on the place. Walnut woodwork set off the inside of the house, and a carved wooden balcony originally adorned the exterior.

America was a land of trees, and the continual exploitation of these sylvan resources kept the price of building with wood low. The constant experimentation with structural engineering that allowed the use of less and less material also contributed to the increasing domination of the domestic building industry by frame construction. The efficiency and economy of light frame construction would prove to be irresistible to builders of the second half of the nineteenth century.

INDUSTRIALIZATION AND VERNACULAR TRADITIONS, 1850–1920

As the railroads extended their network across Tennessee in the mid- to late nineteenth century, they carried along not only new building technology and

Decorative Interior Painting and Vernacular Traditions

HISTORIC EXAMPLES OF DECORATIVELY PAINTED INTERIORS IN EIGHTEENTH- AND NINETEENTH-CENTURY homes exist across Tennessee, indicating the wide variety of techniques, styles, and motivations for adorning private interiors with architectural paintings. Using painters' manuals and their own imagination, both itinerant and local artists employed the common and inexpensive techniques of wood graining, stenciling, and marbling to imitate rare and costly woods and marbles. While involving different methods and tools, these various techniques were usually combined within individual rooms and executed by a single painter. In a few cases, the decorators painted landscapes to serve as a focal point of the room, often in the form of an overmantel painting or fire screen.

Some of Tennessee's earliest examples of painted interiors indicate the transference of New England decorative traditions to Tennessee. The John and Landon Carter Mansion in Elizabethton is one of Tennessee's oldest residences, dating to about 1780. The mansion has two rare over-mantel paintings depicting pastoral scenes. The "Stencil House" (c. 1840), built near Clifton in Wayne County and moved in 2002 to the grounds of the Ames Plantation in Hardeman County, is the earliest known completely painted interior to retain its original decoration. This log dogtrot house contains stenciling in both the parlor and entrance hall. The anonymous artist painted such common nineteenth-century motifs as flowers, leaves, vines, weeping willow trees, pineapples, and swags and tassels.

Freed House, Trenton. Courtesy of Center for Historic Preservation, Middle Tennessee State University.

Many Tennessee houses contain fine examples of Victorian-era decorative painting. Together they serve to illustrate the varied and changing interior fashions of the late nineteenth century. In East Tennessee, the Acquilla Lane House in Whitesburg once contained at least two decoratively painted rooms: the parlor and a second floor bedroom. These rooms were the work of W. Bakar, who signed and dated the bedroom in 1861. The parlor design is composed of colored blocks in a stretcher bond pattern. The bedroom, dismantled and transferred to the Tennessee State Museum in Nashville in 1981, features tulips, birds, heart-shaped leaves, urns, vines, pomegranates, baskets, and a woman and man holding fish. Set on a bright blue background, these Pennsylvania Dutch–style motifs may indicate that Bakar was of German descent, although no written documentation exists to support this.

In Middle Tennessee, The Beeches outside Springfield contains elegant tromp l'oeil paintings on the ceilings of both the entrance hall and dining room, said to be the work of an itinerant French artist. The Italianate Campbell House outside of Spring Hill has a painted and grained interior, featuring a decoratively painted border on the parlor's floor.

In West Tennessee, the Meady White House in Saltillo and the Julius Freed House in Trenton feature geometric designs and floral motifs similar to those recommended by painters' manuals and household critics of the late 1870s. The Meady White House contains graining, marbling, and stenciled ceiling paintings attributed to John Joseph Christie, an Irish artist. At the Julius Freed House, an anonymous artist painted landscape scenes, flowers, and geometric designs on a marbled background in the parlor and a second floor bedroom.

Anne-Leslie Owens, Middle Tennessee State University

Cantilevered Barns

THE DISTINCTIVE CANTILEVERED BARN IS FOUND IN THE APPALACHIANS OF TENNESSEE. MOST ARE located in the East Tennessee counties of Blount and Sevier, though some cantilevered barns have been documented as far west as the Cumberland Plateau. Both the Museum of Appalachia at Norris and Cades Cove at the Great Smoky Mountains National Park exhibit examples of cantilevered barns. A cantilever barn features a huge, overhanging gable-roof loft, supported by long hand-hewn logs and usually resting on two hand-hewn log cribs. Typically used for livestock, the two cribs were rectangular in shape, measuring roughly twelve feet by eighteen feet, and were separated by a large open space, or driveway, that measured between fourteen to sixteenth feet in width. Depending on the pitch of the roof and the length of the cantilevered logs, the loft used for grain and hay storage could be quite large. Self-sufficient farmers built most of the extant cantilevered barns between 1870 and 1915, according to the research of Marian Moffett and Lawrence Wodehouse. The barns met well the dual needs of livestock protection and grain storage found on southern Appalachian farms, where the climate was generally humid and rainy. While architectural historians once thought that cantilevered barns were always constructed early in the settlement period, some scholars now believe that they were a post–Civil War adaptation of the earlier Pennsylvania barn (also called a forebay bank barn), found in Pennsylvania and western Maryland and Virginia.

Cantilever barn, Officer Farm, Overton County. Photograph by Carroll Van West.

Carroll Van West, Middle Tennessee State University

Suggested Reading

Moffett, Marian, and Lawrence Wodehouse. *East Tennessee Cantilever Barns*. Knoxville: Univ. of Tennessee Press, 1986.

tools but also illustrated catalogs that advertised new ways of living and homemaking. The market economy that was reshaping so much of American life also began to transform the built environment of Tennessee, where standardized, mass-produced architectural plans and building components would eventually supplant many of the vernacular building traditions of the state.

The key to this revolution in domestic architecture was the development of the "balloon frame" house, which became possible only because of the simultaneous appearance of standardized sawn lumber and cheap, mass-produced nails. The balloon frame was an innovation that maximized the support capacity of a structure to the fullest. Comparatively wispy, standard-sized bearing members with nailed,

George Franklin Barber

AT THE END OF THE NINETEENTH CENTURY, American society underwent rapid growth and development as evinced in the power of advertising, the ability to deliver goods to market easily, and the change in residential patterns away from the central city to the newly developing suburbs. George Franklin Barber (1854–1917) recognized the conjunction of these forces and became one of the world's most successful merchandisers of architecture.

A Kansan by birth, Barber migrated to Dekalb, Illinois, in 1884 with his wife and family and established the firm of Barber and Boardman. As local contractors and builders the firm's most notable work was the Congregational Church. Barber also began writing and circulating plan books and designs for houses, hotels, and other buildings.

Knoxville residence designed by George F. Barber. Courtesy of Tennessee Historical Commission.

In 1888, the Barber family moved to Knoxville, Tennessee. Between 1880 and 1890, the small town of Knoxville quadrupled its population and established itself as the fourth largest market in the South due to the quick rebuilding of its rail system after the Civil War. The region's abundant natural resources, as potential power sources, also encouraged the expansion of all types of manufacturing plants. Improvements in the economic life-style of citizens created a demand for new housing. Barber, the entrepreneur, already had the germ of an idea to mass produce and ship homes across the country. Seeking to expand his influence, he viewed Knoxville as a logical choice for relocation.

Soon after moving, Barber and Martin E. Parmelee opened an architectural firm. While the firm struggled to attract clients, inquiries for Barber's plan books grew. Among the titles circulated were *Modern Artistic Cottage, or The Cottage Souvenir Designed to Meet the Wants of Mechanics and Home Builders* (1891), *New Model Dwellings and How Best to Build Them* (1894), and *Modern Dwellings* (1901–1907). His advertising savvy had led him in 1889 to offer the first complete customized homes in the popular Queen Anne style shipped by rail. In 1898, Barber opened his own publishing company, the American Home, and launched an illustrated monthly magazine, *American Homes,* which became the second most widely circulated architectural publication in the United States. Architectural historian James Patrick estimated that at least ten thousand Barber homes were constructed in the United States, Canada, and Japan.

Although partners came and went over the decades, the relationship with Parmelee proved important for Knoxville and Barber. Parmelee was a member of the Edgewood Land Improvement Company, developers of a streetcar suburb now known as the Park City Historic District, where the Barber family reportedly lived in at least two homes along Washington

[Continued on next page]

Avenue. Barber's ostentatious designs appealed to the city's rising professional class and also complemented the Victorian era's cult of domesticity and the concomitant need to shelter women and children from urban ills. Personalized expression realized through mass-produced design elements, such as fish-scale shingles, turned spindles, latticework, and other adornments, was a selling point to builders and buyers of Barber houses and plans.

In the twentieth century, Barber offered Classical Revival–style architecture to his clients through plan books and his magazine. In Knoxville, his Laurence D. Tyson House (1907) stood as a fine example of American architecture inspired by, and borrowed from, European villa prototypes.

Barber remained a prolific architect, builder, publisher, and developer until his death in 1917. Barber homes dot the landscape of twenty-first-century America. His son, Charles, continued the family architectural tradition through the firm of Barber and McMurray that designed numerous buildings in Knoxville and on the University of Tennessee campus.

Jeri Hasselbring, Adventure Science Center

overlapped joints replaced the cumbersome mortise-and-tenoned post-and-beam system that had existed for centuries. By the 1840s, the use of these lightweight pieces had created a new building gestalt in which the whole was considerably stronger than sum of its parts.

The balloon frame also allowed maximum freedom in the layout and design of a house. Until then, the loading capacity of large wooden beams limited the size of any room. This new system freed the designer from many of the limitations of the past. Walls could be built any length and height. Trusses formed from small pieces of lumber could now span large distances, supplanting the older rafter systems. This new flexibility allowed the development of novel and complicated floor plans in response to society's demand for increased privacy within the domestic sphere. The new configurations effectively broke up the compact square that had been hearth and home for all members of the household, and set the stage for the more complex arrangements of the Victorian era.

Better transportation, the ability to mass produce architectural elements, balloon-frame construction, and the proliferation of mail order catalogs combined to give professional architects and contractors more influence on the housing choices of Tennesseans. Turn-of-the-century firms, such as George F. Barber's in Knoxville, for example, designed residences in a variety of Victorian styles and price ranges and distributed their designs in the form of pattern books and mail-order catalogs for house kits. "Barber" houses appeared not only across Tennessee, but the nation as well. Several firms mass produced "shotgun" houses, typically one room wide and three rooms long with a gable entrance, and sold them to planters, who used them to house tenants, and to industrialists, who needed cheap housing for factory workers. The success of Barber, and other architects/builders like him, encouraged larger, better-capitalized commercial enterprises, such as Sears and Roebuck and Montgomery Ward, to enter the prefabricated housing business. By 1920, Tennessee towns and suburbs had their share of Sears homes, often designed in the popular Bungalow, Colonial Revival, and Tudor Revival styles.

Domestic architecture also changed in rural Tennessee. The shotgun house and the simple box, or plank, house became the common housing stock for most tenants and sharecroppers. The highly economical box-type construction utilized a spare carpentry technique that eliminated most of the ordinary fram-

Exterior of R. B. Johnson's residence, Knoxville, built about 1900 by George F. Barber. Johnson was owner of Knoxville Poultry and Egg Company. The house was torn down in the 1950s. "Looking Back at Tennessee Collection," No. BT 239. Manuscripts Division, Tennessee State Library and Archives. Courtesy of Tennessee State Library and Archives.

ing elements. This ancient method depended on vertical boards nailed to top and bottom plates to support the roof load. The idea had descended from stave construction, in which round or split logs were embedded in the ground to form the walls of the building. Eventually, the log staves evolved into sawn planks. This system was greatly improved by the introduction of a horizontal sill, rather than the earth, to support the bottom of the staves. The small box house eventually supplanted the traditional log cabin as the primary housing option for the rural poor by the early twentieth century.

The acceptance of the box house in the countryside was predicated on the destruction of many of the old ways. It was an efficient building method for men with little spare time; it was easy to construct without much help; the materials could be paid for with earned wages; and it fulfilled a new sense of aesthetics. The soon-to-be ubiquitous box house thrived on changing values and represented the new rural economic order.[10]

By the early twentieth century, the increased interconnectedness among the Volunteer State's residents fostered by exposure to the mass culture largely ended the state's vernacular traditions of building with log, brick, and stone. Outside opinions about what was necessary and correct at many levels of the popular culture would doom the more individualistic vernacular architectural expressions to the past. Yet a few scattered survivors of log, brick, and stone remain on the cultural landscape, and they are not forgotten, for they have served us well.

Notes

1. Patricia I. Cooper, "Cabins and Deerskins: Log Building and the Charles Town Indian Trade," *Tennessee Historical Quarterly* 53 (Winter 1994): 272–79.
2. James A. Crutchfield, "Pioneer Architecture in Tennessee," *Tennessee Historical Quarterly* 35 (Summer 1976): 162.
3. J. G. M. Ramsey, *The Annals of Tennessee* (Charleston, S.C.: Walker and Jones, 1853; reprint, Johnson City, Tenn.: Overmountain Press, 1999), 94.
4. Some of the old soldiers' descriptions of their childhood homes in Colleen M. Elliot and Louise A. Moxley, eds., *The Tennessee Civil War Veterans Questionnaires,* 5 vols. (Easley, S.C.: Southern Historical Press, 1985) are illuminating. See especially those of D. S. M. Bodenhamer, I. Griffith, N. E. Harris, L. C. Howes, and J. F. Ponder.
5. James R. Gilmore, *The Rear Guard of the Revolution* (New York: D. Appleton, 1886), 56.
6. J. Frazer Smith, *White Pillars: The Architecture of the South* (New York: Bramhall House, 1941), 26–27.
7. Nathan Vaught, "Youth and Old Age," in Nancy C. Tinker, "Nathan Vaught, Master Builder of Maury County: A Study of Middle Tennessee Greek Revival Architecture" (master's thesis, Middle Tennessee State Univ., 1983), 116.

8. Caneta S. Hankins, "Hugh Rogan of Counties Donegal and Sumner: Irish Acculturation in Frontier Tennessee," *Tennessee Historical Quarterly* 54 (Winter 1995): 317.
9. James Phelan, *History of Tennessee: The Making of a State* (Cambridge, Mass.: Riverside Press, 1888), 175.
10. Walter R. Nelson, "Some Examples of Plank House Construction and Their Origin," *Pioneer America* 1, no. 2 (1969): 18–29; Charles E. Martin, *Hollybush: Folk Building and Change in an Appalachian Community* (Knoxville: Univ. of Tennessee Press, 1984), 93; Michael Ann Williams, *Homeplace: The Social Use and Meaning of the Folk Dwelling in Southwestern North Carolina* (Athens: Univ. of Georgia Press, 1991).

Suggested Readings

Brumbaugh, Thomas B., Martha I. Strayhorn, and Gary G. Gore, eds. *Architecture of Middle Tennessee: The Historic American Buildings Survey.* Nashville: Vanderbilt Univ. Press, 1974.

Crutchfield, James A. "Pioneer Architecture in Tennessee." *Tennessee Historical Quarterly* 35 (Summer 1976): 162–74.

Glassie, Henry. *Pattern in the Material Folk Culture of the Eastern United States.* Philadelphia: Univ. of Pennsylvania Press, 1968.

Jordan, Terry G., and Matti Kaups. "Folk Architecture in Cultural and Ecological Context." *Geographical Review* 77, no. 1 (1987): 52–75.

Magness, Perre. *Good Abode: Nineteenth Century Architecture in Memphis and Shelby County, Tennessee.* Memphis: Towery Press, 1983.

Martin, Charles E. *Hollybush: Folk Building and Change in an Appalachian Community.* Knoxville: Univ. of Tennessee Press, 1984.

Morgan, John. *The Log House in East Tennessee.* Knoxville: Univ. of Tennessee Press, 1990.

Patrick, James. *Architecture in Tennessee: 1768–1897.* Knoxville: Univ. of Tennessee Press, 1981.

Ramsey, J. G. M. *The Annals of Tennessee.* Charleston, S.C.: Walker and Jones, 1853. Reprint, Johnson City, Tenn.: Overmountain Press, 1999.

Smith, J. Frazer. *White Pillars: The Architecture of the South.* New York: Bramhall House, 1941.

Williams, Michael Ann. *Homeplace: The Social Use and Meaning of the Folk Dwelling in Southwestern North Carolina.* Athens: Univ. of Georgia Press, 1991.

Three

Classic Traditions
Tennessee's Academic Architecture

Leslie Noel Sharp
Middle Tennessee State University

Tennessee's legacy of academic architecture (buildings designed by professional architects trained formally in either apprenticeships with master builders or in university programs) is limited when compared to the larger architectural centers of the United States, such as New York, Philadelphia, San Francisco, and Chicago. The state's urban centers—Knoxville, Chattanooga, Nashville, and Memphis—have their fair share of community landmark architecture, designed by architects of regional, and in some cases national, significance. There are even buildings of note, mostly public buildings, in the smaller towns and county seats of Tennessee. But the number of Tennessee structures regularly found in American architectural history textbooks may be counted on the fingers of one hand, and no architect of national importance can be considered a Tennessean. Yet this is not to say that Tennessee's architecture lacks significance. On the contrary, its architecture is beautiful, interesting, and in many cases unique.

If one had to give a one-word description of Tennessee's built environment, the word chosen would be classic, used in both senses of the word—timeless and relying upon the classical forms of the Greeks and Romans. The best symbol of this is the Tennessee State Capitol, designed by nationally recognized architect William Strickland.[1] The capitol building is a Greek Revival masterpiece that embodies the democratic ideologies associated with the classical orders of the columns.

Tennessee State Capitol. Manuscripts Division, Tennessee State Library and Archives. Courtesy of TSLA.

The construction of Strickland's capitol from the mid-1840s to the mid-1850s capped fifty years of evolution in the state's architectural traditions. Apprenticed-trained builders designed a range of early formally styled landmarks, from the Georgian influence found in such landmark East Tennessee houses as the Embree House (1780s), the Gillespie house (c. 1792), and Blount Mansion (c. 1792–1834) to the magnificent carpentry of Cragfont (c. 1798–1811), the Winchester House in Middle Tennessee.

Cragfont's symmetrical five-bay, two-story facade became a common architectural vocabulary for Tennessee's domestic architecture for the next sixty years. These dwellings reflect the conservative building practices of Tennessee's early house builders that architectural historian James Patrick describes in *Architecture in Tennessee:* "The first settlers and house carpenters brought with them architectural ideals firmly rooted in pre-industrial carpentry and in the lively Georgian building tradition of the seaboard."[2] Although architectural historians generally consider the Georgian period in Tennessee as being 1780–1820, Carroll Van West observes that the Late Georgian style "remained influential until 1860" and is "often described as 'Tennessee Federal' to reflect the period of its greatest popularity."[3] This conservative nature and adherence to traditional building methods and styles in Tennessee is also present throughout the South and will be seen again and again over the course of Tennessee's architectural history.

By the time Andrew Jackson was in the White House, classicism had begun to redefine the maturing state's architectural traditions. In the late 1820s and early 1830s the work of David Morrison at Jackson's own Hermitage mansion and especially at Fairvue, the Sumner County plantation home of Isaac Franklin, created new architectural models. Here was the beginning of Tennessee's love affair with the Greek Revival style linked to democratic principles and the rise of the common man. "The local success of the Greek Revival," James Patrick explains, "was the result in part of the regional acceptance of political and educational theories which seemed to the typical southerner to perpetuate the classical ideal. Many apologists for southern civilization saw the South as a society of tradition and unchanging principles and an architecture that rested on precedent seemed to echo that unvarying order."[4]

In East Tennessee, the first important public building in a classical idiom, the Hawkins County Courthouse in Rogersville, was built in the mid-1830s. Designed by John Dameron, the courthouse is one of the earliest courthouses still in use in Tennessee. Although altered in 1929, the building still has a Federal-style entrance and Palladian windows in combination with a Greek Revival portico. The commanding two-story portico, most often highlighted by Ionic or Doric capitals, became a new common trait of the state's architectural traditions.

Not everything new and formal in Tennessee architecture in the 1830s had pediments and Ionic columns. The Gothic Revival made a brief but significant appearance from the mid-1820s to the mid-1850s. Hiram Masonic Lodge (1823) and St. Paul's Church (1834) in Franklin, along with Brownsville's Christ Episcopal Church (1846), are representative of the early Gothic Revival style with their castellated towers and pointed-arch windows. Their overall form, building methods, simple detailing, and buttressing more closely resemble the Old Brick Church in Virginia, which was then almost two centuries old, rather than the nineteenth-century early Gothic Revival–style churches in New England. Designed by New York architect Patrick C. Keeley, St. Peter's Catholic Church and Parish House (1852) in Memphis are the best examples of true early Gothic Revival architecture in antebellum Tennessee. St. Peter's is a stucco-covered building with two towers topped with crenellation and pinnacles. An excellent Middle Tennessee example is Columbia's Anthenaeum Rectory (1835), the only surviving building of a female academy designed entirely in Gothic style. The rectory is notable for its castellation and Moorish arches.

No matter its picturesque qualities, Gothic style held a decidedly minor role in antebellum Tennessee architecture compared to the many classically styled buildings of that era. Hundreds of large and small buildings were constructed with temple fronts and Doric columns. James Patrick writes that "Greek Revival, or Grecian as antebellum architects called it, was favored for public buildings in the interior South after about 1830 to the near exclusion of Gothic and other styles."[5] Some of the most notable extant Greek Revival buildings include the Knoxville City Hall (1848, 1905, formerly the Tennessee

St. Peter's Roman Catholic Church, Memphis. Courtesy of Memphis/Shelby County Public Library and Information Center–Memphis and Shelby County Room.

Asylum for the Deaf and Dumb) built by Jacob Newman, the Jefferson County Courthouse (1845) designed by the Hickman Brothers, and the Bank of Tennessee Building (1838–39) in Columbia designed by Nathan Vaught.

Known for his Greek Revival designs, Nathan Vaught (1799–1880) was a master builder who primarily practiced in Maury County. He began his training as an apprentice for cabinetmaker James Purcell until 1811, when Purcell began building houses. Vaught then worked under Purcell as a carpenter until 1821, when Purcell died and Vaught began to design and construct his own buildings. Vaught is best known for his grand and impressive Greek Revival mansions in the plantation country of Maury County. He designed over fifty houses and many commercial and public buildings. Some of his other extant Maury County designs include the Greek Revival–style Clifton Place (1838–39), Rose Hill (1845), and the Vaught Block (1858).

Many of Vaught's later designs were undoubtedly influenced by the grand classical edifice—the state capitol—under construction in Nashville. Its architect, William Strickland (1788–1854), was the first architect of national standing to receive a Tennessee commission. Strickland was born in New Jersey and trained with architect/engineer Benjamin Henry Latrobe. Although some of his early designs were Gothic, Strickland specialized in the classical styles and is most associated with the Greek Revival style. His best work was in Philadelphia, including the influential temple-style Second Bank of the United States (1818–24) and the Merchants Exchange Building (1832–37). During his years in Nashville, Strickland also accepted a commission from the wealthy and politically well connected congregation of First Presbyterian Church. He designed for that congregation another American landmark, his Egyptian Revival–style First Presbyterian Church (1851). This exotic style enjoyed limited popularity in the middle decades of the century, and today few Egyptian revival buildings still exist. Although Strickland's time in Tennessee was relatively short and his commissions not large in number, he has perhaps had the greatest influence of any single architect on the built environment in Tennessee. His state capitol design symbolized Tennessee's emergence from its raw-edged frontier to a mature state with some pretense to sophistication, especially in the growing urban center of Nashville.

A contemporary of William Strickland, Adolphus Heiman (1809–1862) was born in Potsdam, Prussia, and trained as a stonecutter before coming to United States in 1834. After working in New Orleans, he was in Nashville employed as a builder and architect by the late 1830s. He served with distinction in the Mexican War, which extended his connections with the state's elite, and developed a local reputation as an engineer. In addition to various engineering works, he designed churches, government buildings, schools, elaborate grave markers, private homes, and other community landmark buildings—mostly classical with a scattering of Gothic and Italianate-influenced designs—until 1860, when he left Nashville to serve as an officer in the Confederate army, where he died in service in Mississippi. Heiman's major extant landmarks are the Greek Revival–style St. Mary's Catholic Church (1847), the Gothic

Belmont Mansion (Nashville), historic photograph. Courtesy of Belmont University, Nashville.

Revival–style Literary Department at the University of Nashville (1853), and the superb blending of classicism and Italian villa styles at Nashville's Belmont Mansion (1850s). While the latter two exhibit the influence of the romantic movement on Heiman's work, overall his buildings possess a strict formality and classical undertone that reflect Tennessee's adherence to more conservative detailing and a preference for the Greek and Roman forms. Despite his achievements, many aspects of Heiman's career are either poorly understood or not even recognized. Indeed, national architectural scholars, such as Talbot Hamlin, once attributed several of his buildings to Strickland.

Heiman's Belmont was one of the state's great achievements in domestic environments, complete with its gazebos, the engineering marvel of its water tower, and many ornamental plantings and statuary that complemented the great manor house. But there were others across Tennessee, most built in the 1850s when better railroad access, urban growth, plantation prosperity, and a more sophisticated clientele combined to create the state's golden age of classical domestic architecture. These examples range from the austere two-story portico of the Hunt-Phelan House (1832) in downtown Memphis to the grandiose and flamboyant Corinthian front of Rattle and Snap (1854–56) in Maury County. These Greek Revival domestic masterpieces demonstrate how the Grecian style reflected the virtues of southern life and the growing prosperity of Tennesseans prior to the Civil War.

The Civil War (1861–65) interrupted many architects' careers and brought building—outside of military-related structures—to a standstill. The Reconstruction years soon yielded, however, to the boom of the New South, and academic architecture broke away from its classical preoccupation to embrace Victorian architecture in all of its eclectic diversity.

The Italianate style, with its hooded windows, prominent cornices, and bracketing, was popular before and after the Civil War. McNeal Place (1858–61) in Bolivar is an excellent example of the late antebellum style in a cotton-belt urban setting. After the war, several courthouses were built in a vernacular adaptation of Italianate style, including the Coffee County Courthouse (1871), the Loudon

Adolphus Heiman

NASHVILLE'S PROMINENT ANTEBELLUM ARCHITECT, ADOLPHUS HEIMAN, WAS BORN ON APRIL 17, 1809, in Potsdam, Prussia, where his father was grounds superintendent of the summer palace Sanssouci. After attending school to learn the sciences he felt were important to the art of building, Heiman began his career in building at the age of fourteen. It is unknown if he received any formal training, but he was an able draftsman.

With a letter of recommendation from Alexander Von Humbolt, the Prussian naturalist, Heiman sailed to New York in April 1834. Fluent in English and a qualified stonecutter, he found employment with the noted engineer Albert Stein, the former builder of Nashville's first water works in 1832, who was now constructing the water works in New Orleans. When Stein built the Lake Pontchartrain Canal, Heiman was his assistant engineer. Heiman stayed in New Orleans until 1836, when he moved to Nashville and was soon hired to build the First Baptist Church in the Gothic style, the first of several church commissions Heiman would receive in the next ten years. His St. Mary's Cathedral in Nashville is extant and considered one of the city's outstanding Greek Revival monuments. He also continued to work as a stonecutter designing tombstones and vaults. Among his most notable cemetery works were Nancy Maynor's tombstone in Nashville's Old City Cemetery and Isaac Franklin's mausoleum at Fairvue in Sumner County. The latter's frontispiece was of Egyptian design with an orb flanked by winged serpents. He also designed a cast-iron fence to encircle it.

Tennessee State Asylum, Nashville. Photograph by Calvert Studio, Nashville, n.d. Library Picture Collection, Tennessee State Library and Archives. Courtesy of TSLA.

After returning with a hero's welcome from the Mexican War in 1847, Heiman's status as an architect grew. In 1849, he designed the first cable suspension bridge in the South, connecting East Nashville with Edgefield. The cables, made in Wheeling, West Virginia, were shipped to Nashville. When Heiman's suggestions to the builder for proper anchorage were ignored, he disassociated himself from the project. His concerns were realized when the bridge fell in 1855. Rebuilt, it stood until damaged in 1862 and was demolished in 1886.

The Tennessee Insane Asylum (1851–57) was another of Heiman's triumphs. He had corresponded with noted social reformer Dorothea Dix for advice and visited hospitals in five northern states. Contemporaries rated this Gothic-style building (razed) as the finest such

[Continued on next page]

structure in the South, complete with running water and a central heating and cooling system. Unique for its day, Heiman used steel rails in the floor construction to provide a light, fireproof material.

Heiman also designed Nashville's Adelphi Theater, reputed to be the second largest stage in America. He also received many public commissions, including Nashville's Hume School, Davidson County Jail, Deluge Company 3 Firehall, and several buildings at the University of Nashville as well as the Giles County Courthouse in Pulaski. Of those commissions, only the Gothic Revival–style Literary Department of the University of Nashville is extant.

His most outstanding achievement in domestic architecture is Belmont, a country estate in Nashville. When completed in 1860, this eclectic Italian villa–style house was the largest private residence in Tennessee and boasted the most elaborate formal grounds in the state. A 105-foot water tower erected on the grounds supplied the running water.

While initially opposed to secession, Heiman joined the Confederate army as colonel of the Tenth Tennessee and was placed in charge of the construction of Fort Henry, Fort Heiman, and Fort Donelson in 1861. With a heavy German accent and a serious bearing, he earned the respect of his men and the nickname "Uncle Dolph." After capture and six months' imprisonment, he and his men reorganized in Mississippi. Marching in unusually warm, wet weather caused many to get the "fever," including Heiman, who died in Jackson, Mississippi, on November 16, 1862, at the age of fifty-three.

John Lancaster, Belmont Mansion

County Courthouse (c. 1872), designed by architect A. C. Bruce of Knoxville, and the Moore County Courthouse (1885).

In its time, the Second Empire style was considered modern architecture that reflected the recent international influence of the 1852–53 major addition to the Palace of the Louvre in Paris, France. Mansard roofs, dormer windows, and elaborate detailing, rather than the historicism associated with classical forms, identified the new style. Although conceived for public buildings, the style found its way into many elite Tennessee homes, such as the Collier-Crichlow House (1878–79) in Murfreesboro. Examples of community landmark buildings designed in the Second Empire style are Benjamin Fahnestock's Anderson Hall (1869) on the Maryville College campus, the Smith County Courthouse (1879), and the Robertson County Courthouse (1881), the latter designed by Nashville architect William C. Smith and expanded by Nashville architects Doughtery and Gardner in 1930. Craigmiles Hall is an attached commercial building in Cleveland that was modernized in 1880 with an elaborate Second Empire cast-iron facade.

Although a loose description of almost all architecture built during the second half of the nineteenth century, including the Italianate and Gothic forms, High Victorian architecture more specifically can be used to describe many of the more elaborate vertical buildings associated with the principles of John Ruskin in his influential book *Seven Lamps of Architecture* (1849). Referred to as High Victorian Gothic or Ruskinian Gothic, these buildings generally have polychromatic brick, patterned-roof shingles, and Gothic detailing. Perhaps the most-celebrated high Victorian Gothic building in Tennessee is Fisk University's Jubilee Hall (1873–75). Designed by New York architect Stephen Hatch, Jubilee Hall is best remembered for the Fisk Jubilee Singers, for whom the building was named. They traveled around the country singing to raise money for the financially destitute college and making

Jubilee Hall, Fisk University, Nashville. Courtesy of Library of Congress, Music Division, American nineteenth-century sheet music collection (call number M1629).

famous a new form of music called the "American Negro Spiritual."[6]

The Romanesque style is most often characterized by its red brick construction, asymmetrical form, and round-arched openings. A popular style for public buildings during the late nineteenth century, important examples include the Broad Street United Methodist Church (1893) in Cleveland, the Warren County Courthouse (1897) designed by Reuben H. Hunt, and Temperance Hall (1893), formerly a part of the American Temperance University in Harriman. Henry Hobson Richardson is the only American architect to have his name given to an architectural style, as buildings in the Richardsonian Romanesque style are so readily identified as antecedents of Richardson's Crane Memorial Library (1880–83) in Quincy, Massachusetts, the Allegheny Courthouse and Jail (1884) in Pittsburgh, Pennsylvania, and the Marshall Field Building (1885–87, razed) in Chicago. Tennessee has an impressive array of Richardsonian Romanesque buildings, including the Morristown City School (1892, now known as the Rose Cultural Center), St. John's Episcopal Cathedral (1892) in Knoxville, and Union Station (1900) in Nashville.

Three architects in particular represent the quality of design coming from the state's three Grand Divisions by the end of the Victorian era. Peter J. Williamson of Nashville was a native of Holland who immigrated to Wisconsin, where he joined the Union army and rose to the rank of major during the Civil War. Afterward, he settled in Nashville and served as a partner in the firm of Dobson and Williamson before striking out on his own. Williamson created impressive, lasting High Victorian Gothic designs for the ornate St. Luke's Episcopal Church (1873) in Cleveland, the Vanderbilt Gymnasium (1880, now art museum), the McClung Mansion (1875–76) in Knoxville, and the First Baptist (Eighth Street) Church (1888–91) in Chattanooga. His Nashville office also produced the architect Hugh C. Thompson, who is best recognized for his understated Gothic design for the Union Gospel Tabernacle (1889), later renamed the Ryman Auditorium, in Nashville.

A prominent Memphis architect during the late nineteenth century was Edward Culliat Jones (1822–1902), who was born in Charleston, South Carolina, where he practiced architecture before moving to Memphis after serving in the Civil War. His best-known designs are the Second Empire–style Woodruff-Fontaine House (1871), the Italianate J. J. Busby House (1882), and the D. T. Porter Building (1895, formerly the Continental Bank Building). Jones also designed the eclectic Beale Street Baptist Church (1867–71) that is "said to be the first built in the South by blacks for blacks."[7] Noteworthy in the church's design is the classical interior. It features plain two-story columns supporting a balcony and the appearance of arched buttressing created by curved wooden beams. This trait is a vernacular

Reuben Harrison Hunt

REUBEN HARRISON HUNT (1862–1937) WAS ONE OF THE MOST PROLIFIC ARCHITECTS IN THE Southeast. While not the most original of designers, Hunt was trusted by his many clients for his competency and trustworthiness as an architect, businessman, and community leader. By the time of his death, he had built one of the largest architectural firms in the country, with offices in both Chattanooga and Dallas, and at least one major structure in virtually every state from Virginia to Texas. As early as 1907, three decades before his retirement, Hunt listed over sixty churches, twenty-eight schools, and sixteen municipal buildings among his works. Renowned especially for his public buildings, Hunt was certainly the foremost architect in Chattanooga during his fifty-year career.

Hunt was born in 1862 in Elbert County, Georgia, the son of a Civil War veteran and farmer. Trained initially as a carpenter, he moved in 1882 to Chattanooga and found work with Adams and Bearden, a firm of local architects and contractors. This was a time of growth for Chattanooga, as Reconstruction-era industry took advantage of the city's status as a rail and river hub. Hunt spent five years as an apprentice/draftsman with Adams and Bearden before establishing an independent practice in Chattanooga in 1886, at the height of a building boom.

A devout Baptist (who often began client meetings with a prayer), Hunt's first major commission was for a new edifice for his congregation, First Baptist Church in Chattanooga. Completed in 1889 (destroyed 1968), the church was a massive pink sandstone structure, the design of which was largely influenced by the Romanesque Revival work of H. H. Richardson. Richardson's influence dominated Hunt's ecclesiastic work through the end of the century, seen, for instance, in his earliest extant building, Second Presbyterian Church in Chattanooga (1890–91).

After 1900, during the "American Renaissance," Hunt changed to a more neoclassical style, evidenced in his designs for the Chattanooga Public Library (1903–5) and Hamilton County Courthouse (1911–13). At the same time, Hunt was also influenced by the new skyscrapers of Chicago; indeed, his design for the first major office building in Chattanooga, the James Building of 1907, is worthy of Louis Sullivan.

Hunt was adept at combining his civic activities with his architectural work. A vice president of the YMCA, he designed an eight-story building in Chattanooga for the organization in 1908. He also served as Director of the Board of the Provident Insurance Company, a firm for which he designed a major office building in 1923. Noted for his political contacts, which perhaps explains his many civic contracts, Hunt was also celebrated for generosity; he sponsored several college scholarships and regularly donated to smaller congregations designs for churches, many of which were published in his three-volume series *Modern Church Designs* (1916).

One of Hunt's last buildings brought him national fame. The Federal Building in Chattanooga (1933), a fine example of a WPA Art Deco courthouse, was selected by the American Institute of Architects as one of the 150 best American buildings constructed between 1918 and 1938.

Gavin Townsend, University of Tennessee at Chattanooga

D. T. Porter Building, Memphis. Courtesy of Memphis/Shelby County Public Library and Information Center–Memphis and Shelby County Room.

adaptation of English architect James Gibbs's model of interior church design that was popular in the late-eighteenth- and early-nineteenth-century American ecclesiastical designs.

The most important of the three was Rueben H. Hunt (1862–1937), who was born in Georgia and trained as a builder and carpenter. He arrived in Chattanooga in 1882 and worked as a builder, contractor, and architect. By 1900 he had formed his third architecture company, R. H. Hunt Company, and was concentrating on designing rather than constructing buildings. He designed mostly community landmark and commercial buildings. His firm was well known throughout the South and had branch offices in Jackson, Mississippi, and Dallas, Texas. "While Hunt was not inclined toward the development of architectural theory," architectural historian Sara A. Butler wrote, "he was extremely alert to new ideas and fashion, and prompt to exploit their practical values to the fullest."[8] His firm was one of the most prominent and prolific firms in the South, designing hundreds of buildings in the Beaux Arts, Classical Revival, and Stripped Classical styles. The larger architectural community recognized his work in journals such as *Architecture and Building, The Inland Architect, Pencil Points,* and *The Architectural Record.* Toward the end of his career his firm concentrated on designing churches, and produced an influential pattern book about church architecture. His best-known designs are in Chattanooga, including the Second Presbyterian Church (1891), the Beaux Arts–style Hamilton County Courthouse (1911), the early skyscrapers of the James Building and MacClellan Buildings, and the Solomon Federal Building (1932–35), recognized in the 1930s as one of the state's preeminent modern-style office buildings.

While Hunt's Chattanooga skyscrapers remain downtown architectural anchors, the true early center of the tall building in Tennessee was Memphis, which enjoyed a tremendous business and population boom in the late 1890s and early 1900s after the construction of the Frisco Bridge across the Mississippi River. Memphis's tall buildings provide a glimpse of how this building type evolved in the Volunteer State.

Early tall buildings are all examples of load-bearing masonry construction. The B. Lowenstein and Brothers Building (1882) is a masonry-constructed building with cast-iron and brick piers and cast-iron detailing. Designed by Mathias Harvey Baldwin, this five-story commercial building is comparable to some of New York's early tall buildings in its now famous cast-iron district. Once architects and engineers invented how to build a tall building safely and practically, their next challenge was to ornament it so that the detailing would be in proportion to the scale of the building and not look awkward or overstated. American architect Louis Sullivan promoted ornamenting a building based on the three-part composition of the classical column—base, shaft, and cornice. Constructed in the Beaux Arts classical style, the five-story Joseph N. Oliver Building (1904), designed by Alsup and Woods, is a masonry-constructed building demonstrating a Sullivanesque-like tripartite configuration of the facade. Another building demonstrating the tripartite facade is the Exchange Building (1912), designed by Neander M. Woods Jr.

To be classified as a skyscraper, a building must be tall, have a steel frame, and include an elevator. The first skyscraper in the country was the Home Insurance Building (1883–85, razed) designed by William LeBaron Jenny in Chicago. Only ten years later, the D. T. Porter Building (1895, formerly the Continental Bank Building) designed by Edward Culliat Jones became Memphis's first skyscraper. When built, this eleven-story building was the tallest building south of St. Louis. It was also noteworthy as having the world's tallest hot-water circulating system and one of the first elevators in the South.[9] The twenty-two-story Lincoln-America Tower (1924), designed by Isaac A. Baum of the St. Louis firm Boyer and Baum, is similar in form to Cass Gilbert's Woolworth Building (1913) in New York in its central tower, overall verticality, and historic design references. This well-proportioned and exquisitely detailed building is one of Memphis's most successful designs. The Bluff City also has an excellent example of the concrete, steel, and glass high-rise of the late twentieth century in the Luther Towers (1970–71), designed by Walk Jones and Francis Mah, Architects. This building was constructed as a high rise for the elderly and is notable for its Mah-LeMessurier structural system. This structural system is one that Francis Mah and William LeMessurier perfected to be constructed in eighty-nine days. Architectural historians Eugene J. Johnson and Robert D. Russell Jr. describe the structural system: "The projecting vertical piers, which form the vertical structure, are made up of eight-foot prestressed concrete modules that contain the bathrooms. The horizontal members were then hung on the verticals to produce the floors and also wind bracing. The verticals, clear echoes of Louis Kahn's servant spaces, produce strong shadow patterns that considerably enliven the otherwise plain walls."[10]

The emergence of the modern skylines of both Memphis and Nashville were well underway at the beginning of the twentieth century, and new design ideas were continually coming from a rapidly expanding number of professional architectural firms. If the tradition of the builder and the apprentice architect dominates the first one hundred years of building history in Tennessee, then the rise of the architectural profession—documented in part by the establishment of chapters of the American Institute of Architects in Nashville and Memphis—and the emergence of large professional firms are important trends of twentieth-century Tennessee architecture.

Thomas Marr founded the Nashville-based Marr and Holman firm in 1897. One of Tennessee's first technically trained architects, Marr worked as a draftsman before attending Galludet College, then the Massachusetts Institute of Technology to study architecture. Joseph Holman worked his way up from office boy to partner and contributed to the firm's emergence as an architectural design leader in the Southeast. The firm's commissions ranged from residential architecture to commercial buildings to ecclesiastical buildings, and its architects were comfortable working in both revival styles and the emerging modern movement in American architecture. Marr and Holman became known for its high-profile government commissions in the 1930s and 1940s; it designed nine Tennessee county courthouses, including the Colonial Revival–style Pickett County Courthouse (1935) and Hardin County

Post office lobby, Nashville, n.d. Tennessee Historical Society, Marr-Holman Collection–Addition, Manuscripts Division, Tennessee State Library and Archives. Courtesy of TSLA.

Courthouse (1950) as well as the "Stripped Classicism" or "PWA Moderne" of the Franklin County Courthouse (1935) and the Weakley County Courthouse (1949–50). Another Stripped Classicism landmark was the U.S. post office in Nashville, renovated in 2000–2001 as the home of the Frist Center for Visual Arts. The firm's Streamline Moderne–style Belle Meade Theater and Shopping Center (1940) in Nashville was recognized for its innovative design by the June 1941 issue of *Architectural Record.*

In 1915 Charles Irving Barber (1887–1962), his cousin D. West Barber, and Ben McMurray established the Knoxville firm of Barber and McMurray. A prominent southeastern firm, Barber and McMurray designed residences and community landmark buildings. Charles Barber was formally trained in the Beaux Arts style in Europe and the University of Pennsylvania, but he gained invaluable practical experience, especially in domestic architecture, from work with his father George Franklin Barber. The elder Barber was a successful Knoxville builder and architectural writer, who published popular architectural pattern books and mail-order designs for houses. West Barber and Ben McMurray also attended the University of Pennsylvania; within the firm McMurray ran the office and kept clients happy while West Barber produced the working drawings for Charles Barber's designs. Barber and McMurray have designed many buildings in the changing architectural styles of the twentieth century, with its collegiate

McKissack and McKissack Architects

McKISSACK AND McKISSACK, THE NATION'S OLDEST AFRICAN AMERICAN OWNED ARCHITECTURAL and engineering firm, began its operation in Nashville, where the company was headquartered until moving to Philadelphia in 2001. McKissack men managed the firm in its beginning; however, the McKissack women now own and operate it.

The McKissack family maintains a prolonged building heritage, dating back to the first Moses McKissack (1790–1865), an Ashanti from West Africa who was sold into human bondage to William McKissack of North Carolina. In 1822, he married a Cherokee woman named Mirian (1804–1865), and their union produced fourteen children. Although physically enslaved, McKissack I became a master builder and taught his ninth child, Gabriel Moses McKissack (1840–1922), the building trade. Continuing the family's tradition, the son taught the building trade to his son, Moses McKissack III (1879–1952).

Born in Pulaski and educated in the town's segregated public schools, McKissack III began his career working with his father. In 1890, a Pulaski architect hired McKissack III. Serving as a construction superintendent, he built houses in Pulaski, Mount Pleasant, and Columbia, Tennessee, and Decatur, Alabama. His construction proficiency earned him the reputation as a superb artisan.

In 1905, McKissack III moved to Nashville and opened his construction business in the Napier Court Building. He constructed a home for Vanderbilt University's dean of architecture and engineering. Later, he designed and built other homes in the West End area. His first major commission was Fisk University's Carnegie Library. He and his brother, Calvin Lunsford McKissack (1890–1968), formed McKissack and McKissack and in 1922 became Tennessee's first professional African American architectural firm. They were successful across the southern states with their most notable works being for African American educational and religious institutions.

Gymnasium, Pearl High School, Nashville. Photograph by Carroll Van West.

In the 1930s the firm received various Works Progress Administration and Public Works Administration contracts, including the commission for Pearl High School in Nashville. Later they designed several federal housing complexes. In 1942, the federal government awarded McKissack and McKissack a $5.7 million construction contract for the Ninety-ninth Pursuit Squadron Air Base, a World War II African American combat air unit based in Tuskegee, Alabama. During Franklin Roosevelt's administration, McKissack III received an appointment to the White House Conference on Housing Problems.

Five of McKissack's Nashville buildings are listed in the National Register of Historic Places: the Fisk Carnegie Library (1908); the George W. Hubbard House (1920); the Neoclassical Morris Memorial Building (1924); the Neoclassical Capers C. M. E. Church (1925); and the modernist Pearl High School (1936–37). Additionally, the firm designed several buildings on the campuses of Tennessee State University and Meharry Medical College. Recently artist Red Grooms recognized the McKissacks' contribution to the state's building heritage by featuring a likeness of the brothers on the Tennessee Fox Trot Carousel, located in Nashville's Riverfront Park.

After Calvin McKissack's demise, the scepter passed to Moses III's youngest son, William DeBerry McKissack (1925–1988). He directed the company until 1983, when an incapacitating stroke caused him to relinquish his post. Subsequent to his resignation, the firm's management shifted to his spouse, Leatrice Buchanan McKissack. In 1987, the Tennessee Building Commission awarded McKissack and McKissack the design contract for the National Civil Rights Museum in Memphis. Following her husband's death, McKissack's daughters, who were professional engineers, joined the company. Together these women opened satellite offices in several cities.

Over the years, the firm has designed approximately 5,000 structures. Today, not only is McKissack and McKissack diversified by gender, it is also a racially diversified architectural and engineering firm.

Linda T. Wynn, Tennessee Historical Commission/Fisk University

Gothic buildings for the University of Tennessee being its best-known landmarks. Their other notable works include the classically inspired Alex Bonnyman House (1916), the Church Street United Methodist Church in Knoxville, and the affordable housing for Norris, Pickwick, and Wheeler Dam sites (1930s) for the Tennessee Valley Authority. The firm has received many national honors and recognition. Although the last original partner died in 1969, the firm remains important in Tennessee's architectural community, with a recent landmark commission being the expansion of the East Tennessee Historical Society in downtown Knoxville.

McKissack and McKissack Architects was Tennessee's first professional African American architectural firm, formed in 1922. The McKissack family's heritage in building began when the first Moses McKissack (1790–1865) became a master builder as a slave in North Carolina. His son Gabriel Moses McKissack II (1840–1922) and grandson Gabriel Moses III (1879–1952) both became builders. Moses McKissack III was born in Pulaski, Tennessee, and by the time he was eleven years old he was working in a Pulaski architectural firm. In 1905, he moved to Nashville to open his own construction firm. The Carnegie Library on Fisk University Campus was his first major commission. His brother Calvin Lunsford McKissack (1890–1968) participated in the business and they both became registered architects in 1921, soon after the state began to require it.

During the twentieth century, McKissack and McKissack designed many private residences, community landmark buildings, and housing projects. Its prominent Tennessee designs include the classically inspired Morris Memorial Building (1923–1925), the Colonial Revival Bridgeforth School (1927) in Pulaski, and the Egyptian Revival– and Art Deco–influenced Universal Life Insurance Company (1949) in Memphis. In 1942, it received the largest government contract ever granted to an African American firm for the construction of the Ninety-ninth Pursuit Squadron Air Base in Tuskegee, Alabama. The firm remained Nashville-based until it moved its corporate offices to Philadelphia in 2001.

The professionalization of architecture in Tennessee during the first half of the twentieth century brought sophistication and technological improvements, but it did little to alter most architectural tastes in the state. Most Tennesseans still viewed classicism, as celebrated at the Tennessee Centennial Exposition of 1897, as proper architectural expression, especially for public buildings. The exposition's centerpiece was a careful reconstruction of the Parthenon, the ancient temple of Athens. Although originally built of impermanent materials, in 1920 the city decided to reconstruct the Parthenon in reinforced concrete under the supervision of Nashville architect Russell Hart and architectural historian William Bell Dinsmoor. As the focus of Nashville's Centennial Park, the Parthenon remains the only exact-sized replica ever built of the temple and the only building that remained in its original location after the exposition. Like the Parthenon, most of the buildings in the exposition reflected the classical influence to some degree, including the classical design of the Woman's Building (1897) by Nashville artist Sara Ward Conley. The only building Conley designed, it was purportedly styled after Andrew Jackson's Hermitage. Judging from photographs of the building, however, it was actually a Beaux Arts-style building with elaborate details. Conley received high praise for its beautiful and spacious design, which included a salesroom, restaurant, model kitchen, grand staircase, rotunda, and gardens. Early-twentieth-century government buildings of all shapes, sizes, and purposes embraced and celebrated the classical tradition. In 1901, for instance, the federal government's supervising architect of the Treasury, James Knox Taylor, announced the return to classical style of architecture in federal building design. Styles such as Beaux Arts, Renaissance Revival, Classical Revival, and Colonial Revival then dominated federal buildings. Designs attributed to Knox in Tennessee include the Renaissance Revival style of the Murfreesboro Post Office (now the Center for the Arts) and the colonial revival-style post offices in Paris and Union City. Newly constructed county courthouses in Tennessee soon mirrored the architectural styles of the federal buildings as interpreted by local and regional architects.

The Beaux Arts style is found in the Henry County Courthouse (c. 1897) and the Hamilton County Courthouse (1911) by Rueben H. Hunt and is especially strongly expressed in the Giles County Courthouse. Constructed in 1909 and designed by Alabama architect Benjamin N. Smith, this landmark building embodies the ornate classicism associated with the École des Beaux Arts in Paris. More popular was the Classical Revival style, characterized by dominant porticos, prominent columns, and monumentality. Four representative examples are the Blount County Courthouse (1909) designed by the Knoxville firm of Baumann and Baumann, the massive Shelby County Courthouse (1909) designed by New York City architect James Gamble Rogers, the Washington County Courthouse (1912) by Baumann and Baumann, and the Carroll County Courthouse (1930) by the Nashville firm of Hart, Freeland, and Roberts.

The Colonial Revival style was generally based on the Georgian style of architecture that was popular in the eighteenth century and was associated with a return to the nation's historical roots. In the South, the influence of the architectural restoration of Williamsburg, Virginia, in the late 1920s and 1930s influenced the design of both public and residential architecture. Colonial Revival courthouses range from the understated to the ornate. At first glance, the Hickman County Courthouse (1926) and the Jackson County Courthouse (1927), designed by the Nashville firm Tisdale, Pinson and Stone, are restrained interpretations of the style reflecting the tastes and budgets of rural counties. But then the Hancock County Courthouse (1930), by Knoxville architect Allen Dryden, and the Cannon County Courthouse (1934–35), by Nashville architect George D. Waller, are almost textbook-perfect examples of Colonial Revival style from two other rural Tennessee counties. The popularity of Colonial Revival style for public buildings has waned at times, but never disappeared in the state as evident in the post–World War II county courthouses in Savannah, Athens, Fayetteville, and Altamont.

The master of the middle-class Colonial Revival dwelling was Memphis architect J. Frazer Smith, who popularized the style not only in his own commissions but also through his work for the Federal Housing Administration in the 1930s. Wealthy Tennesseans preferred the more ornate Georgian Revival style, which harkened to the English tradition of the Country House. Bryant Fleming, a landscape architect and scholar from Ithaca, New York, designed the grandest country estates in the new suburbs outside of Memphis in his Carrier House (1926) and Cheekwood (1929–32) in Nashville.

The Colonial Revival was not the only architectural revival shaping the state's built environment in the first half of the twentieth century. Among the buildings that represent this eclectic period of historicism in Tennessee design are the Spanish Colonial Revival–style Scates Hall (1921) designed by Everett Woods at the University of Memphis, the Mediterranean Revival–style Dyersburg United Methodist Church (1923), and the Egyptian Revival–style Ballard and Ballard Obelisk Flour Company (1924) in Memphis. The Collegiate Gothic style greatly influenced school and college architecture in hundreds of school buildings across the state. Coherent, expressive, and consistent campuses of Collegiate Gothic style developed at Rhodes College in Memphis, Scarritt College (now the Scarritt-Bennett Center) in Nashville, and the University of the South in Sewanee. Other campuses, such as the University of Tennessee, the University of Chattanooga, Fisk University, and Vanderbilt University, had new Collegiate Gothic–style classrooms, dormitories, and administration buildings added to their earlier Victorian and Classical structures.

Scaritt College for Christian Workers. Courtesy of Peabody Collection, Photographic Archives, Vanderbilt University.

One of the best Collegiate Gothic designers was architect Henry Clossen Hibbs (1882–1949), who was born in New Jersey and received his architectural training at the University of Pennsylvania. Hibbs made his first mark on the state's colleges as the supervising architect (for the Boston firm of Ludlow and Peabody) of the George Peabody College for Teachers in Nashville. The Peabody campus, recognized as a National Historical Landmark for its architecture, is an impressive statement of classicism, inspired by and

J. Frazer Smith

JOE FRAZER SMITH OF MEMPHIS HAD A DISTINGUISHED CAREER AS AN ARCHITECT WITH A HIGHLY diversified practice. Born in 1897 in Canton, Mississippi, and educated at the Georgia Institute of Technology and the Naval School of Architectural and Steel Construction at Newport News, Virginia, Smith completed his studies in 1921. After three years with an established firm, he broke away and began a meteoric rise to the top of the architectural profession in Memphis. From 1924 to 1927, he was responsible for a number of residential commissions, culminating with the design of the Kimbrough Place Subdivision, a large-scale residential development which included the home of its developer, J. F. Kimbrough Jr.

Despite the economic ravages of the Great Depression, the decade of the 1930s was the most productive period in Smith's life. He was active on the local, state, and national levels of the American Institute of Architects. He helped create an employment program for the nation's architects called the Historic American Buildings Survey (HABS) and was appointed regional director of HABS in 1935.

Smith won commissions to design the first public housing projects for Memphis. Lauderdale Courts and Dixie Homes, begun in 1935, and Foote Homes and Lamar Terrace, from 1938, had campuslike settings, with low, residential-scale buildings not unlike the atmosphere of single-family neighborhoods. Among the first in the nation funded by the Public Works Administration, the Memphis projects instantly became a standard for the country.

B. W. Horner, director of the Federal Housing Administration (FHA) in Tennessee, approached Smith in 1936. The FHA was charged with stimulating economic growth by building new houses for low- to moderate-income families. Smith formed the Memphis Small House Construction Bureau, a consortium of mortgage lenders, building supply houses, home builders, and architects, loosely based on the model of the Architect's Small House Service Bureau of Minnesota, begun in 1919. Member architects provided plans and specifications for a variety of houses. The potential homeowner selected a plan to fit his budget, knowing that the mortgage lender could approve the project and be guaranteed mortgage insurance through the FHA. The architect who designed each plan oversaw construction and ensured that the house was built according to specifications. The program was a huge success, having an immediate effect in Memphis and copied by other cities. While the number of houses developed to the Bureau's plans is not known, the FHA reported in 1938 that twelve hundred houses had been insured in the previous year, and of these, 85 percent were architect-designed, as opposed to 15 percent in the year before.

Smith's experience in subdivision design took an important new turn in 1938, when developer William C. Chandler retained him to design two radically different Memphis subdivisions that set a new standard for housing developments over the next several decades. The Rosemary Lane Subdivision, with thirty-three small but distinctive houses sited along curving streets, demonstrated that a quality residential environment could be created for low- and middle-income homeowners. In the Village subdivision, Smith created a neighborhood of more expensive houses on large lots, with an intimate scale reminiscent of a quaint colonial village and strongly influenced by the namesake of its principal street, Williamsburg Lane. The one-story brick cottage with Colonial Revival details became the archetype of residential architecture in Memphis's eastern suburbs for decades after the development of the Village.

Smith's interest in historical buildings emerged early in his career, perhaps following his travels to Europe in the mid-1920s. Beginning around 1931, he made extended trips throughout the South to sketch some of the region's most significant historical properties. Smith continued to study antebellum plantation houses of Tennessee and its neighboring states for years, compiling his materials into his book, *White Pillars,* published in 1941. While not the first architectural history of Southern places, it was innovative in its examination of architecture on a regional basis. A standard reference for many years, it remains a useful and reliable source. Smith continued his successful architectural practice until 1957. He died while on a business trip in Little Rock.

John Linn Hopkins and Marsha R. Oates
Hopkins and Associates Preservation Consultants

modeled after the work of Thomas Jefferson and Benjamin H. Latrobe at the University of Virginia. Due to the success of Peabody, Hibbs received commissions from the Meharry Medical School, Fisk University, Middle Tennessee State University, Vanderbilt University, and Ward-Belmont College. His campus plan and designs for Scarritt College in Nashville won the American Institute of Architects gold medal in 1929. One of Hibbs's most lasting legacies is the Collegiate Gothic campus of Memphis's Rhodes College and its original six buildings constructed between 1923 and 1925. Considered by architectural historians Eugene J. Johnson and Robert D. Russell Jr. as one of the city's "real architectural surprises," Rhodes College reflects "the architectural and social ideals that lay behind the Gothic Revival style of building for American college campuses in the early part of this century."[11]

The 1930s interjected both the New Deal and modernism into Tennessee architecture. While a few Prairie-style houses were constructed in urban suburbs, and a new roadside aesthetic began to develop along the state's new highway system during the 1920s, modern styles such as the International, Art Deco, and Art Moderne did not appear in any numbers until the Depression decade. During the early 1930s, the Treasury Department sponsored the construction of three huge new federal buildings—combination post offices, courthouses, and offices—in Knoxville, Chattanooga, and Nashville. All three introduced urban Tennesseans to the "Stripped Classical" style, originated by architect Paul Cret. The new style was a transition between classical architecture, with its pediments and pilasters, and modern architecture, especially the Art Deco and International styles, in its sleek, hard-edged surfaces. It represented the synthesis of the "traditionalists," who favored the use of classical details, and the "modernists," who favored streamlined, smooth, unadorned buildings and rejected historical antecedents. The Stripped Classical style remained popular through the 1950s, as demonstrated by architect George Awsumb's design for Baron Hirsch Synagogue (1955) in Memphis. The synagogue is a modern interpretation of the Greek Revival, constructed in limestone with few windows to produce a flat and smooth wall surface usually associated with the International style.

The closely related Art Deco and Art Moderne styles were most popular in the cities and were used for all types of buildings. In Memphis, E. L. Harris designed the Fairview High School (1930) while Walk C. Jones incorporated Art Deco designs into the downtown Mid-South Cotton Growers Building (1936). Another Memphis architect, Noland Van Powell, used the Streamlined Moderne style for a number of Greyhound bus stations along the new federal highways, including the stations in Jackson and Waverly, still extant. The Nashville skyscraper, the Sukeham Building with its Tennessee Theater

Norris Dam. Courtesy of the Tennessee Valley Authority.

(razed), was an instant modern landmark, designed by Marr and Holman. Bristol's Paramount Theater (1931) is an excellent example of how the entertainment industry rapidly embraced modernism, and many Art Deco/Art Moderne theaters were built across the state during the decade, including the extant Crockett Theater in Lawrenceburg, the Oldham Theater in Winchester, and the Ruffin Theater in Covington.

Tennesseans gave comparatively little attention to the International style—the epitome of modernism—but in its handful of examples, Tennessee boasts some nationally important landmarks. Dixie Homes in Memphis is a New Deal model public housing project funded by the Public Works Administration. An impressive consortium of Memphis design talent, including J. Frazer Smith, Walk C. Jones Sr., Everett Woods, R. J. Regan, and Herbert M. Burnham, produced an International-style neighborhood of twenty-eight one-story and forty-eight two-story housing units scattered on a forty-two-acre site. Critics then and now have praised the project's plan of blending human-scale apartments into a larger urbanscape of public parks and open space. The modern comprehensive planning associated with the Tennessee Valley Authority was nowhere better demonstrated than at the Norris project in Anderson County. TVA architects and engineers produced a striking complex of modernity, where architects and engineers were "given tens of thousands of acres to redesign as a nature reserve, as long as they placed a huge modern machine in the middle of it."[12] That huge modern machine was Norris Dam, designed by Roland Wank, which measures 1,860 feet in length and 265 feet in height. The powerhouse was another marvel of modern engineering, with a generating capacity of 100,800 kilowatts of electricity. On the other side of Anderson County, developing almost overnight it seemed in 1942–43, was a second massive technological wonderland, the Clinton Engineering Works, better known as Oak Ridge, whose city plan and residences came from the important New York firm of Skidmore and Owings (later Skimore, Owings and Merrill).

In the cities, the most significant statement of modernism at midcentury was the Life and Casualty Tower (1956) in Nashville. Its architect, Edwin A. Keeble (1905–1979), was born in Monteagle and raised in Nashville. He studied engineering at Vanderbilt University and then architecture at the University of Pennsylvania, the École des Hautes Études Aristiques at Fountainebleau, and the École des Beaux Arts in Paris. Upon completing his education, he returned to Nashville to practice alone and then in partnership with Francis B. Warfield. The firm of Keeble and Warfield designed many residences and public buildings over the next fifteen years, including for the Works Progress Administration several National Guard armories such as the identical stone Murfreesboro Armory (1940) and Shelbyville Armory (1941), both on the Old Dixie Highway. Keeble joined the Navy as a lieutenant in 1944. After World War II, he returned to Nashville to practice architecture until he retired in 1970. Keeble worked statewide—witness his Stripped Classical–style McLean Baptist Church (1953) in Memphis—but his best work remained in Nashville.

By 1960, the architectural profession had achieved a level of success and prominence unmatched by any other period in Tennessee history. The state even had its first—and only—building designed by master American architect Frank Lloyd Wright. The Shavin House (1950) on Missionary Ridge in Chattanooga is a good example of one of Wright's Usonian houses. Wright, who favored blending buildings with the surroundings, constructed the house in Tennessee limestone and Crab Orchard Stone.

Wright was the first of the acknowledged masters of modern American architecture to receive a Tennessee commission. Over the next generation, the firm Skidmore, Owings and Merrill designed office buildings for both Memphis and Nashville. Edward Larrabee Barnes (b. 1922), best known for his design of the Burlington Vermont Cathedral, was the architect of the Knoxville Museum of Art (1990) encased in pink Tennessee marble and located in downtown Knoxville's World's Fair Park. The firm Kohn Pederson Fox designed Nashville's postmodern-style Third National (now SunTrust) Financial Center (1983–86), which "combines historical details with the modern shine of glass and steel skyscraper. In this case, the building reflects the architectural traditions of Strickland's earlier Egyptian Revival church,"[13] which is across the street. Boston architect Robert A. M. Stern designed one of the first landmark buildings of the twenty-first century, the new Metropolitan Nashville and Davidson County Public Library (2001), in a modern revival of classical style.

Even more important, Tennessee firms produced their own significant designs of modern American architecture. Miesian style, named for master architect Ludwig Mies van der Rohe, is characterized by regularity and precision of rectangular forms where structural framing (usually steel or concrete-clad steel) and glass walls create a modular pattern. An excellent example of a Miesian-style building is the First Tennessee Bank Building in Memphis. Designed by the Memphis architectural firm of Walk C. Jones Jr., this building incorporates the same design principles as those found in Mies's and Phillip Johnson's New York Seagrams Building (1961–64) but on a more modest scale. The Lawrence County Courthouse (1974), designed by Hart, Freeland, Roberts Architects of Nashville, is an excellent but rare example of New Formalism style set in a rural county seat. Another Nashville firm, Yearwood and Johnson, designed the Wayne County Courthouse in 1975. It came almost a decade after influential Philadelphia architect Robert Venturi wrote his book *Complexity and Contradiction in Architecture,* in which he promoted a new style that has become known as postmodern where there is an abstract reinterpretation of historical forms using modern materials. Constructed of reinforced fireproof concrete, the Wayne County Courthouse's overall form is that of a geometric broken pediment with a modern clock tower protruding from the center portion. A recent modernist landmark is the Eskind Biomedical Library at the Vanderbilt Medical Center. Designed by Davis, Broady and Associates of New York in association with Thomas, Miller and Partners of Brentwood, the library features a forty-nine-foot-high glass tensile curtain wall, which, at the time of its construction, was the nation's first self-supported tensile curtain wall. The Bicentennial Mall State Park, an urban landscape by Tuck Hinton Architects and Ross/ Fowler Landscape Architects, memorializes state history while creating a new vista of the north elevation of the state capitol. The prominence of the L&C Tower on the Nashville skyline has been eclipsed by the soaring twin spires of the BellSouth Headquarters (1992–94), one of several modern Nashville landmarks (Opryland Hotel and Centennial Medical Center are others) designed by Earl Swensson Associates.

The rise of the architectural profession to a place of prominence and achievement also, finally, reintroduced women to the field of academic architecture in Tennessee. There were a handful of women architects in 1900. Elizabeth Pritz (1879–?),[14] for example, trained at Columbia University in architecture and worked with several firms in New York and Nashville, including Dougherty and Gardner in Nashville. Pritz concentrated mostly on designing residences, but unfortunately none of her extant buildings have been identified. A new generation of women architects, who emerged largely from the state's architectural schools in the last thirty years, is now adding its own legacies to the state's design traditions. For example, in 1998 architect Harriet Hall Cates, the granddaughter of Henry Hibbs, was in charge of the rehabilitation of Fisk University's Cravath Hall, a building her grandfather had designed in 1930. Diane Dixson in 1987 helped to establish and remains a principal of the Memphis firm of Clark Dixson Associates, which has designed the University of Memphis Student Center, the museum at the Chucalissa Archaeological Park in Memphis, and other public and private buildings in the region.

By the end of the twentieth century, Tennessee architecture was more diverse, professional, and sophisticated. Yet the introduction of many new styles, forms, and building materials had not moved many Tennesseans away from their assumption that Tennessee design was best expressed by classicism, like that of the state Capitol. Tennessee's architectural future will be built out of the design legacies of its past.

NOTES

1. The dates of construction were generally obtained from secondary sources. Whenever a date is an estimate of the authors, it will be noted with *circa* (i.e., c. 1900).
2. James Patrick, *Architecture in Tennessee, 1768–1897* (Knoxville: Univ. of Tennessee Press, 1981), 7.
3. Carroll Van West, *Tennessee's Historic Landscapes: A Traveler's Guide* (Knoxville: Univ. of Tennessee Press, 1995), 78.
4. Patrick, *Architecture in Tennessee,* 118.
5. Ibid.
6. Eleanor Graham, *Nashville: A Short History and Selected Buildings* (Nashville: Historical Commission of Metropolitan Nashville–Davidson County, 1973), 97.
7. Eugene J. Johnson and Robert D. Russell Jr., *Memphis: An Architectural Guide* (Knoxville: Univ. of Tennessee Press, 1990), 145.
8. Sara A. Butler, "Rueben Harrison Hunt," in *The Tennessee Encyclopedia of History and Culture,* ed. Carroll Van West (Nashville: Tennessee Historical Society, 1998), 452.
9. Johnson and Russell, *Memphis,* 21.
10. Ibid, 300.
11. Ibid, 188, 189.
12. Carroll Van West, *The New Deal Landscape of Tennessee* (Knoxville: Univ. of Tennessee Press, 2001), 221.
13. West, *Tennessee's Historic Landscapes,* 98.
14. Many thanks to Anne-Leslie Owens at Middle Tennessee State University for allowing me to use her research on Conley and Pritz.

Suggested Readings

Brumbaugh, Thomas, et. al. *Architecture of Middle Tennessee.* Nashville: Vanderbilt Univ. Press, 1974.

Johnson, Eugene J., and Robert D. Russell Jr. *Memphis: An Architectural Guide.* Knoxville: Univ. of Tennessee Press, 1990.

Kreyling, Christine M., Wesley Paine, Charles W. Warterfield, Jr., and Susan Ford Wiltshire. *Classical Nashville: Athens of the South.* Nashville: Vanderbilt Univ. Press, 1996.

McNabb, William R. *Tradition, Innovation and Romantic Images: The Architecture of Historic Knoxville.* Knoxville: Frank H. McClung Museum, 1991.

Morgan, William. *Collegiate Gothic: The Architecture of Rhodes College.* Columbia: Univ. of Missouri Press, 1989.

Patrick, James. *Architecture in Tennessee, 1768–1897.* Knoxville: Univ. of Tennessee Press, 1981.

West, Carroll Van. *Tennessee's Historical Landscapes: A Traveler's Guide.* Knoxville: Univ. of Tennessee Press, 1995.

West, Carroll Van, Connie L. Lester, Anne-Leslie Owens, and Margaret D. Binnicker, eds. *Tennessee Encyclopedia of History and Culture.* Nashville: Rutledge Hill, 1998. Online ed. at http://tennesseeencyclopedia.net, Univ. of Tennessee Press, 2002.

Four

Sculpture in Tennessee
2000 Years

Susan W. Knowles
Pikeville, Tennessee

Before the first exploration of what is now Tennessee by foreign adventurers, before the first Tennessee history was "written" in letters sent back to sponsors of the overland expeditions, before the first European settlers arrived, before Tennessee war heroes were commemorated by portraits in marble and bronze, before the establishment of art societies, academies, and museums, the original inhabitants of Tennessee recorded observations and reflected rituals of everyday life in artistic objects made from materials close at hand. Sculpture is one of the most ancient cultural traditions in Tennessee.

Early Artisans of the Tennessee Country

A small stone smoking pipe, uncovered in West Tennessee by the Tennessee Division of Archeology, depicts a crouching rabbit. An artist of the Woodland Period (1000 B.C. to A.D. 900) gracefully incised the rabbit ears so that they lay back against the head and carved eyes that look out unblinking. The sculpture so successfully captures the completely motionless posture of a rabbit trying not to be noticed that it rings true to contemporary experience. The limestone, which has been chipped and carved into a relatively smooth form by a confident hand, bears no identifiable tool marks.

From the artisans of the Mississippian period (A.D. 900–1600) come images of the human figure, some as tall as four feet. Seated figures made of native sandstone have been found mostly in northern Middle Tennessee. The males sit in a one-raised-knee posture and have a distinctive hairstyle: two coiled plaits above the forehead and a single braid down the back; the females sit back on their feet, both knees on the ground. They have open mouths, long curved noses, and staring, almond-shaped eyes. Examples like this can be found on permanent display at the Frank H. McClung Museum, University of Tennessee, Knoxville, and in the Rockefeller Wing, Metropolitan Museum of Art, New York City.

Numerous pieces of Mississippian Period pottery, made from Tennessee clay lightened (or tempered) with ground freshwater shells, attest to a prolific ceramic tradition. Many of these small bowls and water bottles are effigies, which have stylized human or animal heads. They were found along with small ceramic seated male and female figurines, three to six inches in height, in stone grave burial sites alongside rivers in and around Middle Tennessee. Many depict seated females with severely rounded backs and protruding spinal columns. A number of the vessel forms have painted decorations. Their shapes—distended bellies and open backs—are dictated by their function as bowls or bottles. Images of frogs, owls, turtles, deer, beaver, mountain lions (or

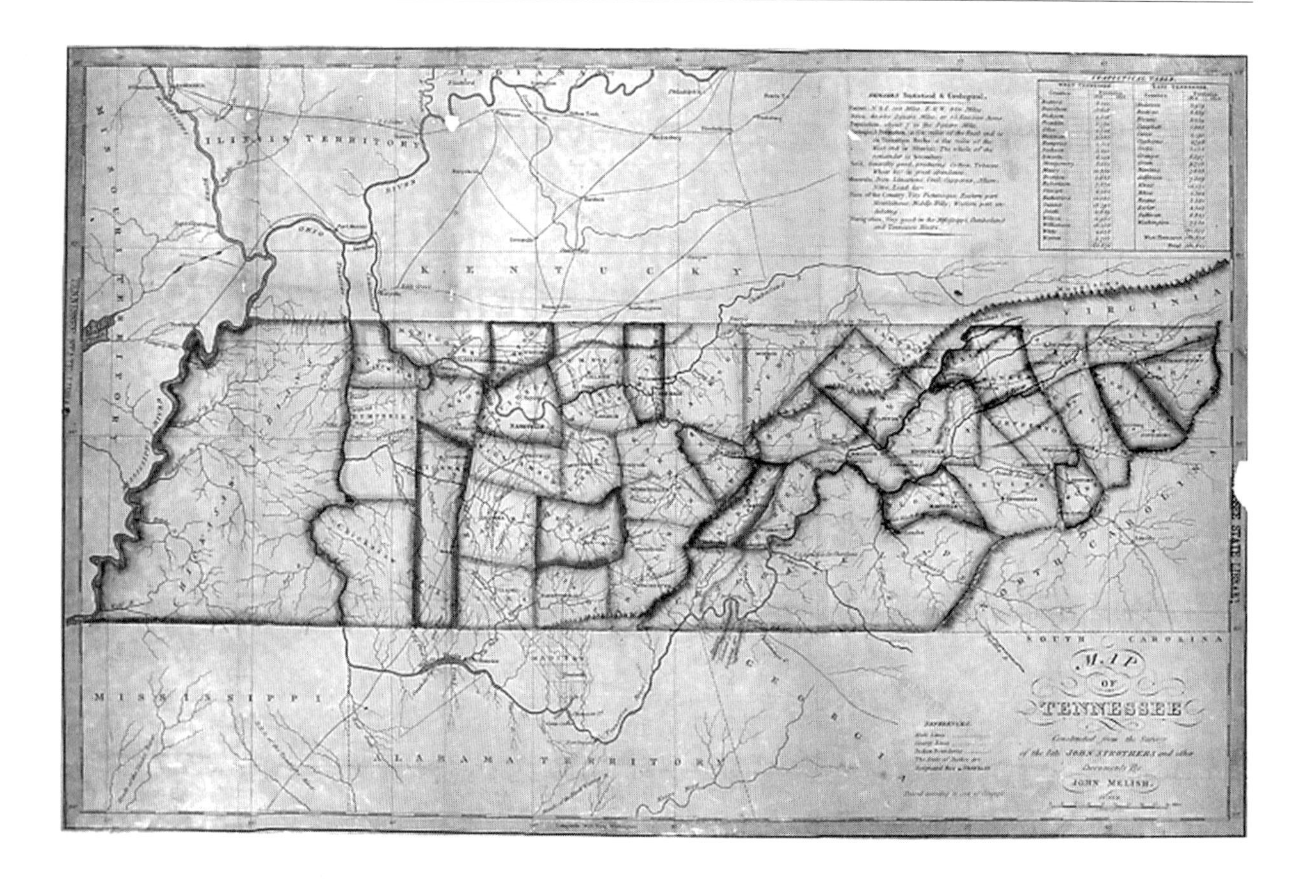

Map of Tennessee by John Melish, c. 1818. Map Collection, No. 1867, Tennessee State Library and Archives. Courtesy of TSLA.

bobcats), fish, and waterfowl are clearly articulated by species, sometimes wearing facial expressions that bear witness to the liveliness of the artist who made them.

Another example of pre-Columbian artistry is a group of two- to four-inch-diameter gorgets (round ornaments made from conch shells once worn suspended by a thong against the chest). Sometimes plain and sometimes incised with symmetrical patterns like the pileated woodpecker circling a sun form, these pieces were carefully and beautifully crafted from non-native shells that may well have been acquired by trade with inhabitants of the Mississippi Gulf Coast.

Few purely decorative objects have thus far been discovered in association with the Overhill Cherokee and Chickasaw peoples who encountered the earliest explorers, trappers, and traders coming into Tennessee during the sixteenth and seventeenth centuries. The making of utilitarian objects, such as log canoes, tools, utensils, and weapons, appears to have taken precedence over sculptural production during the tumultuous period of European settlement. Likewise, Tennessee's pioneer population, arriving at the end of the eighteenth century, had little time for artistic endeavors other than careful craftsmanship in the making of furniture and useful items for their log and brick houses. Some wealthier early Tennesseans, moving from eastern colonial cities, brought along family portraits, or, later, commissioned paintings from artists or itinerant portrait painters. Sculptural works in Tennessee from this period are all but nonexistent.

While there was little painting or sculpture in Tennessee's first museum collection (founded in 1818 by portrait painter Ralph E. W. Earl, who lived for many years at The Hermitage), there was a great

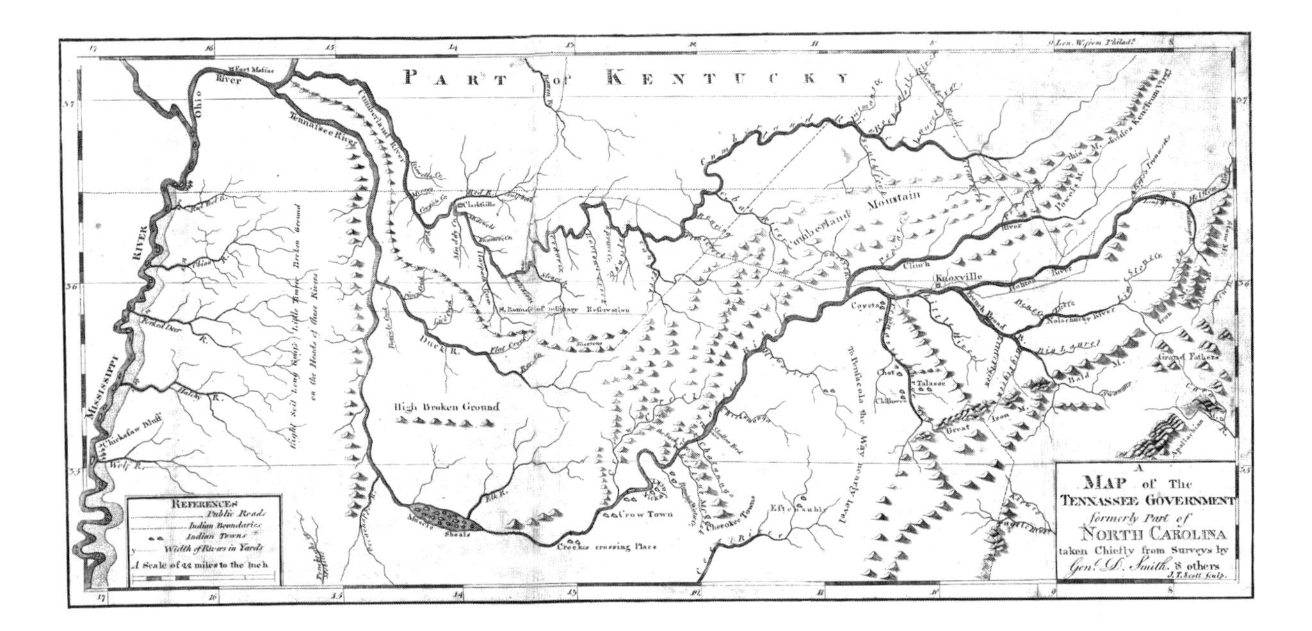

Map of the Tennessee Government by Gen'l D. Smith and Others, 1795. Map Collection, No. 1862, Tennessee State Library and Archives. Courtesy of TSLA.

deal of interest in assembling a collection of aboriginal artifacts for the museum. The impetus to preserve and study Tennessee's Indian antiquities, along with other objects reflecting the natural history, technological achievements, and civic history of the state, was a major factor in the founding of the Tennessee Historical Society in 1849.

The Age of Portrait Sculpture

During the mid-nineteenth century the thread of sculptural tradition appeared once again in Tennessee. Adelicia Acklen, Nashville's wealthiest woman at the time of the Civil War and mistress of Belmont Mansion, was one of the few local citizens who had the means to acquire as well as commission works of art. In the 1860s or 1870s, Acklen purchased two substantial pieces of white marble sculpture in Rome by expatriate sculptors Chauncey Bradley Ives and Randolph Rogers, two prominent American artists working in the romantic Neoclassical style of the 1850s.

Tennessee's first significant piece of public sculpture memorialized an earlier war hero. In 1880, the Tennessee Historical Society erected Clark Mills's bronze of Andrew Jackson on the grounds of the state capitol in honor of the city of Nashville's centennial anniversary. It is based on Mills's popular Jackson Memorial of 1853, commissioned by the Jackson Memorial Committee, which stands today in the District of Columbia's Lafayette Square. The statue depicts Jackson as the victorious commander of American forces at the 1815 Battle of New Orleans. Shown as a dashing hero, he tips his hat while sitting astride a rearing horse whose nostrils flare and veins bulge with effort. Mills (1801–1883), who was a self-taught artist, cast the first equestrian statue in the United States at his foundry in Washington. Although he did an equestrian portrait of George Washington in 1860 and created many portrait busts throughout his career, the Jackson statue proved to be Mills's most popular work. The cities of Nashville and New Orleans both commissioned replicas of the statue.

After the Civil War, communities and organizations often relied on sculpture to commemorate the

Andrew Jackson, bronze, by Clark Mills, 1880, on the grounds of the state capitol. Photograph by J. Clarence Hankins, 1931. Library Picture Collection, Tennessee State Library and Archives. Courtesy of TSLA.

valor, sacrifice, and struggle of their local citizens. The first southern monuments to the war did not rely on traditional models of the conquering hero, but instead placed their emphasis primarily on the architectural landmark or the place itself. These commemorations in Tennessee began modestly with headstones and memorial obelisks in cemeteries, such as those in Union City (1869) and Farmington (1873).

Throughout the 1880s and 1890s many Tennessee communities rushed to build public monuments to memorialize the "Lost Cause" of the Civil War. The obelisks or prominent markers were enhanced with generic sculptural elements intended to carry the message of the Lost Cause to the public. In fact, it appears that cities and towns throughout both North and South erected similar monuments, which differed only in details of uniform and insignia. As the demand for them grew, such statues became available in ready-made packages at granite or marble quarries and metal foundries. The iconography most commonly employed depicted the ordinary citizen as soldier, with an emphasis on anonymity, duty, and sacrifice, in order to show the Confederate forces as heroic volunteers. One of the most public, and artistic, of Tennessee's cemetery monuments is Knoxville's forty-eight-foot obelisk topped by the image of a Confederate soldier. Erected in Bethel Cemetery in 1892, its model for the eight-foot, six-inch soldier at parade rest was created by Lloyd Branson (1854–1925), Knoxville's most prominent painter at the time. He supervised the carving of the statue, from gray Tennessee marble, by an artisan at a Knoxville quarry.

By far, the historical event that had the most impact on public sculpture in Tennessee was the Tennessee Centennial Exposition of 1897. A full-scale replica of the Athenian Parthenon was erected to serve as the festival's fine arts building and a large-scale pyramid was built to represent Memphis at the fair. Twenty-eight-year-old Enid Yandell, who had worked with prominent sculptor Lorado Taft at the World's Columbian Exposition in Chicago in 1893, was commissioned to create a monumental *Pallas Athena* to stand in front of the Parthenon. Yandell, a Louisville sculptor whose mother was from Nashville, was studying with Frederick MacMonnies (whose Paris studio was one of the first to admit women) when she received the commission. She copied the Classical Greek *Pallas de Velletrie* in the Louvre and built it of staff (a mixture of plaster, hemp and concrete) in three large-scale sections. When assembled on its base in Nashville, it reached a height of forty feet. Yandell had several other pieces on the exposition grounds, including a replica of her first major commission, a heroic-scale plaster *Daniel Boone* garbed in buckskin clothing, which had been done four years earlier for the Kentucky building at the World's Columbian Exposition.

George Julian Zolnay, a Hungarian artist trained in Paris and Vienna, who had also worked at the Columbian Exposition, came to Nashville to help create the pediment sculptures for the full-scale replica of the Parthenon. Giuseppe Moretti, an Italian artist living in New York, was invited to exhibit five works in the sculpture section of the exposition's Fine Art Exhibit, including a bronze statue, *Commodore Cornelius Vanderbilt,* that was displayed temporarily on the west side of the Parthenon. American sculptor Lorado Taft, guest juror for the student art section, praised the work of a local ten year old, Belle Kinney, and later assisted her in gaining entrance to the School of the Art Institute of Chicago

Compared to the tremendous number of painters—of regional, national, and international reputations—whose works were shown at the Tennessee Centennial in both juried and loaned exhibits, the twenty-three sculptors represented an odd group. Zolnay and Yandell found themselves in the company of such well-known artists as Auguste Rodin and Lorado Taft in the exhibits. The medals in sculpture went to R. P. Bringhurst of St. Louis and Bessie O. Potter of Chicago. Potter's plaster version of her award-winning piece, *The Young Mother,* is now in the collection of the Cheekwood Museum of Art. The piece, a smoothly curved tabletop sculpture, is, essentially, a "Madonna and Child" depicting a seated mother with head tilted down toward the child in her arms. It proved to be a very popular subject for Potter, and bronze versions can be found in museum collections around the United States.

The centennial also increased demand for portrait sculpture. Few portrait sculptures are known to have been executed in Tennessee until Zolnay came to Nashville in 1896 to work on the sculptural programs for the centennial's temporary buildings. Already an accomplished portrait sculptor, Zolnay soon gained commissions from William Hicks Jackson, owner of Belle Meade Plantation, and several other prominent Nashville civic leaders.

Over the next thirty years, special-interest citizen groups and public-minded corporate commissions were primarily responsible for sculptural monuments in Tennessee cities. Several of the participating sculptors at the Centennial Exposition received commissions for public pieces in Nashville. Some commissions reflected the Lost Cause mentality of the age. Others reflected the politics of a confident and progressive state and city. In 1897, the officers of the Tennessee Centennial purchased Moretti's full-length bronze statue of Commodore Cornelius Vanderbilt, whose newly founded university stood across the street from Centennial Park. At the exposition's close, the sculpture was moved onto the Vanderbilt campus, where it faces the West End Avenue entrance today. The seventeen-foot-tall bronze *Mercury,* a replica of Giovanni da Bologna's mid-sixteenth-century sculpture of the Roman messenger that had topped the exposition's Commerce Building, became the spire on the clock tower of Nashville's new Union Station when it opened in 1900. In 1904, then seventeen-year-old Belle Kinney was commissioned to do a posthumous monumental portrait of Jere Baxter, president of the Tennessee Central Railroad, that would be placed at the intersection of Broad Street and West End Avenue in Nashville. Baxter had waged a futile fight against the monopolistic practices of the Nashville, Chattanooga, and St. Louis Railroad, and died suddenly of a gallstone attack. As if to counter the hero-making impulse of Baxter's supporters, Enid Yandell's *Major John W. Thomas Monument* (1907), paid for by the Nashville, Chattanooga, and St. Louis Railroad to commemorate the past president of the Tennessee Centennial, was soon mounted in Centennial Park.

Around the same time, Memphians commissioned an equestrian monument to Confederate general Nathan Bedford Forrest (1904) by noted American sculptor Charles Henry Niehaus. Niehaus, originally from Cincinnati, had trained at the Royal Academy in Munich and lived in Rome. The over-life-sized monument, located above Forrest's tomb in Forrest Park on Union Avenue, is a naturalistic likeness of Forrest at ease, hat off and sword sheathed, seated astride his horse King Philip, standing alert and still, with pricked ears and flowing tail. Memphis Brooks Museum of Art owns small models in bronze and plaster that were done as preparatory studies for the piece, for which monies began to be raised in 1887 by the Forrest Memorial Association.

After a long public campaign by S. A. Cunningham, editor of the Nashville-based *Confederate Veteran* magazine, the Fifty-first Tennessee General Assembly commissioned George Julian Zolnay's *Sam Davis* (1908). The statue is a full-length bronze of the "boy hero of the Confederacy," a young soldier from Smyrna, Tennessee, who risked his life to carry a message across the battle lines. Davis's famous words when captured, "I would rather die a thousand deaths than betray a friend or be false to duty," are inscribed on the statue's base. Scholars now believe, however, that Cunningham may have fashioned the words after a similar quotation attributed to Robert E. Lee. Zolnay depicts the youthful Davis as a dashing figure in a short jacket, arms crossed, staring unafraid at the far horizon. This handsome, well-sited piece, which stands today at the base of Capitol Hill, is a prime example of the sympathetic power of the "Lost Cause" theme.[1]

Sam Davis, bronze, by George Zolnay, 1908, on the grounds of the state capitol. Photograph by Carroll Van West.

Nashville's most impressive Civil War–theme monuments—Zolnay's *Sam Davis,* Belle Kinney's *Monument to Confederate Women,* and Giuseppe Moretti's *Battle of Nashville Monument*—were commissioned in the early twentieth century. Because these commissions took place long after the fact, works like these are often somewhat confusing combinations of heroic style, contemporary dress, and historical symbolism. *The Battle of Nashville Monument,* for example, while it commemorates the decisive 1864 battle, also symbolically depicts the "re-union" of North and South during World War I in the form of a Greek youth leading two horses.

Zolnay was invited to return to Nashville once again, for the rebuilding of the Parthenon in the early 1920s, this time to work on the ninety-two metopes in the frieze that surround the upper level of the building. He brought with him a model for what would prove to be his finest work in Nashville, the *Gold Star* monument, commissioned by the Kiwanis Club and erected at the southeast corner of Centennial Park in 1922. In tribute to those who lost sons in World War I, Zolnay created a dramatic grouping: a mother bending over her dying son, her cloak and skirts spreading around him in a protective manner and her bent form conveying the extremity of her grief. The massive bronze, which has taken on a beautiful green patina over the years, is inscribed with the words, "I gave my best to make a better world."

Belle Kinney, after graduating from the Art Institute of Chicago, moved to New York City, where she married fellow sculptor and Prix de Rome winner Leopold Scholz in 1921. In the mid-1920s, they returned to Nashville so she could complete her *Monument to Confederate Women,* and together they helped recreate the pediment sculptures for the rebuilding of the Parthenon. The United Confederate Veterans' commission, originally awarded to Kinney in 1909, was said to be the largest monetary award given to a woman sculptor. But fund raising did not meet expectations, and the piece could not be completed until 1926. The graceful bronze memorial located on Legislative Plaza today features three figures, mounted atop a rectangular base. The over-life-sized monument depicts the Lost Cause as the dashed hopes of southern men and women. It is an image of noble defeat. The Confederate flag is furled and an overturned cannon has lost a wheel. The kneeling woman in period clothing and the slumped soldier in uniform are handsome and youthful. They are accorded sympathetic recognition by the serene, classically dressed figure representing "Fame," who towers over the scene, supporting the wounded man and holding a laurel wreath over the woman's head.

Once Kinney and Scholz completed the Parthenon sculptures in 1925, they received the commission for a monumental courtyard figure for the new War Memorial Building being built on the plaza below the state capitol. Completed in 1929 "in memory of the sons of Tennessee who gave their lives in the great war," the tall bronze *Victory* is a handsome idealized male with billowing cloak, clad only in sandals. He wears a laurel wreath and holds aloft a small standing figure of Athena, goddess of war. Once their Nashville projects were completed, Scholz and Kinney together created a World War I memorial column for New York City's Pelham Parkway and received joint commissions to do portrait busts of John Sevier and Andrew Jackson for the U.S. Capitol.

Also in the mid-1920s, the Tennessee Legislature decided to make good on a 1909 resolution creating a memorial to Edward Ward Carmack, the young newspaper editor who became a martyr to the cause of Prohibition in Tennessee after he was assassinated by a member of the anti-Prohibitionists. Nancy Cox McCormack, a Nashville-born sculptor who had trained in St. Louis and Chicago, portrayed young Carmack, with his trademark bushy mustache, standing disapprovingly, fists clenched, above Legislative Plaza. The bronze, cast in Rome, was erected at the bottom of the capitol steps in 1925. Its base bears a plaque from the Women's Christian Temperance Union.

Harking back to the tradition of depicting anonymous ordinary citizens as heroes, the Shelby County Daughters of the American Revolution raised funds for *The Doughboy* (1926), a memorial to the young men of Shelby County who gave their lives in World War I. Now standing in Memphis' Overton Park, American sculptor Nancy Coonsman Hahn's rendition of a dashing young soldier charging out of a foxhole is an impressive and moving tribute to wartime bravery.

Modern Sculpture for Modern Times

Even the turn-of-the-century art associations founded by art patrons and artists interested in promoting the visual arts paid little attention to sculpture, other than as architectural decoration or as monument, until the formation of the Memphis Art Association in 1914. Founding member Florence McIntyre initiated the organization by showing works of painting and sculpture borrowed from New York's Macbeth Galleries (made famous by the 1908 exhibition of "The Eight" American painters). Those early sculpture exhibitions made a strong impression on supporter C. P. J. Mooney, editor of the *Commercial Appeal.* Mooney stated in 1915,

> Unfortunately we have paid for our soldiers' monuments through our ignorance of good sculpture, and while we were at the mercy of the

> most enterprising commercial agents, who made good business by attending our annual reunions, the highest price was paid for the worst sculpture in the world. We know better now and have real works of art to show the world that we appreciate our heroes; such as the monument of General [Nathan B.] Forrest, and the noble groups of statuary decorating our [Shelby County] Court House.[2]

The Memphis Art Association was incorporated into the charter of the new Brooks Gallery, donated by association member Bessie Vance Brooks as a memorial to her husband, which opened in May 1916. In 1917, the Brooks Memorial Art Gallery sponsored a show of notable American artists' bronzes cast by the Gorham Company of New York City. Included were works by some of the best known sculptors of the day, including Harriet Whitney Frishmuth, Evelyn Beatrice Longman, Gutzon Borglum, Anna Vaughn Hyatt, Malvina Hoffman, Daniel Chester French, and Augustus St. Gaudens. Similar showings must have been held in Nashville a decade or so later. Evelyn Beatrice Longman's graceful bronze of a young girl, *The Future* (1925, cast in 1929), which had been purchased by individual members of the Centennial Club from a show at the Parthenon Galleries in 1925, was placed on long-term loan to the Parthenon at its rededication in 1931 as a tribute to the Centennial Ladies of 1897.[3]

Ironically, two notable pieces of sculpture from this same period, by two of the more prominent artists of the 1920s, were placed on the campus of the University of Tennessee in Knoxville long after their creation. Harriet Frishmuth's bronze, *The Vine* (1923), a classic Art Nouveau design of curving form and sinuous line, the central focus of the lobby at the McClung Museum and a prominent work in the Metropolitan Museum of Arts American Wing, was donated to the museum in 1958. Carl Milles's *Europa* (1926), a powerful bronze of a cavorting nude female on the back of a massive bull, was cast in Denmark in 1967 and installed on the McClung Tower plaza in 1968.

The decade following the onset of the Great Depression witnessed the return to Tennessee of several modernist sculptors who had been active on the national and international art scene during the 1920s and 1930s. Harold Cash, a Chattanooga-born sculptor who had studied in New York, moved to Paris in 1928. Guggenheim Fellowships supported his artistic development there until 1932, when he returned to New York and, later, Chattanooga. His figurative bronze sculptures display a simplified and modern, yet still recognizable, approach to the human form. In 1939, Memphian Marie Craig, trained at Memphis' James Lee Memorial Academy before winning a scholarship to the Boston Museum School and, later, to the Fontainebleau School of Art outside of Paris, exhibited *Seated Nude* (A Study in Marble), which was carved in sinuous lines with noticeably geometric angles, at the Architectural League of New York. Craig's *Autumn* (or Boy with Grapes), a more conventionally modeled piece with rounded, naturalistic limbs, was shown that same year at the New York World's Fair. Craig returned to Memphis in 1940 and taught for two years at the Memphis Academy of Art before enlisting in the Women's Army Corps. She died in military service, and her parents presented *Seated Nude* to the Memphis Brooks Museum of Art in 1945.

Thomas Puryear Mims, born in Nashville, studied under William Zorach and Robert Laurent at the Art Students League in New York from 1930 to 1935, worked one summer with sculptor Gutzon Borglum on Mount Rushmore, and took private studio lessons from Zorach in 1936–37. After his return to Nashville, he received a Julius Rosenwald Foundation Fellowship to support travel in the South, creating a sculptural chronicle of people he met. Mims, who was at heart a modernist, did many traditional portrait busts during his lifetime, leaving a well-observed record of Nashville's lively literary scene of the 1930s and 1940s. But Mims was at his best when working in stone, with simple rounded volumes, cubist-inspired angles meant to be seen from all sides, and contrasting textures of smooth and rough stone. A founding member of the Nashville Artist Guild, Mims was active in the fledgling Nashville art scene. In the early 1950s, he received a commission from the state of Tennessee for a group of four monumental figurative bronzes to be placed in front of the Cordell Hull building. The massive human figures, symbolizing Tennessee's pioneers, farmers, laborers, and soldiers, were criticized as heavy and awkward looking. Mims's *Founding of Nashville* (1962), stiff-looking heroic figures of buckskin-clad city fathers James Robertson and John Donelson created in copper, was first placed inside Fort Nashborough in Riverfront Park on the Cumberland River, and not moved into public view on First Avenue until 1980.

Also during the 1930s, Burton Callicott, a graduate of the Cleveland School of Art (now Cleveland Institute of Art), returned home to Memphis rather than risk trying to make a living as an artist in Depression-stricken New York City. Callicott's stepfather, Michael Abt, who ran a commercial display business, had been appointed to direct the western division of Tennessee's short-lived Federal Works of Art Project. While he put the young Callicott to work immediately creating cast stone ornaments and elaborate Memphis Cotton Carnival floats, he also helped him secure a Public Works of Art mural proposal. Callicott's mural, titled *The Coming of De Soto,* now in the Memphis Pink Palace Museum, was quickly funded by local civic leaders. It proved so successful that prominent regionalist painter Thomas Hart Benton, himself the creator of many mural projects for public buildings around the United States, urged Callicott to continue painting the narratives of American history. Abt had other plans, however, having already arranged a sculptural commission for Callicott—this time a pair of bas-reliefs for a private manufacturing firm. Callicott's ten-foot-square relief panels, done in plaster and inspired by the social realism of Diego Rivera and José Clemente Orozco, gave particular prominence to the position of African Americans as a disenfranchised labor force in the cotton industry, an unpopular stance in what was still a racially separated society. Callicott's so-called socialist intentions created a schism between father and stepson. The client accepted the panels, and they were successfully exhibited at the client's Memphis Fairgrounds convention. Although Callicott later credited Abt with having profound artistic influence on him, this incident brought an end to Callicott's collaboration with Abt.[4] In 1937, Callicott became a founding faculty member of the Memphis Academy of Art, Tennessee's first professional art school (now the Memphis College of Art). Although he began at the academy as a teacher of sculpture and ceramics, he is best known today as a painter.

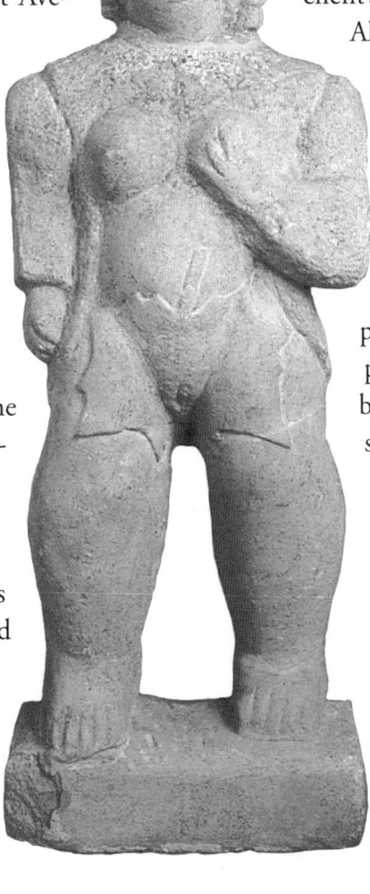

Eve, limestone, by William Edmondson, c. 1935. 1964.10. Collection of Cheekwood Museum of Art, Nashville, Tennessee.

The most prominent Tennessee sculptor of those years, however, was Nashvillian William Edmondson, the state's first nationally recognized African American sculptor. Edmondson was a self-taught artist, son of freed slaves on two Nashville plantations, who carved limestone into simple blocky forms depicting animals and small human figures. Edmondson began working as an artist only after ill health forced his retirement from janitorial work at age fifty-nine, claiming to have received divine instruction that told him to begin carving in stone. While his works were included in the 1948 Spring Arts Festival at Fisk University, he did not have a solo exhibit in Nashville until the Nashville Artist Guild organized a show immediately following his death in 1951. The Tennessee State Museum opened its new facilities in 1981 with a major Edmondson retrospective, selections from which were organized into a small traveling exhibit by the Southern Arts Federation in Atlanta. The Cheekwood Museum of Art's traveling exhibit of his work (2000–2001) is the first comprehensive show to tour the country.[5]

Tennessee Federal Relief Programs

In the late 1930s, a number of artists were employed by various federal programs to create works of art for public places in Tennessee. Most of these were murals whose narrative programs reflected the idealization of America's rural culture, but a few sculptors also received commissions. In 1938, the Federal Works of Art Project tapped Leopold Scholz to create *The Mail Carrier,* a cast-aluminum bust of an anonymous postal worker, for Chattanooga's modernist Federal Building. Another notable sculptural offering from the Treasury Section of Fine Arts is William Zorach's pair of seven-foot-tall teak relief carvings for the Federal Courthouse and Post Office at Greeneville. Zorach was a well-known sculptor in the prime of his career when *Man Power,* a solidly built bare-chested man leaning on a shovel standing in front of a Tennessee Valley Authority dam, and *The Resources of Nature,* a similarly built bare-breasted female holding an active baby and pictured against trees and hills, were completed in 1940. Due to his reputation, Zorach received a relatively sizeable amount of money for the commission. Recognizing that the commission was one of the major works of his career, he arranged to exhibit the panels at the Whitney Museum of American Art before delivering them to the small Tennessee town for permanent installation.

Other sculptural projects done under the auspices of the Federal Relief programs for Tennessee include Enea Biafora's *News on the Job* (1940), a carved-wood relief depicting a woodcutter with his son and daughter, installed at the Decherd Post Office in Franklin County; Christian Heinrich's cast ceramic relief sculpture of three deer, titled *Wild Life* (1939), for the Rockwood Post Office in Roane County in 1939; and Sidney Waugh's nine-foot-tall, cast-stone *American Eagle* (1940), placed on the facade of the Federal Courthouse and Post Office in Columbia in Maury County.

Puryear Mims benefited from a commission by the Works Progress Administration while living in New York City, creating cast-plaster portrait busts of nine American Presidents for Manhattan high schools. Upon returning to Nashville, Mims set up a studio for WPA-supported lessons. Sculptor William Edmondson was also supported by the WPA for Project service during 1939–41. While General Service Administration records show that he received financial assistance for several years, it is not known whether he actually taught classes or merely developed new projects on his own at this time. Thus far, no publicly commissioned works from this period have been identified.

Within Tennessee, a short-lived Public Works of Art program spearheaded by Edward E. Dougherty of Nashville employed thirty-five painters and sculptors for approximately three months in late 1933 and early 1934. While some works of art were actually created, most of the commissions resulted only in models for planned public projects, many never to be executed after government funding was curtailed. Among the sculptural projects were Belle Kinney Scholz's designs for nine marble low relief panels intended to adorn the exterior of Nashville's War Memorial Auditorium. Leopold Scholz created a three-foot model for a proposed *Goddess Athena,* which was planned for large-scale realization at the Parthenon once sufficient funds could be raised.

Other sculptural works in the program were by Mary Hooper Donelson of Nashville, who submitted a design for a public fountain employing a female figure, and Knoxville artist Gilbert H. Switzer, whose bust of Admiral Farragut can be found today in the collection of the East Tennessee Historical Society.

ACADEMIC ART PROGRAMS AND PRIVATE PATRONAGE

After World War II, the Memphis art scene, which had been building its audience for several decades, showed a strong interest in nurturing contemporary sculpture in Tennessee. Important sculptors came one after another to lecture in Memphis: Paul Manship in 1946, Wheeler Williams in 1948, George Rickey in 1949, and Alexander Archipenko in 1950. In 1948, the Memphis Academy of Art showed both political courage and allegiance to the language of modernism by holding an exhibit of the work of Leo Amino, an avant-garde Japanese American sculptor. Soon afterward, the academy hired Edwin Cooper Rust, a graduate of Yale University, who had exhibited at the Whitney Museum, the Metropolitan Museum of Art, and the Carnegie Institute, to serve as its director. During World War II, Rust had been assigned to administer the Arts and Crafts Department of the American Red Cross. As the new director of the Memphis Academy of Art, Rust reinforced curricular offerings by bringing in sculptor Brian Watkins, a graduate of Yale and Cranbrook, who worked in wood, stone, clay, and small metals, and John Wylie, who had studied design with Richard Neutra at Cranbrook. In 1952, painter Ted Faiers joined the faculty. The academy's program, which included weaving, drawing, and advertising design in addition to painting and sculpture, was a rigorous one, only slightly less demanding than that of the Cleveland Institute of Art, where faculty member Burton Callicott had trained. It stressed experience in all media, with no delineation between the fine and applied arts.

Portrait of an Architect, bronze, by Ted Rust, 1948. Courtesy of Memphis Brooks Museum of Art; Eugenia Buxton Whitnel Funds 73.25.

In 1948, Wheeler Williams, a sculptor whose work had been featured in the 1937 Exposition Internationale in Paris, came to Memphis to speak under the auspices of the Memphis Garden Club. In his remarks, Williams decried the fact that "American cities have too few monuments and too many signs," pointing out that there was no important public sculpture in Memphis and hoping that the Garden Club might be able to help the situation. They did, in 1961, by commissioning him to do sculptures of the four seasons for the Brooks Museum. Today, *Spring, Summer,* and *Fall,* carved in white marble, grace the south garden of the Memphis Brooks Museum of Art. *Winter,* created on a smaller scale from bronze covered with a gold patina, is in the museum's permanent collection.[6]

Private patronage of contemporary art in Tennessee seems to have gotten its start in Memphis with the founding in 1953 of Art Today. This group of art patrons is still actively dedicated to supporting museum acquisitions of the works of contemporary artists of "notable or growing reputation" by the Memphis Brooks Museum of Art. A quick glance at the Brooks' Art Today Collection, with an eye toward the dates of acquisition for the works included, is strong testament to assembling museum collections in sync with the history of contemporary art. The collection includes works by such prominent American sculptors as Louise Nevelson, Richard Lippold, George Rickey, and James Surls. Also in this prestigious collection is *Shag,* a cast cobalt-blue glass head by Hank Murta Adams, one of the stars of the current American art glass movement, who was in residence at the Joe L. Evins Appalachian Center for Crafts, near Smithville, Tennessee, in the late 1980s.

In contrast, building an audience for the art of the times in Nashville seems to have fallen almost entirely to the artists. In 1950, a core group of twenty-six members established the Nashville Artist Guild in an effort to forge a place for themselves and their work in a city long taken up with politics and heritage. One of the first and most influential exhibits to come to Nashville under guild sponsorship was *Sculpture in Time and Place* (1952), an American Federation of the Arts exhibit organized by the New York Sculptor's Guild. Featuring the work of Puryear Mims's mentor, William Zorach, the show made Nashville its first stop. The Nashville Artist Guild unified the Nashville arts community into a cohesive body that continues to this day. Notable sculptor members from the 1960s and early 1970s include African American artists Earl Hooks (Fisk University), Gregory Ridley (Fisk University), and Bill Johnson (Nashville Public Schools), as well as Mims, Sylvia Hyman (George Peabody College for Teachers), Olen Bryant (Austin Peay State University), and Philbrick Crouch (Nashville Children's Museum). Other influential guild members were painting teachers Louise LeQuire, Joseph Van Sickle, and Phillip Perkins. Budding artist Charles "Red" Grooms was admitted to the guild as a voting member while he was a high school student.

Not until the 1960s and 1970s did Tennessee colleges and universities embrace sculpture as an integral part of their fine arts curriculum. Vanderbilt University hired Puryear Mims as a fine arts lecturer in 1949, but he was not appointed to teach sculpture until 1958. Southwestern at Memphis (now Rhodes College) recruited sculptor Lawrence (Lon) Anthony to run their Art Department in 1961, the University of Tennessee hired Philip Nichols to teach sculpture in 1965, and sculptor Jim Collins came to the University of Tennessee at Chattanooga in the mid-1960s. Although Harris Sorelle had been teaching welded metals for some years, Memphis State University (now University of Memphis) did not add a sculpture major to the curriculum until 1970.

The exhibit *Tennessee Sculpture 1971,* organized by the Chattanooga Art Association in conjunction with the Tennessee Arts Commission, was the first effort to survey sculpture making statewide. Fourteen of the seventeen artists in the show were affiliated with universities or academies; many were graduates of nationally recognized programs. The influence of such pioneer professionals as Ronald Bennett (bronze, East Tennessee State University); Klaus Kallenberger (welded steel, Middle Tennessee

State University); Dennis Peacock (welded steel, University of Tennessee); Robert Pletcher (wood, Peabody College); John Seyfried (mixed media, Memphis Academy of Art); Lewis Snyder (ceramic, Middle Tennessee State University); and Michael Taylor (glass, Tusculum College, Peabody College), many of whom taught the current generation of Tennessee sculptors in public and private schools across the state, still can be felt. Budd H. Bishop, director of the Chattanooga Art Association and later director of Hunter Museum of American Art, remarked that "this exhibit dramatizes some of the turn-arounds in art activities in Tennessee," indicating that the show was a pivotal moment in the history of Tennessee sculpture. Bishop noted that slow public acceptance of contemporary art and the lack of college-level sculpture departments had held Tennessee back in the field of sculpture. By 1971, the proliferation of university sculpture programs and new support in the form of purchase awards and subsidized exhibits from the Tennessee Arts Commission were significant factors beginning to bring Tennessee sculpture into the mainstream of contemporary art.[7]

The Contemporary Scene and a New Wave of Public Art Projects

The 1970s saw a rise in both public and private patronage of the arts in Tennessee. During this period, Chattanooga began to emerge as a major art center due to strong private support. The Hunter Museum of American Art was able to build an important collection of contemporary art through the participation of a collector's group that made annual pilgrimages to New York galleries. The *Hunter Museum Fence* (1975), one of metal sculptor Albert Paley's earliest commissions, was the first major piece of contemporary outdoor sculpture in the state. Progressive museum director Budd H. Bishop brought Paley in for a planning session when the Hunter's new building was under construction. Thirty-five years later, the melting lines and playful curves of this postmodern blacksmith's art still make an elegant and witty statement. A related, early piece by Paley, *Garden Gate* (1976), which was donated to the Hunter by private Chattanooga patrons, now stands outside the museum's main entrance.

Public motivation has also played a significant role in the addition of major sculptural pieces to the Memphis cityscape over the past thirty years. Funds were raised locally for a long-desired monument to the twenty thousand Memphians who died in the yellow fever epidemic of 1878. Sculptor Harris Sorelle completed the twenty-foot-tall concrete and welded bronze piece in 1971. Sited in Martyrs' Park on the bluffs of the Mississippi River, this nearly abstract work consists of a cast concrete frame enclosing a weblike screen of thin metal figures floating one on top of another, as if dissolving into the air. In 1976, a group of businessmen founded the National Ornamental Metals Museum at an auspicious Mississippi river bluff site that houses both a defunct United States Marine hospital and ancient Native American mounds. The museum is a unique concept that incorporates changing exhibits in both formal galleries and out of doors, a permanent collection (inside and out) of artistic metalwork, a working smithy, and a metals conservation laboratory. The museum's founding director, Jim Wallace, has trained a number of up-and-coming metal sculptors and fabricators, has assisted in the creation and repair of major sculpture commissions, and has served on most of the important public art committees for projects in the city of Memphis.

In the mid-1970s, the city of Memphis, like many other urban centers attempting to revive a failing downtown core, began the development of a walking street known as the Mid-America Mall. Jim Wallace and colleagues at the National Ornamental Metal Museum created a series of artistic cast-iron benches for public spaces on the mall. Local sculptors John Seyfried and John McIntire, both teachers at the Memphis College of Art, were commissioned

Edmondson, Harvey, Wickham, and Streeter
Four Self-Taught Sculptors

FOUR SELF-TAUGHT ARTISTS, WILLIAM EDMONDSON, BESSIE WHITE HARVEY, ENOCH TANNER WICKHAM, and Vannoy Streeter, contributed significantly to the diversity of Tennessee sculpture during the twentieth century through their unique visions, techniques, and materials.

Of the three, William Edmondson (c. 1870–1951) is certainly the best known today, documented through several exhibits, articles, and two major books. A railroad worker as a young man, Edmondson worked at a local Nashville hospital until the early 1930s, when he became a stone mason. He specialized in carved images for grave makers, and his carvings represented such common gravestone images as doves and lambs to such creative images as preachers, famous people, lions, imaginary creatures, and abstract designs. After Nashvillians introduced photographer Louise Dahl-Wolfe (who was married to Nashville painter Meyer Wolfe) to Edmondson, Dahl-Wolfe was impressed and championed Edmondson's work, taking photographs to Alfred H. Barr Jr., director of the Museum of Modern Art in New York City. Barr and contemporary critics praised Edmondson's modern minimalist carvings—Edmondson himself always emphasized that divine visions influenced his work while the trends of modern art meant nothing—and with their backing, Edmondson became a star in the modern art world. In 1937 he was the first African American artist to receive a one-man exhibition at the Museum of Modern Art. Barr then arranged for Edmondson's work to be shown in a Paris exhibit. The sculpture division of the fine arts program of the Works Progress Administration further supported Edmondson in the late 1930s and early 1940s. Edmondson continued to carve his visions in limestone until his death in 1951.

Preacher, by William Edmondson. Courtesy of The Frank H. McClung Museum, University of Tennessee.

Bride, by William Edmondson. Courtesy of The Frank H. McClung Museum, University of Tennessee.

While Edmondson was a stone mason, Bessie White Harvey (1929–1994) made evocative sculptures out of sticks. Harvey was born poor in Georgia and her family's fortunes did not improve much after their move to East Tennessee and the industrial town of Alcoa, where Harvey grew up. Like Edmondson, she turned to sculpture later in life, after her mother's death in 1974, when Harvey was forty-five years old. While working at the Blount Memorial Hospital in Maryville, Harvey began to give friends and patients small "healing pieces," made from sticks that she collected, shaped, and decorated with cloth, beads, metals, and other common items. The devout Harvey, who believed strongly in the power of alternative medicine, also believed that her African roots gave her special powers of healing. The spirit sculptures were the best way, in her mind, to convey her healing powers to the physically and spiritually sick.

What began as works of spiritual faith and African identity became works of art in the early 1980s after Harvey's figures were exhibited in the hospital's annual art shows. In 1983, Harvey began a series titled "Africa in America," in which she explored her own history as well as the history of African Americans from slavery to the civil rights movement. Her powerful, emotional images included *Black Church* (1984) and *A Thin Line,* or *The Hanging Tree* (1984), the latter depicting a vicious lynching. "I want the black children not to forget their history," she told state folklorist Robert Cogswell. "Not to make 'em prejudiced or mean, but to see how far God has brought their race of people and to praise and give God thanks for these things."

Moses and the Serpent, mixed media, 88 × 22 × 16 inches, by Bessie Harvey. Collection of the Knoxville Museum of Art; gift of Glady Faires.

The spiritual world also shaped the work of Enoch Tanner Wickham (1883–1970), who left a roadside park, across from his own concrete-and-log home, full of concrete sculpture devoted to famous events and people in American history and left powerful religious imagery at his family cemetery in rural Montgomery County. When he was sixty-nine years old, Tanner turned to building large, concrete memorial statues to represent heroes such as Daniel Boone, Andrew Jackson, and Alvin York at his roadside park. He also expressed his faith, by erecting wing-spread angels and other religious symbols in the family cemetery. Critics did not "discover" Wickham, however, until after his death. The 1982 Knoxville World's Fair featured some of his statues, removed from his property, and later reinstalled at Austin Peay State University. Vandalism has marred the remaining work at the roadside park. In 2000 the National Endowment of the Arts awarded a grant for a combined effort from Austin Peay professors and the Custom House Museum in Clarksville to document and interpret Wickham's legacy to the state's self-taught art traditions. The result was a major exhibit and catalog about Wickham's sculpture at the Custom House Museum in 2001.

Wickham Cemetery, Montgomery County. Funerary sculpture, concrete, by Enoch Tanner Wickham. Photograph by Carroll Van West.

Vannoy Streeter (1919–1999) was better known to Middle Tennesseans as the "Wire Man," due to his many small sculptures made from wire, usually coat hangers. Streeter, a self-taught artist, grew up in Wartrace, where he was a stable boy for the famous Tennessee Walking Horse, Strolling Jim. Many of his sculptures depict Tennessee Walkers, but Streeter also made wire sculptures of trucks, motorcycles, helicopters, various animals, and famous people such as Elvis Presley and Tina Turner. Streeter was discovered in the 1980s, and many of his works are now in museum collections across the South. He was a demonstrating artist at the National Black Arts Festival in 1990 and was named a Heritage Craftsman in 1991.

Carroll Van West, Middle Tennessee State University

Suggested Readings

Crouch, Ned, Michael Hall, Daniel C. Prince, Susan W. Knowles, Janelle S. Aieta, Dixie Webb, and Robert Cogswell. *E. T. Wickham: A Dream Unguarded.* Clarksville, Tenn.: Customs House Museum and Cultural Center, 2001.

Freeman, Rusty, Robert Farris Thompson, Judith McWillie, Grey Gundaker, Lowery S. Sims, and Bobby L. Lovett. *The Art of William Edmondson.* Jackson: Univ. Press of Mississippi; Nashville: Cheekwood Museum of Art, 1999.

to do monumental works for the site. Seyfried's *River* (c. 1976) is an impressive stainless steel piece with water flowing down its ribbed surface. McIntire's *Muse* (c. 1976), created in smoothly shaped cast concrete, is a tall abstract column suggesting the female form of its namesake. In 1977, the Mallory Knights Charitable Organization commissioned nationally prominent African American sculptor Richard Hunt to make a large public sculpture for the mall in commemoration of the death of Reverend Martin Luther King Jr. Hunt's *I've Been to the Mountaintop,* a forty-foot-long, abstract sphinx/pyramid in corten steel symbolizes both the mountain of King's famous speech in Memphis on the night before he died and the aspirations that King fostered in all people. For the Memphis Power and Light Company on Beale Street, Eric Parks created the bronze *Elvis* in 1980. Parks's piece has since been relocated to the Memphis Welcome Center, and Andrea Luger's bronze *Elvis* stands in its place today. In 1979, Ted Faiers, consummate pop artist and professor of painting at the Memphis College of Art for more than twenty-five years, received a commission by First Tennessee Bank for a multipaneled mural telling stories from Tennessee history. Faiers was an innovator who had begun "breaking the picture plane" by building three-dimensional wood stretchers for his canvases in 1969. Filling the downtown bank's lobby today, Faiers's project is an extravaganza of painting and sculpture dominated by simplified silhouettes and splendidly caricatured figures. The mural proved to be his final work. Around this same time, Lon Anthony was invited to create group of attention-grabbing outdoor pieces for the popularly supported Theatre Memphis in midtown. His lively and imaginative sixteen-foot-tall corten steel figures of theatrical characters, completed in 1983, are still fondly regarded by Memphians. In 1985, First Tennessee Bank, which was amassing a corporate art collection now known as the First Tennessee Heritage Collection, commissioned local sculptor Roy Tamboli to create a bronze figure of *Piomingo,* the last chief of the Tennessee Chickasaws. In order to find a model for his seven-and-a-half-foot-tall bronze sculpture, Tamboli traveled to Oklahoma to spend time with some of the remaining Chickasaws whose relatives survived the Trail of Tears. The result is a beautifully detailed standing figure of a noble Indian.

In 1975, Knoxville sculptor Arnold Schwartzbart created one of the first monuments to the Vietnam War to be installed in a Tennessee city and one of Knoxville's first major pieces of public art. Privately financed, it was placed first outside City Hall and later moved to its current location in front of the City County Building in downtown Knoxville. The simple and elegant eight-foot-tall marble piece takes the form of a very simplified eagle, which stands on a concrete and metal base containing the names of about two hundred war casualties from the eight-county region surrounding Knoxville.

At Cheekwood Museum of Art in Nashville, local patrons purchased a major piece of contemporary sculpture by Red Grooms, now one of Tennessee's best-known artists, for the museum's permanent collection. *Mr. and Mrs. Rembrandt* (1971), a life-sized "sculpto-pictorama," was included in the major retrospective of Grooms's work that traveled the country in 1985, stopping at the Tennessee State Museum in 1986. In 1975, Vanderbilt University's Sarratt Student Center became the first campus building project in Tennessee to have a designated budget for art. Evidence of this new policy is Memphis sculptor Lon Anthony's *Campus Types,* a three-quarters life-sized bronze grouping of bellbottom-wearing students, commissioned for the walkway on the Center's north side. When the new Tennessee Performing Arts Center opened in 1979, installed in the lobby was a life-sized bronze figure of a seated woman by Bell Buckle sculptor Russell Faxon. Walking into the lobby, even today, it is often startling to see a living human seated next to the bronze lady.

Nashville's Century III art competition, organized in 1980 to commemorate the two centuries of Nashville's existence, was juried by prominent art critic John Canaday. Bill Ralston, a former student of Puryear Mims at Vanderbilt, took the top award over

University of Tennessee Sculpture Tour

FOR FIFTEEN YEARS THE ANNUAL UNIVERSITY OF TENNESSEE SCULPTURE TOUR ENRICHED THE VISUAL landscape of the University of Tennessee campus in Knoxville. The 1982 world's fair, held on grounds adjacent to the university, provided the impetus for an outdoor exhibition of contemporary sculpture. As vast numbers of world's fair attendees were anticipated, the university's Council for Study in the Arts endorsed the concept of making the campus a more visually stimulating and culturally enriched environment. The plan called for an outdoor sculpture invitational exhibition in which large-scale pieces would be placed at various locations, augmenting the university's modest permanent outdoor collection of two traditional and two contemporary sculptures. There was little time or money to organize the exhibition by the opening date of the fair. However, Professors Dennis Peacock and Sam Yates of the Art Department were able to secure the participation of seven sculptors who recognized this opportunity to exhibit their art. Without financial reimbursement, these artists generously loaned and delivered their sculptures to the University of Tennessee campus. A black-and-white printed brochure included photographs of the sculptures and a map of their locations.

The sculptures inspired an open and robust dialogue on issues of contemporary art and creative expression. While each piece of sculpture may have garnered praise or criticism depending on the individual viewer, the overall tour was well received as it added a creative dimension to the campus. Its success and broad-based support led to the establishment of an annual Sculpture Tour. Through the efforts of Peacock, a sculptor himself, the number of sites in 1983 increased to twelve and the participants hailed from five states and Canada. By 1985, there were twenty-eight sites that required a walk of two miles to view all the sculptures, now presented in a color catalog. In ensuing years, participating artists received reimbursement for their expenses.

The national and international attention that the Sculpture Tour brought to the university helped Peacock, the tour's curator and coordinator, secure an associate curator, LeeAnn Mitchell, for the 1987–88 tour. Together they broadened the range and diversity of the Sculpture Tour and increased its level of recognition and importance. This tour also initiated the practice of purchasing a sculpture annually for permanent installation on the campus. With the 1990–91 tour, the collection of permanent sculptures was dedicated to Chancellor Emeritus Jack Reese, who had enthusiastically supported the tour during his tenure as chancellor of the Knoxville campus. This collection of sculptures remains affectionately known as "Reese's Pieces."

In 1994, Mitchell departed and Monica Thomeczek joined the tour's curatorial team. Because of state budget cuts in higher education, the Sculpture Tour ended in 1996. The tour brought to campus 206 unique sculptures by over one hundred artists from the United States and Canada. The popularity, success, and excellent management of the Sculpture Tour helped it become the model for similar tours in Tennessee, Alabama, Michigan, Pennsylvania, Louisiana, and Virginia. Its legacy lives through the continuation of these other tours, the Reese Collection, and the memories of students who attended the University of Tennessee during the years when art became part of their daily lives.

The commitment shown by Don Kurka, Harry Rutledge, John Parker, Homer Fisher, Phil Scheurer, Jack Reese, Don Eastman, and others helped establish the Tour, but it was Dennis Peacock's vision, tenacity, and tireless efforts that made the Sculpture Tour a model of innovation and excellence for which it is remembered.

Sam Yates, Ewing Gallery of Art, University of Tennessee

575 entrants for a simple, Brancusi-like bird carved in marble. The Century III collection forms part of the permanent museum collections of the Parthenon. Nashville's Metropolitan Parks Commission took a bold step in 1981 when it sponsored one of the first neighborhood art projects in Tennessee. Fannie Mae Dees Park, in the Hillsboro Village section of the city, was the site of a lively workshop with New York artist Pedro Silva, who invited parents, children, neighborhood residents, and local artists to help complete a large-scale mosaic-tile dragon. One of the city of Nashville's first civic sculpture commissions was awarded to Nashvillian Alan LeQuire in 1982. Once a student of Puryear Mims at Vanderbilt University, LeQuire was hired to create a permanent *Athena Parthenos* for the Parthenon. The sculpture, which had been the dream of the original supporters of the rebuilding of the Parthenon in the mid-1920s, was funded almost entirely by the Parthenon Patrons, a group of private donors. Rather than copy previous versions of *Athena,* as imagined by Enid Yandell at the Tennessee Centennial or Leopold Scholz under the Federal Works of Art project, LeQuire did extensive research, consulting both scholarly and literary resources, before creating his own interpretation of the monumental Athenian goddess, for which there is no known model. The statue, completed in 1990, faces toward the rising sun in the east, stands forty-two feet tall and is considered the tallest indoor sculpture in the world.

The Long Distance Driver, mild steel, by Dennis Peacock, 1992, in Ardmore, Lincoln County. Photograph by Carroll Van West, 2004. Courtesy of Tennessee Arts Commission.

The 1982 World's Fair in Knoxville proved to be another turning point in the history of Tennessee sculpture. It prompted several notable events, the first of which was a special showing at the fair of concrete statuary by self-taught artist Enoch Tanner Wickham, who once lived just outside of Clarksville. Sponsored by the Tennessee State Museum, Austin Peay State University, and sculpture professor Olen Bryant, who had visited Wickham's outdoor sculpture park many times, the world's fair show gave Wickham, who died in 1970, a wide new audience for the folk-style sculpture that was little appreciated during his lifetime. At the University of Tennessee, an outdoor sculpture exhibit was placed on the campus for fair visitors by professor of sculpture Dennis Peacock and Ewing Gallery director Sam Yates. Participating were sculptors James Gibson (Middle Tennessee State University), Jim Collins (University of Tennessee–Chattanooga), and Greely Myatt (then at Arkansas State University, now at University of Memphis). The show formed the nucleus of the University of Tennessee Sculpture Tour, an innovative temporary show of large-scale sculpture from around the United States, which grew over the next ten years to encompass as many as twenty-five pieces per year. The tour, which the University of Tennessee generously shared with other locations, such as Walters State Community College, Cleveland State Community College, the Metropolitan Nashville Arts Commission, and the National Ornamental Metals Museum in Memphis, had a wide impact on public awareness of outdoor sculpture. The printed catalogues that accompanied the ten-year project, which was directed by Dennis Peacock and LeeAnn Mitchell, are some of the only publications reflecting sculptural activity in Tennessee during the 1980s.

Also created with world's fair visitors in mind was the first phase of the Tennessee Arts Commission's

Interstate Welcome Center Sculpture Program, which effectively signaled the dawn of large-scale, contemporary public art projects in the state. Welcome Centers at Bristol (I-81 East) and Chattanooga (I-75 North) received bold new works by Joe Falsetti and Jack Hastings in 1982. Nine others, located at every border where an interstate highway enters the state, have since been funded by the Tennessee Arts Commission, in cooperation with the Tennessee Department of Tourist Development and the Tennessee Department of Transportation. The works range in subject from figurative to abstract and are made of metal, stone, concrete, or mosaic tile—materials that can last indefinitely through Tennessee's regular change of seasons. As a group, the Welcome Center sculptures convey an impressive range of skill and originality. The list of competition winners, which, in addition to Falsetti and Hastings, includes Lanie Gannon, Sherri Warner Hunter, Al Keim, Greely Myatt, Philip Nichols, Dennis Peacock, Bill Ralston, Phillip Vander Weg, and Tom Wuchina, reads like an honor roll of contemporary Tennessee sculptors. A map-brochure with locations and descriptions for all of the works is available at Tennessee Welcome Centers and at the Tennessee Arts Commission.

Citizens, corten steel, by Joe Falsetti, 1982, in Bristol, Sullivan County. Photograph by Timothy Weber, 2001. Courtesy of TAC.

Another important development during the mid-1980s was the inauguration of the Tennessee Valley Authority's Regional Arts Program, which conducted competitions for major sculpture commissions. Artist Jack Hastings's colorful aluminum mobile *Homage to Calder* was floated out into the inner atrium of TVA's Chattanooga headquarters in 1986, and his *Eight Elements of Energy*, a twenty-foot-long metal screen divided into eight colorful sections, was mounted outdoors at Watts Bar in 1987. Al Keim and Joe Falsetti were among other artists receiving TVA commissions for large-scale works.

Downtown Knoxville has continued to add public pieces of art as funds have been made available from both public and private sources. In the City County Building can be found an impressive wall sculpture titled *Roman Quilt* (1989) by Joe Falsetti. The wall-mounted panels weave carved and turned-wood architectural fragments with mirror-like metal squares in a checkerboard pattern that reflects the movements of passersbys and animates the building's lobby. An oversized bronze man in a rowboat was the choice of a public panel of art experts when Triad Development funded a public art competition for a piece of figurative sculpture on Gay Street. Oklahoma artist David Phelps completed the massive piece in 1989. Showing a man and a boat seeming to sink into the pavement, the sculpture continues to surprise and delight downtown visitors.

With the opening of the new Nashville International Airport Terminal in 1988, Tennessee's first "Art in Public Places" exhibition program was started by the Metropolitan Nashville Airport Authority in partnership with the Metropolitan Nashville Arts Commission. What began as an innovative temporary exhibit involving the installation of light-diffraction panels in the terminal's rafters, the *Airport Sun Project* (1989) by Kansas City artist Dale Eldred proved so popular that the Airport Authority paid the artist to make it a permanent piece. In the intervening years, two permanent sculptures by Tennessee artists have been commissioned for the airport: *Flights of Fantasy* (1995), a mosaic bench and play area by Sherri Warner Hunter, and *Dancing on Air* (1999), a pair of colorful aluminum mobiles by Jack Hastings.

During the late 1980s, private investors in Chattanooga created the Bluff View Arts District, a complex of restaurants and outdoor sculpture spaces adjacent to the Hunter Museum of American Art. Sculpture by Tennessee artists and others is placed on temporary display in garden settings overlooking the Tennessee River. In an exemplary partnership, the privately owned River Gallery works with the Hunter Museum of American Art to sponsor talks in Chattanooga by major contemporary sculptors. Equally unusual is a partnership between Chattanooga's Association of Visual Artists (AVA) and local professional masons, in which masonry benches, designed by artists and created by masonry artisans, have been produced for downtown sidewalk locations.

Since 1989, when private and public funds were raised to build the Knoxville Museum of Art, visitors have turned out in force to see a wide range of exhibits. Knoxville's art community, bolstered by the presence of the University of Tennessee's impressive Art Department, has proven itself to be as interested in the sculpture of Rodin as in the inspired assemblages of Alcoa artist Bessie Harvey, a self-taught artist whose imagery deals with such painful topics as slavery, lynching, and rape. The renewal of urban riverfront areas in Knoxville is cutting an impressive swath through previously neglected real estate and providing an impetus for the addition of public art to the Knoxville cityscape. Raymond Kaskey's *Treaty of the Holston Monument* (1999), a dramatic sculpture that incorporates an impressive granite boulder, is located in a small park where a freshwater creek drains into the Tennessee River, just below the James White Fort in downtown Knoxville. The image of a dignified Indian chief, carved in full-round relief, is flanked by low-relief figures of James White and his men on one side and additional representatives of the Cherokee people on the other. The location is authentic to the 1791 event, and the powerfully drawn portraits of the individuals present at the treaty signing lend the piece an aura of historical truth that makes it truly moving. Another recent large-scale sculpture in Knoxville is the enormous bronze portrait *Alex Haley* at Morningside Park. Artist Tina Allen depicts Haley as storyteller, seated comfortably, wearing a sweater, jacket, and cap and holding a book while looking out at his listeners through a pair of glasses. Dedicated in 1998, it was funded through the joint efforts of African American Appalachian Arts and the city of Knoxville.

Even though one can find bronze statues of Jefferson Davis, E. H. "Boss" Crump, W. C. Handy, and Elvis Presley in downtown Memphis, the state's capital city continues to be a magnet for monumental figurative sculpture. In 1968, the Tennessee General Assembly commissioned a bronze portrait of World War I hero Alvin York for a prominent location on Capitol Hill. Sculptor Felix de Weldon's convincing portrayal shows York with feet planted wide apart, aiming a rifle at an unseen enemy. In the early 1990s Jim Gray, a prominent nature painter with a studio in Gatlinburg, was asked to create a full-length bronze of President Andrew Johnson for Capitol Hill. In 1985, the War Memorial Plaza added a narrative bronze figural grouping in honor of the Vietnam War by Alan LeQuire; in 1992, a bronze sculptural relief panel telling the story of the Korean War by Russell Faxon was added. After securing a piece of appropriate city property for its placement, the descendants of Timothé de Montbrun (Demonbreun) engaged Alan LeQuire to create a bronze statue of their ancestor in 1996. The slightly larger-than-life-sized bronze of the French trapper, who inhabited the environs of Nashville prior to its actual settlement, is located near the Davidson County courthouse on a bluff overlooking the Cumberland River. Recent additions to other public spaces in downtown Nashville include Russell Faxon's life-sized bronze statues of Grand Ole Opry stars Roy Acuff and Minnie Pearl on the Ryman Auditorium plaza, and his bronze portrait of country guitarist Chet Atkins (2000) outside Bank of America's downtown Nashville offices.

Recent efforts by local arts groups and similarly motivated private individuals in both Nashville and

Memphis have resulted in important local government initiatives in both cities. Memphis has formed an Urban Arts Commission to oversee a spate of private and publicly funded projects such as the Memphis Shelby County Public Library, which contains impressive pieces of permanent architectural art, including a terrazzo floor by Memphis artists Alonzo Davis and Pinkney Herbert, and a mosaic garden by Sherri Warner Hunter. The new Memphis Shelby County Convention Center upon completion will house a major sculptural installation by American artist Vito Acconci. In Nashville, the Metropolitan Arts Commission undertook a campaign to achieve a "percent for art" ordinance for city-sponsored building projects in the future. Nashville's new Public Library features commissioned works of art, including sculptural relief panels by Tennessee sculptors Gregory Ridley and Alan LeQuire.

Another recent piece of public art in Nashville is a fun and frivolous history lesson: Red Grooms's *Tennessee Fox Trot Carousel,* a working carousel with characters from Tennessee history. The majority of funds for its construction were raised privately and proceeds from carousel rides go toward public art education for Nashville schoolchildren. The most extensive offering of contemporary public sculpture currently in Tennessee is Cheekwood Museum of Art's Carell Woodland Sculpture Trail (1999), which contains nearly twenty works. This unique presentation of outdoor sculpture interprets and interacts with the natural setting. The trail yields surprises at every turn, including British artist Sophie Ryder's huge and magical wire sculpture *Crawling Lady Hare* and American artist James Turrell's *Blue Pesher,* a round meditation chamber where one can gaze out at a blue sky long after dark. Nearly hidden in the woods is a piece by Tennessean Yone Sinor, a direct descendant of Major Ridge, a chief of the Cherokee, which recreates an Indian dwelling in the woods. Sinor's angle-cut cedar logs stand on end, forming an uneven roofline. The poles have been inserted into the ground in a spiral pattern, marking the area in between rows as an entryway. At the center of the spiral stands a cold hearth, with pottery shards scattered in its ashes. In the trees above flutter solitary prayer feathers. Sinor's imaginative artistry creates an implied narrative that prompts viewers to reexamine what they think they know about Tennessee's early inhabitants. The now deserted place is being taken back into nature by climbing vines. Sinor dedicated the piece, created in the final

A Memorial to the Aboriginal People of this Land who Lived in and with These Forests, by Yone Sinor, 1997, mixed media. 1997.13. Collection of Cheekwood Museum of Art, Nashville, Tennessee.

year of her life, to the Woodland Indians. It is "a memorial to the aboriginal people of this land, who lived in and with these forests," who first made pleasing objects from the materials of nature. They who were Tennessee's first sculptors.[8]

Notes

1. John A. Simpson, *S. A. Cunningham and the Confederate Heritage* (Athens: Univ. of Georgia Press, 1994), 152–53.
2. Florence McIntyre, *Art and Life* (Memphis: S. C. Toof, 1952), 10.
3. Charlotte A. Williams, *The Centennial Club of Nashville: A History from 1905–77* (Nashville: Centennial Club, 1978), 155.
4. Ray Kass, "Sharing a Vision: The Paintings of Burton Callicott," in *Burton Callicott: A Retrospective* (Memphis: Memphis Brooks Museum of Art, 1991), 15.
5. Bobby L. Lovett, "From Plantation to the City: William Edmondson and the African American Community," in *The Art of William Edmondson,* Rusty Freeman, Robert Farris Thompson, Judith McWillie, Grey Gundaker, Lowery S. Sims, Bobby L. Lovett (Jackson: Univ. Press of Mississippi and Nashville: Cheekwood Museum of Art, 1999), 15.
6. Scrapbook, Memphis College of Art, vol. 3, 1948–52.
7. Budd H. Bishop, *Tennessee Sculpture 1971* (Chattanooga: Chattanooga Art Association, 1971), 1 (unpaginated).
8. Yone Sinor, "Woodland Sculpture Path Proposal," for Cheekwood Museum of Art, 1997.

Suggested Readings

Bishop, Budd H. *Tennessee Sculpture, 1971.* Chattanooga: Chattanooga Art Association, 1971.

Chapman, Jefferson. *Tellico Archaeology: 1200 Years of Native American History.* Knoxville: Univ. of Tennessee Press, 1995.

Cox, Stephen D., ed. *Art and Artisans of Prehistoric Middle Tennessee.* Nashville: Tennessee State Museum, 1985.

Crouch, Ned, Michael Hall, Daniel C. Prince, Susan W. Knowles, Janelle S. Aieta, Dixie Webb, and Robert Cogswell. *E. T. Wickham: A Dream Unguarded.* Clarksville, Tenn.: Customs House Museum and Cultural Center, 2001.

Crown, Carol J. *"I've Been to the Mountaintop": Prints and Sculpture by Richard Hunt.* Exhibition pamphlet. Memphis: Memphis Brooks Museum of Art, 1990.

Darst, Stephanie. *The Sculpture of Enid Yandell.* Louisville: J. B. Speed Art Museum, 1993.

Freeman, Rusty, Robert Farris Thompson, Judith McWillie, Grey Gundaker, Lowery S. Sims, and Bobby L. Lovett. *The Art of William Edmondson.* Jackson: Univ. Press of Mississippi; Nashville: Cheekwood Museum of Art, 1999.

Holder, Philancy. *Thomas Puryear Mims.* Nashville: Cheekwood Museum of Art, 1977.

Hull, Howard. *Tennessee Post Office Murals.* Johnson City, Tenn.: Overmountain Press, 1996.

Memphis Brooks Museum of Art. *The Art Today Collection.* Memphis: Memphis Brooks Museum of Art, 1991.

Moffatt, Frederick C. "Painting, Sculpture and Photography." In *Heart of the Valley: A History of Knoxville, Tennessee,* ed. Lucille Deaderick, 424–38. Knoxville: East Tennessee Historical Society, 1976.

Simak, Ellen, and William T. Henning Jr. *A Catalogue of the American Collection: Hunter Museum of American Art.* Chattanooga: Hunter Museum of American Art, 1985.

Smith, Elise L. "Belle Kinney and the Confederate Women's Monument." *Southern Quarterly* 32, no. 4 (1994): 6–32.

Tennessee Centennial Exposition, Fine Arts Department. *An Album of the Tennessee Centennial and International Exposition.* Nashville: Marshall and Bruce, 1897.

West, Carroll Van, et al, eds. *The Tennessee Encyclopedia of History and Culture.* Nashville: Tennessee Historical Society, 1998.

Archival Sources

East Tennessee Historical Society.
Memphis Brooks Museum of Art.
Memphis College of Art.
Memphis Room, Public Library of Memphis and Shelby County.
Nashville Artist Guild.
Tennessee State Library and Archives.

Five

Painting in Nineteenth-Century Tennessee

MARILYN MASLER
Memphis Brooks Museum of Art

The story of painting in Tennessee over the course of the nineteenth century tells of its progression from the early antebellum portraitists to the expatriate students of the Gilded Age. It unfolds within the broader context of nineteenth-century American art, which itself went through many significant and dramatic changes during these years. And it encompasses not only native talent, but artists from out of state and abroad whose activities within Tennessee began the artistic evolution which continues today.

How the aesthetics of painting and a basis for its development and support were woven into the fabric of the state as it grew from a wilderness is a history in two distinct chapters—the pages that separate them, the Civil War. The first chapter is defined almost exclusively by portraiture. The second, characterized by a zeal for international style and methods, chronicles the work and the activities of expatriate painters within Tennessee. Their influence contributed to the advancement and refinement of Tennessee's painting tradition during its postwar years, and brought about the establishment of art institutions statewide as the Victorian era drew to a close.

Portraiture was the foundation of the painting profession in America at the start of the nineteenth century. The demand for good likenesses seemed inexhaustible, and business was available for painters at every level of skill. The best-trained artists remained along the eastern seaboard, where they catered to wealthy and influential citizens while hoping for more lofty commissions. As many artists still considered portrait painting to be the occupation of a menial craftsman, "on par with the commonest barterers of goods," most American academic painters preferred to use their talents in creating European-influenced genre scenes or historical tableaus.[1] However, few Americans wanted such canvases, a market

Hunters, watercolor, by Martha Gillespie Fain, age twelve, Jefferson County. This watercolor is possibly a school-girl's interpretation of a contemporary print of the legend of Francis Marion entertaining a British officer with a feast of sweet potatoes during the American Revolution. Courtesy of East Tennessee Historical Society, Knoxville.

reality that most artists attributed to the new republic's lack of sophistication in the arts. Samuel Morse of the National Academy of Design cautioned that an educated artist returning from abroad would "perish by neglect."[2] But if a painter could not build and maintain a satisfactory career in the east, how could frontier states like Tennessee expect to attract painters of merit?

Most newly settled areas waited decades before any distinguished artists visited their towns. Small populations without an established society had little to offer painters. Except for the occasional documentary artist who stopped to record the terrain or the indigenous plants and animals, only itinerant portrait painters would venture into these areas. Just as portraiture had been the preference in the east during its formative years, it would remain the most desired form of painting throughout Tennessee's antebellum period, a trend found in most developing states during the wave of westward expansion.

General Andrew Jackson, by Ralph E. W. Earl. Courtesy of Memphis Brooks Museum of Art; Memphis Park Commission Purchase 46.2.

What was the typical profile of the early portraitist in Tennessee? The range of talent and the level of education were broad and their backgrounds were varied. Some were primitive limners who used their unschooled abilities to build their trade and were usually anonymous and fleeting with no real home or direction. Others, who migrated from the East along the Ohio-Mississippi Rivers circuit from Cincinnati, Louisville, Philadelphia, and New York, could generally boast of artistic instruction, if not in Paris, London, or Munich, then usually the academies in New York or Philadelphia. Often these men were inclined to travel because their talent could not match the fierce competition back East, while others traveled for reasons of health, seeking the warmer and more temperate climate in the south. Lastly, there were Tennessee-born artists who received their education elsewhere but chose to return and pursue their careers in their native state.

Although these general characteristics define the vast majority of early Tennessee artists, there were also instances where luck and unforeseen circumstances played a part in bringing an artist to Tennessee, such as Ralph E. W. Earl (1785–1838). Earl, the son of respected Connecticut painter Ralph Earl and student of the prominent artist Benjamin West, arrived in Nashville in 1817 anxious to have Gen. Andrew Jackson sit for a portrait. What better enticement than a national hero? Earl had planned to stay only long enough to secure a likeness to use as a study for a large work representing the Battle of New Orleans, but he befriended Jackson, married his niece, and subsequently remained working in the city until he followed newly elected President Andrew Jackson to Washington in 1829. Earl's career was primarily based on producing likenesses of Jackson, but he also took commissions from the public. As fate would have it, Earl became Tennessee's first resident portrait painter. And in another twist of fate, Auguste Hervieu

(1794–1858), a well-trained French artist, became one of the first artists to take portrait commissions in Memphis in 1830—only because he was stranded there while awaiting a steamboat to Cincinnati.

The most successful portrait painters in Tennessee were those, like Earl, who had a personal reason for working here: family, marriage, inherited land, legal matters, or illness. Because pioneer communities were not encouraging to artists—the clientele was limited and there was little inspiration, camaraderie, or instruction—it took some type of anchor to keep a talented artist from eventually abandoning these young communities for better opportunities elsewhere. Tennessee, like most states during their formative years, was not particularly encouraging to the arts; here painters did the best they could under the circumstances. Through their determination and ingenuity art began to take root on the frontier.

Two native Tennesseans, Washington Bogart Cooper (1802–1888) and his brother William Browning Cooper (1811–1900), maintained two of the longest running portrait businesses in the state. After refining his painting skills in the east under the guidance of the New York painter Henry Inman, Washington Cooper established a studio in Nashville in 1832. The younger William, tutored at the National Academy (under Henry Inman) and in Europe, initially set up business in Memphis in 1846 and later worked in Nashville. The Coopers, both respected Southern gentlemen with moderate skill and good business sense, received loyal patronage through the 1880s.

During the second quarter of the nineteenth century, other artists established themselves, from Knoxville and Chattanooga in East Tennessee to Clarksville in Middle Tennessee and to Somerville in West Tennessee, but by midcentury most concentrated their focus on Nashville and Memphis, the state's fasting growing cities. While expanding cotton and tobacco markets, along with steamboat, railroad, and industrial development, fueled their growth, these two urban centers lured more and more artists in the decades prior to the Civil War.

With its older established families, concentrated wealth, political associations, and strong ties to the eastern seaboard states, Nashville could attract painters by its reputation. Memphis, settled at a later date, was still only one-third the size of Nashville by 1840 and subsequently lagged behind in civic and cultural amenities. But unlike Nashville, it had the advantage of being conveniently located along the busy Ohio-Mississippi Rivers circuit and benefited from artists who were passing up and downriver to New Orleans. Without much investment of time or expense a painter could investigate the market in Memphis and then catch a steamer to the next desired location.

Tennessee's prosperity during its antebellum boom years created a new crop of landowners in all corners of the state along with upwardly mobile merchants, bankers, and politicians who wished to have an image of themselves that reflected their hard-earned success and social status. An aristocratic heritage was no longer needed to justify one's desire for a portrait; America's new democracy had endowed each citizen with nobility regardless of class. Yet whether full scale or miniature, these likenesses contained the conventions of European formal portraiture, with style varying according to the skill of the artist and the preferences of the sitter.

Southern estates and plantations were particularly well suited to house the American "aristocratic" portrait, which, aside from recording the features of a loved one, showcased his or her property and position. The most ambitious presentations of this sort can be found in the portrait work of East and Middle Tennessee. Native Samuel Shaver (c. 1816–1878), who catered to the counties of Sullivan, Hawkins, Washington, and Carter, painted some of their earliest and most prominent families. Although his early work is simple and austere, his later presentations included highly personalized backgrounds. Typical is his *Portrait of John Roper Branner* (c. 1866), in which the subject is seated before a customized vista of his estate and his home in Jefferson County with the addition of a smoking train alluding to his presidency of the East Tennessee and Virginia Railroad.

Colonel and Mrs. James A. Whiteside, Son Charles and Servants, oil on canvas, by James Cameron, c. 1858–59. Courtesy of Hunter Museum of American Art, Chattanooga, Tennessee, Gift of Mr. and Mrs. Thomas B. Whiteside.

Scotsman James Cameron (1817–1882), who worked primarily in Chattanooga and Knoxville, was not to be outdone in his presentation of the family of Col. James A. Whiteside, a railroad magnate who was also his primary patron. In this elaborate composition, the figures are seated on an Italianate terrace complete with columns and a tiled floor, while a house-servant cradles their child and the Chattanooga valley sprawls out behind them. William Wallace Warfield of Robertson County commissioned Robert Loftin Newman (1827–1912) of Clarksville to paint two full-length, life-sized portraits. This format, which in Europe had been reserved for royal or noble patrons, was generally employed in colonial America for government or public use. But in the nineteenth century, wealthy country gentlemen, such as Warfield, proclaimed themselves as the new elite in America. They had no reservations striking a

Portrait of William Wallace Warfield and Son, by Robert Loftin Newman. Collection of Cheekwood Museum of Art, Nashville, Tennessee.

royal pose complete with the trappings of columns, tasseled drapery, and urns.

By far the most common presentation was the seated figure, waist length, with a simple background—usually a drapery or a column with just a suggestion of sky and clouds. Even the most provincial painters in the state produced this format countless times. Whether done by the competent hand of James Hart (1812–1870), or with the high technical skill and sophistication of William Edward West (1788–1857), it found its place in many Tennessee homes. Miniatures, by artists such as John Wood Dodge (1807–1893) or John O'Brien Inman (1828–1896), also were popular. A recent study of Dodge's work found that the artist painted over one hundred Tennesseans in the two decades before the Civil War. In painting portraits, followers of the renowned Gilbert Stuart had advocated his method of modeling the face before a plain background in order to depict the essential character of the sitter with no indication of class or property. Although this format was also frequently employed, few frontier painters had the consummate skill and sensitivity necessary to distill into a simple image the depth of a complex personality with intrinsic human qualities.

Technical flaws in perspective, anatomy, and proportion were commonplace in early Tennessee portraits, but this was inherent in most frontier painting. To properly render the human figure required intensive studio training with live models, and this was simply unavailable to most artists working in America in the first half of the nineteenth century. Many taught themselves to correct their shortcomings through trial and error and often times relied on engravings and mezzotints as learning aids. A trip to Philadelphia or New York to study quality pictures firsthand might also serve as refresher course. Even pictures that contained some distortions could often present an impressive portrait that ranged from charming to decorative to surreal. Kentuckian William S. Shackelford (c. 1814–1878), who worked in Clarksville in the 1850s, received no formal art

Shackelford Children, by William Shackelford. Courtesy of TSM.

training, yet his portrait of the *Shackelford Children* (c. 1857–60) possesses an enchanting quality due to his simple, unsophisticated shading technique. Although the softened edges of the bodies make them appear as cutouts set before a theatrical backdrop, it also lends a doll-like charm to the young boy and girl.

The wide range in quality of the portraits produced in antebellum Tennessee indicates that the desire to have one's image captured for posterity crossed economic lines. At midcentury, as the standard of living rose, and with the introduction of photography, the primitive painter lost much of his livelihood. A small daguerreotype would suffice for those with limited income. As for the middle and upper classes, where the appeal of a fine hand-painted portrait would not be lost, the perception of painting, and of the painter, slowly began to change.

The tide had already turned along the Atlantic seaboard where the Hudson River School had revitalized the eastern art market. These paintings made in and of the Catskill Mountains in upper New York state spoke of the grandeur and divinity inherent in America's virgin wilderness. These American painters received newfound respect from the public and from a new group of self-made patrons who were eager to purchase their work. In the era of Jacksonian Democracy the painter moved from artisan to gentleman, and the pantheistic view of nature revealed in these landscapes moved painting onto a higher contemplative plane. Documentary portraiture was now left to the daguerreotypists and to less innovative painters, while the work of artists such as Thomas Cole (1801–1848), Asher B. Durand (1796–1886), and John Frederick Kensett (1816–1872) led American painters in a new direction and developed a market for native landscapes.

Before this movement significantly influenced Tennessee painting the Civil War took place, and its hardship and devastation consumed the South and the nation. During the initial years of recovery in Tennessee, as the New South struggled with the problems of industry, immigration, education, and civil rights, the fine arts languished. Aside from the countless commissions executed for portraits of politicians and Confederate heroes, the earliest signs of artistic regeneration were found in the careers of Carl Gutherz, Kate Carl, Lloyd Branson, Mary Solari, and Edwin N. Gardner; they were the first artists in Tennessee to join the wave of American expatriate painters in France, Germany, and Italy in the 1870s. The number of expatriates reached its peak in the 1890s, and as this national exodus grew, it continued to draw men and women from Memphis, Knoxville, and Nashville, as Paris became the undisputed center of the art world. For those American painters prepared to compete with the finest continental painters in the marketplace as well as in the salons, not only was European art training essential but they also needed a well-rounded education in literature, religion, history, and philosophy. No longer could the illiterate and self-taught, or those lacking knowledge in the basic elements of art techniques and theory, find critical success in a now-sophisticated arena in which painting was considered an intellectual pursuit. The standard for an artist was to be "well trained, well informed, scholarly and accomplished."[3]

The expatriate movement was one factor that contributed to the rising standard of art throughout the United States. In Tennessee, it was the impetus behind the establishment of art schools and an enlightened approach to the appreciation and practice of painting as many artists returned home anxious to exhibit their newly acquired knowledge and skills and to replicate European teaching methods used in the academies and the ateliers. Although Tennessee would not produce its own signature style of painting by the century's end, stylistic influences from abroad significantly raised the quality of regional painting. By no means a quick transformation, it took successive waves of painters, learning abroad then returning home to paint or instruct, in order to establish a strong base of support. Although the length of their trips varied—some a few years, others over ten—the experience proved invaluable.

Civil War Illustrations

Drawings of Tennessee in the Civil War fall into three categories: soldier art, works by "special artists" employed by northern newspapers, and art done after the war to illustrate books, such as Benson Lossing's *Pictorial History of the Civil War* and the Century Company's *Battles and Leaders of the Civil War.* The categories overlap because, when Century called in the 1880s for illustrative material for its project, soldiers' eyewitness sketches and wartime works by "specials" were forwarded to New York and reworked by Century's team of professional illustrators. In some cases those copies made for *Battles and Leaders* are all that survive.

All the known soldier art from Tennessee is from the Union side. One drawing groups seven images of camp life in Decherd, Franklin County, in the summer of 1863. A view of Nashville by the same artist, H. B. Huebner, shows the Sixteenth Illinois Volunteer Infantry, perhaps his unit, camped in Edgefield. An unknown Ohio soldier depicts the Sixty-fourth Ohio Volunteers encamped on the battlefield of Stones River in March 1863. In the same year William Blanton of the 117th Illinois Volunteers drew a plan view of Fort Pickering in Memphis. So did William D. Ferree, an enlisted man in the Eighty-ninth Indiana Infantry. Henry Domon of the Twenty-first Battery Ohio Light Artillery, on guard duty in Knoxville, drew a bird's-eye view of the town and surroundings in April 1864. John Gaddis of the Twelfth Wisconsin Infantry drew three watercolors in Tennessee, one showing a Union troop train crossing the Obion River and two depicting a Confederate attack on the Union occupiers of Humboldt, Tennessee, on July 28, 1862.

[Continued on next page]

Gunboats at Fort Donelson, watercolor on paper heightened with white, 11 × 15¼ inches, by Harry Fenn (1838–1911), for *Battles and Leaders of the Civil War,* after an 1862 eyewitness sketch by Capt. Henry N. Walke. Photograph by June Dorman. Courtesy of TSM.

The landscape around Chattanooga enticed H. Bambrick, a New Englander, to produce a watercolor called *Blue Coats in Bivouac on Lookout Mountain.* James Hope, a topographic officer in the Second Vermont, did sketches of the region that after the war were translated into oil paintings such as *View from Lookout Mountain.* H. E. Brown, an enlisted man in Gen. Joseph Hooker's Twelfth Corps, drew at least two action scenes—*Bridging Lookout Creek* and *The Battle of Lookout Mountain.*

Magazines such as *Leslie's, Harper's Weekly, New York Illustrated,* and the *Illustrated London News* employed about fifty "special artists" who were sent into combat zones to produce pictures to satisfy the insatiable public demand. Only one, Frank Vizitelly of the *Illustrated London News,* operated on the Confederate side, but he never reached Tennessee. The first "specials" in Tennessee accompanied General Grant and Commodore Foote in the campaign against Forts Henry and Donelson. Alexander Simplot was one of this "Bohemian Brigade," the label given to Civil War correspondents and artists. He sketched Fort Henry on the Tennessee soon after its capitulation, and his sketch of the naval battle of Memphis in 1862 later was converted to a painting. Capt. Henry N. Walke, captain of the Yankee gunboat *Carondelet,* also sketched that engagement, and many other scenes on the western waters, including *Gunboats at Fort Donelson* and *The Carondolet Passing Island Number Ten.* Henry Mosler of *Harper's Weekly* sketched the stockade protecting the railroad bridge at Franklin.

Alfred E. Mathews of the Thirty-first Ohio Volunteer Infantry drew *Federal Reinforcements at Murfreesboro* and *The Federal Right at Murfreesboro.* Mathews's original drawings were copied by Walton Taber, a professional illustrator for *Battles and Leaders of the Civil War,* who reworked many drawings submitted by aging soldiers or specials. Because there were no specials with General Thomas during 1864, Taber generated drawings of Nashville by copying wartime photographs by George Barnard. Harry Fenn, another Century artist, copied *Lookout Mountain* from a wartime photograph and *Cumberland River from Fort Donelson* from a 1884 photograph. *Battle of Shiloh* by Allen C. Redwood raises hope because he was a Confederate soldier, but we know that he never left the Virginia theater, so his drawing for Century is merely conjectural, as is Thure de Thulstrup's moonlit view of *Buell's Troops Arriving at Pittsburg Landing.*

Benson J. Lossing won considerable renown in the 1850s for his *Pictorial Field Book of the Revolution.* His *Pictorial History of the Civil War* appeared in three volumes between 1866 and 1868. In April and May of 1866, he traveled across Tennessee doing sketches for the projected volumes. Among his surviving Tennessee sketches are "Parson" Brownlow's *Office of the Knoxville Whig, Fort Zollicoffer near Nashville and Fort Bruce near Clarksville, Headquarters of Bragg and Thomas at Murfreesboro, Rosecrans' Headquarters at Murfreesboro, Blockhouse at Normandy, Place of Longstreet's Charge near Chattanooga, The Crozier House at Knoxville,* and *Morgan's Headquarters at Greeneville.*

James C. Kelly, Virginia Historical Society

Carl Gutherz (1844–1907) was the first in the state to begin this pattern, returning to his family in Memphis in 1872 after studying at the École des Beaux Arts in Paris and at the Academies in Munich and Rome. Later associated with the American Symbolist movement, Gutherz introduced Memphians to the current European academic aesthetic with the local viewing of his first allegorical work, *Awakening of Spring* (1872). Unable to support himself financially in Memphis, shortly after his return he took up teaching in St. Louis and later returned to Paris.

When Lloyd Branson (1854–1925) returned to Knoxville in 1878, he encountered similar conditions. After receiving an education at the University of Tennessee and the National Academy of Design, his three-year sojourn abroad brought him back to a city that was geared to industrial development with little sentiment for the arts. He generated his own artistic core working in partnership with a photographer and establishing the firm of McCrary and Branson in Knoxville. The firm's building eventually evolved into a community art center, where Branson offered instruction to Knoxville's next generation of artists.

Edwin M. Gardner (1845–1935) also found employment as a teacher upon his return in 1875. After six years of instruction at the National Academy and in Europe he was employed at several female colleges before moving to Nashville in 1885. There, he made his living as a painter and illustrator and eventually took up teaching once again.

When Kate Carl (1854–1938) and Mary Solari (1849–1929) left Memphis to study art in the 1870s, Tennessee society had not yet advocated an acceptable role for women in the arts. In the following decades, the fine arts became a hallmark of urban culture and women were encouraged to take up painting and drawing as part of a genteel lady's education. Carl and Solari took an early lead in pursuing serious painting careers at a time when the profession was predominantly male and extremely competitive. After two years of instruction in Paris, Carl returned to Memphis and taught studio art. Not content in this role, she returned to Paris in 1884 to work and live for the next nineteen years. Solari, who chose to study in Florence, Italy, because of her Italian heritage, also took up a teaching career upon her return to Memphis when she opened an art school in 1894.

Solari and Branson spent more time actually living and teaching in Tennessee than Gutherz or Carl, but all four continued to serve as significant role models throughout the last three decades of the nineteenth century. Solari had made history, after six years of persistence, by becoming the first woman admitted to the Florence School of Fine Arts. She also reaped an impressive group of awards and notices for her work while abroad. Gutherz and Carl, who both resided in Paris for an extended second period, accumulated extensive exhibition records—each having been accepted annually into the Paris salon during their tenure there in the 1880s and 1890s. Branson, who exhibited primarily in the United States at the National Academy of Design and in various southern expositions, became the premiere painter in Knoxville. With local press consistently reporting on their progress at home and abroad, the activities of these artists became a source of pride, and their paintings could be found in many Tennessee homes and businesses. Gutherz and Carl, who were known to have welcomed visitors from home into their Paris studios, would maintain the most prominent careers, and no other Tennessee painters would eclipse them by century's end.

As the 1880s unfolded and the 1890s ushered in the Gilded Age, the next group of painters in Tennessee found the state more receptive and encouraging to their artistic pursuits. The late Victorian era saw an increase in art organizations, art schools, and art exhibitions that reflected a nationwide trend. Within this twenty-year period, the Nashville Art Association and the Memphis School of Art and Music were established. Independent artists, including Solari and the brothers Peter (1855–1931) and Ebenezer Calvert (1850–1924), opened studios for instruction while Branson continued his tutoring in Knoxville. The newly formed Ossoli Circle, Knoxville Art Circle, and the Memphis Art League provided further incentive and instruction. Female academies in Memphis and Nashville also began promoting their art departments as women took the lead in the proliferation of the arts.

It was a small group of painters who taught in Tennessee's art schools, participated in the state's art associations, lectured, and regularly exhibited nationally and internationally. Among them were Memphian

Le Pain Beni (Passing the Holy Bread), by Willie Betty Newman. Courtesy of Centennial Club, Nashville.

John B. Longman (1860– n.d.) and his wife Fannie May Longman (birth and death dates unknown), who both had European training. Fanny May opened an art school in Memphis in 1885, but after her marriage to John Longman in 1890, the two operated the school together. They eventually relocated it to Nashville in the mid-1890s. St. Louis painter George Chambers (1856–1929) was recruited to head the Nashville School of Fine Arts in 1886. Chambers was aptly qualified, having attended the St. Louis School of Fine Arts and the École des Beaux Arts and the Académie Julian in Paris. Along with Solari and Branson, Chambers and the Longmans comprised the state's leading art instructors at the end of the century.

These five artists, together with Gutherz and Carl, represented the primary group of active Tennessee painters, who influenced the next wave of rising Tennessee artists from about 1885 to 1900. The majority of these young art students were women, of whom Willie Betty Newman (1863–1935) was the most prominent. Others working within this era included Frank W. Stokes (1858–1955), Sara Ward Conley (1859–1944), Charles Frederick Naegele (1857–1944), Robert Lee McComb (1860–?), Minnie Gattinger (birth and death dates unknown), and Katherine Huger (birth and death dates unknown). All continued on the expatriate path, receiving training in Paris in addition to their initial art instruction in the United States, but nearly half, at some point, returned home to Tennessee.

A review of the work of this entire ensemble of late-nineteenth-century artists indicates that each had assimilated elements of contemporary European imagery and theory into their paintings. Aside from portraiture (which was an economic necessity for each of them), they produced paintings which, although not particularly innovative, reflected trends within the artistic mainstream. Absorbing what was taught by the French masters of the day, such as Jean-Léon Gérôme, Jules Lefebreve, Jules Dupré, and William Bourguereau, the work of these Tennessee painters was often accepted into the Paris salons. At the time, European folk life was one of the most popular subjects. Based upon the successful work of Jean-François Millet (1814–1875) and Jules Breton (1827–1906), these pictures, which filled the exhibition halls, "ranged from anecdotal tableaux to observations of daily life," and the "painting techniques varied from exacting detail to impressionist brushwork."[4] Close ties to the earth and a sense of tradi-

École des Beaux Arts and the Paris Salons

"WHO WOULD NOT BE A STUDENT IN PARIS?" AMERICAN ARTIST ROBERT HENRI ASKED IN 1888. From the mid-1860s until 1900, thousands of Americans echoed his sentiment and traveled to Paris to seek art instruction.

They studied in Paris for several reasons. Although American art schools provided solid art instruction, Paris remained the leading center for professional training. Further, the taste in art among American patrons, artists, and critics had shifted from the Hudson River School to a preference for French painting. Where better to learn French painting than in Paris?

When they got to Paris, American students had several options. They could seek entrance to the government-run, tuition-free École des Beaux Arts (School of Fine Arts); they would, however, have to pass a rigorous entrance examination conducted in French. An artist could also train outside of the École by studying with a particular artist in his atelier, or studio. Leading artists of the day, including Jean-Léon Gérôme, Leon Bonnat, and Carolus Duran, offered such classes. Finally, some private art schools, notably the Académie Julian, provided drawing classes.

The heart of study at the École was drawing, particularly life drawing, or drawing a nude model. Students began by copying engravings, moved on to sketching plaster casts of antique sculpture, and culminated in drawing from the live model. To French academicians, the human form was the foundation of their art, so a mastery of depicting the body was essential. Along with classes in drawing, students at the École could also take such courses as anatomy, aesthetics, and art history. The only way a student could receive instruction in painting or sculpture was to enroll in one of the private ateliers affiliated with the École or to work in an independent atelier.

Like the École, the ateliers and private art schools emphasized life drawing. They differed from the École, however, in several important respects: they charged tuition, they did not offer anything other than life-drawing classes, and they allowed women to attend the classes. The École opened its doors to women only in 1897, whereas other schools had begun to offer classes to female art students almost twenty years earlier.

The opportunity to display work in the annual international salons, or art exhibitions, in Paris was also of great importance to Americans studying abroad. Such juried exhibitions allowed Americans to show their work in an international context and to prove they could hold their own with the best artists in France.

The number of Americans studying in Paris academies waned as modernism and abstraction increased in importance, but the impact of Parisian academic art training lived on in American art schools. When these artists returned to the United States, they helped craft the curriculum of schools and taught a generation of young American artists.

Ellen Simak, Curator of Collections, Hunter Museum of American Art

tion and spirituality made the European peasant an appealing subject that evolved into a variety of domestic scenes of mother and child as well as landscapes of the Normandy and Brittany countryside. This genre, which brought into focus "the significance of the commonplace,"[5] was the basis for much of the painting produced by Tennessee's artists during the latter part of the century.

This theme was particularly inspirational to Willie Betty Newman of Murfreesboro, who spent

The Orphans, by Frank Stokes, painting destroyed by fire in 1896.

the 1890s studying and painting in France and Holland. For over ten years her canvases focused on various aspects of peasant society, many containing religious themes or overtones—an element that was frequently woven into this type of imagery. Her *Le Pain Béni,* shown in the 1894 salon, depicts Finistere (France) villagers in regional costume, receiving the Eucharist with piety and devotion in a simple stone church. *Le Neuvine* (c. 1895), another depiction of Catholic ritual, shows two devout women praying by the light of nine candles. Other works by Newman titled *Head of a Madonna* (c. 1899) and *The Young Virgin* (c. 1889) imply a sacred association with the woman figure, another outgrowth of this genre. A glimpse at an intimate moment in *En Pénitence* (c. 1895) lends quiet significance to the relationship of child and caregiver.

In the same vein, Frank Stokes (1858–1955) of Nashville produced Paris salon works such as *Procession of the Virgin* (c. 1890), also focusing on religious celebrations in rural France. *The Orphans* (c. 1888), in which two French peasant children embrace each other in grief before their mother's grave, is Stokes's sympathetic rendering of the eternal bond between mother and child.

Unfortunately, the present locations of many late-nineteenth-century paintings by Tennessee artists remain unknown. Judging from a compilation of the known titles of these works, however, the works shared the same interest in European provincial images: *The Shoemakers, A Good Sermon,* and *An Interior at Etaples* (Stokes); *Bretonne* (Carl); *A Dutch Peasant Reading* (Gattinger); *A Brittany Fishing Village* and *Au Bord du Loing* (McComb); and *Dutch Mother, Normandy Farm, The Wayfarers,* and *Eventide* (Huger).

Upon their return to the United States, some painters began to integrate American imagery into these same European themes. In a simple composition, *Our Daily Bread* (c. 1897) by former Memphian John Longman, the sanctity of the family meal is depicted as mother and child sit at their table, in prayer, before their food while the title adds further religious implication. Longman's figures, in contrast to Newman's, have been "Americanized," denoting Victorian costume and hairstyle.

While in Paris, George Chambers had painted and exhibited Normandy genre such as *The Dunes* (c. 1884) and *The Shepherdess* (c. 1883) at the salon. Chambers's *In the Tennessee Mountains* (1887), painted on site at the Sumner farm in Middle Tennessee, replaced the Brittonne and Normandy folk peasants with images of rural American culture, using the same stylistic formulas he had absorbed in Paris. The bonnet and dress of the elderly woman and the architecture of the barn and cabin indicate

Left: In the Tennessee Mountains, by George Chambers, location unknown.

Below: Our Daily Bread, by John Longman, location unknown.

American roots yet the stance of the figure, her placement in the cabbage field, and her gaze speak of the same weariness and humility found in Millet's timeless figures.

Even while artists such as Winslow Homer (1836–1910) were proving the strength and appeal of familiar native subjects, artists and critics alike complained that American images lacked the depth of character and history that made European folk images so compelling. Once back in the United States, if painters working in this genre were to continue the practice of rendering from firsthand observation, as was the preferred method abroad, they had little choice but to integrate national subject matter into their work.

Painting directly from nature in the open air was an activity that was encouraged in summer schools across America during the last decades of the nineteenth century. In Tennessee, Chambers, the Longmans, and others taught classes at the Monteagle Assembly, a popular summer resort area in Middle Tennessee. Like the well-known Shinnecock School conducted in New York by William Merritt Chase, pupils at Monteagle were comprised mainly of women, and sketching and painting were often practiced *en plein air* in the scenic surroundings. During these summer sessions, which often promoted the use of local rustic imagery, Katherine Huger of Knoxville produced *Washday in the Tennessee Mountains* (c. 1887). Elizabeth Nourse (1859–1938) of Cincinnati, who spent three summers in the Smoky Mountains after graduating from the McMicken School, also portrayed a southern folk scene in *Tennessee Woman Weaving* (c. 1885), a precursor to her later peasant-based work produced in France and Belgium.

Above: Woman Weaving, watercolor on paper, 17 × 14 inches, by Elizabeth Nourse, Tenn. Mts., 1885. Courtesy of Ran Gallery, Cincinnati.

Below: Hauling Marble, by Lloyd Branson. Courtesy of The Frank H. McClung Museum, University of Tennessee.

Also capturing slices of rural life in Tennessee was Lloyd Branson, who took notice of the day-to-day activities in and around Knoxville. *The Marble Haulers* (c. 1890) and his later *Hauling Marble* (c. 1910), two paintings Branson based upon the region's stone quarry industry, depict horse-drawn wagons loaded with excavated stone lumbering through the hills. In three other canvases, *The Fruit Driers* (c. 1890), *Women at Work* (1891), and *Over the Hills* (c. 1891), he also portrays women in common activities associated with the local agricultural community.

Although the majority of these late-nineteenth-century painters employed highly popular peasantry themes and related genre in their work, Carl Gutherz and Mary Solari remained outside this particular Parisian current. Solari, as a result of her Italian roots and her high regard for the heritage of Italian painting, had studied, exhibited, and taught almost exclusively in Italy during her fifteen years abroad. This isolation and her conservative approach to painting prevented her from being consumed by the latest European trends and her work consisted mainly of architectural renderings and scenic studies

in watercolor. During her Tennessee years, her painting became secondary to her strong role as a teacher and advocate for art education.

Gutherz, whose passion was allegorical work, had tried his hand at a few French genre paintings such as *Normandy Cider* (1889) and *The Gleaners* (1888), but he found his greatest success and satisfaction in producing large canvases with religious symbolism. *Light of the Incarnation* (1888), the birth of Christ from an angelic perspective, and *Arcessita Ab Angelis* (1889), an interpretation of the soul's journey at death, both reflect his strong interest in the connection between the real and the ideal. *Memorialis* (1888), *Angel of the Tomb* (1892), and *Evening of the Sixth Day* (1893), all shown in Paris salons, were not as marketable as the peasantry being produced by his peers, but they led to three mural commissions in the United States, including one in the Library of Congress.

After his twelve-year residency abroad, Gutherz was fortunate to establish a painting career in

Top: Women at Work, by Lloyd Branson. Courtesy of Namuni Hale Young.

Above: Normandy Cider, by Carl Gutherz, 1889. Courtesy of Memphis Brooks Museum of Art; gift of Mr. and Mrs. Marshall F. Goodheart 67.9.

Light of the Incarnation, by Carl Gutherz, 1888. Courtesy of Memphis Brooks Museum of Art; gift of Mr. and Mrs. Marshall F. Goodheart 68.11.1.

Washington, D.C., in 1896. Transition back into the American art scene was difficult for some expatriates, and many, like Gutherz, settled in larger urban areas rather than returning to Tennessee. Opportunities were greater in eastern cities where established art institutions offered instruction and incentive, and where population density and wealth offered a more enthusiastic marketplace.

Katherine Huger of Knoxville and Charles Naegele of Memphis, for example, worked primarily in New York City after returning from Europe, producing portraits and genre scenes and showing regularly at the National Academy's exhibitions. Anna Weaver Jones of Nashville returned to Chicago where she had initially attended the Chicago Academy of Design before studying in New York and Paris. For years she remained well represented in the Art Institute's annual exhibits. Two others, Kate Carl and Frank W. Stokes, followed two very different and fascinating paths.

Through connections with her brother, Carl had visited China and was given the great honor of painting a portrait of the Empress Dowager in 1903. This painting, which was sent to the St. Louis World's Fair the following year, made Carl a celebrity of sorts. One of the few foreigners welcomed as a resident guest of the Imperial Court of China, she wrote of her experience in a book, *With the Empress Dowager of China.* Although she continued to live in China for the next twenty-seven years, Carl maintained her ties to Memphis. Stokes, who had shown his work very successfully in Paris, Philadelphia, and Chicago, signed on as an independent member of Admiral Peary's historic Greenland expeditions of 1892 and 1893–94. After accompanying other subsequent Arctic and Antarctic expeditions, his work became primarily focused on capturing the beauty and isolation of these regions. Very much removed from his earlier work under Thomas Eakins or his later salon work, Stokes's landscapes took on an impressionist quality as he attempted to capture the light and color unique to these areas.

Among those who did return to live in Tennessee were Sara Ward Conley and Willie Betty Newman. Conley, who specialized in portraits and murals, taught in Nashville for many years after her studies in Paris and Rome. Although Nashville was also fortunate to have a painter of Newman's experience and skill residing in the city, the art school she created proved unsuccessful and she turned to portraiture for the remainder of her career. Regrettably, as was

The Empress Dowager, Tze Hsi, of China, by Katherine Augusta Carl. Courtesy of the Smithsonian American Art Museum; gift of the Imperial Chinese Government.

the case with many expatriates, Newman's painting career never regained the success and momentum of her twelve years abroad.

Gilbert Gaul (1855–1919) of New Jersey was a Tennessee-associated painter in the second half of the nineteenth century who did not take up an expatriate life in Europe but nonetheless left his mark. Gaul, an alumnus of the National Academy, spent short periods in Van Buren County throughout the 1880s and 1890s. Although he painted some landscapes of the area, his specialty was military scenes from which he also profited as an illustrator. It could be argued that his canvases such *Rafting on the Cumberland River* (n.d.) or his Civil War depictions contain a greater sense of regional identity than anything produced by local painters under the influence of the French masters. Yet it was imperative for artists native to this area, in order to shed their "provincialism," to acquire unquestionable validity in the European ateliers and salons.

By century's end, as "American art came to be seen and estimated in an international context,"[6] Tennessee expatriate painters had joined with other artists from across the country to contribute to the new perception of the American artist both at home and abroad. Newfound respect had grown through the display of American competitive spirit and skill in the European schools as well as participation and success in international salons and expositions. Evidence of this would come home to Tennessee through the Fine Arts Exhibition at the Tennessee Centennial in 1897, where paintings of the majority of these artists could be viewed in context with their peers and alongside a selection of early masterworks. The exhibition exposed Tennesseans to an unprecedented standard and scope of painting—with the inclusion of their native sons and daughters (as well as resident instructors) as professional participants.

Locally known painters John Longman, Carl Gutherz, and George Chambers also had been called upon to serve in various capacities to help organize the exhibition, which included over a thousand paintings obtained from artists and institutions around the world. The private purchase of the juried works had been encouraged so that when the exposition closed there might be enough significant paintings within the state to form a permanent gallery or museum. But sales were not as great as anticipated—less than 20 percent of the 669 artworks were sold—and these did not go exclusively to patrons in Tennessee.

With the Fine Arts Exhibition also came the hope that a deeper awareness of the arts would develop in Tennessee as the new century dawned. The organizers had hoped that each citizen "would

Rafting on the Cumberland River, by Gilbert Gaul. Courtesy of TSM.

The Ephraim Hubbard Foster Family, by Ralph E.W. Earl Jr., oil on mattress ticking, 1824. 1969.2. Collection of Cheekwood Museum of Art, Nashville, Tennessee.

cultivate an appreciation for the art of his day" through the study of the broad range of paintings represented in the Parthenon building.[7] Furthermore, by witnessing the stylistic changes that had occurred throughout the centuries and within their own region or vicinity, visitors to the exposition would come to understand that "art can never stand still."[8]

By 1900, painting traditions in Tennessee had evolved beyond the narrow terms of a picture reflective of subject matter in or about Tennessee to encompass work produced by painters who had studied and worked abroad and whose paintings embodied foreign subject matter and style. The painters were not only native-born artists, but included those who had come into the state to teach and work.

In areas such as Tennessee, where no strong native style had yet found its voice and where advancement of the arts needed a strong push, the technical expertise and inspiration provided by the expatriates was a welcome spark to the development of painting. Through their paintings, their careers, and their teaching they formed a bridge between Tennessee and the artistic mainstream. These men and women not only brought recognition to Tennessee in art circles outside of the state, but they elevated the local standard of painting from the function of documentary portraiture to a purer aesthetic experience. The consideration of "art for art's sake" was one of the crucial lessons underlying the work of these painters—a lesson that set the stage for

Memphis, Tennessee, by John Hazelhurst Boneval Latrobe, 1832, watercolor on paper, 5½ × 8¼ inches, negative number 49711, accession number 1969.445. Collection of the New-York Historical Society. Courtesy of The New-York Historical Society.

what would follow as the twentieth century unfolded and as modernism was introduced to America and the South.

Notes

1. James Thomas Flexner, *History of American Painting: The Light of Distant Skies* (New York: Dover Publications, 1969), 245.
2. Ibid., 231.
3. Michael Quick, *American Expatriate Painters of the Late Nineteenth Century* (Dayton, Ohio: Dayton Art Institute, 1976), 21.
4. Lois Marie Fink, *American Art at the Nineteenth-Century Paris Salons* (New York: Cambridge Univ. Press, 1983), 204.
5. Mary Alice Heekin Burke and Lois Marie Fink, *Elizabeth Nourse, 1859–1938: A Salon Career* (Washington, D.C.: Smithsonian Institution Press, 1983), 101.
6. Quick, *American Expatriate Painters,* 15.
7. *Tennessee Centennial and International Exposition, Catalogue, Fine Arts Department Tennessee Centennial* (Nashville: Brandon, 1897), 80.
8. Ibid., 20.

Suggested Readings

Bishop, Budd H. "Art in Tennessee; The Early 19th Century." *Tennessee Historical Quarterly* 29 (Winter 1970): 379–89.

———. "Three Tennessee Painters: Samuel M. Shaver, Washington B. Cooper, and James Cameron." *Antiques* 100 (Sept. 1971): 432–37.

Burke, Mary Alice Heekin, and Lois Marie Fink. *Elizabeth Nourse, 1859–1938: A Salon Career.* Washington, D.C.: Smithsonian Institution Press, 1983.

Chambers, Bruce W. *Art and Artists of the South.* Columbia: Univ. of South Carolina Press, 1984.

Deaderick, Lucille, ed. *The Heart of the Valley.* Knoxville: East Tennessee Historical Society, 1976.

Fink, Lois Marie. *American Art at the Nineteenth-Century Paris Salons.* New York: Cambridge Univ. Press, 1990.

Gerdts, William H. *Art Across America: Two Centuries of Regional Painting, 1710–1920.* Vol. 2. New York: Abbeville Press, 1990.

Kelly, James C. "Landscape and Genre Painting in Tennessee." *Tennessee Historical Quarterly* 44 (Summer 1985): 1–52.

———. "Portrait Painting in Tennessee." *Tennessee Historical Quarterly* 46 (Winter 1987): 193–276.

MacBeth, Jerome R. "Portraits by Ralph E. W. Earl." *Antiques* 100 (Sept. 1971): 390–93.

Masler, Marilyn. "Art and Artists in Antebellum Memphis." *Tennessee Historical Quarterly* 57 (Winter 1998): 219–35.

———. "Carl Gutherz: Memphis Beginnings." *West Tennessee Historical Society Papers* 46 (Dec. 1992): 59–72.

Painting in the South: 1564–1980. Richmond: Virginia Museum of Fine Arts, 1983.

Price, Prentiss. "Samuel Shaver: Portrait Painter." *East Tennessee Historical Society Publications* 24 (1952): 92–105.

Quick, Michael. *American Expatriate Painters of the Late Nineteenth Century.* Dayton, Ohio: Dayton Art Institute, 1976.

———. *American Portraiture in the Grand Manner: 1720–1920.* Los Angeles: Los Angeles County Museum of Art, 1981.

Strass, Stephanie A., and Susan E. Schockley, "The Art of Willie Betty Newman." *American Art Review* 14 (Jan.–Feb. 2002): 102–9.

Tennessee in the Nineteenth Century. Knoxville: Dulin Gallery of Art, 1971.

White, Raymond D. "John Wood Dodge and Portrait Miniatures in Nineteenth-Century Middle Tennessee." *Tennessee Historical Quarterly* 59 (Spring 2000): 20–37.

Six

Painting in Twentieth-Century Tennessee

Celia Walker
Vanderbilt University

In this global age, painting in Tennessee is rich in stylistic and thematic diversity. There is a wealth of avant-garde art in the state, particularly in the major cities, alongside a longstanding more popular tradition of regional realism. Regionalism, once it emerged in the 1930s in response to the influx of European modernism, became and remains a constant in the state's art market. When the cultural upheaval of the 1960s and 1970s prompted many of the nation's artists to create strongly politicized artworks, few Tennessee painters followed suit. This was due, in part, to the lack of patronage for political art in Tennessee and, in larger part, to the homeward focus of many Tennessee painters, who are still connected to the land.

Certainly, the prominent landforms in our elongated state are the subjects of many regional painters, from Memphians who paint the Mississippi River to Knoxvillians who paint the Smoky Mountains. The state's topography has also shaped our preferences for certain media. Since the late nineteenth century, we find a predilection for watercolors in the east where artists traveled rough terrain to find scenic views and were forced to pack lightly. Similarly, available land in downtown Memphis has encouraged the creation of experimental co-ops and installation art, both of which require a lot of space. But beyond regional subjects and the physical constraints of location, little differentiates Tennessee painting from that found elsewhere in the Southeast. The story of Tennessee painting follows the main patterns of style, institution building, and increasing professionalism found throughout the Southeast.

Despite the tremendous increase in venues and opportunities for painters over the last one hundred years, most artists must seek representation in a major art center outside of the state to make a living because there are just not enough patrons for art outside of the Regionalist tradition. At the same time, art in Tennessee improved significantly during the twentieth century. The number of art schools in the state has increased and today's artists have the opportunity and materials to create work that rivals anything found elsewhere in the country. That was not true in 1900, and the development of a support system of schools, museums, galleries, associations, and patrons frames the picture of Tennessee painting in the twentieth century.

Imported Goods

The art exhibition of the 1897 Tennessee Centennial, an exposition honoring the state's admission to the Union, was the first event to open new opportunities for painting and art in Tennessee. Based on the highly successful 1893 Columbian Exposition in Chicago and Atlanta's 1895 Cotton States Exposition, the Tennessee Centennial Exposition drew large crowds to Nashville and brought the state's industrial achievements onto the national stage. The exposition promoted art appreciation among the thousands of Tennesseans who attended the six-month-long event. The centennial's Parthenon pavilion housed over one thousand artworks on loan from collections outside of the state and from around the world. Paintings by such Gilded Age artists as Cecilia Beaux, J. Carroll Beckwith, and Thomas Anshutz highlighted the exhibitions. The five primary displays of the Parthenon exhibition contained the work of more than five hundred artists, of whom only eighteen were born or worked in Tennessee.

Of the 321 artists represented in the *Paintings by American Artists Exhibit,* fifteen had lived or worked in Tennessee. From Knoxville came Enoch Lloyd Branson (1854–1925) and Charles Frederick Naegele (1857–1944), who spent his early years in Memphis. Memphis residents included Robert Lee McComb (1860–?) and Mary Magdelene Solari (1849–1929), who curated the art exhibit in the Memphis building. Also with Bluff City associations were Kate Augusta Carl (1854–1938), who was living in Neiully, Paris, France, and exhibiting in the Paris Salons after leaving Memphis in 1884, and Carl Gutherz (1844–1907), who was working on a mural for the Library of Congress in Washington, but who had spent the mid-1860s in Memphis. Work from Myrtle Nickels, a Bristol native, was shown, along with paintings by seven Nashvillians: Sara Ward Conley (1859–1944), the architect of the Women's Pavilion, Cornelius Hankins (1863–1946), Minnie Gattinger (1857–1944), Louise E. Jennings, Anna Weaver Jones (and birth and death dates not known for these latter artists), and former Memphians Fannie M. Longman and John B. Longman (b. 1860?). Johannes A. Oertel (1823–1909), who earlier had taught and painted in Sewanee and Nashville, was by then a resident of Bel-Air, Maryland. The paintings of George W. Chambers (1856–1929), a recent resident of Nashville, were displayed in the Loan Collection, and two works in the watercolor exhibition came from Louise Lewis, another Nashville artist. Elizabeth Nourse (1859–1938), who won a medal at the exposition for her painting, *The Reading Lesson,* had visited the Smoky Mountains during the latter part of the century but was a resident of Cincinnati. Other Tennessee artists were represented in the less prestigious exhibit at the Women's Pavilion, although little information is available about that exhibition. Tennessee-born George de Forest Brush (1855–1941) was a juror for the exhibition.

Nashville art patron Sarah (Mrs. James C.) Bradford remarked, "As the Philadelphia centennial marks the first period in American art, so does the Tennessee centennial mark the first period in our art."[1] More than any other event of its time, the Tennessee centennial inspired local interest in art education and patronage and launched tremendous growth in the visual arts. James M. Cowan of Chicago eventually donated his prestigious collection of sixty-three turn-of-the-century American paintings to the Nashville Parthenon due to his fond memories of the Centennial Exposition. More immediately, exhibition venues would increase for the state's artists following the rise of art galleries, museums, and associations.[2] Moreover, art schools were established, creating greater opportunities for female artists.

Stylistically, however, the Centennial Exhibition was mired in the past, a shadow of what had been happening in Europe over the last fifty years. The surviving images of the galleries reveal paintings and sculpture by both the Victorian masters of academic painting, the Barbizon school, and a small number of Impressionists, reflecting the influences of the exhibition's jurors and current popular taste. Americans in the mid- to late nineteenth century were still enamored with the picturesque classicism of the French and German academies that had taken the lead over London's schools in the early part of the century. American artists were encouraged to study in Europe—Munich and Paris were favorite destinations—following the completion of class work in an American art school. "'Imported goods," noted a midstate reporter, "even when they are no better than, or not so good as, the home products, are held in more popular esteem than American goods. And so it is with art. To the unthinking many foreign art is the only art and foreign artists are held without distinction to be the only masters, to the disparagement of American artists whose achievements have won suitable recognition in the world."[3]

Those Americans who studied in Paris typically came away with a deep appreciation of the Barbizon painters, whose romantic landscapes emphasized mood over detail, or of the bright, spontaneous paintings of the Impressionists. Enoch Lloyd Branson, for example, became best known for his Barbizon-influenced landscapes and portraits. He had studied at the National Academy of Design, where he won first prize in 1875 for a classically inspired drawing. A Tennessee patron, John M. Boyd, sponsored Branson's attendance at the University of Tennessee and on a subsequent trip to Europe for further study. After returning to Knoxville, he and Frank McCrary opened a Gay Street photography studio and art gallery that became a gathering point for Knoxville artists. Branson's dramatic lighting and controlled brushwork suited the tastes of the country at the turn of the century, and he received many portrait commissions. He also influenced a generation of Knoxville artists. Landscape painter Charles Christopher Krutch (1849–1934) worked for McCrary and Branson. Often Branson took his students on sketching trips into the Smoky Mountains, an arduous journey that required a succession of train trips and hikes. These expeditions, which necessitated portable media, encouraged a propensity for watercolors among future generations of East Tennessee artists.

Lloyd Branson also taught many members of the Nicholson Art League, including C. Mortimer Thompson (1858–1939) and Anna Catherine Wiley (1879–1958). The league was an art association formed in 1898 out of the Knoxville Art Circle. Named for Maj. Calvin Hunter Nicholson, a former league officer and patron, the Nicholson Art League was the guiding light for Knoxville artists during the first quarter of the century. At the 1910 Appalachian Exposition in Knoxville, Branson curated the art exhibition, which contained paintings by many of the Nicholson Art League members, including Adelia Armstrong Lutz (1859–1931), Catherine Wiley, James W. Wallace (1852–1921), and Thomas Campbell (1834–1914). It was the first Knoxville exhibit to include artists from outside of East Tennessee. Branson's best-known painting, *Hauling Marble,* won the exposition's gold medal.[4]

Self-portrait, Catherine Wiley, pencil on paper. Courtesy of Special Collections, University of Tennessee, Knoxville.

New Opportunities for Women

The 1910 exposition's award for the "Most Meritorious Collection" went to Catherine Wiley's *Girl with Red Bow.* Wiley, like Branson, had studied in New York. She attended the Art Students League in 1903 and studied under Frank Vincent Dumond, augmented by several summers studying in New

England with Robert Henri, Jonas Lie, John Johannson, and Robert Reid. A member of the American Impressionist group known as The Ten, Reid was the teacher who most influenced Wiley's work. Reid's light, impressionist palette and loose brushwork also are characteristics of Wiley's painting. Her favorite subjects were women, like *Girl with Red Bow,* and interiors. Between 1905 and 1918 Wiley taught drawing in the Home Economics Department at the University of Tennessee before it had an art department. During the early 1920s she exhibited at the Pennsylvania Academy of Design, the National Academy of Design, and the Cincinnati Museum of Art, but was hospitalized in 1926 with what was diagnosed as a "mental breakdown" following the death of her father and that of Lloyd Branson, a close friend. Hospitalized for the remaining thirty-two years of her life, she never painted again.

Emma Bell Miles (1879–1919), like Wiley, was working in East Tennessee when illness cut short her promising career. She had studied at the St. Louis School of Art in 1899 and 1901 before returning to her home at Walden's Ridge on the Cumberland Plateau. There she supported a family of five children by writing essays for *Harper's Monthly* and the *Chattanooga News* and by painting. She was diagnosed with tuberculosis in 1917 and spent the last two years of her life completing a book on regional birds.

Water and Boats, oil on canvas, 14¼ × 16⅓ inches, by Catherine Wiley. Collection of Knoxville Museum of Art; gift of the Wiley Family in Memory of Catherine Wiley.

A third important woman artist of the early twentieth century, Willie Betty Newman (1863–1935), was born near Murfreesboro. She had studied locally before going to Cincinnati to study at the Art Academy under T. S. Noble. A series of academy scholarships allowed Newman to spend twelve years in France, where she studied at the Académie Julian, one of the top European art schools that would accept women as students. Rigorous training there involved drawing and painting from models, both cast and live, for years. Newman learned to paint idealized, classical figures in the manner of her teachers, William Adolphe Bouguereau, Benjamin Constant, Jean-Paul Laurens, and Robert Fleury. Newman's *Le Pain Béni* (Passing the Holy Bread, 1894), one of her scenes of "picturesque Brittany," typifies Bouguereau's highly finished style of painting. The artist became known for sentimental paintings of turn-of-the-century Breton peasants, whose style owed so much to Académie Julian but whose subjects are pure Barbizon. The Impressionists' palette also influenced Newman, as seen in her large painting, *En Pénitence,*[5] a portrayal of a group of school children that utilizes rapid brushstrokes and bright colors.

Newman returned to the United States around 1900 and settled in Nashville, becoming a member of the Nashville Art Association. She painted portraits of many of the city's residents and established the Newman School of Art, where painting was taught in the European manner, working from models. Newman's studio, outfitted with furniture and accessories purchased in Paris, must have seemed a bohemian retreat for Nashville's art students, who were accustomed to painting from chromolithographic reproductions.

Newman was just one of several important artists connected with the Nashville Art Association. Established in 1883 under the leadership of Dr. J. P. Dake and General Gates P. Thruston, the association served as an ardent advocate for two generations of Nashville painters. Its first members included Peter Ross Calvert (1855–1931), a miniature painter and photographer, and painter George Dury (1817–1894). Later members included painters Mayna Treanor Avent (1868–1959); William Gilbert Gaul (1855–1919); Pearl Saunders (dates unknown); Cornelius Hankins (1863–1946) and his artist wife, Maude Hankins (1861–1946); and William Brantley Smith (1874–1947).

Although men founded the association, female artists and civic leaders, especially Willie Betty Newman and Sarah Bradford, dominated it in the early twentieth century. Newman served on the executive committee of the association and had a one-person exhibit in 1916 at the Nashville Art Association's art gallery, housed in the downtown Carnegie Library. She won the association's first gold medal in the visual arts—the Tiffany-designed Parthenon gold medal—in the Arts and Crafts Exhibition. Newman eventually sold most of her work to Bradford, then president of the Nashville Art Association. One of Nashville's leading art patrons, Sarah Bradford was a key link to a second important Nashville organization, the Centennial Club.

The Centennial Club, founded in 1894 as a vehicle for the development of the Woman's Building at the Centennial Exposition, was reorganized in 1904 and supported a variety of civic projects in an effort to beautify Nashville and enlighten its citizens. While its focus was broader than that of the Nashville Art Association, it did offer a venue for art exhibits. Along with loan exhibits arranged through the American Federation of the Arts, the Southern States Art League, and eastern galleries and museums, the club showed art by Studio Club members, and drew from Nashville's art schools and colleges, such as Watkins, Vanderbilt and Peabody, for exhibits and lectures. The club purchased Willie Betty Newman's *Le Pain Béni* in 1915 after the Nashville Art Association failed to raise the funds necessary to purchase it. Newman regularly exhibited at the Centennial Club in the last years of her career, when she became noted for her many portraits of the leading dignitaries of the day. Her subjects included Sarah Bradford, Elizabeth Rhodes Eakin (president and founder of the Centennial Club), Governor James Frazier, Joel Cheek, James E. Caldwell, John Trotwood Moore, Austin Peay, and Oscar F. Noel (her last portrait). In 1911, she received a commission from Congress to paint a posthumous portrait of Senator John C. Bell, a founder of the Whig Party in Tennessee and a presidential candidate in 1860.

Sarah Bradford also remained extremely active, and worked tirelessly to create a permanent art gallery in the old Nashville Parthenon. In 1925 she and artist Bertha Herbert (Mrs. Edward Jr.) Potter hosted an exhibition from the Grand Central Art Galleries at the Parthenon under the auspices of the Centennial Club. It is likely that the positive response to the exhibit convinced James M. Cowan to donate his collection in January 1927. The donation persuaded Nashville's city council to fund needed repairs that enabled the Parthenon to reopen its doors in May 1931. By this time, the name of the Nashville Art Association had been changed to the Nashville Museum of Art. In the late 1950s its collections and resources were deeded to the newly founded Tennessee Fine Arts Center at Cheekwood.

Painter and printmaker Ella Sophonisba Hergesheimer (1873–1943) also found professional support in Nashville. Hergesheimer came to Nashville in 1907 to paint a portrait of Bishop Holland M. McTyeire, the Methodist clergyman who had convinced Cornelius Vanderbilt in 1873 to endow Vanderbilt University. Hergesheimer's paintings had come to the attention of Nashville art patrons when she submitted five works to a traveling exhibition organized by the Nashville Art Association. She was a great-great-granddaughter of Charles Willson Peale (1741–1827), the painter and founder of the country's first museum, and had studied with William

Self-Portrait, by Ella Sophonisba Hergesheimer, 1931, oil on canvas, 1960.2.12. Collection of Cheekwood Museum of Art, Nashville, Tennessee.

Merritt Chase (1849–1916) at his Shinnecock School of Art and at the Pennsylvania Academy of the Fine Arts under Cecilia Beaux (1863–1942).

The Pennsylvania Academy was a center for Impressionism at the turn of the century, and Hergesheimer responded to the school's emphasis on color and light. She excelled at the academy, winning student competitions in each of her four years, followed by a Cresson traveling scholarship in her final term. Hergesheimer used the funds to spend three years in Europe, studying at the Colarossi School in Paris (with Muche and Privett) and copying master paintings in Normandy, Madrid, Germany, Italy, and Holland. Her teacher, Cecilia Beaux, had followed much the same pattern thirty years earlier, going from the Pennsylvania Academy to Colarossi, and must have influenced the younger artist in her travel plans. Like Beaux and Willie Betty Newman, Hergesheimer also exhibited in the Paris Salon.

Soon after Hergesheimer returned to Pennsylvania, she received the McTyeire commission and she was off to Nashville, where she spent the rest of her life, painting portraits and still lifes, mainly, and printing lithographs. The success of the Bishop McTyeire portrait led to a commission to paint McTyeire's wife, Amelia Townsend McTyeire, and other portraits soon followed. Her favorite still-life subjects were magnolia blossoms. By 1910, she was exhibiting her work with members of the Nashville Art Association at the Carnegie Library and she showed her first painting at the Centennial Club in 1915. Hergesheimer found a group of kindred spirits in the Studio Club. It included fellow members Cornelius Hankins and Clarence Stagg (who lived from 1902 to 1942), who were both former students of William Merritt Chase; Mayna Treanor Avent, who attended the Cincinnati Art Academy and the Académie Julian; Charles Cagle (1907–1968), who studied at the Pennsylvania Academy of Fine Art; Philip Perkins (1907–1970); and Bertha Herbert Potter. They met monthly to exhibit, share information, and offer mutual support. The group exhibited in the 1920s and 1930s at the Studio Club, the Parthenon, the Centennial Club, the Woman's Club, and Watkins Institute. In 1939, Hergesheimer was one of six Tennesseans representing the state in the New York World's Fair.[6]

As in Nashville, women were at the forefront of the Memphis art scene in the early twentieth century. Mary Solari, who was among the first women admitted to the Academy of Art in Florence, Italy, returned to the United States determined to raise interest in art education in Memphis. Solari taught and wrote articles urging city leaders to improve art education and to create an art league. But it was Florence

The Studio Club and the Nashville Artist Guild

Bertha Herbert Potter, a leading Nashville artist in the 1920s, realized that the large number of nationally and internationally trained local artists needed some means by which they could come together for comradeship and a stimulating exchange of ideas within their profession. In 1932 Potter and other professional artists in Nashville formed the Studio Club. Lasting until the end of the decade, the Studio Club offered that exchange between artists and a public exhibition space for their work. The gallery for the club, at 514 Cedar Street (now Sixth Avenue North), held group shows each season, with special events to coincide, and planned individual exhibitions for each member, to last at least a month.

Ella Sophonisba Hergesheimer was a strong component in the early group. Others, whose work has remained in local collections, were Clarence Stagg, Charles Cagle, Pearl Saunders, and Ernest Pickup. Potter served as president of the organization, as did Pickup, a graphic artist whose woodcut prints became widely known in local and national exhibitions. Additional members of the Studio Club were Cornelia Park Byrns, Marie Barton, Aline Wharton, Marie Woolwine, Susan Wilkes, Jeanette Gillespie, John Richardson, and Sara Ward Conley.

Potter also served as art chairman for the Centennial Club on Eighth Avenue in the downtown area and arranged regular showings there by members of the Studio Club, as well as one-man shows for individual artists. Cagle, Saunders, and Richardson taught at Watkins Institute on Church Street, the local downtown school of art. Ward-Belmont College offered the only other local art classes during the 1930s. Some artists in the Studio Club moved away; others may have become discouraged or were enticed away by employment in larger institutions, and the Studio Club ceased to exist by the 1940s.

In the fall of 1950 Puryear Mims and Walter Sharp at Vanderbilt University, along with Joseph Van Sickle of Ward-Belmont College and Philip Perkins of the University of Tennessee Extension School, brought together some of their students and any professional artists exhibiting locally into a new organization called the Nashville Artist Guild. Thirty joined at that time. The rules established at the beginning included high standards for the work of the applicants, and in succeeding years a long parade of local artists, many who served on the faculties of nearby schools and universities, were accepted as members.

Unfortunately, some artists who were teaching and exhibiting were excluded from the guild at the time of its inception; they banded together to form another artists' organization, the Tennessee Art League, which offered open membership. Soon the league had enough strength to buy its own gallery location, and it is still in use today. The gallery for the league has served its members well, as a place to exhibit their own work on a regular basis and as a studio space for groups producing art. Its membership list of several hundred includes both professional and amateur artists from Nashville and surrounding communities.

The Nashville Artist Guild began to exhibit in 1951, when local architect Victor Stromquist donated space in his building at 1618 Church Street, where an attractive courtyard extended the possibility of displaying sculpture and entertaining. The guild's primary interest was educational programs for the public, such as a children's art workshop continuing from 1956 until 1966; forums with discussion of new trends; and special exhibitions such as the first of any size that presented the work of sculptor William Edmondson—in the year of his death, 1951. The guild brought art from many outside sources or locations to Nashville, since there was no museum to do this.

[Continued on next page]

The guild operated a gallery in seven different locations during the first forty years of its existence. The loss of exhibition space at the Silver Dollar Saloon on Broadway in 1988, combined with a dwindling membership and the appearance of a strong new open group called the Visual Arts Alliance of Nashville, led some guild leaders to consider ending the organization. This idea, however, was resisted, and in the twenty-first century the guild's forty or so members maintain a close relationship, though no longer a physical space of their own.

Today Nashville has several artists' organizations, for the needs Potter recognized in 1932 have not changed. An artist's work is by nature a very personal endeavor, but pursuing that work is better accomplished with support—both from one's peers and from the community as a whole.

Louise LeQuire, Nashville

McIntyre, who had studied in Philadelphia and returned to Memphis and aspired to create an organization on the pattern of the Pennsylvania Society of Miniature Painters, who founded the Memphis Art Association in 1914. The group, led by McIntyre, Mrs. Alston Boyd, Mrs. Daniel Grant, and others, held its first exhibitions at the Nineteenth Century Club, a woman's civic organization, on Third Street. Artworks were borrowed from New York's Macbeth and Kraushaar Galleries, including paintings by American Impressionists Willard Metcalf, Childe Hassam, and John Twachtman; traditional landscape painters Henry Ward Ranger and Alexander Wyant; and Robert Henri and Ernest Lawson, who were members of a group known as The Eight. The Eight were urban realists and progressive thinkers who organized one of the first independent art exhibitions in the United States, in 1908 at the Macbeth Gallery in New York City.

The year 1914 was also when Bessie Vance Brooks established the Brooks Memorial Museum Gallery with a $100,000 donation in memory of her late husband, Samuel Hamilton Brooks.[7] When the gallery (now the Memphis Brooks Museum of Art) was opened in May 1916, Florence McIntyre became the first director of the institution, which was housed in a striking neoclassical building designed by New York architect James Gamble Rogers. This was a sweet story of nearly instant success as compared to the years in which the Nashville Art Association struggled for a permanent display space.

Director McIntyre produced a series of exhibits on a shoestring budget by networking with the National Association of Women Painters and Sculptors, the Metropolitan Museum of Art, and commercial art galleries. In 1919 Edward Robinson, director of the Metropolitan Museum in New York City, introduced her to the American Federation of Arts and she began a long relationship with that institution. She also invited the Southern States Art League to hold their first exhibition at the Brooks in 1922. At about that time, McIntyre left the Brooks to pursue the idea of a free art school in conjunction with the Memphis Art Association. The school grew to an enrollment of about six hundred students and became the site for the Memphis Academy of Arts (now Memphis College of Art) in July 1936. Once again, women led this important artistic endeavor.

THE GROWTH OF ART SCHOOLS AND THE ART PROFESSION

The seeds planted by the state's art associations began to take root in the 1940s with the establishment of professional art schools and university art departments across the state. Organized by Mrs. Sidney Farnsworth, Rosalee Cohn, and Mildred Hudson, who served as director from 1943 to 1949, the Memphis Academy of Arts drew art students with its offerings in sculpture, painting, drawing, clay, weaving,

Brooks Memorial Art Gallery, Memphis (original structure). Courtesy of Memphis/Shelby County Public Library and Information Center–Memphis and Shelby County Room.

and design. Saturday School was offered for children and adult night classes were available. During the war years, the school's enrollment increased and after the war the GI Bill brought another wave of students. Teachers at the academy included Marjorie Liebman (oil painting), Pillow Lewis (oil painting), Dorothy Sturm (life drawing, history of art), and Burton Callicott (drawing, lettering, and sculpture).

Callicott (b. 1907) was trained at the Cleveland School of Art, where his stepfather, Michael Abt, had studied. Abt ran out of money in Memphis while on a sketching trip down the Mississippi. He came ashore, found work, and met and later married Callicott's mother. Abt was an inspiration to Callicott, who studied figure drawing and clay with him. But in Cleveland Callicott found perhaps his greatest inspiration in the work of Albert Pinkham Ryder. Ryder's powerful use of light and dark led Callicott to a lifelong investigation of illumination.

Callicott's early career was spent as a float fabricator for the Memphis Cotton Carnival and Christmas parades during the early 1930s. He continued to paint and received a Public Works of Art commission in 1933 to paint a mural about Hernando De Soto's exploration of West Tennessee, which is still on view at the Memphis Pink Palace Museum. Callicott's painting, *The Gleaners* (1936), was included in the 1939 World's Fair, where it received much attention. Meanwhile, Callicott was moving away from the representation of volume and toward the flattened perspective of modern art. During the 1940s, he was exposed to the tenets of Abstract Expressionism through his peers at the Memphis Academy of Arts. His breakthrough came in 1950 with the painting *Tree in the Sun,* in which he explored abstracted pattern in the forms of nature. Over the next fifty years, Callicott explored light and pattern in nature, moving from natural shadows to the intersecting sunspots between shadows and then to rainbows. Led by a belief that visual art can best express the spiritual, Callicott's rainbows are a natural progression in his search for a purely abstracted form.

Callicott joined the Memphis Academy of Arts in 1937, the same year that Dorothy Sturm

(1911–1988) was hired to teach book illustration. Sturm had studied with Florence McIntyre and later attended the Art Students League. While in New York, she looked through a microscope for the first time, a seemingly insignificant action that actually expanded her artistic vision. By the 1940s, when their colleague Worden Day introduced Sturm and Callicott to the teachings of abstract expressionist Hans Hoffman, Sturm was able to connect Hoffman's theories with the abstracted forms of the microscopic world. Sturm was affiliated with the Memphis College of Art for nearly forty years. She expanded her media to include enamels, metal, and glass, leading her into the age-old controversy over fine art and crafts. Sturm worked to break down the barriers between the terms by working in a range of media.

Chattanooga was the last of the state's major urban centers to establish an institution for the exhibition and encouragement of painting. The Chattanooga Art Association was formed in 1924 under the leadership of Mrs. Lucius Mansfield and a group of prominent citizens, including Adolph Ochs, owner of the *Chattanooga Times* and *New York Times* newspapers. Like the Nashville Art Association, the group held their exhibitions in the local Carnegie Library. They worked closely with Frank Baisden, head of the Art Department at the University of Chattanooga (now University of Tennessee at Chattanooga). The Art Study Club, established in 1913 and already affiliated with the American Federation of Arts, supported the association with guidance and funding. The University of Chattanooga further supported local artists by hosting a WPA Federal Art Gallery in the 1930s.

In the 1930s and early 1940s, many artists working in the major art centers rejected such European avant-garde styles as Cubism and Post-Impressionism and turned back to the realist tradition espoused by the Ashcan school. As those urban realists had explored Manhattan, so a generation of painters explored life in the growing South. Two African American brothers born in Knoxville, Beauford Delaney (1901–1979) and Joseph Delaney (1904–1991), created individualized views of the urban landscape after they left Knoxville in the 1920s. Beauford Delaney, after his initial studies with Lloyd Branson, went to Boston in 1924, then settled in Greenwich Village where he associated with Palmer Hayden, Ellis Wilson, and other members of the Harlem Artists Guild. He exhibited under the auspices of the Harmon Foundation (1931, 1933, and 1935) and most notably in *The Negro in Contemporary Art,* a groundbreaking exhibition at the Baltimore Museum in 1944. Delaney left New York in 1953, spending the last twenty-six years of his life in Paris. Beauford Delaney's city scenes are isolated landscapes, reflecting the country's disillusion with the American dream felt in the aftermath of the Great Depression. He eventually abandoned all subject matter in his later work, which is characterized by its free-flowing curves and bright colors.

After leaving Knoxville in the early 1920s, Joseph Delaney eventually settled in Manhattan, where he attended the Art Students League, studying under the Regionalist Thomas Hart Benton in 1932. Benton, well known for his images of the American Midwest, encouraged Delaney to paint from his own experience as an American. He found his subjects in Manhattan's bustling urban scenes. Joseph Delaney once observed that the "main difference between us is that Beauford likes deserted streets for his pictures, while I like crowds and more crowds—just as many people as I can get onto a canvas."[8] Joseph Delaney eventually returned to Knoxville in 1986 where, at age eighty-two, he worked as artist-in-residence at the University of Tennessee. In that same year his work was the subject of a traveling exhibition organized by the university's Ewing Gallery.

The New Deal's various arts projects shaped the career of several Tennessee artists from 1933 to 1943, although most government funding went to established art centers such as New York. Joseph Delaney worked with Norman Lewis (1909–1979) on a mural for the New York Public Library. Likewise, George Oberteuffer's son, Karl Oberteuffer

Macy's Parade, acrylic and pastel, 81½ × 121⅛ inches, by Joseph Delaney. Collection of Knoxville Museum of Art; gift of the Artist.

(1908–1958), was commissioned to paint a mural for the post office in McKenzie, Tennessee, in 1938. His painting, *Early United States Post Village,* is typical of the historic subject matter approved by the Treasury Department's Section of Fine Arts in its depiction of pioneers settling the state. The Treasury Section also commissioned other murals by Edwin Boyd Johnson (b. 1904 in Watertown, Tennessee) and Memphians John R. Pickett (b. 1896) and Burton Callicott.

Carroll Cloar (1913–1993) was another young Tennessee artist to emerge during the Depression decade. Cloar moved to Memphis in 1930 from his hometown in nearby Earle, Arkansas. He studied at Southwestern at Memphis (now Rhodes College) and at the Memphis Academy of Arts under Académie Julian–trained Impressionist George Oberteuffer before attending the Art Students League in 1936. While there, Cloar printed a series of lithographs with fellow artist Will Barnet that drew the attention of *Life* magazine's editors. Their publication of his prints established young Cloar in the national art community. Cloar found his subjects in childhood images, taken from his family scrapbooks. He combined a pointillist background with flat foreground figures to create a collage effect that reflected the fragmented character of the scrapbooks. The unshaded, flattened subjects give his work a surreal, isolated character that aligns his work with the Social Realists of the 1930s and 1940s.

Cloar's paintings are examples of Regionalism at its best: family memories, combined in a surreal format that belies their specific associations, give viewers the opportunity to explore their own remembrances.

Federal Art Commissions during the New Deal

THE NEW DEAL OF THE 1930S FUNDED VARIOUS FEDERAL ARTS PROJECTS TO COMMISSION ARTISTS AND sculptors to produce works for public buildings. According to a mid-1990s survey of twenty-eight extant Tennessee public art works by Howard Hull, a professor of art education at the University of Tennessee, the most important agency was the Treasury Department's Section of Painting and Sculpture, later the Section of Fine Arts. Between its creation in 1934 and its dissolution in 1943, it commissioned and funded most of the murals and art found at Tennessee's post offices. Its national leaders—Edward Bruce, Edward Rowan, and Forbes Watson—came from art backgrounds, and its competitive jury-selection process emphasized quality and diversity. In Tennessee, for example, eleven women artists received post office mural commissions. Anne Poor's 1942 depiction of the sweet potato industry in Weakley County, complete with a border composed of sweet potato vines, adorns the post office wall in Gleason.

Eastern Tennessee, by Wendell C. Jones. Courtesy of East Tennessee State University.

Other important agencies that funded art projects in Tennessee included the Public Works of Art Project of the Civil Works Administration, the Treasury Relief Art Project, and the Federal Art Project of the Works Progress Administration. The Public Works of Art Project only lasted for six months in 1933–34, although later federal agencies often took over its unfinished projects. One of its notable projects was the lobby murals of Hernando De Soto's arrival in Memphis executed by Burton Callicott for the Memphis Museum of Natural History, now the Memphis Pink Palace Museum. Since its art funding came from a percentage of federal appropriations for new building construction, the Treasury Relief Art Project was much more substantial and lasted until 1939. The WPA's Federal Art Project was extremely varied, funding all types of visual arts as well as performance arts. In a limited way, its projects were even color-blind; African American sculptor William Edmondson of Nashville, for example, received WPA grants in 1937 and 1939. Women artists received commissions too. Laura Woolsey Daily, associated with the well-regarded arts project at the University of Chattanooga (now University of Tennessee at Chattanooga), produced a series of woodcuts depicting Hamilton County sites and landscapes, including the Chickamauga Dam. This collection is now at the Chattanooga Regional History Museum.

[Continued on next page]

These federal art commissions "were a uniquely American blend, combining an elitist belief in the value of high culture with the democratic ideal that everyone in the society could and should be the beneficiary of such efforts," observed historians Marlene Park and Gerald E. Markowitz.[1] Most of this art could be classified as part of the American Scene movement, which historian Barbara Melosh defines as a "contemporary movement to express a distinctive national culture" by aiming "squarely for the artistic center, endorsing a representational style updated with modernist gestures."[2] That observation certainly holds true for the Tennessee mural art. The general theme of the Tennessee post office art is the significance and meaning of place in each individual community. In rural towns, scenes of early settlement and the frontier, where ordinary people are working together for mutual goals, represent this theme. In larger, more industrial towns, images of the past often are blended with those from technology and development to represent a community's sense of place and achievement.

Carroll Van West, Middle Tennessee State University

Notes

1. Marlene Park and Gerald E. Markowitz, *Democratic Vistas: Post Offices and Public Art in the New Deal* (Philadelphia: Temple Univ. Press, 1984), 5.
2. Barbara Melosh, *Engendering Culture: Manhood and Womanhood in New Deal Public Art and Theater* (Washington, D.C.: Smithsonian Institution Press, 1991), 7.

As Cloar created a universal expression out of his own history, his peer and friend, Burton Callicott, conversely used the universal idea of light as spirit to allow viewers to reflect on their own experiences.

During the late 1930s and 1940s, the immigration of several artists who left Europe in the wake of World War II brought new talent to Tennessee art circles. Jack Grué (1896–1956) established a reputation as a miniaturist in Memphis. A native of Kiev, Russia, Grué came to Memphis in 1939 in advance of the German expansion into Vienna, where he had worked as a set designer for Max Reinhardt. Though best known in Memphis for his mural at the Immaculate Conception Catholic Church, Grué also painted exquisite miniatures on masonite and ivory, utilizing a magnifying glass, and, like many other artists, painted watercolors of exotic locales while on summer vacations. His work was the subject of a memorial exhibition at the Memphis Brooks Museum in 1956, the year of his death. Werner Wildner (b. 1925) left Witten, Germany, as a child, settling in Nashville in 1940. After working as an American interpreter during the war, Wildner returned to Nashville where he established a reputation for his macabre, highly finished paintings and reclusive life-style. Austrian-born Eugene V. Biel-Bienne (1902–1969) escaped to the United States in 1942, later serving as chair of the Art Department of Vanderbilt University in the early 1960s.

African American artists also shaped Nashville's art traditions in new directions beginning in the 1930s. Under the leadership of Charles Spurgeon Johnson (1893–1956), a brilliant sociologist and African American art patron, Fisk University commissioned the Harlem Renaissance artist Aaron Douglas (1898–1979) to paint a series of murals telling the story of African American history for the walls of the Erastus Milo Cravath Memorial Library (now the Administration Building). In 1925, Douglas went to New York City to be a part of the cultural renaissance taking place in Harlem. He studied mural decoration with Winold Reiss (1886–1953), who

Mountain Summer Schools

By 1860, Tennessee was beginning to take realistic strides toward making education available to the general population. But the destructive forces of civil war brought this, like so many other promises of the future, to an abrupt halt. Perhaps nowhere was this more pronounced than in the mountains that coursed through the eastern sections of the state. The divisions and acrimony of the Civil War had been particularly acute in these mountains, characterized by guerrilla warfare and enduring animosities that brought hardship and deprivation to future generations. Education, particularly in the arts, became a luxury.

As a general rule, the people of the mountains had remained loyal to the Union cause even as Tennessee joined the ranks of the Confederacy, so in the postwar era there was a sympathetic response to their distressed status from many in the northern states. That sympathy manifested itself in many ways, including the establishment of mission and settlement schools beginning in the 1870s, and by the 1930s there were nineteen mission schools in East Tennessee. One of the ways these schools sought to pull the mountain people out of poverty was by encouraging traditional crafts, and by providing outlets for the sale of these handiworks. These efforts were often paternalistic or condescending, but there were notable successes.

One of the best of these was the settlement school established in Gatlinburg in 1912 by the Pi Beta Phi Women's Fraternity, which developed a program that emphasized manual labor and crafts and, in 1926, established the Arrowcraft Shop as a retail outlet. By the 1940s there were over a hundred artisans providing wares to Arrowcraft, and in 1945 Pi Beta Phi joined with the University of Tennessee to offer summer craft workshops. These classes attracted students from many other states as well as from a number of foreign countries, reflecting a national trend that saw trained professionals beginning to dominate what had been traditional crafts. The legacy of Pi Beta Phi has continued as the Arrowmont School of Arts and Crafts, a name it assumed in the 1960s.

Education and assistance in traditional mountain crafts came from other sources, with particular impetus from the federal government during the 1930s, in the wake of the Depression. The Southern Guild and Federal Art Project, the Anderson County Federal Art Project in Norris, the WPA Federal Art Gallery at the University of Chattanooga, and TVA's Southern Highlanders were among those which included lectures and classes.

A mountain summer program of another sort began at Monteagle in 1882, which was more of a learning retreat for the upper and middle classes from neighboring towns and cities. But it had a healthy arts education emphasis, with a significant long-term effect on Tennessee arts. It was chartered as the Monteagle Sunday School Assembly, inspired by the Chautauqua movement from the north and conceived as the Chautauqua for the South. It was to be non-denominational, and, among its purposes, was "the promotion of the broadest possible culture."[1] This immediately translated into a summer program involving vocal and instrumental music, and lectures by some of the nation's leading authors. In 1901, Peabody College held its summer school there, including courses in art, drawing, and music. After 1912 the substance of the Monteagle program began to decline, but it has continued to the present day, offering lectures and classes in art, music, and crafts.

There were intermittent Chautauqua-style programs in other mountain communities, such as Bristol in 1909 and Knoxville in 1912, but they were narrowly focused and did not last. The Summer School of the South, at the University of Tennessee from 1902 until 1918, was organized primarily for teachers and was initially very popular. While it did not offer much in the way of specific art training, it did expose the participants to significant arts programming,

[Continued on next page]

which undoubtedly had impact in other communities. In 1905, for example, the Summer School featured Maude Powell, "the world's greatest woman violinist," and G. Campanari, baritone from the Metropolitan Opera.[2]

The modern embodiment of this mountain legacy can be found at the Joe L. Evins Appalachian Center for Crafts, which was built as a federal project near Smithville in 1979. It is now affiliated with Tennessee Technological University, offering a BFA degree and certificates in crafts, as well as a robust summer program designed to appeal to all ages.

Dan Pomeroy, Tennessee State Museum

Notes

1. Curt Porter, "Chautauqua and Tennessee," *Tennessee Historical Quarterly* 22 (1963): 351.
2. James R. Montgomery, "A Summer School for the South," ibid., 370.

encouraged Douglas to explore his African heritage. Douglas developed a bold, geometric style in his illustrations and his mural painting that owed much to African motifs and Art Deco design, as seen in his *Drama* (1930) from the Fisk murals. The two silhouetted figures stand on either side of a Doric column on which the masks of comedy and tragedy are seen. The seated figure, an older man, represents the vernacular storytelling tradition while the standing female figure strikes a classical Shakespearean pose. A modern city, frequently found in Douglas's paintings, forms the rest of the stage set, all of which is framed by a raised theatrical curtain.

In 1937, Charles S. Johnson convinced Douglas to accept a teaching position at Fisk. Douglas chaired its Art Department for the next twenty-nine years, teaching the next generation of artists, including Gregory Ridley, Jacqueline Bontemps, and LiFran Fort. Douglas produced many of the annual Fisk Festivals of Music and Fine Arts, which brought important art collections and lecturers to Nashville. He oversaw the donations of important art collections to the university, including the George Gershwin Collection of photographs and ephemera, donated in 1947 by photographer Carl Van Vechten; twenty-one drawings of Harlem and St. Helena Island subjects by Douglas's teacher, Winold Reiss, donated in 1952; and 252 pieces of African art donated by Irene McCoy Gaines, also given in 1952.

Alta, by Aaron Douglas. Courtesy of Fisk University Galleries, Nashville, Tennessee.

Douglas's and Johnson's most important acquisition, by far, came in 1949, when American painter Georgia O'Keefe donated a portion of the modern art collection of her late husband, photographer

Aaron Douglas

AARON DOUGLAS WAS THE LEADING VISUAL ARTIST OF THE HARLEM RENAISSANCE. WITHIN WEEKS OF his arrival in New York in 1925, Douglas was recruited by the NAACP's W. E. B. Du Bois, editor of *The Crisis,* and Charles S. Johnson, the Urban League's editor of *Opportunity,* to create illustrations to accompany their editorials on lynching, segregation, theater, jazz, poems, stories, and political issues. Douglas, a Kansas City high school teacher, had decided to join the young artists of the Harlem Renaissance after viewing a copy of *Survey Graphic's* special issue devoted to Harlem. Bavarian artist Winold Reiss had created the cover for the magazine, and his portrayal of blacks in a forthright manner and with dignity impressed Douglas.

Within this largely literary movement, Douglas was hired to create a visual message for a public that had grown dramatically with the increase of black migration to the North during World War I. Douglas tried to reach this new black middle-class public with the language of African art as one of his most important tools. Before Douglas, some American artists had begun to include African motifs in their work, but not on a regular basis. Douglas, who believed his work could touch the black audience in a unique way, wanted to change the way blacks were depicted. As one of his most important tools he brought the language of African art to Harlem, and then across the United States.

We can see Douglas's growth and experimentation through his magazine illustrations. Here he created some of his most forceful and interesting works and his artistic language evolved, immersed in African art in a way no other American artist had been to date. These illustrations are clean and bold, often just a few simple figures, illustrating a basic idea or just showing images of African Americans.

Douglas came to Nashville in 1930 for a commission at Fisk University's library to create murals that represented a panorama of the history of black people in the New World. The cycle began with life in Africa, then depicted slavery, emancipation, and freedom, which Douglas symbolized by Fisk's Jubilee Hall. Through this extensive project, Douglas hoped to make Fisk students realize the important contributions black Americans had made in the building of America. The final cycle of the murals, still visible today, represents philosophy, drama, music, poetry, and science, with depictions of night and day.

Douglas permanently joined the Fisk University faculty in 1940 and founded its Art Department. His students recalled him as a sensitive, caring, and thorough teacher, strongly classical in his training and academic in his teaching style. Teaching was one of the greatest commitments of his lifetime and his greatest joy. Douglas retired in 1969 and died in Nashville in 1979.

Douglas remains unique in his efforts, providing crucial links between the literary figures of the Harlem Renaissance, that movement's ideas about Africa, and the thinking of blacks throughout the world. He was a black artist in the United States creating racial art, and as an illustrator he reached a large readership through black magazines. During a time of limited artistic freedom for African Americans, he based his works on studies of African heritage. Douglas confronted the problem of trying to reach a public that was still difficult to define and locate, with limited patronage and a geographically isolated audience. Despite these challenges, Douglas successfully addressed issues of importance to a growing black middle class. Black leaders sought his work to illustrate their message, and he received regular commissions until his departure from Harlem in 1937.

Douglas brought African art to Harlem in a new, accessible, immediate way, then through his illustrations to Americans, both black and white, across the country.

Amy H. Kirschke, Vanderbilt University

Suggested Reading

Kirschke, Amy H. *Aaron Douglas: Art, Race and the Harlem Renaissance.* Oxford: Univ. Press of Mississippi, 1995.

Alfred Stieglitz, to the university. The Alfred Stieglitz Collection of Modern Art contains 101 works of paintings, sculpture, photographs, and prints, including works from Picasso, Renoir, and Cezanne. In 1949, Douglas also directed the renovation and dedication of the Van Vechten Gallery and O'Keefe came to Fisk to personally supervise the original installation of the Stieglitz Collection. For his many contributions, Fisk University's library gallery was named after Aaron Douglas when it opened in 1969.

Throughout these years of institution building and collection development, Douglas continued to paint, creating psychologically introspective portraits of many of Nashville's leading citizens, including John W. Work and Charles S. Johnson. One of his most sensitive portraits is that of his wife *Alta* (1936). The painting's broad brushstrokes are gradually refined as the viewer's eye moves from the dark background to Alta's bright face. The subject's V-necked red dress and pattern also act as foils to direct attention upward to Alta's serene gaze.

Tennessee at Midcentury

Tennesseans at midcentury were filled with the optimism and self-confidence felt by many Americans in the aftermath of World War II. The decade of the 1950s, in fact, would prove significant to the history of Tennessee painting as the state's academies, art departments, and museums blossomed into new directions and new programs. During this golden age of art production in the 1950s and 1960s, artists bonded in search of venues and there was a pervasive feeling of optimism that education could raise interest in the arts. The Tennessee Arts Commission was founded, along with city arts councils, and art festivals flourished across the state. It was a time of stylistic experimentation and creative collaboration.

Like Nashville in the wake of the Centennial Exposition fifty years earlier, Memphis was at the forefront of these various developments. Prior to the 1950s the state's universities had rarely supported the arts—the Art Gallery of the University of the South at Sewanee was one of the first university-supported museums in the region when it opened in 1938. But in the 1950s the Art Department at Memphis State University was established under the leadership of Dana Johnson and Charles Allgood; by 1961 the faculty would increase to twelve. Also during the 1950s Southwestern at Memphis instituted its artist-in-residence program and a degree was offered in art, following the department's founding in 1942.

The center of artistic activity was the Memphis Academy of Arts. Mario Bacchelli (1893–1951) came to Memphis in 1948 to lecture at the academy. He stayed to teach there and at Southwestern and to paint picturesque scenes of Memphis in a confident, expressive manner. Bacchelli joined an already distinguished group of artists, including the painters Marjorie Liebman and Adele Lemm. Liebman, who taught at the Memphis Academy of Art between 1940 and 1950, was working in an Abstract Expressionist mode in the 1950s. After traveling in the early 1960s, principally to Mexico, Liebman returned to Memphis, developing a keen interest in the local landscape. Adele Lemm, who first studied at the academy from 1934 to 1940 and then taught there for twenty-three years, combined her love of landscapes, seascapes, and interiors with an impressionist's interest in sunlight. She painted her figures with a loose expressive brush, creating abstracted subjects. Tragically, Bacchelli did not have such a long Memphis career; he died in a motorcycle accident in 1951.

In 1952 academy director Ted Rust hired British-born Edward (Ted) Faiers (1908–1985) to replace Bacchelli. Faiers had taught at the University of Alberta in 1947–48 after studying there in the early 1940s. He moved to Memphis on the recommendation of Will Barnet, whom Faiers had known at the Art Students League. During the 1950s, Faiers worked through a period of abstract experimentation, developing his signature figurative style in the 1960s and 1970s. He developed a friendship with Burton Callicott at the academy, and later served as chairman of its Painting Department, becoming professor emeritus. In 1979, the First Tennessee Bank commissioned Faiers to paint the First Tennessee Heritage Mural in its Memphis headquarters. The subject of the momentous undertaking is the history of the state, depicted in fifty-one panels. Faiers's mural utilizes three-dimensional projections that bring the subjects out into the viewer's space. Ted Faiers died in 1985 before finishing his "Big Wall." His former student, Betty Gilow, completed the remaining fourteen panels.

Another 1950s product of the Academy was Veda Reed (b. 1934), who arrived as a student in 1952. Burton Callicott's interest in light and his use of glazes to add luminosity influenced her early work. Reed began teaching at the academy in 1963, retiring as senior professor in 1995. While the Memphis landscape had been the subject of her early series of paintings, she has focused on the southwestern skies since a summer visit to Taos. Reed's abstracted landscapes evoke a spiritual quality in their dramatic coloration and reduced format.

The Memphis Brooks Museum of Art also helped to open new horizons for modern art in Bluff City. In 1953, Majorie Liebman, Adele Lemm, and Dorothy Sturm joined with Mildred Hudson and Nancy Glazer to form Art Today, a program dedicated to the advancement of contemporary art, at the Brooks Museum.

At the same time in Chattanooga, arts advocates, civic leaders, and artists worked together to create a major museum dedicated to American art. In 1951, the Chattanooga Art Association moved its headquarters to the home of the late George Thomas Hunter, a gift to the association from the Benwood Foundation. The George Thomas Hunter Gallery of Art opened in July 1952, with an impressive exhibition of works loaned from the National Gallery of Art, the Metropolitan Museum of Art, and other prestigious institutions. It was the city's first permanent exhibiting art institution. A mid-1970s expansion not only increased gallery space, but it also led museum trustees to change the name and the focus of the institution to the collection and exhibition of work by American artists. Now connected to the city's downtown attractions by the Riverwalk, the Hunter Museum of American Art is a landmark arts institution in the Southeast.

Artists, academies, and institutions of higher education combined efforts to advance contemporary art in both Nashville, Chattanooga, and Knoxville during the 1950s and 1960s. George Ayers Cress (b. 1921) moved to Chattanooga from Knoxville in 1951 to chair the art department of the University of Chattanooga. Cress led the department for thirty-two years, during which time his colorful landscapes would influence generations of art students. Myron King opened his commercial gallery in 1948, becoming an important resource for artists in the 1950s and 1960s. Two years later, professors associated with three Nashville schools, Joseph Van Sickle from Ward-Belmont College, Puryear Mims from Vanderbilt University, and the University of Tennessee, Nashville's Philip Perkins, joined together to form the Nashville Artist Guild, an organization dedicated to promoting the art of its members. Establishing its first gallery in the Stromquist Building (named for one of the guild's great patrons, architect Victor Stromquist), the guild launched a series of exhibitions and challenging programs. In its first year, the guild brought an Abstract Expressionist show to the Parthenon. Lectures were equally challenging: topics in 1951–52 included the "Primitive Origins of Modern Art" and the "Relationship of Psychiatry to Art." This was not the type of art seen at the earlier, more conservative-in-taste Nashville Museum of Art.

In 1955, the guild accepted into its membership a young artist who would go on to become an internationally recognized figure: Charles (Red) Grooms (b. 1937). A Nashville native, Grooms had just graduated from Hillsboro High School when he became a guild member in June 1955. "The Guild gave me a sense of being a professional artist when I was just getting started," Grooms noted. "They made me a member when I was 17, and included my work in a show at the Guild's first gallery in the Victor Stromquist Building on Church Street."[9] Grooms spent the summer of 1956 in Provincetown, Massachusetts, studying with Hans Hofmann. In 1957, his oil *Two Crackers* was one of the one hundred works by Nashvillians exhibited in the first Nashville Arts Festival. By the following year, Grooms had moved to Manhattan, working odd jobs during the day and painting at night. During the late 1950s, he experimented with Happenings such as *The Burning Building* (1958) at the Reuben Gallery on the Lower East Side.

Grooms continued to experiment, first with film and then with large constructions that he called "sculptopictoramas." Constructed out of mainly found objects and painted with bright colors in a bravura manner, these oversized creations built on Grooms's theater and films toward a truly interactive art, like a cartoon coming to life. One of the first of these constructions was *Mr. and Mrs. Rembrandt* (1971). Honoring the seventeenth-century Dutch painter, the work is composed of materials found in the attic of his parents' home. Grooms would return to Nashville to visit family and to exhibit on occasion with the Nashville Artist Guild. The Tennessee State Museum featured his work in a 1986 exhibit. Ten years later, Grooms participated in Tennessee's Bicentennial Celebration, a three-day-long event that included three art exhibitions in downtown Nashville.

Although not so well represented in Tennessee's museums as Grooms, native Nashvillian Robert Ryman (b. 1930) is another major artist who began his career in the 1950s. Like Grooms, Ryman studied at George Peabody College for Teachers, but he worked in music during the late 1940s. Whereas Grooms knew from a very early age that he wanted to paint, Ryman was first interested in jazz. After moving to Manhattan, Ryman began to paint in the early 1950s while working as a guard at the Museum of Modern Art. In 1958, the year Grooms moved to New York, art patron Gertrude A. Mellon purchased Ryman's work in a staff exhibition and Ryman was on his way. By 1961 he was painting full time.

Where Grooms's work is interactive, Ryman's non-objective paintings are introspective. Grooms is more concerned with what the painting portrays; Ryman focuses on how the painting is made. His subject is his method. Ryman's work has been the subject of only one Nashville exhibition to date, at Cheekwood Museum of Art. "Seldom has less been said or generally known about the background of a major contemporary painter," notes Robert Storrs. "In America, this is especially striking given the role—most often distracting and distorting—that personality cults have played in the estimation of comparably important artists. The paucity of information about Ryman's life reflects his desire to forestall such myth-making and follows from his insistence that we focus exclusively on the painting as painting."[10]

Compared to Ryman, Grooms's work is well recognized in his native state. His *Tennessee Foxtrot Carousel* in downtown Nashville is a popular tourist attraction, and his work has been the subject of several large exhibits at the Tennessee State Museum, the Knoxville Museum of Art, and Cheekwood Museum of Art.

The creation of the latter institution capped a decade of significant development in the capitol city's art history. In 1957 Walter Sharp, a founder of the influential Nashville Arts Council a year earlier, and his wife Huldah Cheek Sharp donated her family's "Cheekwood" estate as the newly established Tennessee Botanical Gardens and Fine Arts Center. The fine arts center, led by director Harry Lowe, opened in 1960 with two important exhibits: *Tennessee Painting—The Past* and *Tennessee Artists Now,* arguably the first exhibits to portray the history of Tennessee painting up to the present time.[11]

Nashville's universities also became regular contributors to the diversity of the city's art scene in the 1960s. August Freundlich became chair of the Art Department at the George Peabody College for Teachers in the late 1950s. He hired creative artists Arthur Orr and Alfred Pounders, who transformed the department by joining the industrial arts with the Art Department. In 1960, the college's renovated Cohen Gallery reopened with a series of challenging shows, highlighted by an exhibition of works by Wassily Kandinsky, Paul Klee, and other non-objective painters from the collection of the Soloman R. Guggenheim Museum in New York City. At Fisk University, Aaron Douglas retired in 1966 and was succeeded by David Driskell (b. 1931). Driskell served as chair of the Art Department for a decade, leaving behind a legacy in the collections that he brought to the university, the exhibitions that he organized and the students he taught (including such prominent artists as Stephanie Pogue and Jacqueline Bontemps). Driskell's own painting flourished at Fisk, where he found inspiration in the university collections.[12] His earlier work at Howard University exhibited the influence of French painters Paul Cézanne and Henri Matisse. However, exposure to the work of social realist Jack Levine (b. 1915) during a summer of study in 1953 at Maine's Skowhegan School of Painting and Sculpture and the advice of Howard professor James A. Porter (1905–1970) encouraged Driskell to "define the role that our people have played in art."[13] A series of trips to Africa beginning in 1969 gave Driskell the opportunity to deepen his exploration of his African heritage. His paintings and collages speak to his forty-year spiritual journey. Biblical themes are interspersed with African masks and contemporary subjects; a series of landscape paintings done at Driskell's home in Maine evoke a personal closeness to nature. Driskell's style is eclectic, ranging from loose, expressive brushwork to the flat linearity of collage.

Art instruction also expanded at Vanderbilt University during the 1950s and 1960s; the university held its first exhibition, a selection of work from twenty-one Nashville artists, in the remodeled Old Gym Gallery in 1962. Among the artists were several winners of the Nashville Arts Festivals: Werner Wildner (whose surreal drawings and paintings of somewhat sinister dream images are meticulously detailed), Harry Lowe, Robert Marks, Peggy Smith, and Gus Baker.

Yaddo Circle, by David Driskell, 1980. Courtesy of the artist.

Nature Series #390, watercolor, 30 × 40 inches, by Carl Sublett. Collection of Knoxville Museum of Art; gift of Mr. Robert Van Deventer.

Gus Baker and Avery Handly (1913–1958), both natives of Winchester, exhibited together several times; in 1946, after both returned from duty in, respectively, the army and navy; in 1948; and again in 1950 at the Sewanee Art Gallery. Baker had studied at the University of the South before moving to Dallas to work at the Dallas Museum of Fine Arts. Handly had majored in English at Vanderbilt University, where he was influenced by the Agrarians, and then gone on to study with the Regionalists Thomas Hart Benton and Grant Wood at the Kansas City Art Institute. Handly came back to Winchester to farm and paint what he knew best, the subjects of his hometown. His interpretations of familiar Winchester scenes, painted with expressive exaggeration, were the subject of a memorial exhibit at the 1960 Nashville Arts Festival. Louise LeQuire, writer for the *Nashville Banner,* noted in the exhibit catalogue, "It is almost unheard of now for a confessed regionalist in painting to receive nationwide honors. Those who do not feel that residence in New York will help them to realize their greatest work, rarely receive full mention there. But in Tennessee, where Handly chose to remain and live and work, those who have been concerned with art have always been cognizant of the talent in their midst, and deeply saddened at its going."[14]

Art in Knoxville between 1950 and 1970 was a story of growth and greater sophistication centered at the University of Tennessee. Its Department of Art expanded under the leadership of C. Kermit Ewing (1910–1976), who came to Knoxville in 1948 from the Carnegie Institute of Technology in Pittsburgh. In 1957, he hired Walter Hollis Stevens (1927–1980), Richard Clarke, and Philip Nichols, who would set the course for the next generation of Knoxville painters. In the early 1960s, together with their colleagues, Joanna Higgs and Robert Birdwell, hired in 1963, and Carl Sublett (b. 1919), hired in 1966, they became known as the Knoxville Seven. The seven shared a common interest in the spiritual as found in nature, interpreted in abstracted form in paint. Stevens, leader of the group, summed up his intentions: "We often are wonderfully aware that we are actually a meaningful part of that which we view, and that it in turn is an integral part of us. The moment of 'becoming' is magnificent, no matter how brief, for we are strangely assured that our lives

Fissure III, oil on linen, 25½ × 39⅝ inches, by Walter Hollis Stevens. Collection of Knoxville Museum of Art; gift of Carolyn Preston.

are immeasurably enriched even though this enrichment is intangible."[15]

During these years, the campus at Knoxville became a refuge for Abstract painters in Tennessee. Stevens had first experimented with abstract Expressionism in the mid-1950s. New York was on the verge of becoming the art capital of the world, and Stevens found inspiration in art magazine articles about Wilhelm de Kooning, Joan Mitchell, and other abstract painters. Stevens and Carl Sublett combined their interest in Abstract Expressionism with their love of watercolor, creating nature-inspired paintings on sketching trips to the Smokies, following in the footsteps of Lloyd Branson and his students. In the late 1960s, Stevens became more introspective and his subject changed from the ridges of East Tennessee to interior scenes and still lifes. Stevens experimented with the new acrylic-polymer paints developed in the mid-1960s that required less preparation and drying than oils. In his *Windows* series of the mid-1960s and his *Island* series of the early 1970s, Stevens heightened his palette and manipulated his medium. In 1976, Sublett became a full professor at the University of Tennessee and was elected as a member of the National Academy of Design. While Sublett continues to exhibit his work around the country, he remains in Knoxville, creating an enormous oeuvre. In 1960 he remarked, "The true value of a man's art, I believe, does not depend upon the capacity with which it is received by others but rather the degree of personal conviction exercised in a lifetime of creating it."[16] His work was the subject of a major retrospective exhibition, organized by Louise LeQuire for the Tennessee State Museum in 1984.

The Rise of Private Art Galleries, New Art Venues, and New Art Organizations

Three distinctive phases mark the development of painting in Tennessee during the twentieth century. From 1900 to 1930 came the creation, largely under the guidance of women artists and women arts leaders, of the state's major urban art associations and the beginnings of an institutional structure for the permanent exhibiting of art. From the Depression decade to the 1970s came further institutional development and the expansion of art departments and the support for artists at colleges and universities across Tennessee. We are still in the most recent phase, which is especially characterized by the creation and growth of new art venues and organizations as well as private galleries, related to but independent of the state's major museums and university programs.

In Memphis, major expansions took place at the Memphis Brooks Museum in 1972 and 1990. The Dixon Gallery opened its doors in 1976. Established by the Hugo Dixon Foundation, the museum assembled an impressive collection of paintings by French and American Impressionists and Post-Impressionists under the guidance of expert John Rewald. The Alice Bingham Gallery opened on Cooper Street in 1979, specializing in work by twentieth-century Memphians. Bingham eventually established a gallery in New York, where she continued to showcase art by Tennesseans. Also opening in 1979 was the Lisa Kurts Gallery, which includes work from established artists and promising newcomers. Albers Fine Art Gallery opened in Memphis in 1984, followed by Cooper Street Gallery (which shows emerging artists), and, in 1995, Ledbetter Lusk (now David Lusk) Gallery (which features a mixture of established and emerging artists). A number of alternative venues have emerged in the last ten years, most notably Delta Axis Contemporary Arts Center and Marshall Arts, the latter operated by artist Pinkney Herbert. A graduate of Rhodes College and the University of Memphis, Herbert paints canvases full of biomorphic, centripetal shapes that suggest microscopic organisms.

In Knoxville the major development of the past generation has been the Knoxville Museum of Art. Founded in 1961 as the Dulin Gallery of Art, the museum moved from its cramped facilities in a historic mansion, designed by architect John Russell Pope, on Kingston Pike into a contemporary building, designed by architect Edward Larabee Barnes, at the site of the 1982 world's fair, after an interim period occupying an old candy factory building. Recent exhibitions curated by the museum staff have highlighted Nashville's Red Grooms and the work of Bessie Harvey (1929–1994), an Alcoa sculptor. The museum, in collaboration with other Knoxville schools and institutions, maintains the Bessie Harvey Homepage on the internet to document and interpret Harvey's sculpture and other artistic contributions. Knoxville's art galleries have emerged out of a tradition of framing galleries. Today, Bennett Galleries exhibits fine arts and crafts, including painters Andrew Saftel and Carl Sublett. Saftel's richly worked surfaces reflect his early training as a printmaker. Found objects and calligraphic excerpts from centuries-old sailing journals give viewers a foothold to begin their own personal interpretation.

In Nashville, the late twentieth century witnessed the creation of an array of private galleries. The Cumberland Gallery, founded in April 1980 by Carol Stein, Susan Hammond, and Susan O'Neil, joined the earlier Lyzon Gallery. Still owned and run by Stein, Cumberland Gallery represents close to fifty American artists, approximately half of whom are from the Southeast, including nationally established painters John Baeder and Barry Buxkamper. Baeder, known for his exactingly beautiful paintings of America's diners, moved to Nashville from New York and has become an active part of the arts community. Buxkamper also is interested in the urban environment. However, where Baeder's images are a paean to a disappearing icon, Buxkamper questions our contemporary suburban culture. Both artists possess superior skill in rendering their subjects, which usually incorporate an unnatural stillness that connects them to the social realist tradition. Barry Buxkamper worked as a graphic designer for twenty years before turning full time to painting and teaching at Middle Tennessee State University in Murfreesboro. Another significant late-twentieth-century Nashville gallery was the Zimmerman/Saturn Gallery, established by Alice Zimmerman. Local Color Gallery, In the Gallery, Zeitgeist Gallery, and Williams Fine Art joined the city's art scene in later years. These venues

Passed Time, mixed media 47⅝ × 58¾ inches, by Andrew Saftel. Collection of Knoxville Museum of Art; Collector's Circle purchase.

offer a range of choices, from contemporary art by Tennessee painters to turn-of-the-century works by Gilbert Gaul and Ella S. Hergesheimer. Together with local restaurants, the metropolitan airport, and local nightspots, an estimated one hundred exhibition spaces currently exist in the Nashville area. In addition, new arts organizations have sprung up as alternatives to the Nashville Artist Guild and the Arts League: VAAN (Visual Artist Alliance of Nashville), N4Art (Nashville African American Arts Association), and Untitled.

Among the capitol city's art institutions, Cheekwood Museum of Art completed a major renovation in 1999, including the conversion of the Cheek's stables into a center for contemporary art. The Frist Center for the Visual Arts opened in what had been Nashville's New Deal–era post office in 2001. One of the Frist's initial exhibits, *An Enduring Legacy: Art of the Americas from Nashville Collections,* presented the city's long history of acquiring and showing a wide range of art through 145 different works. As the state's largest visual arts organization, the Frist's education and outreach programs involved thousands of children and adults. The Parthenon has presented a major exhibition on the art of Winslow Homer in addition to an important retrospective on the work of Willie Betty Newman. The Tennessee State Museum hosted the 1990 Masterworks exhibit of paintings from the Bridgestone Museum of Art, and has curated numerous important exhibitions of Tennessee artists. Its 1993 exhibit, *From the Mountains to the Mississippi,* pointed to another development in the work of Barbara Bullock, whose brightly colored canvases explored relations between races and sexes in a sometimes challenging way.

Bullock's controversial and confrontational style reflects well the maturation of the subject matter and skill exhibited by Tennessee's painters since the 1897 Centennial Exposition. Her career also speaks volumes about growing opportunities for women and minorities in the arts. Tennessee's painters began the century with their eyes trained on Europe, where centuries of artistic tradition had created a well-developed network of schools, galleries, critics, dealers, patrons, and exhibitions. Struggling in the twentieth century to establish standards for their profession, Tennessee's artists searched for venues and worked to educate and develop a sophisticated art audience.

Their labors have not gone unrewarded. Today, Tennessee's galleries and museums jostle for position in an increasingly crowded calendar of art openings, lectures, and workshops. Painters enjoy a freedom of expression that was unheard of in 1900, when American Impressionism was considered avant-garde. The number of venues for local display (not counting the ever-expanding Internet) has grown exponentially, including an impressive number of artist-run cooperative spaces. There are signs of change in the contemporary art audience, which has gone from a small, select elite to an enormous population that cuts across socioeconomic lines. These patrons may turn the tide of support from the conservative preference of many Tennesseans for realism alone, encouraging a greater range of expression. All of these things were among the goals of the early art associations; they knew that a large audience was critical to the attraction and survival of professional artists in our state.

Dorothy and Lillian Gish Aboard a Steamship Bound for Europe, mixed media, by Charles "Red" Grooms, c. 1992. Courtesy of Wilhelmina Grooms.

The challenge of the twenty-first century will be to maintain our meaningful traditions yet remain open to emerging forms of art. Regional painting may go the way of the southern accent in the information age. The last century has witnessed great strides in the development of an arts support system in Tennessee. Minority artists once outside the art world are moving into the mainstream. New exhibition venues, challenging art schools, and a growing patronage system nurture the arts community. Tennessee's painters must take these accomplishments into the next century, where technological advances will challenge them to use their creative abilities to have their voices heard amid the information onslaught.

NOTES

1. Mrs. James C. Bradford, *The Nashville Art Association Minutes* 1:385.
2. The first state art associations of the late nineteenth and early twentieth centuries, like the East Tennessee Art Association (founded 1852), the Memphis Art Association (1914), and the Nashville Art Association (1883), were created out of the desire to develop a public art audience through school programs and exhibits. Lectures on a diverse range of topics were offered on a regular basis and membership was open to both males and females. Members endeavored to improve themselves and their communities through the efforts of these organizations in a manner that echoed England's Victorian ambitions. The associations also created a support group of like-minded individuals for struggling artists during a period when many had little time or appreciation for fine art.
3. *Nashville Banner*, Aug. 26, 1905, p. 10.
4. The art exhibitions at the Knoxville Appalachian expositions were different from those at the Tennessee Centennial in that they drew heavily from Tennessee artists. In 1910, the first incarnation of the Knoxville exposition, over half of the paintings were by artists from the state, as compared with approximately 3 percent of the

1897 Nashville exposition. Like the earlier exhibit, the Knoxville exposition contained artwork on loan from major American centers, but the Nashville exhibit relied more heavily on out-of-state work.

5. Newman exhibited *En Pénitence* at the 1895 Paris Salon, the prestigious government-sponsored exhibition dating back to the eighteenth century. Acceptance in the salon conferred professional status among one's peers and patrons. Newman exhibited work at eight of the twelve salons between 1891 and 1902 and was honored by the French government in 1900 for her portrait of Fanny Alice Gowdy, daughter of the American consulate.
6. Other Tennesseans listed as such at the fair were Burton Callicott; Marion Junkin, who became the first art teacher at Vanderbilt University in 1942; Will Henry Stevens, who spent his summers in the Smokies in the 1910s; Carroll Cloar; and sculptor Harold Cash. Cash was the only Tennessean listed in both the 1933 and 1939 world's fairs.
7. Situated in Overton Park, the Memphis Brooks Museum is the oldest extant museum in the state, holding a strong collection of Italian Renaissance and baroque paintings and sculpture, many of which were given to the museum by the Kress Foundation in 1952. The earliest donations to the museum were a portrait of Mr. Brooks by Cecilia Beaux, a portrait of Samuel Hamilton Brooks by William Cooper, and a portrait of Mrs. Brooks by Kate Augusta Carl.
8. "N.Y. Shows May Exhibit Sketch of Blount Home," *Knoxville News Sentinel,* Aug. 8, 1948.
9. Clara Hieronymus, "Red Grooms Painting in Artist Guild Show," *Nashville Tennessean,* Feb. 6, 1983.
10. Robert Storr, *Robert Ryman* (New York: Harry N. Abrams, 1993), 11.
11. Over the years, Cheekwood would build an impressive collection of paintings by Tennesseans, a subsection of their collection of American and contemporary painting.
12. See Keith Morrison, "Introduction: Driskell the Collector," *Narrative of African American Art and Identity: The David C. Driskell Collection,* exhibition catalogue (College Park: Art Gallery and the Department of Art History and Archaeology at the University of Maryland, 1998).
13. James A. Porter to David Driskell as related in a gallery talk by the artist for the exhibit "Echoes: The Art of David Driskell," Fisk University's Van Vechten Gallery, Dec. 11, 1999.
14. Gus Baker, ed., *Avery Handly Memorial Exhibition of Paintings,* exhibit catalogue, the Parthenon, Nashville, May 8–29, 1960.
15. *One Hundred Works from the Permanent Collection,* Tennessee Fine Arts Center at Cheekwood, Nashville exhibition catalogue, Oct. 14–Nov. 28, 1965, 31.
16. *Knoxville Artists,* exhibition catalogue, Univ. of Tennessee, 1960.

Suggested Readings

Callicott, Burton. *10 Years @ Brooks.* Memphis: Memphis Brooks Museum of Art, 1998.

Faiers, Edward S. *Burton Callicott: Retrospective Exhibition of Paintings.* Memphis: Memphis Academy of Arts, 1961.

Fine Arts Department. *An Album of the Tennessee Centennial and International Exposition.* Nashville: Marshall & Bruce, 1897.

Gerdts, William H. *Art Across America: Two Centuries of Regional Painting, 1710–1920.* New York: Abbeville Press, 1990.

Haskell, Barbara. *The American Century: Art and Culture, 1900–1950.* New York: W. W. Norton, 1999.

Holland, Juanita Marie. *Narratives of African American Art and Identity: The David C. Driskell Collection.* San Francisco: Pomegranate Communications, 1998.

Hull, Howard. *Tennessee Post Office Murals.* Johnson City, Tenn.: Overmountain Press, 1996.

Kelly, James C. "Landscape and Genre Painting in Tennessee, 1810–1985." *Tennessee Historical Quarterly* 44 (Summer 1985): 1–152.

———. "Portrait Painting in Tennessee." *Tennessee Historical Quarterly* 46 (Winter 1987): 193–285.

Kirschke, Amy Helene. *Aaron Douglas: Art, Race, and the Harlem Renaissance.* Jackson: Univ. Press of Mississippi, 1995.

McIntyre, Florence M. *Art and Life.* Memphis: S. C. Toof, 1952.

Nosanow, Barbara Shissler. *More than Land or Sky: Art from Appalachia.* Washington, D.C.: Smithsonian Institution Press, 1981.

Phillips, Lisa. *The American Century: Art & Culture, 1950–2000.* New York: W. W. Norton, 1999.
Powell, Richard J., and Jock Reynolds. *To Conserve a Legacy: American Art from Historically Black Colleges and Universities.* Cambridge: MIT Press, 1999.
Probasco, Zane. *An American Collection.* Chattanooga: Hunter Museum of Art, 1978.
Young, Namuni Hale. *Art & Furniture of East Tennessee.* Knoxville: East Tennessee Historical Society, 1997.

Archival Sources

Cheekwood Museum of Art, Nashville. Artist files.
East Tennessee Historical Society Archives, Knoxville.
Knoxville Museum of Art. Artist files.
Memphis Brooks Museum of Art. Library files.
Memphis College of Art. Scrapbooks.
The Nashville Artist Guild. Guild scrapbooks, lent by Louise LeQuire, Nashville.
Nashville Room, Public Library of Nashville and Davidson County.

Seven

Tennessee Photography and Its Documentary Traditions

Beverly Brannan
Library of Congress

Tennessee has a long but disaggregate history of photography. This chapter is a preliminary effort to pull together the different themes, individuals, and events that shaped the practice of photography in the state. The essay also identifies Tennessee's major collections of photographic images for viewing and researching the state's visual tradition.

The photographic record of Tennessee, once it began in the 1840s with portraits, or "likenesses," became diverse in both subject and technology over the next fifty years. As it diversified, Tennessee photography also developed distinct local, perhaps regional, themes. Photographs of people include individuals, groups, people demonstrating processes or displaying prized possessions, and people depicting ethnic or racial stereotypes. Portraits of animals like fine horses and favorite hunting dogs complement human portraits. Other emblematic Tennessee photographs show special places, like the Great Smoky Mountains, Lookout Mountain, homes of state and national leaders, country cabins, and representative sites like farms, quarries, or major construction such as Norris Dam. Transportation photographs abound—from steamboats at the levee to trains on the track, from building battleships to flying airplanes. As both the country music capital and the birthplace of one form of the Blues, Tennessee has an extraordinary wealth of photographs of musicians and performances. These people, places, and events are captured in all photographic formats, from daguerreotypes to digital images. Styles range from the personal snapshot to the news photo for international distribution.

Historical Patterns and Significant Photographers

Frenchman Louis Jacques Mandé Daguerre was the first to publicize and capitalize on his form of photography, daguerreotypes, the finely detailed, one-of-a-kind, mirror-like images on silver-plated copper, protected by a cover glass in a case with a hinged lid. While Samuel F. B. Morse was in France in early 1839, promoting his own invention of the telegraph, Daguerre personally demonstrated his photographic technique for him. When Morse returned to New York, he created an expectant audience for the new medium by heralding the process to scientists, inventors and fellow Americans. The French government purchased and published Daguerre's formula on August 9 and in late September a ship from Paris arrived in New York harbor with the formula, thus introducing to America the form of photography that would become popular beyond anticipation.[1]

By spring 1840, daguerreotypy had already begun to develop as a profession in New York and Philadelphia. In 1842, a Morse-trained New York photographer, Edward Anthony, recognized the importance of making a portrait of Andrew Jackson, the only former president living when photography was introduced. Anthony went to The Hermitage, Jackson's home outside Nashville, where he made a daguerreotype of the elderly statesman, an image that proved essential to the gallery of images of important Americans that Anthony and his brother opened in New York in 1844. The Anthonys soon shifted to the photo supply business and the enterprising New York jewel- and miniature-case maker Mathew Brady opened his own photography gallery of celebrity portraiture in 1845. Brady began collecting daguerreotypes of famous people, including Anthony's daguerreotype of Andrew Jackson, and relied heavily on the celebrity value of the portrait to attract visitors to what became Brady's National Portrait Gallery.[2]

Daguerreotype of Mary Smythe Magevney. On April 7, 1843, Fredrick Clark placed the earliest advertisement for a commercial photographer in Memphis. He became part owner of Merriman and Clark studio there. Magevney sat for this likeness in 1843, according to the date scratched on the back. A posthumous painting based on this image belongs to the Pink Palace Museum in Memphis. Attributed to Fredrick Harvey Clark. Courtesy Pink Palace Museum, Memphis.

Future research may determine whether Jackson's portrait is the first Tennessee-made daguerreotype, but the earliest known in the Memphis area has the date 1843 scratched on it and is attributed to Frederick Harvey Clark, originally of New York. The 1850 Memphis city directory lists four daguerreotypists and a total of eight people employed in photography in this port city of 8,841 people. Each daguerreotype cost about one dollar, or approximately one week's wages for an ordinary man at that time.[3] The often static-looking daguerreotype portrait resulted from sitters having to maintain their poses for a minute or more. Less expensive than the hand-painted miniature portraits they replaced, daguerreotypes were presented in elaborately embellished same-size cases. Besides Clark, other early Tennessee photographers include James Cameron in Chattanooga; Samuel Shaver, an itinerant who worked in several upper East Tennessee counties; Thomas Jefferson Dobyns in Nashville and New Orleans; and a Mr. Shaw of Memphis.

The Talbotype or calotype process, introduced in England by William Henry Fox Talbot in late 1839, produced multiple copies of the same image in a negative-to-positive process, using a paper negative. The technique failed to catch on as the fibers in the paper negative could produce only soft focus images that never appealed to popular taste and left practitioners unable to pay for the expensive licenses required to reimburse the inventor. The process became obsolete by the 1850s when cheaper methods for making sharp photographs became available. These cheaper methods included two forms of the collodion wet-plate process: ambrotypes (negative images made in gelatin that, on darkened glass, appear as positive pictures) and tintypes (gelatinous negative images that appear positive on thin black-lacquered iron). Like the daguerreotypes they replaced, these forms are known as "cased objects." The cases protect the delicate image surface and imitate as closely as possible the presentation of the more expensive daguerreotypes.

In 1850, Englishman Frederick Scott Archer introduced collotypes, fine-detailed photographs on

Portrait of Pvt. Robert Patterson, Company D, Twelfth Tennessee Infantry, CSA. When a negative is formed on a glass plate by using a light-sensitive collodion emulsion, a positive image appears when viewed against a dark background. Photographed between 1860 and 1865; rephotographed 1961. Courtesy of Library of Congress, Prints & Photographs Division, Selected Civil War photographs, 1861–1865, Collection (reproduction number LC-B8184-10038).

paper, printed from glass negatives coated with light-sensitive chemicals dissolved in collodion. Finally, it was possible to produce multiple identical clear, sharp salted-paper prints, images exactly alike on a paper base. When the reduced production costs of the quick, inexpensive albumen (egg white) image emulsion for printing the negatives came along in 1853, the era of mass distribution of images arrived, making ownership of portraits and pictures of significant events affordable to all but the poorest citizens.

Initially photographs were printed on very thin paper and adhered to card stock to prevent curling. Cardstock sizes quickly became standardized: the carte-de-visite (2½ by 4 inches, approximately calling card size) was in common use by 1860. Technological improvements made it possible to increase print sizes and provided photographers with a rationale to draw people back to their studios and to accommodate increasingly elaborate backgrounds. Prints about 8 by 10 inches, mounted on 11-by-14-inch paper boards, could be produced after the mid-1850s, for display on walls or in albums. The cabinet card (initially 4¼ by 6½ inches) started in the 1860s and the Imperial cards (approximately 6 by 10 inches) came into vogue in the 1870s for celebrity photographs and to permit photographers to display their skills. In another marketing ploy of the 1870s through 1890s, photographers touched up photographs with charcoal, pencil, or pastel, to render them more like paintings.[4]

The Civil War proved a great impetus to the documentary tradition of American photography. Probably tintype or cartes-de-visite portraits of soldiers, alone or with buddies, are the most common photographs of the Civil War. Photographers set up portable studios at registration and muster sites and where armies camped. One journalist observed that the standard outbuildings to an army camp were those of the photographer and the coffin maker. In addition to portraits, photographs from this era picture buildings, fields vacant or decimated after a battle, soldiers at rest in camps, weapon stockpiles, railroads, and bridges. Technology did not exist for "battle action shots" until the twentieth century.

War scarcities limited production of war photographs by Confederate and border state photographers but photographs made in Tennessee by Union and Confederate camera operators now coexist in repositories such as the Tennessee State Museum, the Tennessee State Archives and Library, Nathan Bedford Forrest State Park's Tennessee Folklife Center, the Shiloh National Battlefield Park, Fort Pillow State Park, and Fort Donelson National Battlefield. Important out-of-state collections are at Pennsylvania's Carlisle Army Barracks; and in the collections of the National Archives and Library of Congress in Washington, D.C.

Federal forces relied on photographs of railroads for logistical planning and made photos of military structures to document accomplishments. George

Top: Running Water Creek. Gelatin silver photograph from wet-plate collodion negative on glass. On verso: "Running Water Bridge & Raccoon Valley between Chattanooga, Tenn. & Bridgeport, Ala." Photograph by George N. Barnard, 1864. Courtesy of Library of Congress, Prints & Photographs Division, Orlando M. Poe Collection (reproduction number LC-USZ62-115234).

Above: Stereo card from Woodward's Photo-Tent Gallery. Courtesy of Library of Congress, Prints & Photographs Division, Verson, Stereo File—U.S. Geography—Tennessee.

N. Barnard (1819–1902) was the most capable of the Union army photographers. His images from the federal occupation of Tennessee, made between 1862 and 1864, include the cleared, vacated site of the 1863 bloody battle at Missionary Ridge in Chattanooga and the largely demolished Nashville of late 1864. As official photographer for Gen. William Tecumseh Sherman's "March to the Sea" in late 1864 through early 1865, Barnard photographed ruins and Union-held bridges and fortifications en route to Atlanta. Back in Washington, these photographs communicated to Congress and the administration that the infrastructure of the South had been effectively demolished. The National Archives is the principal repository for these images. Other photographers working during the Civil War in Tennessee include Theodore M. Schleier of New Orleans and a Nashville photographer known only as "Mr. Bailey."

Resumption of trade after the Civil War permitted widespread use of the glass negative process in Tennessee. Temperamental wet-plate glass negatives had to be coated with solutions immediately before exposure, limiting the number of images made at any opportunity. Dry-plate glass negatives (invented in 1871) eliminated much of the chemical experimentation from photography and made it possible to photograph timely events "on location."

During the 1850s, stereographic photographs came into being, but few were produced in Tennessee until the late 1860s. Stereographs consist of two nearly identical photographs made with a double-lens camera, then mounted side-by-side on a card that, after the 1880s, curved gently to heighten their visual impact. Viewed through a stereoscope, they give the illusion of depth. From the 1860s through the 1920s stereos were popular for entertainment and education because they made views of faraway places accessible at affordable prices to ordinary Americans. A series of narrative scenes on two or more cards were almost like short movies.

Tennessee photographers produced and copyrighted stereographs that appealed to both local and national markets. For instance, in 1875, when former president Andrew Johnson died at his home in Greeneville, Jonesboro photographer L. W. Keen produced stereographs of the funeral of the former president, the Greeneville Court House where his remains lay in state, the hill on which he was buried, and the old tailor shop that he had once occupied.

It is difficult to trace distribution of stereographs made by general photographers, but some sold their photographs to companies that specialized in making and distributing nationally stereographs on many topics. From late in the Civil War until the early twentieth century, when most veterans had died, a lucrative market existed for images of Civil War battle sites, regimental reunions, and military cemeteries in Tennessee and other states where combat had occurred. Both local photographers and national photographic companies supplied this need. Edward and H. T. Anthony of New York dedicated much of their practice to producing Civil War images in the 1890s for the thirtieth-anniversary observances. The B. W. Kilburn Stereographic View Company and the Keystone View Company produced photographs of Chattanooga's National Cemetery repeatedly between 1891 and 1905.

Lantern slides, introduced in 1849, are three-by-three-inch pieces of glass supporting the photographic emulsion (often hand-colored), with a same-size protective cover glass held in place by paper tape. After the Civil War, leisure travel by rail, stagecoach, and boat created a market for lantern slides of sites for individual viewing and, once gaslights could produce a sufficiently bright light, for projection at lectures to large audiences.

As inventors and innovators continued to refine photographic technology, more photographic studios were established, especially in cities and larger towns. Shopkeepers could add photography to services already offered: John Glenn of Newport stamped his photographs "Jeweler and Stationer," and in 1878, J. Fletch. Woodward, M.D., of McMinnville, stamped the backs of his stereocards with information about his medical background and "Woodward's Photo-Tent Gallery and Dark Room Trunk" to advertise his services as both a physician and a photographer. As a young man, Edward Emerson Barnard worked as an assistant in the photographic gallery of Van Stavoren in Nashville, where he learned skills that helped him photograph the Milky Way in his later career in astronomy. Studio photographers R. S. Patterson in Nashville and Bingham Brothers in Memphis, like their counterparts throughout the state, produced individual and group portraits, recorded social and civic events, documented natural and built environments, and photographed the occupations of the local economy. In Tennessee as elsewhere, surviving studio photographs form the backbone of most photographic archives.

During the New South era (1870 to 1900), the number of Tennessee photographs dealing with mining, logging, industrialization, and urbanization rapidly multiplied. The Tennessee Division of Geology Archives show that photographs have been successful tools in topographical surveys conducted for mapmaking, waging war, economic development, flood control, road construction, and forestry management since the late 1860s. U.S. Army Corps of Engineers photographs at the National Archives document federal river dredging, flood control, and transportation projects from the late nineteenth through the late twentieth century. The James Goforth photographs at the Archives of Appalachia at East Tennessee State University document railroad construction and routes on the Carolina, Clinchfield and Ohio Railway in North and South Carolina, Tennessee, and Virginia between 1906 and 1915. Photographs at the Tennessee State Archives and Library are especially rich in images of the state's economic development between the Civil War and World War I. These photographs document coal mining, timbering, chemical and steel production; the quarrying of ore, copper, limestone, and marble in East Tennessee; tobacco and horse farming near Nashville; and cotton growing in West Tennessee. National photo companies continued to provide informative views. The Keystone View Company, for instance, photographed the Memphis area and its cotton combing machinery in 1899 and twice in the 1920s, producing stereographic images of bales of raw cotton; loading cotton onto steamboats; machinery for carding, spinning, and weaving cotton; and making cotton cloth.

Souvenir booklets, panoramic photographs, and stereographs document a booster mentality that thrived during the New South era. In the late 1880s, Chattanooga, Knoxville, Nashville, and Memphis produced souvenir booklets to show their churches, colleges, arts and music centers, fine homes, landscaped parks, and major industries, both as tourist mementoes and to attract additional businesses. In the decades that followed, many other towns produced similar promotional materials, including panoramic photographs. Introduction of flexible roll film in the 1880s made it possible to produce a long

Edward Emerson Barnard

ASTRONOMER AND PHOTOGRAPHER of the Milky Way, Edward Emerson Barnard (1857–1923), rose from an impoverished youth in post–Civil War Nashville to international acclaim. To support his invalid mother, Barnard worked as a photographer's assistant in the shop of John H. Van Stavoren, where he operated the gigantic solar Jupiter camera. This early experience instilled in Barnard the patience and persistence that later enabled him to spend long hours in telescopic observation. Working with photographers Rodney Poole and Peter Calvert, Barnard acquired the photographic skills that garnered future accolades. Barnard's interest in comets attracted the attention of Nashville's business and scholastic elite. In 1883, Bishop Holland N. McTyeire notified Barnard of his election to a fellowship at Vanderbilt University, where he would also take charge of the school's observatory. His success enhanced his reputation and led to positions first at California's Lick Observatory and then Chicago's Yerkes Observatory.

Barnard first photographed the Milky Way in August 1889. Over the next three decades he produced more than four thousand photographs and wrote some 840 addresses and articles. He published two books of photographs, *Publications of the Lick Observatory*, volume 11 (1913), and *Atlas of the Milky Way* (1923–24). Barnard's many honors included the French Academy of Sciences Gold Medal, the Janssen Prize of the French Astronomical Society, the Royal Astronomical Gold Medal, and the Bruce Medal of the Astronomical Society of the Pacific.

At his death, Barnard was buried in Nashville's Mount Olivet Cemetery.

Connie L. Lester, Mississippi State University

Suggested Reading

Sheehan, William. *The Immortal Fire Within: The Life and Work of Edward Emerson Barnard.* Cambridge: Cambridge University Press, 1995.

Boy working on warping machine in Elk Cotton Mills, Fayetteville. Gelatin silver photograph by Lewis W. Hine, 1910, mounted in an album by the Library of Congress. This is one of ten photographs made of children working at a textile mill and of their superintendent and overseers. Courtesy of Library of Congress, Prints and Photographs Division, National Child Labor Committee Collection (reproduction number LC-USZ62-96801).

"pan" from a single continuous negative. The panoramic camera had a long curved back and the lens actually turned while making the picture, enabling jokesters to run from one end of the picture to the other so they could appear twice in the same image. Pans, usually at least twice as long as wide, were very trendy from about 1880 until about 1930 for popularizing landscapes and cityscapes, and for recording groups such as military regiments, sports teams, or high school classes. Several Tennessee cities have turn-of-the-century panoramic photographs that monumentalize their railroad stations, skylines, and tall office buildings. Industrial and urban stereographs served a similar purpose: the B. W. Kilburn Company produced stereographs of the Memphis area in 1891 and 1892, and William Henry Jackson and the Detroit Photo Company in 1902 made some of the best-known lantern slides and stereographs of the state's urban landscape.

The Progressive era (1900–1930) witnessed the continuation of booster photography, but documentary photographers also began to focus on the "other" side of the new industrial and urban changes in Tennessee. Photography to support the Progressive movement combined realistic images with factual text to inform the educated middle class about the need for child labor reform, government protection of workers, rural uplift, improved education and health services, and conservation activities for natural resources, as well as to motivate them to support reform.

In 1907, New York photographer Lewis W. Hine, hired by the National Child Labor Committee, began to photographically document children in the workplace throughout the nation. Assigned to search out abusive labor practices, he crisscrossed America reporting the practices in various industries. Between 1910 and 1911, he photographed child workers in the textile mills and mines of Athens, Chattanooga, Cleveland, Coal Creek, Elizabethton, Fayetteville, Jellico, Knoxville, Loudon, Nashville, and Sweetwater. Hine made most of his portraits outside the factories or mines where his subjects worked. The youngest workers were seven year olds who helped their sisters or mothers, but an eight-year-old boy told Hine, "No, I don't help sister or mother. Just myself." The National Child Labor Committee was the first organization, public or private, to sponsor the production of a large quantity of social documentary photographs over a long period of time and to use the images to convey information and to persuade. Hine's Tennessee

Major Public Photographic Collections

TENNESSEE'S THREE MAJOR GEOGRAPHIC REGIONS MAINTAIN COLLECTIONS OF HISTORICAL PHOtographs, collections either generated by photographers or gathered by history-minded individuals or organizations and corporations. They generally show local life from the last quarter of the nineteenth century to the present, documenting both continuity in family and civic institutions, and change, such as through railroad construction and the extractive industries of coal mining and lumbering.

Principal Collections in East Tennessee

The Archives of Appalachia at East Tennessee State University in Johnson City contain collections made by local photographers such as Bristol's Kelly and Green Photo Craftsmen Company's photographs of stores, churches, city scenes, and schools dating from 1905 to 1940; Burr Harrison's extensive 1920 to 1950 documentation of the Johnson City business district, industries, residences, and public buildings and activities in the East Tennessee State University area, as well as some turn-of-the-century photographs that Harrison probably copied from an older photographer; Clifford A. Maxwell's photographs of Washington County between the 1950s and the 1970s; and Kenneth Maynard Murray's photographs of people, landscapes, mining, crafts, and musical performances in southern Appalachia. Collections gathered by concerned citizens such as Erlene Ledford record late-nineteenth- and early-twentieth-century individuals, families, and landscapes of East Tennessee. Other examples are Anne Newton's photographs from 1910 to 1939 of Johnson City schools and Jane Dulaney Hilbert's collection of photographs from 1936 to 1970 of herself and other female aviators in eastern Tennessee.

In Knoxville, the Public Library photography collection includes work by Frank McCrary, who opened a studio around 1880 and by Charles and Joseph Knaffl of Knoxville, who created painterly portraits, staged folk narratives, and produced racial stereotype images from the 1880s through the early twentieth century and exhibited at the Photographer's Association of America Convention in New Orleans in 1899. Knoxville's Beck Cultural Exchange Center maintains a black history research collection with photographs by local photographers such as George H. Anderson, Boyd B. Browders, Claud's Studio, and Thompson and Welch Photography Studio. The Frank H. McClung Museum of the University of Tennessee in Knoxville has photographs relating to Tennessee archeology, ethnology and paleoethnobotany, as well as local historical materials.

The Chattanooga African-American History Museum contains images of Chattanoogan vocalist Bessie Smith, called "Empress of the Blues," as well as musicians and instruments in Africa that may have influenced Tennessee's musical traditions. The Special Collections portion of the University of Tennessee at Chattanooga is expanding its already valuable collection of regional photographs.

Principal Collections in Middle Tennessee

Nashville is home to several important archives, including the Tennessee State Library and Archives, the Public Library of Nashville and Davidson County, Special Collections at the Vanderbilt University Library, and Special Collections at the Fisk University Library.

Tennessee State Library and Archives holds the state's most extensive historical photograph collections. Its Manuscript Section houses photographs as well as manuscripts. Among the individual objects are portraits of social and civic organization leaders, such as a carte-de-visite photograph by local photographer Carl Casper Giers of John Snyder Dashiell (1807–1877), a member of the Freemasons Knights Templar of Nashville. It also holds entire studio archives, such as the collection of brothers Ebenezer and Peter Ross Calvert who took up photography in 1896 to supplement their painting careers. One of the earliest large Middle Tennessee collections, it is housed in four notebooks arranged by subject and date, and is searchable through a computer database. The *Looking Back at Tennessee* Collection consists of ten thousand images copied between 1985 and 1986 from privately held photographs in thirty-six counties throughout the state. The Manuscript Section also has photographs from Verne and Nonie Sabin, who worked in the Reelfoot Lake vicinity of Obion County.

The Tennessee State Museum collects photographs that complement its manuscripts, art, and artifacts collections having to do with the state, its history, and its place in the region and the nation.

Principal Collections in West Tennessee

The Memphis Public Library has the Coovert and Poland Collections, two major local photo archives, interfiled in its general Memphis and Shelby County image file. Photographer J. Charles Coovert documented rivers, floods, packet boats, refugees on levees with their belongings, bridges, cotton culture, waterfront activities, and plantation scenes. He operated out of Greenville, Mississippi, from about 1890 until he moved in 1895 to Memphis where he maintained a studio until his death in 1937. He covered northern Mississippi, western Tennessee, and northeastern Arkansas, documenting the lumber industry that shipped 90 percent of Mississippi's hardwood to Memphis in the early part of the twentieth century. Work by photographer Clifford H. Poland (1882–1939), active from 1912 to 1939, shows similar scenes

[Continued on next page]

Martin Luther King Jr. and Daisy Bates address Freedom Rally, July 31, 1959, in Mason Temple, Memphis. Behind King and Bates hang photographs of political candidates *left to right:* Russell Sugarman, Benjamin Hooks, Roy Love, and Henry C. Burton. Photograph by Ernest C. Withers. Courtesy of Memphis/Shelby County Public Library and Information Center–Memphis and Shelby County Room.

with more emphasis on street life and local string bands. The Library also has B. B. King and Elvis Presley photos from the 1950s by professional photographer Ernest Withers. Graceland, the Memphis home of Elvis Presley, has an archive of thousands of photographs relating to his musical career.

The Memphis Pink Palace Museum photographic holdings range from informal portraits by Robert Hooks, its leading black photographer in the late 1920s, to construction photographs by Walter Angier (1863–1928), and photographs of local events by J. Mack Moore (1869–1954). The Center for Southern Folklore on Beale Street in Memphis has more than fifty thousand photographs relating to local history and music, including works by Clarence Blakeley (1898–1976), Ernest Withers, and Rev. L. O. Taylor, who made and showed movies of community and church events.

The University of Tennessee–Memphis photography collections include the West Tennessee farm photograph collection, documenting farm life in West Tennessee from the 1880s to the 1960s; and the Estelle Wells collection of class photographs and pictures of rural school buildings in Weakley County, Tennessee, where she taught, 1900 to 1918. LeMoyne-Owen College in Memphis has work by photojournalists George E. Hardin, Bobby Sengstacke, and Ernest C. Withers that show African American perspectives on the civil rights movement.

The many public collections of photography in Tennessee reflect the nature of the people they serve. The vast majority of the images, whether made by professional or amateur, document the life and times of the Volunteer State.

Beverly Brannan, Library of Congress

photographs from 1910–11 are housed in archives at the University of Maryland–Baltimore and the Library of Congress, which also holds his field notes and reports of his findings. His images contributed to passage of America's first child labor laws.

A local set of motivational photographs were either made or collected in the 1920s by Dr. Harry Mustard, one of the national pioneers of the public health movement in the United States, when he supervised a Rutherford County rural health demonstration project that was supported by the Commonwealth Fund of New York State. Mustard made photographs of both well-known and not-so-well-known places in Murfreesboro; portraits of poor families (black and white) who benefited from the project; and photographs of classroom public health activities. The Mustard Collection is at the Tennessee State Library and Archives. An important collection of progressive education photographs, made by agents working with Julius Rosenwald Fund's school building program, documented the construction of rural African American schools across the South in the 1920s. The program was headquartered in Nashville throughout the 1920s and early 1930s and its numerous "before" and "after" photographs of rural black schools are now available at both the Rosenwald Collection at Fisk University Archives and the Tennessee State Library and Archives.

The national conservation movement also developed during the Progressive era. Tennessee photographers had long capitalized on natural beauty such as Lookout Mountain and the Great Smoky Mountains and the resorts around them, but in the 1890s, photo companies with national and international distribution systems began photographing in Tennessee and selling lantern slides, stereos, and later, picture postcards of scenes from the state. The Keystone View Company, for example, photographed Lookout Mountain in 1898, 1905, 1920, 1926, 1928, and 1930. William Henry Jackson and the Detroit

Smoky Mountains with snow and clouds. Photograph by Jim Thompson. Courtesy of Library of Congress, Prints & Photographs Division (reproduction number LC-USZ62-71850).

Photo Company in 1902 made some of the best-known lantern slides and stereographs of Chattanooga and the Tennessee River from Lookout Mountain.

The movement to conserve the natural environment overlapped with the popular art photography style known as pictorialism. Soft focus, romantic, pictorial-style images of people, genre scenes, and nature were popular periodically between the 1880s and the 1940s. Conservationists contrasted artistic photographs of natural landscapes with stark photographs of industrially blighted areas to produce scenic testimonials that helped gain federal designation for the Great Smoky Mountains National Park in the 1930s. Knoxville photographer James Thompson was one of the photographers who supplied the conservation movement with pictorialist postcards, panoramas, and souvenir photographs of pine forests in the area during the 1920s. Across the state in Memphis, Lawrence Hunt Wyckoff made and sold pictorialist landscape photographs of the Delta area of Tennessee and Arkansas.

Inventions during the final quarter of the nineteenth century resulted in lighter-weight cameras, flexible film, and the snapshot camera, all of which further democratized photography. In 1889, Kodak gave ordinary citizens the means to create their own photographs. "You take the picture, we do the rest," Kodak proclaimed when it released lightweight cameras already loaded with film that the photographers mailed back to the company for developing. In return, customers received their photographs and another camera reloaded with film. Often used to hastily record informal gatherings and activities, snapshot photography characteristics include odd perspectives from unexpected vantage points, distracting backgrounds, and key elements partially outside the image area, an aesthetic that painters came to emulate to convey a sense of spontaneity.

Snapshot photography became widespread in Tennessee only in the 1920s, but Memphis cotton agent Abe Frank provided an early example of how families incorporated amateur photography into their traditions. Near the turn of the nineteenth century, he obtained a camera that he shared with sons Godfrey and Henry. The Frank family collection at the University of Tennessee–Memphis includes 547 photographs. From about 1880 to 1905, studio portraits predominate but after that date, very good snapshots by Abe and Henry Frank make up the bulk of the collection. The snapshots show friends and family, the

Southern School of Photography

THE ART OF MODERN PHOTOGRAPHY AND WILLIAM SPENCER "DAD" LIVELY OF MCMINNVILLE BOTH came of age in the last half of the nineteenth century. One of the first professional artists to experiment with the marvels of "picture taking," Lively based his work primarily in his native Warren County, but his contributions to the burgeoning field brought national and international recognition. Through the Southern School of Photography, founded by Lively in 1903, the artistry, skill, and possibilities of photographic art and documentation were taught to a generation of twentieth-century practitioners.

Southern School of Photography. Courtesy of Charles Nunley and the Warren County Historical Society.

Lively recalled that a visit to a photographer's studio in 1865 was his first encounter with the art and science that would be his lifelong obsession and vocation. During the 1870s he studied the craft first as an itinerant portraitist traveling in Middle Tennessee and then as an apprentice to a Nashville photographer. In 1878 he moved to Scottsboro, Alabama, and established his own business. While in Alabama, he married Lela Jones and they had three children. With his family, Lively returned to McMinnville in 1883 to manage the family furniture business, but he soon opened a studio on the top floor of the family store. His sons, Joe and Lee, worked regularly in the studio and also became professional photographers.

Lively was well known across the nation, exhibiting and winning many awards, and he founded the Kentucky-Tennessee Association in 1900. Observing the increasing demand by the public for pictures that, because of the complexity of the equipment and skills could be provided only by photographers who had some formal training, Lively planned a school that would teach photography.

Enlisting the assistance of longtime friend and colleague, W. G. McFadden of Paducah, Kentucky, who was also a respected and experienced photographer, Lively launched his new venture in August 1903. The officers of the incorporated business included Lively as president; McFadden as first vice president; Joe Lively, second vice president; J. J. Morford, secretary; and Huel R. Walling, treasurer. The Southern School of Photography opened in the renovated and impressive former Cumberland Female College. With sixty-four rooms surrounded by four acres, an early advertisement described the Southern School of Photography as the "largest building in the world devoted to the teaching of this art."

When the school opened for its first session in January 1904, state-of-the-art equipment was in place, skylights had been added to the studios, and the darkroom fitted into the cellar had a maze entrance to eliminate the possibility of light reaching the picture developing area. All was ready, but only one student enrolled on opening day.

Recognizing the need for getting the word out, a publicity campaign was launched with brochures and information mailed to photographic studios across the country. By the fall session of 1904, twenty-two were enrolled. Many of the first students were from Kentucky and Tennessee, but over more than two decades of operation the alumni represented every state and several foreign countries. Women were an important and welcome part of the student body from the beginning and in some sessions made up 50 percent of the enrollment.

Students could enroll for sessions that lasted three, six, or nine months. The curriculum offered basic and advanced studies in lighting, developing, exposing, finishing, retouching, and enlarging. Lively and his teachers, drawing on their own considerable experience, also taught proven business practices for operating and managing a photographic shop. As the profession evolved, so did the courses, equipment, techniques, and methods at the school.

Lively used the critical assessment of a student's work by instructors and peers as a primary teaching tool for instilling not only technical skill but also artistic conception and realization. Student pictures that Lively considered exceptional were often exhibited in the large parlor of the school building along with many of his own renowned examples and those collected from around the nation and world.

For more than twenty years, the school gained in reputation and students, though it never achieved the expected enrollment of 350 per session. Beginning in 1908, the school offered a four-week postgraduate course for professional photographers that proved quite successful. In 1912, for example, forty established photographers from nineteen states and Canada journeyed to McMinnville for intensive training and practice.

After World War I, the Southern School of Photography qualified as a veteran training institution and steady enrollment continued without constant recruitment and concern over tuition payment. In the mid-1920s, however, the military support diminished and, with no other publicity strategy in place, enrollment plummeted. In January 1928, only one student registered. Lively was then seventy years old, and his sons, who might have succeeded him as president, ran successful studios in other towns. Whatever plans might have been in the making for revitalizing the school abruptly ended on January 4, 1928, when fire destroyed most of the school building.

Lively continued to practice his profession and to receive accolades and honors throughout his long life. He died at the age of eighty-eight in McMinnville in 1944 and, as he was often described as the Dean of American Photographers, his death was reported in the November 6 issue of *Time* magazine. Under W. S. Lively's vision and direction, the Southern School of Photography was a highly respected and innovative educational institution.

Caneta Skelley Hankins, Middle Tennessee State University

Suggested Reading

Bonner, Pat, and Charles Nunley. *W. S. Lively and the Southern School of Photography.* McMinnville: Womack Printing, 1984.

family business, and their original home in Raleigh, Tennessee, presenting both the public and private lives of an upper-middle-class family; the transition from buggies to cars, and from streetcars to busses; as well as views of the 1912 flood on the Mississippi.

By marketing these lightweight snapshot cameras to women, Kodak catered to a previously untapped market. Suddenly, any amateur could photograph friends and family, but some young women took up photography along with the painting classes then required for proper ladies. Still others embarked on careers in photography. The Southern School of Photography, operated by William Spencer "Dad" Lively at McMinnville during the first half of the twentieth century, welcomed women to its program. Early women photographers in Tennessee include Fannie J. Thompson, an African American schoolteacher active in Memphis in the mid-1880s, who devoted her 1886 school vacation to the study of photography, and professional photographers Miss Sue Fox and Mrs. J. W. Holcomb of Paris and Sparta, Tennessee, respectively, who attended a national professional photographic conference in St. Louis in 1909.

The complex color photography processes evolved much later than those for black and white. The first "color" photographs were the hand-colored cased photographs (1840s-1910s in Tennessee) and paper prints (1840s–early 1950s). Autochromes, invented in 1907, used a thin potato paste on glass to hold dyes that react when exposed to light through a photographic lens. The Southern School of Photography taught this high-skill, labor-intensive technique but the most practical color photographs came somewhat later from color film that Kodak introduced on the commercial market in the late 1930s and the amateur market in the late 1940s. Memphis's Vance Color Lab, which maintains a collection showing the downtown area from the 1930s through the 1950s, provides but a single important example of the excitement color photography can provide. Photographer Larry McPherson has wedded documentation with artistic expression in his color photographs published as *Memphis: A Work in Progress,* which evokes a sense of the locale from earliest times to 2000.

A golden age of Tennessee photography—when photographers of national reputation as well as locally based photographers of similar intent—worked to document and depict the ordinary and the extraordinary in the Volunteer State ironically began around the Depression decade of the 1930s, when Americans individually and collectively reassessed themselves and their country. Several significant photographers now associated with self-expression and art worked in Tennessee during this period. In an effort to record the ethnic groups that made America, New York heiress Doris Ullman photographed Appalachian people of English and Scottish-Irish ancestry who she dressed in old-fashioned costumes she carried with her. Louise Dahl-Wolfe, whose photographs of her neighbors at Pigeon Forge brought her to the attention of New York magazine publishers in 1929, returned from New York to photograph Nashville stone carver William Edmondson in the 1930s. Marion Post (later Post Wolcott) accompanied Frontier Films Company as a still photographer on the set of the movie *People of the Cumberlands,* which was shot on location in Tennessee in 1937. Edward Weston, a pioneer of the Group f/64, a group of California photographers named for the extremely narrow lens opening needed for their sharp-focus pictures, used part of his Guggenheim Fellowship in 1941 to photographically illustrate Walt Whitman's *Leaves of Grass,* and to again photograph William Edmondson and his work. Weston's friend, and fellow Group f/64 founder Ansel Adams, photographed in the Great Smoky Mountains for the National Park Service in the 1940s. After World War II, modernist photographer Consuelo Kanaga came from New York to photograph Edmondson in 1950, toward the end of the stone carver's life.

Another group of photographers who worked in Tennessee during this era to inform the public and gain support for New Deal programs were employed by state and federal agencies to document photographically the need for and results of the federal programs. The straightforward black-and-white images, usually with spare explanatory texts, convey the photographer's humanitarian concerns for the subjects and are intended to motivate ameliorative action from viewers. Made as social documents, these Tennessee photographs form part of the zenith of the documentary style, the internationally predominant expressive form in arts and letters for the era.

The Tennessee Valley Authority (TVA), the Historic American Buildings Survey (HABS), and the Farm Security Administration (FSA) were the primary federal agencies sponsoring documentary photography in Tennessee during the 1930s. Photographers for federal projects traveled throughout the country while state programs usually hired locally. Together, these projects produced some of the most comprehensive visual documentation of life that exists. (Increasingly, descriptions of these photographic projects are available online, sometimes to the level of individual images that can be viewed and downloaded.)

Top right: Beale Street, Memphis, Tennessee. Gelatin silver photograph by Marion Post Wolcott, October 1939. Courtesy of Library of Congress, Prints & Photographs Division, Farm Security Administration—Office of War Information Collection (reproduction number LC-USF33-030638-M3).

Above: Murfreesboro. Photograph by Ben Shahn, 1935. Courtesy of Library of Congress, Prints & Photographs Division, FSA-OWI Collection (reproduction number LC-USF33-006143-M3 DLC).

Mrs. Jacob Stooksbury Family, Loyston. Photograph by Lewis W. Hine. Courtesy of the Tennessee Valley Authority.

The Tennessee Valley Authority (TVA), one of the most challenging, exciting experiments of the New Deal, represented an attempt to go beyond mere flood control and hydroelectric power to establish long-term regional planning and development. In 1933 Lewis Hine returned to Tennessee to photographically document communities the new river courses would soon submerge, especially in the vicinity of the Norris project. He produced an invaluable set of images of a place and life-style now vanished. Later TVA images show electrification, use of electrical appliances, dams, and power plants.

The Historic American Buildings Survey (HABS) began as a federal program to employ a thousand professional architects nationwide put out of work by the near-cessation of new construction during the Great Depression. In its documentary work, HABS also employed many gifted photographers. J. E. Butterworth, Edouard E. Exline, Charles S. Grossman, and Lester Jones were some of the initial HABS photographers in Tennessee. Formally initiated in 1933 and made permanent in 1934, its mission is to document America's built environment with measured drawings, written reports, and photographs. Structures selected include buildings both humble and grand. At the millennium, records for Tennessee showed some 340 projects, including the Ramsey House outside of Knoxville, pioneer barns at Cades Cove in the Great Smoky Mountains National Park, and Ryman Auditorium—the "mother church" of the Grand Ole Opry—in Nashville. In 1969 the

Major Photographic Exhibit Venues

THE IMAGES FROM MORE THAN A CENTURY AND A HALF OF PHOTOGRAPHY IN TENNESSEE, ALONG WITH PHOtographic works from a wide array of national and international photographers, are exhibited at diverse venues. The Tennessee State Museum in Nashville concentrates on photographs from studios that have operated in the greater Nashville area and images of historic events. Cheekwood Museum of Art in Nashville holds works by European and American art photographers, including Berenice Abbott and her French mentor Eugène Atget, Antoine Beato, Dumas, George Hurrell, Barbara Morgan, and W. Eugene Smith, with large holdings for Felix Bonfils, Edward S. Curtis, and fashion photographer Louise Dahl-Wolfe. Nashville's Country Music Hall of Fame and the Grand Ole Opry Collection have photographic portraits of Grand Old Opry members, other stars of country and western music, and performances from the Grand Old Opry stage. Photographs of these artists also appear on posters, book and recording jackets, and magazines in the Hall of Fame's collections. Fisk University at its Special Collections and Carl Van Vechten Art Gallery in Nashville houses one of the most important modern art collections in the South, building on the school's strength since the 1870s in African and African American art. Since the 1930s, Fisk has incorporated art into its educational program and benefited from the talent of its faculty, including painter Aaron Douglas, as well as from major gifts from Douglas's teacher, Winold Reiss; the Harmon Foundation; Alfred Stieglitz through his widow, painter Georgia O'Keeffe; and Carl Van Vechten. Its holdings of photographs by African Americans include those of James Latimer Allen; Earl Hooks; Robert Sengstacke; George Walker, III; and Carlton Wilkinson.[1] The Baldwin Photo Gallery at Middle Tennessee State University in Murfreesboro is strong in contemporary photography, such as works by Jerry Uelsmann, Garry Winogrand, and Barbara Crane, as well as vintage photographs by masters from the previous generation, including Edward Weston, Aaron Siskind, Harry Callahan, and Ansel Adams.

The Frank H. McClung Museum of the University of Tennessee in Knoxville has photographs relating to Tennessee archaeology, ethnology, and paleoethnobotany, as well as local historical materials. The Museum of East Tennessee History of the East Tennessee Historical Society exhibits photographs from its own collections as well as from the McClung Collection and the Knox County Archives. The LeNoir Museum at Norris displays images from the vast collections of the Tennessee Valley Authority. In Chattanooga, the Hunter Museum of American Art has a growing photography collection and the gallery of the Art Department at East Tennessee State University regularly hosts photographic exhibits.

Memphis Brooks Museum has more than six hundred photographs by well-known photographers, principally American, from the 1860s to the present. The photographers best represented are specialists in interpreting the West Tennessee culture, such as Ernest Withers, William Christenberry (born in Alabama), and William Eggleston, all three of whom have risen to international fame for their work. The Memphis Music and Blues Museum collections document the area's distinctive forms of musical expression growing out of the interactions of its racial groups and its crossroads location. Examples include musicians W. C. Handy and B. B. King as well as Elvis Presley, the king of rock and roll. The museum has more than one hundred thousand photographs from the Hooks Brothers Studio (Henry Sr. and Robert, before their sons Henry Jr. and Charles took over the family business) that document the African American community from 1908 to the 1960s, and portraits of Stax Record musicians by that label's photographer, Don Nix.

Beverly Brannan, Library of Congress

Note

1. Richard Powell, Jock Reynolds, Studio Museum in Harlem, *To Conserve a Legacy: Art from Historically Black Colleges and Universities* (Boston: MIT Press, 1999), 22–23.

project extended to systematically documenting engineering and industrial sites in the Historic American Engineering Record (HAER) project.

The largest and most familiar New Deal photography effort operated from 1935 until 1943, when the Historical Section of the federal Resettlement Administration, and later the Farm Security Administration (FSA), sent photographers throughout the nation to photograph results of the Dust Bowl, the effects of the Great Depression, the shift from agriculture to industry, and America's preparations for entry into World War II. In Tennessee, nationally acclaimed photographers Ben Shahn (1935), Carl Mydans (1936), Walker Evans, Edwin Locke, and Dorothea Lange (1937), Marion Post Wolcott (1939 and 1940), Peter Sekaer (1941), and Jack Delano and Arthur Rothstein (1942) documented agriculture, results of relief programs, local life, street shows and racism, picturesque riverboats and flooding, Cotton Carnival activities in Memphis, copper mining and labor injustices in the Copper Basin, transportation and electrification systems, and the inevitable preparations for war. Together the photographers made hundreds of black-and-white photographs in Tennessee and seventy-five color transparencies. Interior photographs, which became practical during the 1930s with the introduction of flash bulbs, bring an element of intimacy almost impossible in earlier photo surveys.

After 1939, national objectives changed from farm recovery to military preparedness. Project director Roy Stryker's FSA photographic section shifted in 1942 to the Office of War Information (OWI) until 1943, when another office superseded it. Esther Bubley's 1943 bus trip through Tennessee that called attention to race relations and rural-to-urban migration was among Stryker's last assignments. Alfred T. Palmer, an OWI News Bureau photographer, captured pictures of war preparations in Tennessee, including construction and operation of TVA's Douglas, Wilson, and Chickamauga Dams, munitions work at Vultee-Nashville airplane manufacturing factory, and shipbuilding at Combustion Engineering Company. Stripped of specific identification for national security reasons, Palmer's images were released free to publications vaunting American military strength.

Two books are enduring legacies of the federal New Deal programs: *Scenic Resources of Tennessee,* a TVA-sponsored report of 1937, and *Tennessee: A Guide to the State* (1939) compiled by the Federal Writers' Project under the auspices of the Works Projects Administration (WPA). *Scenic Resources* identifies valuable natural and cultural resources while the WPA guide addresses the geologic, social, business, and geographic history of the state. Both books include photographs from national and local photographers along with images from both state and federal

The Lone Sentinel, Reelfoot Lake, 1922. Photograph by Verne Sabin. Verne Sabin Photographic Collection, No. 2888. Manuscripts Division, Tennessee State Library and Archives. Courtesy of TSLA.

Outside Watts Bar Steam Plant, 1940–42. Courtesy of the Tennessee Valley Authority.

projects such as the Tennessee Department of Conservation and the Farm Security Administration. Photographers include W. Lincoln Highton, Lewis W. Hine, E. C. McGlynnan, Clifford Poland, and Thompson's Studio of Knoxville. Complete sets of photographs from the REA, TVA, and other federally programs are available at the National Archives in Washington, D.C. The HABS and FSA photographs are at the Library of Congress and on its web site. Selections also are available at the Tennessee State Museum.

In addition to the massive federal documentary efforts, Tennessee established state-level development, assistance, and documentation projects during the 1930s. Among the Tennessee photographers working in the state then, Marshall Wilson photographed the removal of citizens from the Tennessee Basin for the TVA, and Tennessee photographer Rell Clement made pictures of the Civilian Conservation Corps (CCC) projects and the TVA in the 1930s and 1940s. Examples of their photographs are at the LeNoir Museum at Norris Dam State Park. In 1937 the Tennessee Department of Conservation—spurred by the federal documentary effort—began a project to document the state's natural, recreational, commercial, and cultural resources. When the project ended in 1965, photographers William H. Cox, Wallace Dauley, and Paul Moore had made thousands of images that parallel those produced by the FSA.

Ed Clark

INTERNATIONALLY RECOGNIZED *LIFE* PHOTOGRAPHER, ED CLARK (1911–2000) WAS RAISED IN NASHville. Clark dropped out of Hume-Fogg High School to pursue an early interest in photography and work as a photographer's assistant at the Nashville *Tennessean.* For thirteen years he served as staff photographer, photographing such events as the Shelbyville Riot of 1934, which destroyed the local courthouse.

Clark's work attracted the attention of the new picture-oriented magazine, *Life,* and in 1936 he began working for the publication as a stringer. A Tennessee photo opportunity came his way in 1942, when Sergeant Alvin York, famed World War I hero, registered for the "old man's draft" in Pall Mall. Clark's photo of York so impressed *Life* editors that they invited him to New York and hired him as a staff photographer. During World War II, Clark covered the home front and later served as a correspondent in postwar Europe, covering the Nüremberg Trials.

Clark's photographic exposés captured the prosperity and change of postwar America. The best known Clark image is that of a grieving Graham W. Jackson playing *Goin' Home* on his accordion in honor of President Franklin Roosevelt's funeral procession in 1945. His 1946 image *The Harvest that Saved the World* portrayed the abundant fields of the Midwest. A series of 1948 photographs brought attention to the West Memphis School District in Arkansas and led to construction of a new building for African American students.

In the 1950s and early 1960s, Clark's work took him from Washington to Hollywood and around the world. He photographed Presidents Franklin Roosevelt, Harry Truman, Dwight Eisenhower, John Kennedy, Lyndon Johnson, and Richard Nixon, as well as such Hollywood celebrities as Marilyn Monroe, Humphrey Bogart, and Clark Gable. In 1955 an unexpected invitation to Russia gave him the distinction of being the first Western photographer in the Soviet state in thirty years.

Retrospective shows in Birmingham, Nashville, Jackson, Mississippi, and New York showcased his thirty years of work. In 1990, Clark received the Photographic Society of America's Understanding Through Photography Award.

Anne-Leslie Owens, Middle Tennessee State University

Suggested Reading

Herrera, Frank. *Ed Clark; Decades: A Photographic Retrospective, 1930–1960.* Yardley, Pa.: Publishers at Yardleyville, 1992.

World War II rapidly altered Tennessee's demographics and economy. In 1940, 65 percent of Tennessee's population lived on farms; five years later, 60 percent lived in towns and cities. The production of goods and services eclipsed the once-dominant extractive industries of Tennessee. The new companies manufactured tires, electrical equipment, glass, chemicals, aluminum, trucks, and automobiles. Product and promotional photography for those industries now accounts for much of Tennessee's commercial photography, although extractive industries continue operating, as Jeanne M. Rasmussen's images of coal-mining life in the Appalachian coalfields in the mid- to late-twentieth century testify. Architectural photographs by Samuel H. Gottscho in 1948 and 1955 show structures in Tennessee designed by New York firms such as the renowned Raymond Loewy Associates for both production and sales of manufactured

Downtown Memphis lunch counter, early 1960s. Students from LeMoyne College and Owen College conduct a "sit-in." Photograph by Ernest C. Withers. Courtesy of Memphis/Shelby County Public Library and Information Center–Memphis and Shelby County Room.

goods. Aerial photography, used to a limited degree before World War II, is now a mainstay for all types of business and government endeavors.

Fundamental political and cultural change came during the civil rights movement. Photographers from national magazines, newspapers, and photo agencies joined in reporting on civil disobedience and the conditions that caused it. Ernest Withers photographed segregation and the civil rights movement from the African American perspective, along with the local way of life, such as cotton bales across Main Street in the 1950s, documenting a major cornerstone of the Memphis economy. *Look* magazine photographer James Karales photographed a Southern Christian Leadership Congress at Memphis in 1962.

From 1979 to 1986, the Tennessee State Parks Folklife Project, supported by a grant from the National Endowment for the Arts, ran a program to document the state's wealth of traditional crafts. Folklore graduate students documented and photographed participating local artists and craftspeople

Howard Baker. Courtesy of Special Collections, University of Tennessee, Knoxville.

Contemporary Photography in Memphis

CONTEMPORARY PHOTOGRAPHY FLOURISHES ACROSS TENNESSEE. TWO OF THE FINEST ARTISTS ARE Memphis photographers William Eggleston (born 1939) and Ernest C. Withers (born 1922), who have achieved international fame by creating images that are crucial to understanding the art of their time, a definition of value consistently applied by art historians. The two friends have often exhibited and published together, most recently in the Whitney Museum of American Art's important survey of twentieth-century masters, *The American Century: Art & Culture, 1900–2000.* Other than the Knoxville artist Beauford Delaney, they were the only Tennesseans so honored.

Eggleston and Withers came to prominence in vastly different circumstances. Withers was a fearless African American photojournalist. His camera took him from Montgomery and Dr. Martin Luther King's first predawn bus ride marking the end of the bus boycott in 1956 to the entry of black students at Central High School in Little Rock in 1957 to King's last march in Memphis on behalf of the striking Sanitation Workers in 1968. Two recent books and a traveling museum exhibition highlighted Withers's significant contribution to documentary photography in the South and African American history. Through his work, a new audience for the life and culture of the mid-South has evolved, from Atlanta's High Museum to New York City's International Center for Photography.

From his base on Beale Street (to which he has recently returned), Withers chronicled pathbreaking events, including the 1955 Emmett Till murder trial in Mississippi, B. B. King's first traveling tour bus, and the rise of Stax Records recording artists in the 1960s. At the same time, Withers documented daily life along one of the South's most storied thoroughfares. Recognizing what was unique and visually important in his everyday life and preserving those moments photographically is one of the hallmarks of Ernest Withers's work. As the events he witnessed faded into history, the photographs of Ernest C. Withers became art.

In contrast, William Eggleston emerged from a privileged Mississippi Delta existence to become one of the most important photographers of the twentieth century by pioneering color photography. In an era when color was linked exclusively to advertising, Eggleston adopted it exclusively, transforming the history of photography. His first exhibition was a one-person show at New York's Museum of Modern Art in 1976. It provoked immediate controversy. Eggleston melded the crassly commercial medium of brilliantly colored dye-transfer prints with his sleepy, everyday surroundings, expanding on the observational skills of his great photographic forebears, Walker Evans and Robert Frank.

William Eggleston's Guide (New York: Museum of Modern Art, 1976), the now-rare book that chronicled Eggleston's debut, was the museum's first publication to feature forty-eight color reproductions. Neither Picasso or Matisse had been the subject of such effusive treatment. Perhaps Eggleston's most important body of work, the photographs are drawn from Memphis and the surrounding Delta, eloquently evoking the "sense of place" often identified with the great southern writers.

Eggleston has been the subject of countless international exhibitions and retrospectives, including important shows at London's Barbizon Gallery, Paris's Fondation Cartier, and the J. Paul Getty Museum. He continues to receive numerous awards, including the prestigious

Hasselblad Foundation International Award in Photography. Over the years, he has produced a host of acclaimed photographic books, including the 1986 Doubleday publication, *The Democratic Forest*, which features numerous Tennessee images.

Eggleston's influence is felt throughout the world, with large-scale color photographs seeming to dominate contemporary photography.

Carole Thompson, Memphis

and their works statewide. They generated approximately fourteen thousand black-and-white and color images now available for research and reproduction at the Tennessee State Library and Archives.

In the twenty-first century, electronic technology provides the most democratic arena to date for individuals and institutions alike to display and disseminate images. The Tennessee Genealogy Web Project (TNGenWeb) is an all-volunteer effort sponsored by a Tennessee communications firm. It provides single entry points for all counties in the state where collected databases are stored, indexed, and cross-linked. The information posted includes county histories, major maps, genealogy, biographical sketches of leading citizens, and presentations about unique local features. The Tennessee State Library and Archives maintains a postcard web site with pages for each Tennessee county, with public domain images of local sites and landscapes that offer a sense of each locale. Extended texts explain the significance of select images. Through improved access to and the proliferation of photography, the broadening public record continues to democratize image making and access. Due to its dual nature as a record and an art, the photographic medium can sustain an expanding body of both documentation and creative expression.

NOTES

I thank the following individuals for their assistance: Mary Jane Appel, Harold Baldwin, Robert Cogswell, Jim Cole, Pete Daniel, Winston Eggleston, Bobby Fulcher, Tim Jimison, Steve Knoblock, Tom Rankin, Frances Robb, Mike Smith, and Carroll Van West. I also acknowledge the assistance of staff from the following institutions: Archives of Appalachia, Memphis Public Library, Nashville Room at Nashville Public Library, and the Tennessee State Library and Archives.

1. Jeff L. Rosenheim, "'A Palace for the Sun': Early Photography in New York City," in *Art and the Empire City: New York, 1825–1861,* ed. Catherine Hoover Voorsanger and John K. Howat (New Haven, Conn.: Yale Univ. Press, 2000), 227–41.
2. Mary Panzer, *Mathew Brady and the Image of History* (Washington, D.C.: Smithsonian Institution Press, 1997).
3. Bill Cupo, Memphis Pink Palace Museum, correspondence with the author, May 12, 2000.
4. Richard E. Blodgett, *Photographs: A Collector's Guide* (New York: Ballantine Books, 1979).

SUGGESTED READINGS

Bonner, Pat, and Charles Nunley. *W. S. Lively and the Southern School of Photography.* McMinnville, Tenn.: Womack Printing, 1984.

Booker, Robert J. *Two Hundred Years of Black Culture in Knoxville, Tennessee, 1791 to 1991.* Virginia Beach, Va.: Donning, 1993.

Hinton, Kem G. *A Long Path: The Search for a Tennessee Bicentennial Landmark.* Franklin, Tenn.: Hillsboro Press, 1997.

History of Photography 17 (Spring 1993):1.

Hoobler, James A. *Cities Under the Gun: Images of Occupied Nashville and Chattanooga.* Nashville: Rutledge Hill Press, 1986.

Kollar, Robert (photographs), and Kelly Leiter (text). *The Tennessee Valley.* Lexington: Univ. Press of Kentucky, 1998.

McPherson, Larry. *Memphis: A Work in Progress.* Oxford: Univ. Press of Mississippi, 2001.

Moore, Wayne C., and Mark Herbison. *Looking Back at Tennessee: A Photographic Retrospective.* Franklin, Tenn.: Hillsboro Press, 1996.

Netherton, John, ed. *Tennessee: A Homecoming.* [Nashville]: Third National, 1985.

Plunkett, Kitty. *Memphis: A Pictorial History.* Norfolk, Va.: Donning, 1976.

Riss, Murray. *Southern Eye, Southern Mind: A Photographic Inquiry, Catalogue of a Joint Exhibit, Memphis, Tennessee, 29 March–30 April, 1981.* Memphis: First Tennessee Bank, 1981.

Wilson, Peggy Stephenson, comp. *Nolensville, 1797–1987: Reflections of a Tennessee Town.* Nolensville, Tenn.: Nolensville Recreation Center, 1989.

Withers, Ernest C. *Let Us March On! Selected Civil Rights Photographs of Ernest C. Withers, 1955–1968.* Boston: Massachusetts College of Art; Afro Scholar Press, 1992.

Part Two

THE CRAFT ARTS

Eight

From Frontier to Revival
The Evolution of Woodcraft in Tennessee

Lisa Norwood Oakley
East Tennessee Historical Society

Tennesseans have always crafted many of the things of their lives from wood. Wood was the basis of much prehistoric material culture: baskets, tools, weapons, and ceremonial objects. Later, Cherokee, Chickasaw, and Creek artisans utilized the beautiful woods of the area in their traditional forms, especially in basketmaking. When the first colonists came to settle permanently in Tennessee, they moved into a richly forested region, and most quickly became woodworkers by necessity. In their homes, furniture, and everyday objects, their own cultural patterns of construction and design blended with other migrant influences to create design trends. Hard woods such as cherry and walnut abounded, which made large jobs possible, while soft woods like dogwood and holly provided flexibility and beautiful detail. The result is a long tradition of woodcraft that still flourishes, although in an altered form, today.

Shifting consumer tastes, industrialization, and urbanization influenced the state's woodcrafters from the beginning of statehood into the twentieth century. The opening of new railroad routes and the coming of industrialization from 1850 to 1880 led more and more Tennesseans to favor mass-manufactured, "store-bought" products from new wood-based manufacturers. Industries also provided urban woodworkers with opportunities to use their skills in such wood products centers as Claiborne, White, and Shelby Counties. Woodcraft as a family trade declined markedly statewide between the Civil War and World War I. By the 1920s, however, rural woodcraftsmen experienced a new demand for their handcrafted pieces as the impact of the national Arts and Crafts movement filtered down to the upper South as an interest in "handicraft revival." Fed by various reform impulses—from the vocational education movement to home

Tool chest and cabinetmaker's tools, c. 1848. The chest, 22 × 39 × 22 inches, was made by Joseph Daniel in Knoxville (tools are his) and descended to Gaines Caswell Emmett, then to his son, Robert George Emmett (1902–1983). These men were all cabinetmakers. Courtesy of East Tennessee Historical Society, Knoxville.

economics movement to the early-twentieth-century search for "folk" roots—this revival reached its zenith in the late 1940s with the establishment of the Southern Highland Handicraft Guild's Craftsman's Fair in Gatlinburg. Schools specialized in training new generations of woodcrafters and, in large part, the classroom replaced the process of one generation teaching the next. For families who carried on the folk tradition, however, craft became business to a degree never imagined, and forms and processes were adapted to meet the demands of the new consumer market.

Early Traditions, 1770–1860

In *The Handcraft Revival in Southern Appalachia,* Garry Barker observes that "every handcrafted piece tells a story, evokes a memory of a very real person, adds a special warmth and character to daily life."[1] Those stories began when the first settlers came down the Shenandoah Valley from Pennsylvania and Virginia or crossed the mountains from North Carolina.

Most items used on a pioneer homestead were made of wood. House, furnishings, tools, utensils, games, toys, canes, and all other useful items were crafted from the trees surrounding the home. Families themselves produced many of these items, but typically, select individuals in the community were identified as having a special skill and ability in crafting furnishings, tools, utensils, wagons, casks, and other wooden implements. Neighbors traded with these community crafters when possible. The families of the artisans frequently learned different aspects of the craft, and together families operated sheds and sold or exchanged products within close proximity of their farms. Most were farmers first, then cabinetmakers, chairmakers, wheelwrights, rifle makers, and coopers. Examples from the artifact collection of the East Tennessee Historical Society (ETHS) illustrate the capabilities of many of these often unidentified part-time craftsmen. A white oak spinning wheel, decoratively punched with "WM 1818" and with surrounding flower pattern, testifies to skill at the lathe and awl of a Smith family craftsman of Whitesburg, Hamblen County. There are other examples of the same type of detailed punching used as decoration on simple wooden items, such as two flax hackle bases in the collection of the Carroll B. Reece Museum at East Tennessee State University in Johnson City. Yet another sample of the work of farmer artisans from the ETHS collection is Blountville, Sullivan County, farmer G. G. Cox, who added his talented hand to a simple blanket chest by finishing his piece with a red over yellow faux graining; he was obviously pleased with his effort as he signed and dated his work "G. G. Cox 1857." It is possible that Cox made chests for others as there is at least one other example of similar form and technique known to exist in private hands.

The stylistic influences shaping these early Tennessee woodcrafters came from various sources. The recent research of Anne S. McPherson suggests that early Tennessee furniture reflects a strong influence of Delaware Valley styles, as adapted by cabinetmakers in the Winchester area of Virginia's Shenandoah Valley and then further regionalized by craftsmen in East and Middle Tennessee in the late eighteenth and early nineteenth centuries. At The Hermitage in Nashville, for example, a desk-and-bookcase (c. 1800) that Jackson once owned shows the impact of Winchester furniture style in its central prospect doors and fluted document drawers. By 1802 in Knoxville four different cabinetmaking shops produced furniture in the Delaware Valley style; one beautifully crafted desk-and-bookcase from one of the Knoxville shops is in the collections of the Museum of Early Southern Decorative Arts (MESDA) in Winston-Salem, North Carolina.

The makers of fine furniture typically lived in and near towns, where there would be enough demand for their work. Full-time woodcrafters, however, were the exception in early Tennessee. Most were craftsmen who spent much of their extra time in their shops but could never depend on woodcraft as their livelihood. And their numbers were small. In Bledsoe County in 1850, for instance, there were 13

The Southern Mountain Rifle

In the first half of the nineteenth century, gunsmiths in Upper East Tennessee developed a distinctive Tennessee-associated rifle type known as the Tennessee or Southern Mountain rifle. Compared to the stylish, intricate carvings and metal work of Pennsylvania rifle makers in the late eighteenth and early nineteenth century, the Southern Mountain rifle reflected its origins as a practical shooting piece for families who relied on hunting as an important part of their sustenance. The Tennessee rifle stock was typically made of walnut or maple (and cherry in rare cases) while bar-and-sheet iron, which was locally abundant, provided the metal for the barrel, buttplate, thimble, and trigger guard. The Beans of Sullivan County were notable gunmakers; a fine rifle dated c. 1850 by Charlie Bean is part of the East Tennessee Historical Society collections. But most early gunmakers were blacksmiths, or farmers, first. The Museum of Appalachia in Norris has an excellent collection of Southern Mountain rifles and the museum's founder, John Rice Irwin, has written extensively on this rifle type.

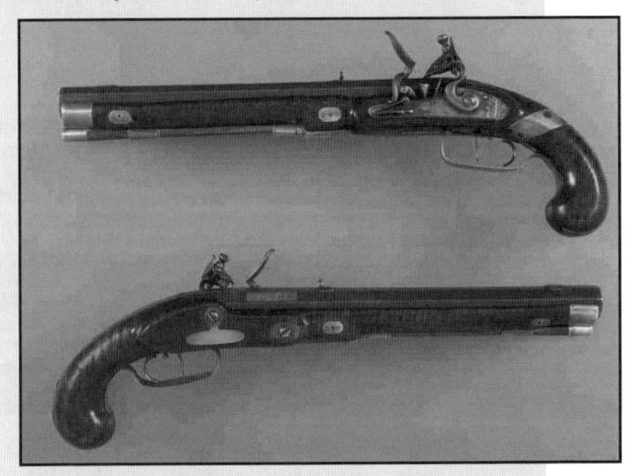

Baxter Bean pistols. Matching pair of flintlock pistols made by Baxter Bean of Jonesborough, late eighteenth century to early nineteenth century. Photograph by June Dorman. Courtesy of TSM.

Gunsmiths also remained craft specialists in an age of industrial standardization and mass production. Veterans returning home from the Civil War brought along any rifles and pistols they could acquire, and factory-made guns became commonplace throughout the state. Traditional gunsmiths remained, however, and they received steady patronage from hunters who had learned to trust their plain, sturdy, and accurate pieces. Hacker Martin in Washington County was an important gunsmith of the early twentieth century. When Allen Eaton explored the Appalachian craft heritage in the 1930s, he found Mary Ownby making rifle barrels with tools and techniques learned from her father.

In the late twentieth century, a revival in traditional gunsmithing created a new generation of crafters for a rather different modern market of consumers, including frontier-era or Overmountain reenactors and collectors, who display beautifully designed and decorated rifles as works of art. Adapting traditional designs to the tastes of modern collectors, Greg S. Murry makes flintlocks at his shop in Leipers Fork. Dixie Gun Works in Union City also sells a popular kit where reenactors and others can make their own version of the Pennsylvania long rifle. Grant Hardin has used these kits to teach a course in gunsmithing at the Rocky Mount historic site in Sullivan County.

Carroll Van West, Middle Tennessee State University

carpenters, 6 millwrights, 6 cabinetmakers, 4 wagon makers, 4 coopers, 1 staymaker, 1 wheelwright, 1 gunsmith, and 1 chairmaker out of 854 families. Statewide, the census takers of 1850 counted 784 cabinetmakers, or cabinetworkmen (both terms were used), and an additional 126 chairmakers.

For most families, woodcraft was part of their overall economic strategy to achieve self-sufficiency

Early Furniture Makers and Cabinetmakers

TENNESSEE FURNITURE HAS BEEN AN OVERLOOKED AND FORGOTTEN REGIONAL TREASURE. THE SIMPLE AND straightforward functional pieces produced by Tennessee craftsmen before 1850 reflect an era of outstanding craftsmanship. The furniture of this period exhibits dignity and the worth of material objects from everyday life.

Early furniture making was not limited to cabinetmakers in major settlements like Greeneville, Knoxville, Memphis, and Nashville. Many craftsmen lived in rural areas and combined their craft with farming and carpentry. Other craftsmen—turners, joiners, chairmakers, carpenters, upholsterers—produced furniture for Tennessee homes. For cabinetmakers and related craftsmen, the growing towns offered more opportunities for successful businesses.

Above: 1851 Portrait of Richard M. Fisher, pen and ink, watercolor, chalk, by Edmund Hacker. Fisher was the son of Jacob Fisher, a cabinetmaker from Wytheville, Virginia. The family moved to Athens in the 1830s, and Richard was working as a cabinetmaker there by 1837. Courtesy of East Tennessee Historical Society, Knoxville.

Nineteenth-century craftsmen had to be versatile in order to survive, prosper, and satisfy the needs of their community. Rural and urban cabinetmakers served as coffin makers, which established them in the undertaking business. These craftsmen adapted their skills to the needs of their patrons.

The 1820 Manufacturers' Census from East and Middle Tennessee counties contains important information about cabinetmakers. Craftsmen listed information about the materials used, the quantity and cost of materials, and the names and pieces of finished products. Gross production ranged from less than one hundred dollars annually to as much as six thousand dollars. The average shop operated with no more than three craftsmen, though one Nashville cabinetmaker employed five men and nine boys.

Left: Pie safe, c. 1840–60, Sullivan County. The primary wood is cherry, the secondary wood, tulip poplar. The design of the tin is a cornstalk with ears of corn. Courtesy of East Tennessee Historical Society, Knoxville.

Right: Tall chest of drawers. Courtesy of East Tennessee Historical Society, Knoxville.

The apprenticeship system, in which boys in their early teens were bound to craftsmen by the quarterly court or by parental consent, provided necessary help in the cabinet shops. The wide variety of furniture forms mentioned in the 1820 census included chests, chairs, cupboards, tables, dining tables, clock cases, sideboards, desks, secretaries, bedsteads, presses, bookcases, and candlesticks. In one year, James Bray, a Knoxville cabinetmaker, and the four craftsmen in his shop produced sixty pieces, ranging from square tables (sold for three dollars each) to secretaries and cherry presses (sold at fifty dollars each).

Above: Blanket chest, Sullivan County, c. 1857. Courtesy of East Tennessee Historical Society, Knoxville.

Right: Blanket chest, detail. Faux grain created by red over yellow paint. Signed on the left back post, "G. G. Cox, 1857." Courtesy of East Tennessee Historical Society, Knoxville.

Apart from the 1820 census, the most important estate inventory is that of cabinetmaker Daniel McBean. His inventory and sale accounts provide a vivid picture of a Nashville shop in 1815. Forty-three furniture items, made in advance for sale, were on hand at the time of his death. The items, ranging from cradles to dining tables to bookcases and sideboards, were sold by the administrator of McBean's estate.

Tennessee furniture reflects the heritage of the westward migration and the individualism of the early pioneers. While isolated from the eastern mainstream influences, frontier craftsmen inherited Old World craft traditions and often showed some familiarity with academic styles. Their work was shaped, however, by their new environment and the peculiar circumstances and needs of a frontier society. The result was an individualistic combination of stylistic elements and an unconventional use of construction techniques that gave backcountry furniture the distinctive character so attractive to the collector and challenging to the historian of material culture. Identifying furniture made in Tennessee can be difficult. Cabinetmakers signed few pieces of furniture. Instead, artisans let style and craftsmanship identify their work. Many years later, this practice is puzzling when trying to identify regional pieces.

The patrons of Tennessee furniture makers were primarily Anglo-Americans of English, Scots, and Scots-Irish descent. They arrived from Virginia, Maryland, North Carolina, and Pennsylvania, the products of diverse economic and social backgrounds. As they poured over the mountains, the settlers furnished their homes as their means allowed, using design concepts brought from eastern areas.

[Continued on next page]

The difficulty of the journey to Tennessee often precluded the inclusion of furniture. As a consequence, settlers purchased locally made furniture after their arrival in the new region. As wagon roads became better, and river shipping became easier, Tennessee craftsmen found themselves in competition with the skills and stylistic influences of manufacturers in Pennsylvania, Virginia, and North Carolina. Cincinnati, one of the largest furniture manufacturing cities, began shipping large assortments of furniture down river to Tennessee in the nineteenth century. Prominent citizens, like Andrew Jackson, selected wares from Philadelphia, which were shipped upriver from New Orleans.

The use of woods is useful in designating Tennessee furniture. The distinguishing characteristics of the grain and color of cherry made it the favored wood for furniture. The mellow brown color made walnut the second most frequently used wood. Other woods used for furniture included maple, mahogany, and rosewood. Two regionally abundant woods—tulip poplar and yellow pine—were used for secondary parts like drawer bottoms and sides and backboards. Tulip poplar was used in pieces made throughout the state, but yellow pine was used in the geographic regions of higher altitudes, where these trees were plentiful. Occasionally cedar and cypress were used as secondary woods.

Tennessee furniture has a simplicity in both form and decoration. Craftsmen of the region inlaid lighter woods into the native cherry and walnut for decorative appeal. An array of motifs can be found: rope and tassel, gamecocks, geometric forms, running vine, eagles, compass stars, simple line, diamond, and quarter-fans. The largest number of inlaid pieces originated in upper East Tennessee. The use of inlay declined in Middle Tennessee and is found least frequently in West Tennessee.

The most distinguishable Tennessee forms include the sugar chest and the Jackson press. The sugar chest was developed to safeguard large quantities of sugar, a commodity of great value. Fairly simple in design, a sugar chest consisted of a large wooden storage bin set on legs. The majority of chests featured a small drawer below the bin. Since only the most affluent nineteenth-century households could afford sugar in bulk, a sugar chest was a status symbol that was displayed in public areas of the home like the dining room.

The Jackson press is also indigenous to the Tennessee region. Although the form and name were contemporary with Andrew Jackson, the exact origins of the press remain unknown. As early as 1825, the term appeared in an estate inventory in Davidson County, where Andrew Jackson lived. Most presses consisted of a shaped back splash over a rectangular top above two projecting drawers over cupboard doors set on turned feet. In the small area of Good Spring, the cabinet shop of Levi Cochran is known to have produced three Jackson presses between 1833 and 1835, charging from twenty to twenty-three dollars for each.

Other forms of furniture produced in Tennessee included desks, secretaries, bookcases, candlestands, work tables, tables, cellarets, sideboards, slabs, safes, cupboards, presses, dressers, tall case clocks, tall chests, bureaus, chests, clothes presses, wardrobes, bedsteads, chairs, settees, and sofas. According to the 1820 Manufacturer's Census, desks were among the most expensive articles produced, though most settlers would not have needed a desk. Necessary pieces of the nineteenth-century home included candlestands and work tables. These were found in abundance in inventories of the period.

The rise of the plantation culture sparked demand for high style furniture like elaborate sideboards. In 1815, cabinetmaker Capt. James G. Hicks produced a cherry sideboard for

Art and Furniture of East Tennessee, a 1993 major exhibition on regional furniture hosted by the East Tennessee Historical Society. Photograph by Carroll Van West.

$129.99. Advertisements often proudly listed sideboards. Another related form was the slab or slab-sideboard, which was a tall table, sometimes fitted with drawers. The safe was a piece used for storage of food, usually placed in the kitchen area. The safe consisted of a wooden case with two drawers over two doors fitted with punched tin panels. The tin varied from simplistic designs to the more elaborately punched with designs of tulips, hearts, stars, candlesticks, urns, and other geometric shapes.

Two forms of furniture necessary for storage were the cupboard—flatback or corner—and the bureau. Both of these forms survive in large numbers. The continued functional aspect of these pieces may explain why they have survived.

Three major categories of chairs appeared in Tennessee inventories—Windsor, fancy, and common chairs. Nineteenth-century household accounts referred to chair sets in half dozen and one dozen lots. Most households had a half dozen Windsor or common chairs. Chairs were usually painted in a variety of colors ranging from yellow, red, green, and black to conceal a variety of woods used in their production.

The furniture produced in Tennessee during the nineteenth century imparts a sense of pride and respect for our forbears who struggled to create homes of comfort and beauty in a new territory.

Derita Coleman Williams, Memphis

and produce some things that could be traded or sold. The situation would be similar across the state. In Hardin County, for example, James Graham was not designated as a carpenter or cabinetmaker in the 1850 census; however, he is known to have built his circa 1822 brick home and crafted all the interior woodwork and much of the furniture for the house. He continued to build furniture for family and friends through his life. Many pieces still survive and are prized pieces of the family's history. In 1850, Graham also appeared to be training craftsmen. In that year, Winfield Scott, then twenty-four years old, and his wife Elizabeth, were living with the sixty-three-year-old Graham. The census taker listed Scott as a carpenter, which hints that he was apprenticing under Graham.

Another example of this versatility is the story of the renowned Stewart family of Hancock County. Made famous in the 1970s and 1980s by third-generation master craftsman Alex Stewart, the family's woodworking tradition began with Alex's grandfather, Boyd, who arrived in Hancock County between 1850 and 1860 and was designated a "wheelwright" in both the 1870 and 1880 Hancock County census. In the 1920 Hancock County census, Boyd's son Joseph and grandson Alex headed neighboring households; in the occupation column, both were listed as "farmer." While the official record illustrates that the primary endeavor was agricultural, for the Stewart family the woodcraft tradition learned at Boyd's side remained an important economic supplement. Today, through the acclaim awarded Alex Stewart's work, the three generations are given credit primarily for their coopering; however, they were expert in many areas including, but not limited to blacksmithing, cabinetmaking, logging, milling, mining, masonry, weaving, and turning.

It was not uncommon to find that the largest number of artisans were carpenters. Staff at the Museum of Early Southern Decorative Arts has researched Tennessee records for mention of artisans in the pre–Civil War era. There are at least thirty-three titles for workers of wood. Everything is represented, from bandbox maker to millwright and toymaker to Venetian blind maker. The most common title throughout the records of the nineteenth century, however, is carpenter.

Rural woodcrafters in the early nineteenth century were fairly conservative in the variety and basic form of their wood items. However, the detail in their work was often remarkable, especially the inlays, with furniture from Greene County in the early nineteenth century being especially spectacular in that regard. Case furniture in particular, such as chests and cupboards, featured inlays of cherry, dogwood, and holly in patterns of rope and tassels, bands and string, and leaves and berries, just to name a few. A chest of drawers (c. 1805–15) from Greene County, for example, has chamfered corners with an inlaid vase of cherry with trailing vine and leaves ending in a three-pronged flower. In one case, these decorative inlays were even replicated in paint on a Sevier County miniature blanket chest made by cabinetmaker John Catlett.

The story was somewhat different in Tennessee's early towns. The closer the woodcrafter lived to town, the larger the consumer market. Woodcrafters who lived in larger communities by the early 1800s could often claim their trade as their primary profession. If they did not own their own shop, they generally could find employment in a larger shop. In the 1830s, R. W. Wilson operated from a large shop in Jackson, until an accidental fire destroyed the building in 1835. The signature and date on a wonderfully crafted fall front cherry desk in the ETHS collection testifies to the presence of William Cannon in Knoxville in 1844. Six years later, according to the 1850 census, the thirty-year-old Cannon was living with cabinetmaker John Garvin and obviously working in his shop. The largest furniture-making shop in Tennessee at midcentury, however, probably belonged to James W. McCombs of Nashville, who employed sixteen people. By the 1850s numerous woodworking businesses existed in towns across the state. In order to compete with the amount of imported goods coming from commercial centers

Sugar Chests

ONE OF THE MOST EVOCATIVE PIECES OF EARLY TENNESSEE MATERIAL CULTURE IS THE SUGAR CHEST, popular among elite families in Middle and West Tennessee in the first half of the nineteenth century. (Relatively few sugar chests have been identified as East Tennessee–made, although several East Tennessee museums have sugar chests in their collections.) The creation of this specialized piece of furniture to store the family's sugar and coffee under lock and key emphasizes the scarcity and value of sugar in the settlement era. It perhaps also hints that prosperous white families, who could afford this extra piece of furniture, believed that their domestic servants and slaves would pilfer some of the precious items unless they were kept locked in a primary room of the house. When the family needed sugar, the mistress of the house, or a trusted servant, would unlock the chest, take nippers or a knife stored in a small drawer at the bottom of the chest, and cut the amount the family required. Some families also kept ledger books in the chest drawer to record the amount taken.

Fountain B. Carter cherry sugar chest, c. 1830. Courtesy of Rick Warwick.

Cabinetmakers from small towns and the state's major cities crafted sugar chests. Typically using cherry as the primary wood and tulip poplar as the secondary wood, cabinetmakers often chose cherry, maple, and tulip popular for the chest interiors, so the woods would not impart a distinctive flavor to the sugar. A sugar chest is typically a rectangular-shaped wooden box, with a hinged top lid, that rests on four legs that rise approximately twelve inches from the floor (so to protect the contents from vermin and insects). The interior of the chest typically has one large compartment, but some have three separate sections: one each for brown sugar and loaf sugar and another compartment for coffee.

A rare variation of the sugar chest is the sugar desk, where the top lid would be slanted, and could be opened to serve as a desk. One example from Sumner County (c. 1810–20) opens to display concealed pigeonholes and drawers for papers and writing tools.

Carroll Van West, Middle Tennessee State University

outside the region, these businesses employed increasing numbers of woodcrafters and produced a variety of forms competitive in quality and style to those items from more established eastern markets. In some cases artisans could afford to concentrate on just one form, such as case furniture, wagons, or chairs. Most often, however, woodcrafters found themselves offering a variety of items. The craftsman's specialty was often defined, however, by the tools used. For example, wheelwrights might second as chairmakers, since so much of their skill was perfected on the lathe.

Many early Tennessee woodcrafters were African American slaves. While they were not able to compete on an economic basis with free white artisans, they were equally capable as craftsmen. Many of the surviving furnishings, tools, and implements found in museums and at historic houses testify to the skills and abilities of the anonymous African Americans who used and made them. One such example is the handcrafted toolbox owned by William Ballard Lenoir's head carpenter. Lenoir was a prominent businessman and landowner in Roane (now Loudon) County. His estate included rich farmland as well as a textile mill. Lenoir's large slave holdings—sixty-three slaves were listed in the 1850 slave schedule—ensured the need for a number of those slaves to be skilled at woodcraft as well as many other trades and arts. The inventory from the Sumner County estate settlement of Isaac Franklin lists the most valuable slaves as the bricklayers and John Jennings, carpenter. The town of Franklin, according to the 1870 census, had eight chair and cabinetmakers, some of whom were undoubtedly slaves before emancipation. The town's best-known craftsman was Dick Poynor, who had learned chair making from his white owner, Robert Poynor, before acquiring his own freedom and establishing his own chair-making shop before 1860.

Early Tennessee woodcrafters, both in town and country, were trained in the traditional manner of passing on learned skills from generation to generation with the novice training at the side of the master. This method of training, often formalized in an apprenticeship, largely defined preindustrial life of Tennessee. In his 1873 account of early life in Rutherford County, John C. Spence recorded how all of the antebellum trades relied on apprentices, who either stayed to open their own shops or became journeymen crafters. A representative example is the story of a toolbox built by woodcrafter Joseph Daniel in the 1840s. The toolbox was handed down to his ward Gaines Caswell Emmett, then to his son Robert George Emmett, a Knox County cabinetmaker. Today the chest continues its mission and is used daily by master craftsman James Hooper, a student of Robert Emmett's.

THE INDUSTRIAL ERA, 1860–1920

The Civil War laid ruin to the physical and economic landscape of Tennessee. In order to rebuild both, Tennessee leaders looked to industrial development. While foundries and other small industries existed in antebellum Tennessee, a cash-based industrial economy increasingly dominated postwar Tennessee life. Memphis, Nashville, Chattanooga, and Knoxville grew from towns to manufacturing and wholesale urban centers. Outlying regions boasted new mining and milling industries. The key to success was outside capital investment and the expansion of the railroad system throughout the state. No longer did business depend on limited local markets.

As cities grew and the economy became based on cash-purchased "ready-made" items, urban woodcrafters adapted in a number of ways. There was still a demand for Tennessee furniture, casks, wagons, and other goods, but the level of investment and production had to increase to compete with imported items from other regions.

Established woodcrafters competed by incorporating new machinery to increase efficiency, as well as increasing their payroll for additional woodcrafters to staff their growing shops. Artisans who could not compete individually continued to find jobs with these larger companies and in the shops of the new manufacturers that needed pattern and form makers, repairmen, millwrights, and lumbermen for the growing timber industries. Examples of the types of wooden products being manufactured in New South Tennessee included boxes, caskets, tool handles, ice boxes, wooden pumps, baskets, gun stocks, and building supplies, not to mention the traditional production of furniture, wagons, and a growing interest in carriages and other conveyances. Businesses such as White County's Sparta Spoke Factory, established by James Richardson Tubb in 1896, provided job opportunities in the factory as well as for the lumbering companies in the region which supplied the needed timber. West Tennessee was a booming lumber market throughout the late nineteenth and early

Richard "Dick" Poynor

RICHARD "DICK" POYNOR WAS BORN A SLAVE IN HALIFAX COUNTY, VIRGINIA, ON JUNE 22, 1802. HE immigrated to Williamson County in 1816 with the Robert Poynor family, settling on the Little Harpeth near the present-day Cool Springs Galleria. Since the estate inventory of Robert Poynor included chair-making tools, it appears likely that Robert taught Dick the art of chair making. Upon Robert's death in 1848, Dick, valued at $450, became the property of A. B. Poynor, Robert's son, while his children were valued at $2,700 and divided among the other heirs. The Bible (purchased for three dollars on May 27, 1835) of the Richard Poynor family recorded the death of Loucinda, Dick's first wife, on February 29, 1840, shortly after the birth of their seventh child.

Dick Poynor chairs. Courtesy of Rick Warwick.

Sometime between 1850 and 1860, Dick obtained his freedom and, if tradition is correct, purchased the freedom of his second wife, Millie. By 1860 Dick, a free man, was working at his horse-powered chair factory and hillside farm of 150 acres off Pinewood Road in western Williamson County, twelve miles from Franklin. Dick Poynor with the help of his son James (1833–1893) produced hundreds of chairs at their factory. His chair construction was simple. With the knowledge that green wood shrinks as it dries, Poynor was able to drive dry rungs into green posts and be assured the joint would remain tight without nails or glue. The classic signature of a Poynor chair is found in the graceful arching mule-eared post secured with a wooden peg in the top maple slat. Dick made rockers in several sizes, high chairs for infants, and youth chairs for children. Mostly he made standard straight chairs in three sizes. The Poynor chair could be purchased as a rosewood-grained yellow-striped "fancy chair" or in the solid hues of red, blue, black, brown, and green, all bottomed in finely woven patterns of white oak–splits. The advertisement by John D. Miller of Main Street, Franklin, Tennessee, in the *Review-Appeal* of April 18, 1861, which stated, "Poynor's chairs—kept constantly on hand for sale" may illustrate the large market Poynor enjoyed. Traditionally cherished by many Williamson County families, the Poynor chairs' simple style and famous durability have rendered them highly collectable today.

Dick Poynor the man is as interesting as his famous chair. Despite the racial strife following the Civil War, he remained an honored citizen of the community as evidenced by his membership from April 1865 until his death in 1882 in the Leiper's Fork Primitive Baptist Church, a predominately white congregation. He was buried in the Garrison cemetery near his home, next to his second wife, Millie, and among his white neighbors. His homestead remained

[Continued on next page]

in the family until 1976. Though he died over a century ago, Dick Poynor is still revered as a craftsman and a gentleman in the Leiper's Fork area.

In 1990 the Tennessee Historical Commission placed a marker near the site of his home and chair factory in Williamson County. His highest honor and recognition came in February 1999, when the Tennessee State Museum exhibited a collection of his chairs.

Richard Warwick, Franklin, Tennessee

twentieth centuries. In Martin, Ed King operated a blacksmith and woodworking business from the turn of the century until the 1940s while in the town of Sardis during the 1930s, J. T. Hanna operated a workworking shop that produced cedar chests, cabinets, swings, and truck beds, in a design that he called Hannabilt. Another interesting example is the evolution of Louis C. Berney's Knoxville blacksmith shop and wagon making business. When established in 1889, plenty of wagon, buggy, and hack businesses were available. By the 1920s, Louis's son had converted the business to an automobile repair shop—a commonsense decision.

The city directories of the 1890s in East, Middle, and West Tennessee cities reflect the transition between the need for nineteenth-century tradesmen and new industrial demands. At the time of the Tennessee Centennial, the profession of carpenter was still as common as was the blacksmith, but the size of the operations in which these individuals were employed were much larger and more numerous than in previous years. Dual professions still existed in some towns, however. In Bristol, for example, you could trade with W. B. Pemberton, who advertised in the 1896–97 city directory as "cabinet maker and undertaker" and advertised "furniture repaired and teeth extracted."[2]

A study of Sevier County architecture exhibits ways in which urban woodcrafters adjusted to the new economic world. For example, the Sevierville Lumber Company advertised in the November 13, 1886, edition of the *Sevier County Republican* that it "will ship to the North East and North Western markets," and concluded with "orders for house patterns solicited."[3] The reference to house plans highlights one of the ways that the growing timber and rail business was supporting the national phenomenon of catalogue sales. In this case, house plans—not actual houses—were the product being advertised and delivered by mail. But in another catalogue, consumers could order the timber and other materials needed to construct any house. Knoxville architect and builder George F. Barber was successful in the late nineteenth century drawing house plans and marketing them nationally through his catalogues. Barber's designs and plans for his Victorian-style homes were clear and detailed as to the design features—especially the millwork that companies such as the Sevierville Lumber Company could, and often did, provide.

Sevier County craftsman Lewis Buckner exemplifies how individual artisans adapted to the new economy. Born a slave in the 1850s, Buckner became a highly skilled African American carpenter, carver, and furniture maker who probably apprenticed with Christian Stump of Sevierville. Buckner designed many houses for Sevier County's finest families in the late nineteenth and early twentieth centuries. Buckner not only built the house in the style of the day but also designed and crafted the interiors, from moldings to furniture. While he worked in the accepted style of the period, Buckner incorporated unique and distinctive design details as did many African American craftsmen. Lewis Buckner's career also testifies to the difficulties of making a living on your own after the turn of the century. The years from 1880 to 1910 were most productive for Buckner. He was listed as a cabinetmaker in the 1880 Sevier

Musical Instrument Makers

THE QUESTION OF WHERE AND FROM WHOM EARLY TENNESSEE MUSICIANS ACQUIRED THEIR instruments, simple as it may seem, is not easily answered. Did the interest in music and singing of our ancestors initiate a demand for the fiddle, banjo, the dulcimer, and other instruments, thereby prompting innovative souls to start making them? Or did the availability of such instruments constitute an invitation for so many of our folks to take up playing, picking, and singing? Various aspects of early and rural America tended to thwart the specialization of arts and crafts, such as the making of musical instruments. Most villages in Europe had a stone and brick mason, a tanner, a butcher, a wagon maker, carpenters, thatchers, and so forth. Often, there was also a luthier, who made violins and other instruments as an occupation, or at least as an avocation. The village of Cremona in northern Italy, for example, was as early as the 1600s the home of specialized musical instrument makers, including such masters as Nicolo Amati and the incomparable Antonio Stradivari.

Renda Whitaker with a banjo she and her husband made. This instrument has been loaned temporarily by the Museum of Appalachia to the Country Music Hall of Fame in Nashville. Photograph by John Rice Irwin. Courtesy of John Rice Irwin and the Museum of Appalachia, Norris.

Such specialization could not develop in frontier and rural America, especially in the South, because of the sparse population of the region. Neighbors were often few and far away. Every head of family had to become a farmer, a tanner, a furniture maker, a carpenter, a tool maker, a blacksmith, an herb doctor, and indeed a jack of all trades, and, consequently, a master of none. If he wanted a musical instrument, he likely would make it himself. This custom was more profound in pioneer times but continued largely intact well into the twentieth century.

Those who made instruments, for themselves and for family members, were often of the logger-farmer-hunter type who whittled out the semblance of a banjo as they sat before the fire in ill-lit cabins at night or on rainy days. Some of the young boys and old men who were not fully engaged in making a living for their families and who had more idle time also made crude instruments—and the older folk more often added decorative and non-utilitarian designs to their creations. Since these artisans were self-taught and often without patterns, templates, or other instruments as guides, the shape, form, and fashion varied greatly. Hence, the intrinsic nature of these instruments reflected true folk art qualities. Additionally, these instruments encouraged and shaped the native music as an art form—which was soon to be heard literally around the world.

Renda Whittaker's story is somewhat typical of the musical instrument maker of the region. She and her husband lived in an isolated section of the Cumberland Plateau in a community called Lick Skillet, near Monterey in Middle Tennessee:

[Continued on next page]

> When me and my husband Vetter got married, we worked hard clearing the land, planting crops and such, trying to get a start. After supper, we'd set on the porch and rest a little until it got dark, and sometimes we'd sing. We'd sing them old songs, and one day Vetter said to me: "Renda, we need us a banjar. If we had us a banjar we could play a little music while we sing."
>
> Well, the very next day we went out here in the woods behind the house and cut a poplar sapling and commenced whittling out the neck for a banjar, and we split a piece of white oak for the rim. In a day or two, Vetter went down there to the corn patch early one morning, and he killed a big ground hog. He skinned him and he dug a hole in the ground, put the hide down in it, and covered the hide with hickory ashes ... to take off the hair. We kept it wet, poured water on it every once in a while for a few days, and then we took it out and rubbed it in corn meal. Just kept working it, pulling, and twisting it, until it was good and soft, just like a dish rag. Then we used the hide for the head of the banjo; and when we got it strung up, it sounded pretty good. Law, at the good times me and Vetter had playing that old banjar![1]

Renda's old banjo can be veiwed in a display of folk art and contemporary musical instruments at the Country Music Hall of Fame in Nashville. This simple crude piece has been one of the most popular items in the extensive exhibit.

Many other colorful and innovative makers of fiddles, banjos, dulcimers, mouth bows, guitars, and mandolins could be mentioned, and each would be different and unique. But all would reflect a construction involving throwaway items. Usually they were devoid of any store-bought items except for the strings. They also reflected a remarkable variation in shape, style, construction technique, and materials. Interestingly, the musical instruments of southern Appalachia and rural Tennessee, different as they may have been, had an intrinsically basic "look" which experienced and studious observers could readily identify and differentiate from instruments made in New England, the Pennsylvania Dutch region, the Midwest, or other sections of the country.

John Rice Irwin, Museum of Appalachia

Note

1. John Rice Irwin, *A People and Their Music: The Story Behind the Story of Country Music* (Atglen, Pa.: Schiffer Publishing, 2000), 11.

County census, and most of his surviving work dates from the pre-1910 period. By 1910, however, he no longer worked for himself, but for the Burchfield Lumber Company and, later, Rawling's Coffin Manufacturing Company. Even for this highly respected craftsman, the world was no longer suited for his sole endeavor.

Charles Luther Crump is also an example of the town woodcrafter adjusting to changes. Born in 1880, Luther Crump was listed independent of his father, Robert, in the 1901 Nashville city directory. Crump's occupation was listed as carpenter. He continued to be designated as a carpenter until the 1930s, when he began working for the new Davis Cabinet Company as a spindle carver. Luther's son Milton learned the trade alongside his father at the cabinet company in the 1930s and 1940s. After World War II, father and son left Davis to establish their own business, Crump Carving, in Gallatin.

By 1900 change also came in the lives of rural woodworkers as they adapted to urbanization and new consumer demands for stylish rather than traditional pieces and as they grew accustomed to a cash-based rather than exchange-based economy. In the aftermath of a pattern of panics and recessions culminating in the depression of 1893–94, many men and women moved to growing towns and industries to find work. This migration from the rural areas not only had a direct impact on those who chose to stay home and on their county's economies but also on folk traditions. As the nation changed to a cash economy, even the local market was using cash to buy the new "ready-made" goods in the stores and catalogues. The general store became the focus for local spending. This emphasis on "factory-made" goods included baskets, tools, implements, furniture, wagons, and other products. Now, if the store did not have the desired items you wanted, you could mail in an order and have it brought to your door through Rural Free Delivery. By the early 1900s, traditional crafts were an economic alternative and fewer and fewer woodcrafters plied their trade. Many artisans found that moving on to new things made more sense than staying with the old. For example, in Woodbury the two most prominent late-nineteenth-century woodcrafters were R. H. Robertson and John Williams, who made furniture from surrounding stands of walnut and cherry but found their market niche in crafting hexagonal-shaped walnut coffins.

In the early 1900s, the aesthetic principles of the Arts and Crafts movement, introduced from England a generation earlier, finally took center stage in American architecture and decorative arts. The movement reacted against the mass production and standardization of modern industry by celebrating individual crafters and the products they made using traditional methods, tools, and artistic conventions. In England, arts and crafts devotees looked to the medieval guilds and their apprenticeship programs as models for the proper relationship between art and labor. In the American South, there was no medieval tradition, but there was the persistence of traditional crafts in Appalachia, and soon was born the Appalachian handicraft revival.

It is not surprising that Americans sensitive to the movement's philosophy looked to the Appalachian region as a source for hand-produced traditional crafts, and their interest motivated crafters to once again practice their trade. Woodworking and weaving were two crafts in demand. Ironically, the timber and textile industries were also major industries in Tennessee cities, employing many who had moved on from their rural homes to apply their skills in the city.

The same sentiment that sparked the Arts and Crafts movement also was related to the progressive reform movement to uplift the "uncorrupted" mountain people. Protestant and educational mission societies from outside the region established mountain missions and settlement schools throughout the Appalachian region. The Pi Beta Phi Settlement School and the Pittman Community Center in Sevier County, Alpine Institute in Overton County, and Pleasant Hill Academy in Cumberland County are examples of these endeavors. The purpose of these institutions was to educate and provide economic aid to the mountain people. A primary focus was on "preserving" the traditional crafts that were now in demand all over the country, but the new outside experts were the ones who decided which crafts were "traditional" and which were worthy of study and preservation.

Other voices of rural uplift came from the state's newly expanded county extension programs and public education system as most counties finally established public high schools in the early twentieth century. Woodworking often figured into vocational education curriculums in the new high schools, either as handicraft or industrial education. Yet some young craftsmen let their traditional training prevail when placed in the new progressive classrooms. One example of this is Henry Hoover from Cannon County. When he attended the new high school with its vocational

Shop of the Woodcrafters and Carvers, Gatlinburg. Dick Whaley, manager, and Charley Huskey carry on this little rural shop and employ at times several of the local workers. This view of the shop shows them working on a drop-leaf table. Photograph by Lewis W. Hine, 1933. Courtesy of the Tennessee Valley Authority.

education program in the 1920s, Hoover soon discovered—as did the other students—that he knew more than his teachers. The teachers, to their credit, realized this too and soon put him to work on "adult" projects such as building bleachers for the athletic field. Hoover shaped Cannon County architecture and decorative arts for fifty years, building commercial, medical, and domestic buildings as well as an impressive array of furniture.

These educational reforms also shaped the lives of rural African Americans. Throughout the South, the black leader and educator Booker T. Washington created a great deal of interest in skill training for the betterment of African Americans of all ages. Wood shop was an important element to a young man's education at Washington's Tuskegee Institute, which served as model for many black colleges and training schools in Tennessee. Education reformers in Tennessee also saw industrial education, including woodwork, as an aspect of African American education in the state's public schools. Many of the more than three hundred Rosenwald schools built for Tennessee's African Americans from the late 1910s to the early 1930s contained a specific room for industrial training.

The settlement schools and the vocational education programs changed the training method for most Tennessee woodcrafters. Due to post–Civil War shifts in the social and economic life of Tennesseans, many woodcrafters did not practice their trade as they had in previous years, and if they did, the next generation was often not interested in the craft. Even in the mountain communities where a demand was growing for handcrafted items, many of the younger craftsmen were trained in the shop environment by teachers, often from outside the region. Otto J. Mattil, for example, moved from Chattanooga in 1922 to the Pi Beta Phi Settlement School in Gatlinburg to teach, among other things, woodworking. Mattil's position was funded by the Smith-Hughes Act, one in a series of federal legislative acts that provided funds for vocational education. Teaching what was basically a traditional craft in a classroom setting was a major departure from the "folk" method of instruction of the nineteenth century in which artisans trained at the side of a master craftsman. There were still cases in which schools hired local master craftsmen to work with students—Henry Hoover, for instance, returned to his Cannon County high school and taught building trades and woodcrafts for four years—but such instances were the exception to the rule.

Traditional woodcraft training in a family setting most often survived in the realm of chairmakers, such as Isaac Ogle of Sevier County whose grandson, Randy, is still making chairs as his grandfather did. Several chair-making families continued their business in the Upper Cumberland region into the late twentieth century. In Cumberland County, Frank Tabor and his family established a thriving business in the 1930s, even gaining WPA support in those years. John Hicks and his son Hague Hicks from Pickett County made rockers and ladderback chairs from the late 1800s into the mid-twentieth century. Also in the middle decades of the twentieth century, the Macon County chair business of Amos Hicks and Dallas Newberry produced hundreds of pieces of furniture, a tradition continued at the end of the century by Dallas Newberry's son, Louis, and Louis's two sons, Terry and Mark Newberry. As recorded by forklorist Lynwood Montell, the Newberrys select trees from their farm and cut them into lengths to season the wood. The brothers use a motor-powered handmade lathe, rather than the foot-powered type used by their father and grandfather, to prepare the chair parts. They next use smoke to season the back and chair rounds before driving them into the chair posts, which tighten as the chair timbers continue to dry out (they do not use nails). Another master craftsman chronicled by Montell was Clarence Hawkins, who operated a mid-twentieth-century furniture shop at Red Boiling Springs. He worked in locally available woods such as wild red cherry, black walnut, and curly maple. The second fundamental change in the nature of woodcraft was that the new handicraft revival did not distinguish between different types of woodcrafts. In the craft revival economy, whittlers and carvers of figures, canes, and toys shared equal market status for the first time with carpenters, cabinetmakers, and chairmakers. Aesthetic values replaced function as the key measuring stick for the worth of woodcrafts. This shift unsettled many woodcrafters, but almost all recognized that the craft revival provided a way that rural people could receive cash rather than exchange for their work, and increasingly cash was necessary to survive in the rural economy. They vigorously participated in the new markets. During the 1920s the family of Jim Hughes, makers of chairs, furniture, and baskets in Warren County, for example, opened a chair shop (that still operates) along the recently completed Memphis-to-Bristol Highway. A few miles to the west the Davis family and Prater family in Cannon County also have used their proximity to the new highway to help sell their chairs. In many instances these chair and basket makers continued the "folk" method of training subsequent generations, as their success "peddling" their chairs and baskets made it economically important to keep the tradition alive. There are instances of relations retiring from their factory jobs and learning the chair-making business from family. This is the case with Arthur Mitchell, a chairmaker from Warren County who left the lumber mill in the 1960s to learn the craft from a brother-in-law from Cannon County, Willie Thomas, and continued making chairs until his death.

Good intentions and results must be weighed against the stress of having well-meaning teachers and ministers from outside the community come in and work to "improve" things at a time of economic and social change in the mountains. These groups did recognize, however, the value of the crafts of the mountain folk they came to tutor and live among. By the 1920s, with the arrival of ever-growing numbers of tourists in the Tennessee Appalachians, the combined efforts of teachers and craftsmen resulted

Mrs. Matt Ownby, Roaring Forks. Making baskets, November 1926. Mary Ownby of the Glades community near Gatlinburg holds items on which she is working: a turned chair post and a partially completed basket. Photograph by Laura Thornborough. Courtesy of the Great Smoky Mountains National Park.

in economic prosperity in such communities as Gatlinburg, where the popularity and reputation of the Pi Beta Phi Settlement School and its marketing efforts made more business for all.

In 1924 the Pi Beta Phi Sorority established the Arrowcraft store in Gatlinburg. The store served as a showcase for the crafts produced by families in the surrounding area, as well as those produced in the school's loom house and woodshop. O. J. Mattil left Pi Beta Phi school a few years later and established Mattil's Woodcrafters and Carvers shop. The experience and education gained in Mattil's shop inspired the custom woodwork of the noted Compton and Huskey families. Brothers Shirl and Roy Compton and Carl Huskey were only a few of the young men trained and motivated to begin careers in woodworking, primarily in building custom designed furniture. Carl Huskey, not only started his own furniture business, but also taught woodworking at Pi Beta Phi school for more than twenty years. The success of Mattil's shop, featuring the work of these young craftsmen, led to the establishment of individual businesses for each. The sons of both families learned from their fathers and continued the business on into the later twentieth century. The renewed interest in the crafts and the success of Mattil's Woodcrafters and Carvers shop helped other woodworkers in Gatlinburg reestablish their businesses, with most adapting to the custom furniture model. The most notable example was E. L. Reagan, whose 1910 woodworking business predated Mattil's arrival by twelve years. Reagan had earlier trained not only his sons in the craft, but also O. G. Ward, who in turn trained his own brother Don. But Reagan recognized that Mattil's targeted custom market was desirable and profitable and his family adapted the old patterns and forms of furniture to meet the different demands of the individual consumer or collector. Thus was born the long and respected furniture tradition that served as a Gatlinburg hallmark, along with weaving, through most of the twentieth century.

In 1930, craftsmen, educators, and reformers established the Southern Highland Handicraft Guild at the annual conference of the Southern Mountain Workers in Knoxville. Leaders in the craft revival movement came together to work as a cooperative. Not all groups joined, but guild cooperative shops and marketing efforts strengthened demand for all craftspeople. The wood products which were often exhibited in guild shops included "early American"-style furniture, traditional ladder-back chairs, bowls, and carved miniatures. Garry Barker asserts that the guild "is the basis for all subsequent development of the Appalachian handcraft industry."[4]

The federal government expressed an interest in the economic development efforts of the guild in 1934. In 1935, the Tennessee Valley Authority

Toqua, a Late Prehistoric Town, c. A.D. 1450. A life-sized mural showing the leaders of the Late Mississippian town assembled in front of the civic buildings on the summit of Mound A. On the plaza before them a single-pole stick-ball game is in progress. The standard with the cross served as a fan and sunshade and was an emblem of rank and importance, not a Christian symbol. The name Toqua comes from the historic Cherokee town of that name that later occupied the same location. Painting by Greg Harlin. Courtesy of The Frank H. McClung Museum, University of Tennessee.

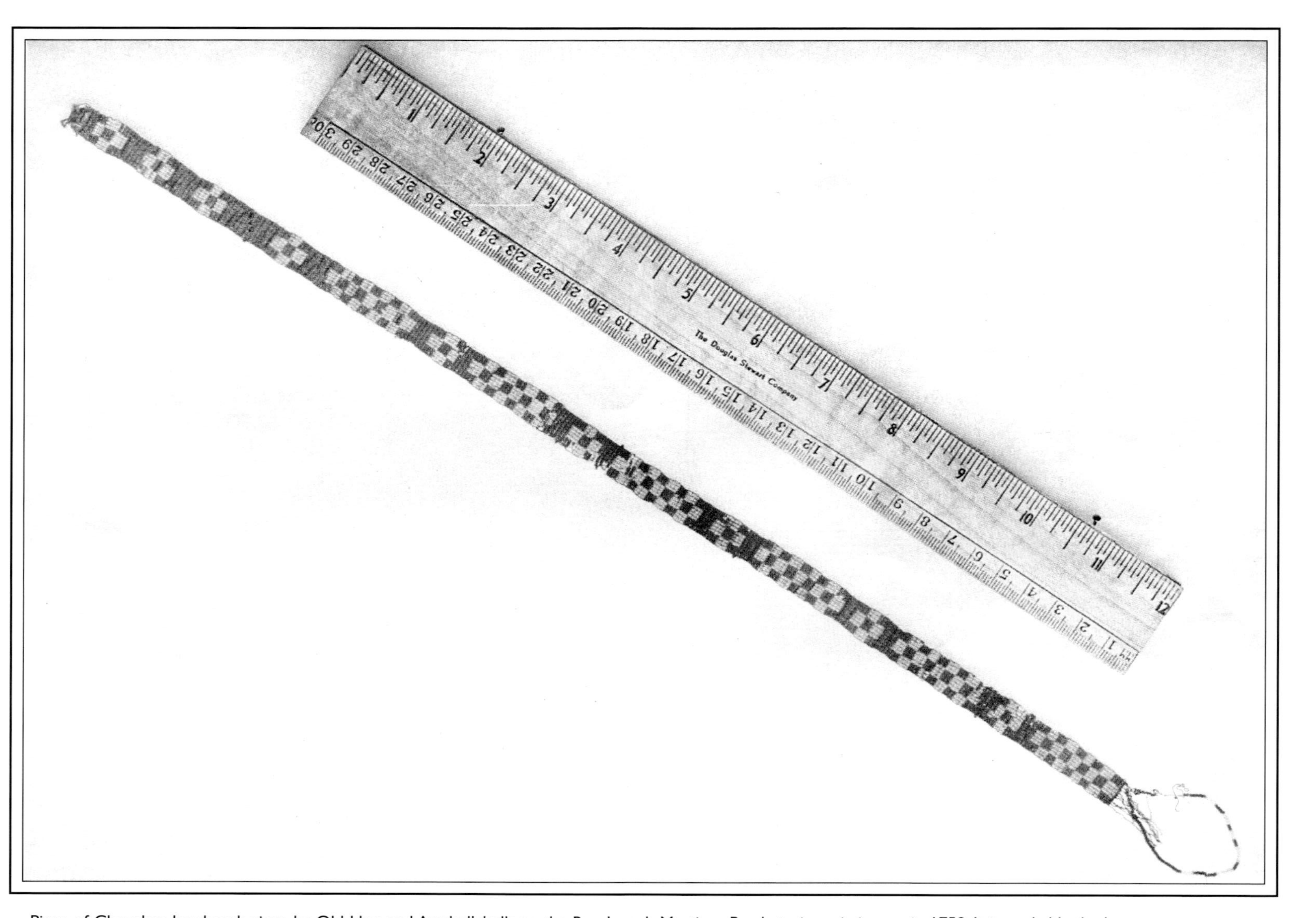

Piece of Cherokee beadwork given by Old Hop and Attakullakulla to the Rev. Joseph Martin, a Presbyterian missionary, in 1758. It is probably the best documented and authenticated piece of beadwork from presettlement times. The beads are Venetian glass and incorporate patterns of 4 and 7, symbolic parts of the Cherokee cosmology. Photograph by Clark Pittman. Courtesy of Patrick Meguiar.

Landon Carter Mansion, first floor parlor. Photograph by Louis Jackson, 2001.
Courtesy of Tennessee Historical Commission.

Hamilton County Courthouse, Chattanooga. Photograph by Carroll Van West.

Chet Atkins detail from the *Tennessee Fox Trot Carousel* by Red Grooms. Photograph by Gary Layda, 2000.
Courtesy of Metropolitan Government of Nashville and Davidson County.

Cumberland, steel, painted orange, by Ned Crouch, 1983. Courtesy of School of Art, University of Tennessee, Knoxville.

En Pénitence, by Willie Betty Newman, oil on canvas, 1894. 1960.2.57. Collection of Cheekwood Museum of Art, Nashville, Tennessee.

Redstart, watercolor on paper, by Emma Bell Miles. Courtesy of Hunter Museum of American Art, Chattanooga, Tennessee; gift of the Authors and Artists Club.

(TVA) and Southern Highland Handicraft Guild joined forces to create Southern Highlanders, a craft-marketing program funded by TVA. Initial programs were introduced at Norris in Anderson County. O. J. Mattil was recruited to start a woodshop similar to the one he established at Gatlinburg. Not only did this effort bring vocational education in handicrafts to new areas of East Tennessee, but programs were developed across the TVA region, spreading the craft revival through the state. In 1935 a salesroom was opened in the concourse of the International Building at New York City's Rockefeller Center. Stores were also located in the town of Norris and Chickamauga Dam and in the Patten Hotel in Chattanooga. The efforts of TVA continued until 1951, when Southern Highlanders merged with the guild.

By the 1940s, the guild included individual members, and its mission had broadened to focus on educating craftspeople about production technique and business. The organization also made efforts to survey and identify artisans in the region. Historian David E. Whisnant sees the guild as a direct extension or result of the earlier reform efforts of the rural missionaries and educators. While the purpose of these organizations and their craft endeavors was to preserve past traditions, Whisnant interprets the impact of these groups and the later guild as undermining those same craft traditions. As in the case of the Gatlinburg woodcrafters, many of the early skills were certainly drawn upon but were adapted to new methods and tools for a new market. The forms also changed to meet the demand of that market—in this case, traditional forms of furniture were replaced by more contemporary custom pieces. Whisnant thus concludes that the guild was an agent of change as opposed to conservator of local traditions. But Garry Barker's study of the handicraft revival emphasizes that the revival's economic success—putting money into the pockets of artisans—would not have happened without the efforts of the guild and its predecessors in the mission and settlement schools.

Another major contribution of the Southern Highland Handicraft Guild was the creation of the Craftsman's Fair in 1948. The July fair was initially held in Gatlinburg, where the popularity of the Arrowcraft Shop, Mattil's Woodcrafters and Carvers shop, and the shops of Mattill's students had grown as tourism increased to Gatlinburg, the western gateway to the Great Smoky Mountains National Park. The Craftsman's Fair moved to Asheville, North Carolina, a few years later, but beginning in the 1950s, an October fair returned to Gatlinburg. The Asheville and Gatlinburg shows continue today. Craft shows remain a vital way for woodcrafters to present their products to the public. The format and size of the shows has changed over the years, but the result is the same: recognition and sales. Craftsmen such as the Compton, Huskey, Reagan, and Ward families found the shows helped strengthen their growing role in the business.

The popularity and success of the craft revival movement serves as the foundation for the woodcrafter's world today. Craft shows continue to be an important part of the economic success of artisans. More so than any other time in the past, however, woodcrafters interact with consumers who have little, or no, interest in function. Consumers are collecting craft art—decorative items which symbolize the past. Today items are being purchased not to use but for their value as collectors' items or their beauty. For many contemporary artisans, the idea of "craft as art and craft as economics" is of critical importance. Craig Nutt of Kingston Springs is one of the state's acclaimed contemporary woodcrafters and has used—and advocated—the use of computer-aided drawing (CAD) programs in such innovative designs as the *Helical Dance.* His furniture and wood sculptures are found in major collections across the state and nation and were part of the important 2001 exhibit North American Wood Turning Since 1930, which showed in Minneapolis, Washington, D.C., and New Haven, Connecticut. Wood turner John Jordan of Antioch also has staked out a national reputation through his work as a teacher and crafter. Jordan's designs may be found in the collections of the Museum of Fine Arts in Boston, the Arkansas Arts Center in Little Rock, the High Museum of Art in Atlanta, the Hunter Museum of American Art in

Chattanooga, and the Renwick Gallery of the Smithsonian Institution. He also sells lathes through his Internet web site, stubbylathe.com.

Throughout the state, others preserve the family tradition of woodcrafting. Rick and Renee Stewart of Hancock County are examples of this effort, as are the Ownby family of Gatlinburg and the Calhouns of Obion and Lake Counties. Alex Stewart, Rick's and Renee's grandfather, inspired them to learn the art of coopering and carving which he had learned from his father and grandfather. While it is necessary for them to concentrate on the appearance, not the utility of their pieces, they also feel a great responsibility "to family, to tradition, to history." It is their obligation to "keep alive at least some small part of a vanishing way of life."[5]

James Colombus "Lum" and Janavee Ogle Ownby opened Ownby Woodcrafts in 1974. Lum

Boat Building and the Reelfoot Lake Boat

UNTIL WORLD WAR II, LOCALLY MADE WOODEN BOATS WERE IN WIDE USE ON TENNESSEE WATERWAYS. Early flatboats or keelboats were the first larger crafts to bear freight and passengers, but by the mid-1800s they had been displaced by sternwheelers, ferry boats, and barges specially manufactured in industrial shipyards. Into the first decades of the 1900s, handmade houseboats or shantyboats commonly provided residence for people who made their living from the water throughout the Tennessee and Cumberland River basins.

Boat building was most widely practiced, however, in the construction of smaller crafts used for fishing and local transport, the most common variety in Tennessee being the jonboat, a versatile design characterized by a flat bottom and squared bow and stern. The skiff, featuring a keel and pointed bow, was also built in some parts of the state by local woodworkers. Both these types made the transition to mass manufacture with the introduction of aluminum and fiberglass technology, which rendered handmade boats largely obsolete.

The boat builder's craft survives, however, in a living tradition unique to northwest Tennessee's Reelfoot Lake. A submerged cypress forest created by the flooding of the Mississippi River during the New Madrid earthquake of 1811, this distinctive environment became known as an exceptional hunting and fishing locale. During the 1800s, a local vernacular boat type emerged with features suited to the lake's navigational needs. Variously called the Reelfoot Lake boat, duck boat, or stumpjumper, it is sturdily built of cypress to endure collisions with underwater obstacles. Akin to the Louisiana pirogue, it has a shallow draft, flat bottom, and pointed bow and stern, and it is usually thirteen to eighteen feet long.

The craft's early history is poorly documented, but its design and features were clearly refined at the hands of different craftsmen, not all of whom are now remembered. Its oddest element, a bow-facing oar mechanism that allows the rower to see where the boat is going, was patented in 1884. The 1930s brought experimentation with the use of gasoline engines, leading to an ingenious inboard motor, guarded prop, and rudder system that also became standard. Hundreds of lake boats with these features crowded local docks during Reelfoot's heyday as a commercial fishery and popular sportsman's paradise through the mid-1900s.

During the past century, the Reelfoot boat-building tradition became exclusively associated with the Calhoun family. Joseph Marion Calhoun (1852–1927) was a blacksmith who started building boats in his shop near the lake by the early 1900s. The family boatworks was passed generationally through Boone Calhoun (1889–1965) and W. W. "Bill" Calhoun (1913–1990) to and Janavee came from woodcrafting families—Ownbys, McCarters, and Ogles. Chairs, baskets, and other woodcrafts were produced during quiet times on the farm and sold to neighbors. As a result of the craft revival, the families found new interest in their products. Mary McCarter Ownby, a first cousin of Lum's father, was one of the woodcrafters featured in author Allen Eaton's 1937 study on Southern Highland crafts. After making items for area shops for a number of years, the Ownbys decided to make woodcraft a full-time business. Son David and grandson David Richard Ownby are craftsmen, and intend to keep the family tradition of quality woodcrafts alive in the mountains. Daughter Jody Ownby Penny manages the business side. Thanks to tourism in the Gatlinburg area and regional craft shows, the old ways are providing economically for the family's newest generation of woodcrafters.

Dale Calhoun working on Reelfoot Lake stumpjumper at the 1986 Smithsonian Festival of American Folklife, Washington, D.C. Photograph by Robert G. Cogswell. Courtesy of TAC.

Dale Calhoun (1935–), who now keeps the legacy alive in his shop near Tiptonville. Though adjusting to modern times in some techniques—fiberglass rather than tin, for example, now comprises the protective skin of his boats—Dale still applies extraordinary folk knowledge and skill in his work. As stumpjumpers no longer dominate boat traffic on the lake, the historic significance of this heritage and the artistry of the handcraft underlying it have been increasingly recognized. In 1998, Dale Calhoun was presented with a National Heritage Fellowship award from the National Endowment for the Arts, America's highest honor, both to him as a master craftsman and to the Tennessee tradition that he preserves.

Robert Cogswell, Tennessee Arts Commission

Suggested Reading

Cogswell, Robert. "Dale Calhoun and the Reelfoot Lake Boat." Tennessee Folklore Society *Bulletin* 59 (1999): 48–60.

Dale Calhoun of Tiptonville, Lake County, is concentrating on cultivating a new generation of Calhouns to continue in the family's boat-building business. Dale's great-grandfather, Joseph Marion Calhoun, was a man of many talents, including blacksmithing and woodworking. Joseph's son, Boone, worked in his father's shop and soon learned about the lake boats that were made in the area. By the 1930s, Boone began specializing in building "stumpjumpers," so named because of the cedar boats' design, which made them able to ply the obstacles of the lake. Boat building became a family business, employing Dale by the 1950s. However, after cheaper mass-produced boats became available, the market dwindled and fewer and fewer craftsmen could continue their trade. Today, Dale Calhoun is the only craftsman who continues producing "stumpjumpers." He now hopes for a grandchild to continue the family's craft tradition.

The folk method of woodcraft instruction perseveres, even if what constitutes the folk tradition in woodcrafting has changed over the last two hundred years. Indeed, the world of woodcrafters will be ever evolving as taste and demand changes the markets served by these artisans. Woodcrafters will continue to play a significant role in the development of Tennessee's craft story, as they always have in the past.

NOTES

1. Garry G. Barker, *The Handcraft Revival in Southern Appalachia, 1930–1990* (Knoxville: Univ. of Tennessee Press, 1991), xvii.
2. *Johnson's Directory of Bristol, Tenn. & Va. for 1896–97* (Wilmington, Del.: Johnson's Publishing, 1896), ii.
3. Robbie D. Jones, *The Historic Architecture of Sevier County, Tennessee* (Sevierville, Tenn.: Smoky Mountain Historical Society, 1996), 49.
4. Barker, *Handcraft Revival,* 16.
5. Jane Harris Woodside, "From Farm to Festivals: Crafts in the Clinch River Valley," Tennessee Folklore Society *Bulletin* 43, no. 4 (1989): 128.

SUGGESTED READINGS

Barker, Garry G. *The Handcraft Revival in Southern Appalachia, 1930–1990.* Knoxville: Univ. of Tennessee Press, 1990.

Bullard, Helen. *Crafts and Craftsmen of the Tennessee Mountains.* Falls Church, Va.: Summit Press, 1976.

Eaton, Allen. *Handicrafts of the Southern Highlands.* New York: Russell Sage Foundation, 1937.

Holland, Ruth Adams. *Henry Hoover: Cannon County Craftsman.* Woodbury, Tenn.: Adams Memorial Association, 1984.

Irwin, John Rice. *Alex Stewart: Portrait of a Pioneer.* Atglen, Penn.: Schiffer Publishing, 1985.

McPherson, Anne S. "Adaptation and Reinterpretation: The Transfer of Furniture Styles from Philadelphia to Winchester to Tennessee." In *American Furniture,* ed. Luke Beckerdite, 298–334. Hanover, N.H.: Chipstone Foundation, 1997.

Montell, Lynwood. *Upper Cumberland Country.* Jackson, Miss.: Univ. Press of Mississippi, 1993.

Weaver, Emma. *Crafts in the Southern Highlands.* Asheville, N.C.: Southern Highland Handicraft Guild, 1958.

Whisnant, David. *All That Is Native and Fine: The Politics of Culture in an American Region.* Chapel Hill: Univ. of North Carolina Press, 1983.

Williams, Derita Coleman, and Nathan Harsh. *The Art and Mystery of Tennessee Furniture and Its Makers Through 1850.* Nashville: Tennessee Historical Society, 1988.

Young, Namuni Hale. *Art and Furniture of East Tennessee.* Knoxville: East Tennessee Historical Society, 1997.

Nine

Tennessee Basketmaking

Carroll Van West
Middle Tennessee State University

Crafting baskets is one of the state's oldest arts traditions, and one that has enjoyed a considerable resurgence in the past thirty years, with basket makers appearing at most of the annual crafts festivals across Tennessee. Although today's baskets are rarely used for their original utilitarian purposes, many modern basket makers still identify their work through the old names: egg basket, berry baskets, clothes baskets, laundry baskets, market baskets, sewing baskets, and the like. Since cheap plastic and metal boxes have replaced the baskets' original storage and carrying functions, baskets have become folk art, prized by collectors and recognized nationally as one of the most distinctive forms of Tennessee craft arts.

Making baskets attracts woodcrafters because they can typically control the process from the selection of the wood to the final decorative touches, adding immeasurably to their sense of individual achievement and expression. As Allen Eaton memorably observed in 1937,

> The experienced basket maker knows where to find the tree and when the rising of the sap makes the time right to assure the best quality of strips and thongs to which he must reduce it; he has learned how to quarter the wood and subdivide the quarters to break right with the grain, and with simple tools to work it into narrow, pliable but durable strips. These, by methods as old as history, he bends and weaves into shape, and with notches, splices, pegs, and thongs produces a basket that will hold together for years of hard use. This intimate association endows the maker with a feeling for quality and a pride of workmanship not experienced by one who does only a small part of the entire process.[1]

Basketmaking also is a craft that is taught through family networks, with one generation training the

Lidded doubleweave basket, c. late eighteenth century to 1838, Knox County. Courtesy of The Frank H. McClung Museum, University of Tennessee.

next, although many contemporary makers learned the craft through classes and workshops sponsored by such institutions as the Tennessee Arts Commission, John C. Campbell Folk School, Arrowmont School of Arts and Crafts, and Joe L. Evins Center for Appalachian Crafts.

Whether one is taught by their parents or by trained experts, the fundamental process of making baskets has changed little over the centuries. Native Americans were the first basket makers in Tennessee. Archaeological excavations carried out in the nineteenth and twentieth centuries found evidence of woven baskets used for a variety of purposes by native peoples. In the historic period, early travelers, explorers, and settlers noted the various types of Native American baskets used for storage, hunting, and fishing. Cherokee and Choctaw women gained reputations as master basket weavers, making intricate patterns with strips of rivercane (and to lesser degrees with hickory and white oak) colored with natural dyes such as bloodroot (yellow), butternut (black), and black walnut (brown). Double woven (also called double-wall) baskets—where baskets "are woven with back-to-back inside and outside fabrics, such that the surface of the basket is glossy and smooth both inside and out"—are viewed as the finest achievements of prehistoric Native American basketry since they combine the beauty of their geometric designs with the practicality of a lightweight, yet strong, carrier.[2] Today basket makers from the Eastern Band of Cher-

Joe L. Evins Appalachian Center for Crafts

THE JOE L. EVINS APPALACHIAN CENTER FOR CRAFTS (ACC) WAS CREATED IN THE 1970S TO MAINTAIN traditional Appalachian crafts while also encouraging contemporary art applications based on those traditions. The center includes studios and gallery space as part of a complex between Silver Point and Smithville, Tennessee, on Center Hill Lake. In many ways the center is heir to the revival of Appalachian crafts that began in the mountain settlement school movement of the early 1900s and ran through institutions such as the Arrowmont School of Arts and Crafts in Gatlinburg (1926) and the Southern Highland Handicraft Guild (1930).

The center's name honors Joseph L. Evins (1910–1984), a Smithville resident and member of the house of representatives from Tennessee's Fourth District from 1946 to 1977. Evins was instrumental in the creation of the Appalachian Regional Commission (ARC) and the inclusion of several Middle Tennessee counties, including DeKalb, in the ARC's thirteen-state region. With Evins's encouragement, the ARC made the largest single federal grant given for crafts, $5 million, for construction of the center near his hometown. The Joe L. Evins Appalachian Center for Crafts opened on December 9, 1979.

The ACC campus sits on 562 acres owned by U.S. Army Corps of Engineers as part of the Center Hill Lake reservoir area on the Caney Fork River. The center provides 50,000 square feet of studio space for instructors, artists, and students and 4,000 square feet of exhibit and retail space. The center complex also contains administrative offices, a cafeteria, library, conference room, lecture space, recreational areas, supplies store, and several housing units. The Appalachian Crafts Gallery provides an exhibition venue and sales center for the traditional and contemporary crafts produced in the region as well as in the Appalachian tradition nationally. The Appalachian Center for Crafts averages one hundred thousand visitors yearly.

The Tennessee Arts Commission, a state agency, originally funded management of the ACC through a contract with Tennessee Technological University, located in Cookeville, about okees are recognized for their colorful baskets made with the natural dyes of their elders as well as commercial dyes.

The early settlers of Tennessee were like the Native Americans in that they used baskets for all types of storage needs. Typically each settlement had one or more families who were skilled basket makers, and they used a wide assortment of materials to make their wares. Mixing techniques and basket forms from England, Scotland, and Ireland, some early Tennessee crafters may have followed the Cherokee tradition of using rivercane—certainly they used white oak in most cases—while in rare cases basket makers used hickory and maple. Over time most Tennessee makers became known for their skill in

Singleweave storage basket, pre-1838, Knox County. Courtesy of The Frank H. McClung Museum, University of Tennessee.

twenty miles northeast of the center. In July 1985, the center became Tennessee Tech's direct responsibility as a division of its Department of Music and Art. In the years since the center's administrative move to the university, the Tennessee General Assembly has frequently debated the level of state funding that should be given to the center and whether it should be a part of Tennessee Tech or a self-supporting institution. As of the 2001–2002 state fiscal year, the Appalachian Center for Crafts remained part of the university.

As cited on the ACC's Internet web site, its original mission, "to develop, stimulate, and preserve the tradition of crafts in the Appalachian region, providing instruction in traditional as well as contemporary crafts," continues, with the addition of goals to educate artists and designers not only in craft techniques but in marketing and exhibition skills and in documenting the crafts and ethnic traditions of Appalachia.

The ACC faculty in 2001 consisted of a full-time instructor and an artist in residence for each of five fields: ceramics, metals, wood, glass, and fibers. The center's programs are integrated into the bachelor of fine arts degree program at Tennessee Tech, and there are certificate and emerging professional artist programs. Non-degree-seeking students and aspiring craftsmen can take part in evening, weekend, and summer workshops offered on such varied topics as blacksmithing, ancient clay techniques, furniture making, weaving, glass blowing, and basketmaking, among many others. Instructors for workshops are local and Appalachian artists, graduates of the most prestigious folk arts schools in the United States, and ACC faculty and artists in residence. The workshop series offer a rich opportunity to learn from some of the premier traditional and contemporary artisans connected with Appalachian crafts. For more than twenty years, the Evins Appalachian Center for Crafts has played a vital role in shaping and promoting the decorative arts of Tennessee and the region.

Ann Toplovich, Tennessee Historical Society

making white oak baskets, with rib baskets and split baskets being the most popular varieties, produced in different sizes and shapes.

Whatever the type of basket produced, the process begins, as it did hundreds of years ago for the Native Americans, with selecting the right tree. "You want one about four inches in diameter," recommends one Union County maker. "I like my trees to come from a brushy thicket, where they can shoot up fast and put on lots of growth wood. A white oak growin' in the woods usually ain't no good. It doesn't get enough sunlight to grow fast enough."[3] Louis Dunn, a late-twentieth-century basket maker in DeKalb County, cut his white oak trees when "the rising of the sap assure[d] the best quality of strips and thongs."[4] The next step is to prepare the wood splits. A Cannon County maker first cut the heartwood out of a white oak log, "then stripped off the bark. The heartwood was quartered, then halved, and then split parallel to the grain to make the long narrow strips," which were then moistened and wove into the desired shape.[5]

Lydia Whaley. Courtesy of Arrowmont School of Arts and Crafts, Gatlinburg.

Crafting a rib basket demanded an ability to construct an intricate framework of ribs, hoops, and splits, but the end result was a basket of strength and durability as well as striking beauty due to graceful curves inherent in its ribbed design. The rib basket is closely associated with the basketmaking traditions of the eastern half of the state, from the Appalachian Mountains to the Highland Rim of eastern Middle Tennessee. West Tennessee makers, especially for cotton and work baskets, are more associated with split baskets, comparatively simple constructions made of long flat strips of wood woven together with often "skillfully carved handles or elaborate top rim treatments."[6] One of the leading twentieth-century makers of split baskets was Emanuel Dupree, an African American woodcrafter in Fayette County.

Several basket designs possessed enough unique traits to be identified through their maker. "Aunt Lydia" or "Whaley" baskets made of willow came from the work of Lydia Whaley, who was active in Sevier County from the Civil War era into the early 1900s. According to Eaton, the Whaley basket possessed a "harmony between the bowl of the basket and the handle," the result of "a consistent working out of bark and branch in combination."[7] Whaley's daughter, Mrs. J. V. Huskey, still made Aunt Lydia baskets in the 1930s and described the process of making them: the willow bark "is gathered in the summer when there is a nice smooth spa on it. It is skinned from the willow tree, the hard outside part of the bark is removed before it is left to dry. When dry the rough side is smoothed with a knife—the side which is seen on the inside of the basket—and the bark is then cut in splits and woven into the basket."[8]

The necessity of baskets was a constant in rural Tennessee for most of the nineteenth and early twentieth centuries. In several communities, baskets were treated much like cash and were commonly accepted in exchange for goods and services well into the twentieth century. Rural and small town merchants often kept a corner of the store for the sale of baskets—or hung them from the store's rafters by the dozens to encourage their sale. In an interview with Rachel Nash Law and Cynthia Taylor, Earlean and Lawson Thomas of Cannon County recalled, "We made baskets. We had to make 'em, take 'em to the store for our living. They wouldn't give you no money on 'em. So you had to take 'em to the store and trade 'em for groceries to live on." Si Pearce and Louis Thomas of Pickett County made baskets starting in the 1920s, trading them in exchange for the baskets being filled with shelled corn.[9]

Cannon County resident Ida Pearl Underwood Davis, who came from a generations-old tradition of making baskets, recalled trading her first basket "at the store for a toboggan cap. It was a little round egg basket . . . about a gallon size." Her family often "carried them over the country, all over Stone's River, up and down, through the hollers, trading 'em for meat, used clothes, lard, turnips, potatoes, or anything we could get to eat or wear." The expanding use of mail-order catalogues and Rural Free Delivery, along with the continued infusion of mass-produced consumer goods into rural trade networks, eventually marginalized local demand for baskets, and the number of basket makers diminished accordingly. The crafters themselves felt marginalized, and associated basketmaking with the poverty of their youth. Ida Pearl Davis told her daughter Thelma, "I was made to feel ashamed, mighty little, looked down on. I don't know just how to explain. I was made to feel so I knowed I didn't want to teach my kids to do it. That's the reason I never would make you'uns make 'em."[10]

But basketmaking never disappeared; in fact, the advent of automobile touring and new highway construction gave the craft a greater visibility than before. In the early twentieth century, the market for baskets as folk art multiplied. In 1908, Olive Dame Campbell, later instrumental in establishing the John C. Campbell Folk School in North Carolina, bought three baskets at Pleasant Hill Academy in Cumberland County and noted that the items held money-making potential for their makers. Like Campbell, teachers and officials at Appalachian settlement schools treasured basketmaking and continued to nurture the craft. Pine Mountain and Hindman schools were important in Kentucky while the Pi Beta Phi Settlement School at Gatlinburg and the Pittman Center in Sevier County, the Alpine Institute in Overton County, and the Pleasant Hill school in Cumberland County played similar roles in Tennessee. The Pi Beta Phi basketry program at Gatlinburg produced baskets for sale at its Arrow Craft Shop in the mid-1920s

Ida Pearl Davis and Bill Davis making white oak baskets. Photograph given to author by Thelma Davis Hisdon.

as it also created a market for the work of Huskey, Mac McCarter, and others.

The role of the settlement schools in the handicraft revival has been well documented. There is no doubt that the handicraft revival expanded what had been a local appreciation of and market for baskets into a larger regional, even national, market for these items. In reaction, makers often changed baskets to meet new consumer expectations. Baskets became more colorful (also due in part to the greater availability of cheap, effective commercial dyes) and individual artistic expression—compared to the earlier attention to the function and use of the basket—drove the design of basket shapes. The baskets gained a conscious aesthetic look and became smaller generally; makers and buyers alike called them "fancy baskets" in comparison to the earlier utilitarian types.

During the 1920s improved transportation systems enabled several rural communities of basket makers to extend their reputation across the region. Roadside stands for craft sales became commonplace in the upper Cumberland during the 1920s and 1930s. The completion of the Memphis-to-Bristol Highway, the first modern road to link the state's northeast and southwest corners, passed through what had been isolated, small farms in the Cumberland Plateau and Highland Rim of Middle Tennessee. Between Crossville and Sparta, the Pleasant Hill Craft Shop sold woodcrafts, including the baskets of Laura Blaylock of White County, to highway travelers. Currently Kathleen Dunn Palmer and Roger Dunn keep the White County tradition alive. As the highway passed through western Warren County and Cannon County, it allowed a large community of family basket makers, who mostly lived in the Thomas Town and Manus Town settlements and around Short Mountain, to sell their goods to a much wider audience. "All of these families," county historian Robert Mason pointed out, "were closely knit through intermarriage and through their close association preserved the crafts."[11] From these families would emerge what is now considered the greatest concentration of traditional basket makers in the state.

Top: Rib basket by Josie Jones. Photograph by Robert G. Cogswell, 1985. Courtesy of TAC.

Above: Splint baskets by Kathleen Dunn Palmer. Photograph by Robert G. Cogswell, 1987. Courtesy of TAC.

The Thomas, Davis, Youngblood, Mathis, Manus, and Murphy families had been making baskets for generations, supplementing their meager incomes as subsistence or tenant farmers. Neighbors still recall that most of the families were poor, but by making baskets, they could trade for food and other necessary items. The better highways of the 1920s and 1930s encouraged families to travel extensively to sell their baskets in towns and cities. While Law and Taylor's study of Appalachian white oak basketmaking concluded that the craft declined after World War II, many of the Cannon County makers continued making baskets. A good example is the work of William

Jessee (Bill) Davis and his wife Ida Pearl Underwood Davis, both of whom descended from notable local basketmaking families. Married in 1941, the Davises lived in the Center Hill community. They were farmers who used woodcrafts as a cash income, working the farm by day and crafting baskets and chairs at night. As a farmer, Billy raised livestock and used his mules to tend row crops. As a woodcrafter, he made stools, chairs, and basket materials; his family recalls that "when his brothers Jake, Don, Thomas, or any of them would go basket and chair peddling with their families to other cities like Memphis, Bill always had ham or shoulder meat to carry along."[12] Ida Pearl Davis was the family's great basket maker; she had learned the craft from her mother and grandmother and made her first basket when only a child.

By the late 1950s, the farm generated so little income that the Davises took jobs in the local textile factory in Woodbury, but Ida Pearl still made baskets at nights and on weekends. As the new interest in basketmaking appeared in the late 1960s and early 1970s, spurred on in part by folk arts initiatives from the Tennessee Arts Commission, Ida Pearl Davis became a full-time basket maker, with her work recorded in such books as Law and Taylor's *Appalachian White Oak Basketmaking* and in such collections as those of the American Folklife Center and the Museum of Appalachia. She eventually passed on her skills to the next generation, training her daughter Thelma Davis Hibdon and son-in-law Billy Hibdon, as her own eyesight began to fail her. In May 2001, Ida Pearl Davis and Thelma Davis Hibdon received a Folklife Heritage Award at the annual Governor's Awards in the Arts ceremony, where the mother and daughter were commended for being "ambassadors for the important craft legacy of their county."[13]

Another Cannon County family whose work was highlighted by the Tennessee Arts Commission a generation earlier was Willie and Maggie Murphy of the Short Mountain community. Again, both came from families of basket makers, but in this case, Willie's mother—not Maggie's own mother—taught Maggie Murphy the craft. Making and selling baskets was one way the family could make ends meet—by all accounts they were poor and their small home did not have electricity until 1972. By the early 1970s, the arts commission hired Maggie Murphy to conduct demonstration workshops in basketmaking at her Short Mountain home. According to a newspaper account of 1973, the workshops attracted teachers, folklorists, and "a number of young people, most of whom had migrated to this beautiful area in the back-to-the-land spirit of recent years." Murphy's rib baskets, recognized for the fancy braiding along the handle, basket edge, and bottom rib, were considered among the best of the Cannon County tradition. Her husband Willie Murphy, who made baskets infrequently, once had located and prepared the white oak for his wife's work. But as demand for Maggie's work increased, Willie let another neighbor, Howard Blair, supply the wood and then market the baskets. The Murphys produced generalized and special order baskets—she described her types as including bushel, round, feed, corn, egg, magazine, berry, cake, spring, half-wall (flat on the back to be hung on a wall), and toy baskets. She could weave two egg baskets a day.[14]

Maggie Murphy was not the only Cannon County maker training the next generation of basket makers. Trevle Wood taught the craft at the Campbell Folk School and at Arrowmont (she now lives in nearby Murfreesboro) while sisters Gertie and Mildred Youngblood have given lessons at the Evins Center for Appalachian Crafts. Josie Jones still makes and sells baskets from her home in Smithville. Now that the broader community is interested in their craft, the older basket makers eagerly pass on the art and necessity of basketmaking to younger generations. In 2002, for example, a group of Cannon County high school students who were collecting oral histories from older residents interviewed Gertie Youngblood—then in her mid-eighties—about her story and traditions of basketmaking. Interviews such as these, as well as the various arts programs, shape not only the lives of younger Tennesseans, but they also touch older Tennesseans who have always been intrigued by basketmaking. Jesse Butcher, a former game warden with

Fine Craft/Fine Art

THE STUDIO CRAFT MOVEMENT, WHICH HAS GROWN STEADILY SINCE THE BEGINNING OF THE TWENTIETH century, has become closely intertwined with the world of contemporary art during the last thirty years. Ask anyone at the leading craft museums and organizations in the United States, such as the American Craft Museum, The Renwick Gallery of the Smithsonian Museum of American Art, or the American Craft Council, to draw a line between craft and fine art, and they will do it only on the basis of the materials used. Artists working in the traditional materials of craft—wood, clay, metal, glass, or fiber—may be found showing at crafts fairs and craft museums if their technique is competent and their work convincingly executed. Craftspersons, once they have mastered a medium, are expanding their works into expressive original statements, which are happily welcomed by art galleries and art museums.

Dedicated craft schools, such as the Penland School of Crafts in North Carolina, the Haystack Mountain School of Crafts in Maine, and Tennessee's Arrowmont School of Arts and Crafts in Gatlinburg and the Appalachian Center for Crafts in Smithville, often employ visual artists, writers, and architects as instructors, and recruit their students equally from both the craft and art worlds.

Today's craft objects, once by definition utilitarian, now span the spectrum. While many are functional, based on traditional, handed-down design and technique, others are playful experiments in nonfunctional design that carry ironic commentaries on their former usefulness. Many craft objects have been admitted into the art world for the aesthetic pleasure of their materials: the brilliance and translucency of colored glass, the glitter of precious metals in clothing and jewelry, the exotic patterns and mirror-like surfaces of polished wood, or the astonishing variety of textures and dyeing techniques in fiber.

What is also true is that some of the most exciting and original art in the southeastern United States today involves the methods and materials of craft. The works of several outstanding Tennesseans exemplify this potent mixture of craft and art. Sculptor Lanie Gannon (Nashville) is a graduate of both the Memphis College of Art and the Appalachian Center for Crafts. Nationally recognized studio furnituremakers Rob Ogilvie (Nashville) and Craig Nutt (Kingston Springs) have put their woodworking skills to unusual purpose. Gannon's quirky and colorful figures and Nutt's humorous vegetable tables and chairs are virtuoso performances in smoothly planed and turned wood, while Ogilvie's material-led design has prompted his invention of new forms for tables, desks, and chairs.

Artists Richard Jolley (Knoxville) and Curtiss Brock (Smithville), pioneers in the field of American glass, have pursued separate paths to international recognition. Jolley's sensual forms in clear and colored glass range in size from tabletop to totem pole, embracing the classical nude, capturing the jaunty attitude of the baseball-cap-wearing male, and taking on existential and geopolitical issues. Brock's works encompass not only exemplary and showy blown glass vessels but also a serene "stone" series of rounded forms with pebbled textures that are like geodes whose rough exteriors have been sawn in half to reveal dazzling interiors penetrated by bold slashes of light. These artists, and many others currently living within Tennessee's borders, continue to forge ahead unbounded into new creative frontiers.

Susan W. Knowles, Pikeville, Tennessee

the Tennessee Game and Fish Commission, took classes from the Youngbloods at the Evins Center as part of his physical therapy from a terrible accident that almost cost him one of his hands. Today, Butcher gathers wood with another Union County basket maker, Ralph Chesney, and produces prize-winning rib baskets. Lonnie Taliaferro of Hawkins County learned basketmaking from older residents of his community and incorporates locally available materials such as grapevines, honeysuckle, and white oak into his wild plum hollow baskets.

No matter the age of the maker, the enduring values of basketmaking still permeate the craft traditions of Tennessee. To recognize the craft, and to continue the traditions, the Cannon County Arts Center hosts the White Oak Country Fair each August in Woodbury.

Notes

1. Allen H. Eaton, *Handicrafts of the Southern Highlands* (New York: Russell Sage Foundation, 1937), 168.
2. Charles Hudson, *The Southeastern Indians* (Knoxville: Univ. of Tennessee Press, 1976), 385.
3. Sam Venable, *Mountain Hands: A Portrait of Southern Appalachia* (Knoxville: Univ. of Tennessee Press, 2000), 88.
4. Sally Crain, "Handmade in Tennessee: Arts and Crafts in the Upper Cumberland," in *Lend an Ear: Heritage of the Tennessee Upper Cumberland,* ed. Calvin Dickinson, Homer Kemp, and Larry Whiteaker (Lanham, Md.: Univ. Press of America, 1983), 92.
5. Clara Hieronymus, "Maggie's Baskets," *Nashville Tennessean,* Nov. 18, 1973, p. E-3.
6. Rachel Nash Law and Cynthia W. Taylor, *Appalachian White Oak Basketmaking: Handing Down the Basket* (Knoxville: Univ. of Tennessee Press, 1991), 5.
7. Eaton, *Handicrafts of the Southern Highlands,* 170.
8. Huskey cited in Eaton, *Handicrafts of the Southern Highlands,* 170.
9. Thomas interview cited in Law and Taylor, *Appalachian White Oak Basketmaking,* 9.
10. Interview with Ida Pearl Davis by Thelma Hibdon, 1988, typescript copy provided to the author by Ida Pearl Davis and Thelma Hibdon. In the spirit of full disclosure, Mrs. Davis's late husband, Bill Davis, was a close friend of my father, W C West, as both grew up as neighbors in Cannon County.
11. Robert L. Mason, *History of Cannon County, Tennessee* (Woodbury, Tenn.: Cannon County Historical Society, 1984), 161.
12. *Cannon County, Tennessee: History and Families* (Paducah, Ky.: Turner Publishing, 1995), 105.
13. Quote given in booklet provided at the Governor's Awards ceremony by Tennessee Arts Commission, May 15, 2001, at the Ryman Auditorium, Nashville; also see Trish Milburn, "Weaving by Heart," *Tennessee Magazine* (Sept. 2001): 18–20; David LeDoux, "Proud to Make Good Baskets," *Cannon County Courier,* June 13, 1990, pp. 1–2; and Mary Ellen Glasco, "Ida Pearl Davis Weaves Baskets of Pride," *Tennessee Magazine* (Sept. 1989): 8–9, 20.
14. Hieronymus, "Maggie's Baskets," pp. E-1 and E-3.

Suggested Readings

Alexander, Lawrence. "Basketmakers of Cannon County: An Overview." Tennessee Folklore Society *Bulletin* 52, no. 4 (1987): 110–20.

Bullard, Helen. *Crafts and Craftsmen of the Tennessee Mountains.* Falls Church, Va.: Summit Press, 1976.

Duggan, Betty J., and Brett H. Riggs. *Studies in Cherokee Basketry.* Occasional Paper No. 9. Knoxville: Frank H. McClung Museum, 1991.

Eaton, Allen H. *Handicrafts of the Southern Highlands.* New York: Russell Sage Foundation, 1937.

Irwin, John R. *Baskets and Basket Makers in Southern Appalachia.* Exton, Pa.: Schiffer Press, 1982.

Law, Rachel Nash, and Cynthia W. Taylor. *Appalachian White Oak Basketmaking: Handing Down the Basket.* Knoxville: Univ. of Tennessee Press, 1991.

Leftwich, Rodney L. *Arts and Crafts of the Cherokee.* Cullowhee, N.C.: Western Carolina Univ., 1970.

Overcast, Roy M., Jr. "Basketmaking." In *Tennessee Encyclopedia of History and Culture,* edited by Carroll Van West, Connie L. Lester, Anne-Leslie Owens, and Margaret D. Binnicker, 49–50. Nashville: Tennessee Historical Society, 1998.

Venable, Sam. *Mountain Hands: A Portrait of Southern Appalachia.* Knoxville: Univ. of Tennessee Press, 2000.

Ten

Iron in a Golden Age
Ornamental Blacksmithy in Tennessee

F. Jack Hurley
The University of Memphis

In the myth that has developed concerning America's past we are led to assume that 150 years ago every community had its blacksmith who was capable of shoeing a horse or turning out a great wrought iron gate with equal ease. In fact, although blacksmiths were certainly common in Tennessee in the nineteenth century, they were practical men and few had either the time or the ability to turn out first-class ornamental work. Shoeing horses and sharpening plow points were far more familiar to them than any sort of "fancy work." The ironwork that decorates our antebellum homes was generally brought in from New Orleans, Charleston, Savannah, or even, in a few cases, Europe. Today there are more fine ornamental smiths working in the state than there were in Andrew Jackson's time.

The Nineteenth-Century Iron Industry

In the nineteenth century, Tennessee was a major iron-producing state, but the product was pig iron, a crude first-level refinement of iron that needed further

Hand-forged iron driveway gate in midtown Memphis. The gate was created by Jim Wallace, National Ornamental Metal Museum. Photograph by F. Jack Hurley.

work if it was to be of much use to anyone. Using a technology that had been worked out in Europe between about 1300 and 1650, Tennessee iron men built stone pyramids some thirty to thirty-five feet high with their hollow cores, shaped rather like an inverted bottle, lined in fire brick. These can still be seen in Stewart, Houston, and Montgomery Counties and in a few other parts of the state, mostly in Middle Tennessee. Often referred to as "hillside furnaces" they depended on manpower that toiled up the hills into which they were built and filled them from the top.

Early settlers recognized that Middle Tennessee had excellent deposits of iron ore. Gen. James Robertson built what was probably the first real iron-making operation in the area that would later become Dickson County in 1795. By 1802, Montgomery County had a furnace "in blast," and in 1820 Dover Furnace began operations in Stewart County. All of Tennessee's nineteenth-century ironworks hugged the river system. Without railroads or even roads worthy of the name, river transportation was a necessity.

Running a furnace was hard work. Ore had to be mined and crushed, as did limestone. Thousands of trees had to be felled and slow-burned to make charcoal. All this took dozens or in some cases hundreds of men. Most of these people were slaves. When it was time to put the furnace "in blast," workers filled the entire unit with some 250 bushels of charcoal, set the mass afire, and began pumping air into it with a water-powered bellows. The result was a very hot mass of burning material into which were introduced crushed iron ore and limestone. The iron ore and limestone melted and ran down through the burning charcoal, which was constantly replenished by workers. The molten limestone formed a flux that surrounded the iron ore, keeping oxygen out and cleansing it of impurities. Eventually everything gathered in the bottom of the "bottle" where the ironmaster could break a clay seal and allow the molten iron to run out into trenches that had been prepared in a deep sandy casting bed. Ironworkers called the main trench the "sow" and the smaller trenches that fed off from it "pigs." The metal held by each pig weighed about 150 pounds and was named "pig" as well. Once cooled, the pigs were broken in two, allowing graders to view their interior grain structure. These seventy-five pound pigs were a standard trade item and could easily be sold anywhere that iron was being finished into more refined forms.

By the mid-nineteenth century, Tennessee iron was highly regarded. It commanded good prices and made a few men very wealthy. Montgomery Bell's iron operations eventually grew to the point where he required the services of 332 slaves plus more than 100 free workers. Moving beyond mere production of pig iron, Bell re-refined the product into much more valuable bar iron that local and regional blacksmiths could "work up" into horseshoes, hinges, agricultural tools, and perhaps the occasional ornamental item. In fact, Bell even manufactured some of the cannon balls that Andrew Jackson used in the Battle of New Orleans! Other iron men created empires as large or larger than Bell's. By the 1850s, the Cumberland Iron Works in Stewart County, owned by Woods, Lewis and Company, was operating four furnaces and a rolling mill. They owned over fifty-one thousand acres of land and operated vast farms that fed and clothed a community of nearly three thousand people, both free and slave.

Most iron-making operations were smaller than Bell's or the Cumberland operation and most concentrated on the crude pig-iron product. A 1988 archaeological survey of Tennessee's primary iron-producing region, the Tennessee and Cumberland river valleys in the north-central part of the state, found thirty-four furnaces in 1854 operating in eight counties (although not all operated simultaneously). Some prospered, some struggled, but Tennessee furnaces smelted a lot of iron—until the Civil War.

As was the case in so many areas, the war changed everything. The capture of Forts Henry on the Tennessee River and Donelson on the Cumberland was a tremendous blow to the iron industry, since it cut them off from their only practical means of transportation, the river route north to the Ohio.

The Western Highland Rim Iron Industry

The manufacture of iron in America predated settlement of the Middle South, and eighteenth-century Pennsylvania iron production, in particular, had a major influence on developments in Tennessee. Though some of the earliest iron furnaces were in upper East Tennessee, the longest and most unified regional industry was in Tennessee's Western Highland Rim. A 1980s survey of this industry found and recorded most of the sites for sixty-one furnaces, thirty-three forges, two rolling mills, two foundries, and one nail making operation. This same study identified thirty-four still-standing buildings constructed for some purpose directly associated with the Western Highland Rim iron industry.

Tombstone of Stephen Eleazer, Dickson County. The tombstone's relief carving is of a furnace stack with attached bridge house and casting shed and shows that Eleazer died July 6, 1835, at age thirty-five. Photograph by Samuel D. Smith. Courtesy of the Tennessee Division of Archaeology

Iron making in the Western Highland Rim began with the mid-1790s construction of Cumberland Furnace, which grew into the town of the same name in Dickson County. Iron manufacture continued at Cumberland Furnace into the 1930s, undergoing several phases of technological change. A majority of the early furnaces were located in Stewart, Montgomery, Dickson, and Hickman Counties. These were large pyramidal-shaped stone structures set in an operating context that included numerous buildings and sometimes thousands of acres of land from which the necessary raw materials were obtained. They were cold-blast charcoal furnaces that used a mixture of iron ore, charcoal, and a fluxing agent such as limestone to produce pig iron and a variety of cast iron products. Initially the industry depended on water-powered devices, but by the mid-nineteenth century, steam power was used for purposes such as supplying blast to the furnaces. Following the Civil War, Western Highland Rim furnaces became increasingly mechanized and dependent on railways for transporting raw materials and products. By the late nineteenth to early twentieth century, only a few still operated, but these were highly productive, hot-blast furnaces that, instead of charcoal, used coke made from East Tennessee coal. Though demand for Western Highland Rim pig iron remained strong during the early 1900s, unfavorable economic factors forced the closing of most operations by the 1920s. The industry was essentially dead by the 1940s.

While early Western Highland Rim furnaces were sometimes used for the direct production of cast iron items such as kitchenware and architectural components, their main product was bars of cast pig iron. Pig iron was too brittle to be used without further refinement, and in the

[Continued on next page]

Western Highland Rim it was often reprocessed in a refinery forge. These produced malleable wrought iron, which was then used by blacksmiths and others to make a multitude of every day farm and household items. During the first half of the nineteenth century, refinery forges became increasingly common, with the greatest number operating in the 1830s and 1840s. Few Western Highland Rim forges resumed operation after the Civil War, and all of them were gone by the 1880s.

Pig iron could also be made into other products by other means, including reprocessing in foundries. There were few foundries in the Western Highland Rim, but after the Civil War Nashville became a major center for such operations. Here large quantities of iron, much of it from the Western Highland Rim, were cast into many different kinds of household items, farm implements, and architectural materials. The latter ranged from purely functional objects, such as door parts, to elaborate decorative structures, such as cast iron garden fountains.

Throughout its history there was a degree of overlap between the functional aspects of the Western Highland Rim iron industry and the artistic and decorative aspects of its implements and products. Some furnace structures were works of great aesthetic appeal, with fine quality stonework, to which some builders added carved stone embellishments. One striking piece of "folk art" on the upper front surface of Bear Spring Furnace in Stewart County includes the incised name of the 1870s owner "WOODS, YEATMAN, & CO," a relief carving of a bear followed by the word "SPRING," an incised carving of a rifle and powder horn, some other decorative elements, and the names of the furnace superintendent and architect. The 1980s survey encountered a number of cemeteries where Western Highland Rim iron makers are buried, and some of these exhibit interesting interplays between decorative work in iron and stone. Some graves have elaborate stone and cast iron, fence-like enclosures. A number of iron master tombstones bear carved images of furnaces. The one shown marks the Dickson County grave of Stephen Eleazer. It has a relief carving of a furnace stack with attached bridge house and casting shed and shows that the deceased "Died July 6, 1835—Aged 35 Years."

Samuel D. Smith, Tennessee Division of Archaeology

Lacking railroad connections, most of the furnaces were forced to close. The end of slavery destroyed a major competitive advantage that southern iron men had enjoyed over their northern counterparts. To make matters worse, northern iron men like Andrew Carnegie were learning to use highly efficient new methods such as the Bessemer and open-hearth processes to manufacture tremendous amounts of steel, a stronger product than either the cast or wrought iron that the southerners were still trying to make. As a result, the southerners were forced to the wall. By the end of the 1870s, most Tennessee furnaces were cold. While a few held on as late as the 1920s, finding small niche markets that needed their products, the last indigenous iron-making operation in Tennessee was gone by 1927.

The last third of the nineteenth century was not an easy time for many Tennesseans. The end of the Civil War brought a period of readjustment during which money tended to be in short supply and credit expensive. Memphis went bankrupt in 1879 as a result of bad management and the infamous yellow fever epidemics of the decade. Other cities, Nashville included, found themselves struggling. Both cities saw the building of stately homes, but far fewer than would come a generation later and, as before the war, opportunities

Left: Half of Philip Kerrigan's inner gates at Cheekwood, Nashville. The gates show the traditional scrolls and acanthus leaves that Kerrigan favored. Photograph by F. Jack Hurley.

Below: Side panel detail of Cheekwood inner gates. Photograph by F. Jack Hurley.

for local ornamental smiths were thin on the ground. Victorians loved ornate cast iron but were unwilling to pay the considerably higher cost of employing a skilled smith to create beautiful ironwork by hand and eye.

This situation began to change shortly after the turn of the twentieth century. The first two decades brought good times for many. Agriculture was more profitable than it had been in a generation, and money flowed from the farms to the cities of Tennessee. With money in their pockets, well-off Tennesseans read about the Arts and Crafts movement and found in it much to admire. The first generation of well-informed professional architects developed to serve the needs of the affluent. By the 1920s, in Nashville, the development of an appreciation for good, European-based design gave rise to some of the finest handmade art-smithing available in the United States.

KERRIGAN IRON WORKS

Middle Tennesseans learned to love fine art metal-smithing from Philip Kerrigan Jr. His story comes close to the classic American version of "rags to riches." Born in Nashville in 1904 into a large Irish Catholic

Kerrigan at Cheekwood

PHILIP KERRIGAN ACCEPTED A CHALLENGING task when Bryant Fleming offered him the commission for a new Belle Meade estate, Cheekwood. Fleming had proposed an ambitious English Georgian estate as the residence of Leslie and Mabel Cheek of Nashville. The Cheeks provided Fleming with extensive funds and one hundred pristine acres of woodland in Harpeth Hills. Although Fleming intended to purchase antique architectural elements, he relied on regional craftsmen for work exclusive to the house and gardens. He charged Kerrigan to create interior and exterior ironwork in the eighteenth-century style. In a few years, The Forges of Kerrigan fashioned a range of ornamental iron at Cheekwood that secured Philip Kerrigan's reputation as a master of the craft.

Construction started in 1929 as Fleming and the Cheeks finished a buying trip through Great Britain. They returned with railroad cars of treasures such as doors, mantels, and some ironwork. These pieces perhaps served as design inspiration for Kerrigan; however, other sources existed. In the early twentieth century, the English Georgian style underwent a revival throughout England and America.

Cheekwood's Queen Charlotte staircase, c. 1934, by Philip Kerrigan. Courtesy of Cheekwood Museum of Art, Nashville, Tennessee.

family of limited means, young Philip irritated the nuns at his school by constantly sketching during class. At age eighteen, however, he put his artistic impulses to use, becoming a mechanical draftsman at a local engineering company that did some ornamental ironwork. While at the Englert Engineering Company, Kerrigan worked on the side gates to St. Mary's Church and the ornamental iron detailing for Nashville's Far Hills estate, which now serves as the Governor's residence.

In 1929, at age twenty-five, Kerrigan borrowed $1,700 and went into business for himself. What began as an enterprise with three employees employed over five hundred by 1950 and became one of the largest metal companies in the South with a value of over $10 million in 1958. As is often the case, a combination of luck, good timing, and very hard work brought about this pattern of impressive growth.

The stock market crash of 1929 rocked the nation, but it took another year for hard times to reach Tennessee. In Nashville, there was money, both inherited and made, and that money stretched farther than it had ever done before. People with money could afford to build, and they could afford to ornament their homes and office buildings with hand wrought art-smithing. The 1930s became the great

Magazines and books promoted it with large photographic essays of old and new houses. Tunstall Small and Christopher Woodbridge's *Houses of the Wren and Early Georgian Period*, published in 1928, provided photographs and measured drawings of ironwork.

With antique ironwork and historical publications, Kerrigan reproduced objects with the Georgian language of scrolls, leaves, and classical symbols. For the mansion, Kerrigan manufactured two staircases. The first staircase dominates the two-story entrance. Cast iron eagles alternate with classical lyres as faceted pineapples link them to the brass handrail. The effect is massive, a definite contrast to the delicate scrolls and leaves of Kerrigan's second staircase. Named Queen Charlotte's staircase, tradition maintains that Kerrigan reproduced it with antique pieces from her palace near London. Installed below a rotunda, it is a spiral of open urn shapes in wrought iron.

For the terraced gardens, Kerrigan executed numerous ornaments ranging from simple iron railings to cast balustrades of heavy acanthus leaves. Ornate lampposts, constructed of perpendicular panels, line the drive to the mansion. Intricate grills protect the windows on the ground floor and a shallow balcony extends from the large Palladian window above.

Kerrigan's Wisteria Arbor is the iron masterpiece at Cheekwood. It skillfully combines knowledge of materials with sensitivity to aesthetic effect. From the mansion, glass doors open onto this stone balcony. Overhead, a vault of iron spans the entire space, creating the frame for a roof of wisteria. At its end, a panel bears an open globe flanked by two heraldic devices with ancient gods and winged dragons. The arbor commands a vital position in Fleming's landscape design as a transition between house and garden. From its wall, a view runs over a pool, another Kerrigan balustrade, through an allée, and into Warner Park.

Kerrigan's ornamental iron at Cheekwood explores fully the vocabulary of Georgian ironwork. It testifies not only to his skill in design but also to Kerrigan's absolute mastery of and passion for his craft.

Lisa A. Porter, Cheekwood Museum of Art

era of growth for the "Forges of Kerrigan." Sometime during the 1920s Kerrigan met and became friends with Nashville architect, Bryant Fleming. It was a symbiotic relationship. Fleming admired Kerrigan's commitment to high quality craftsmanship and design while Kerrigan later acknowledged that Fleming had taught him the importance of closely observing nature and had introduced him to historical European traditions in ironwork.

The Belle Meade section of Nashville was filling with great estates during the 1930s, and the team of Fleming and Kerrigan worked on many of them. One of the best places to see Kerrigan's work today is at Cheekwood, the great estate of the Cheek family on the edge of Belle Meade. Now open to the public as a museum and botanical garden, Cheekwood is also a virtual catalogue of Kerrigan's ideas concerning design in iron. The undulating lines and natural motifs of acanthus leaves, vines, and flowers can be seen in the great gates that lead to the inner gardens. Beautiful use of scrolls and geometrical forms are featured in the exterior light fixtures. The bannister to the great stairway in the entrance hall uses a combination of wrought iron and cast brass to dramatic effect.

Philip Kerrigan exterior lamp stand, Cheekwood, Nashville. Note the strong nineteenth-century French influence on Kerrigan's work. Photograph by F. Jack Hurley.

Due to Fleming's influence, Kerrigan's work was always couched firmly within traditional European styles. This was art for affluent customers who had been abroad and had come to associate what they had seen in Paris and London with "high culture." In a 1930 issue of *Southern Architect and Building News,* a monthly journal steeped in the Arts and Crafts movement, Helen Dahnke saluted the young Nashvillian whose work was having such a powerful impact on regional architecture. "He is the center of a real revival in Tennessee of old wrought iron arts," she wrote. "Today Nashville architects and others of an ever-widening territory look to him with increasing respect. They know that for an intimate bit of detail they are executing for a discriminating client, he may be depended upon to supply an authentic and artistic piece of work."[1] Two years later, in the same journal, an artist named A. C. Webb Jr. added to the contemporary praise for Kerrigan's craftsmanship: "The hand-wrought iron of Philip Kerrigan, Jr. is not inferior to that of . . . the grills and screens made by those master craftsmen of the Middle Ages. . . . It was a revelation to me to see wrought iron of such beauty being produced here in New America, and a further revelation that his work is appreciated to the extent that his forges at Nashville are being kept constantly busy."[2]

By the late 1930s Bryant Fleming and Philip Kerrigan were receiving commissions in Memphis, Louisville, Kentucky, and as far away as the affluent community of Grosse Point, Michigan. Always, however, the bulk of their work was in Middle Tennessee, and it is here that Kerrigan's influence on public taste in ironwork has been the most lasting.

With the coming of World War II the whole nature of Kerrigan's business changed. By the end of 1942 he was making landing mats for airstrips for the

Army Corps of Engineers. Roll wire mesh was turned out for the Navy and large orders of pontoons were fabricated for the Bureau of Yards and Docks. Kerrigan Iron Works (as it was now known) built ship mast booms for the Navy, large truck cabs and even locomotive cabs for the Army's Ordinance Department, plus many miles of welded flat sheets of wire for the Seabees. None of this material was in the least "ornamental" but that did not matter. There was a war to be won and men who knew how to work iron on a fairly large scale found plenty to do. When the war ended, Kerrigan faced the challenge of reconversion to a peacetime economy in which returning his business to an art-smithing shop offered poor prospects. Although Kerrigan Iron would continue to do some ornamental work on a small, special order basis, for the country as a whole, and for the southern region, architectural tastes were changing. By the late 1940s the International School of architecture with its emphasis on the unadorned white box was becoming dominant. The influence of this style only intensified in the 1950s and 1960s. Work for the ornamental smith virtually disappeared. Kerrigan's company manufactured steel grating and bridge floors.

Kerrigan's own taste remained wedded to historic European styles, however. When he built his own estate, Longacres, in 1947, he designed and had the specialty shop build a beautiful gateway and other architectural details that many consider his finest work. Just over ten years later, in 1958, Phillip Kerrigan Jr. died at age fifty-four. A revival of interest in fine art metalsmithing eventually emerged, but a virtual vacuum for architectural blacksmithy existed for thirty years after Kerrigan's death. The demand for art-blacksmithy did not reappear until the late twentieth century.

Herndon and Merry

William Merry, of the firm of Herndon and Merry in Nashville, understood these realities very well. His own shop, which opened in 1959, the year after Kerrigan's death, took in all sorts of work in the early days but specialized in carports and patio shelters made with welded tubing and featuring cast iron ornamentation. No one would have ever accused these projects of being art or even high craft, but they were what the market demanded in the 1960s, 1970s, and even the 1980s. "Those carports put food on my table and educated my children," Merry recalls. In the early 1990s, however, Merry began to sense a change in public taste. He knew that a few specialized shops, such as that of the National Ornamental Metal Museum in Memphis, were getting orders for fine gates and railings, and he realized that the handmade market was coming alive again: "We started advertising a better line of iron work in *Southern Accents* and, later, *Veranda* magazines and all sorts of requests for literature began arriving in the mail."[3]

During the last decade, Merry, with the help of his sons Bill Jr., Kevin, and Keith, has transformed the firm of Herndon and Merry into the logical successor of The Forges of Kerrigan, as that firm operated in the 1930s. Today two in-house blacksmiths are kept busy, and Randy Jacoby, a fine Middle Tennessee smith, is employed as a subcontractor to do much of the hand detailing for which Herndon and Merry has become known in the Middle and East Tennessee regions. Merry acknowledges his aesthetic debt to Kerrigan and to Kerrigan's European influences: "Oh yes indeed, we like Philip's work and our customers like his work. He knew about Europe's ironworking traditions and we do too. I go to Europe and take hundreds of pictures. When I can show a prospective customer a balcony from Vienna and tell him, 'we can make you one just like this,' they love it."[4]

The firm of Herndon and Merry has dressed the homes of some of Nashville's most affluent entertainers, among them Eddy Arnold, Crystal Gayle, and Waylon Jennings. But in recent years, the middle Merry son, Keith, has executed some of the most interesting work in the firm. With formal training in interior design, Keith Merry has founded his own company, Garden Park Antiques, and has pioneered

Andirons made at Cumberland Homesteads, Crossville. Photograph by Ben Shahn, 1937. Courtesy of Library of Congress, Prints & Photographs Division, Farm Security Administration–Office of War Information Photograph Collection (reproduction number LC-USF33-006259-M3 DLC).

in readapting bits and pieces of fine antique European and American ironwork to stunning new uses that are popular in national markets.

Jim Wallace and the National Ornamental Metal Museum

There are many reasons why fine art-smithing has become a favorite way of decorating both the exteriors and the interiors of our homes and public buildings in recent years. Increased affluence has made the higher costs of good work affordable, and the public has become tired of the unadorned-white-box style of architecture demanded by the International School. At the same time some taste-makers have also worked hard for the past twenty years to change public tastes and bring back fine art-smithy. One of the key people in the hand wrought-iron revival in Tennessee is Jim "Wally" Wallace of the National Ornamental Metal Museum in Memphis.

Although he has lived in the South for the last generation, Jim Wallace is a midwesterner, born in Rapid City, South Dakota, in 1947. He grew up as an Army brat, moving around the country and even Europe, but home was always the family ranch in South Dakota and nearly every summer was spent there. By the time he was in college at Western State College in Gunnison, Colorado, he was fascinated with blacksmithy and had apprenticed himself to a local smith who sported the intensely western name of "Slim" Sperling. A degree in engineering won Wallace a series of jobs in deep mines in northwestern Colorado, but hitting iron had become his passion. "I would come home to my little house at Crested Butte and go out to my little blacksmith shop in the alley and work away," he recalled. "It was a great time to be working because nobody in Crested Butte cared who you were—only what you could do."[5]

Wallace met Francis Whitacre, one of the genuine legends of twentieth-century fine-art blacksmithing, who was working in the then small town of Vail, Colorado, and Wallace began to make contact with the tiny handful of men scattered around the country still forging iron into wonderful shapes by hand. In 1974, after meeting Brent Kington, Wallace's work took a new direction. Kington, a professor of art at Southern Illinois University at Carbondale, was a trained metalsmith who had studied at Cranbrook Academy in Detroit, Michigan, one of the great centers of the Arts and Crafts movement in the United States. Kington invited Wallace to Carbondale and a few months later, Jim found himself in southern Illinois. "I talked to Brent and saw his shop," Wallace explains. "There wasn't a whole lot to see. Basically it was a little room in a basement. They had a twenty-five pound Little Giant trip hammer that was 'beat up' and not running too well and some forges and not much else. But they were nice people there and I enjoyed talking to them and of course Brent was doing work that I was interested in. Frankly, at that stage I was a far better smith than he was, but I knew there were things I could learn from him."[6]

Wallace completed a master's in fine arts (MFA) degree at Carbondale in 1978. The next year he was invited to Memphis to become the director of the National Ornamental Metal Museum, which was in the process of being established. Becoming the director of a brand new, fiercely underfunded museum had its good and bad points. The good part was that Wallace was able to start with a clean slate and build the museum in his own unique way; the bad part was that the museum had few financial resources. To make ends meet, Wallace established a blacksmith shop in a miserable shack on the museum's grounds. There, with the help of an apprentice named Mike Weeks, he began building beautiful architectural iron in a style that was different from anything anyone in Tennessee had seen before. His gates did not contain recognizable acanthus leaves or even the sort of regular scrolls that had been imported from Europe to Middle Tennessee. Influenced as much by modern jewelry makers as by traditional ironwork, Wallace's work might fairly be described as organic but not specific. Using fairly heavy dimensions of iron and powerful mechanical hammers Wallace pounded and twisted iron into shapes that suggested the Art Nouveau style and yet also made a modern statement.

By pricing his work initially at or below costs, patrons were found and Wallace gates began to appear around Memphis. Today the National Ornamental Metal Museum continues to train fine smiths as well as to contribute to its own support through sales of its apprentices' work at the museum shop. Because of Wallace's influence, the ironwork of Memphis has a distinctly different look from that of Middle or East Tennessee. There are fewer traditional, European influenced scrolls and acanthus leaves and more rough-formed S curves and smooth, contrasting tendrils. Other art-smithy shops are open and functioning in the Memphis area, helping to meet the growing demand for fine work. Brian Russell, as much a sculptor as a blacksmith, lives near Arlington, Tennessee, where his interests have led him into woodworking as well as metalworking and even casting of glass. Jerry Cuillard, former artist-in-residence at the Metal Museum, keeps from three to ten employees busy doing a broad assortment of metal work that ranges from tall, thin candlesticks to large railings and staircases. Russell's work is strongly modern while Cuillard's runs the gamut from modern to traditional. Other smiths such as Tim and Jill Brogdan, with their shop in the rapidly redeveloping South Main area of Memphis, specialize in furniture and lighting fixtures in styles ranging from traditional to modern. California-trained Jill Brogdan acknowledges the role of Wallace and the Metal Museum: "There is no question that Wally and the Museum have made my work here possible."[7]

Wallace's influence extends beyond the Memphis area. In 1981, as a young geology student at Tennessee Technological University, Ray Spiller saw Wallace demonstrate basic blacksmithing techniques at the nearby Joe L. Evins Appalachian Center for Crafts and was hooked for life on blacksmithing. "I went down there and fell in love with it," he recalls. "I was worthless as a geologist after that." Spiller worked with Herndon and Merry for a while in the 1980s and then went into business for himself, doing contract work for another large commercial iron company, Tennessee Iron Works of Clarksville. Today Spiller lives north of Nashville where he operates the Mount Sharon Forge, specializing in beautiful floral and bird motifs. Spiller's love for flowers is reflected in his careful attention to detail. He insists on hand forging every detail of this work, even leaves, in order to avoid the "cookie cutter" look of die-cut materials.[8]

It is significant that when Ray Spiller wanted to learn about ironwork, he went to the Joe L. Evins Appalachian Center for Crafts, where Bob Coogan is the resident expert in metal work. With an MFA from the Cranbrook Academy of Art, Coogan has the training to match his inclination to work on the cutting edge of metalsmithing. Some of his work is large, as in the case of a beautiful stone and iron bench that he recently completed. Some of it is as small as a pocket knife. In between he has experimented with raised vessels in such materials as silver, copper, and mokume gane, a spectacular material developed in Japan through the fusion of copper, brass, and silver. Most of his knives sport

National Ornamental Metal Museum

THE NATIONAL ORNAMENTAL METAL MUSEUM, LOCATED JUST SOUTH OF DOWNTOWN MEMPHIS and directly across from the Chickasaw Heritage Park, is a collection of classically structured buildings comprising the former U.S. Marine hospital. The massive pair of entry gates designed by Richard Quinnell of Surrey, England, in the traditional Renaissance style commemorates the museum's tenth anniversary in 1989. Comprised of repeated S scrolls, the gate's design suggests the inclusive approach of the museum. Each scroll terminates in a rosette unique to the artist who created it, and 180 smiths from eighteen nations donated both scrolls and rosettes.

Tenth Anniversary Gates. Dedicated on May 3, 1979, these gates were designed by Richard Quinell of Surrey, England. Courtesy of the National Ornamental Metal Museum, Memphis.

The Memphis chapter of the National Ornamental and Miscellaneous Metals Association proposed an industry museum in 1975, and a year later a charter was filed in the state of Tennessee. The property in Memphis was located, and the museum doors opened in 1979. On entering the grounds the first of four buildings is the gallery, where changing exhibitions feature both historic and contemporary metal work. The range of exhibitions illustrates that idea of inclusion. From classic exhibitions of silver and gold jewelry and hollowware to *Pig Iron: Art Cookers,* celebrating the American art of barbecue, exhibits encompass every aspect of the field. The gallery also hosts exhibitions organized by other museums.

Under the guidance of its director, Jim Wallace, the museum has grown and prospered. Its unique focus on ironwork of all kinds ranges from architectural work to swords. While serving the field by covering the entire range of metal work, the museum always returns to its focus on iron. A grant from Schering-Plough transformed one structure into a proper working blacksmith's shop and demonstration facility. Now one of the finest-working smithies in the country open to the public, the facility is used for classes, demonstrations, and staff projects and also houses a restoration lab.

The hard work of the museum staff, volunteers, and artist-craftsmen to improve the facilities and give back to the Memphis community that supports them is typified in the annual fundraiser known as Repair Days. One featured artist mounts a solo exhibition and gives a lecture open to the community. Then for three days more than fifty metalsmiths work as volunteers repairing treasures brought in by the public. Many of the metal artists have traveled distances at their own expense in order to participate and give back to a museum that has done so much for their field. Visitors are invited to walk around the tents and work areas to ask questions as the work is being done on almost any form of metal that passes through the gates.

Robert Coogan, Tennessee Technological University Appalachian Center for Crafts beautiful damascus steel blades, made by folding and welding two different steels together into patterns. Coogan learned the techniques of making damascus blades back in 1979, in Vail, Colorado, at a class taught by Jim Wallace. The two men have been friends ever since. For Coogan, however, the main emphasis of his professional life has been teaching. "I teach everything from small-scale jewelry to blacksmithing and hollow ware, and I also teach three dimensional design," he notes. He insists that his students be exposed to a wide variety of techniques:

> All my students take everything. If they want to be a jeweler they still have to take blacksmithing and if they want to be a blacksmith they take jewelry making. It offers a better range of possibilities. The blacksmith learns that he can do more detailed work and the jeweler learns hand-eye skills, especially with the hammer. It offers potential that these people don't know they have. A good eye for design is important and in some cases it may be all you need, but if you have knowledge of lots of different techniques, maybe you can combine them and find that unique sphere that is yours.[9]

Robert Coogan demonstrates hammer planishing techniques for two students during the 1999 Repair Days event at the National Ornamental Metal Museum, Memphis. Photograph by F. Jack Hurley.

Pulpit, Ascension Episcopal Church, Knoxville. Crozier and pulpit handrail balusters by Charlie Fuller, Broken Anvil Forge. Photograph by F. Jack Hurley.

Above: Steven Williamson, president of the Appalachian Chapter of the Artist Blacksmiths Association of North America and a skilled amateur smith, demonstrates the technique of hand-forging a baroque dragon's head. Photograph by F. Jack Hurley.

Top: Dale Davis works 1020 hot roll metal in Manchester, Coffee County. Photograph by Jennifer C. Core, 2001. Courtesy of TAC.

Coogan's students participate in the annual "Repair Days" at the National Ornamental Metal Museum in Memphis. Along with smiths and students from as far away as Detroit, St. Louis, and Carbondale, he and his students tackle an amazing variety of problems brought in for repair and/or restoration. "You come in contact with so many different problems," Coogan asserts. "I mean, I've done things at Repair Days that I was told in graduate school could not be done. Solder pot metal? They tell you it can't be done but it is done all the time at Repair Days."[10]

One of the interesting things about fine blacksmithy in Tennessee is the network that has developed within the field. Bob Coogan in Smithville and Jim Wallace in Memphis are good friends and between the two of them they know practically everyone in the field in the state. This has promoted the free exchange of information. If a church group in West Tennessee needed some beautiful iron detailing for their sanctuary, Wallace often put them in touch with Charlie

Fuller, outside Pigeon Forge, who was known for some of the finest liturgical work in the state. Fuller, a self-taught smith from Florida who died in 2001, became so caught up in his work with churches around the state and around the country that he went back to school and completed a ministry education program at the University of the South at Sewanee. Fuller's shop utilized tools from the most traditional to very modern. The work rivals Kerrigan's best.

In addition to the many professional smiths discussed in this chapter, Tennessee is studded with amateur blacksmiths, many of whom are astonishingly good. One count in 2000 of known amateur and professional smiths in the state listed 156 names, but that may not represent a comprehensive tally. The Artist Blacksmith Association of North America (ABANA) is active in the state and forms a meeting point for amateurs and professionals. Networking, sharing ideas and techniques, helping each other over the rough spots, blacksmiths and ornamental metal workers in Tennessee continue to work within and enlarge a tradition of iron making and ironworking that began two hundred years ago. No longer is pig iron wrestled from the hills of Middle Tennessee by slave labor. But hard, hot work involving muscle and, most of all, the human eye and heart does go on in what may well turn out to be the golden age of fine art-blacksmithy in Tennessee.

Notes

1. Helen Dahnke, "Hand Wrought Iron: Exemplifying the Work of Philip Kerrigan, Jr.," *Southern Architect and Building News* (Oct. 1930): 37.
2. Webb is cited in Elizabeth R. Cunningham, "The Art of Philip Kerrigan, Jr.," *1994 Antiques and Garden Show of Nashville,* pamphlet (Nashville, 1994), 38–39.
3. Bill Merry, interview with the author, Jan. 14, 2000, Nashville. Notes in possession of the author.
4. Mary Hance, "Old Bridge Getting New Life in Furniture," *Nashville Banner,* Sept. 15, 1990, p. D-1; "Ironwork's Restored and Put to Use in Nashville," *Knoxville News Sentinel,* Nov. 1, 1992, p. E-11; "Nashville's Garden Park Antiques," *Colonial Homes,* June 1996, 70–73; Liz Seymour, "Salvage Connoisseur: Alchemist of Style," *Renovation Style,* Spring 1996, 24–28.
5. James Wallace, interview with the author, Jan. 6, 2000, Memphis. Notes in possession of the author.
6. Ibid.
7. Jill Brogdan, interview with the author, Jan. 21, 2000, Memphis. Notes in possession of the author.
8. Raymond Spiller, interview with the author, Nov. 17, 1999. Notes in possession of the author.
9. Robert Coogan, interview with the author, Dec. 13, 1999. Notes in possession of the author.
10. Ibid.

Suggested Readings

Bining, Arthur C. *Pennsylvania Iron Manufacturing in the Eighteenth Century.* Harrisburg: Pennsylvania Historical Commission, 1938.

Carpenter, Jim, and Daniel Schaffer, eds. *Tennessee's Iron Industry Revisited: The Stewart County Story.* TVA's Land Between the Lakes Cultural Resources Program, n.d.

Dalton, Robert E. "Montgomery Bell and the Narrows of Harpeth." *Tennessee Historical Quarterly* 35 (Spring 1976): 3–28.

Dew, Charles B. *Bond of Iron: Master and Slave at Buffalo Forge.* New York: W. W. Norton, 1994.

Smith, Samuel D., Charles P. Stripling, and James M. Brannon. *Tennessee's Western Rim Iron Industry: A Cultural Resource Survey.* Research Series No. 8. Nashville: Tennessee Department of Conservation, Division of Archaeology, 1988.

Vlach, John M. *Charleston Blacksmith: The Work of Philip Simmons.* Columbia: Univ. of South Carolina Press, 1992.

Watson, Aldren A. *The Blacksmith: Ironworker and Farrier.* New York: W. W. Norton, 1990.

Eleven

Tennessee Silversmiths

Benjamin H. Caldwell Jr.
Nashville

From the earliest of times and in most ancient societies, people have made and prized vessels and ornaments of gold and silver. However, history has not been kind to the people who have come to Tennessee to practice the craft of silversmithing, leaving their records hard to locate and their achievements difficult to assess.

Silversmiths from Statehood to 1850

The Territory South of the Ohio River (1790–96) contained the area that is known now as Tennessee. William Bean and Lydia Russell Bean settled with their young son, George, at "Bean's Station" in Hawkins County (later Grainger County) at a place where the Baltimore-Nashville and Louisville-Charleston Roads crossed. George Bean would be Tennessee's first silversmith. He advertised in 1792 his services as goldsmith, jeweler, and gunsmith. His services as gunsmith were probably more useful to him than silversmithing, as there was little need for large amounts of silver, sitting on the table or sideboards to impress the guests of their wealth and importance as had been done in Boston, New York, Philadelphia, and Charleston for the previous 150 years. At the same time, there were no banks in which to put accumulated wealth, so silver often was made into useful objects, marked by the maker, engraved with the owner's initials, and therefore not very negotiable for any thieves. Tennessee was then a frontier with little place for grandiosity.

Above: Hallmark on tablespoon, "R.T.," c. 1825, Knoxville. Photograph courtesy of the Museum of Early Southern Decorative Arts, Winston-Salem, North Carolina. Courtesy of Benjamin H. Caldwell Jr.

Left: Punch ladle marked "F. H. Clark & Co., 1855" and engraved "Bankhead," Memphis. Photograph courtesy of the Museum of Early Southern Decorative Arts, Winston-Salem, North Carolina. Courtesy of Benjamin H. Caldwell Jr.

Andrew Jackson and Silver

ANDREW JACKSON WAS BORN MARCH 15, 1767, INTO A POOR FAMILY OF SCOTS-IRISH DESCENT IN the Waxhaw settlement in western Carolina. The available inventories from that time of families similar to his show little, if any, silver in their possession. Jackson would have grown up eating from a spoon made either of horn or, at most, from pewter. Still, Jackson was literate and attended a school conducted by Dr. William Humphreys. In 1784 Jackson moved to Salisbury, North Carolina, and read law under prominent attorneys Spruce McKay and John Stokes. As a young man, Jackson associated with people of wealth and education, just as he had when residing with a family in Charleston, South Carolina, after his mother's death in 1781. Licensed in law in September 1787, he almost immediately was appointed public prosecutor for the Mero District of Tennessee, with Nashville as its only town.

One of a pair of candelabra that Tammany Hall presented Andrew Jackson during his presidency. These were later given by Jackson to Andrew Jackson Donelson. Courtesy of Benjamin H. Caldwell Jr.

Jackson has often been presented as a pioneering, rough and ready individual who let few people tread on him. He was aggressive and raucous; he dueled. Jackson met the challenges of a frontier society, but he wanted more, and as he advanced in positions of power so did his material holdings. Elected to the U.S. House of Representatives in 1796, Jackson was then elected to the U.S. Senate to replace the impeached William Blount in 1797. During these few years in Philadelphia Jackson probably purchased the first silver—a tea set made by A. Dubois—for his home.

In 1804, he formed a business partnership with John Coffee and John Hutchings. They operated a mercantile store in the vicinity of Jackson's log home, The Hermitage. Agents in Philadelphia and New Orleans supplied the store's needs, and Jackson must have been aware of the decorative pieces available in china and silver. Seven teaspoons and a pair of sugar tongs by Nashville's first silversmith, Joseph Thorp Elliston, and now in The Hermitage collection, no doubt were made to go with the tea service Jackson had purchased while in Congress.

Rachel Donelson Jackson had some formal education and was probably at ease serving tea. She succeeded at running a complicated household during her husband's absences. The Jacksons' next major silver purchase came in 1816 when they purchased two punch ladles made by Nashville silversmiths Richmond and Flint who came to Nashville in 1816 from Providence, Rhode Island. In July 1821, President James Monroe appointed Jackson territorial governor of Florida. While traveling to his post, Jackson purchased from Anthony Rasch in New Orleans a coin silver ladle as well as a large old Sheffield caster.

The inventories of homes in Tennessee between 1810 and 1825 list very little silver. Even a man as wealthy as John Overton had much less silver than Jackson, in part because people trying to honor Jackson often gave him silver. The state of South Carolina presented him a

[Continued on next page]

large trophy made by Fletcher and Gardiner of Philadelphia. Jackson's will returned this fine example of the silversmith's art to South Carolina after his death, and it resides in Columbia at the state capitol.

After an unsuccessful bid for the presidency in 1824, Jackson was elected president of the United States in November 1828. During his eight years at the White House, Jackson possibly added more silver to the president's house than any individual before him. In fact, of all the presidents, Monroe, Jackson, and John F. Kennedy made the most important additions to the silver collection of the White House. Jackson acquired approximately a thousand pieces of silver, mainly through a purchase from the Baron de Twyll, the Russian ambassador to the United States, that consisted of many pieces of flatware as well as hollowware, decanter stands, covered dishes, tea pots, castors, and plateaus. Over six hundred pieces are still in existence. Jackson also purchased silver for himself from Stephen Decatur's widow, who lived nearby the White House. Several of these covered dishes remain at The Hermitage, and one is in the Smithsonian's holdings.

Tammany Hall gave Jackson a pair of large candelabra. Used at the White House and later given to his secretary and nephew, Andrew Jackson Donelson, these pieces descended in the Donelson family and were exhibited at the Tennessee Centennial in 1897 in Nashville. At Betty Donelson's sale in 1940, Stanley Horn, then Tennessee state historian, purchased the candelabra, and after Horn's death I purchased them from his daughter.

Jackson continued to collect silver despite his wife's death in 1828, and his last buying spree occurred after The Hermitage burned in 1834. He purchased a large amount of silver from agent Lewis Veron of Philadelphia, including a coin silver tea and coffee set, tray, and coffee urn, all of excellent quality. Of the Jackson silver artifacts, many remain at the White House, at The Hermitage, or in private collections. Together they remind us of an interest Jackson had which, while not well known to the public, reveals another facet of this great president.

Benjamin H. Caldwell Jr., Nashville

Most of the earliest Tennessee settlers were from what we would identify as the middle class. Their household inventories contained very little silver except maybe a few spoons. These people more likely used horn or pewter for their tableware. They traveled to the new territory on horseback, often on trails too narrow to allow a wagon. Many had only a change or two of clothes and some wore clothing of dressed skins. They often arrived carrying only the barest of necessities. Their wills and inventories reveal a paucity of possessions, maybe just a quilt, bedding, a "kittle" (kettle), and perhaps a horse. Jedediah Morse's *American Geography,* published in London in 1789, noted that a simplicity of manner prevailed among the men and women who came to work the land of early Tennessee.

Nashville's first silversmith was Joseph T. Elliston, a native of Virginia. He was sixteen years old when his family apprenticed him to his uncle Samuel Ayres of Lexington, Kentucky, to learn silversmithing and clockmaking. Two years later Elliston established himself in Nashville as that city's first silversmith as well as a jeweler, and a clock and watchmaker. A normal apprenticeship was seven years but there is no record of previous training for young Elliston. He was very successful, nonetheless. He was one of Nashville's five incorporators and served for at least three one-year terms as an alderman (1808, 1810, 1820) as well as being mayor between 1814 and 1816. He made silver for Andrew Jackson and Nashville's wealthy. Elliston made so much money in the real estate business in Nashville (which was booming) that he retired sometime after 1815 from the silversmithing trade. His nephew, John Elliston, entered the silversmithing business with him about that date.

There is some silver bearing the hallmark "J. T. Elliston," some marked "Elliston," and even some marked "I.T.E." ("I" being used occasionally in the eighteenth century rather than "J"). These pieces are rare, but enough exist to indicate that he had a profitable business.

A tall case clock with "I.T. Elliston, Nashville" printed on the dial also exists, but the works of the clock were made in Birmingham, England. Most likely early Tennessee silversmiths or clockmakers marked on the dials of case clocks as a guarantee of the product they sold; it is extremely doubtful that any tall case clocks were made by early Tennessee artisans. Elliston advertised in the *Tennessee Gazette* of August 2, 1802, of his first attempt at the clockmaking business in the Mero district. He also had taken a partner named Henner. They state that they will warrant clocks made by them equal to any. No known locally manufactured watches or clocks have been found. That is not to exclude the possibility that some might have been manufactured. Later as a member of the commission for building the Tennessee State Capitol, Elliston served on the committee that chose William Strickland as the architect. J. T. Elliston died in 1856.

Sugar tongs by Joseph T. Elliston. H1925.05.039. Courtesy of The Hermitage: Home of President Andrew Jackson, Nashville.

Elliston is just one of several significant silversmiths from the early settlement era. In the period between statehood in 1796 and outbreak of war in 1861, many silversmiths arrived in Tennessee. They came overland by old Indian and hunting trails as well as by the rivers (which were heavily traveled even before the steamboat era). Silversmiths working in Tennessee came mainly from North Carolina, South Carolina, Virginia, Georgia, New York, Pennsylvania, Maryland, and Rhode Island, but some arrived from Ireland, France, and the Dominican Republic. The towns of Jonesboro, Greeneville, Kingston, Knoxville, Carthage, Murfreesboro, Nashville, Clarksville, Shelbyville, Jackson, and Memphis and many others made a home for silversmiths during this early period. Between 1796 and 1861, as many as 535 people, such as John Garner and Thomas Cain of Knoxville, Benjamin Barton of Carthage, and Jonesboro's Matthew and William Atkinson (who created our first Great Seal of the State of Tennessee), listed themselves as silversmiths or goldsmiths. The arrival of the craft of silversmithing reveals the growth of the local economy, the expansion of the cities, and the increased complexity of the household, which then needed forks, spoons, julep cups, trophies, and even a few tea services to fill the desires in the lives of this prospering economy. The number of silversmiths also reflects Tennessee's population boom, expanding from 105,802 in 1800 to 261,727 by 1810, and to 422,813 by 1820. With the purchase of Western Tennessee and Kentucky by Andrew Jackson and Isaac Shelby from the Chickasaws, the state lines were complete. West Tennessee towns such as Memphis and Jackson were soon supporting silversmiths by the 1820s. The availability of good silver at many places across the state allowed the middle class and elites to make a "show" on their sideboards and tables just as the silver had been a way to show wealth and influence in the colonies.

As silversmithing became a craft found statewide—around 1820—the business of selling silver

Above: Sauce ladle by Richmond and Flint. L1982.03.002. Courtesy of the National Park Service, Morristown National Historical Park, Morristown, New Jersey, and The Hermitage: Home of President Andrew Jackson, Nashville, Tennessee.

also changed. Bell, Dye and Simpson of Knoxville advertised as "watch and clock makers, silversmith, gilders and jewelers, and sword and dirk makers" at their shop formerly owned by another Knoxville silversmith, G. G. Garner. Also in Nashville, F. P. Flint and Barton Richmond advertised in 1817 "a great variety of gold seals, keys and chains . . . silverware, plated candlesticks, plated snuffers and trays" as well as "a few elegant sets of Britanniaware; plated and gilt mounted swords, epaulettes, plumes and lace" were available from their firm.[1] Later they advertised that they had received from Boston, Providence, and Baltimore a number of similar items. These advertisements indicate that northeastern manufactured goods were being marketed in large numbers by 1830. These goods were not merely imported; they also were produced by machines rather than the handcrafted silver items that dominated the early silver markets of the state. Andrew Jackson at the Hermitage used a ladle with the "Richmond and Flint" mark. In a December 1823 newspaper advertisement, Paul Negrin, watchmaker and jeweler from France, informed the citizens of Nashville that he offered gold and silversmithing service as well as jewelry, cut glass, china, sheet music, perfumes, buttons, and military items. Silversmithing shops were slowly changing to "jewelry stores" and the wares were being made elsewhere as well as Tennessee.

The influx of these wares was hastened by the advent of steamboat transportation, which much reduced the time and cost of goods arriving from the northeast. A steamboat could reach New Orleans in a week rather than in a month by keelboat, and return in about seventeen days rather than three to six months. An advertisement in the *Gallatin Examiner* for July 2, 1830, informed local readers of a change of address by Bailey and Company, a silversmithing and jewelry firm located within the Philadelphia city limits. The purchase of the advertisement in a local paper indicates that this Philadelphia company either had a good business with Tennesseans or wanted to encourage new business in the state.

The Age of Jackson, from 1820 to 1840, was also largely an age of silver in Tennessee. Jackson himself loved and purchased much silver, not only from local Nashville silversmiths but from silversmiths in New Orleans, Philadelphia, and New York. As trade, wealth, and population increased, so did the number of skilled urban silversmiths, who moved from New York City, Boston, Baltimore, Philadelphia, and Charleston. They came not only to take advantage of frontier opportunities but also because market changes in the East left them with few options to practice their craft. The mechanization revolution in silver in northeastern and coastal cities threatened their jobs, but in states like Tennessee they could still do business as usual. Silversmiths such as John Campbell, W. H. Calhoun, Paul Negrin, Samuel Bell, Calvin Guiteau, John Hodge, and others found plenty of customers who wanted handcrafted silver pieces, judging by the amount of silver found marked by these men and other Tennessee silversmiths. Their silver appears to be made locally by old techniques, evidence of eighteenth-century craftsmanship still existing in antebellum Tennessee.

Boom to Bust, 1850–1870

By the 1850s, silversmithing was a well-established business in both large cities and many small towns in Tennessee. Records of the 1840–60 period document 354 men working in silversmithing and related trades. Of that number, 73 called themselves silversmiths; 74 were watchmakers and clockmakers; 55 referred to themselves as jewelers, and the remainder used a combination of these terms.

These artisans and merchants found plenty of demand for their products. The planter class, busily either building or expanding upon such famous Middle Tennessee estates as Belle Meade, "Rattle and Snap," Belmont, and Oaklands, particularly fueled demand for silver items. They required tea services, coffee urns, and other large pieces of silver to furnish their new homes properly. The planters as well as urban consumers turned not only to the traditional silversmiths for goods, but also to a new generation of merchants who sold electroplated silver.

Electroplating allowed factories to shape large pieces from brass, copper, or Britannia metal and then to plate them in silver for only a small portion of the cost of solid silver. These pieces were sturdy, fashionable, and affordable. The English had discovered electroplating about 1840, and by 1845 it was in use in America. But electroplated silver did not immediately overwhelm the Tennessee market. An advertisement by J. Fowlkes and Company in the *Memphis Weekly Appeal*, July 7, 1843, states that they have on hand for silversmiths and jewelers an extensive assortment of sand and black lead crucibles used for the casting of silver. This indicates that many were still using their old methods for production of their wares.

By the end of the decade, however, electroplated silver items were listed in the inventories of Nashville silversmith Thomas Gowdey and Memphis silversmith F. H. Clark, who found these products well received by their clients. The new industrial-produced silver gained another competitive advantage as the state's railroad network neared completion in the 1850s. By the mid-1850s, nine rail lines in Tennessee used about four hundred miles of track and seven hundred additional miles were under construction. The railroads made transportation of manufactured items from the factories in the Northeast even cheaper and quicker. The value of electroplated wares surpassed the production of solid silver by 1860 in the United States. Within twenty years that same trend characterized the silver business in Tennessee. By 1860, just before the Civil War, mechanization of silver production is very evident by the wide variety of wares advertised in the daily newspapers. Their advertisements reveal many items, as well as "the newest fashion" from Boston, Baltimore, Philadelphia, and New York.

Then came the Civil War, which destroyed the state's economy and did lasting harm to its property. Whether silver was taken, stolen, or bartered away, many items disappeared or were altered to hide their origins. In fact, engraver Daniel Adams of Nashville, who was captured and imprisoned in the battle of Nashville in late 1864, is said to have first refused a Union officer's request to remove some engraving from silver in the officer's possession. Adams, being a practical man, later consented to the task in exchange for his release. After the Civil War the city directories of Nashville list him as an engraver, daguerreotypist, and later a photographer. There is one known piece of marked silver made by him remaining in his family. Adams was hardly the only silver artisan whose career was wrecked by the war. George Washington Donigan of Nashville was imprisoned during the war for unknown reasons. He was wounded by a stray bullet on the streets of Nashville just after his release and died January 15, 1864. An inventory of his accounts receivables published after his death in April 12, 1864, list among his patrons some of the wealthiest and most influential people of Tennessee.

Many silversmiths left the war-torn state for safer havens. Those who left sometimes reappear in the artisan records of Indiana, Missouri, Arkansas, Texas, and other western or midwestern states. Swannee Bennett in his book *Arkansas Made* (1991), for instance, states that over 10 percent of the silversmiths

Silver Trophies by Tennessee Silversmiths at Belle Meade Plantation

BY THE 1850S GENERAL WILLIAM GILES HARDING, THE OWNER OF BELLE MEADE PLANTATION IN Nashville, had accumulated one of the largest collections of silver in the state. The silver consisted mainly of trophies won for the farm's thoroughbreds and livestock. Trophies were often functional items in the nineteenth century, so the mint julep cups, goblets, and pitchers were actually used. When the Union army occupied Nashville during the Civil War, Harding asked two of his slaves, Susanna Carter and Bob Green, to hide the silver. All of it was successfully recovered in 1865, but neither Bob nor Susanna ever revealed its hiding place. Susanna feared another war and did not want the Yankees to know where to look for it.

After Reconstruction, Harding and his son-in-law, Gen. William Hicks Jackson, won many more trophies. The collection grew to several hundred pieces, worth thousands of dollars, and was displayed in three mahogany cases in the sitting room and a trophy desk in the entry hall. The desk and some of the silver can still be seen at Belle Meade today.

The trophies were made in Philadelphia, Boston, and Tennessee. Those made in Tennessee are simple classical revival designs. Among them are two coin silver mint julep cups made by C. Guiteau, a watchmaker, jeweler, silversmith, and engraver who operated in Nashville from 1836 to 1845. He was in partnership with John Peabody in 1839, but Guiteau was on his own by 1841 when the cups were made. They were awarded by the Agricultural Association of Davidson County. One is engraved "To W. G. Harding / For his 2 year old Heifer Queen of Scots." The other is inscribed "To W. G. Harding for his aged Bull Sam Patch Imptd." They stand three and a half inches high.

Left to right: two mint julep cups made by Campbell & Donigan, a goblet by William H. Calhoun, and two julep cups by C. Guiteau, all of Nashville. Courtesy of Belle Meade Plantation, Nashville.

Another pair of julep cups was made by Campbell and Donigan of Nashville. John Campbell, a Scottish immigrant, apprenticed in Fayetteville, North Carolina, before moving to Tennessee in 1836. George Washington Donigan came to the city in 1850 from New York. The two partners operated at the corner of College and Union streets from 1853 to 1855. Campbell and Donigan marked their silver with either "C & D" or "Campbell and Donigan" and an elephant hallmark. One of the Belle Meade cups is engraved "M.C.A. & M.L. to Leda 1855." The other is marked "M.C.A. & M.L. to Castor 1855." "M.C.A. & M.L." stands for the Maury County Agricultural and Mechanical League.

William H. Calhoun, the most prolific silversmith in Nashville, made three matching silver goblets at Belle Meade. Trained in Philadelphia, Calhoun opened a jewelry store in Nashville in 1835. After a partnership with J. Flowers from 1841 to 1846, Calhoun was on his own again by 1847. He sold wares from New York and Philadelphia as well as items that he or his journeymen made. The five-inch goblets have a Greek key band around the base. They were won for Epsilon and Castor, two of Belle Meade's prize horses.

Janet S. Hasson, Belle Meade Plantation

found in Arkansas before 1870 were born in Tennessee; many others had worked in Tennessee prior to moving to Arkansas. Records in the Federal Census, the Manufacturer's Census, and the *Tennessee State Gazetteer* reveal only a few of the silversmiths known prior to war as practicing their trade after the war. Most had become "jewelry stores" carrying all sorts of silver, silver plate, and Britanniaware, which was imported from the northern manufacturing center.

A few artisans stayed in the Volunteer State and tried to make a go of it. Ernest Wiggers can first be documented as producing silver in Nashville in 1866. The 1870 census reveals that Wiggers was born in "Hanover Kingdom" (Germany) about 1836. His surviving silver appears to be hand made. Ten percent of the nation's work force at that time was immigrant labor, with the newly arrived German workers being especially competitive.

Silversmiths in the Late Victorian Era

The impact of mechanization, which had so influenced Tennessee silver from 1840 to 1860, became even more pronounced in the late nineteenth century as traditional silver artistry largely disappeared. The number of silversmiths declined markedly. In 1876–77 the Nashville *Tennessee Gazetteer* listed only E. Wiggers, B. H. Stief, and F. A. Fallen as jewelers, and Memphis only had F. J. Bowman and VanBuren Thayer as jewelers. The only reference following the Civil War to anyone manufacturing solid silver is S. O. Merrill of Memphis, who advertised he had available "solid silver goods" at his store at 4 North Summer Street.[2]

In the Victorian era, silversmithing was further mechanized with the casting of spoons, forks, and multiple service pieces as well as the machine spinning (raising) of cups, beakers, and other pieces of holloware. The new techniques of silver-plating replaced the old methods of making solid silver items. Sterling silver, a standard in England for many centuries, became the standard in America after 1865 with silver ingots replacing the Spanish milled dollar as a source for the silversmith's raw material. The Spanish milled dollar (the source of "coin" silver) was about 900 parts silver out of 1,000, while sterling was 925 parts silver out of 1,000.

Mechanization also brought technological advances in silversmithing to Tennessee. The rolling machine produced a flat piece of silver from the ingot. Another mechanical development employed rolling dies capable of producing decorative banding or beading on strips of silver. Also the spinning of thin rolled silver on a lathe superceded the time-consuming process of raising hollowware by hand. The nation's expanded national market networks further hurt traditional silversmithing in Tennessee. The South could not compete with Gorham, Tiffany, Whiting, and many other northeastern silver manufacturers.

Yet consumer demand for silver products never lessened. New fashions in foods and furnishings created the demand for new silver items. Castors, tea sets, large covered dishes, mechanical pots for coffee, tea or water, and the number of forks, spoons, and other pieces for special foods and occasions added to the demand for plated and more ornamental, less costly items which suited the life-styles of the late nineteenth century.

Silversmiths in the Twentieth Century

In 1897, the Tennessee Centennial Exposition demonstrated the acceptance of the machine as a positive and creative force, marking the beginning of what we identify as the modern era of silversmithing. At the same time in England, the Arts and Crafts philosophy of William Morris—that industrialization was killing the crafts—was starting to take hold. It took another generation beyond the Arts and Crafts and the Art Nouveau movements to make effective use of machines, especially in an artistically expressive way, and reintroduce the craftmanship of silversmithing to Tennessee's craft arts.

Extensive research found only a handful of silversmiths producing their wares in the last one hundred years. Others must exist; perhaps this chapter will encourage others to bring their names and work to light.

One of the best-known twentieth-century silversmiths is James David Andrews Jr., who brought an Arts and Crafts sensibility to his work. Born in 1887 in Nashville, a colonel in the Corps of Engineers, he practiced the art of hand hammering flat sheets of sterling silver into bowls, cups, plates, and other shaped containers. He had a distinguished military career, which included overseas service in World War I and World War II, and was the recipient of the French Croix de Guerre. He was the victim of war injuries during World War I and spent months recuperating in various army hospitals. At the Walter Reed Rehabilitation Center, he was introduced to the art of hand hammering metals, primarily copper. The tools were simple but the execution was difficult. Colonel Andrews fashioned silver objects ranging from coasters to large punch bowls. Much of the beauty of his work is found in the free flowing bowls of all shapes and sizes.

Andrews never sold any of his silver, although he would often swap for another artist's work—usually a painting. Most of his work survives with his family. He taught his son Nashvillian Nelson Andrews, a prominent city leader, his craft but Nelson has made only a few pieces.

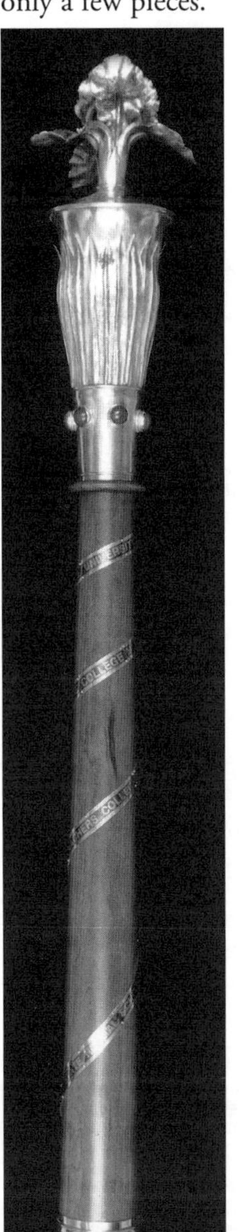

Klaus Kallenberger, who was born in the 1930s, has taught gold and silversmithing at Middle Tennessee State University (MTSU) since the late 1960s. Early influences in the development of Kallenberger's style came from the work of silversmith Georg Jensen. Kallenberger felt himself very much a child of the modernist aesthetic in which less is more. During this time, he has been active as a practicing artist/craftsman and has a regional reputation. His pieces are collected by many individuals and museums. These pieces can be seen at the Tennessee State Museum as well as in other collections.

Far left: Silver plates by James Andrews. Photograph by Nan Andrews. Courtesy of Benjamin H. Caldwell Jr.

Near left: Official mace for Middle Tennessee State University, by Klaus Kallenberger. Silver, cherry wood, lapis lazuli gems, and fresh water pearls; 36 inches high. Courtesy of the artist.

Earl Pardon

ACCLAIMED METALSMITH AND JEWELRY DESIGNER, EARL PARDON (1926–1991) WAS A MAJOR CONtributor to the rise of American studio jewelry in the second half of the twentieth century. Born in Memphis in 1926, Pardon served in World War II and then attended the Memphis Academy of Art for his undergraduate degree in painting and his initial training in metalsmithing. After graduating from the academy in 1951, he joined the faculty of Skidmore College in Saratoga Springs, New York, where he remained an influential art professor until his retirement in 1989. In the 1950s, Pardon began designing silver items for commercial firms such as Towle Silversmiths of Newburyport, Massachusetts. In 1959, he received his master of fine arts from Syracuse University.

Pardon brought the sensitivity of a modernist painter to his metalwork and jewelry—certainly he gained his greater reputation in the latter. He often described his bracelets and necklaces as portable works of art. Some biographers credit Pardon with having played a significant role in the revival of the art of enameling, since he incorporated enamel-colored stones and beads to create the effect of costly gems in his jewelry. His obituary in the *New York Times* of May 4, 1991, noted, "He used enamel like an artist's canvas, painting abstract patterns on it."

The first major retrospective exhibit about Pardon's design legacies—some three hundred works—took place at Skidmore College in 1980. After his death in 1991, a series of commemorative exhibitions about Pardon's work took place in such prominent New York galleries as the Aaron Faber Gallery. His designs may be found in major national collections, such as the Renwick Gallery in Washington, D.C., and the Metropolitan Museum of Art in New York City. Pardon's work also was highlighted in the influential traveling exhibit, *Messengers of Modernism: American Studio Jewelry, 1940–1960,* which was curated by the Montreal Museum of Decorative Arts in the late 1990s.

Carroll Van West, Middle Tennessee State University

Another important late-twentieth-century silversmith was Terry Don Talley (c. 1948–2001) from Bradyville, Tennessee, who learned his techniques at MTSU under Kallenberger's guidance. He made objects in copper, silver, and gold, as well as many serving pieces such as trays, bowls, and spoons in silver and copper. He made beautiful jewelry in all metals. Talley apprenticed Ben Caldwell (the author's son) and passed the silversmithing trade to another generation. Caldwell has made trays, bowls, serving pieces, candelabra, and other pieces from silver and copper. His style reflects the present-day renewed interest of the Arts and Crafts revival movement and he often incorporates natural materials such as antler or bone into his work. His work is represented in the collection of the Tennessee State Museum.

Another silversmith working at the beginning of the twenty-first century is Bob Coogan, who teaches at the Tennessee Technological University through the Joe L. Evins Appalachian Center for Crafts in Smithville. He graduated from Cranbrook Academy of Art in Michigan with a master of fine arts in metalsmithing. He has worked from 1981 to present at the Evins Center. In 1988, he received a Fulbright Scholarship to South Devon College in Torquay, United Kingdom. He is in many public collections and has received many honors and awards for his metal work.

One of Coogan's students is Kimberly Moore, who presently resides in Bowling Green, Ohio, where she is working toward a master's degree in fine arts in metals at Bowling Green State University. Other Tennessee silversmiths working presently are Richard Prilaman of Memphis, who is at the Memphis College of Art; Marci Margolin of Memphis; and Ramsey Hall of Murfreesboro, as well as others overlooked.

Circumstances have not always been kind to the silversmith working in Tennessee. Despite the hardships of war, industrialization, and stiff competition, though, today's silversmith seems to be making a comeback. The realization that the beauty of a handmade and finished object cannot always be exactly duplicated by a machine has allowed a few silversmiths to earn a livelihood doing what they love best—producing silver by traditional methods and earning a living in the process. They also teach their apprentices thus perpetuating their craft for another millennium.

NOTES

1. Jane H. Thomas, *Old Days in Nashville: Reminiscences* (1897; reprint, Nashville: Elder Books, 1969, 49).
2. *Tennessee Gazetteer and Business Directory* (Nashville: R. L. Polk, 1876).

SUGGESTED READINGS

Beckman, Elizabeth D. *Cincinnati Silversmiths, Jewelers, Watch and Clockmakers Through 1850, Also Listing the More Prominent Men in Their Trades from 1851–1900.* Cincinnati: B. B. and Company, 1975.

Bennett, Swannee, and William B. Worthen. *Arkansas Made 1819–1870.* Fayetteville: Univ. of Arkansas Press, 1991.

Boltinghouse, Marquis. *Silversmiths of Kentucky, 1785–1900: Jewelers, Watch and Clock Makers.* Lexington, Ky.: Privately published, 1980.

Bryding, Adams E. *Made in Alabama: A State Legacy.* Birmingham, Ala.: Birmingham Museum of Art, 1995.

Burton, E. Milby. *South Carolina Silversmiths.* Charleston, S.C.: Charleston Museum, 1942.

Caldwell, Benjamin H., Jr. "Tennessee Silversmiths." *Antiques* 100 (Sept. 1971): 382–85.

———. *Tennessee Silversmiths.* Chapel Hill: Museum of Early Southern Decorative Arts, Univ. of North Carolina Press, 1988.

From top:

Winged Cups, by Robert Coogan, 2000. Sterling silver and mokume-gane, 4½ × 3 × 2 inches. Courtesy of the artist.

Sterling cup, by Kimerlen Moore. Sterling silver, 6 × 3 inches. Courtesy of the artist.

A pair of ladles with silver ginko-leaf bowls and horn handles by Ben Caldwell. Courtesy of Benjamin H. Caldwell Jr.

Cutten, George Barton. *The Silversmiths of Georgia, Together with Watchmakers and Jewelers, 1833–1850.* Savannah, Ga.: Pigeonhole Press, 1958.

———. *Silversmiths of North Carolina, 1696–1850.* Raleigh: North Carolina Department of Cultural Resources, Division of Archives and History, 1973.

———. *The Silversmiths of Virginia.* Richmond, Va.: Dutz Press, 1952.

Fales, Martha Gandy. *Early American Silver for the Cautious Collector.* New York: Funk and Wagnalls, 1970.

Fink, Paul M. "The Great Seal of the State of Tennessee: An Inquiry Into Its Makers." *Tennessee Historical Quarterly* 20 (Winter 1961): 381–83.

Hood, Graham Hood. *American Silver: A History of Style, 1650–1900.* New York: Praeger Publishers, 1971.

Williams, Samuel Cole. *Dawn of the Tennessee Valley and Tennessee History.* Johnson City, Tenn.: Watauga Press, 1937.

Twelve

Jugs, Jars, Bowls, and Churns
Tennessee's Ceramic Crafts and Potters

Stephen T. Rogers
Tennessee Historical Commission

Tennessee's ceramic history is rich with fine examples of the expertise and beauty of the potter's craft. The recent fascination and interest in southern pottery in general and Tennessee-made pottery in particular are reflected in a continued level of scholarship, a growing interest by ceramic collectors, and the accompanying rise in values of these pieces on the collectors' market. Although the end products of the potter's craft are held in high regard, little is known about the individual potters who produced these vessels. This chapter discusses the changes and trends that shaped the pottery industry at the state and regional levels, highlights Tennessee potters who made significant contributions to the craft, and establishes a context by which to judge and evaluate Tennessee's pottery industry.

Eli Lafever Pottery, Putnam County, showing the semisubterranean updraft kiln under a shed roof. An assortment of churns, pitchers, and jars are shown in the foreground, and a potter's wheel lies on the ground in the lower right corner. Courtesy of the Tennessee Division of Archaeology.

When trying to record Tennessee's ceramic heritage, one is often left with a blurred image of the individual potters, and perhaps only a small sample of their work to evaluate and critique. Who were these people who searched for the specialized potting clays, then labored to dig them out of the ground? Who were the potters who had the strength to chop the many cords of wood needed to fire the kilns, but also the talent to transform a ball of clay into a beautiful ten gallon churn? Who were these craftsmen, often with little formal education, who understood the complexities of kiln construction, the chemistry of glaze and slip formulation, and the precision needed to fire these clay vessels to the correct temperature for an exacting amount of time?

In trying to answer the question "Who were the potters?" several generalizations can be made. Most of the early potters of the nineteenth century followed the earlier lead-glazed earthenware and salt-glazed stoneware traditions established in North Carolina and Virginia. The great migration of people into Tennessee from those two states brought with them family traditions of pottery making. Potters such as Thomas Cravens Jr. moved his family from Randolph

Charles F. Decker, Keystone Pottery, Washington County, turning a stoneware jar on the potter's wheel. Members of the Decker family are shown along with an assortment of ceramic vessels in the foreground; potter's tools and implements are suspended from the wall. Courtesy of the Tennessee Division of Archaeology.

County, North Carolina, to Henderson County, Tennessee, in 1829, and passed along a ceramic tradition that extended back to his grandfather, Peter Cravens, born in Staffordshire, England. Thomas Cravens's sons and grandsons continued this tradition of salt-glazed stoneware production into the last quarter of the nineteenth century. Andrew Lafever, the patriarch of the potters in White, Putnam, and DeKalb Counties, had six sons, five who were potters. He established a salt-glazed stoneware tradition that lasted six generations over a period of a century. Leonard Cain's pottery in Sullivan County was one of Tennessee's earliest. Cain's children and grandchildren continued a lead-glazed earthenware tradition that lasted throughout the nineteenth century.

By the 1880s factory stoneware operations located in cities had replaced many of the small rural family potteries. The potters employed in these factories typically had a European background, often from Germany or England, and produced slip-glazed stoneware for commercial consumption. Whiskey jugs, large-mouth churns, and jars were the predominant vessel forms produced at these potteries. A good example is the businesses of potter James Steele. Born in Scotland, Steele established a pottery in Louisville, Kentucky, by 1858. By 1876, he moved to Memphis and established the Bluff City Terra Cotta Works. There he employed several Irish- and German-born potters who produced a wide range of home and commercial vessels. Charles Decker, born in Baden, Germany, established the Keystone Pottery in Chucky Valley, Washington County, Tennessee, by 1872. Decker's stoneware pottery evolved from a family pottery into a larger factory operation employing six people by 1880. Making some of the most decorative stoneware in the state with the use of cobalt blue inks, Decker's pottery produced both utilitarian and ceremonial vessels. During the late 1800s, Decker used flatboats to float his pottery down the Nolichucky and Tennessee Rivers to markets in Chattanooga.

The trends in the factory stoneware operations changed somewhat by 1910, as the closing of potteries in Ohio and Illinois brought potters from the Midwest into Tennessee. Typical of the change was Torrence Connor, a potter born in Illinois, who operated potteries in Toone, Hardeman County, by 1910, and another in Grand Junction by 1920. The largest and perhaps the best-known pottery in Tennessee emerged at the end of this factory stoneware period with the establishment of Southern Potteries in Erwin, the county seat of Unicoi County, in 1917. The migration of potters from East Liverpool and Minerva, Ohio, into Erwin produced decaled and hand-painted dinnerwares that had nationwide distribution. Employing over five hundred women to hand paint fifteen hundred different floral designs and motifs, the Blue Ridge line of dinnerware is one of the most recognized and collectable in the country.

Although Tennessee potters were not recognized for establishing unique or defining ceramic traditions, the development of the state's pottery industry generally mirrored that of the South, emulating regional and national trends. Vessel forms in Tennessee changed in keeping with the general styles of the period. Use of common glazes was typical; however, alkaline glazes used in neighboring southern states were relatively rare in Tennessee. Decorations and embellishments to Tennessee pottery were uncommon as the utilitarian nature of the vessels gave testimony to the simplicity of design and form. This lack of significant decorative elements does not, however, detract from the overall quality and beauty of the craft. The large ovoid-shaped wide-mouth earthenware storage jars made in the Potterstown area of Greene County by Christopher A. Haun demonstrate a high degree of sophistication and craftsmanship. Charles Decker's large stoneware presentation pieces reflect the potter's dexterity and the artist's decorative skills.

Tennessee's ceramic history can be divided into a chronology of four broad categories: family potters, factory stoneware potters, art potters, and early studio potters. Each of these categories differs in the type of ceramics produced, acquisition of raw materials, expected uses for the vessels, and marketing strategies.

Family Potters, 1800–1880

The family pottery was typically a small rural business that produced utilitarian vessels for local consumption and largely belonged to the male sphere of work. To quote John Burrison, "With the typically large rural family, the likelihood of a succession of sons to serve as labor force and chain of continuity was good, and it was usually assumed that a potter's sons would follow in his muddy footsteps. . . . They were born with clay in their veins."[1] These craftsmen constructed kilns designed by their fathers and grandfathers and used local raw materials. Their vessel forms and glaze formulas were passed down from father to son. In the era before mechanization, one to three people would operate a family pottery.

Continuing research on Tennessee's ceramic heritage has identified over 275 individuals who can be described as family potters working on 140 potteries throughout the state. These craftsmen typically combined work at the pottery with other general farming activities. Many potters, when asked their occupation by census takers in the nineteenth century, described themselves as farmers or laborers. They often viewed their pottery production as part-time work to supplement their farm income and tried to schedule pottery making during periods of slow farm activities.

Initially making lead-glazed earthenware vessels, the family potters produced an assortment of items used around the farm or home for food storage and preservation. The vessel forms were traditional, ranging from ovoid-shaped wide-mouth jars to churns, jugs, bowls, bottles, plates, and pitchers. Traditional manufacturing methods were often slow to change. Perhaps the best example of resistance to change was demonstrated by the continued use of lead to glaze the earthenware vessels. The dangers of lead glazes were well known in Tennessee by 1817, yet William Grimm, a family potter in Greene County, continued this type of manufacture into the 1880s.

The sale and distribution methods used by the family potters were also traditional. Typically they sold their wares locally as neighbors visited the kiln sites to purchase assorted items, or a family member might organize a horse and wagon peddling excursion through the countryside trading or bartering pottery for needed supplies and foodstuffs. Efforts to sell and distribute the potter's wares were directly dependent on the established transportation systems. While the rough, bumpy roads of most overland routes proved to be an obstacle in transporting manufactured goods such as pottery, the Great Road, a name given to a section of the primary route from Philadelphia west to Tennessee and Kentucky, was the exception. Earthenware produced in Greene and Sullivan Counties in the 1850s and 1860s found its way into southwest Virginia via this route.

The shift from producing lead-glazed earthenware to salt-glazed stoneware was a gradual but significant evolution. This transformation, beginning in the 1820s, marked a change of emphasis from more English traditions of earthenware production to that of salt-glaze stoneware of German traditions. As the dangers of lead glazing became more obvious, the production of salt-glazed stoneware began to dominate the pottery industry. Stronger and more durable, the early stoneware vessel forms followed the earthenware traditions. Generally ovoid in profile, these stoneware vessels evolved into a more straight-sided shape by the 1860s. Stoneware potters continued producing items necessary for food storage and preservation, but they also produced smoking pipes, ink wells, grease lamps, and even ceramic tombstones. Whimsical items such as ceramic animal figurines and marbles were produced for children.

Redware pot, Sullivan County, made by William M. Cain, signed and dated 1857. Courtesy of East Tennessee Historical Society.

In Tennessee, Andrew Lafever is representative of the shift to stoneware production. Born in Pennsylvania in 1774, Lafever moved into Middle Tennessee about 1824, after living in Virginia and Kentucky. Andrew was the son of Abraham Lafever, of French Huguenot descent. Andrew Lefever and his sons, Zachariah, John, Asher, Andrew, and James, created an extended pottery family that dominated the midstate. With more than two dozen family members directly associated with the pottery industry, the Lafevers' ceramic legacy was unsurpassed. The Lafevers continued as family potters into the mid-1930s, decades longer than other pottery operations.

An anomaly of Tennessee's ceramic history is the scarcity of family potters producing alkaline-glazed stoneware. Use of this distinctive glaze was first employed in the Edgefield District, South Carolina, near the end of the eighteenth century and quickly spread west throughout the southern tier of states as far as Texas. Potters combined wood ash, clay, and silica (either sand or ground glass) to create this unique stoneware glaze. Given the popularity of this glaze in surrounding states, and the migration pattern of potters, it seemed very unusual that an alkaline-glaze stoneware tradition did not take root in Tennessee. Research has identified only three potters in Tennessee who attempted making stoneware with this characteristic glaze. The best-known potter using alkaline glazes in Tennessee was Benjamin F. Ussery, who was born in North Carolina in 1825, but by 1850 he moved to Randolph County, Alabama, where he developed his abilities as a potter. After a

Andrew Lafever

ANDREW WESLEY LAFEVER, THE PATRIARCH OF THE LAFEVER FAMILY IN WHITE, PUTNAM, AND DEKALB Counties, was born in Pennsylvania in 1774, the son of Abraham Lafever and Catherina Zink. The Lafever family was of French Huguenot descent, having migrated from France to Holland and then into New York by 1685. The spelling of the family name varied through time from LaFavre, LeFeber, to LeFaber and Lafever. After living in Augusta County, Virginia, Hawkins County, Tennessee, and Wayne County, Kentucky, Andrew Lafever moved in about 1824 to White County, Tennessee, where good quality stoneware clays were readily available. There he established a potting legacy unsurpassed in Tennessee. It is not known from whom Lafever learned the art and skill of the pottery trade. The German potters in Pennsylvania were well established by the beginning of the nineteenth century, and they may have served as Lafever's mentors. While the Staunton area of Augusta County, Virginia, was a center for pottery production in the mid-nineteenth century, this period of ceramic activity was well after Lafever moved out of the area. As a result of Lafever's training, he passed along a ceramic heritage steeped in the German tradition of producing salt-glazed stoneware.

Andrew married Nancy Ard (1776–1845), the daughter of John Ard and Sarah McHenry from Anson County, North Carolina, about 1796. Andrew and his wife had a large family that included six sons, Zachariah, John, Eli, Asher, Andrew, and James. Five became potters. The Lafever family established a ceramic industry in Middle Tennessee that lasted over 120 years through six generations of potters. The large number of Lafever family members actively engaged in the production of pottery is unequaled in Tennessee and served as a role model for the term "family or folk potter." No less than twenty-three Lafever family members were potters, and at least a dozen other individuals who married into the Lafever family worked in the pottery profession. Members of the Dunn, Spears, Elrod, and Hitchcock (Hedgecough) families were all part of the extended Lafever pottery lineage.

The Lafever pottery clan produced salt-glazed stoneware in a variety of vessel forms. Fired in a semisubterranean circular updraft brick kiln, the pottery produced by the Lafevers was utilitarian in nature and sold throughout Middle Tennessee. The unmarked churns, bowls, jars, and jugs have a distinctive vessel shape and decorative style that can be attributed to Middle Tennessee and the Lafever family. The marked or signed Lafever vessels found in private collections attest to the beauty and artistic skill of the family. The whimsical pieces made by the Lafevers included animal figurines, marbles, and pipes.

Andrew Lafever died in 1849 in White County, but his legacy of pottery production lasted another hundred years through the efforts of his large extended pottery family.

Stephen T. Rogers, Tennessee Historical Commission

brief stay in Georgia, Ussery moved to Hardeman County, Tennessee, by 1860, and established two potteries producing alkaline-glazed stoneware. Both Alabama and Georgia are known to have strong alkaline-glaze stoneware traditions, and Ussery probably acquired the skills to produce the glaze while he lived in these states. Ussery moved again in 1875 to Yallobusha County, Mississippi, where he established another pottery operation.

Perhaps the most difficult aspect of evaluating the state's early pottery traditions was determining the role of African Americans. Few historical documents

Christopher Alexander Haun

CHRISTOPHER ALEXANDER HAUN, ONE OF TENNESSEE'S FINEST EARLY POTTERS, DIED SHORTLY AFTER HIS fortieth birthday, when his considerable talent was probably just reaching its peak. Haun was executed at Knoxville on December 11, 1861, charged by a Confederate drum-head court-martial with "bridge-burning," a crime punishable by public hanging.

Christopher A. Haun, Greene County, made this ovoid-shaped lead-glazed earthenware jar with copper and iron oxide splashes on the sides. The jar, 13¼ inches high, has a coggle-wheeled decoration on the ends of the strap handles and is stamped "C.A. HAUN No.1" on the shoulder. Private collection. Courtesy of the Tennessee Division of Archaeology.

In November 1861, early in the American Civil War, "Alex" Haun, as he was known to his family, joined a large group of his neighbors in burning a strategic railroad bridge in western Greene County in East Tennessee. The bridge, located near Haun's home, carried the tracks of the newly built East Tennessee and Virginia Railroad across Lick Creek. The men involved were from a small settlement known locally as "Pottertown." The area was home to several potters who produced utility-grade crocks and jars from the local clay along Lick Creek. Most households of the period used these wares for storage or food preservation.

Pottertown was a Union stronghold in a Confederate state. Haun and the majority of his neighbors were ardent Union men. They had quietly opposed secession, but their county was being "occupied" by Confederate troops sent in anticipation that "Lincolnites," as the Union men were called, would attempt an uprising or damage to the important railroad line.

On the night of November 8, 1861, the men from Pottertown surprised seven Confederate bridge guards and burned the Lick Creek Bridge. The guards were released after taking an oath of allegiance to the Union, but they immediately notified Confederate authorities of the destruction of the bridge, and on the following day arrests began. Haun was one of the first seized, and along with others arrested, he was transported to the Knoxville jail.

On December 10, Haun wrote two letters to his wife Elizabeth, bidding his family goodbye and instructing them regarding the sale of his personal property. He told Elizabeth, "Have Bohannon, Hinshaw, or Low [all local potters] to finish off that ware and do the best you can with it for your support." Later in the letter Haun directed his wife, "Sell my shop-tools, lead oven, glazing mill, clay mill and lathe which will be some help to you and the children."

The content of those letters reveals that Christopher Alexander Haun, the "bridge-burner," was also C. A. Haun, the great potter. Haun's family, like the families of the other executed men, had been reviled by the Confederates and told that the men were "traitors." The terrified widows and children seldom spoke of the execution, even among themselves. Until recent years none of Haun's descendants knew that he had been a noted potter.

Further research has revealed that the executed men were sworn in as members of the Union Army shortly before the bridge burning. Their graves are now marked with the official grave markers furnished by the United States government.

Donahue Bible, Mohawk, Tennessee

identify specific African American slaves who worked in the pottery industry. While most of the antebellum potteries in Tennessee were small, family-based operations, slaves could have been a part of the labor force. To date, only one document has been found that suggested the involvement of an enslaved African American in the antebellum pottery industry. In 1826, Samuel Smith Jr., a stoneware potter in Knox County, placed an advertisement in the local newspaper wishing to hire an African American man of about sixteen years old. Examples such as the alkaline-glazed stoneware produced by the slave and master potter named Dave in the Edgefield District of South Carolina are rare, but they testify to the skill and craftsmanship developed in antebellum times. Census data taken in Tennessee after the Civil War identified a number of African Americans who were active at some level in the factory stoneware potteries. The challenge to researchers and ceramic historians will be to develop and expand the undocumented presence of African American potters.

Although the success of the family potters can, in some measure, be attributed to the traditions established by previous generations of potters, its decline can be linked to the changing technology in glass production that led to improved methods for canning foods. Another more dramatic and more immediate event—the Civil War—also contributed to the decline of the family potter. The Civil War caused pottery families to become dispersed and disrupted trading networks and economic systems. Perhaps the most interesting and tragic episode affecting the family potters occurred in Greene County, Tennessee, in November and December 1861. Union resistance to Confederate control in upper East Tennessee escalated into a series of bridge burnings along the East Tennessee and Virginia Railroad. Hoping to disrupt communications lines and initiate the invasion of Union troops, a small group of pro-Union loyalists planned and burned a number of trestles and bridges. The Lick Creek Bridge in western Greene County was set ablaze on November 9, 1861. Within weeks five men who participated in the guerrilla activities were executed. Four of the five men were family potters. With the deaths of Jacob M. Hinshaw, Christopher A. Haun, and Jacob and Henry Harmon, the vigor and spirit of the family potters in Greene County were forever dampened. Jacob Harmon was forced to witness the execution of his son Henry before he suffered a similar fate. Few letters are more poignant than the last words written by potter Christopher A. Haun to his wife from a Knoxville jail cell on the day he was hanged:

> I have the promise that my body will be sent
> home to you.
> O live for heaven
> Oh my bosom friend and children
> Live for heaven, I pray.
> My time is almost out, dear friend, farewell to this
> world—farewell to earth and earthly troubles.[2]

A fifth potter, J. A. Low, whose Confederate sympathies did not allow him to participate in the bridge burning, enlisted in the Confederate army. Fearing retribution from his pro-Union neighbors, Low moved to Arkansas after the war's end.

Factory Stoneware Potters, 1860–1930

The evolution from family to factory stoneware potters reflected general economic trends throughout the South. The factory stoneware potteries were usually centered in the major metropolitan areas of the state. These potteries were "usually large, typically employing a number of non-family workers hired by the owners; that used industrial, mechanized techniques; and that operated independently of local clay resources, relying on railway lines for hauling in clay and exporting the ware produced."[3] Ongoing research has identified over one hundred individuals associated with factory stoneware potteries in Tennessee. These potters worked at over thirty-five separate properties from the 1880s until circa 1930. The urban setting of these potteries directly changed

Pinson Pottery, Madison County, 1891. Henry F. Weist, potter and future owner of Pinson Pottery, is shown center right wearing a derby hat. Also pictured are Wiest's wife Mary; their four children, Amelia, Laura, Cora, and Charles; four turners (in aprons); and several other workers, including three African Americans. Courtesy of the Tennessee Division of Archaeology.

the entire nature of the pottery business. No longer gathered locally, raw materials were shipped into the cities, usually by railroad. The focus of ceramic products shifted from the local household needs of the farmer to commercial needs, primarily of the liquor industry. Stoneware whiskey jugs and wide-mouth jars were the most prevalent items produced. The sale and distribution of these products were wide ranging as the railroad shipped items throughout the entire southern region of the country.

The most visible changes demonstrated by the factory stoneware potter involved a transition in the shape and style of the vessels and the glaze or surface treatment of the pottery. After the 1860s, the popularity of most vessel forms slowly began to change from a rounded ovoid form to one that was much more straight-sided. The change in vessel forms resulted from new mechanization and techniques developed by the pottery industry. The use of steam or gasoline engines changed the way power turned the potter's wheel and replaced the horse-powered pug mills that family potters had used to mix and prepare the clays. Jiggers, machines in which soft clay was formed in a spinning mold, standardized vessel shapes and greatly increased the production capacity of the potter. Jiggers also enabled seemingly unskilled workers to produce vessels of standard size and quality. Author Charles Zug recounted potter Javan Brown's dislike of the jigger and the men who operated them: "They call themselves potters! I told them there one day, I says, 'Any potter can jigger, but,' I says, 'Any jigger can't pot.'"[4] Slip casting, the formation of vessels by using a watery suspension of clay poured into an absorbent mold, usually made of plaster of paris, also greatly changed the manner in which pottery was produced.

Decorative changes took place as well in the factory stoneware potteries. The traditional salt glaze on vessels was being replaced by commercially purchased slips and glazes, the two most popular during this time period being the Albany slip and Bristol glaze. Potters first used Albany slip in the latter half of the nineteenth century. Found along the Hudson

River valley in New York, this clay formed a rich brown color when fired to stoneware temperatures. By the last quarter of the century, the cream-colored Bristol glaze became very popular. Use of the Albany slip was prevalent on whiskey jugs in the 1880s, when the names of saloons or liquor distributors were scratched into the surface of the vessel. Known by collectors as scratch jugs, these stoneware vessels were an important product of the potter's craft.

Often potters combined the use of the Albany slip and Bristol glaze to decorate the same vessels, as seen notably in shouldered stoneware whiskey jugs. The white-colored Bristol glaze was used on the bottom and sides of the jug while the Albany slip was used on the vessel's shoulder and neck. Liquor distilleries usually sold their products to wholesalers in large wooden casks or barrels. Local saloons or liquor distributors repackaged the whiskey for sale into gallon jugs. These jugs often contained stenciled lettering in black or blue cobalt ink that advertised the names and addresses of the local taverns, saloons, or whiskey dealers. Very popular between 1890 and 1910, these stenciled stoneware jugs were a major source of advertising. For example, the Jackson Pottery made and shipped whiskey jugs as far away as Aberdeen, Mississippi, and New Orleans, Louisiana.

Economic trends of the late 1800s often required these factory stoneware operations to shift focus from the production of pottery to the manufacture of bricks or other ceramic products. Agricultural drainage tiles and architectural items such as chimney tops, sewer pipes, and house ornaments were commonly produced. The Tennessee Terra Cotta Works and Pottery located in Germantown even claimed that their production of earthen cooking pots was superior to any metallic pot for cooking vegetables or fruits.

The extended Weaver family was very important in the development and diffusion of factory stoneware potteries in Tennessee. Descended from several generations of family potters in Pennsylvania, Virginia, and Ohio, potter George C. Weaver brought his family's potting traditions to Tennessee. Three of his four sons, David H., William H., and George W. Weaver, became potters who established numerous businesses throughout the state. David H. Weaver arrived in Knoxville in 1869, and three years later he and his brother William purchased a pottery in the North Knoxville suburb of Mechanicsville. By 1880, their father, George C., and brother George joined them in a family operation. Producing an assortment of stoneware jars, jugs, churns, and bowls, the Weaver Brothers Pottery was one of the few potteries to mark a large percentage of their wares. This firm ceased operations by 1888, as the brothers moved to various parts of the state to establish new businesses. William moved to West Tennessee where he was associated with potteries in Paris and Jackson. Meanwhile, David Weaver and his son Carl moved to Mohawk, in Greene County, to begin a pottery business that specialized in drain and sewer tile. This business continued until 1912. David A. Weaver, son of Carl and grandson of David, embodied the longevity of the Weaver ceramic tradition. He moved the ceramic business from Mohawk to McCloud in neighboring Hawkins County and produced bricks. This business operated until 1952.

Another factory stoneware pottery that had significant influence in West Tennessee was the Pinson Pottery in Madison County. The Pinson Pottery began in the 1880s and bore witness to the migration of Midwest potters into Tennessee. Henry Cline and Henry F. Weist, potters born in Illinois whose fathers had immigrated from Germany, managed the Pinson Pottery from about 1900 to 1910. The firm employed a number of skilled and semiskilled workers, and vessels made at the Pinson Pottery were distributed through West Tennessee, Alabama and Mississippi.

Though few pottery families in Tennessee can boast a longevity and successful adaptation to change that spanned three distinct ceramic traditions, the Russell potteries in Henry County can make such a claim. Begun in the mid-1800s as a family pottery near the Tennessee state line in Calloway County, Kentucky, the Russell family established a series of potteries. John Wesley Russell, the family patriarch,

Southern Potteries Incorporated

THE DISTINCTIVE FORTY-YEAR HISTORY OF SOUTHERN POTTERIES EXEMPLIFIES SEVERAL SIGNIFICANT regional and national trends of the first half of the twentieth century.

Ted Owens brought skilled potters from Minerva and East Liverpool, Ohio, to upper East Tennessee in 1917 and founded a dinnerware factory in Erwin, Unicoi County. The enterprise hired unskilled local workers (both men and women), trained them in the manufacturing of decalcomania stoneware, and became the second largest employer in Erwin, following the Clinchfield Railroad, which had its shop, yards, and headquarters there. From the beginning, the pottery labor force belonged to the National Brotherhood of Operative Potters, and during the Depression years the union's presence ensured cooperation of Southern Potteries' management to help save jobs.

Late in the 1930s, the pottery factory developed a method of hand-painting patterns and labeled this dinnerware "Blue Ridge." Management committed to this new look with its bright

Warehouse and showroom of Southern Potteries, Erwin, October 9, 1952. The photograph shows the large volume and varied patterns of the Blue Ridge line of dinnerware as well as the sample board on the back wall depicting the wide range of patterns for sale. *Center:* E. C. Sellers, assistant sales manager, examines a plate. Record Group 82, Box 48-176, Department of Conservation Collection, Manuscripts Division, Tennessee State Library and Archives. Courtesy of TSLA.

Right: Blue Ridge plate in the Stanhome Ivy pattern. Photograph by Margaret D. Binnicker *Below right:* Blue Ridge Floral Wreath pattern produced by Southern Potteries, Erwin. Photograph by Margaret D. Binnicker.

flowers that suggested a folk-art spontaneity. The public's apparent approval through increased sales helped make Southern Potteries the largest hand-painted pottery in the nation by the mid-1940s. To meet consumer demands, the full-time decorator work force, all women, increased to over five hundred, and they created distinctive, identifiable products sold by the mail catalogues of Sears, Roebuck and Company and Montgomery Ward, in department stores, including Gimbel's in New York, and through eleven sales rooms, among them ones in New York, Toronto, Chicago, Dallas, and San Francisco.

A falling off of consumer sales in the 1950s, when peacetime allowed the reintroduction of Japanese ceramic imports, led to a descent as mercurial as the pottery's assent had been. In 1957, Southern Potteries' stockholders voted to close the factory and liquidate its assets.

Southern Potteries provides one example of outside capital using Appalachian resources, both materials and humans, to produce goods sold in other parts of the country. The women workers the factory employed were essential to the company's success. Teams of four women would work on decorating a plate in an assembly-line sequence that allowed completion of one piece after another in rapid succession. The first decorator painted the central elements on the blank glazed surface, "setting" the pattern. The next painter put in leaves. The third added stems and outlining, and the fourth finished with the border and tidied any smudges. The best crews could decorate one-hundred dozen plates a day.

The appearance of their Blue Ridge hand-painted patterns occurred during the years of great interest nationally in acquiring and displaying Appalachian crafts. The resurgence in popularity of the Blue Ridge pieces among collectors forty years after the factory's demise reflects another surge in consumer desire for the look of hand-crafted goods. Originally intended for the tables of middle- and lower-middle-class families, the Blue Ridge dinnerware from Southern Potteries has attained more recently a status that surprises but pleases those former employees who made it.

Margaret D. Binnicker, Tennessee Historical Society

married Susan Bonner, daughter of potter James Bonner, and learned the pottery trade. Russell's son, William Kirkman Russell, and his grandson, William David Russell, continued the family pottery tradition, operating potteries in Pottertown and Bell City, Kentucky. In 1924, W. D. Russell, assisted by his sons Thad, George, Paul, and Duell, moved his pottery to Paris, Tennessee. Their work emphasized a more commercial operation, producing straight-sided jars and jugs. By the mid-1940s Paul and Thad Russell again shifted the product line of the pottery to create a range of art pottery forms.

Nonconnah Pottery cameo ware pitcher, Shelby County. Made by Walter B. Stephen, c. 1910, it has a green body with brown grape vines and white leaves and is 12¼ inches high. Private collection. Courtesy of the Tennessee Division of Archaeology.

ART POTTERS, 1875–1930

Production of American art pottery began about 1875 and continued until 1930. This type of ceramics developed out of the American Arts and Crafts movement and catered primarily to aesthetic and decorative purposes. Compared to the family pottery tradition, which males dominated, women played a key role in the early period of Tennessee art pottery.

The hands and talents of Elizabeth J. Scovel were very important to the emergence of this new pottery tradition. Her establishment of the Nashville Art Pottery in 1884 utilized local clays and sought to produce a high-fired earthenware of high artistic merit. Scovel developed several decorative glazes for her pottery. "*Goldstone,* a rich, dark brown glaze over a red body, had a brilliant golden appearance as a result of high firing," and *Pomegranate,* a "white body [that] was decorated with a red-veined effect on a mottled pink and blue-gray background," were perhaps her two best examples.[5] Newspaper accounts of the time applauded Scovel for the beauty of her pottery, the fine subtlety of the vessel shapes, and her low prices. One writer claimed: "People of Nashville and Tennessee will make a sad mistake if they do not see to it their little art pottery is the foundation of a great industry in that state, and thus make the practical discoveries of Miss Scovel a permanent benefit to the people. . . . It is evident that at Nashville there is a clay of extraordinary value for artistic products in pottery, and there is a lady potter of remarkable skill and taste."[6] Despite the glowing review of Scovel's work, her art pottery ceased operations about 1889. Examples of her pottery are extremely rare, as only two marked examples of her high-fired earthenware are known.

A later chapter of the art pottery phase in Tennessee's ceramic history began in 1901 with the work of Nellie Randall Stephen and her son Walter B. Stephen. Living in eastern Shelby County, the Stephens established the Nonconnah Pottery and produced the most intricate and decorative art pottery in the state. Using local clays discovered while digging a well, the Stephens initially produced vessels that relied on the potting skills of Walter and the decorative art skills of Nellie. Their work evolved into the production of a type of cameo ware (pate-sur-pate) that was not only technically intricate, but also artistically demanding. Pate-sur-pate is a delicate bas-relief design built up by painting layer upon layer of porcelain slip or liquid clay, allowing each layer to dry before the next application. The relief work is usually tooled.

Nellie Stephen died in 1910, ending the Tennessee phase of the Nonconnah Pottery. Walter Stephen left West Tennessee, moved his pottery over the mountains, and reestablished the Nonconnah Pottery in Skyland, North Carolina, in 1913. Stephen stayed at that location until 1920, when he moved again to Arden, North Carolina, and established the nationally known Pisgah Forest Pottery. Stephen made his national reputation producing cameo ware that depicted figures and actions of pioneer America, especially cowboys and covered wagon scenes. His devotion to experimentation with ceramic shapes and surface treatment (in both glaze and design) produced an original and exceptional product. Walter Stephen died in 1961, leaving a sixty-year legacy and tradition as one of America's most gifted and inventive art potters.

Studio Potters, 1930–present

The least researched and understood aspect of Tennessee's ceramic heritage resides in the early studio potters that developed out of the Arts and Crafts tradition in the 1930s. Economic and political forces in the 1910s and 1920s forever changed the course of pottery activities in Tennessee. Temperance interests and the passage of the Eighteenth Amendment to the U.S. Constitution spelled the doom for the factory stoneware potteries, which specialized in the production of whiskey jugs. The onset of the Great Depression forced potteries to close their kilns as the economy constricted and demand for ceramic products lessened. In response, the newly created Tennessee Valley Authority established a ceramics research laboratory in Norris in April 1934, and helped establish the early phase of the studio potteries in Tennessee.

TVA hired Robert E. Gould as its chief ceramic engineer to test the feasibility of developing a local ceramics industry using kaolin clays from western North Carolina and TVA-produced power. TVA hired its first potter, George W. Fichter, in May 1936. The following year, it hired Ohio-trained potter Ernest Wilson, who spent several years working at Southern Pottery in Erwin, Tennessee, before moving to the TVA facility in Norris. In 1946, Wilson's son-in-law, Douglas Ferguson, moved from Norris to Sevier County to establish the Pigeon Forge Pottery. Following the interest generated by the establishment of the Arrowmont craft shop in nearby Gatlinburg in the mid-1920s, Ferguson was among the first group of potters to create a line of ceramics marketed primarily for the growing tourist industry. Capitalizing on the popularity of the newly created Great Smoky Mountains National Park in 1940, the Pigeon Forge Pottery prospered as thousands of tourist and campers flocked into the area.

While Ferguson can be considered one of the better-known studio potters, he was certainly not the only potter continuing Tennessee's ceramic traditions. The Tennessee Association of Craft Artists (TACA) was established in 1965, in response to renewed interest in revitalizing local crafts. Two of TACA's founding members were important potters, Sylvia Hyman of Nashville and Lewis Snyder of Murfreesboro. Hyman took her undergraduate degree in art education from Buffalo (New York) State College in 1938 and later added her master's in art education from the George Peabody College for Teachers in 1963. Important as a teacher and contemporary clay artist, Hyman's work is in the permanent collections of national and international museums. She received the Lifetime Achievement Award from the National Museum of Women in the Arts in 1993, followed by the Tennessee Governor's Award in the Arts in 1993, and a thirty-year retrospective exhibit of her work at the Tennessee State Museum in 2000. Lewis Snyder, who holds a MFA from Ohio University, opened the Studio S shop in Murfreesboro in 1970 and has taught in the Art Department at Middle Tennessee State University. His works too are held in national and international collections. Both Hyman and Snyder have been elected members of the prestigious International Academy of Ceramics at the Ariana Museum in Switzerland. Through their efforts a juried crafts fair was established in Tennessee in 1972 as a means to develop markets for craft products. TACA's purpose is to encourage, document, and promote crafts and craft persons in Tennessee. Today over 130 potters who are members of TACA do their part to keep alive the craftsmanship established by Tennessee's historic potters.

CONCLUSION

> Once more within the Potter's house alone
> I stood, surrounded by the shapes of Clay.
> Shapes of all Sorts and Sizes, great and small,
> that stood along the floor and by the wall;
> And some loquacious Vessels were; and some
> Listened perhaps, but never talked at all.
>
> *The Rubaiyat of Omar Khayyam,*
> Translated by Edward FitzGerald, 1857

Surviving examples of Tennessee's rich ceramic history can indeed speak if one chooses to listen and has the diligence to explore. These vessels can demonstrate the value of hard work and the skill of the potter in transforming lumps of clay into objects of beauty we now define as art. Because of the utilitarian nature of the pottery, most vessels produced by Tennessee potters are gone, discarded or broken by the everyday activities associated with their general use, or unrecognized because most Tennessee potters failed to mark or identify their products. Through the skills of the historian, talents of the genealogist, and deftness of the archaeologist, many of the styles and characteristics of individual potters have been identified. While the finished product of the potter's craft remains fragile at best, the pottery sites where craftsmen produced these vessels are severely endangered. Encroachment of commercial development, urban sprawl, and continued farming practices makes the likelihood of learning more about these pottery sites rather difficult. Important information on kiln construction and vessel production is being lost as the context to research and study the sites is being compromised. Some consolation can be offered to those who appreciate the art and craftsmanship of the Tennessee potters. Current research has documented a sizable pottery industry producing vessels that today are admired and appreciated by a myriad of people. Several museum exhibits have highlighted Tennessee-made pottery and brought attention of the craft to ceramic collectors and the general public. As additional cemeteries are transcribed, census data compiled, and family histories published, the evaluation and assessment of significant individual potters and their wares becomes easier. This new data will allow ceramic historians and archaeologists to place Tennessee's pottery heritage into the broader context of the South.

NOTES

1. John A. Burrison, *Brothers in Clay: The Story of Georgia Folk Pottery* (Athens: Univ. of Georgia Press, 1983), 44.
2. Records of East Tennessee, Civil War Records, vol. 1, Prepared by the Historical Records Survey Transcription Unit, Division of Women's and Professional Projects, Works Progress Administration, Mrs. John Trotwood Moore, State Librarian and Archivist, Nashville, Tennessee, June 1, 1939, p. 40-a.
3. Samuel D. Smith and Stephen T. Rogers, *A Survey of Historic Pottery Making in Tennessee,* Research Series No. 3 (Nashville: Tennessee Department of Conservation, Division of Archaeology, 1979), 8.
4. Charles G. Zug III, *Turners and Burners: The Folk Potters of North Carolina* (Chapel Hill: Univ. of North Carolina Press, 1986), 282.

5. Paul Evans, *Art Pottery of the United States: An Encyclopedia of Producers and Their Marks* (New York: Scribner, 1974), 178.
6. "The Art Pottery Established by Miss Bettie J. Scovel," *Nashville Daily American,* June 16, 1887, p. 7.

Suggested Readings

Baldwin, Cinda K. *Great and Noble Jar: Traditional Stoneware of South Carolina.* Athens: Univ. of Georgia Press, 1993.

Bridges, Daisy Wade, and Kathryn C. Preyer, ed. "The Pottery of Walter Stephen." *Journal of Studies Ceramic Circle* 3 (1978).

Burrison, John A. *Brothers in Clay: The Story of Georgia Folk Pottery.* Athens: Univ. of Georgia Press, 1983.

Comstock, H. E. *The Pottery of the Shenandoah Valley Region.* Winston-Salem, N.C.: Museum of Early Southern Decorative Arts, 1994.

Koverman, Jill Beute. *I Made This Jar . . . Dave: The Life and Works of the Enslaved African American Potter, Dave.* Columbia, S.C.: McKissick Museum, 1998.

Moore, J. Roderick. "Earthenware Potters along the Great Road in Virginia and Tennessee." *Antiques* (Sept. 1983): 528–37.

Rogers, Stephen T. "Family Potters: Tennessee's Forgotten Craftsmen." *Courier* 18 (Feb. 1980): 2–3.

Smith, Samuel D., and Stephen T. Rogers. *A Survey of Historic Pottery Making in Tennessee.* Research Series No. 3. Nashville: Tennessee Department of Conservation, Division of Archaeology, 1979.

Sweezy, Nancy. *Raised in Clay: The Southern Pottery Tradition.* Washington, D.C.: Smithsonian Institution Press, 1984.

Webb, Thomas G. "The Pottery Industry of DeKalb, White and Putnam Counties." *Tennessee Historical Quarterly* 30 (Spring 1971): 110–12.

Willett, E. Henry, and Joey Brackner. *The Traditional Pottery of Alabama.* Montgomery, Ala.: Montgomery Museum of Fine Arts, 1983.

Zug, Charles G., III. *Turners and Burners: The Folk Potters of North Carolina.* Chapel Hill: Univ. of North Carolina Press, 1986.

Thirteen

Tennessee Textiles

Christi Teasley
Monteagle, Tennessee

Humble yet rich, Tennessee's textile tradition sets the stage for the distinct variety of contemporary fiber work created by the state's artists and craftspeople. Slightly more than two hundred years since statehood, the process and product of the textile arts have evolved naturally from the unpretentious decorative design of the functional object to a powerful vehicle of artistic expression. The fiber art of Tennessee is as diverse as the culture and geography. High esteem for the functional roots of textile production has inspired many to preserve and continue creating within these traditions. Their labors assure a continued familiarity of the beauty of these early methods and an appreciation of the handmade. Honoring the Appalachian traditions and fresh on the heels of the craft revival's second and third generations, many of these artists are building upon this abundant heritage. Other contemporary fiber workers are challenging our sense of nostalgia by linking familiar techniques with unaccustomed messages. Tennessee's textile story embraces a sturdy history and celebrates the meandering path leading toward her dynamic current voice.

Early textile production stemmed from necessity, yet the aesthetic decisions and the chosen design elements have spoken for their makers from the beginning. Rarely are the earliest textiles preserved; however, Tennessee enjoys a number of archaeological discoveries indicating cloth production as early as the Mississippian period. Chards of pottery carrying the imprint of fabrics and twisted cords reveal the making of cloth long after the actual textiles have rotted. Ironically, textures impressed on little pieces of earth describe a wealth of patterns and structures, clues to the cords and bindings used, and notions of life-style, all of which disintegrated back to the land that made the clay. Textile archaeologists Jenna Tedrick Kuttruff and Carl Kuttruff observe that the 510 impressed chards from Mound Bottom, a Mississippian period village site in Cheatham County, exhibit predominantly twined textiles. While it is uncertain whether the textiles were constructed specifically for the production of pottery, it is likely that they served both functional and decorative purposes. The textiles eased the removal of the clay vessels from their molds while imprinting pattern and texture to the surface of the pottery. A prehistoric twined bag from Big Bone Cave in Van Buren County is dated between A.D. 335 and 1510, the earlier date belonging to the Middle Woodland period and the later date placing the bag in the Late Mississippian period. Because of the dry conditions, lack of light, and constant temperature in the cave, the rectangular bag was preserved. Jenna Kuttruff concludes that the bag was highly valued because of the numerous repairs to it. Its fabric was of local fibers that required little or no processing and it was constructed with skilled care, so that the ends of the twining are not visible when joined. The maker of this finely crafted utilitarian work of cloth shares common ground with the fiber workers to follow centuries later.

Very little textile work that can be attributed to Eastern Woodland Cherokees has survived. Once again, pottery vessels bearing the marks of textiles provide a clue to the early Cherokee cloth industry. Wooden paddles wrapped with cord were used to shape and create textures on the clay. The range of coarse and fine cordage and complete weaves indicates that the Cherokees possessed an advanced level of weaving skill. The technical excellence of the Cherokees is documented in travel accounts of the Spaniards in the mid-sixteenth century. The whitened cloth that was woven of tightly spun, pounded, bast fibers was mistakenly admired as the "fine weave of their cotton mantles."[1] These early Cherokee methods and traditions, however, failed to influence the work of the incoming white settlers from England and Europe. What could have been an intriguing cultural exchange between two different weaving traditions proved to be a missed opportunity. After white settlers introduced English looms and spinning wheels, traditional Cherokee methods and designs faded away, although the wealth of patterns recorded through the Cherokee basketmaking tradition provides clues to the imagery probably once found in the earlier weaving. After Removal in 1837–38, a small number of Cherokees remained in the eastern mountains. The regional weaving revival of the 1920s, initiated by missionaries and reformers, triggered renewed Cherokee interest in their ancient craft. Encouraged by the Indian Arts and Craft Board and the establishment of a craft guild in Qualla, North Carolina, contemporary Cherokee weavers have developed designs for shawls, table linens, and bedcovers based on traditional patterns.

Two-thousand-year-old woven bag from dry cave in Middle Tennessee. Courtesy of The Frank H. McClung Museum, University of Tennessee.

Tennessee in 1796 was the western edge of the American frontier, but it was also an industrious, bustling, and diverse place. For town residents, a wide variety of store-bought cloth was available, supplementing home production. In an advertisement in the *Knoxville Gazette* of December 12, 1791, merchants Summerville and Ore announced that they would sell "well chosen goods" from Philadelphia and Baltimore while at the same time they offered "the highest price: for "good lynsey" and "seven hundred linen," indicating a local demand for these indigenous materials. A month later, in the *Knoxville Gazette* of January 14, 1792, John Hague sought "a number of GOOD WEAVERS," encouraged particularly those "acquainted with the weaving of Velvets, Corduroys, and Calicoes," and announced that his machines for carding and spinning were ready to use. David Deadrick's advertisement in the *Knoxville Gazette* of July 11, 1792, proclaimed goods from Philadelphia and Baltimore on sale at his stores in Jonesborough and Greeneville, including "fine and colorful cloths, velvets, royal ribs, Fustian, a handsome assortment of Chintzes, Calicoes and printed linens, Turkey cotton . . . Cambric, lawn and muslin." In exchange, Deadrick would accept for trade "SKINS, FURS, BEESWAX AND FLAX." These ads from 1791 to 1792 indicate that homespun and imported cloth were available to sewing customers on the Tennessee frontier. Other newspaper advertisements listed sewing notions, dyestuff, spinning wheels, carding combs, and shuttles for sale as well as calls for raw fiber, yarn, and finished cloth. Merchants regularly sought flax for barter; cotton, wool, and occasionally hemp also were mentioned in early Tennessee newspapers.

Other sources reveal the diversity of early Tennessee textiles. Estate inventories in Washington County list fine fabrics, looms, and spinning wheels. The cloth made in home production was typically humble and serviceable—fabric for bed linens and everyday clothes. While fancy garments were often constructed at the homes of town dwellers and plantation owners (with slave women doing much of the work), the cloth of which they were made was more often than not imported from Philadelphia, Baltimore, and Richmond. The flax grown and the yarn spun in early households were viable tender at the mercantile, for notions and fancier cloth. In her transcription of early ledgers of the Amis family, who operated a rural store and farm in Hawkins County, Lucy Gump found that imported cloth and notions were available in the outlying communities as well as the emerging towns of East Tennessee. From Amis's store, residents could purchase or trade for imported calico, silk skeins, local linen, and osnaburg, which was a yarn dyed cloth of flax and tow often in blue or brown and white stripes. Ledgers from early businesses suggest that locally produced goods served as the commodities that allowed for the purchase of imported finery.

Primarily working with flax fiber, East Tennessee weavers produced both fine linen and a coarser grade of tow linen for everyday use. The production of cloth was labor intensive and involved a vast array of tools and processes. Early inventories listed farming and harvesting equipment, rippling combs, flax brakes, scotching boards and knives, hackles, and a variety of flax wheels. After harvest, processes to ready the fiber for spinning included rippling, to remove seeds; retting, to dissolve gummy sap by soaking the stalks; braking, to separate the pulpy core from the fiber; scotching, to remove hard pieces and to make the fiber tender by scraping the fiber; hackling, to separate the long fine linen fibers from the coarser tow fibers by raking the fibers over sharp combs; spinning, to create yarn, and finally weaving, to create cloth. Finished cloth was valued highly for domestic use as well as for barter for other merchandise. The home weavers of fine cloth were well respected for their extraordinary work and skill.

Early affluent farms throughout the state had rooms or small buildings devoted to cloth production. Rocky Mount, the Sullivan County home of William Cobb, had a small outbuilding devoted to spinning and weaving. It was equipped with both wool and flax wheels, the loom, fireplace, and a sleeping loft for two slave children, who helped with the weaving. Travellers Rest was the Davidson County home of John Overton, who in 1820 married Mary McConnell White May, a widow with five children and a gifted herbalist. Many of the plants grown in her gardens were useful for dyeing as well as healing. The mistress of a household of this scale would delegate the production of cloth and household items to competent and often apprentice-trained slaves. One Overton slave, Matilda, was recognized as an expert weaver, and Overton sometimes hired her out to other families. The McGavock family at Carnton plantation in Williamson County also had an outbuilding devoted to weaving. Later, as the bulk of cotton grown in the state shifted to West Tennessee, many of these new cotton farms also produced cloth on-site for use of the plantation residents. While a major supplier of cotton, the Tennessee delta did not create significant amounts of cotton cloth for other regions before the Civil War (although some Tennessee textile mills, such as the Lenoir Mill in Loudon County, were in operation). The bulk of raw cotton was exported to New England and England, where it would be spun and woven in huge mills.

The majority of Tennesseans could not devote whole buildings or rooms to making cloth or hire a staff for such production. Yet many homes had a spinning wheel or even a loom set up in a corner. Laodicea "Aunt Dicie" Fletcher (1830–1913) was a weaving legend from Morgan County. She wove the patterns that she designed on an old loom that her family brought across the mountains from Virginia through Cumberland Gap. Well versed in literature and ballads, she copied her intricate weaving patterns on parchment. Her niece, Minnie Fletcher Kidd, remembers that "she would spin and weave all the time: she took time off to milk her cows, but seldom took time off to cook."[2] While the slaves raised sheep, sheared them, prepared the wool, and spun and dyed the thread, Betty Gleaves of Dickson County worked with her slave Cindy to weave cloth, which they cut and sewed clothing, linens, and other items for both the white family and the slaves. Many households spun the yarn used for their daily cloth and it was not unusual for young children to contribute their efforts. Sometimes the yarn was delivered to a local dyer; other yarn was dyed at home. Finished yarn might be taken to a professional weaver or knitted into socks. Itinerant weavers ventured to a community to weave for a few weeks or even months before moving on. Nancy Osbourne Greer (1833–1934), from the village of Trade in Johnson County, spun and wove until the age of ninety-five. As a professional craftsperson, it was not unusual for Nancy Greer to travel as far as Virginia and North Carolina, where she would stay for a month or more to weave for a family. She continued to spin wool for the weaving of Taft Greer, her grandson, at the age of one hundred.

Granny Nancy Osbourne Greer of Trade, Johnson County. Photograph by Doris Ulmann. Used with special permission from the Berea College Art Department, Berea, Kentucky.

Professional weavers like Greer took in work of local households as well as created work for the general mercantile. In her diary on November 26, 1863, Fannie Fain of Sullivan County complained about one such weaver: "Mr. Fain went out to Mrs. Hawks, for a piece of Lynsey, brought it home, not nice or well done by any means. I am much disappointed in it. She wove for sixpence a yard, 16 and ¾ yards, $2.00 for the whole, 50 cts for edging, paid in flour."[3] Other mid-nineteenth-century diarists recorded their own cloth production. Jane Jones of Hardeman County wove in her early years of marriage, but as the family plantation prospered by the late 1850s, she began to purchase all of her cloth and acquired a sewing machine. She stitched regularly, making most of her family's clothing, her children's diapers, and winter and summer clothes for the slaves who worked the plantation. Myra Inman of Bradley County kept a diary from 1859 to 1866, from her teen years to the age of twenty-one. She recorded daily sewing of garments for herself, her family, their slaves, and, during the Civil War, soldiers. On September 16, 1861, for example, she wrote that "Rhoda, Mother and Sister have been making drawers for the soldiers all day."[4] Sewing machines were not uncommon and the bulk of the household textiles and clothing were made at home. While Myra's sister wove periodically, and everyone knitted, the Inmans purchased the bulk of their gingham and calico for household clothing from the local mercantile.

The ordinary textile is not well preserved (unlike the more often carefully preserved wedding dress imported from St. Louis), and is typically "worn out." Thus, much Tennessee-produced cloth and tex-

Mrs. Leah Dougherty, weaver. Photograph by Doris Ulmann. Used with special permission from the Berea College Art Department, Berea, Kentucky.

tile art never appear in collections outside of those of their family of origin. While ordinary cloth rarely survived, such locally produced, everyday goods still can be found in the backing of a quilt or the lining of a jacket. Such is the case of the bedcover woven by a slave for Mrs. William Winfrey of Memphis in 1840. The backing is a heavy cottonade with ribbed grid, reminiscent of the Acadian weaving of Louisiana. Wholecloth quilts, appliquéd bed covers, and patchwork quilts may have examples of native cloth on the back, if not on the top as well. The worn linen towels used to pack china, mattress ticking, and pillow covers provide other clues to the breadth of locally woven cloth. While most everyday textiles were used until threadbare, the one exception is bedcovers. The maker and the family who owned them treasured these blankets, coverlets, quilts, counterpanes, and afghans. Due to the labor involved in the creation of these large textiles, the personal aesthetic investment made in such pieces, and the durability of these household staples, bedcovers have survived to tell a large part of the textile story in Tennessee.

Throughout the nineteenth century, cloth production tended toward simple weaves since much of the home sewing was from necessity. But within many remaining works, the pleasure of making something personal and beautiful is evident. A bit of tatted lace for the collar, a stitched monogram for the pillowcase, or an embroidered posy for a child's pocket added variety to the chore of sewing, providing an outlet for creative expression. Moore County's Eunice Ophelia Evans Motlow (1885–1983) created extraordinary crewel work, almost Jacobean in nature. These Old World designs were not noted on paper, but rather they had been passed from one generation of needleworkers to the next. Ophelia and her sister, Mary Evans Bobo, learned these designs from their mother Bird Evans. By the time granddaughter Elizabeth Motlow knew her, Ophelia's sight had diminished, yet she still called stitching "her work."[5] Granddaughter Elizabeth Motlow now prizes two crocheted dishrags as well as the more decorative embroideries of Ophelia Motlow. Pieces such as these gather nostalgia as they are passed down through a family, a process that would probably shock the original maker, who never would have suspected the charm that a handmade, everyday object could hold for a future generation.

The sampler is one of the most cherished combinations of the utilitarian and the decorative in Tennessee textiles. Created by young girls in order to learn and record embroidery stitches and designs, early samplers have charmed audiences of all eras. The sampler served not only as a means of learning stitches, it was also an exhibition piece for the young woman. With name and date carefully rendered with her needle, these samplers became works of accomplishment as well as reference for future needlework. Generally, mothers, aunts, and older sisters introduced embroidery skills to young girls. Many

Grape shawl by Elmira Lewis Warwick, Williamson County, c. 1850s. Handspun, home-dyed, and handwoven, embroidered wool; 54 × 57 inches. Collection of Elaine and Rick Warwick. Courtesy of Rick Warwick.

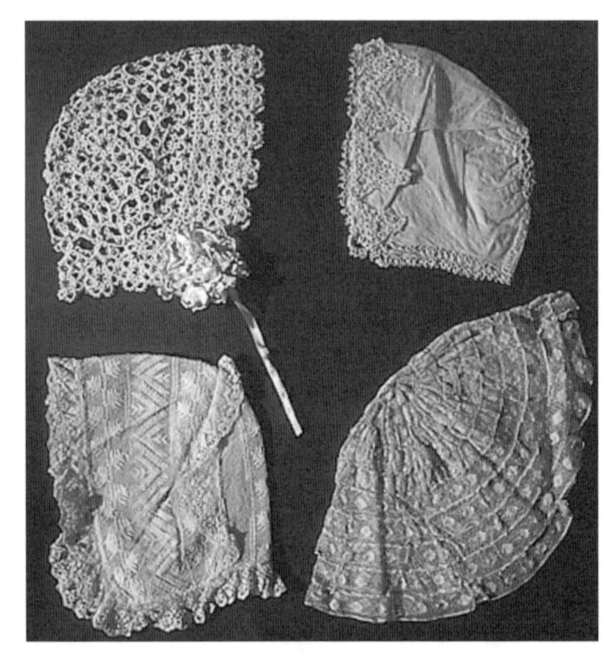

Baby caps from the Priest and Waters families, Davidson and Wilson Counties, 1870–1920. Ranging from hand-tatted to manipulated store-bought lace. Courtesy of Bettie Hill.

women, however, learned the skills at the increasingly accessible and popular female academies, where the sampler became part of a formal education. While attending Spring Hill Academy in Williamson County in 1845, Eliza Jane Graham made a Tennessee map sampler, perhaps a school project to combine geography and needlework lessons.

Common themes wind through the sampler tradition, yet in many cases the personality of the needleworker surfaces with clarity. Young Sarah Gooch of Beechville began her sampler in 1822, and continued to add family initials to the work as late 1849, documenting the expanding family tree until thirty initials appeared on the sampler.

Young women used the stitches and techniques learned through the sampler process to create utilitarian garments, label household items, ornament their linens with decorative monograms, and embellish their "Sunday best" clothes. Elmira Lewis Warwick of Chesnut Ridge in Anderson County created her "grape" shawl from start to finish, probably in the 1850s. After shearing her sheep, carding the wool, spinning the yarn, weaving the fabric, and dyeing her handwoven cloth with walnut hulls, she embroidered corner motifs of grapes in crewel wool. In the nineteenth century, both baby boys and girls wore elaborate bonnets and long white dresses until they could walk. Even at the turn of the twentieth century, the prevailing belief was that a baby's layette should be made by hand. Exhibiting a wide range of white work, tatting, bobbin lace, French embroidery, and pin-tucking, exquisite hand sewing on infant clothing and christening garments has been preserved and cherished by generations. Although many of these same techniques were employed on women's shirtwaists, they were not frequently preserved. Later, as industry created more household textiles, these embroidery skills were utilized to personalize and decorate the store-bought pillowcases and aprons.

The influential *Godey's Lady's Book and Magazine* (1830–1898) offered the expanding audience of middle-class and elite women a collection of short poems, comments on lady's fashion, instructions for knitting and crochet patterns, and commentary on various social and fashion trends. As magazines such as *Godey's* gained in popularity and distribution from the mid- to late nineteenth century, needlework inevitably became more homogenized. As prescribed in an endless array of advice manuals, magazines, and books, Victorian women took up handwork as a fashionable pastime for ladies, even though they no longer had to be concerned about home production of clothing and linens. Tatting, bobbin lace, knitting, crochet, hair work, beading, needlepoint, and crewel embroidery all cycled in and out of fashion as pleasant and rewarding pastimes for middle-class and elite women, especially in the nation's booming urban and suburban areas. In rural areas, however, home production remained common well into the twentieth century until a combination of mail-order catalogues, Rural Free Delivery, and the home economics movement interjected a degree of standardization into textile work on family farms.

Weaving at Cumberland Homesteads, Crossville. Photograph by Ben Shahn, 1937. Courtesy of Library of Congress, Prints & Photographs Division, Farm Security Administration—Office of War Information Photograph Collection (reproduction number LC-USF33-006261-M3 DLC).

Two developments in the second decade of the twentieth century shaped the future course of Tennessee textiles for the next three generations. In 1913, the first issues of the Nashville-based *Southern Women's Magazine* included patterns for needlework projects designed by Anne Orr, the magazine's art editor and the operator of the Anne Orr Studio in Nashville. Stylized floral motifs, bonneted babies, and crisp revisions of traditional patterns became her trademark. Orr enjoyed a long and successful career and her work was published in prominent national women's periodicals, including a monthly column in *Good Housekeeping*. In 1917 Coats Thread Company, then of England, sponsored the publication of her needlework pattern booklets. Orr's patterns reached a large and wide audience, and many awards were given nationally to needleworkers for their renditions of her designs. Her booklets served as guides for tatting, knitting, embroidery, crochet, quilts, needlepoint, and cross-stitch, and were reproduced on playing cards, dishware, and toys. Immensely popular from 1920 through the early 1940s, Orr's designs continue today to be published individually and in various collections. In 2000, Travellers Rest sponsored an exhibition of her work, Quilts and Ephemera from the Anne Orr Studio of Nashville, curated by Tennessee textile historian, Merikay Waldvogel.

The second and more important development was the handicraft revival that swept through Tennessee craft and design arts in the middle decades of the twentieth century. The settlement school movement of the turn of the century aimed to help mountain communities and families to become self-sufficient and to uplift rural life. The reformers, often women associated with various church missions, saw themselves as saving and preserving an almost lost tradition of craft and design arts through their revival of Appalachian and Southern Highland crafts. Mountain families typically accepted the "revival" more as another stage in their evolution of craft traditions and anticipated the economic benefits of increased interest in their work. As craft historian Jane Kessler observed, the efforts of the mission women "were fueled by both practicality and deeply rooted spiritual beliefs. Although termed a revival, the [settlement school] movement did not so much revive the traditional crafts as create a new tradition. Objects originally made to meet specific needs were transformed into objects with a mission."[6]

The Pi Beta Phi Settlement School in Gatlinburg was one of over 150 similar settlement schools in Appalachia. Established in 1912 by the women of the Pi Beta Phi sorority, the school's mission was "to show the mountain people how to use their own resources, to develop industries suitable to their environment, and to lead more happy, healthful lives."[7] While initially teachers focused their attention on mountain children, they soon learned that education of the child was impossible without uplifting rural life, especially in light of the poverty they saw all around them. In 1915, the school's head teacher, Mary O. Pollard, observed that "many of the women make exquisite patchwork quilts, and some still make the handwoven coverlets and blankets. If a sale could be found for these articles, many might undertake the work."[8] The school acquired four looms by 1916, and under the direction of teacher Caroline McKnight Hughes and others, the school launched a weaving program. The effort to reteach mountain women forgotten textile arts involved a combination of the teachers' energies and the knowledge of older women in the traditional skills of spinning and weaving. The teachers encouraged production of traditional woven household items. The school paid the weavers for their work, and then sought to market the items in a northeastern market, appealing to the middle class interest in handwork earlier generated by the Arts and Crafts movement, which had been particularly influential in the Northeast. The creation of this outside market for handmade goods gave mountain women "pin money" for household needs in an era of general hard times and an economic reason to revive the almost forgotten skills.

Winogene Redding, a Canadian weaver, rejuvenated the settlement school's program with new designs for the weavers and alternative colorways for traditional patterns. Redding solicited the work of home weavers from the surrounding areas in addition to the pupils at the school. She remembered going by horseback "up the creeks and hollows to see the women in their homes, where the looms were . . . sometimes in the old days I helped them make their warp with pegs stuck in the logs on the outside of their cabins."[9] Redding recruited thirty weavers, and also inspired the school's other teachers to take up weaving when their classroom duties were over. For many years she published "Reddigraphs," loose-leaf instructions for weaving projects. She returned to Gatlinburg over the years for lengthy leadership stints as well as short visits until her retirement to Pigeon Forge in 1962.

Ruth Clements Bond, interior and textile designer, relocated to Chattanooga in 1934 with her husband J. Max Bonds, the top African American administrator in the Tennessee Valley Authority during the years of dam construction in the Chattanooga area. Despite their education and accomplishments, the Bondses lived in segregated TVA construction-site housing, where most every item for the home had to be created on site. Ruth Bonds soon started working with other African American women in neighboring TVA construction communities. Curtains made from flour sacks and rugs made from cornshucks and rags were designed by Bonds and created by women throughout these communities. Skilled in traditional needlework, the women were already able to crochet, quilt, knit, and make braided rugs. Ruth Bonds taught them color and design, concepts that they incorporated in their dye making from local plants. The resulting quilts, rugs, and home furnishings were intended to make the home more desirable and were not created for an external market.

The weaving movement of Gatlinburg in the mid-1920s was replicated in several other Tennessee rural communities. As the research of historian Mary Hoffschwelle has shown, the rural reform movement, led by home economics teachers and home demonstration agents, became interested in the potential of weaving as a way rural women could raise their family income. Beginning in 1915, home demonstration clubs sold crocheted items, along with canned goods, at the Chattanooga market house. They also took special orders for homemade rugs, and by 1922, according to one agricultural official, many women supplemented their incomes with rug making. Around the town of Apison, about one hundred women made rugs for sale, selling fifteen hundred dollars' worth in 1923; two years later, sales reached four thousand dollars, as the women prepared handmade rugs, wall hangings, table linens, dresser scarves, and draperies. Similar ventures proved successful for the Knox County community of Asbury, which sold rugs at a 4-H Shop in Knoxville, and for Union County women, who in 1929 established a shop along the eastern branch of the Dixie Highway in Maynardville. Along with quilts and linens, the women sold baskets, vases, and pottery.

In all of these settings, women were producing textiles not for themselves or their communities, but for an external clientele who nostalgically sought the work as a reminder of earlier eras and took pride in the social consciousness demonstrated by their purchases. As completion of the Great Smoky Mountains National Park neared in the 1930s, an influx of tourists descended on Gatlinburg, and many snapped up the available mountain crafts. The years 1935 to 1945 were significant for the Gatlinburg area weavers. Sales from tourists, Pi Beta Phi alumnae, organized urban marketing, and a mail-order catalogue broadened the customer base, encouraging weavers to bring out new products. Items such as placemats, decorative guest towels, bibs, aprons, and baby blankets were uncommon in mountain homes, but in demand by middle-class tourists. Inspired by traditional patterns, the new household items "were not represented as authentic mountain crafts, but as produced by mountain people."[10]

The single most important institution in shaping these new markets and products of the handicraft movement was the Southern Highland Handicraft Guild, which was founded in 1930. Over fifty years later, Charles Counts, a quilter and crafts activist, commented, "The social movement that created such an organization as the Guild, was, I believe, a part of a vast international effort to save the world from too much materialism and greedy industrialization."[11] The guild's original philosophy, linked with marketing savvy and a high aesthetic code, continues to strengthen the role of craft and the craft artist today.

In the early days of the guild, weavers played an important leadership role. The Shuttle-Crafters, a weaving cooperative in Hamblen County, enjoyed a proud heritage, dating back to six generations of weavers in the Doughtery family. Organized by Sarah Doughtery in 1923, Shuttle-Crafters involved area weavers in their remote cabins as well as local weavers who joined the Doughtery family for work in their Russelville home, Forest Hill. Sarah and her sister Ella Doughtery Wall had an old log structure moved to their property in 1930 and restored it as a loom house and a show room of their finely colored work inspired by traditional designs. At the log house, community weavers also gathered and rediscovered lost family traditions. In 1934, the Doughtery sisters hosted a two-day meeting of the Southern Highland Handicraft Guild at their property. The sisters exhibited a linen bed sheet by Elizabeth Cable Mart, their great-grandmother; coverlets by their grandmother Betsy Flannery Adams and their mother Leah Adams, a coverlet by Sarah Doughtery, and another coverlet by their niece Mary Doughtery. Leah Adams Doughtery was considered an authority on natural dyes and dye lore, dating to the days of the Cherokees and early settlers. Sarah Doughtery stated that they dyed all of the Shuttle-Crafters' colors, except indigo, which was dyed by "Mrs. Alice Greer, whose large iron pot has contained blue dye yeast for the last ninety years."[12] The Doughterys collected an extraordinary assortment of equipment from all eras of cloth production, including looms, spinning wheels, and a wide variety of devices for skeining yarn such as "swifts" and "niddy-noddies." The Shuttle-Crafters' reputation for fine and prolific work continued until Sarah Doughtery's death in 1965.

A renewed interest in the potential of regional dyes, as exemplified by the Shuttle-Crafters, paralleled the excitement generated by local weaving. Most eighteenth- and early-nineteenth-century American dyers received formal training and relied on tested, time-honored materials rather than experimenting with natural materials found in the United States. Home dyers in Tennessee found the old colonial recipes to be useful guides, but they were convinced that the best way to assure quality dyed goods was from careful experimentation with local plants and the sharing of successful recipes through family and friends. They found that yellow dyes from black-eyed Susans, coreopsis, goldenrod, and onion skins were available in the back yard, while the general store provided indigo and madder, the plant base for the remarkable Turkey-red color. Home dyeing varied from excellent to poor, depending on the dedication, knowledge, and experience of the dyer.

Most of Tennessee's indigenous plants, or those from anywhere else for that matter, will only stain unless the dyer adds a mordant, usually a mineral or tannin, to create a chemical bond with the fibers. The resulting color of dyed goods from a single species varies according to the mordant chosen. Occasionally, the metal of the iron pot used to heat the dye served as the mordant. More often, such mordants as alum, copper, chrome, or tin were added to the dye pot. Indigo and black walnut hulls were the region's substantive dyes, meaning that they contain their own mordant. The finest black dyed cloth is said to come from dyeing black walnut brown on a deep indigo bottom. Well into the first part of the twentieth century, indigo used in the Southern Highlands was usually fermented in vats with limewater, urine, or wood ash lye. But most indigo came from local general stores. Synthetic indigo was invented in 1880, but it was not until the early 1900s that its price was cheaper than natural indigo, which mostly came from the Bengal region of India. Once the cost was down, dyers made the shift to synthetic dyes for economy and for the intense colors they produced. Like weaving itself, the craft revival of the 1920s reintroduced traditional methods of natural dyeing, mostly by spinners, weavers, and knitters, for use in their finished products. Two Tennesseans, Mary Frances Davidson and Jim Liles, have contributed significantly to the rejuvenation of natural dyeing through their extensive research and scholarship.

Davidson learned about the beauty of naturally dyed yarns during a visit to the John C. Campbell Folk School, in Brasstown, North Carolina, in the late 1940s. Her studies led to work with Mrs. Wilma Stone Viner, who then created the widest range of naturally dyed colors in the Southern Highlands. Davidson summarized her research in the influential book, *The Dye-Pot* (1950). Davidson's collection of recipes, science, and lore is regarded as the authoritative, natural dye recipe book for wool. Her lively descriptions of regional plants and the dyeing processes, from harvest to dye-pot, provide both the novice and experienced dyer a guide to the diverse hues found in the fields and woods. Crafts advocate and educator Marion G. Heard described Mary Frances Davidson as "one of the pioneers in preserving this age old craft—an extender of knowledge through scientific research, a promoter, and an inspirational teacher."[13]

Jim Liles is a modern counterpart to Davidson. His research began in 1977, inspired by his wife Dale Liles's experiments with natural dyes, spinning, and felting, as well as his own interest in East Tennessee history. Liles found that much of the cloth used in the region's early clothing contained primarily cellulosic, or plant-based, fibers: linen, fustian, and cotton. Wanting to experiment with dyeing these types of cloth, Liles found that most dyeing literature was geared toward wool. Thus he began to experiment and record his findings about using natural dyes with cellulosic fibers. His friend and mentor Mary Frances Davidson supported his investigations with enthusiasm. In 1990 Liles published the fruits of research and experimentation in *The Art and Craft of Natural Dyeing: Traditional Recipes for Modern Use.*

Other Tennesseans have contributed significantly to an understanding of Tennessee's vastly layered textile traditions. Sadye Tune Wilson and Doris Finch Kennedy embarked on an extraordinary quest for the history of the Tennessee coverlet when they began their 1978 Tennessee Textile History Project. Over four hundred of the one thousand coverlets they documented are included in their 1983 publication, *Of Coverlets: The Legacies, the Weavers.* This generous volume offers precise notation of the weaving drafts, analyses of patterns, and their evolution. Many of the entries include photographs and lore about the weavers gathered from the weavers themselves, or in most cases, their descendants.

The goal of Helen Bullard's 1976 book *Crafts and Craftsmen of the Tennessee Mountains* was to continue the story of East Tennessee crafts where Allen Eaton's *Handicrafts of the Southern Highlands* left off in 1937. Bullard represents well the textile artists and their art, including weaving, spinning, natural dyeing, embroidery, needlework, and rug making. She also includes textile design processes that were introduced to the region since Eaton's day, such as screen printing, batik, and macramé. A friend of many of the artists and an artist herself, she provides a familiar account of the state of crafts in the region.

Through their work and through their teaching, many of the textile artists included in Bullard's overview have had lasting effects on fiber arts in Tennessee. The traditional methods continued to be preserved, yet these artists took the processes a few steps further by using timeless methods to communicate contemporary ideas. Weavers began to make weavings for the sake of weavings, to be hung on the wall as one would hang a painting. The notion that handwoven cloth was created solely for functional items was dismissed. Weaving, off-loom fiber constructions, and experiments with nontraditional forms echoed the trends of the country and the gypsy aesthetic of the 1960s and early 1970s. The artists, teachers, and centers for textile learning evolved to reflect the changes occurring in this creative climate.

Out of the reform movement, three craft schools grew, adapted, and survived: Arrowmont School of Arts and Crafts, which evolved from the Pi Beta Phi Settlement School of Gatlinburg, and both the Penland School of Crafts and the John C. Campbell Folk School in North Carolina. The three schools continue to offer course work in the traditional and contemporary crafts, and each offers resources and out-reach projects to their communities. In addition, many Tennessee colleges and universities established fiber art curriculums over the years. Often the textile offerings were housed in the home economic departments until moving into art departments as the role of hand-worked textiles changed. The University of Tennessee offers undergraduate and graduate coursework at Arrowmont, and Penland's courses are credited through East Tennessee State University (ETSU) in Johnson City as well as Western Carolina University in Cullowhee. ETSU continues to offer a degree in Fiber Arts, as does Tennessee Technological University through its affiliation with the Joe L. Evins Appalachian Center for the Crafts in Smithville.

The fiber tradition of Memphis College of Art and Design (MCAD) has produced a strong web of artists, including many contemporary fiber artists both of Tennessee and throughout the nation. Viola-Joyce Welliver Quigley opened MCAD's Weaving Department and served as the weaving instructor from 1945 to 1959. Trained in Chicago, Norway, and England, she led a technically precise curriculum. Her own work included yardage and liturgical textiles, research of Peruvian weaving techniques, and the publication of a weaving manual, *The Unit Repeat.* Upon her retirement, her former student, Henry Easterwood, provided direction for the fiber curriculum as chair of the department through 1999. Continuing the department's tradition of emphasizing technical excellence, he encouraged and promoted knowledge of new directions in contemporary fiber art, both through his own work and his work with students. Easterwood's abstract tapestry work has received wide acclaim and is well represented in private and public collections nationally, among them, the collections of the Mayo Clinic, the Tupperware International Corporation, IBM, and *U.S. News & World Report.* Since 1979, an additional body of his

Arrowmont School of Arts and Crafts

ARROWMONT SCHOOL OF ARTS AND CRAFTS IS LOCATED IN GATLINBURG ON A WOODED SITE BORdering the Great Smoky Mountains National Park. It opened in 1912 as the Pi Beta Phi Settlement School, in a borrowed building with thirteen students. Pi Beta Phi, the first women's social "fraternity," founded in 1867, had voted at its 1910 national convention to establish a philanthropy in Appalachia. Following in the distinguished tradition of Hull House, the neighborhood settlement school started by social worker Jane Addams in Chicago, the sponsors were concerned not only with providing basic education, but also with sustaining the life of the small mountain community. After two years of operation, with support from grateful local citizens, land was purchased and the first official school building constructed. Pi Beta Phi realized the need for a basic medical clinic in 1920, opened a shop through which to market mountain handicrafts in 1926, and soon added a high school. Recognizing that area residents possessed a wealth of practical knowledge in weaving and woodworking, the school offered both academic and vocational classes for children and employed a weaving teacher who worked in the community instructing women at their looms. The school created a cottage industry of "Arrow"-craft design, named after the symbolic Pi Phi arrow, which is still marketed through alumnae clubs around the country.

In 1945, the Pi Beta Phi School was transformed for six weeks into a summer craft school offering one- and two-week sessions taught by faculty members from the University of Tennessee Department of Home Economics. Fifty students from nineteen states attended, sharing room and board in the Pi Phi School teacher cottages and in the elementary school classrooms. The success of the summer program created a working partnership between the university and Pi Beta Phi that would chart a course for the future. Permanent studios were to be built on the school campus by the 1960s. The Jennie Nicol Health Center closed in 1965, and when the Sevier County Board of Education assumed control of the school in 1968, Gatlinburg's elementary school retained the name Pi Beta Phi Elementary in honor of its founding mothers.

For Pi Beta Phi's Centennial in 1967, members voted to create a major craft complex called Arrowmont on the former settlement school grounds. The centerpiece would be a new thirty-eight-thousand-square-foot building containing a gallery, an auditorium, teaching studios, and a library named after founding director Marian Heard, a University of Tennessee faculty member who had assisted with the first summer workshop in 1945.

Arrowmont's growth has paralleled the rise of the studio craft movement, many of whose finest practitioners have passed through Arrowmont studios. Today's Arrowmont School of Arts and Crafts is internationally known, sponsoring innovative year-round craft workshops, popular Elderhostel classes, progressive craft conferences and exemplary rotating exhibitions. True to its original mission, Arrowmont offers artist-in-residence support to young artist-teachers just beginning their careers, and provides outreach classes to Sevier County public schools. Students attending workshops at Arrowmont now earn credit through the University of Tennessee's Fine Arts Department. Major financial support comes from the Pi Beta Phi Fraternity, with regular grants from the Tennessee Arts Commission, the city of Gatlinburg, and local and national foundations and corporations.

Susan W. Knowles, Pikeville, Tennessee

work has emerged which explores textile structures in three-dimensional bamboo constructions, confirming his conviction that "innovation and tradition are mutually compatible."[14]

The other faculty and alumni of the MCAD fiber program have represented it well and in great variety over the years. Martha Beacon Turner taught silkscreen, batik, and surface design from 1950 to 1975. Her sewn, fabric collages were exhibited widely and were represented by Betty Parson's Gallery in New York. William Roberson followed Turner as instructor of Surface Design and creates large printed and collaged textiles. He is currently the assistant dean of the college as well as an active studio artist.

Contemporary Nashville weaver Martha Christian taught at Rhodes College in Memphis before its fiber program closed. She did graduate work at MCAD under Easterwood and is known for her large-scale tapestries and extraordinary color work. Martha Christian notes with great respect that her work with weaver Margaret Windekencht significantly influenced her ability to mesh her painting aesthetic with her technically expert weaving. Windekencht, an articulate scholar, designer, and colorist, came to Memphis from Michigan. She played a significant role in the Memphis Handweavers Guild and brought a new level of innovation to the art conversation surrounding contemporary weaving. Pidge Cash, a Murfreesboro metals artist, applies her graduate fiber training from MCAD to huge metal weavings. Creating metaphors for her notions of quantum theory, her work pushes the boundaries of fiber art through her choice of materials, while maintaining a woven structure. The MCAD Fiber Department has joined the twenty-first century by adding three AVL computer looms to the traditional studio equipment, and the Complex Weavers Internet group supplements an already rich, critical discussion exploring the role of fiber in the contemporary art world.

Another Memphian, Hilton McConnico, has made his mark in the fashion world with his haute couture garments created with fabric of his designs. McConnico's splashy, screen-printed fabrics are used both in his apparel designs as well as his home furnishings. Stephen Blumrich of Tullahoma, formerly the editor of the national textile publication *Surface Design Journal,* also designs textiles for production. His designs are represented in a wide variety of retail venues including Neiman Marcus, Sundance, and Pottery Barn. The combination of handmade, artist-designed work with mass-production methods allows these artists a broader audience than they might reach in the "one-of-a-kind," fine art and craft market.

Tennessee textile artists have enjoyed a variety of venues for networking, exhibiting, and sharing their work. Local chapters of the Handweavers Guild have played significant roles in the work of many of the state's weavers. The Southern Highlands Craft Guild and other regional guilds have provided educational and marketing opportunities for artists. The TVA created and funded Southern Highlanders, a new craft-marketing program, in 1935. Clementine Douglas, a weaver, a designer, and an early player in the North Carolina craft scene, was chosen to direct the new program, which included opening a craft shop in Tennessee near the Norris Dam and preparing a study of ways to assist with craft and design production. Though the Southern Highlands Craft Guild helped create Southern Highlands, and many craft artists were members of both groups, the organizations were distinctly separate until their merger in 1951.[15]

The advent of the craft fair played an important role in the marketing of textile arts in Tennessee. Miss Fannie Mennen's Plum Nelly Clothesline Art Show drew thousands of visitors to Lookout Mountain, "plum" out of Tennessee and "nelly" in Georgia. The Plum Nelly Shows started in 1948 and continued for over twenty-five years, helping to establish a group of art and craft professionals and led to a gallery by the same name in Chattanooga. In 1964, a new cooperative gallery, 12 Designer Craftsmen, opened in Gatlinburg on Roaring Fork Road and featured the prints of Fannie Mennen as well as Tina McMorran's stitched weavings. Founded in 1965, the Tennessee Association of Craft Artists (TACA) serves

TAPETA, by Arlyn Ende, 1986. Collection of UnumProvident Corporation, Chattanooga. Courtesy of the artist and UnumProvident Corporation, Chattanooga.

the craft community of the entire state. Sponsoring exceptional craft fairs, exhibitions of fine craft, and professional development workshops, TACA's mission is to "encourage, develop and promote crafts and craftspeople in Tennessee."[16]

The role of artist as teacher and mentor resoundingly recurs throughout the legacy of contemporary Tennessee fiber arts. When contemporary fiber artists in Tennessee were asked what influence working in Tennessee has had on their art, their answers pointed to people as well as to the actual place. Claudia Lee, a papermaker whose work evolved from her early work as a weaver, credits renowned weaver and teacher Persis Grayson, of Kingsport, for providing her with inspiration and technical grounding. Respected for her spinning as well as her commissioned weavings, Grayson served as the first national president of the Handweavers Guild of America and as president of the Southern Highlands Handicraft Guild. From her Smithville studio, Claudia Lee works with a variety of fibers in her cast paper works, and incorporates small weavings into her handmade books.

The Tennessee landscape provides the visual departure point for many of the state's fiber artists. Batik artists Betty Kershner, of Sewanee, and Judith Bills Williams, of Shelbyville, incorporate the local landscape and fauna. Kershner's silk wall hangings depict the mountains of the Cumberland Plateau and much of William's imagery is derived from the plants growing in Tennessee. Franklin County weaver Larry Carden describes the Southern Highlands as an ongoing influence on his work. "The natural colors and textures of the terrain"[17] guide his contemporary variations on traditional weave structures such as summer and winter, double weaves, and turned twills.

Textile arts in Tennessee have emerged with a contemporary voice while continuing to honor the craft of the past. Creating significant art that is recognized far beyond the region, Tennessee artist's work ranges from the concrete to the conceptual, demonstrates technical expertise and holds its own in the field of current fiber. Darla Beverage creates sculptural clothing from her weaving studio in Gray, Tennessee. In her Breast Plate Series, Beverage floats loose threads through her work while her weaving is still under the tension of the loom. The grace of Beverage's garments only becomes evident and three-dimensional when draped on a live model. Arlyn Ende, noted for her large-scaled textile hangings, has invented both methods and tools for the expansion of

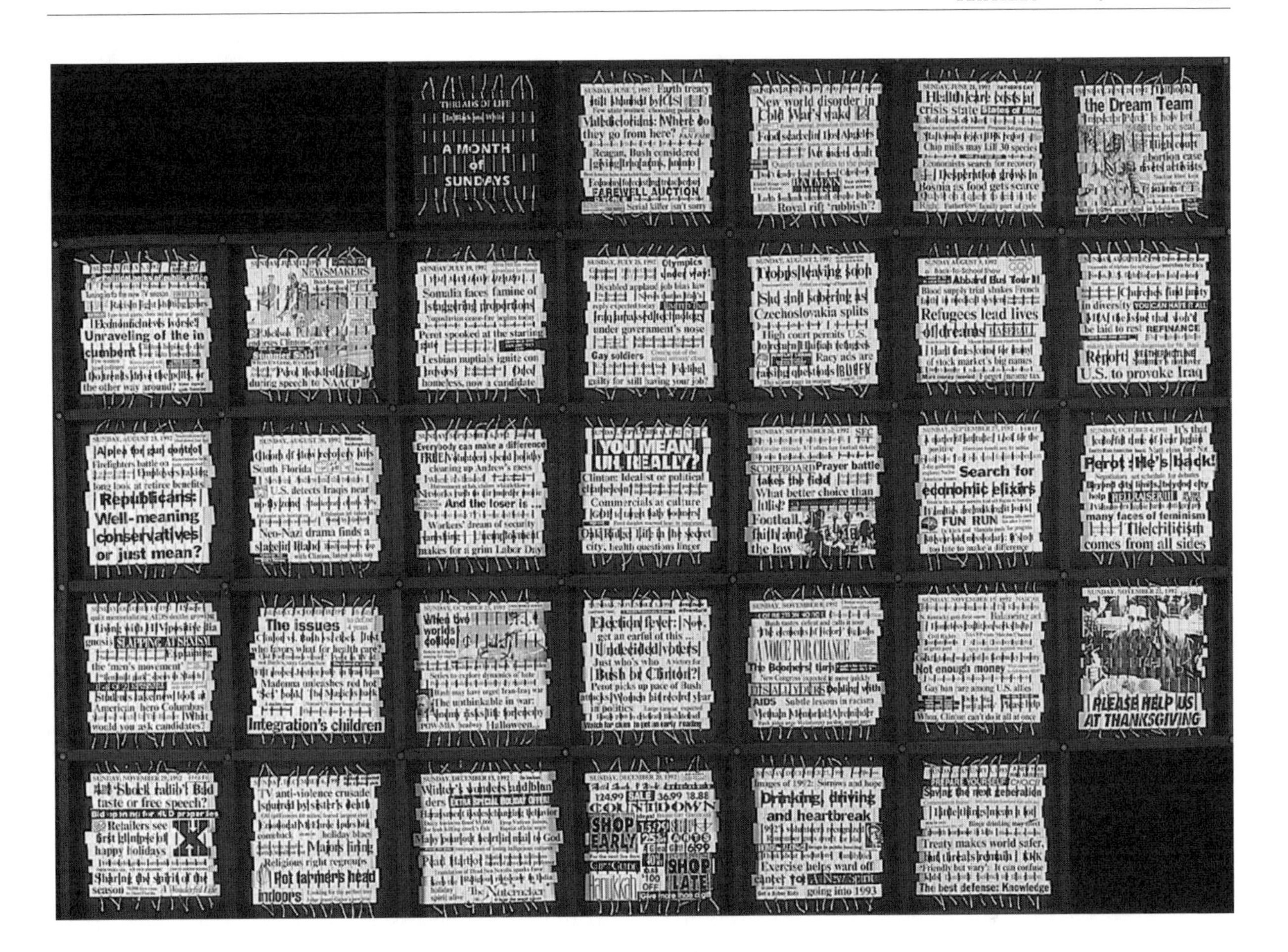

A Month of Sundays, by Vickie Vipperman, 1993. Woven from the Sunday paper headlines from thirty-one consecutive weeks. Courtesy of the artist.

traditional rug-hooking techniques. Ende's work for public spaces ranges from a large hooked hanging for Union Planters Bank in Cannon County, inspired by regional quilt patterns, to a sixty-four-foot-long, geometric abstraction for Provident Life and Accident Insurance Company in Chattanooga. Both Beverage and Ende exemplify expressive innovations, while expanding upon traditional processes.

In their collaborative work, Maxine Strawder and Harriet Ann Buckley employ multiple textile techniques and materials. Their two-sided quilt, *Got to Be Natural,* explores notions of beauty impressed upon their generation of African American women in their youth. Incorporating three-dimensional elements, yarn, stitching, and dyed fabrics, these artists also create spirited, narrative work individually.

The installation work of fiber artist Adrienne Outlaw transforms an environment by grouping life-sized figures molded from discarded bedsheets. The body-shaped shells are seam-stitched with nontraditional materials: barbed wire, staples, and nails. Exploring the "basis and the complexities of trust . . . referencing handwork, domesticity, and the female voice,"[18] Outlaw utilizes the public's familiarity with domestic cloth to initiate dialogue surrounding contemporary social issues.

The weavings of Nashville artist Vickie Vipperman initially were based upon traditional overshot patterns. After discovering thickened dyes and the techniques of ikat warp painting, her work shifted to nontraditional landscapes in the late 1980s. More recently, Vipperman has experimented with weaving headlines from newspapers, and is intrigued

The Hunt, by Adrienne Outlaw, 2000. Courtesy of the artist.

by the new meanings created through oddly juxtaposed words. This new body of work addresses social and political issues as well as the media's relationship with the public. Doris Louie, professor of fiber in ETSU's Art Department in 1999–2001, incorporates words into her tapestry-woven, bright yellow renditions of caution tape. Long trails of clichés that have become mental barriers in daily life are meticulously woven into a familiar physical barrier of the cloth "caution tape." Both Vipperman's *Word Weavings* and Louie's *Text as Textile* cross into the conceptual arena of the contemporary art world.

Steeped in a rich heritage, textile arts of Tennessee continue to evolve, honoring their sturdy roots and rising to the challenge of innovation. Early functional work was created both out of necessity and as an outlet for personal expression. Not surprisingly, early citizens of the state were intrigued with the exotic, often reserving such imported goods for special occasions. The textile objects made by Tennesseans were meant for everyday use; however, utilitarian, "ordinary," they were not. Homespun lynsey-woolsey—subtly colored cloth woven from wool for warmth and linen for strength—inherently possesses simple integrity. Corded cottonade, a ribbed, textured cloth made from doubling up the weft or warp at regular intervals, constructs an architectural elegance. These admirable qualities of simplicity and grace persist in the works produced by textile artists throughout Tennessee's history. Current artists choosing to work with fiber are revisiting the ordinary, embellishing the familiar, and making work that reflects the processes that created it, assuring both the continuity and quality of the Tennessee textile tradition.

NOTES

1. Frederick J. Dockstader, *Weaving Arts of the North American Indian,* 4th ed. (New York: HarperCollins, 1993), 173.
2. Sadye Tune Wilson and Doris Finch Kennedy, *Of Coverlets: The Legacies, the Weavers* (Nashville: Tunsteede Press, 1983), 76–77.
3. Fannie Fain Diaries, folder 1, p. 20, Archives of Appalachia and Special Collections, East Tennessee State Univ.
4. William R. Snell, ed. *Myra Inman: A Diary of the Civil War in East Tennessee* (Macon, Ga.: Mercer Univ. Press, 2000), 114–15.

5. Elizabeth Motlow, telephone conversation with author, Aug. and Nov. 2000.
6. Jane Kessler, "From Mission to Market: Craft in Southern Appalachia." *Revivals! Diverse Traditions: The History of the American Craft Tradition, 1929–1945,* ed. Janet Kardon (New York: Henry N. Abrams, 1994), 124.
7. Philis Alvic, *Weavers of the Southern Highlands: The Early Years at Gatlinburg* (Murray, Ky.: Privately published, 1991), 3.
8. Ibid., 2.
9. Edward L. Dupuy and Emma Weaver, *Artisans of the Appalachians: A Folio of Southern Mountain Craftsmen* (Asheville: Miller Printing, 1967), 120.
10. Alvic, *Weavers of the Southern Highlands,* 7.
11. *Gifts of the Spirit* (Asheville, N.C.: Southern Highlands Handicraft Guild, 1984), 5.
12. Allen Eaton, *Handicrafts of the Southern Highlands* (New York: Russell Sage Foundation, 1937), 142.
13. Cited in Mary Frances Davidson, *The Dye-Pot,* 4th ed. (Gatlinburg, Tenn.: Privately published, 1986), ii.
14. Patricia Bladon Lawrence, "Henry Easterwood: Tradition and Innovation," in *Tapestry Constructions,* ed. Henry Easterwood (Memphis: Memphis College of Art, 2000), 6.
15. Garry G. Barker, *The Handcraft Revival of Southern Appalachia* (Knoxville: Univ. of Tennessee Press, 1991), 21 and 49.
16. Tennessee Association of Craft Artists, Directory 2000, p 3.
17. Larry Carden, correspondence with the author, Dec. 2000.
18. Adrienne Outlaw, correspondence with author, Dec. 2000.

Suggested Readings

Alvic, Philis. *Weavers of the Southern Highlands: The Early Years at Gatlinburg.* Murray, Ky.: Privately published, 1991.

Davidson, Mary Frances. *The Dye-Pot.* 4th ed. Gatlinburg, Tenn.: Privately published, 1986.

Dupuy, Edward L., and Emma Weaver. *Artisans of the Appalachians: A Folio of Southern Mountain Craftsmen.* Asheville, N.C.: Miller Printing, 1967.

Eaton, Allen. *Handicrafts of the Southern Highlands.* New York: Russell Sage Foundation, 1937.

Hulan, Richard. "Tennessee Textiles." *Antiques* 100 (1971): 386.

Kessler, Jane. "From Mission to Market: Craft in Southern Appalachia." In *Revivals! Diverse Traditions: The History of the American Craft Tradition, 1929–1945,* edited by Janet Kardon. New York: Henry N. Abrams, 1994.

Liles, Jim N. *The Art and Craft of Natural Dyeing: Traditional Recipes for Modern Use.* 4th ed. Knoxville: Univ. of Tennessee Press, 1999.

Warwick, Rick. *Tennessee Stitches: An Exhibit of 19th-Century Williamson County Samplers.* Franklin, Tenn.: Carter House, 1993.

Wilson, Sadye Tune, and Doris Finch Kennedy. *Of Coverlets: The Legacies, the Weavers.* Nashville: Tunsteede Press, 1983.

Fourteen

Tennessee Quilts as Art

BETS RAMSEY
Nashville

The knowledge of quilt making that came to Tennessee with the first pioneer settlers can be considered both as a craft and as a form of art. Ranging from the simplest scrap utility quilt to the most exquisitely stitched, quilted, and stuffed bride's quilt to quilts made for the wall as pieces of art, all types of quilts can be judged for their artistic merits regardless of their intended function.

A quilt can be categorized as art when, even as an ordinary object in daily use, it meets the usual criteria for judging any artwork: by its composition, color, design, craftsmanship, originality, and possession of a quality to set it apart from similar objects. Some kinds of quiltwork, however, preclude utilitarian use: fine chintzwork; quilted and stuffed work; some types of album quilts; embroidered silk and velvet crazy quilts; designer appliqué quilts; and quilts made as wall hangings. Such quilts demonstrate the makers' skills in needlework and creativity even as they vary in the success of artistic achievement.

Crown of Thorns, by Mrs. D. P. Walker, Sweetwater Valley, Monroe County, c. 1840. Walker made this quilt for her daughter's wedding. Courtesy of Quilts of Tennessee.

Prior to the nineteenth century a woman may have had no other opportunity for self-expression than through her quilts. Her thoughts, her longings and passions, even her grief, were stitched into the fibers of the quilts, and they were the vehicles for her message. Whether she expressed herself in a simple, everyday quilt put together in an original way or made an extraordinary and elaborate appliquéd bedspread, she may have created a work of art. The quilt becomes a statement of its maker's individuality, her uniqueness, and may even be more lasting than her weathered gravestone.

As a traditional art, no barriers separate quilt making by geographic location, wealth, social standing, gender, race, age, or other circumstance. Quilts are familiar objects. Scarcely a person has not had contact with them in some way, at some time in life, and for that reason quilts can be called America's most available art form, understood and appreciated by many who do not relate to other types of art. Whether making a work of art or a utility object, Tennessee women, and men, have enjoyed the craft and art of making all kinds of quilts during the more than two hundred years of our history.

ESTABLISHING TRADITIONS, 1775–1860

The state's earliest settlers brought with them the necessities for establishing new homes and cultivating the land and, perhaps, they brought a few treasures. Household inventories of the period record their scanty possessions but seldom list quilts among the household linens. Quilts were luxury items made of expensive imported fabric, or purchased ready made, and found in the homes of the more affluent families. By its very nature, hand-sewn quiltwork was labor-intensive, more suitable for a leisure activity. The more practical feather beds and woven blankets took less time to make and could be produced from one's own fowl and sheep.

Quilts brought into the new state reflected the national backgrounds of their owners whose origins were primarily from Great Britain and Western Europe and, therefore, followed European styles. The bedchambers of the well-to-do households were furnished in the latest fashion, just as styles of dress changed from season to season. There were wholecloth quilts in glazed wool, silk, linen, or cotton, some with embroidered motifs, some ornamented solely by the quilting. Block printed and copperplate printed cottons from India, France, and England, and later, America, were favored for furnishing fabrics and bedcovers and hangings.

Indian palampores—wholecloth block printed and painted panels with Tree of Life motifs—were the design source for many appliqué quilts of the period. Cutout motifs from glazed cotton chintz fabrics were arranged in imaginative tree patterns and, if one wished, could carry religious significance.

The medallion quilt—a center panel surrounded by borders and other appliqué or pieced work—was another style for chintz quilt making, and there were other variations. Because the chintz quilts were favored for their beauty and fine workmanship, they were saved for special occasions when guests were entertained or other events were taking place and, thus, they became family heirlooms for succeeding generations.

Fashions changed periodically, but the all-white wholecloth quilt of linen or cotton retained its popularity over an extended length of time. Variations of the handmade all-white wholecloth quilt continued to be made in Tennessee as late as 1900, unlike other locales where they were seldom made after the mid-1800s.

A few simple shapes, clamshell and mosaic, for instance, were piecework styles familiar to eighteenth-century quilters and many of them continued to follow the English template method of basting the patch over a paper pattern and whipping the turned edges together. Contrary to popular belief that the first immigrants began at once to make patchwork quilts, the pieced block did not come into its own until the nineteenth century.

Shopkeepers and peddler merchants were quick to include fabric and sewing supplies in their inventories for it was a woman's duty to supply or oversee the production of all textile requirements: bedding, clothing, linens, and furnishings. Those who needed textiles included her immediate family, extended family in residence, and servants, slaves, or hired help. Since a practical model of the sewing machine was not produced until 1848, all sewing had to be done by hand. Quilt making was but one of the seemingly endless duties for the needleworker but, perhaps, it was the most pleasurable.

Before long American mills rapidly increased production of cloth made from domestically grown cotton and lessened the need for imported fabric. The decrease in cost made fabric affordable to more people and led to increased activity in quilt making. In Tennessee's largely rural population, it was practiced in the majority of households prior to the Civil War. Some were able to raise their own cotton or wool for quilt filler and weave cloth for backing.

Following fashion of the time, some of the quilts were made in the whitework style for a show piece or bride's quilt. Several panels were seamed together to make the top, then quilted in designs of flowers, leaves, feathers, or urns, with close quilting filling in the background. Extra cotton was sometimes added to certain areas from the underside of the quilt to heighten the sculptural effect. With fine quilting and stuffed work, plain white material was turned into a masterpiece quilt.

Silk embroidered floral medallion quilts were favored in England in the seventeenth and eighteenth centuries and that theme was later transposed to chintz floral appliqué work. Chintz, a cotton fabric with a glazed finish, was popular for a furnishing fabric in the early nineteenth century and became a part of the quilter's repertoire. The all-over Tree of Life design and the medallion-bordered quilt, mentioned previously, evolved into block construction format. Instead of making the top from a single unit of seamed panels that produced a whole cloth, a transition occurred whereby smaller units—blocks—were joined together to make the top. Cutouts of flowers, leaves, birds, and other emblems were appliquéd to the single blocks before joining them together. Working in smaller units was practical, especially if more than one person was working on a quilt. The pieced block became more popular during this period as new patterns were invented and shared with acquaintances. The collecting mania of the time included collecting quilt blocks from one's friends and relatives to be made into friendship or album quilts. The blocks were signed, dated, and inscribed by their makers or a chosen scribe and became valuable historical notations.

With cloth readily available, quilt-making activity increased in the years preceding the Civil War. Many Tennessee quilt makers favored the appliqué style, using red and green small-patterned prints and solids, with smaller amounts of pink and yellow. There were floral and leaf designs: Rose of Sharon, Whig Rose, Rose Wreath, Rose Tree, Prince's Feather, Washington's Plume, Cockscomb and Currant, Tulip, Oak Leaf and Acorn, and Oak Leaf and Cherries, to name a few. At first the quilts were made of four large blocks; eventually the blocks became smaller and more numerous. The number of patterns for piecing increased rapidly and quilt makers were challenged to try as many as possible. With discriminating selection of fabric and color combinations, with fine quilting and even additional stuffing, a pieced quilt could become as elegant as any showpiece. Many of the patterns for piecing are adaptable for the use of scraps and allowed makers to create economical bedcovers for everyday wear. No longer was the quilt a luxury item.

Few quilt patterns were published prior to the Civil War. Patterns were exchanged among families and friends, sent in letters, along with snippets of fabric from the writer's latest project. When visiting, guests might depart with a sketch of a new design

Floral Applique, by "Aunt" Lisa McKenzie, Meigs County, c. 1860. Courtesy of Quilts of Tennessee.

from their hostess's handiwork. It was a pleasant diversion to invent a pattern, try it out, and call it one's own.

Young girls were required to learn needlework in anticipation of their future duties as wives and mothers. At an early age girls learned the simplest steps to sewing and quilt making. Starting with Four Patch and Nine Patch patterns, then Irish Chain, Basket, and Windmill, gradually they progressed to more complex projects. By the time they were adolescents, the girls were expected to have completed several tops for their hope chests and to begin to quilt them. Their collection might include Variable Star, Young Man's Fancy, Turkey Tracks, North Carolina Lily, Melon Patch, or Spinning Ball.

A quilting bee was a splendid social occasion that sometimes accompanied a barn-raising or corn-husking neighborhood event. Plentiful food was prepared for a noon meal and a day of quilting and outdoor work might be followed by games and dancing. More commonly quilting took place in the home with family members, hired help, and friends putting in the stitches. Scarcely a home, whether cabin or plantation house, was without a quilting frame to provide the needed bedding. The frames were of many styles, usually homemade, ranging from single rails hung from the ceiling with rope and pulleys to well-crafted fine furniture on upright legs.

Quilt making in various stages was an ongoing process in most homes. While a grandmother was cutting pieces from scraps and piecing blocks, her daughter might be dyeing cotton yardage for a quilt back, using bark and walnuts gathered by her children. On a cotton-producing farm, boys and/or slave children, as well as adults, had to chop cotton, pick it in the fall, carry it to the gin for processing, and return with a batch for quilt making. The young girls, and sometimes boys, were occupied learning the rudiments of piecing while the older girls spent time at the quilt frame. A great deal of cooperation was required to make a quilt.

Because it took time and energy to produce quilts and other textile goods, much attention was given to their care. Periodic airing and washing was given to bedding. When a quilt became worn, its life was prolonged by covering the top and back with new material, or another pieced top, and adding tacking stitches. A worn blanket or coverlet made an acceptable filler and even more unlikely materials found their way into quilts. Complicated as it was, quilt making was only one aspect of the busy life of a nineteenth-century homemaker.

Whig Rose, pieced, by Susan G. Courtesy of Quilts of Tennessee.

Transitions in an Age of Industrialization, 1860–1920

When the Civil War began, Tennessee was a prospering state with established towns and a thriving agricultural base. The pioneer days were past; homes were furnished with taste and style, according to one's means, but then the Civil War came and brought widespread suffering and devastation, leaving scars that were to last for decades. Many women were left to manage families, households, and property as best they could.

The quilts of the period serve as diaries for their experiences. Quilts were sent with loved ones when they departed for service. As the war continued, soldiers also stole quilts, although at the time some claimed that they merely "borrowed" them from housewives. Quilts were used in makeshift hospitals or torn up for bandages. Quilts were auctioned to raise money for war relief or equipment. Quilts were hidden to prevent pillaging. And quilts were made while battles raged and anxious hours passed. Many thoughts were stitched into the seams of the pieces.

Friendship, by Elizabeth M. Baxter, Cocke County. Courtesy of Quilts of Tennessee.

After the war, normalcy was slowly restored to the lives and homes of Tennesseans. Industrialization brought an increase in consumer goods and the country moved into a new era. The sewing machine was one of the life-changing inventions to affect women. It eliminated the necessity for hand sewing of all garments and household textile furnishings. It freed a certain amount of women's time for other activities.

Quilt makers quickly adopted the sewing machine for their quilt work, particularly in piecing the blocks and assembling the top. The more adventurous succeeded in maneuvering the machine for quilting. In the last part of the nineteenth century, a surge in quilt-making activity can be attributed in large measure to the use of the sewing machine and cheaper cloth produced by the expanding textile mills of the United States. In addition, various ladies magazines and homemaker literature encouraged women to take up handcrafts. More quilt designs were being invented and published in national and regional magazines and newspapers. The Ladies' Art Company catalogue offered a dazzling selection of quilt patterns: Arabic Lattice, Chimney Swallows, Twinkling Star, Royal Japanese Fan, Swing in the Center, Mrs. Cleveland's Choice, and Storm At Sea, to name a few. *The Southern Agriculturalist* and *Southern Woman's Magazine,* both published in Nashville, informed women readers of the latest trends in decorative arts and handicrafts, especially the articles written in the latter magazine by Nashville's Anne Orr. With designs like those provided by Orr in hand, women also found other materials much easier to obtain. Ready-made batting, for example, eliminated the need to prepare batts at home. Quilt making was becoming less laborious and more enjoyable than ever.

The newly published patterns offered a challenge to quilters and some endeavored to try as many as possible in rapid succession. Competitions also increased quilt-making activity. State and regional fair organizers encouraged needleworkers to enter work in a variety of categories. Quilts, by their very size, dominated the displays and viewers were eager to see the latest designs, to see the styles and fads that changed just as rapidly as did fashion. After the Philadelphia Centennial Fair of 1876 where Japanese articles were displayed, the crazy quilt ("crazed," as in pottery) came into vogue. It was interpreted in endless ways, worked in the finest silk and brocade fabrics down to the humblest of discarded woolen and work-clothes materials. The crazy quilt appeared in competition in nearly every fair for twenty-five years. Entrants brought pieced quilts and appliqué quilts, many that were made with the sole intention of competing for the fair's ribbons and prizes. An expert quilt maker could garner enough ribbons through the years eventually to be able to join them together for an unusual quilt top.

The interest in making quilts continued for the remainder of the nineteenth century, especially in the rural areas where it was an accepted part of the women's life on the farm. Once Rural Free Delivery came into existence in 1906, every rural home had mail-order buying power that made fabric and quilting supplies easy to obtain. With better transportation and less arduous household duties, women found time to attend outside gatherings and be part of the developing communities. As churches became centers for activities relating to local improvement and missionary work, quilting circles raised money for building programs, church educational programs, and mission support by staging quilt auctions and by quilting for payment. Group-made quilts were given to departing ministers, to victims of fires and disasters, and to overseas relief work. During World War I quilts were made as fund-raisers for the Red Cross and for soldiers' aid. The infrequent and occasional quilting bee of the past became a monthly or weekly activity for many quilters.

Top: Soule College Crazy Quilt. Courtesy of Quilts of Tennessee.

Above: Dutch Tulips. Courtesy of Quilts of Tennessee.

QUILTS AND THE HANDICRAFT REVIVAL, 1920–1945

Efforts in the early twentieth century to improve rural life in the South, often grouped together and described as the Progressive Movement, resulted in a number of agencies being formed. Ideally, improvement programs were envisioned as creating better homes, better farms, and more contented farm families. Notable among the programs in Tennessee was the creation of the Knapp School of Country Life at the George Peabody College For Teachers between 1912 and 1915 and Peabody's launch of a bachelor of science degree in home economics in 1918. With the passage of the federal Smith-Lever Act in 1913, the University of Tennessee soon established several important home economics programs. The formation of the United States Department of Agriculture Extension Service reached even more directly into the rural communities and continued to do so through most of the twentieth century. In the late 1910s and 1920s, the Extension Service's Home Demonstration Clubs encouraged quilting projects and workshops on the local level. Once a year a statewide assembly of quilt makers took place at the 4-H camp near Crossville where members had an opportunity to display their quilts, take classes, attend lectures, and have a good time away from home.

The quilts produced in the classroom were like those produced at home: they were diverse in materials and designs. Quilters might use feed sacks, tobacco sacks, or the bottom of men's trouser legs. Many produced string quilts made of blocks utilizing the narrowest of scraps sewn to a base square, triangle, or other shape, and quilted in fan (concentric quarter-circles) design. Simultaneously, the fashion-conscious were making floral appliqué quilts or the pieced quilts featured in women's magazines, in accord with the latest style of interior decoration.

The popularity of quilt making spread to the urban and suburban middle-class women. Quilts were designed to accompany the Colonial Revival decorating style of the 1920s. Batting and thread companies also distributed books and pamphlets. Magazines included instructions for making the newest fashions in home decorating. The Boudoir style, featuring roses and lace, soft quilted satin or sateen comforters, and feathers on slippers and dressing gowns, was an alternate choice to the colonial style. Some middle-class women, however, bought quilts rather than made them. Rural women in Hamilton, Knox, and Union Counties established shops in which, among other handicrafts, they sold rugs, quilts, and linens.

As the handicraft revival in southern Appalachia was gathering momentum, Allen Eaton came to the South in 1926 through the support of the Russell Sage Foundation to conduct a survey of Appalachian crafts. At his urging, and after discussions lasting

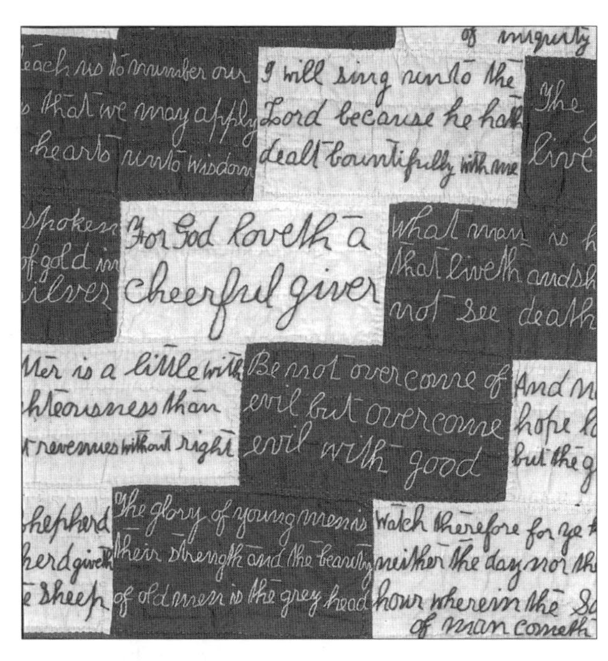

Bible Verses, by J. P. Clark, c. 1922. Courtesy of Quilts of Tennessee.

three years, the Southern Highland Handicraft Guild, encompassing southern Appalachian mountain regions, was formed in 1930. In 1935, the guild joined with the Tennessee Valley Authority in initiating Southern Highlanders, a craft-marketing program. A craft shop opened at the TVA's Norris Dam, Rockefeller Center in New York, and Chickamauga Dam and the Hotel Patten in Chattanooga, where it remained in business for fifteen years. Cumberland Mountain Crafts near Crossville was another outlet for handmade goods.

The Great Depression brought dramatic change for many people. Quilts made from scraps were viewed as an economical measure and prompted a variety of patterns employing assorted fabric: Grandmother's Flower Garden, Dresden Plate, Double Wedding Ring, and the novelty Yo-Yo quilts. The Sears Quilt Contest for the 1933 Chicago World's Fair motivated hundreds of quilt makers to compete for the prize money that could alleviate depression woes. At the same time women saw the fancier appliqué quilts as a way of lifting their spirits from economic concerns. Anne Orr's pattern business in

Anne Champe Orr

ONE OF THE MOST EVOCATIVE NEEDLEWORK DESIGNERS OF THE TWENTIETH CENTURY, ANNE CHAMPE Orr (1869–1946) gained worldwide acclaim while living her entire life in Nashville. Her mother, Emma Claiborne Champe, nurtured Anne's obvious artistic abilities, providing private tutorials with Nashville artist Sara Ward Conley and sending her to Cincinnati, Chicago, and New York for further study.

Anne Orr in her Packard at 130 Twenty-first Avenue South in 1930. Courtesy of J. Scott Grigsby.

Anne, who married John Hunter Orr in 1894, helped raise funds for a Woman's Pavilion at the 1897 Tennessee Centennial Exposition. The success of this campaign led to formation of the Centennial Club, a woman's organization that spearheaded initiatives in civic pride, cultural enrichment, and social services in Nashville.

Anne and John Hunter Orr raised three daughters in the family home at 130 Twenty-First Avenue South while Orr began her publishing career. From 1913 to 1918, the *Southern Woman's Magazine* was published in Nashville, and Orr provided monthly columns on antiques and needlework. In 1915, she wrote her first booklet, *Centerpieces and Lunch Sets in Crochet Work,* and sold copies through the Anne Orr Design Studio, located in the lower level of the family home. Coats Thread Company of England hired her in 1917 to produce a needlework series for worldwide distribution. The *Nashville Banner* reported that Orr received an advance order for five hundred thousand booklets.

Orr quickly made a name for herself, and from 1920 to 1940, she wrote a monthly needlework feature for *Good Housekeeping.* While well known for her tatting, crochet, needlepoint, and cross-stitch designs, Orr's original quilt patterns based on charted cross-stitch patterns are considered her signature pieces. One of her pattern books described her ideas as "young, fresh, alive, and firmly grounded upon experience." She knows "the mechanics of her craft. She is a creative pioneer, who can interpret needlework for the novice as well as the expert."[1]

Interestingly, Orr did not do needlework or make quilts herself. Her strength was her ability to design simple, appealing patterns. Her studio employed women to produce needlework to ensure the instructions were correct. They also produced and sold quilt patterns, basted tops, or completely quilted quilts. In 1933, Orr was chosen to judge the final round of the Sears National Quilt Contest held at the Chicago World's Fair. The contest attracted over twenty-four thousand entries at local and regional venues. Four of the thirty final-round quilts were Anne Orr patterns—proof of the esteem lower-round judges held for her quilt designs. The one-thousand-dollar grand prize went, however, to a traditional eight-pointed-star quilt.

In 1940, Orr retired her column for *Good Housekeeping,* but she kept her business going with the help of two daughters. She died in 1946 and is buried in Mount Olivet Cemetery in Nashville.

Daughter Mary Hunter Orr Grigsby kept the Studio open until 1956. Since the late 1970s, reprints of Anne Orr's needlework and quilt patterns have ensured an even wider audience of appreciative needle workers—novice as well as expert.

Merikay Waldvogel, Knoxville

Note

1. *Pattern Book Anne Orr Quilts—Book 5* (Nashville: Anne Orr Studio, 1944), 2.

Suggested Reading

Waldvogel, Merikay. "Historical View: Anne Orr." American Patchwork & Quilting, Feb. 1999, 8, 10–11. Also in her *Soft Covers for Hard Times: Quiltmaking and the Great Depression.* Nashville: Rutledge Hill Press, 1990.

Nashville and the column she wrote on beautifying the home environment for *Good Housekeeping* reached readers across the country.

The Rise of Art Quilts, 1945–1970

By the mid-1940s, the Southern Highland Handicraft Guild (later changed to the Southern Highland Craft Guild) was a major contributor to the craft revival. Two members, Marian Heard and Clem Douglas, through a Rockefeller grant, conducted a survey of regional craftsmen to further implement the Eaton study and organize workshops and other forms of instruction for better quality products. In 1945 the first summer classes were presented at the Arrowmont School (the earlier Pi Beta Phi Settlement School) in Gatlinburg where Heard soon became the enduring director and led the school to world prominence. Three years later the guild held its first craft fair in Gatlinburg, becoming extremely popular and continuing until 1975 when the location was changed to Asheville, North Carolina. The quilts and pottery of Charles and Rubynelle Counts were frequently exhibited at the fairs and introduced

String-pieced quilt, Sevier County, c. 1940. Courtesy of Quilts of Tennessee.

a new style of quilt, the art quilt. Hundreds of visitors became acquainted with crafts and bought work to enjoy in their homes.

Interest in quilt making gradually declined as more and more women joined the work force during World War II and the years following. Business and commerce seemed more desirable than housework and domestic arts. Quilting was left for a few to quietly pursue individually. An occasional church group managed to maintain quilting groups through the years. The Northside Presbyterian Church in Chattanooga, for example, had a quilting group that began in the early 1900s and has never missed a regular day except for Pearl Harbor Day and major holidays.

In the 1960s, the back-to-the-earth movement activated new interests in handcrafts and homemaking, coinciding with the establishment of university-based arts and crafts departments, craft centers, and greater acceptance of crafts as art. After adapting to a mechanical age for several decades, people seemed to long for a connection to the past. Handmade items having a human imprint provided that association. Even when quilts left the bed and became wall hangings exhibited in museums and art galleries, they retained the familiarity of home and family.

Many women were searching for a new definition of their lives. There seemed to be the need to make a personal statement, to relieve the hardness of machines with softness of textiles, to make a gift for succeeding generations, to be joined to other women in a similar and sharing experience. Quilting, alone or in a group, was a way of meeting these needs and desires.

Since membership in the guild was limited to craftsmen residing in the mountain regions, the Tennessee Artist-Craftsmen's Association (TACA) was founded in 1965, led by Lewis Snyder. It organized exhibitions and workshops and presented its first Craftsmen's Fair in Centennial Park, Nashville in 1972. Later the name was changed to the Tennessee Association of Craft Artists and the fairs and exhibits continue.

THE MODERN ERA, 1970–2000

The modern quilt explosion is often linked to a major quilt exhibition, *The American Quilt,* held in 1971 at the Whitney Museum in New York and presented by Jonathan Holstein and Gail van der Hoof. Other museums had exhibited quilts, more or less in the context of Americana or needle art, but at the Whitney the quilts were shown as Art. The collection, gathered primarily from Pennsylvania and New York state, caught the attention of the press and launched quilts as a favorite topic for years to come. A proliferation of magazine articles fueled the public's increasing interest in things handmade and created activities relating to quilts: quilt making, quilt collecting, and quilt research and history.

In the wake of the Whitney exhibit followed formation of quilt guilds and groups, presentation of workshops and seminars, and competitive and invitational exhibitions of all kinds. If one lacked skills with the needle but admired the complexity and artistic quality of quilts, one might become a collector. To appreciate quilts more fully, it was helpful to learn about their history, traditions, makers, and other circumstances and connections. These investigations and research projects led to seminar meetings and more and more publications about quilts. By the end of the decade, according to the *Wall Street Journal,* quilt making had become a billion-dollar industry.

By a fortunate circumstance, an exhibition titled *The American Quilt* came to Chattanooga's Hunter Museum of American Art during its limited tour of the country. Budd Bishop, the museum's director, asked the present author to present a lecture and organize a two-day workshop to attract quilt enthusiasts. It was to be a serious study of quilts as an art form and, thus, he initiated a weighty title: The Southern Quilt Symposium.

The symposium attracted an audience from several states and became the first such quilt seminar of national scope. For the next sixteen years thereafter, the author curated an annual exhibition of quilts from outstanding, recognized artists and collectors coinciding with two days of lectures and workshops. Many people from Tennessee, and beyond, benefited from the association with experienced teachers and lecturers. They made lasting friendships and saw quilts as an art form in both traditional and original designs.

The media emphasis given to quilts and collecting in the 1970s strongly increased quilt marketability. New quilt groups and guilds were formed and teachers had full schedules instructing beginners. Textile and gadget manufacturers produced an astonishing array of lines designed primarily for quilters. Museum and continuing education departments added quilt-making classes to their curricula. It took little time for teachers to become experts, writing books, introducing their methods, traveling the world to share their enthusiasm with eager learners. The craft revival of the 1930s to 1960s increased appreciation for crafts, including quilts, that led some women to make quilts for family use or study quilt history or take lessons to improve needlework and machine skills. Others enjoy viewing exhibitions or displaying their work and competing for awards. Some prefer to be collectors of other people's work. Many organizations statewide offer opportunities to quilt lovers for every interest and level of experience.

State and regional fairs originating in the nineteenth century were, and are, favorite places to exhibit handwork, compete for awards, and observe trends and styles of fashion. At one time serious competitors sent their work to selected out-of-state fairs in hopes of capturing ribbon awards. That competitive spirit is still alive and the rules have changed but the ribbons are just as treasured. Now to enter a quilt in the state fair, it must have been made in Tennessee within the last five years. Luckily for beginners there is a separate category for first quilts.

By the 1970s the crafts coordinator for the Tennessee Arts Commission, Roy Overcast, was working with quilt makers in the nine economic development districts of the state to increase individual earning capacity from their craftwork. He arranged regional workshops to introduce marketing guidelines emphasizing trends in color, design, style, and preferred size that would increase sale of quilts. In addition to occasional regional sales that were held, a limited number of antique quilts were distributed to a New York department store for sale. As local guilds increased and other opportunities arose, guidance from the arts commission was discontinued.

The Appalachian Regional Commission, established by Congress and appointed by President Lyndon Johnson in 1965, supported certain Southern Highland Craft Guild activities and in 1975 the commission appropriated funds for the Joe L. Evins Appalachian Center for Crafts near Smithville, completed four years later. The center is intended to attract folk and university-trained artists as well as beginning students in a variety of media, including quilt making.

Another important part of the institutional support for quilting in Tennessee was the formation of the Tennessee Valley Quilters' Association in 1980 through the leadership of Mildred Locke, a quilt teacher and shop owner in Bell Buckle. According to its mission statement, the purpose of the Quilters' Association is "to promote interest in, and to develop the appreciation of, quilts and quilt making; to sponsor and support quilting activities; to encourage quilt making and collecting; to expand knowledge of quilting techniques, textiles, and patterns; and to foster fellowship, mutual aid and common interests." The organization unites local guilds and presents statewide exhibitions and workshops. It supports publication of research papers by the American Quilt Study Group. Its affiliation with the National Quilters Association allows members to enter and attend national competitions and events.

After the creation of the Quilters' Association, several other institutions and groups either sponsored annual quilting events or established their own regional associations and partnerships. East Tennessee State University offered several sessions of quilt workshops and exhibits that attracted a wide audience in the 1980s. When the program was discontinued, Polly Taylor, a quilt-shop owner of Jonesborough, arranged quilt workshops and exhibits held each summer in

August. The Smoky Mountain Quilt Guild incorporated its annual quilt competition as part of the Knoxville Dogwood Arts Festival in 1991. The McMinn County Living Heritage Museum's annual quilt festival and show began with a few local entries in 1982 when the museum was housed in a building on the campus of the Tennessee Wesleyan College. Each year the event attracts an ever-increasing number of entries and visitors to Athens. When the museum moved to new quarters in a former high school, exhibition space greatly increased, as did the permanent collection. Special events, lectures, and work-shops are presented during the three-month duration of the exhibition of more than three hundred quilts, making it one of the largest displays in the South.

Diverse Opinions, Bets Ramsey, 1988. Courtesy of Quilts of Tennessee.

IDENTIFYING AND DEFINING THE TENNESSEE QUILT

The flowering of modern quilt making in Tennessee led to an effort, starting in 1983 and led by Merikay Waldvogel and the author, to conduct a statewide survey of quilts to determine what might distinguish Tennessee quilts from those of other states or regions. With several volunteers and the cooperation of local quilt guilds, churches, museums, and other public facilities, we crossed the state to conduct Quilt Days. On a typical day, quilt owners, makers, and collectors brought their quilts to be included in the survey, supplying us with family history, quilt provenance, and any pertinent stories. A detailed examination, including measurements, construction, pattern, fabric, age, technique, condition, and quality of design, was entered on the prepared form, and finally, the quilt was photographed. The survey had two stipulations: quilts were to predate 1930 and were to have been made in Tennessee or brought to the state before the Civil War. Quilt Days provided a sampling of regional quilts and emphasized the historic value of preserving family quilts as part of one's heritage. After summarizing the findings, representative quilts were chosen for exhibition in eight museums across the state. The survey is housed in the Tennessee State Library and Archives in Nashville.

This study gave an overview of domestic life as recorded in an everyday object. Quilt style reflects fashion and influences, choice of fabric often indicates the economic circumstances of the family and its relation to commerce, and the block pattern may have a political, religious, or regional theme. The workmanship hints at a maker's ability, age, situation, and personality. "Reading" the characteristics of the artifact—the quilt—is to learn of the past and women's history in a new way. Some men, too, make quilts, but primarily it is a woman's art.

Initially the study was a search for the characteristics of Tennessee quilts but it became apparent that the stories of the quilts and their makers were far more interesting than all the statistics. The purpose, then, became twofold and greatly enriched the original plan. The book, *The Quilts of Tennessee: Images of Domestic Life Prior to 1930,* summarizes the project, presenting the distinguishing characteristics and differences of these quilts and makes comparisons with quilts in a broader context. Adding personal stories to the factual analysis allows a far more comprehensive view of quilt history.

The state is often characterized as having three distinct divisions and the quilts seemed to have a similar pattern. The oldest quilts were found in East Tennessee and suggest that they came from well-established homes of the early nineteenth century, were well crafted, and similar to quilts made in Virginia, North Carolina, Pennsylvania, and even Europe. Pre–Civil War quilts tended to have white fabric used in combination with red, green, pink, and yellow; or white and blue; or white, red, and blue. Sometimes natural dyes were used to color the cloth.

From 1790 to 1850, there were wholecloth, appliqué, and pieced quilts: whitework quilting and stuffing on a wholecloth top; chintz appliqué and piecework; appliquéd roses and other flowers, plumes, and leaves; and pieced quilts in patterns such as Delectable Mountains, Stars, Rocky Mountain, Rose Tree, and Orange Peel. Four large squares set off with borders made a favorite format for appliqué. The "best" quilts were used sparingly and passed down in families, while everyday quilts were seldom saved.

In Middle Tennessee, elegant pre–Civil War quilts indicate that many homemakers had generous resources for quilt making. Lucy Virginia Smith French of McMinnville states in a letter of 1858 that her husband has purchased silk material for a quilt while on a business trip to New Orleans. She sketched the flowers in her garden and embroidered them on the silk, taking two premiums at a fair competition. Slaves on the Batey plantation near Murfreesboro wove woolen blankets and made quilts for the big house. Even on a small farm such as that of the Gleaves near Ashland City, the same work was performed. Betty Gleaves wrote in her 1858 diary, now at the Tennessee State Library and Archives, "Work some among my flowers. Plant tomatoes & pepper seeds. Cut some squares for Lizzy May's hexigon [*sic*] quilt. . . . Get quilt out and hem it."

From the last of the nineteenth century on, many fine quilts were made in the central part of the state—fancy quilts inspired by magazine and newspaper articles, crazy quilts of all kinds, and plain utility quilts.

In West Tennessee, the quilts brought to Quilt Days were not so old as those found in other parts of the state. Fabric came from a different market source and the styles were less refined. Published patterns accounted for many of the designs where, in other areas, a single pattern may have circulated through the community and been repeated by a number of quilters. Styles and customs from adjoining states have an effect on those living near the Mississippi River where there is little contact with the eastern part of the state.

The quilt survey uncovered two important Tennessee trends. More than two dozen examples of rose quilts, made in the mid-nineteenth century or later, were found to have been pieced rather than appliquéd, as was first assumed. The technique had apparently gone out of favor in the twentieth century, and quilt historians were unaware of its practice until the Tennessee project brought it to attention.

The second discovery was more obvious. A number of beautifully quilted and stuffed quilts were recorded from primarily one area, Rhea County, long after the style had been abandoned elsewhere. It was not an uncommon fashion in the middle of the nineteenth century, but it continued until the beginning of the twentieth century in that one county. The extra cotton stuffed into the quilting from the underside of the quilt creates a more sculptural effect than in plain quilting.

Although not limited to Tennessee quilters, quilts made here in the Rocky Mountain pattern had a refinement not found in quilts from other regions. The design (sometimes also called New York Beauty) is demanding even for an experienced quilter, and the survey found the Tennessee makers's workmanship was generally of excellent quality.

Thousands of quilts have been made in this state, and the survey findings offer only an approximate profile of that total. Pieced quilts are the most popular by far and account for three-fourths of those reviewed. One-seventh of the quilts were appliqué. Next came crazy quilts and a small number of quilts combining both piecing and appliqué, followed by wholecloth, embroidered, and novelty quilts in lesser numbers. The pieced quilts had the largest variety, ranging from elegant Feathered Star, Friendship, Rocky Mountain, and Basket quilts to simple Four Patch, Nine Patch, Brick, and String Quilt examples.

Appliqué work was usually reserved for "best" quilts. The Dutch Doll or Sunbonnet Sue was less refined in both design and execution but laden with family sentiment and familiar sewing scraps. The Crazy Quilt category included heavily embroidered silks and velvets as well as wool and cotton Crazy Quilts with simple embroidery for more practical use.

Tennessee quilters, historians, and collectors are part of a global network, and teachers and lecturers travel a worldwide circuit. Guilds, fairs, and museums within the state present numerous exhibitions and competitions where an astounding variety of work is shown. Quilts from Tennessee have received awards and recognition in national and international exhibitions. Local authors and historians contribute outstanding books and articles that reach a wide audience. Individuals and groups support research, present papers, and actively participate in the American Quilt Study Group, an organization that authenticated quilt scholarship. At this point, no one can predict the duration of the quilt revival phenomenon but one thing is certain, the next generation will be covered with quilts.

Quilts are made for many reasons: for personal growth and expression; for gifts to commemorate births, weddings, anniversaries, deaths, or other occasions of one's family and friends; for income; for competitions and exhibitions; for solace or therapy; for group activity; or simply for the pleasure of making a quilt. In the process, the quilt maker receives a sense of accomplishment and self-esteem, praise and thanks. She, or he, has created an object to cherish. "Remember me / When this you see," a favorite phrase inscribed on nineteenth-century quilts, remains the desire of every quilt maker. Today, as in the past, each quilter leaves something of herself in her quilt, her monument.

Suggested Readings

Barker, Garry B. *The Handcraft Revival in Southern Appalachia, 1930–1990.* Knoxville: Univ. of Tennessee Press, 1991.

Eaton, Allen H. *Handicrafts of the Southern Highlands.* New York: Russell Sage Foundation, 1937.

Freeman, Roland L. *A Communion of the Spirits: African-American Quilters, Preservers, and Their Stories.* Nashville: Rutledge Hill Press, 1996.

Hoffschwelle, Mary. *Rebuilding the Rural Southern Community.* Knoxville: Univ. of Tennessee Press, 1998.

Ramsey, Bets. *Old and New Quilt Patterns in the Southern Tradition.* Nashville: Rutledge Hill Press, 1987.

Ramsey, Bets, and Gail Trechsel. *Southern Quilts: A New View.* McLean, Va.: EPM Publications, 1991.

Ramsey, Bets, and Merikay Waldvogel. *Quilts of Tennessee: Images of Domestic Life Prior to 1930.* Nashville: Rutledge Hill Press, 1986.

———. *Southern Quilts: Surviving Relics of the Civil War.* Nashville: Rutledge Hill Press, 1998.

Waldvogel, Merikay. *Soft Covers for Hard Times: Quiltmaking and the Great Depression.* Nashville: Rutledge Hill Press, 1990.

Waldvogel, Merikay, and Barbara Brackman. *Patchwork Souvenirs of the 1933 World's Fair.* Nashville: Rutledge Hill Press, 1993.

Part Three

The Literary Arts

Fifteen

Establishing a Literary Tradition
Tennessee Literature to 1920

Allison Ensor

University of Tennessee

Where does Tennessee literature begin? Some would want to go back to the myths, legends, and tales of the Cherokees and other Native Americans who lived here before the coming of the Europeans. Others might begin with accounts of Spanish explorations led by Hernando De Soto (1540) and Juan Pardo (1566) or the diaries and letters of early British traders and military men such as Lt. Henry Timberlake. Still more would include the narratives of travelers who passed through the wilderness between Nashville and Knoxville in the late eighteenth and early nineteenth centuries: André Michaux, the French botanist; Louis Phillipe, duke of Orleans and future king of France; the Moravian missionaries Abraham Steiner and Frederick Schweinitz; Francis Asbury, one of the first bishops of the Methodist Church in America; and Lorenzo Dow, popular Methodist preacher who came from New England to minister in the South.

More obviously literary is John Robinson's collection of essays, *The Savage,* first published in Philadelphia in 1810 and reprinted in Knoxville by F. S. Heiskell in 1833. The writer presents himself as "Piomingo, Headman and Warrior of the Muscogulgee Nation." (The real Piomingo was a Chickasaw, a friend of James Robertson, a founder of Nashville.) Under this pseudonym, Robinson, who lived in Tennessee before and after 1810, offers observations on "the manners and customs, vices and virtues" of those claiming to be more refined and civilized than Native Americans.

Other writings soon followed, their chief significance lying in their primacy. A novel largely based on the Bible, *The Life of Joseph,* was published in Nashville in 1811; *The Englishman; or Letters Found in the State of Tennessee,* an imitation of William Wirt's *Letters of the British Spy,* appeared in Rogersville in 1815. The first drama printed in the state, Josiah P. Smith's *Who Ever Saw the Like* (Knoxville, 1827), concerned the race for state senate in Knoxville.

Commonly cited as Tennessee's first novel, Charles W. Todd's *Woodville; or, The Anchoret Reclaimed,* was printed in Knoxville by F. S. Heiskell in 1832, preceded by the first novel to use a Tennessee setting, Anne Newport Royall's *The Tennessean* (New Haven, Conn., 1827). Todd's Gothic romance, heavily influenced by Lord Byron, disguises its settings, identifying towns only as S—— or L——, but it is commonly supposed that part of it takes place at the "——— Springs," presumably Montvale Springs, south of Maryville. (The author, about whom little is known, may have been a student or teacher at Maryville.) The overly romantic plot has the title character, Allison Woodville, in love with Matilda, who marries another man instead, causing Woodville to travel to Europe, where, like Byron, he becomes involved in the struggle for Greek independence. There he meets his rival and kills him in a duel. Alas, there is no happiness for Woodville, as it turns out that his beloved is his half sister! He retreats to the woods with his dog Trajan and an African American servant, Ned. Though it was praised by the *Knoxville Register*, other papers were less kind to Todd's tale.

In 1833, William Field's *Literary and Miscellaneous Scrap Book*, an anthology of poetry and prose, was published in Knoxville, to favorable reviews, and went through several subsequent revisions. Tennessee writers contributed only a few of its many moralistic and sentimental pieces, but it did include an essay, "Recollections of Infancy," from Robinson's book *The Savage*. Four years later, Walter Marshall McGill published a long narrative poem in ten books, *The Western World* (Maryville, 1837), presenting the story of America from 1492 to 1781, the end of the Revolutionary War. Like Joel Barlow's *Columbiad*, it may have been another attempt to write the great American epic.

Davy Crockett, charcoal, artist unknown, c. 1835. Courtesy of Special Collections, University of Tennessee, Knoxville.

A more popular book than any of these, though not literary, was *Gunn's Domestic Medicine, or Poor Man's Friend* (Knoxville, 1830), editions of which continued to appear into the twentieth century. Mark Twain's Huckleberry Finn was able to spot a copy in the parlor of the Grangerford family and examined it enough to know that it "told you all about what to do if a body was sick or dead."

None of the authors and works mentioned thus far has been able to hold a place in the public mind across the years. Not so David "Davy" Crockett (1786–1836), the subject of his own "narrative" and of many other books, including a series of popular almanacs, most of them published after his death. Born in Greene County and an Indian fighter under Andrew Jackson in the Creek War of 1813–14, Crockett served in the Tennessee General Assembly (1821–22, 1823–24), and then as a Tennessee member of the U.S. House of Representatives. Defeated for reelection in 1835, he moved to Texas, where he died at the Battle of the Alamo the following year.

Crockett's own account of his adventures, *A Narrative of the Life of David Crockett of the State of Tennessee* (Philadelphia, 1834), is not completely reliable but was considerably more so than other books about him that were published in the 1830s. Its title page contains what is probably Crockett's most often quoted maxim: "I leave this rule for others when I'm dead. / Be always sure you're right—THEN GO AHEAD!"

The *Narrative* appeared a year after Seba Smith's *Life and Writings of Major Jack Downing of Downingville* (Boston, 1833), one of the earliest pieces of American humor which did not rely on a European model. Crockett's book preceded A. B. Longstreet's *Georgia Scenes, Characters, Incidents, Etc. in the First Half Century of the Republic* (1835) by a year, and so is one of the earliest examples of the literature of the southern frontier. In some respects, Crockett was a real-life version of James Fenimore Cooper's hero Natty Bumpo, first introduced in *The Pioneers* (New York, 1823).

Seven Crockett almanacs were published between 1835 and 1856, beginning with *Davy Crockett's Almanack, or Wild Sports of the West, And Life in the Backwoods* (1835). In the almanacs Crockett appears as a superhero able to tangle with a grizzly bear or any other ferocious man or beast he might encounter. Although readers were surely aware that Crockett had been killed in Texas in 1836, some almanac prefaces insisted that he was still alive as a prisoner in a Mexican salt mine. Other prefaces admitted Crockett's death but asserted that he had left behind a great deal of manuscript material, which was being printed in the almanacs. The stories for the most part were presented as if by Crockett himself, told in a thick dialect. Ben Harding, the supposed editor of the tales of "Kurnel Krockett," also addresses the reader in dialect. The mode is usually comic, though there are occasional stories that are more sentimental. Profusely illustrated, the almanacs provided in addition to the Crockett stories, the time of sunrise and sunset, the length of the day, phases of the moon, and the time of high tide at New York, Boston, and Charleston.

Another Tennessee writer with even more significant contributions to the humor from the southern frontier was George Washington Harris (1814–1869), the creator of Sut Lovingood. Harris is the one Tennessee writer before the 1920s regularly included in college-level anthologies of American literature. By the time Harris began his Sut stories, southern humor had been enriched not only by Longstreet's *Georgia Scenes* but also by Thomas Bangs Thorpe's "The Big Bear of Arkansas" (1841) and Johnson Jones Hooper's *Some Adventures of Simon Suggs, Late of the Tallapoosa Volunteers* (1845). To a large extent these stories reflected the roughness of the southern frontier, written by males for a male audience. Harris's work now seems the culmination of antebellum southern humor and the best American dialect humor before Mark Twain.

Harris, a native of Allegheny City (now part of Pittsburgh), Pennsylvania, came to live in Knoxville in 1819 with his half-brother Samuel Bell and lived in the city until shortly before the Civil War. Writing was by no means his only employment: at one time or another he was a steamboat captain, Blount County farmer, operator of a metalworking shop, railroad employee, superintendent of the Holston Glass Works, and postmaster of Knoxville. While working for the Hiwassee Mining Company in the Ducktown and Copperhill copper mines of southeastern Tennessee, Harris became acquainted with William S. "Sut" Miller, said to have been the model for Sut Lovingood.

Harris's earliest writings appeared in William T. Porter's *Spirit of the Times,* published in New York, which described itself as a "Chronicle of the Turf, Agriculture, Field Sports, Literature, and the Stage." In 1843, he contributed four "sporting epistles" to the *Spirit* and his first full-length story, "The Knob Dance—A Tennessee Frolic," appeared August 2, 1845. The character of Sut Lovingood first appeared in *The Spirit of the Times,* November 4, 1854, in a story called "Sut Lovengood's [*sic*] Daddy 'Acting Horse.'" This was Harris's last contribution to the *Spirit;* many of his later Sut stories ran in the *Nashville Union and American,* including three that satirized Abraham Lincoln.

Though Harris hoped for years to publish a collection of his stories, the book did not come out until 1867, when the New York firm of Dick and Fitzgerald published *Sut Lovingood. Yarns Spun by a "Nat'ral Born Durn'd Fool." Warped and Wove for Public Wear.* The quotation is Sut's characterization of himself in "Sicily Burns's Wedding": "Hit am an orful thing, George, tu be a natral born durn'd fool. . . . Hits made pow'fully agin our famerly, an all owin tu dad."

Harris planned a second book, to be called "High Times and Hard Times," and in 1869 took the manuscript with him to Lynchburg, Virginia, supposedly in an attempt to arrange for its publication. On his return trip, however, he became ill on the train, was removed at Knoxville, and, before he died, said only the single word, "Poisoned." The manuscript was never found.

The best known and now most frequently reprinted stories from *Sut Lovingood* are "Parson John Bullen's Lizards," "Mrs. Yardley's Quilting," "Blown Up with Soda" with its sequel "Sicily Burns's Wedding," and "Rare Ripe Garden Seed," the first in a series of connected stories. Most of the tales are set in the Copper Basin area before the Civil War. They take the form of overheard conversations between Sut

Lovingood and a more refined urban dweller called George, whose standard English contrasts markedly with the extreme dialect of his mountain friend. After a few preliminaries Sut typically takes over to narrate some incident that he has witnessed or event in which he has played a major part. Frequently Sut's tales involve fighting, suffering, embarrassment, and general chaos of which he himself has been the chief instigator.

Over the years Harris's book has earned both praise and condemnation. Twain and William Faulkner liked the stories, but critic Edmund Wilson in the *New Yorker* of May 7, 1955, memorably denounced *Sut Lovingood* as "by far the most repellent book of any real merit in American literature. . . . It is all as offensive as possible." Wilson saw Sut as "a peasant squatting in his own filth," and he lamented that "all that was lowest in the lowest of the South found expression in Harris's book."

Though Sut still has his admirers, many readers have had problems with the book, beginning with its heavy dialect, so much more difficult to read than Mark Twain's or that of any other southern frontier humorist. Harris likes to change the spelling of a great many words so as to indicate their pronunciation. To write "fight" seems to him a distortion, an inadequate representation; only "fite" satisfies him. Harris's admirers may delight in such spellings as "dimunt" for "diamond," while other readers may simply be puzzled. The stories are too violent, too ribald for some tastes, and many readers have been made uncomfortable by the prejudice shown in them against African Americans, Jews, and Native Americans. Women are clearly subordinate, since Sut believed they "wer made tu cook the vittils, mix the sperits, an' help the men du the stayin awake," the last a reference to sex. Despite all of this, Harris's stories continue to attract readers and inspire scholarly endeavors. He will always be ranked as one of the finest of the southern frontier humorists, one of the most important in a tradition out of which Mark Twain would arise.

Appearing in the same year as the Sut Lovingood *Yarns* was a very different book, *Tiger-Lilies* (1867), the only novel by Georgia poet Sidney Lanier (1842–1881). It was set at Knoxville, Cades Cove, along the Little Tennessee River, at Montvale Springs, and at a house called Thalberg (a German version of the name "Montvale"). Lanier's grandfather owned the seven-gabled, one-hundred-room hotel built at Montvale Springs by a previous owner in 1853. Lanier spent several summers there before the Civil War, a conflict in which he was captured and imprisoned at Point Lookout, Maryland, where he developed the tuberculosis that shortened his life. Later critics singled out *Tiger-Lilies* as the first novel in which the mountaineer is treated as a distinct regional type.

The Civil War plays a large part in *Tiger-Lilies,* with the malevolent, Mephistophelean John Cranston joining the Union army, while its hero Philip Sterling and his friend Paul Rubetsahl join the Confederates fighting in Virginia. Hardly remembered today, the novel's reputation quickly paled alongside such poems as "The Song of the Chattahoochee" (1877) and "The Marshes of Glynn" (1878), and even they have been largely neglected, in part because of the low regard of Lanier held by the Vanderbilt critics, especially Allen Tate and Robert Penn Warren.

Surely there are few better accounts of the Civil War by a participant than *Co. Aytch: A Side Show of the Big Show,* published serially by Sam R. Watkins (1839–1901) in the *Columbia Herald* in 1881–82 and then later published in book form. Watkins, twenty-one years old when he joined the Maury Grays of the First Tennessee Regiment, looks back on his experiences as a "humble private." While admitting there were "glorious times," he concludes that "the glory of war was at home among the ladies and not upon the field of blood and carnage of death, where our comrades were mutilated and torn by shot and shell." The carnage at Franklin appalled him: "My flesh trembles, and creeps, and crawls when I think of it today. My heart almost ceases to beat at the horrid recollection. Would to God I had never witnessed such a scene!"

The war inspired a good amount of poetry, though now the best known poems about Tennessee

Nineteenth-Century Poetry

IN THE 1920S, ALLEN TATE, JOHN CROWE RANSOM, AND OTHERS PUBLISHED THEIR POEMS IN *THE Fugitive* magazine and made Tennessee one of the centers of modern poetry. It would have been hard, however, to anticipate this development in the nineteenth century; the age boasted few poets of any sort and none who enjoys any critical reputation today. Still, a few of these poets deserve to be recalled, if only for the historical interest their careers embody.

Among the first of these was Walter Marshall McGill, whose poem *The Western World* was published in Maryville in 1837. McGill's epic, 381 pages of unvarying rhymed couplets, celebrated the history of the United States in terms particularly resonant for a Tennessean of the 1830s. His George Washington, for instance, was not the stiff but kindly moral exemplar described by Parson Weems but a furiously warlike Achilles resembling no one so much as Tennessee's own Andrew Jackson. Composing an epic about American history was a conventional gesture in nineteenth-century America, and indeed most Tennessee poetry of the century was profoundly conventional, indistinguishable from the poetry of other sections, even when taking its inspiration from Tennessee subjects. Here, for instance, is Clara Cole, a locally popular poet of the 1840s, bidding "Farewell to Nashville":

> Fair city of the hill, adieu,
> With feeling of regret
> Thy fast receding shade I view,
> For how can I forget
> The scenes of youthful hope and joy,
> When all seemed bright and gay,
> When not a grief or care arose
> To cloud my life's young day.

Cole, like most Tennessee poets of her day, published her verse in newspapers or in one of the struggling magazines that appeared during the 1840s, such as *The Parlor Visitor, The Southern Lady's Companion,* or the more ambitious but short lived *South Western Monthly.* These organs relied mainly on local writers, many of whom remained anonymous, for copy. The verse they published tended to be sentimental, didactic, pious, and a bit morbid, like "Dying Charlie" by a poet in the *Companion* who signed herself simply "Katrina":

> Little Charlie's dead, Mother,
> His heart has ceased to beat;
> His spirit's gone to heaven, Mother,
> And is nestling at Jesus' feet.

Reading this verse today reminds us that Emmeline Grangerford, the lugubrious graveyard poet whose odes Huck Finn admires so much in Mark Twain's novel, was not much of an exaggeration. But other writers struck other notes: for instance Clara Cole's principal rival in verse during the 1840s and 1850s, the cheerier and marginally more gifted Lucy Virginia Smith French of McMinnville (1825–1881). French worked with a broader array of themes and benefited from some respectable literary influences, including Poe, Bryant, and Byron. If her

[Continued on next page]

Leonore seems but a poor imitation of a well-known work of Poe, "The Iron Horse," her tribute to the steam locomotive, despite its straining for grandeur, is more original:

> From the cavern of art, in the hills of the North
> Sprang a proud-crested charger exultingly forth,
> By the spirit of steam was his breathing up-born;
> From the strong forest giants his sinews were torn;
> And the gnomes of the mine shouted loud in their ire,
> O're his iron bound bosom and pulses of fire!

Both Cole and French were thought distinguished enough to have their works collected between hard covers at midcentury.

During the Civil War, Tennessee produced its share of poetic celebrations of Confederate valor. But some verse of the period sufficiently escaped the heroic mode to take note of the costs of war (for example, "Melt the Bells" and "The Cotton-Burners Hymn," anonymous works from the *Memphis Appeal*) and eventually became elegiac, as in "All is Gone," composed by "Fadette" and also published in the *Appeal* near the war's end. Indeed, the most famous poetic lament for the defeated South, "The Conquered Banner," was composed by a sometime-Tennessean, Father Abram Ryan (1838–1886), supposedly within an hour of his receiving the news from Appomattox:

Father Abram Ryan, 1862. Courtesy of the McClung Historical Collection.

> Furl that Banner, softly, slowly!
> Treat it gently—it is holy—
> For it droops above the dead.
> Touch it not—unfold it never,
> Let it droop there, furled forever,
> For its people's hopes are dead!

Ryan, a Catholic priest who lived in both Nashville and Knoxville, enjoyed a fame that lasted well beyond the war and rested upon a vast quantity of verse both popular and critically respected. Nearly all of it concerned the two great loves of Ryan's life, the South and the Christian God. These themes resonated powerfully enough in his region to justify a thick volume of his work, which, within two years of Ryan's death in 1886, went through 12 editions. Though Ryan's poems, sentimental, devoid of irony, and ruled absolutely by meter and rhyme, get little respect today, in his own time he was considered a genius rivaled only by Poe.

Several other Tennessee poets of the postbellum period enjoyed critical and popular acclaim. John Trotwood Moore of Columbia (1858–1929), Virginia Fraser Boyle of Chattanooga (1863–1938), and Walter Malone of Memphis (1866–1915) were all well enough respected to be included in several turn-of-the-century anthologies of southern writing. They are now largely forgotten, but their contemporaries George Marion McClellan of Belfast (1860–1934) and Will Allen Dromgoole of Murfreesboro (1860–1934) enjoy some readership even now. McClellan is remembered as the first significant African American poet in Tennessee and among the first in America. Like most African American writers between Reconstruction and the 1920s, McClellan was anxious to demonstrate his mastery of European modes of expression. His verse is therefore carefully conventional in form and subject, but despite those limitations it reveals a genuine talent at work:

> The sun went down in beauty,
> Beyond Mississippi's tide,
> As I stood on the banks of the river,
> And watched its waters glide;
> Its swelling currents resembling
> The longing, restless soul,
> Surging, swelling, and pursuing
> Its ever receding goal.

McClellan's contemporary Will Allen Dromgoole was an indefatigable author of vast amounts of fiction and journalism as well as poetry, literary editor of the *Nashville Banner,* and eventually "poet laureate of the South." She is remembered now as the author of one poem, "The Bridge Builder" (1898), a brief lyric concerning an old man who spends his failing strength building a bridge over a chasm he has already crossed; in reply to the inquiry of a passerby, the old man explains,

> There followeth after me to-day
> A youth, whose feet must pass this way.
> This chasm, that has been naught to me,
> To that fair-haired youth may a pitfall be.
> He, too, must cross in the twilight dim;
> Good friend, I am building the bridge for him.

The poem enjoys an astonishingly vigorous life today. A search for Dromgoole's name on the Internet yields 148 sites, maintained by Earth Day committees, libertarian organizations, "humanist societies," the Black Student Union at the University of North Carolina at Charlotte, and others, nearly all of them quoting "The Bridge Builder" to express their commitment to making a better future. Dromgoole lived into a day when much better poets, such as Tate and Ransom, appeared in Tennessee, and she became, without knowing it, the object of their barbs and the personification of the sort of poetry they were trying to displace. With its broad and lasting appeal, "The Bridge Builder" might stand as a fair representative of Tennessee verse before the modern period. Sentimental, accessible, framed in a rhyme and meter that commended it to memorization, it aimed not to challenge or trouble readers but to "delight and instruct" them by expressing conventional moral ideas in an appealing way. There is little to challenge or trouble any reader in nineteenth-century Tennessee poetry, the reason for what popularity it enjoyed in its own day, and for its obscurity today.

John Grammer, The University of the South

Frontispiece, Lucy Virginia French, *One or Two?* St. Louis, 1883. Library Collection, Tennessee State Library and Archives. Courtesy of TSLA.

battles are probably those in Herman Melville's *Battle Pieces* (1866), in which "Shiloh: A Requiem" is especially memorable, though battles at Murfreesboro, Chattanooga, and elsewhere also were included. Possibly the best known poem of the time written in Tennessee is Father Abram Joseph Ryan's "The Conquered Banner." Ryan (1838–1886) served as priest in both Nashville and Knoxville; he is said to have written his classic requiem for the Lost Cause at the latter.

Until the 1870s, male writers dominated Tennessee literature, but as more and more American women began to write and publish in the latter half of the nineteenth century, it was inevitable that Tennessee women should join them. One of the first was Lucy Virginia Smith French (1825–1881), or L. Virginia French, as her name usually appears. A native of Virginia's eastern shore, French taught school for a time in Memphis but spent much of her life on her husband's plantation near McMinnville.

Using the pen name L'Inconnue (meaning "the unknown"), French wrote for the *Louisville Courier-Journal.* She also edited a number of newspapers and magazines, including *The Southern Ladies Book,* which was "dedicated to Woman, as the symbol of progress" as well as to the advancement of southern literature; the *Southern Homestead,* published in Nashville; the *Georgia Literary and Temperance Crusader,* published in Atlanta; and the *Ladies Home.* Her collection of poems, *Wind Whispers,* was published in 1856, the same year she wrote a five-act tragedy set in Mexico, *Istalilxo: The Lady of Tula.* French was also a novelist, publishing before the Civil War the book *Kernwood; or, After Many Days* (Louisville, 1857), a story about prostitution in New Orleans and writing after the war a historical romance taken from a fictional manuscript of a Confederate spy, *My Roses: The Romance of a June Day* (Philadelphia, 1872). Cross-dressing is a plot element common to both, as a woman disguises herself as a man and then acts heroically. Unable to find a publisher for her third novel, *Darlingtonia: The Eaters and the Eaten,* French sold it to the *Detroit Free Press,* where it ran from April to August in 1879. Set at the resort of Beersheba Springs, south of McMinnville, the novel is partly based on the diaries she kept while living there during the war years.

In the minds of many, Frances Hodgson Burnett (1840–1924) is firmly associated with England, the setting for her children's classics, *Little Lord Fauntleroy* (1886), *A Little Princess* (1905), and *The Secret Garden* (1911). Nevertheless, Burnett spent several years in Tennessee, beginning in 1865, when at age fifteen she arrived from England with her mother, settling in New Market, northeast of Knoxville. Four years later she was in Knoxville, where she lived for six years and married Swan Burnett, a local doctor, in 1873.

Burnett used East Tennessee as a setting for stories such as "Seth," set in the coal-mining community of Black Creek (its characters, however, are all from Lancashire, England). Burnett first published the story in *Lippincott's* and then collected it in her *Surly Tim and Other Stories. Dolly: A Love Story,* later published as *Vagabondia,* obviously reflected her Tennessee experiences. Though its setting is ostensibly

London, the book is based on Knoxville, for Vagabondia was the name of the house near the Tennessee River where Burnett and others lived a rather Bohemian life in the 1870s. Another Tennessee setting appears in the novel *In Connection with the DeWilloughby Claim* (1892), which takes place in a fictional Delisleville, Tennessee, apparently based on Knoxville. Furthermore, Burnett's novel *Louisiana* (1880) is said to have a number of characters inspired by people she had known at New Market.

Another outsider who wrote stories about Tennessee during this time was Mississippi's Katherine Sherwood Bonner McDowell (1849–1883), usually known simply as Sherwood Bonner. The author was perhaps best known for her one novel, *Like Unto Like* (1878), and for such stories as "A Volcanic Interlude," which caused a stir when it appeared in *Lippincott's* in 1880. Before that, in 1875–76, she served as amanuensis to Henry Longfellow, having left her husband and child to go to Boston. She later traveled to Europe and wrote travel letters published in the Boston *Times* and the Memphis *Avalanche.*

Bonner wrote four stories set in the hills of Middle Tennessee, to the west and south of Cookeville, which were published in *Harper's Weekly* during 1881: "Jack and the Mountain Pink," "The Case of Eliza Bleylock," "Lame Jerry," and "The Barn Dance at the Apple Settlement." Two years later these four joined stories of other areas of the South as *Dialect Tales* (1883). Dancing, fiddling, and moonshining—those staples of Appalachian fiction—are prominent in the stories. There is also the "outsider" in the figure of Young Selden in the story "Jack and the Mountain Pink." Selden comes to the "watering place" of Bloomington Springs, northwest of Cookeville, in order to escape the plague then ravaging Nashville and in hopes, perhaps, of becoming romantically involved with a "mountain pink," though nothing develops in that line. Selden instead pronounces Sincerity Hicks, who guides him to the Window Cliffs (near Burgess Falls), a "Cumberland bean stalk."

Current tastes for Tennessee mountain life might prefer Bonner's work as more realistic and less stereotyped, but in the late nineteenth century the supreme depicter of that story was assumed to be Mary Noailles Murfree (1850–1922), who wrote all of her best-known fiction under the pseudonym Charles Egbert Craddock. A native of Murfreesboro, Murfree was not intimately acquainted with the life and people of the Cumberland Plateau and Great Smoky Mountains. Many details of her life suggest just how far she was from the situation, not only of the mountaineer, but of any typical Tennessee woman of the time. She was a member of a prominent well-to-do, cultured family; she had received a good education, first at the Nashville Female Academy and afterward at the Chegary Institute in Philadelphia. Unencumbered by a husband and children, she had the enthusiastic support from her father, brother, and sister.

The Murfree family's closest association with the mountains came during their fifteen summers at the popular resort of Beersheba Springs. The big white frame hotel perched at the top of the mountain, overlooking the Collins River valley hundreds of feet below, was to appear in several of Murfree's stories. Murfree also visited the East Tennessee resort of Montvale Springs, below the mountain that serves as the setting for "The 'Harnt' that Walks Chilhowee," a tale of mountain superstition and of one person's compassion for another. From Montvale Springs she made excursions to Tuckaleechee Cove, Cades Cove, and Gregory's Bald, the last two now part of the Great Smoky Mountains National Park.

Murfree's first ventures in print did not involve the mountains but were satires depicting city sophisticates. "Flirts and Their Ways," which appeared in *Lippincott's* for May 1874, was based on observations from the author's years in Nashville social circles, as was "My Daughter's Admirers" in the July 1875 issue of *Lippincott's.* Both were signed with a masculine pseudonym, R. Emmet Dembry.

Soon, however, Murfree's writing took a very different course, as she turned to the mountains of Tennessee and to the men and women who lived there. While one cannot be sure of the reason for her dramatic change of subject, it has been noted that

Mary Noailles Murfree. Courtesy of TSM.

the issue of *Lippincott's* in which her second story appeared also carried one by Rebecca Harding Davis, "The Yares of the Black Mountains." Davis set her story in the mountains of western North Carolina and included a fair amount of mountain dialect. Too, Murfree must have been aware that writers in other sections of the country—many of them women—were winning fame with their stories of the people and places where they lived. Why should Tennessee not have its representative among these regional writers? And what was the most picturesque element in Tennessee? To her, the answer was obvious: the mountaineers. They had already made an appearance in the Sut Lovingood stories of George Washington Harris and in Sidney Lanier's *Tiger-Lilies.* Mark Twain and Charles Dudley Warner's novel *The Gilded Age* (1873) set its opening chapter in the "knobs of East Tennessee"—a place Twain had never seen and knew only from family stories about their life there before they moved to Missouri. Murfree sought to depict mountain life as it was before the railroads and the industrial revolution reached the people there and changed them forever.

Murfree began her depiction of mountain life by submitting to *Appleton's* two stories: "Taking the Blue Ribbon at the County Fair" and "The Panther of Jolton's Ridge." Both were accepted, but the magazine ceased publication before they could appear and neither saw print until several years later. The failure with *Appleton's* did not discourage Murfree. Her first published mountain story, "The Dancin' Party at Harrison's Cove," appeared in the prestigious *Atlantic Monthly* in May 1878 under the pseudonym Charles Egbert Craddock. In using a male pseudonym, Murfree followed the practice of such well-known female writers as George Eliot, and her editors at the *Atlantic* understood that Craddock was a pseudonym since she signed her letters to them as "M. N. Murfree." Not until considerably later, in 1885, did Murfree, accompanied by her sister and father, go to Boston and reveal her identity to Thomas Bailey Aldrich, then editor of the *Atlantic.* According to all accounts, Aldrich was simply amazed to find that the stories he had been publishing for years were the work of a woman. "But this is impossible," he supposedly exclaimed, "Impossible!" Most early critics assumed that the author was male, though one perceptively noted that Craddock consistently depicted women in a positive light.

Murfree's initial *Atlantic* story, "The Dancin' Party at Harrison's Cove," was one of her best. Set at and near the "New Helvetia Springs," obviously based on Beersheba Springs, it recounts how a shooting between the outlaw Rick Pearson and Kossute Johns, a young man half his age, is averted through the intervention of Mr. Kenyon, a supposed preacher (actually a lay reader in the Episcopal church), who had served with the outlaw in the Civil War. Indeed, Kenyon must have saved his life or at least given him invaluable aid, since Rick leaves the scene with the remark, "Waal, parson. . . . I'll go, jest ter pleasure you-uns. Ye see, I ain't forgot Shiloh." (Incidentally, many Tennesseans would object that "you-uns" is not used when speaking to only one person.)

Over the next several years the *Atlantic* published seven more of Murfree's mountain stories, concluding with the two-part "Drifting Down Lost Creek," set in the eastern part of White County. At the same time Murfree published a series of mountain stories for young people in *Youth's Companion,* beginning with "On a Higher Level" in the issue of January 16, 1879.

After eight mountain stories had appeared in the *Atlantic,* Murfree put them together for a book entitled *In the Tennessee Mountains,* which was published by Houghton, Mifflin in April 1884. Contemporary critics were generally favorable, with many reviewers comparing the volume with the work of other local colorists such as Joel Chandler Harris, George Washington Cable, and Bret Harte. The critical verdict of later years is that this collection was Murfree's best book about the mountains. Prominent among its stories are "The Dancin' Party at Harrison's Cove" and "The 'Harnt' that Walks Chilhowee." The volume also includes "Drifting Down Lost Creek," in which the young Cynthia Ware's devotion, courage, and endurance, manifested in her attempt to free her unjustly imprisoned sweetheart Evander Price, go unrewarded as he rejects both her and the mountains, eagerly embracing the industrialism of the future. Seeing the railroad and the locomotive for the first time, he exclaims, "Ef this ain't the glory o' God revealed in the work o' man, what is?" "He sets more store by metal than by grace," observes Pete Blenkins, adding that "'Vander air a powerful cur'ous critter: he 'lowed ter me ez one year in the forge at the Pen war wuth a hundred years in the mountings ter him." The mountaineers regard "Cynthy" Ware as a "cur'ous critter" too, failing entirely to comprehend her exertions to get justice for an innocent man. Even the accused's mother thinks that Cynthia "never had no call ter meddle with 'Vander."

Of these three stories, the most frequently reprinted is "The 'Harnt' That Walks Chilhowee," though "Drifting Down Lost Creek" is surely of equal merit and now all the more admirable for its portrait of a strong female character. The story's exceptional length—it ran in two issues of the *Atlantic,* March and April 1884—has probably worked against its being chosen for inclusion in anthologies. Since its setting is not the dramatic Great Smoky Mountains nor the Cumberlands near Beersheba Springs, but the hill country east of Sparta, it may seem less characteristic of Murfree's work. It may be said, however, that Murfree's mountaineers talk, think, and act the same, wherever they live.

In the Tennessee Mountains had for many readers the charm of novelty. They were generally delighted with the glimpse of this unknown place and its people, whom they must have looked upon rather condescendingly. Murfree must have felt some distance from the mountain people, and that distance manifests itself all too obviously in the marked contrast between the voice of the sophisticated, urban narrator and the dialect of the illiterate mountain folk.

Murfree's work was not confined to the short story; she wrote a number of novels, though these are not generally read today. Critics favorably reviewed *The Prophet of the Great Smoky Mountains* (1885), *In the Clouds* (1886), and *In the "Stranger People's" Country* (1891), and some believed that Murfree would win recognition as a major American fiction author. Critics usually pick *The Prophet of the Great Smoky Mountains,* with its strong trio of characters in Hiram Kelsey, a mountain preacher who has lost his faith, Rick Tyler, an unjustly accused fugitive, and Dorinda Cayce, as her best novel.

Murfree published twenty-five books, several on historical topics such as *Where the Battle Was Fought* (1884), a tale about the aftermath of the Civil War Battle of Stones River in her native town of Murfreesboro; *The Story of Old Fort Loudon* (1899); and *The Amulet* (1906). But there was only so much that could be done with outlaws, moonshiners, lovely young mountain girls, handsome outsiders, courtships, flights from justice, and seemingly supernatural events which had a rational explanation. Most readers find her novels overly long and filled with stereotypes and overblown description.

In the twenty-first century, Murfree's reputation is not very high. Some local-color fiction still appears in national anthologies, but Murfree's stories do not. The feminist movement, which has rescued so many literary reputations from obscurity, has shown little interest in Murfree. Literary critics complain of Murfree's use of similar plots, stock characters, and overblown description, while historians have attacked her view of Appalachia as a strange place inhabited by backward, ignorant people whose peculiar ways never change and who are entirely outside the mainstream of American life.

Murfree was by no means the only woman local-color writer using the Tennessee landscape as a source of fiction during the late nineteenth century. Will Allen Dromgoole (1860–1934) was, like Murfree, a native of Murfreesboro, born there before the Civil War. Like Murfree she wrote under a masculine name (although it was her own, her parents having named her William), with many of her works being published in Boston. Both women were unmarried, and both received part of their education in the North. If not everyone agreed with her Boston publisher that she was a southern literary genius, Dromgoole was widely admired in her own day, though she is almost forgotten now.

Will Allen Dromgoole. Photograph by W. G. Pruss. Courtesy of Special Collections, University of Tennessee, Knoxville.

Dromgoole began her literary career in 1886, with the publication in Philadelphia of *The Sunny Side of the Cumberland: A Story of the Mountains,* under the name Will Allen. The novel, told in first person by a young female member of the group, is part sentimental love story, part narrative of a journey made by several persons some years earlier, beginning at Sparta and proceeding eastward through Bon Air and Clarktown, eventually swinging westward to Beersheba Springs, Monteagle, and Sewanee. Also in 1886 Dromgoole's first story, "Columbus Tucker's Discontent," set near the Sequatchie Valley, won second prize in a *Youth Companion's* contest and appeared in that magazine on October 13, 1887. About this time Dromgoole built her house, Yellowhammer's Nest, in the rural railroad community of Estill Springs, between Tullahoma and Winchester. Three years later she published a short story called "Fiddling His Way to Fame" in the *Boston Arena* of November 1890. In this work, Tennessee Governor Robert Love "Bob" Taylor recounts in mountain dialect the story of his rise to Congress and the governor's chair, including the famous "War of the Roses" campaign of 1886 against his Republican brother Alf Taylor. A story in the *Boston Arena* of April 1891, "The Heart of Old Hickory," depicted Governor Taylor at the state capitol, talking with a newsboy as he ponders a clemency petition which he eventually signs, despite the criticism which he knows the act will bring him. The piece later served as the title story of her first collection, *The Heart of Old Hickory and Other Stories of Tennessee* (Boston, 1895).

After the books of 1886 and 1895 came a whole series, some appearing very close together, some for children, and some for adults. Her last was *The Island of Beautiful Things: A Romance of the South*

(Boston, 1912). A second collection of short fiction appeared as *Cinch, and Other Stories; Tales of Tennessee* (Boston, 1898). Besides the nineteen stories in the two collections, Dromgoole wrote at least fifteen more for the *Arena,* whose editor, B. O. Flower, was much taken with her work. He wrote a flattering preface for her first story collection and later a review essay on her work for his *Boston Arena* in November 1895.

Dromgoole's stories were more varied than those of Murfree. A number dealt with the mountaineers but more focused on African Americans—though some of these would hardly be acceptable today, as they depict blacks as often lovable but ignorant, superstitious, and dependent on white people. She set some of her stories in rural areas, while placing others, such as "The Heart of Old Hickory," in cities. Unfortunately for her reputation, by today's standards much of her work appears too sentimental, religious, and didactic.

If any of the stories were to find favor today, it would be one like "A Humble Advocate" (*Boston Arena,* 1895), in which Josephine Cary, an abused wife from Sevier County, becomes very excited on hearing Jeff Bynum's unsympathetic account of a women's rights meeting in Knoxville. As Dromgoole's narrator puts it, "The slumbering fires of her nature woke and made response to their effort, those brave few fighting, contesting every inch of the road, their way to freedom—their way, and the way of all womanhood. She was with them as surely as though she had been in their meetings, been one of them." Later Cary offers to a jeering crowd her prophecy: "some o' you-uns'll live ter see the women o' the land castin' o' the'r votes yet. Let them as laugh look ter it." "Prophetic words," observes the narrator, "and big with meaning."

Dromgoole's early work was not confined to fiction. In 1890 she became intrigued with the Melungeons of East Tennessee. She visited Newman's Ridge in Hancock County and stayed with a family there. The experience inspired her to publish two articles about the Melungeons and their mysterious origin in the Nashville *Daily American;* she followed these with two pieces in the *Arena.* Regrettably, her articles were extremely critical. "The Malungeons [*sic*]," she remarked, "are filthy, their home is filthy. They are rogues, natural, 'born rogues,' close, suspicious, inhospitable, untruthful, cowardly, and, to use their own word, 'sneaky.'" It would remain for later writers to speak of the Melungeons more favorably and sympathetically.

Dromgoole also wrote some eight thousand poems (many were quite short), but only one of any real distinction, "Building the Bridge," often called "The Bridge Builder," which has been frequently reprinted and is presently listed on many Internet web pages for its inspirational message. Several of her poems appeared in her regular column, "Song and Story," which, beginning in 1903, ran for more than thirty years in the *Nashville Banner.* In addition to the poems, these columns typically included anecdotes about mountaineers, poor whites, or African Americans. Dromgoole became the *Banner*'s literary editor in 1922. The Poetry Society of the South named her poet laureate in 1930.

Sarah Barnwell Elliott (1848–1928) was another late-nineteenth-century Tennessee woman writer who published some of her work in newspapers. Born in Savannah, Georgia, she was the daughter of Stephen Elliott, the first Episcopal bishop of Georgia, and sister of Robert W. B. Elliott, the first Episcopal bishop of Texas. Both of her parents were from prominent South Carolina families. Bishop Elliott was a leader in the founding of the University of the South at Sewanee, which he served briefly as chancellor. His family had lived at Sewanee before the Civil War and returned there in the early 1870s, after his death.

Elliott's first publication was *The Felmeres* (1879), a novel focusing on religious and moral questions, set along the Carolina-Georgia coast. Her second novel, *A Simple Heart* (1897), was set in frontier Texas. Elliott's trip to Texas in the mid-1880s led to several stories with that setting.

In November 1886, Elliott began a tour of Europe and the Holy Land, accompanied by her brother, which was the subject of sixteen travel letters that were published in the *Louisville Courier-Journal.* Although the author's name was signed "S. B. E.," readers were told at the beginning of the series that these letters were the impressions of "An American woman who keeps her eyes and ears open."

Elliott's best novel is *Jerry* (1891), which was first serialized in *Scribner's.* Sometimes cited as an early example of naturalism, the novel follows the fortunes and misfortunes of a Cumberland mountain boy who leaves home, goes west, and grows up in a mining town. Considerably closer to home was the setting of *The Durket Sperret* (1898), with its picture of the Durket family of Lost Cove, near Sewanee, and its heroine Hannah Warren, who is determined to make her own choice of husband. The "Sperret" of the title is the pride and stubbornness of the family. Elliott published one collection of short stories, *An Incident and Other Happenings* (1899). Her play *His Majesty's Servant* ran for one hundred nights in London in 1904.

In her novel *The Making of Jane* (1901), Elliott showed her interest in the women's movement of the early twentieth century through her leading character, Jane Ormonde, who is portrayed as an intelligent, enterprising, financially independent career woman. Elliott became very active in the woman's suffrage movement, and was elected president of the Tennessee Equal Suffrage Association in 1912. Her petition, "To Law-makers," which called for Tennessee to give women the right to vote, was printed in the *Nashville Banner* of August 17, 1912.

Emma Bell Miles (1879–1919) was one of the few Tennessee local-color writers who actually lived in the mountains. Born in Evansville, Indiana, she moved with her family to Red Bank, north of Chattanooga, and later to nearby Walden's Ridge. At one time she seemed destined for a career as an artist, attending the St. Louis School of Art in 1899–1900 and 1900–1901, but she returned to Walden's Ridge and, against her parents' wishes, married Frank Miles, a mountaineer, by whom she had five children. The relationship was a difficult one, marked by several separations and reconciliations. Frank Miles never held a job for long, leaving the family constantly in bad financial circumstances.

In 1904, Emma Bell Miles began publishing poems, stories, and articles in magazines, including two poems and an article on mountain music in *Harper's Monthly.* Her principal book, *The Spirit of the Mountains* (1905), is a nonfiction account of mountain life as Miles had seen it, dealing with such topics as education, housing, the family and their neighbors, the supernatural, religion, and music. She included illustrations of people and places as well as music for several songs and fiddle tunes. It was one of the earliest of a series of books about the mountains and mountaineers; Horace Kephart's classic *Our Southern Highlanders* (1913) quoted Miles's earlier work.

In the fall of 1913, Miles moved to Chattanooga and soon began working as a staff writer for the *Chattanooga News.* During three months in 1914, she wrote a regular column, "Fountain Square Conversations," in which the White Pigeon, the Gray Pigeon, the Sparrow, and other birds speak, their conversation moderated by the Fireman atop the fountain. Soon afterward Miles contracted tuberculosis and had to enter a sanatorium. She died in 1919, the same year her second major book, *Our Southern Birds,* describing more than one hundred birds, was published in Chicago. A collection of her poetry appeared as *Strains from a Dulcimore* (Atlanta, 1930), eleven years after her death.

Compared to Murfree, Dromgoole, Elliott, and Miles, other turn-of-the-century women writers were less well known. Maria Thompson Daviess (1872–1924) wrote a series of novels, the most popular of which was *Miss Selina Lue* (1908). Like Elliott, she was a strong supporter of women's rights, a charter member of the woman suffrage group at Nashville. Her autobiography *Seven Times Seven* (1923) appeared in the year before her death. Virginia Frazier Boyle (1863–1938) published several books, including *Brokenburne: A Southern Auntie's War Tale* (1897) and *Devil Tales* (1900). A collection of her poetry, *Love Songs and Bugle Calls,* was published in 1906. Supposedly former Confederate President Jefferson Davis pronounced her the "poet laureate of the Confederacy" when she was only ten years old, a title later confirmed by the United Confederate Veterans in 1910. Frances Boyd Calhoun of Covington wrote the classic children's book *Miss Minerva and William Green Hill* in 1909. She died soon after the book's release, and its numerous sequels, appearing between 1918 and 1939, were written by Emma Reed Sampson.

Not all Tennessee writers of the late Victorian era were female. Opie Read (1852–1939), a native of Gallatin, gained fame in the 1880s with his newspaper, the *Arkansas Traveler.* Read, who spent many years in Chicago, wrote more than fifty books, most of which were light, popular titles that have been forgotten today. His novels with Tennessee settings include *A Tennessee Judge* (Chicago, 1893), *The Waters of Caney Fork: A Romance of Tennessee* (Chicago, 1898), and *The Starbucks* (Chicago, 1902). John Trotwood Moore (1858–1929), a native of Alabama, moved to Maury County in the mid-1880s and remained in Tennessee for the rest of his life. Moore collected some of his early writing in *Songs and Stories from Tennessee* (1897) and also wrote novels, including *The Bishop of Cottontown* (1906) and *Hearts of Hickory: A Story of Andrew Jackson and the War of 1812* (1926). The latter arose from Moore's interest in Tennessee history; he became state librarian in 1919 and coedited the four-volume *Tennessee: The Volunteer State* (1923). Moore was also known for his short-lived magazine *Trotwood's Monthly,* which began in 1905 and two years later merged with *Bob Taylor's Magazine* to form the *Taylor-Trotwood Magazine,* a blending of poetry, fiction, and history that lasted until 1911.

Some of the male writers were poets: Walter Malone (1867–1915) was a Memphis attorney and later judge. Though most of his work has been forgotten, his poem "Opportunity" (1905) is still remembered. Malone, like Moore, also wrote on historical subjects, sometimes reaching as far back as De Soto, about whom he wrote a long narrative poem. George Marion McClellan (1860–1934), one of the few African American writers in Tennessee at the turn of the century, published a collection of fifty-seven poems and five sketches simply entitled *Poems* (Nashville, 1895), then reprinted twelve of them as *Songs of a Southerner* (Boston, 1896). Many of his poems, including "The Hills of Sewanee," "A Song of Nashville," and "May along the Cumberland," reflect the Tennessee landscape. In addition to his poetry, McClellan produced one book of fiction, *Old Greenbottom Inn and Other Stories* (1906), in which themes of discrimination and racial injustice are prominent.

In comparison with the writing which followed it—Ransom, Tate, Warren, Lytle, and Davidson lay just ahead, to say nothing of James Agee, Cormac McCarthy, Peter Taylor, and the rest—the literature of Tennessee before 1920 may appear to some rather dull and undistinguished. A few names (Crockett, Harris, Murfree) are reasonably well known; most are not. The anthologies and literary histories have neglected this period in the state's literature. But the nineteenth and turn-of-the-century Tennessee writers did produce work of some value, a tradition that should not be lost. Southern literature did not begin with Faulkner, and there was Tennessee literature before the Fugitives and Agrarians.

Suggested Readings

Cary, Richard. *Mary N. Murfree.* New York: Twayne, 1967.

Ensor, Allison R. "A Tennessee Woman Abroad: The Travel Letters of Sarah Barnwell Elliott, 1886–1887." *Tennessee Historical Quarterly* 52 (Fall 1993): 185–91.

———. "What Is the Place of Mary Noailles Murfree Today?" *Tennessee Historical Quarterly* 47 (Winter 1988): 198–205.

Gaston, Kay Baker. *Emma Bell Miles.* Signal Mountain, Tenn.: Walden Ridge Historical Association, 1985.

Lofaro, Michael A., ed. *Davy Crockett: The Man, the Legend, the Legacy, 1786–1986.* Knoxville: Univ. of Tennessee Press, 1986.

Lyday-Lee, Kathy. "Will Allen Dromgoole: A Biographical Sketch." *Tennessee Historical Quarterly* 51 (Summer 1992): 107–12.

Parks, Edd W. *Charles Egbert Craddock.* Chapel Hill: Univ. of North Carolina Press, 1941.
Rickels, Milton. *George Washington Harris.* New York: Twayne, 1965.
Willbanks, Ray, ed. *Literature of Tennessee.* Macon, Ga.: Mercer Univ. Press, 1984.
Young, Thomas D. *Tennessee Writers.* Knoxville: Univ. of Tennessee Press, 1981.

Sixteen

Tennessee Poetry, the Fugitives and Agrarians, and the Republic of Letters

George Core
The Sewanee Review

The South, Allen Tate declares, is "an immensely complicated region. It begins in the Northeast with southern Maryland; it ends with eastern Texas; it includes to the north a little of Missouri." Tate understands that the diverse geography of the South influences culture in different ways, yet he concludes "that the people in this vast expanse of country have enough in common to bind them in a single culture cannot be denied."[1]

The subregions of the South may partly be defined in terms of literary traditions. As C. Hugh Holman points out in his elegantly original and succinct study, *Three Modes of Southern Writing* (1966), Ellen Glasgow reflects the Tidewater, William Faulkner represents the Gulf South, and Thomas Wolfe comes from the Piedmont. Even then, Holman admits, these three Souths each contain considerable variation, so that Wolfe and the Vanderbilt Agrarians have little in common, even though all derive from the southern Piedmont, as did another notable writer from Tennessee, James Agee, himself a poet, who is closer to Wolfe than to the Vanderbilt writers.

Glasgow, Faulkner, and Wolfe aside, Holman asserts that "the most articulate formulators of . . . Southern distinctiveness were the group at Vanderbilt University who published the *Fugitive* magazine."[2] He mentions their reservations about not only Wolfe (whom Robert Penn Warren criticized for his "attempt to exploit directly and naively the personal experience

THE FUGITIVE

Vol. II. A JOURNAL OF POETRY No. 8

Edited Jointly by
THE FUGITIVES

Walter Clyde Curry
Donald Davidson
William Yandell Elliott
James M. Frank
William Frierson
Sidney Mttron Hirsch
Stanley Johnson
Merrill Moore
Ridley Wills
John Crowe Ransom
Alec Brock Stevenson
Allen Tate
Jesse Wills

Editor for *The Fugitive:*
DONALD DAVIDSON

Associate Editor:
ALLEN TATE

The Fugitives compose a Group meeting fortnightly in Nashville, Tennessee, for the purpose of reading and discussing poetry.

CONTENTS

August-September, 1923

Published every two months at Nashville, Tennessee. Subscription, $1.50 a year; single copies, twenty-five cents. Copyright, 1923, by The Fugitive Publishing Company. Entered as second-class matter, January 20, 1923, at the post office at Nashville, Tennessee, under the Act of March 3, 1879.

MSS. and all other editorial communications must be addressed to *The Fugitive*, 2202 Eighteenth Avenue, South, Nashville, Tennessee.

All business matter should be sent to *The Fugitive,* care The J. Back Agency, Presbyterian Building, Nashville, Tenn.

The Fugitive: A Journal of Poetry, vol. 2 (August–September 1923). Library Collection, Tennessee State Library and Archives. Courtesy of TSLA.

and the self-defined personality in art," adding that "Shakespeare merely wrote *Hamlet;* he was *not* Hamlet") but Ellen Glasgow (whom Tate never praises enthusiastically), and even their differences with Faulkner (whom they all praised, John Crowe Ransom most pointedly in observing that Faulkner reveals man "under the aspect of magnificence").[3] The Fugitives and Agrarians sought, through the agency of myth and history, to create a comprehensive view of the South focused in the Piedmont west of the Appalachian range (Wolfe's Carolina Piedmont is east of these mountains, of course). In their poetry, the Tennessee writers forged a distinctive myth of enduring significance, a myth beginning in Homeric prehistory with Aeneas and extending past the American Civil War well into the twentieth century.

I

Allen Tate has said the most about the South as a mythic entity of any critic, including Louis D. Rubin Jr. and Lewis P. Simpson. In "Faulkner's *Sanctuary* and the Southern Myth," Tate writes of the southern legend (which he deems a "true myth which informed the sensibility and thought . . . of the defeated South"):

> the South, afflicted with the curse of slavery . . . had to be destroyed, the good along with evil. . . . This old order, in which the good could not be salvaged from the bad, was replaced by a new order which was in many ways worse than the old. . . .
>
> The evil of slavery was twofold, for the "peculiar institution" not only used human beings for a purpose for which God had not intended them; it made it possible for the white man to misuse and exploit nature herself for his own power and glory. The exploitation of nature is a theme that runs through all Faulkner's work; it adds a philosophical, even a mystical, dimension to the conventional Southern myth.[4]

Although this myth, as Tate describes it, was created and explored mainly in southern novels written not only by Faulkner but such Kentucky and Tennessee writers as Robert Penn Warren, Caroline Gordon, Andrew Lytle, and Tate himself, it also appears in shadowy outline in the poetry of the leading Fugitives and Agrarians from Ransom through Warren. It can perhaps best be perceived in Tate in such poems as "Aeneas at Washington," "Aeneas at New York," "To the Mediterranean," "To the Lacedemonians," and "Ode to the Confederate Dead." In these and other poems, Tate explores the Greco-Trojan myth of the South. "The Southern culture did not decline," as he tells us, "it was destroyed by outsiders in a Trojan war. The 'older' culture of Troy-South was wiped out by the 'upstart' culture of Greece-North."[5]

From Tate's "Aeneas in Washington," here is the story of Aeneas, the prince of ancient Troy, and his founding a new Rome in the New World:

> . . . I hoisted up
> The old man my father upon my back,
> In the smoke made by sea for a new world
> Saving little—a mind imperishable
> If time is, a love of past things tenuous
> At the hesitation of receding love. . . .
> I saw the thirsty dove
> In the flowing fields of Troy, hemp ripening
> And tawny corn, the thickening Blue Grass
> All lying rich forever in the green sun.

Tate imagines Aeneas coming to the capital of this country and from there envisioning a new civilization taking hold in bluegrass Kentucky, where the poet himself was born in Winchester, near Lexington, in 1899.

Tate, like Ransom, Davidson, and Warren, spent much of his life in Tennessee. Tate, like Warren and Cleanth Brooks, although born in Kentucky, found his true allegiance to Tennessee. Tate might well have said of himself what Warren did in an interview: "I've always felt myself more of a Tennessean than a Kentuckian. . . . I felt it [Tennessee] much more my country than Kentucky." Had it not been for the

Allen Tate. Courtesy of The University of the South Archives, Sewanee.

baleful conduct of Edwin Mims, long the chairman of the Vanderbilt English Department, Ransom and Warren probably would have continued their careers at Vanderbilt—and would not have moved from Nashville. Warren in an early letter wrote of his contentment in "the beautiful country of middle Tennessee," which he was sorry to leave at the instance of Mims, who refused him tenure in the English Department.[6]

Ransom, also thwarted by Mims when he refused to match Kenyon College's offer to Ransom, has a little of the southern myth in his poetry. It appears in such poems as "Antique Harvesters," "Captain Carpenter," and "Old Mansion." The old mansion, for example, suggests chateaux in Europe, especially in the phrase "chateaux on the Loire." It is a mansion drenched in history and crumbling under the weight of the past, like the South itself. The speaker is related to the persona in Tate's famous ode in that he is uneasily poised between two worlds, the one dying, the other struggling to achieve definition; he says at the end, "I went with courage shaken / To dip, alas, into some unseemlier world."

In "Lines Written for Allen Tate on His Sixtieth Anniversary," which should be compared to Tate's "The Oath," Donald Davidson gives us fragments of the Greco-Trojan myth through a conversation between Andrew Lytle and Tate:

> Lytle cried out: "Earth
> Is good, but better yet is land, and best
> A land still fought-for, even in retreat;
> For how else can Aeneas find his rest . . . ?"
> You [Tate] said: "Not Troy is falling now. Time falls
> And the victor locks himself in his victory
> Deeming by that conceit he cancels walls
> To step with Descartes and Comte beyond history. . . ."

In "Old Sailor's Choice" Davidson returns elliptically to the legend of Aeneas's leaving Troy for Rome and beyond, doing so through the story of Odysseus. He has escaped Scylla and Charybdis, and he says:

> What should I say who come with salty lips
> Telling, O King, a tale told yesterday?
> Do I set myself up to tell it again tomorrow?
> I seek my western shore and the house of my fathers.
> I know no softer song.

We are reminded of Tate's "To the Mediterranean," which was prompted by a picnic at Cassis (the original title) at which Ford Madox Ford feasted with the Tates on the shore:

> And we made feast and in our secret need
> Devoured the very plates Aeneas bore. . . .
> What prophecy of eaten plates could landless
> Wanderers fulfill by the ancient sea?
> . . . .
> Let us lie down once more by the breathing side
> Of Ocean, where our live forefathers sleep. . . .

> What country shall we conquer, what fair land
> Unman our conquest and locate our blood?
> We've cracked the hemispheres with careless hand
> Now, from the Gates of Hercules we flood
>
> Westward, westward. . . .

To plumb and measure much of the poetry of these writers in a single essay is impossible, but seeing it steadily and whole through common concerns, themes, and emphases is not. Tracing the Greco-Trojan theme throughout their poetry, especially that of Tate and Davidson, would be worthwhile; instead let us glance at a complementary theme—that of empire—as they seek to define the classic in literature and to forge classics themselves. The line of inquiry that Frank Kermode follows in *The Classic,* prompted by T. S. Eliot's criticism and the general example of Virgil, can be applied to the leading Fugitives and Agrarians. They, like Eliot, perceived "the mind of Europe as changing, but superannuating nothing; of a relation of old to new in which the existing order is modified by new work, the present joining and altering the past in some modality beyond chronological time, so that the poet must live 'in what is not merely the present, but the present moment of the past.' 'Tradition' is the word for the continuum."[7] So Kermode brilliantly argues as he quotes Eliot. Eliot powerfully influenced Tate, who introduced his work in particular and modernism in general to the Fugitives in their early meetings.

Tate, like Warren, was fascinated by time and history. He always sought to escape "time's monotone," as he did fleetingly in "To The Mediterranean": "We for that time might taste the famous age / Eternal here yet hidden from our eyes / When lust of power undid its stuffless rage." In his work, especially his poetry, Tate, like the other Fugitives and Agrarians, wished to achieve the timeless art represented by the classic. That ambition can be inferred from such statements by Tate as "I take the somewhat naive view that the literature of the past began somewhere a few minutes ago and that the literature of the present begins, say, with Homer."[8] Here Tate is alluding to what Kermode deems "the classic *imperium,* Rome and its Empire, which Aeneas founded."[9] The English, French, and other European peoples took up the legend, and the Fugitives and Agrarians modified it for their own purposes in writing poetry about the founding of this country as was westward as Kentucky and Tennessee where those states were on the old southwest frontier. Tate dreams of the new empire as "To The Mediterranean" comes to its powerful close:

> Westward, westward till the barbarous brine
> Whelms us to the tired land where tasseling corn,
> Fat beans, grapes sweeter than muscadine
> Rot on the vine: in that land were we born.

In this poem we see the historical continuum of the Greco-Trojan myth of empire in the Mediterranean, where the cradle of western civilization is located around that "ancient sea."

Robert Penn Warren, in beginning the torrent of poetry that irrupted in *Promises* and ran until his early eighties, wrote poems set in the Mediterranean littoral that unfold in present-day Italy. One of the best is "To a Little Girl, One Year Old, in a Ruined Fortress":

> To a place of ruined stone we brought you,
> and sea-reaches.
> *Rocca:* fortress, hawk-heel, lion-paw, clamped on a hill.
> A hill, no. On a sea cliff, and crag-cocked, the
> embrasures
> commanding the beaches. . . .
> We have brought you where the geometry of a
> military rigor
> survives its own ruined world.

Warren, also like Tate, finds himself caught in the hum and buzz of time's monotone, feeling the burden of the past and wondering what the future holds:

> Let all seasons pace their power,
> As this has paced to this hour.
> Let season and season devise
> Their possibilities.
> Let the future reassess
> All past joy, and past distress,
> Till we know Time's deep intent.

The fascination with the Mediterranean enables Warren to join mythological time with historical time. In "To a Little Girl . . . in a Ruined Fortress," Warren refers not to a Roman emperor but to Philip II of Spain.

In another poem written about twenty-five years later, "Looking Northward, Aegeanward: Nestlings on Seacliff," from *Rumor Verified* (1980), Warren muses:

> You think
> How long ago galleys—slim, black, bronze-flashing—
> bore
> Northward too, and toward that quarter's blue dazzle
> of distance.
> Or of a tale told. . . .
> That was the hour
> When rooftree or keystone of palaces fell. . . .
> The king,
> In his mantle, had buried his face. But even
> That last sacrifice availed naught. Ashes
> Would bury all. Cities beneath sea sank.

This poem is forged in the same vein as "Tiberius on Capri," from *You, Emperors* (1960):

> *All is nothing, nothing all:*
> To tired Tiberius soft sang the sea thus,
> Under his cliff-palace wall.
> The sea, in soft approach and repulse,
> Sings thus, and Tiberius,
> Sea-sad, stares past the dusking sea-pulse. . . .
> For all is nothing, nothing all.

The theme in both poems turns on the tenuousness and transience of power and the decline of empire. Of course Tiberius ruled from Capri at the end of his reign and his long life and was not overthrown or murdered, yet in Warren's words, "darkward he stares in that hour, / Blank now in totality of power."

Through these various depictions of classical civilization we see that the Fugitives and Agrarians imagined the new Aeneas as what Donald Davie calls "one of those Englishmen (Scotsmen, Irishmen, Welshmen) who in history's yesterday crossed the Atlantic to found a new nation cleansed of the errors and evils of . . . Europe."[10] This prince of the fallen Troy recovers himself and his culture in the New World.

Tate has spoken of the Roman role taken up by aristocratic Virginia from the late 1700s until 1861, a form of the lower mythology in what he calls (following Eliot) the historical imagination. He sees the failure of the Old South as resulting for its lack of a higher mythology—and names the religious imagination of the Christian Middle Ages. Tate treats these complex subjects in "What Is a Traditional Society?" as well as in his essay "Remarks on the Southern Religion" in *I'll Take My Stand* (1930). The ideal society he describes in his poetry and prose permitted the planter class to "develop a human character that functioned in every level of life, from the economic process to the country horse race." This traditional man "dominated the means of life; he was not dominated by it."[11]

In re-creating this world, whether that of the Romans or the Christians or both, these writers, working through the southern mode of the imagination, achieved what John Peale Bishop calls "the triumph of the European mind, in its youth and springtime of thought . . . able to adapt the Christian myth to its needs and, extending the human drama to include, not merely lives, but conceivable centuries, to endow it with shape and meaning." For them it would yield under the pressure brought to bear in their writing—poetry, fiction, prose nonfiction—many versions of the fundamental myth of the Aeneas myth sublimated by Christianity. As Bishop points out in "The Golden Bough," Christianity not only added eternity to earthbound time but added to the human drama "an apocalyptic scene."[12] For the southern writer of the generations involving the Fugitives and Agrarians, the apocalypse in southern history was the Civil War; in the time of the prehistory generation the action for much of their poetry and fiction was the Trojan war. "For Southern legend," declares Tate, "is a true myth which informed the sensibility and thought, at various conscious levels of the defeated South . . . so that the myth *is* reality."[13]

II

The major Fugitives and Agrarians—John Crowe Ransom (1888–1973), Donald Davidson (1884–1967), Allen Tate (1899–1979), and Robert Penn Warren (1905–1989)—were all men of letters who shared a profound commitment to literature in the broadest sense and to poetry in particular. Each of them, no matter what else he wrote—essays on economics and religion (Ransom), history (Davidson), biography (Tate and Warren), and criticism and fiction (Davidson, Tate, and Warren)—remained devoted to the craft of poetry and wrote poetry with some regularity. Each also endured long fallow periods, even the most fecund of them all—Warren. "The pursuit of poetry as an art was the conclusion of the whole matter of living, learning, and being. It subsumed everything, but it was also as natural and reasonable an act as conversation on the front porch," Davidson said in 1957.[14] Ten years earlier, Warren, in considering the poetry of Davidson's friend and neighbor Robert Frost, wrote that a poem "defines, if it is a good poem, a sort of strategic point for the spirit from which experience of all sorts may be freshly viewed."[15] With such insights the New Critics, including Ransom, Tate, Warren, and Cleanth Brooks, would forge a criticism that revolutionized the understanding of poetry. As Ransom observes in *The World's Body,* one of the principal books in the canon of that criticism, poetry "only wants to realize the world, to see it better. Poetry is the kind of knowledge by which we must know what we have arranged that we shall not know otherwise." Ransom finds it "a paradox that poetry has to be a technical act, of extreme difficulty, when it wants only to know the untechnical homely fulness of the world."[16]

Such shared attitudes reveal that the Fugitives and Agrarians were a community of writers from the beginning, brought together by their commitment to letters, by their affection for the city of Nashville, and by their connection with Vanderbilt University. The Fugitives met at the home of James Frank, a cultured Nashville businessman who was the brother-in-law of Sidney M. Hirsch, one of the leaders of the group, if a very odd one, who was an autodidact, not a formally educated writer. The joining of town and gown

Woodcut of steamboat on the Tennessee River by Theresa Sherrer Davidson from Donald Davidson's *The Tennessee* (Rinehart and Company, 1946), vol. 1. Courtesy of Photographic Archives, Vanderbilt University.

in the Frank household is essential in understanding how the Fugitives came to be founded and how they functioned and thrived as a group giving and taking one another's poetry and criticizing it. Of Vanderbilt, Davidson writes that it "was then like an Oxford college in its relaxed and casual indifference to what young men like us might be doing with our time." He adds, "The other attachment was to the city, Nashville, superficially one of the least inviting of Southern cities; yet in its jumble of old and new tendencies that both attracted and revolted, it somehow bound us to it." As Davidson makes plain, it is impossible to determine "which one of these attachments was the more important." He explains: "I do know it was possible then for a young southern poet to pass from university to city, from city to university, without any great sense of shock. Both were describable as 'home.'"[17] So the sense of belonging in both the university and the city was essential to the community made by the Fugitives, and the salutary combination of town and gown provided a catalyst that helped them to create poetry. Although the bounds in this community were sometime strained, especially after the group had largely scattered from Nashville, they were never severed.

The Fugitives and Agrarians generally derived from small towns—Ransom from Pulaski and Davidson from Campbellsville; Warren from the little railroad town of Guthrie, Kentucky, near the state line; and Tate from Winchester, Kentucky, in the bluegrass. An Agrarian closely associated with the Fugitives throughout his mature life, Cleanth Brooks, was born in Murray, another western Kentucky town near the state line. Of the close parallels in Brooks's background and his own, Ransom observed, "Brooks and I were about as like as two peas from the same pod in respect to our native region, our stock (we were sons of ministers of the same faith [Methodist], and equally had theology in our blood), the kind of homes we lived in, the kind of small towns; and perhaps were most like in the unusual parallel of our formal educations" at Vanderbilt and Oxford.[18] Davidson made a similar comparison between himself and Ransom. "John Ransom was born at Pulaski, Tennessee, just a few miles from where I was born," noted Davidson, "and my father, who was a teacher, knew John Ransom's father, who was a Methodist preacher."[19]

These parallels in background, education, interests, and values can be traced out almost indefinitely. Further allusions to them appear in Tate's fragmentary memoirs and in Warren's *Jefferson Davis Gets His Citizenship Back* and his "Portrait of a Father," as well as in Malcolm Cowley's wonderfully engaging reminiscence, "The Meriwether Connection," in which he describes life along the Kentucky-Tennessee border near Clarksville during the Great Depression. It was a leisurely world but not necessarily for the artists who visited Allen Tate and his wife, writer Caroline Gordon, a Meriwether, at her family seat, Cloverlands, and at Benfolly, the Tates' home in Clarksville. Cowley described the fading pastoral of the scene of which he was briefly a part: "Looking northward into Kentucky and southward into Tennessee, I could see sheep meadows like immense playgrounds worn bare in patches, then wheatfields already turned a paler green, with hints of gold, then cornfields pin-striped with the first bright-green shoots, and among them level tobacco fields now ready for planting. . . . The east and west horizons were broken lines of forest."[20]

Cowley, like Ford Madox Ford, Robert Lowell, and many other distinguished writers who visited Tate and Gordon at Benfolly, Cloverlands, or elsewhere, was part of the wider literary world constituting the literary imperium or Republic of Letters, a world more fictitious than real, to which the Fugitives and Agrarians—none more so than Tate—gave their allegiance. This republic arose in western civilization and must be understood in that milieu, which Lewis Simpson has brilliantly described in his work on Tate, particularly in *The Man of Letters in New England and the South*. In a letter to John Peale Bishop, Tate claimed that he did his "simple duty by the republic of letters (which is the only republic I believe in, a kind of republic that can't exist in a political republic)." In an earlier letter to Bishop, Tate suggested

The Fugitive

The Fugitive writers and critics. Photograph by Joe Rudis for the *Nashville Tennessean,* May 4, 1956, on the occasion of the Fugitives' reunion. *Front row:* Robert Penn Warren, Dorothy Bethurum (Loomis), Merrill Moore, John Crowe Ransom, Sidney Mttron Hirsch, Donald Davidson, Louise Cowan, William Yandell Elliott. *Second row:* Willard Thorp, Andrew Nelson Lytle, Jesse Ely Wills, Alfred Starr, Louis Rubin. *Third row:* Allen Tate, Cleanth Brooks, William C. Cobb, Rob Roy Purdy, Richmond Croom Beatty, Frank Lawrence Owsley, Randall Stewart, Brainard Cheney, Robert D. Jacobs, Alec Brock Stevenson. Photograph by Joe Rudis. Courtesy of Photographic Archives, Vanderbilt University.

THOUGH THIS JOURNAL OF POETRY EXISTED THROUGH ONLY NINETEEN ISSUES, FROM APRIL 1922 TO December 1925, *The Fugitive* had a role in changing the literature not just of the South but also of the whole country. The magazine achieved such influence in four years because of

the intensity of his allegiance in speaking of the possibility of treason to the Republic of Letters.[21]

Tate's colleagues endorsed his view of the Republic of Letters. Andrew Lytle, in his tribute written for Tate's sixtieth birthday, observed that Tate, "more than any other writer, has upheld this professionalism of letters."[22] Lytle believed that Tate's views were strongly informed by his sense of "our common inheritance" with Europe. In the essay "The New Provincialism," Tate pointed out that "in the West our peculiar civilization was based upon regional autonomy, whose eccentricities were corrected and sublimated by the classical-Christian culture," which was "a nonpolitical or supra-political culture" that allied continuity in two areas: in the poets who participated in the enterprise and in their purpose. Indeed, the magazine emerged in Nashville in the first place because of these factors. A handful or so of men, most with connections to Vanderbilt University, who had met for evenings of discussion since 1915 solidified their focus on poetry by 1921 and began bringing their own poems to fortnightly gatherings for critiques. *The Fugitive* developed, then, out of a mutual interest and respect shared among a group of talented men.

Their meetings occurred in the home of Mr. and Mrs. James M. Frank and were hosted by Sidney Hirsch, Mrs. Frank's brother, who resided with them. Donald Davidson, Stanley Johnson, John Crowe Ransom, Alec B. Stevenson, and Allen Tate regularly attended, and together they produced the first issue of *The Fugitive,* choosing the poems they included by ballot. Their cooperative efforts at critiquing poetry and arguing literary principles remained central to their purpose of producing good poetry throughout the life of the magazine. And while these seven men remained a constant element in the endeavors of the journal, they admitted to their circle additional individuals who are usually labeled Fugitives as well (Walter Clyde Curry, Merrill Moore, William Frierson, William Yandell Elliott, Robert Penn Warren, Alfred Starr, Jesse Wills, Ridley Wills, and Laura Riding Gottschalk). Working as a group they altered the editorial methods they used from time to time, and even the frequency of publication varied from monthly to quarterly.

Their meetings and the magazine proved to be invaluable to these poets not only as a sounding board but also as a spring board. Their intense efforts on *The Fugitive* propelled them into their pursuit of graduate degrees and careers (for the most part) as writers, critics, and teachers of writing and literature. In that way the success of their undertaking made for the magazine's demise, and, by the end of 1925, when because of other commitments no one of the group accepted the responsibility of editorship, the journal ceased.

The Fugitive provided a label, however, to its contributing authors by which they would always be known. Four of the Fugitives, Ransom, Davidson, Tate, and Warren, spent the latter part of the decade involved in a critique of the South that would be published under the title *I'll Take My Stand* and give them another label as Agrarians. Ransom, Tate, and Warren in the following decades would be instrumental in developing and disseminating the New Criticism that changed the way of analyzing literature. As Fugitives these men and their colleagues had appeared less interested in fleeing any one thing than in pursuing their creative ambitions of making good poetry, a legacy that has withstood the test of time in American literature as well or better than that of any other group.

Margaret D. Binnicker, Tennessee Historical Society

"Greek culture and Christian other-worldliness" to hold "Europe together for six hundred years."[23]

Tate was not only an essential citizen in the Republic of Letters but was the linchpin and gadfly of the Fugitives, the Agrarians, and the New Critics. As he wrote "The New Provincialism" in the immediate aftermath of World War II, he was looking at the world in 1945 from the Cumberland Plateau at Sewanee. From that vantage point he clearly saw that regionalism, not world provincialism, was the key to understanding Western culture and society, and he was considering the traditional society of the South as it had undergone the immense strain of World War II, a strain far greater than World War I, which had enabled the

The Agrarians and *I'll Take My Stand*

THE AGRARIANS, MOST ASSOCIATED EITHER DIRECTLY OR INDIRECTLY WITH VANDERBILT UNIVERSITY, shaped southern thought, history, and literature in the decade of the Great Depression. This group of writers and scholars, collectively identified as Twelve Southerners, wrote the classic *I'll Take My Stand: The South and the Agrarian Tradition* in 1930. Four of the twelve—Donald Davidson, Allen Tate, John Crowe Ransom, and Robert Penn Warren—had been key members of the Fugitives and Ransom and Davidson were Vanderbilt English professors. Four more—Lyle Lanier, Herman C. Nixon, Frank L. Owsley, and John D. Wade—also were Vanderbilt professors, of psychology, economics, history, and literature, respectively. Of the last four, Andrew Nelson Lytle and Henry B. Kline were Vanderbilt students while Stark Young and John Gould Fletcher were literary friends of Allen Tate.

I'll Take My Stand was an aggressive manifesto that defended a perceived southern tradition of agrarian life and values while at the same time it vilified the emerging technocrat-guided industrial state of modern America. National critics largely dismissed the Agrarians as backward-looking romantics offering a range of justifications for white supremacy—and several Agrarians wore that label well—but such criticism missed the larger point of the book. The Agrarians, as Louis D. Rubin Jr. once observed, were "thoughtful men who were very much concerned with the erosion of the quality of individual life by the forces of industrialization and the uncritical worship of material progress as an end in itself."[1] And those qualities of the wildly uneven essays are why the book still resonates with southern writers.

Carroll Van West, Middle Tennessee State University

Note

1. Twelve Southerners, *I'll Take My Stand: The South and the Agrarian Tradition,* with an introduction by Louis D. Rubin Jr. (1930; reprint, Baton Rouge: Louisiana State Univ. Press, 1977), xiv.

intense focus of consciousness that brought about the southern renascence, "a literature conscious of the past in the present."[24]

The other historic event that moved Tate and his colleagues to define themselves as southern and to write from the ironic perspective of modernism had been the Scopes trial at Dayton, Tennessee, in 1925. The trial, and the derision it received from outsider commentators, came as *The Fugitive* magazine ceased publication; the cultural criticism aimed at the South pushed these writers toward Agrarianism, which resulted in the publication of *I'll Take My Stand* (1930) and *Who Owns America?* (1935). By the mid-1930s most of the Agrarians, including Ransom, Tate, Warren, and Brooks, had turned their interest toward the making of the New Criticism.

III

In one of the most famous essays in *Poetry and the Age* (1953) Randall Jarrell judged John Crowe Ransom as "one of the best, most original, and most sympathetic poets alive; and it is easy to see that his poetry will always be cared for, since he has written poems that are perfectly realized and occasionally almost perfect—poems that the hypothetical generations of the future will be reading page by page."[25] Jarrell, himself a good poet (and one who might be considered here), was one of the great critics of poetry during his time, and his criticism has worn much better than his poetry. He rated Ransom as an important poet while emphasizing the significance of his influence on his fellow poets of the mid-twentieth-century: Robert Graves, Allen Tate, and Robert Penn Warren.

Jarrell does not consider Ransom as a major poet but properly places him in the company of other established minor poets such as Thomas Campion, Andrew Marvell, and the anonymous author(s) of the Mother Goose rhymes. In fact, Ransom, it is perfectly plain, set out to be a minor poet and succeeded brilliantly at that ambition, as he did at virtually everything he attempted as a writer and an editor. Warren, who has written very persuasively about Ransom's poetry on two occasions, speaks of his place in the literary firmament as a minor poet, a place also occupied by Tate (whose ambition—unrealized—was to be a major poet), and Davidson (who, like Tate, simply did not write enough publishable poetry to be a major figure). This leaves Warren himself, the only writer of genius among the four poets we have been considering, as the only one of them who wrote enough poetry to be considered major. In time he may be thought that, but the odds are against it. His accomplishment as a poet, as well as the general shape of his writing career, superficially resembles those of two writers, Herman Melville and Thomas Hardy, whom he greatly admired. Melville and Hardy also turned from the novel to poetry and applied themselves far more to poetry than to fiction in their old age. Warren attempted the kind of long complicated poems that Melville (in *Clarel*) and Hardy (in *The Dynasts*) wrote as they became more and more involved in the making of poetry. The turning point in Warren's career as a writer occurred when he wrote *Brother to Dragons,* parts of which Ransom would publish in the *Kenyon Review* before Random House published the whole poem. Later Warren would write other book-length poems that are both narrative and dramatic in execution: *Audubon: A Vision* and *Chief Joseph of the Nez Perce.* These poems came from Warren's saturation in American history, including its obscure figures and passages.

As his *Collected Poems* (1998) makes clear, Warren wrote more than enough poetry to be considered a major poet. The selected poems of Ransom, Davidson, and Tate are slighter in bulk and accomplishment. Of the three only Tate reached hard for greatness, and too often, as in the poems written in the early 1950s associated with "The Maimed Man" and "The Buried Lake," he abandoned the larger design of his work and was content to present fragments of the imagined whole. This pattern appears throughout Tate's career; he abandoned far more projects, especially those involving books, beginning with his life of Robert E. Lee, than he brought to fruition. In general, it is fair to say, the disorder in his private life overwhelmed the severe order that he brought to bear in his writing, especially his poetry. The classical severity of his poetry made it too difficult for him to write in sustained flights of the kind that Warren regularly achieved. Warren's narrative poems, beginning with "The Ballad of Billie Potts" (1943) and running through his celebration of Chief Joseph, are among his best. Only Davidson, in such poems at "The Tall Men" and "The Sod of the Battle-fields," achieved anything comparable; and of course Warren's is by far the greater accomplishment so far as the long poem is concerned. All four men wrote brilliant lyric poetry, but Warren attempted—often with great success—more complicated forms. Warren regularly broke the mould of an established form, as in "The Ballad of Billie Potts," and re-created it in a new form based on the old but distinctively different. Warren, in fact, struck a new form in *Brother to Dragons,* one announced in the subtitle, "A Tale in Verse and Voices." The poem brilliantly joins drama with narrative poetry. Here is Thomas Jefferson speaking early in the poem:

> . . . Irony is always, and only a trick of light on
> the late landscape

> . . . we were only ourselves,
> Packed with our own lusts and langours, lost,
> Each man lost, in some blind lobby, hall, enclave,
> Crank cul-de-sac, couloir, or corridor of Time.
> Of Time. Or self: and in that dark no thread . . .
>
> The beast waits. He is the infamy of Crete.
> He is midnight's enormity.

Here is a dazzling instance of one of Tate's insights into the nature of poetry: "A new order of experience—the constant aim of serious poetry—exists in a new order of language."[26] Warren wrote poetry for over thirty years, revising *Brother to Dragons* along the way. At best Warren generates a narrative pace and dramatic power that are seldom matched in American poetry. His range of language, from colloquial and slangy idioms to formal and mannered diction, is astonishing; the range is greater than Eliot's or Ransom's or practically any other poet writing in English but Shakespeare himself.

IV

When one associates a given state with a given writer, the decision is often more nearly arbitrary than a matter of ironclad logic. My inclusion of Tate and Warren in an essay on Tennessee poetry may be questioned, but if we consider the principal roles they played among the Fugitives and the Agrarians, as well as their allegiance to, and affection for, Tennessee, the decision has ample justification. In the same manner it can be argued that George Garrett could be considered a Tennessee poet. Garrett, a native of Florida who has lived for long periods in Virginia, was educated at the old Sewanee Military Academy and has strongly maintained his connection with Sewanee through the *Sewanee Review* since 1957. He is a splendid poet who as a man of letters has done more to enhance and promote poetry in this country, in and out of the South, than anyone since Tate. Two other Tennessee poets of roughly the same age as Garrett—Eleanor Ross Taylor and George Scarbrough—should also be recognized. Both have written especially well over the past decade. Taylor's *Late Leisure* (1999) has created a considerable stir, as did Garrett's *Days of Our Lives Lie in Fragments* (1997).

A younger generation of accomplished contemporary poets associated with Tennessee includes Charles Wright, Richard Tillinghast, Mark Jarman, Wyatt Prunty, and Neal Bowers. All five have written and published good poetry for over twenty years. The recent poetry of Jarman, a Vanderbilt professor, is particularly impressive while Wyatt Prunty continues to inspire poets and writers as director of the Sewanee Writers' Conference. Jarman, Prunty, Wright, and Tillinghast have gotten a considerable amount of recognition, but Bowers, a native of Clarksville who has been at Ames, Iowa, for all of his career, has not received his due. That may change with the publication of Bowers's *Out of the South,* a very impressive work. Bowers, who like Garrett is a man of letters, is a critic of distinction as well as a poet. Lately he has begun writing novels.

Why have the Fugitives and Agrarians had such a lasting impact? They not only held citizenship in the Republic of Letters but established their own offices as men of letters. (Garrett and Bowers are among the few contemporary writers to whom these terms can be accurately applied.) The one woman poet who was associated with the Fugitives, Laura Riding, became a woman of letters as her career developed; that is also true for the woman most closely associated with the Agrarians, Caroline Gordon. The Fugitives and Agrarians in general instinctively knew everything important about the writing life and the profession of letters. In their letters, for instance, Tate and Davidson discussed the importance of publishing outlets of all kinds, including newspapers. Because all the principals came from families of modest means, and had no more than modest livings themselves, they stayed within an academic setting for the most part, often supplementing their incomes not only by writing but by editing magazines and books and by writing textbooks. As Davidson said in "A Mirror for Artists," "an artistic life, in the social

The Sewanee Writers' Conference

When Tennessee Williams died in 1983, he left the residual portion of his estate to the University of the South as a memorial to his grandfather, the Reverend Walter E. Dakin, who had studied at Sewanee's School of Theology in 1895. Williams spent his boyhood summers in Clarksdale, Mississippi, with Dakin, whom he credited with introducing him to the classics of literature and supporting his early efforts at poetry and drama.

In keeping with Williams's wish that the funds be used to encourage "creative writing and creative writers," the university founded the Sewanee Writers' Conference in 1990. Under the direction of poet and critic Wyatt Prunty, the conference soon established itself as one of the nation's foremost literary gatherings. For ten days in July, a distinguished faculty of poets, playwrights, and fiction writers provide instruction and criticism through workshops and lectures. Guest editors, publishers, and literary agents also meet regularly with conference participants, who are aspiring and established writers from around the country. Faculty have included Alice McDermott, winner the 1998 National Book Award for her novel *Charming Billy;* Anthony Hecht, winner of the 1968 Pulitzer Prize for his collection of poems *The Hard Hours;* and Horton Foote, winner of two Oscars for his screenplays of *To Kill a Mockingbird* and *Tender Mercies.* Guests to the conference have included novelist William Styron, short story writer Peter Taylor, and playwright Arthur Miller.

Peter Taylor, Stanley Elkin, and Wyatt Prunty at Rebel's Rest, Sewanee. Photo © Miriam Berkley. Courtesy of Miriam Berkley, the Sewanee Writers' Conference and The University of the South.

Williams's generosity has enabled the conference to attract the highest caliber of participant. Walter E. Dakin Fellowships and Tennessee Williams Scholarships, along with other funds, have ensured that promising writers can attend the conference without financial hardship.

The atmosphere is convivial and supportive, as writers recognize that literary discourse need not be confined to the workshop table. There are ample opportunities for informal readings, candlelight processions to Allen Tate's grave in Sewanee's cemetery for readings of "Ode to the Confederate Dead," and tours of the nearby Monteagle Assembly, where Tate, Andrew Lytle, and Peter Taylor kept summer homes.

The Sewanee Writers' Conference has allowed Sewanee's longstanding literary tradition to flourish. During the academic year, the Tennessee Williams Fellow, a guest writer, teaches undergraduate creative writing courses. The Tennessee Williams Center, which was completed in 1998, houses black-box and studio theaters, along with facilities for dance and scenic design; when suitable, the work of conference participants and faculty is produced. The Sewanee Writers' Series, in conjunction with the Overlook Press in New York, publishes new works of fiction, poetry, and drama. College undergraduates, the Sewanee community, and an increasing number of writers around the country have benefited from the many programs spawned by Williams's gift.

Preston Merchant, New York City

sense, is achievable under the right conditions," that life, for them, was conducted principally within the academy.[27] R. P. Blackmur added that the university's "natural" function is "to take up when society leaves off the preservation, maintenance, and insemination of the *profession* of letters."[28] That development has continued to the present, with all the younger writers whom I have mentioned following the profession of letters within the university.

The only one of the Fugitives and Agrarians who might have made a living as a writer is Robert Penn Warren. But for most of his career he held jobs within the academy, beginning at Vanderbilt. "I am inclined to think, from my own experience, that teaching, or rather the academic environment, may help a writer in keeping him aware of some perspective on his own and on other contemporary writing," he remarked to Granville Hicks in February 1947.[29] Warren maintained such a perspective all his mature life, especially through his role as a Fugitive and Agrarian. His last novel, *A Place to Come To* (1977), reflects many of his lasting attitudes, including a love for the community in and around Nashville and the love of what he called, in a previously quoted letter, "the beautiful country of middle Tennessee." As the Tennessee landscape nurtured the Fugitives and Agrarians, so too did this brilliant group of southern writers enrich Tennessee letters and culture.

NOTES

1. Allen Tate, "The Profession of Letters in the South," in *Essays of Four Decades,* by Allen Tate (Chicago: Swallow Press, 1968), 520.
2. C. Hugh Holman, *Three Modes of Modern Southern Fiction: Ellen Glasgow, William Faulkner, Thomas Wolfe* (Athens: Univ. of Georgia Press, 1966), 8.
3. Robert Penn Warren, "A Note on the Hamlet of Thomas Wolfe," in *Selected Essays,* by Robert Penn Warren (New York: Random House, 1958), 183, and John Crowe Ransom, "William Faulkner: An Impression," *Harvard Advocate* 130 (Nov. 1951): 17.
4. Allen Tate, "Faulkner's *Sanctuary* and the Southern Myth," in *Memoirs and Opinions, 1926–1974,* by Allen Tate (Chicago: Swallow Press, 1975), 151–52.
5. Ibid., 152.
6. Floyd C. Watkins, John T. Hiers, and Mary Louise Weaks, eds., *Talking with Robert Penn Warren* (Athens: Univ. of Georgia Press, 1990), 375–76. On page 272, in an interview with Louis Rubin years later, Warren repeated the sentiment from his earlier letter, saying, "The place I wanted to live, the place I thought was heaven to me, after my years of wandering, was middle Tennessee, which is a beautiful country." See also what Warren says in a letter to Cinini Bescia on October 2, 1927: "The country here is very beautiful, and in many respects similar to Middle Tennessee." William Bedford Clark, ed., *Selected Letters of Robert Penn Warren* (Baton Rouge: Louisiana State Univ. Press, 2000), 1:126.
7. Frank Kermode, *The Classic: Literary Images of Permanence and Change* (New York: Viking, 1975), 21.
8. Allen Tate, "Miss Emily and the Bibliographer," in *Essays of Four Decades,* by Allen Tate (Chicago: Swallow Press, 1968), 152.
9. Kermode, *Classic,* 51–52.
10. Donald Davie, "A Tribute to Allen Tate," in *Two Ways Out of Whitman: American Essays,* ed. Doreen Davie (Manchester, N.H.: Carcanet, 2000), 110.
11. Allen Tate, "What Is a Traditional Society?" in *Essays of Four Decades,* by Allen Tate (Chicago: Swallow Press, 1968), 550 and 556.
12. John Peale Bishop, "The Golden Bough," in *The Collected Essays of John Peale Bishop,* ed. Edmund Wilson (New York: Charles Scribner's Sons, 1948), 35.
13. Tate, "Faulkner's *Sanctuary,*" 151.
14. Donald Davidson, *Southern Writers in the Modern World* (Athens: Univ. of Georgia Press, 1958), 8.
15. Robert Penn Warren, "The Themes of Robert Frost," in *Selected Essays,* by Robert Penn Warren (New York: Random House, 1958), 132.
16. John Crowe Ransom, *The World's Body* (Baton Rouge: Louisiana State Univ. Press, 1968), x and xi.
17. Davidson, *Southern Writers,* 7.
18. John Crowe Ransom, "Why Critics Don't Go Mad," in *Poems and Essays,* by John Crowe Ransom (New York: Vintage Books, 1955), 149.

19. Davidson, *Southern Writers,* 9.
20. Malcolm Cowley, "The Meriwether Connection," in *The Dream of the Golden Mountains: Remembering the 1930s,* by Malcolm Cowley (New York: Viking Press, 1980), 193.
21. Thomas D. Young and John J. Hindle, eds., *The Republic of Letters in America: The Correspondence of John Peale Bishop and Allen Tate* (Lexington: Univ. Press of Kentucky, 1981), 94 and 88 (letters dated Dec. 23 and Dec. 1, 1933).
22. Andrew Lytle, "Allen Tate: Upon the Occasion of His Sixtieth Birthday," *Sewanee Review* 67 (Autumn 1959): 543.
23. Allen Tate, "The New Provincialism," in *Essays of Four Decades,* by Allen Tate (Chicago: Swallow Press, 1968), 542 and 538.
24. Ibid., 545.
25. Randall Jarrell, *Poetry and the Age* (New York: Knopf, 1953), 109.
26. Allen Tate, "Modern Poets and Convention," in *Collected Essays,* by Allen Tate (Denver: Alan Swallow, 1959), 546.
27. Donald Davidson, "A Mirror for Artists," in *I'll Take My Stand: The South and the Agrarian Tradition,* by Twelve Southerners (New York: Harper & Brothers, 1930), 56.
28. R. P. Blackmur, "A Feather-bed for Critics: Notes on the Profession of Writing," in *Language as Gesture: Essays in Poetry,* by R. P. Blackmur (1954; reprint, London: George Allen & Unwin, 1961), 406.
29. William Bedford Clark, "Warren on Teaching, Writing, and Teaching Writing," *Sewanee Review* 107 (Summer 1999): 455.

Suggested Readings

Conkin, Paul K. *The Southern Agrarians.* Knoxville: Univ. of Tennessee Press, 1988.

Fain, John T., and Thomas D. Young, eds. *The Literary Correspondence of Donald Davidson and Allen Tate.* Athens: Univ. of George Press, 1974.

Havard, William C., and Walter Sullivan, eds. *A Band of Prophets: The Nashville Agrarians After Fifty Years.* Baton Rouge: Louisiana State Univ. Press, 1982.

Malvasi, Mark G. *The Unregenerate South: The Agrarian Thought of John Crowe Ransom, Allen Tate, and Donald Davidson.* Baton Rouge: Louisiana State Univ. Press, 1997.

Rubin, Louis D., Jr. *The Wary Fugitives: Four Poets and the South.* Baton Rouge: Louisiana State Univ. Press, 1978.

Sullivan, Walter. *Allen Tate: A Recollection.* Baton Rouge: Louisiana State Univ. Press, 1988.

Winchell, Mark R., ed. *The Vanderbilt Tradition: Essays in Honor of Thomas Daniel Young.* Baton Rouge: Louisiana State Univ. Press, 1991.

Young, Thomas D. *John Crowe Ransom: Critical Essays and a Bibliography.* Baton Rouge: Louisiana State Univ. Press, 1968.

Young, Thomas D., and John J. Hindle, eds. *The Republic of Letters in America: The Correspondence of John Peale Bishop and Allen Tate.* Lexington: Univ. Press of Kentucky, 1981.

Seventeen

Tennessee Fiction since 1920

Walter Sullivan
Vanderbilt University

In 1917, there was, regrettably, some justice in literary critic H. L. Mencken's calling the whole South, including Tennessee, the "Sahara of the Bozart," but even as Mencken wrote, changes were taking place in the South that would lead to a literary renascence. The events that engendered the flowering of southern letters—for the renascence included poetry and literary criticism as well as fiction—are too complicated fully to explore here. World War I, in which southern men participated as Americans, brought an alienated South closer to cultural reintegration into the Union. The South was still mainly agrarian, but following the advice given earlier by Henry W. Grady, some southerners thought it ought not to remain so, and regardless of what anybody thought, cities in the South were growing. The culture of the South, which had changed little since 1865, began to reshape itself as the agrarian economy of the Old South and the values for which the South had entered the Civil War were challenged by urban development and by southern entrepreneurs who thought that the poverty of the South was too great a price to pay for maintaining a traditional society. The struggle between old and new, between tradition and modernity, created a tension out of which the southern literary renascence of the twentieth century was born.

No one was more loyal to southern customs or more acutely aware of the extent to which they were threatened by the urbanization and industrialization of the South than Andrew Nelson Lytle (1902–1995). Born in Murfreesboro, Tennessee, he became friends with some of the Fugitive poets while he was a student at Vanderbilt University, many of whom he later joined as a contributor to the Agrarian manifesto, *I'll Take My Stand* (1930). The basic philosophical and cultural principles enunciated there—the superiority of life lived on the land, the importance of family connections, the significance of place when it is home to succeeding generations—informed his work for the next fifty years. The protagonist of Lytle's first book, *Bedford Forrest and His Critter Company* (1931), which he wrote while performing small parts in plays on and off Broadway, was a frontiersman and farmer before he became a Confederate general. Lytle's biography is deeply sympathetic to Forrest, but of more importance to Lytle's future, the book, which presents Forrest as a mythic hero and emphasizes the most dramatic events in his military career, reads as if it were a novel rather than a biography, and writing it undoubtedly helped Lytle to develop his narrative gifts.

The Long Night (1936), Lytle's first novel, takes place in rural Alabama in the years immediately preceding the Civil War. Cameron McIvor, who has recently moved into the neighborhood, is murdered because he has discovered the identities of a band of thieves who have abused the honest citizens of the community and corrupted the government thereof.

Andrew Nelson Lytle. Courtesy of The University of the South Archives, Sewanee.

To avenge his father's death, Pleasant McIvor, Cameron's son, sets out to kill the members of the outlaw gang, and the first half of the novel is a dramatically rendered story of the murder of the murderers, one by one. In a series of brilliantly written sequences, Pleasant first pursues, then destroys his foes, trying always to make their deaths appear to be accidental. The pattern of his vengeance is soon apparent, particularly to those who know themselves to be threatened. Tension rises with each of Pleasant's executions, and as each enemy is killed, Lytle as novelist must create the character of the next victim. The story gains power because, even though the outlaws are themselves guilty of murder, Lytle makes the reader come to know them as human beings. They have wives who love them, children to be raised, neighbors who arrange their corpses for burial. Lytle, master both of backwoods pathos and backwoods humor, creates a community by bringing to life both the good and the bad people who live in it. But when this part of the narrative reaches its climax, Pleasant learns that the Civil War has begun.

To this point in the story, Pleasant's quest for revenge has coincided, at least in a rough dimension, with what is good for the community at large. But with his enlistment in the Confederate Army, his private and public duty, both of which are always a concern in Lytle's fiction, become inimical to each other. Pleasant's personal vendetta is in all ways divergent from his duties as a scout: to pursue his enemies, he must shirk his responsibilities as a soldier, and now that the South is at war, his private enemies are also his fellow Confederates. At the end, his search for revenge takes him away from his assigned post, which, in turn, brings about the death of his close friend who is another soldier. His allegiance to his private cause has resulted in both private and public evil. Recognizing this, Pleasant deserts the army and retreats to the Alabama hills where later he will pass on his story to a younger relative.

For the setting of his second novel, *At the Moon's Inn* (1940), Lytle moved back in time four hundred years to Hernando de Soto's exploration of the New World which culminated not only in the discovery of the Mississippi River, but in his death and the deaths of most of his soldiers. This is an adventure story, and Lytle develops it as such, but his concerns as a serious novelist are with the clash of cultures that occurs when the Spaniards and the American Indians encounter each other and with the spiritually debilitating effect that exploration and conquest exert on the conquistadores. Lytle's respect for and admiration of the ways and traditions of Native Americans are evident throughout *At the Moon's Inn,* but his primary fidelity is to the Christian values that the Spanish brought into the New World and subsequently lost. Whatever missionary zeal existed in the heart of de Soto—and in that of Francisco Pizarro, hero of *Alchemy* (1941), Lytle's novella based on the conquest of Peru—at the start of their expeditions was soon replaced by pride and greed which resulted in the persecution of the

Caroline Gordon

CAROLINE GORDON (1895–1981) WAS A GIFTED MID-TWENTIETH-CENTURY SOUTHERN NOVELIST, whose years in Tennessee during the 1930s yielded some of her most highly regarded work. Born in Todd County, Kentucky, just north of Clarksville, Tennessee, Gordon attended a private academy in Clarksville before taking her undergraduate degree from Bethany College in 1916. Working initially as a teacher, Gordon joined the staff of the *Chattanooga Times* in 1920, writing stories and reviewing literature for the newspaper until 1924. As literary critic, she wrote in 1922 one of the early (and positive) reviews of the new poetry journal *The Fugitive.* Two years later, Robert Penn Warren, also from Todd County, introduced her to one of the Fugitives, Allen Tate; Gordon and Tate married in 1925.

Caroline Gordon. Courtesy of The University of the South Archives, Sewanee.

In 1930 Gordon and Tate moved to Clarksville, where they entertained and encouraged many of the southern renaissance writers (especially her own mentor Ford Madox Ford) at their home *Benfolly.* The Depression decade also witnessed Gordon's most productive years as a writer. Her literary promise was validated by a Guggenheim Fellowship for creative writing in 1932 and winning the second prize of the O. Henry Awards in 1934. She wrote the novels *Penhally* (1931), *Alex Maury, Sportsman* (1934), *None Shall Look Back* (1937), and *The Garden of Adonis* (1937).

In 1938, Gordon accepted an appointment at the Women's College, Greensboro, of the University of North Carolina. Her later books included *The Woman on the Porch* (1944), *The Strange Children* (1951), and *How to Read a Novel* (1957). In 1973 she accepted a position at the University of Dallas. Gordon died in Mexico in 1981.

Carroll Van West, Middle Tennessee State University

Suggested Readings

Jonza, Nancylee N. *The Underground Stream: The Life and Art of Caroline Gordon.* Athens: Univ. of Georgia Press, 1995.

Makowsky, Veronica A. *Caroline Gordon: A Biography.* New York: Oxford Univ. Press, 1989.

Indians and in the debasement of the conquistadores. For Lytle, the Spaniards' loss of moral and religious purpose was a part of the general spiritual decline of the modern world.

The Velvet Horn (1957), which Lytle considered his best work, takes place in Alabama in the last years of the nineteenth century, which is when, in Lytle's view, the Old South—for him the real South—came to an end. At the beginning of the novel, Joe Cree allows himself to be killed by a falling tree because he has been told that he is not the father of Lucius, whom he has believed to be his son. Lucius is the

Evelyn Scott

NOVELIST AND ESSAYIST EVELYN SCOTT (1893–1963) WAS BORN ELSIE DUNN IN CLARKSVILLE, TENnessee, on January 17, 1893, the only child of Seely and Maude Thomas Dunn. After living in Clarksville as a young child, she moved to New Orleans and enrolled in the Sophie Newcombe Preparatory School and later briefly at Sophie Newcombe College and Tulane University. Dunn rebelled early against the limitations of her class and times, writing at fifteen a controversial letter to the *New Orleans Times-Picayune* advocating the legalization of prostitution as a way to control venereal disease. In 1913, she ran away to Brazil with a married man, Frederick Creighton Wellman, the dean of the School of Tropical Medicine at Tulane. To conceal their identities, they called themselves Cyril and Evelyn Scott.

During the five years she spent in Brazil, where she gave birth to a son named Creighton in 1914, Evelyn Scott emerged as a writer. At first she produced poems and critical essays published in *Poetry*, the *Dial*, and other periodicals. But publication of *The Narrow House* (1921), the first of a trilogy of novels including *Narcissus* (1922) and *The Golden Door* (1923), brought her critical recognition from H. L. Mencken and launched a career that made her a significant American writer in the decades between the two world wars. This first trilogy was followed by a second—*Migrations* (1927), *The Wave* (1929), and *A Calendar of Sin* (1931). *The Wave*, Scott's best novel, deals with the Civil War in an experimental narrative style attempting both epic sweep and accurate psychological analysis. Due to the success of this work, Scott's publisher asked her to write an essay about relative newcomer William Faulkner's *The Sound and the Fury.*

While the Scotts returned to the United States in 1919, they did not settle permanently but spent time in Bermuda, France, North Africa, and England. Evelyn left Cyril for Owen Merton, father of the future Trappist monk Thomas Merton, and ended her common-law marriage to Scott by divorce in 1928. She married British novelist John Metcalfe in 1930 and lived in Canada and England until the end of World War II. Scott continued to write, producing in *Eva Gay* (1932), a fictionalized version of her relationships with Merton and Scott. Her later work did not have the commercial and critical success of her earlier novels. Scott's critical analysis of Soviet communism in *Breathe Upon These Slain* (1934) and *Bread and a Sword* (1937) did not appeal to readers or to a literary establishment flirting with Marxism. Her last novel, *The Shadow of the Hawk* (1941), returned to her earlier focus on family relationships.

Scott's reputation derives from the two trilogies, in particular the individual books *The Narrow House* and *The Wave,* and from her memoir *Background in Tennessee* (1937), a study of her early years. While Scott continued to write after returning to the United States in 1952, she did not find publishers. In ill health, Scott and John Metcalfe lived in a residential hotel in New York City, where she died August 3, 1963.

Robert C. Petersen, Middle Tennessee State University

Note

This biography was previously published in the *Tennessee Encyclopedia of History and Culture* (1998) and is used with the permission of the author and the Tennessee Historical Society.

child not only of adultery but of incest, and his sense of his own confused parentage motivates his marriage to Ada Belle Rutter—the name seems almost Dickensian—an unlettered and unmannered girl who is pregnant with Lucius's child. The novel plays what is left of the Old South, surviving customs of hospitality and love of place and of blood relationships, against the main thrust of the novel which is the sin that has brought Lucius into the world and its consequent damage to the fabric of family and community life. Many of the images of the book become symbols, and they endow the story with a sense of doom. Although Joe Cree chooses his own death, he is felled in a pristine forest, which is being cut for profit and thus is being sacrificed to the mercantile spirit of the New South. The cove where Lucius is conceived is both Freudian and Biblical. Shaped like a womb, it is entered through a narrow passage, which is hidden by a waterfall. It is an image of the female earth goddess, the mythical source of fecundity, and it is Eden wherein man alienates himself from God. As a favorite hunting ground of the Legrand brothers, it is also a place of death. On a visit to the cove, Duncan Legrand lies with his sister Julia, thus reprising the literary convention that joins sex and death and repeating with a modern stress the Ancient Fall. Even the title of the novel is symbolic, suggesting more than the horn of a deer. Many scenes in this book are familiar to readers of Lytle's earlier novels: Joe Cree's wake that brings the community together to cook, drink, and tell stories; Jack Cropleigh witching a well. But it is richer philosophically and thematically than Lytle's other fiction; it is a proper capstone for his work.

Peter Hillsman Taylor (1917–1994) was born in Trenton, Tennessee, the prototype of his fictional town of Thornton. He was educated at Vanderbilt University and Kenyon College, and by the time he entered the army early in World War II he had already begun publishing his fiction in literary journals. The major phase of his career began with the appearance of *A Long Fourth and Other Stories* (1948). In the years that followed, he published twelve more books, including the brilliant short novel *A Woman of Means* (1950), *The Widows of Thornton* (1954), and *The Old Forest* (1984), both collections of stories. Taylor's world, both that to which he was born and that about which he wrote, was the southern upper middle class who lived in Memphis or Nashville or small towns in Tennessee or occasionally in St. Louis or Washington. One of his major strengths as a writer is his ability to create complex and subtle and totally believable characters. He is particularly good at portraying women who are often smarter and more perceptive than men. In "A Wife of Nashville," of all the Lovell family, composed mostly of males, only Helen Ruth understands why their cook, Jess McGhee, has left her job and gone to Chicago. In "The Dark Walk," only Sylvia of all the Harrison family has any

Peter Taylor. Courtesy of The University of the South Archives, Sewanee.

inkling of the cause of the animosities that build between Leander and Mr. Canada and of the attitudes of these two men, one black and one white, toward her and toward each other.

"A Long Fourth," one of Taylor's most successful stories, takes place in Nashville at the beginning of World War II which, like Andrew Lytle's turn of the twentieth century, is a time of change, loss, and dislocation. Harriet Wilson prepares for a visit from her son, now living in New York and soon to be drafted into the army, without realizing that her way of life and the civilization that supports it are moribund. Symptoms of dissolution abound. Son has tried to be discreet about his new beliefs, but he is an intellectual, a publisher of articles, and rumors of his liberal social views have reached Nashville. His sisters, Helena and Kate, both single, living at home, going to parties, drinking too much, are poor examples of the ethical standards that Harriet cherishes, and she is further annoyed by having to endure the presence of the redolent BT, nephew of her black cook, Mattie. Harriet's husband, Sweetheart, a doctor who with BT's help keeps a small farm, is too comfortably established in the status quo ever to examine it. When Son arrives, accompanied by his friend, but not his girl friend, Ann, the sisters, out of a taste for irony or of malice or of simple ennui, remake themselves into caricatures of southern ladies. They trace local kinships; they deplore the recently adopted practice of entertaining at country clubs; worst of all, opposed by the gentle remonstrances of Ann, they mouth all the clichés that are applied in general to black people.

The girls' behavior is counterpoint to a recent rupture of good feelings between Harriet and Mattie. BT, the smell and the presence of whom Harriet cannot abide, has been ordered to work in a defense plant to avoid being drafted, and Mattie, weeping in Harriet's arms, has dared to equate the departure of BT with that of Son. Harriet reprimands Mattie, and one of the major assumptions on which the society that the sisters have been satirizing is built, falls under the weight of Mattie's claim of equality, not of person, but of affection. But Taylor is not quite finished. At the end of the story, Ann confesses that although Son is not in love with her, she is in love with him, and he has used her. He has brought her along to say to his family the things that he believes but that he will not say, preferring to allow Ann to suffer the family's polite opprobrium. Except for Mattie's love for BT and Sweetheart's relaxed acceptance of whatever comes, nothing in this story is what it seems to be: not the attitudes of the sisters toward the culture in which they live; not Harriet's affection for Mattie; not Son's commitment to his liberal causes. Sweetheart's farm, emblem of the agrarian South, is doomed with BT gone and no one to care for it. BT, in his new role as factory worker, is lost to the Old South no matter where he settles. This kind of change, the end of one order of life and the beginning of another, is one of the major and most profitable themes in Taylor's fiction, and he explores it more fully in *A Woman of Means.*

Ten-year-old Quintus Cincinnatus Dudley moves with his widowed father to St. Louis, where his father will marry a divorced woman of substantial wealth. The characters who have most influence on Quint, his father and his stepmother, though happily married, personify the dialectics of southern fiction. Ann is from the city; Gerald is from the country. Gerald cherishes tradition; Ann is a child of the modern age. Ann's wealth is inherited; Gerald, brought up in poverty, refuses to allow her to support him when he loses his job. Quint, who spends his summers on his grandmother's farm before his father's second marriage, is pressed to come to terms with two ways of life, two competing views of the world, which he cannot do. On his twelfth birthday, he receives from his father a large gold watch that belonged to his grandfather, an heirloom that appears to Quint's St. Louis playmates to be a joke. He turns away from the rural South, which the watch symbolizes. His loyalty is to his stepmother and to the marvels of modern technology that are to come. At the end of the book, with the stepmother suffering a severe mental breakdown, her enormous house being closed, her family dispersing, Quint reads in

James Agee

SCREENWRITER, MOVIE CRITIC, JOURNALIST, NOVELIST, AND POET JAMES R. AGEE (1909–1955) WAS A literary artist who was comfortable in many different media—in that sense he was the prototypical modern American writer. Born in Knoxville on November 27, 1909, Agee as a teenager composed fiction, poetry, and reviews for his prep school's literary magazine and then in college he wrote for a literary journal at Harvard University. After graduating from Harvard in 1932, Agee worked for *Fortune* magazine and published a well-received book of poetry, *Permit Me Voyage* (1934). Two years later, *Fortune* editors asked Agee and photographer Walker Evans to document the tenant farmers of Alabama. The project transformed Agee, and he eventually left the magazine in order to spend the time necessary to do justice to his subject. The result was Agee and Evans's lyrical masterpiece, *Let Us Now Praise Famous Men* (1941), in which Agee expanded the bounds of the documentary form through his visual sense, creative organization, and provocative narrative.

James Rufus Agee, New Jersey, 1939. Photograph by Helen Levitt. Courtesy of Helen Levitt and St. Andrew's-Sewanee School.

Agee's reputation as a film critic largely rests on his numerous reviews for the *Nation,* with the first published in 1942. These reviews later were collected in the book *Agee on Film* (1958). In 1950 came his first novel, *The Morning Watch.* By that time he also was writing screenplays for movies such as *The African Queen* (with John Huston, 1951), *The Bride Comes to Yellow Sky* (1953), and *The Night of the Hunter* (1955).

The self-destructive Agee lived hard—and died young, like his own father, who died when Agee was only six years old. His semi-autobiographical novel, *A Death in the Family* (1957), related observations of life in early-twentieth-century Knoxville by a young boy who had lost his father. Published posthumously, the book won the Pulitzer Prize for fiction and was later adapted into the Broadway play, *All the Way Home* (1960). Composer Samuel Barber also took the novel's previously published prologue, "Knoxville: Summer of 1915," and set it to music, creating a concert piece that has been performed and recorded by orchestras worldwide.

Carroll Van West, Middle Tennessee State University

Suggested Readings

Bergreen, Laurence. *James Agee: A Life*. New York: Dutton, 1984.
Lofaro, Michael A., ed. *James Agee: Reconsiderations.* Knoxville: Univ. of Tennessee Press, 1992.
Lowe, James. *The Creative Process of James Agee.* Baton Rouge: Louisiana State Univ. Press, 1994.

the newspaper of Lindbergh's successful flight, which signifies the triumph of the machine, and the defeat of Gerald's antique ways that are rooted in the agrarian culture. Scientific progress and city life are triumphant. This is the kind of story that Taylor tells best.

No other Tennessee writer, and few writers of fiction anywhere, achieve the subtle depth of understanding and feeling that informs Taylor's stories. His sense of manners, of social customs that mask the harsher realities of life, is unsurpassed, and very few writers, particularly men, have created female characters who are as fully realized and as totally convincing as his. A good deal of the richness of his work is a result of his own ambiguous feelings about his material. Unlike Andrew Lytle, whose loyalties were firmly grounded in the agrarian South, Taylor's admiration for the South in which he grew up is tempered by his recognition of its inherent flaws. Although he finds much to deplore in the modern world, he does not condemn it. Such works as *A Summons to Memphis* (1986) and *In the Tennessee Country* (1994) exist in a wonderful—and sometimes wonderfully precarious—balance.

Madison Percy Jones (1925–), a native of Nashville, spent many of his summers on his father's farm in Cheatham County. He studied first under Donald Davidson at Vanderbilt and later under Andrew Lytle at the University of Florida, two masters who never abandoned the agrarian dream. *The Innocent* (1957), Jones's first novel, establishes the basic design of his later books. Duncan Welsh returns to a farm in his native Cheatham County, Tennessee, after a sojourn in Chicago during which he has been disabused of the joys of the city and restored to his belief in the integrity of life on the land. But like all of Jones's characters, Welsh is pessimistic by nature and easily led astray. His marriage goes bad; his attempt to breed horses fails; in the end, he falls under the influence of Aaron McCool, a moonshiner, whose evil nature Welsh recognizes too late. Like several of the main characters in books by Jones, Welsh commits murder and pays for his crime with his own life. The book is saved from developing a sense of despair by Jones's vivid descriptions of the rural world in which his affection for fields and forests, for animals domestic and wild, for the glow of sunlight and the sough of rain, endows his descriptions with a quiet and almost transcendental beauty.

A Cry of Absence (1971), considered by most critics to be Jones's most accomplished novel, concerns Hester Glenn, mother of two grown sons, Ames and Cameron, who has been living as a widow in a small Alabama town since her husband abandoned her years before the action of the novel. Politically and socially conservative, Hester is made increasingly uncomfortable by demands for social justice made both by educated blacks and liberal whites who have arrived with industries recruited from the North. Confrontation leads to violence. The black civil rights leader Otis Stevens, whose name and means of death, the novel makes clear, are intended to suggest the first Christian martyr, is chained to a tree and stoned to death. Shortly thereafter, the Confederate statue on the town square is destroyed with dynamite. Hester discovers that many of her old friends, as well as the Yankee newcomers, are ready to modify the social conventions of their youth. Her feeling of isolation draws her closer to Hollis Handley, the tempter who is a character in all of Jones's books. Handley convinces Hester that, along with his son Pike, her son Cameron has participated in the murder of Stevens. In anger, Hester suggests to Cam that he kill himself, and, probably because he is drunk, he does. Having helped bring about the death of her son, she takes her own life at the end of the novel.

It is easy to see why Allen Tate called Madison Jones "the southern Thomas Hardy." The power of Jones's prose, the sort of dark ambiance that he can develop not only in Handley's decaying house but also in the gazebo of Hester's well-kept garden, seems to authenticate the self-destructive impulses of the characters. Hester's stubborn pursuit of her own disastrous

Alex Haley

INTERNATIONALLY KNOWN AUTHOR ALEX HALEY (1921–1992) WAS BORN IN ITHACA, NEW YORK, ON August 11, 1921, and died in a Tennessee hospital of the complications of diabetes in February 1992. When he was a child, his family moved to his mother's hometown of Henning in West Tennessee, and when his father died young, Haley was brought up by his mother, grandmother, and various aunts whose stories he remembered all his life. In 1939, he entered the United States Coast Guard and served twenty years. In that period he slowly became a writer.

His literary fame rests on two books, *The Autobiography of Malcolm X* (Grove Press, 1964) and *Roots* (Doubleday, 1976). Both were best-sellers.

Roots sold 1.5 million copies in hardback in the United States. Within two years after its publication it had been translated into twenty-six languages and had sold 8.5 million copies. The TV miniseries of *Roots,* aired for a total of twelve hours on eight consecutive nights in January 1977, became a national event. *Roots* won the Pulitzer Prize, and the television version won 145 awards, including 9 Emmys.

Alex Haley at the gravesite of Chicken George. Courtesy of Tennessee Photographic Services.

Haley became an adored national figure, enthralling college audiences with the thrilling story of how he had written his masterwork. He ambled to the platform always with an air of becoming modesty. He faced his audience with a genial reserve, and he spoke in a conversational baritone reeling off stories of his childhood, of women rocking on a front porch, the sound of their rockers going "thump-thump" as they mused over the oral history of their ancestors. Especially the older women remembered tales of an African named Toby who insisted that his real name was Kin-te.

In *Roots*, Haley told of visiting the British Museum on an assignment for *Reader's Digest* and seeing the Rosetta Stone that opened the way to translation of ancient Egyptian hieroglyphics. He remembered the many k sounds in the stories about Kin-te, and he wondered if he might use them as a key to the discovery of his own ancestors.

On a trip to Gambia Haley met a griot, an elder supposedly able to recall in remarkable detail the oral history of the tribe as Homer recalled the *Iliad.* From him, Haley heard the story of his own ancestor, Kunta Kinte, captured by slave traders and not seen again. Haley claimed he had discovered that Kunta was shipped to America in 1767, landed at Annapolis, Maryland, and was sold to a plantation owner in Virginia. He said that further painstaking research provided a remarkably complete story of his ancestors. That story became *Roots.* It appeared in 1976, the bicentennial year, and Haley dedicated it "as a birthday offering to my country within which most of *Roots* happened."

[Continued on next page]

Doubleday marketed the book as a work of nonfiction, and Haley claimed steadfastly that the facts had come out of his research. But the book is clearly cast in the form of a novel with dialogue, thoughts, and acts that could not have come from any historical source. From the beginning, *Roots* was subjected to harsh criticism by historians who found in it numerous errors. Nevertheless, it quickly became required reading in college courses all over America. Literary critics noted its clunky style and its clichés and stereotypes of both whites and blacks.

Behind the national enthusiasm, Haley had troubles. He was sued twice for plagiarism. One case was summarily dismissed, but the other, brought in 1978 by a white specialist in African folklore, Harold Courlander, went to trial. Haley said under oath that he had never read Courlander's novel, *The African,* published in 1967. Haley claimed that eighty-one parallel passages in *Roots* and Courlander's work came from notes intended to be helpful and received from audiences at his lectures. Judge Robert Ward later told *Village Voice* writer Philip Nobile that he would have ruled against Haley and he considered charging him with perjury, but on the eve of Ward's decision, Haley agreed to pay Courlander $650,000, and the case was immediately closed.

Attacks on *Roots* continued while Haley lived extravagantly. When he died in 1992, he was $1.5 million in debt, and his reputation among serious scholars was in ruins. Nobile's long and measured article in the *Village Voice* of February 23, 1993, was a devastating final shot. Nobile used the Haley papers deposited at the University of Tennessee at Knoxville and interviewed a multitude of people connected to the book. One by one Haley's stories collapsed under Nobile's scrutiny. Saddest of all, the story of the griot who allegedly told Haley about Kunta Kinte appears to have been arranged by a collusion between Haley and authorities in Gambia who knew a prospective tourist attraction when they saw one. Haley told them what he needed; they produced the stereotypical old man who, through an interpreter, gave him what he required. A tape of the interview does not resemble Haley's account of the meeting in *Roots.*

Even Haley's authorship is suspect. The manuscript evidence demonstrates that Murray Fisher, Haley's editor at *Playboy,* rewrote huge parts of it, not merely revising Haley's prose but cutting it out altogether.

fate outrages readers because Jones has brought her so fully to life as a character. He is a very skillful writer. His plots develop a sense of inevitability. The reader feels that tragedy can and must be averted, knowing that it will not be. The endings of Jones's novels are far from happy, but they linger memorably in the reader's mind.

Shelby Foote (1916–) was born and raised in Mississippi, which is the locale of his early fiction. But having lived in Memphis for the last half century, Foote qualifies as a Tennessean by choice. A man of great learning and scant advanced formal education—his stint at the University of North Carolina was brief—he is best known for his three-volume history, *The Civil War: A Narrative* (1958, 1963, 1974) and for his numerous appearances on television in connection with that phase of American history, but his fiction is widely admired for its clean story lines and the depth of its characterizations. His mastery of his craft is evident in *Follow Me Down* (1950), which many critics consider his best novel. To a casual reader, this book may appear to be typical southern Gothic, but its sophisticated structure and the bold conception of its main actors endow it with a kind of Old Testament grandeur that few novels achieve.

The book begins with the arraignment of the main character for murder, and much of the narrative is conveyed by the testimony of witnesses and

No one answered Nobile's attack. In a long article in *Critical Quarterly*, Helen Taylor tries to redeem Haley in part, but she does not doubt that he lied habitually. She notes that Haley remained popular with audiences to the end. But among scholars, especially black critics, he is ignored. She calls *Roots* an "autobiography" that like much black autobiography tells a story of community, bondage, flight, and freedom, a tale intended to be didactic and inspirational. Haley came as close to anyone, she says, of becoming the American griot, the custodian of the black community's oral history in America.

It may be more accurate to see Haley, as Nobile suggests, as a writer who created a fictional life for himself and could not escape it once the public had rewarded him so handsomely. Had *Roots* been marketed as the novel it is, and had Haley not spun tall tales about his agonizing "research," the book would have retained an honorable place in southern literature. It is no more inaccurate than William Styron's *Confessions of Nat Turner*. As it is, however, it will always be suspect.

No doubt that during an important period in our history, *Roots* helped white Americans gain a sense of sympathy for what black Americans had suffered in bondage. Unfortunately, the book will be remembered as a phenomenon of popular culture rather than a serious and enduring study of black history.

Richard Marius, Harvard University

Note

This biography first appeared in the *Tennessee Encyclopedia of History and Culture* (1998) and is used with the permission of the Tennessee Historical Society.

Suggested Reading

Helen Taylor. "The Griot from Tennessee: The Saga of Alex Haley's Roots." *Critical Quarterly* 37 (Summer 1995): 46–62.

the assertions of lawyers. Luther Eustis, deeply religious and filled with lust, lives for a few days with Beulah Joyner, whom he knows to be a harlot, on an almost deserted island in the Mississippi River. Thinking that he is following the command of God—Luther hears voices—he kills Beulah and then makes his long way home to his family and to his trial for murder, a strong item of evidence against him being his Bible which he has left on the island after the crime. It may be a given, in fiction as well as in life, that those who believe themselves to be admonished by God or by Satan—Luther changes his mind about who has spoken to him—are crazy, but sacred history holds differently. From the beginning, patriarchs and saints have been on speaking terms with God. Foote does not even suggest that Luther has supernatural power or even that such power exists, but his novel does convey the strong social and psychological influence that fundamentalist Christianity exerted in the South fifty years ago and continues to exert in parts of Tennessee.

In their basic delineations, the characters in *Follow Me Down* are familiar to readers of southern fiction. Like her daughter, Beulah's mother is a nymphomaniac. There are a deaf and dumb boy, a retarded girl who is obliged to wear a chastity belt, a backwoods preacher, and lawyers given to sallies of bucolic wit. At a revival, a woman gets "the Spirit" and goes bumping down a hill on her buttocks. But always, Foote's prose and his firm control of his story lift this book out of the realm of southern grotesque. The angularity of the people, the complicated qualities with which Foote endows them, gives the narrative dignity and power.

In the years between 1949 and 1954, Foote wrote five books of fiction, four of which are set in his mythical Jordan County, Mississippi. Taken together they form a tapestry of Jordan County society. In addition to the characters in *Follow Me Down,* there are the aristocratic Hugh Bart in *Tournament* (1949), the rich but not so aristocratic Amy and Jeff Carruthers in *Love in a Dry Season* (1951), and people of various races and dispositions and degrees of probity in *Jordan County* (1954), a book of interrelated short stories. *Shiloh* (1952) is a novel about the Civil War battle of that name, fought in Tennessee, which is told from the points of view of participants of various ranks on both sides. Although this book preceded Foote's book of stories, it foreshadowed *The Civil War: A Narrative,* a project that would occupy Foote to the exclusion of fiction for the next twenty-three years. *September, September* (1977), Foote's most recent novel, is set in Memphis in 1957—the year of the Russian satellite, *Sputnik,* of the introduction of the Edsel, and of the integration of the public schools in Little Rock, events which develop an ironic counterpoint to the well drawn, but not very smart characters who kidnap the grandson of a rich African American entrepreneur.

Alternating from chapter to chapter, between an omniscient point of view and those of individual characters, the story glosses the struggle over school integration in Little Rock by reversing what had been until then in southern fiction the ordinary roles of blacks and whites. The blacks are bright, hardworking, and honest; the whites are kidnappers, with the possible exception of Reeny, the female of the group, and are rapacious and dumb. Foote avoids the trap that waits for a novelist here: that of creating flat characters who play unrelieved roles of good and bad. The kidnappers, particularly Reeny, are humanized, and the victims, particularly the kidnapped boy's father and grandfather, demonstrate complexity of character and mind in their dealing with the criminals and in their relations with each other. In this return to fiction after an absence of almost a quarter of a century, Foote demonstrated the gifts for narrative that are evident in his early novels as well as an acute consciousness of social and political changes that occurred while he was writing his history of America's most tragic years. His reputation as a novelist is overshadowed not by the work of his contemporaries, but by his own monumental history of the Civil War.

Cormac McCarthy (1933–) was born in Rhode Island, one of six children of an Irish American lawyer who brought his family to Knoxville when Cormac was four. Raised in and around Knoxville, McCarthy attended the University of Tennessee, but did not graduate, and he has continued to maintain his Tennessee connections in the years since. His first book, *The Orchard Keeper* (1965), is in style and to a certain extent in content a frank imitation of the work of William Faulkner, but it is so brilliantly written, the detail so sharp, the dialogue so accurate, the characterization so convincing that, for most readers, the ghost of Faulkner in McCarthy's fiction is soon laid to rest. In the opening pages of *The Orchard Keeper,* the protagonist, Marion Sylder, kills a man, an act that seems increasingly, as McCarthy's career advances, to be a statement of theme for the books that are to follow. The main characters in *Outer Dark* (1968) are violent and incestuous lovers; the leading figure in *Child of God* (1973) is a murderous necrophiliac; one of the miscreants in *Suttree* (1979) blows up a main trunk of the Knoxville sewage system. Violence in McCarthy's work reaches a climax in the aptly named *Blood Meridian* (1985), which is filled with shootings and stabbings, mass scalpings and decapitations, tortures and barehanded engagements, one of which ends when the loser is stuffed head first into the pit of a privy.

All of McCarthy's novels are so magnificently written that almost from the beginning, he began to attract a following, admirers who were more interested

Modern Appalachian Writers

Modern Appalachian writers of Tennessee emerge from a rich literary tradition of distinguishable yet intertwining and overlapping genres. The modern renaissance began with the counterculture in the 1960s. The best symbol for this renaissance in East Tennessee is the quilt, suggesting diversity of literary design and ties with family, community, and the past. Wilma Dykeman of Newport well illustrates these themes in her novels *The Tall Woman* (1962), *The Far Family* (1976), and *Return the Innocent Earth* (1973) and in histories such as *The French Broad* (1955). Similarly Richard Marius, a native of Dixie Lee Junction and distinguished historian, provides a marvelous panorama of family life in the region over several generations. In his series of remarkable novels, *The Coming of Rain* (1971), *Bound for the Promised Land* (1976), *After the War* (1992), and *An Affair of Honor* (2001), the complexities of human relationships abound.

"Ode to My Mountain" appeared in *Now and Then: The Appalachian Magazine* and *Appalachia Inside Out,* vol. 2, 1995. Cartoon by Tony Feathers. Courtesy of the artist.

With considerable effect Marius makes use of the tall tale as does Lisa Alther, a native of Kingsport, in *Kinflicks* (1975), a best-selling, finely crafted novel focusing on conflicts in the female protagonist between her Appalachian background and life in an exclusive eastern college. At present Alther is at work on a novel on the Melungeons whom she counts among her ancestors. Another making broad use of humor is Joe Carson of Johnson City. With her keen ear for dialect and love of folk and family lore, Carson has demonstrated her versatility in poetry, short story, children's literature, and drama, winning the Kesserling award for the play *Daytrips* (1989). The creators of comedy on the frontier were male, but several modern women writers in the region do not let us forget that the muse of comedy, Thalia, is a woman.

One of the most persistent themes in the literature of East Tennessee is that of progress versus nature. The impact of federal dams upon the culture, first mentioned in *This Day and Time* (1930) by Anne Armstrong, finds new and extended expression in the poems in *Watauga Drawdown* (1990) by Don Johnson of East Tennessee State University. The collision of Appalachian-Indian heritage with that of atomic development, made possible by Tennessee Valley Authority dams, is amply reflected by Marilou Awiatka, a native of Knoxville who grew

[Continued on next page]

up in Oak Ridge, in *Abiding Appalachia: Where Mountain and Atom Meet* (1978). Awiatka's "Selu: Seeking the Corn Mother's Wisdom" (1993) applies Cherokee teachings to contemporary issues. Much of the black experience in the region (and out) finds compelling expression in the writings of Ishmael Reed of Chattanooga and Nikki Giovanni of Knoxville. In such verse as *Chattanooga* (1973) by Reed and *Those Who Ride the Night Winds* (1983) by Giovanni both authors remind us that the burdens of history must not only be addressed but redressed.

Nikki Giovanni at Tennessee Arts Commission 1998 Awards Reception, March 1999. Courtesy of Tennessee Photographic Services.

The themes of family, community, and especially the land, are all immediately evident in the finely wrought collections of George Scarbrough, a native of Polk County now living in Oak Ridge, and Jeff Daniel Marion, poet, printer, farmer, and director of the Appalachian Center at Carson-Newman University. "History," appropriately, is the title of a Scarbrough poem in *Invitation to Kim* (1983). Other works include *New and Selected Poems* (1992). Marion's poems, such as those in *Vigils: Selected Poems* (1990), have, like those of Scarbrough, been widely praised and anthologized. Poignant treatment of family relationships emerge in the poems of Linda Parsons, author of *Home Fires* (1997). Lynn Powell, a protégé of Marion, makes original and extraordinary use of another old influence on the region, the Bible, as suggested in the title of her first book of poems, *Old and New Testaments* (1995).

Clear signs of a renaissance of writing in East Tennessee are a wide array of courses in creative writing, annual workshops, little magazines, and writers groups. In southern literature there is a call for a new canon. In modern Appalachian writing no such movement is afoot. Instead, the flowering of prose and poetry in the region suggests a garden where the variety and beauty of each plant may be judged by its special qualities without undue emphasis on comparative ratings to the works of others. Significantly, new growth by emerging writers is always evident and encouraged.

Robert J. Higgs, East Tennessee State University, emeritus

in the brilliance of his prose than they were distressed by the moral degradation of some of his characters. As time passed, and the number of his readers increased, McCarthy began to mellow. Violent scenes continued to appear in his work, but not as frequently as before; villains continued to perform major roles in his narratives, but there were more good people to balance against them. McCarthy's advent as a popular as well as a literary novelist came with the first of his more gentle books, *All the Pretty Horses* (1992). Set in the southwestern United States and Mexico as *Blood Meridian* is—McCarthy moved to that part of the country after receiving a "genius grant" from the MacArthur Foundation in 1981—*All the Pretty Horses* picks up one of the oldest and best of Tennessee literary themes: love of the land which figures so prominently in the work of the Agrarians. Feeling deprived of his birthright when his mother sells his grandfather's ranch on which he was raised, sixteen-year-old John Grady Cole, accompanied by his friend Lacy Rawlins, goes to Mexico, not only in search of adventure, but in search of a traditional world as well, and finds both.

Adventure comes first, precipitated by one of McCarthy's most brilliantly drawn and, in some ways, most annoying characters, Jimmy Blevins, who is too young, and too small, and entirely too impetuous to have been turned loose in the world. John Grady and Lacy risk life and limb to help Blevins recover the horse that has been stolen from him; then they move on to jobs on a ranch, run by a Mexican nobleman where John Grady falls in love with the ranch owner's daughter. Romance is new ground for McCarthy, and to say that he writes of love less skillfully than he writes of violence is not to say that he writes badly about love. Alejandra comes to John Grady's room at night. They lie together; they talk; they take long rides in the moonlight. But there is more than the difference of social rank between them. She is bound by generations to the Old World moral code by which her family lives and which prevents her from finally betraying her father. After his affair with Alejandra, John Grady fails to save Blevins's life and manages barely to save his own in the final, brilliantly realized segments of the novel.

The protagonist of *The Crossing* (1994) is Billy Parham whose self-imposed mission in the early part of the book is to save the life of a pregnant wolf bitch that he has trapped. He wants to return the wolf to the Mexican mountains from whence she came, but he arouses scant sympathy from any quarter. One American asks him if he has been crazy all his life, and another wonders how the Mexicans might be fixed for rattlesnakes. For the Mexicans, the idea of repatriating a wolf is too incomprehensible even to engender irony. Billy's effort fails, and the thrust of the narrative, both thematically and dramatically, is changed when, on returning home, Billy discovers that his parents have been murdered by thieves who took their horses and everything else of value. With his younger brother, Boyd, who avoided the fate of his parents, Billy sets out to find his parent's murderers and to reclaim his father's horses. As was the case in *All the Pretty Horses,* the story of violence and bloodshed plays opposite a story of love.

The male lover is not Billy, but Boyd. He is no more than fifteen, perhaps not even that old, and the girl he desires is not an aristocrat, but a waif whom Billy and Boyd have saved from being raped by bandits. This book contains some of McCarthy's best writing about Mexican peasants, whom he depicts as universally kind and generous, devout and cheerful. Boyd recuperates with a peasant family after he has been shot by outlaws, then escapes from Billy and runs away with the girl. In loving the girl, Boyd opens his heart to the culture that produced her, but he is not Mexican, and his gringo impetuosity causes his death. In the last part of the novel, Billy searches for and finds what is left of Boyd's body, and Billy's final adventures are generated by his successful effort to bring most of his brother's remains home for burial. This segment of the narrative is sufficient to convince seasoned McCarthy admirers that the old master has not lost his touch for the macabre, but the fortitude with which Billy endures the loss of his family and Billy's loyalty to the dead give a sense of purpose to scenes that otherwise might seem to be gratuitously grotesque.

Both Billy and John Grady Cole appear in *Cities of the Plain* (1998), the final volume of the *Border Trilogy,* which resumes McCarthy's earlier themes of love and dispossession. Once more the male lover is John Grady; his beloved is Magdalena whom he meets in a house of prostitution. Although Magdalena is little more than a child, her past and present sufferings are legion. Given away when she was thirteen to settle a gambling debt, she has been betrayed by all from whom she sought help—nuns, the police—and she is now held captive by the owner of the whore house, Eduardo. Magdalena's saintliness is suggested by her name. Strengthened by her past sufferings, she is willing to risk anything, to sacrifice anything to escape her present life and be married to John Grady. But in spite of their past experiences, she and John Grady are still children, and their dreams of love are too fanciful ever to come true. At the end of the novel, only Billy is left, and like John Grady at the beginning of *All the Pretty Horses,* the land on which he lives and works and in which he finds his purpose and identity is to be taken from him, this time by the federal government, for purposes that are not fully clear.

The Border Trilogy did not satisfy all of McCarthy's admirers, many of whom longed for him to return to his more vicious, and in some ways, more morally anarchic characters and plots. But the early books remain in all their bright detail, and by showing that he has been able to move from one mode to another, the trilogy demonstrates the scope of McCarthy's talent. Unlike those written by less skillful novelists, his books do not follow a single pattern. That they have changed in concept and execution as he has grown as an artist is one reason that many critics, even some who are repelled by much of his material, consider him one of the finest writers of his time.

Madison Smartt Bell (1957–), one of the most prolific writers of his, or any other, generation, was born and raised on a farm in Williamson County, Tennessee, and thus came to know early what the Nashville Agrarians had in mind. The beauty of rural landscape, the rhythms of country life were not lost on him, but neither were the Princeton ambiance in which he lived during his college days nor the rundown New York neighborhoods where he made his home for several years after. *The Washington Square Ensemble* (1983), Bell's first book, is set in New York among drug addicts, seedy musicians, and other questionable characters. His subsequent books take place either in New York or other urban centers—Rome, Brussels, London. Although some of the narratives in *Zero Db and Other Stories* (1987) involve Tennessee and Tennesseans, until *Soldier's Joy* (1989), his fifth novel, Bell did not locate a major work in his native state, and his fictional Tennessee is hardly the bucolic land celebrated by the Agrarians. Laidlaw, principal character in *Soldier's Joy,* is a bluegrass musician, a figure familiar enough in fact and fiction set in Middle Tennessee, but Laidlaw is also a Vietnam veteran and a somewhat cynical observer of the southern scene. He resumes contact with Redmon, a black man who has been his best friend since childhood, and the inevitable questions of race and justice and identity are joined. This is a good novel, and the Tennessee landscapes and Nashville cityscapes are done with Bell's usual skill, but Bell's masterpiece, as he reaches midcareer, is *All Souls' Rising* (1995).

Nothing that Bell had written before prepared his readers for the scope and power of this novel. None of his previous books developed so many characters from so many levels of society. None of his earlier novels engaged a story so complex or a theme so grand. *All Souls' Rising* is set in Haiti in the waning years of the eighteenth century, when the unrest generated by the French Revolution impinged on the Haitian social structure that was built partly on a caste system determined by race, partly, and more importantly, on the practice of slavery that seemed sometimes to assume that the most vicious brutality was an end in itself. One of the major actors in this story is Toussaint L'Ouverture, a self-educated, second-generation slave, but it would be wrong to say that L'Ouverture is the main character that he may become in subsequent volumes of what Bell has planned as a trilogy about Haiti (the next volume, *Master of the Crossroads,* was published in 2000). Here there are too many others: landowners, politicians, people of color, rich and poor, slaves in servitude, slaves who have run away to the hills, and, as the book progresses, slaves that have risen against their masters, tortured and killed them, and set fire to the fields. This is a novel on the grand scale, and it marks a turning point in Bell's career. His work is important.

There are many other good Tennessee novelists. Wilma Dykeman (1920–) celebrates the history and culture of East Tennessee in *The Tall Woman* (1962) and *The Far Family* (1966), bringing the families which appear in both novels from the closing days of the Civil War through the first half of the twentieth century. In her loving depiction of mountains and streams, trees and valleys, Dykeman is much like the Agrarians, but she does not romanticize life in the

Richard Marius

RICHARD MARIUS (1933–1999), A NATIVE OF EAST TENNESSEE, WROTE FOUR NOVELS (WITH ONE APpearing posthumously), but he was best known for his biographies of Martin Luther, *Luther* (1974), and Thomas More, *Thomas More: A Biography* (1984). At the insistence of his mother, whom he described as a "religious fanatic," Marius earned a bachelor of divinity degree from Southern Baptist Theological Seminary, but he rejected both a vocation as a clergyman and the Baptist religion in favor of a career as a historian. He was trained at Yale (M.A., 1959; Ph.D., 1962), and he taught history, principally at the University of Tennessee in Knoxville, for sixteen years before becoming director of expository writing at Harvard in 1978. He said that his interest in Luther was engendered by his teaching a course in the Reformation and by his opposition to the war in Vietnam. He discovered parallels between Luther's century and his own, but for many critics, the book, although soundly researched and very well written, was marred by Marius's deep anger at his country's involvement in Vietnam, the "ugly war," as he put it, that engaged much of the author's emotional energy. Nonetheless, even though Marius did not much admire him or the century in which he lived, Luther emerges in the book as a fully drawn character who is an individual as well as a representative of his age.

Thomas More: A Biography, the most widely known book by Marius, is, in part at least, a continuation of Marius's work as coeditor of *The Complete Works of St. Thomas More,* published in several volumes during the 1980s by Yale University Press. Nominated for the National Book Award in nonfiction in 1984, *Thomas More* was widely praised for its depictions of sixteenth-century English society and politics and for new details Marius had discovered concerning More's life. But as had been the case with Marius's Luther, many critics believed that the author lacked sufficient sympathy with his subject, and they disapproved of Marius's severely iconoclastic approach. Until Marius's biography—there had been a previous life of More by R. W. Chambers in 1935—the circumstances of More's death seemed unambiguous. As lord chancellor of England under Henry VIII, he was found guilty of false charges of treason and executed because he refused to sanction Henry's divorce from Catherine of Aragon. Unlike Chambers, whose biography of More is virtually a hagiography, Marius characterizes More not as a saint but as a scheming politician, a clever manipulator who was motivated more by vanity and ambition than by the love of God. But the writing in both Luther and More was almost universally praised for its grace and clarity. Critics judged both books to be well organized and undergirded by sound and accurate research.

Marius's literary skills are abundantly evident in his novels. *The Coming of Rain* (1969), an alternate selection of the Book of the Month Club, is set in East Tennessee during two days in 1885, but much of the story evolves within the memories of its characters. It is a story about the Civil War and Reconstruction that avoids the narrative and historical clichés that are frequently found in novels about that period. In Marius's mind, East Tennessee was not a part of the Confederacy; it was certainly not a part of the Old South, a culture which Marius did not admire and with which he had many disagreements. A significant theme in *The Coming of Rain* is the legacy of slavery which is a guilt that must be expiated, or, as Marius put it, the novel is about "the Confederate myth of the Lost Cause."

[Continued on next page]

Bound for the Promised Land is the story of a family's joumey from East Tennessee to California in the decade before the Civil War. Since much of the action takes place outside the South and involves characters who are not Southerners, this is less a southern novel than either *The Coming of Rain* or *After the War,* Marius's third novel, which takes place in East Tennessee during and immediately after World War I.

Richard Marius. Courtesy of Special Collections, University of Tennessee, Knoxville.

An Affair of Honor, his fourth and best novel, posthumously published by Knopf in September 2001, is a southern novel in every respect and is drenched in the qualities that often are associated with southern fiction: a strong sense of place, the sense of the concrete and specific, a well-defined community, a profound religious dimension, passionate behavior (including abundant violence), and much else. The novel is set in the fictional town of Bourbonville (perhaps Maryville) in East Tennessee and is located near Pigeon Forge and Knoxville.

Marius packs the learning and experience of a lifetime into this sprawling novel, which has a huge cast of characters; many plots and subplots; the life histories of most of its actors, major and minor; themes that involve the clash of religion, race, culture, tradition, and modernity, as well as sexual and material values; and action unfolding in the European and Asian theaters of World War II in addition to small-town Tennessee from the 1930s through the 1950s and up to the present. The pace is swift; the action, gripping; the detail, exact; and the characters, memorable. But the novel is too long and loose and is far closer to the huge fluid puddings of Tolstoy about which Henry James complains than to the well-made novels of James himself. *An Affair of Honor* has the prodigality of another writer who celebrates the Piedmont and mountain South: Thomas Wolfe.

Whatever the settings of his novels, Marius did not think of himself as a southern writer, and he did not want to be thought of as such by his critics. Marius was only partly right about himself. Like it or not, he could not change the reality of his own life. He had been born in Tennessee, which is a part of the South, and although he was at odds with his culture, he wrote about his own place, his own people. His is a minority point of view, but it adds scope to Tennessee fiction viewed in its totality.

Walter Sullivan, Vanderbilt University

mountains where jobs are scarce and schools are poor and modern medical care is virtually nonexistent. This will change as industry moves into the mountain communities, but then the landscape and the nature of life will change. Men who once farmed will punch time clocks. Trees will be cut and streams will be polluted. The characters in *The Far Family* who move to Knoxville pursue lives different from those of their forebears and from those of their relatives who remain in the country, but they seem no less fulfilled. Dykeman's ability to present both urban and rural worlds in a fair juxtaposition to each other is a part of her narrative talent, and her sense of the importance of family to city and country dwellers alike gives depth to her well constructed and interesting novels.

Evelyn Scott (1893–1963) was an early feminist whose work is now being reexamined. James Agee (1909–1955) wrote only one novel, but his posthumously published *A Death in the Family* (1957) has earned a niche for itself in southern literature. *Big Ballad Jamboree* (1996) was also published after the death of its author, Donald Davidson (1893–1968). It is probably the best novel by a Tennessean about country music. And like Agee, Tennessee poet Randall Jarrell (1914–1965) wrote only one novel, *Pictures In an Institution* (1986), but it too survives in the southern literary canon.

Suggested Readings

Bell, Vereen M. *The Achievement of Cormac McCarthy.* Baton Rouge: Louisiana State Univ. Press, 1988.

Bradford, M. E., ed. *The Form Discovered: Essays on the Achievement of Andrew Lytle.* Jackson: Univ. Press of Mississippi, 1973.

Lucas, Mark. *The Southern Vision of Andrew Lytle.* Baton Rouge: Louisiana State Univ. Press, 1986.

Robinson, David M. *World of Relations: The Achievement of Peter Taylor.* Lexington: Univ. Press of Kentucky, 1998.

Stephens, C. Ralph, and Lynda B. Salamon, eds. *The Craft of Peter Taylor.* Tuscaloosa: Univ. of Alabama Press, 1995.

Sullivan, Walter. *Death by Melancholy: Essays on Modern Southern Fiction.* Baton Rouge: Louisiana State Univ. Press, 1972.

Young, Thomas D. *The Past in the Present: A Thematic Study of Modern Southern Fiction.* Baton Rouge: Louisiana State Univ. Press, 1981.

Part Four

The Performance Arts

Speech, Theater, Dance, and Film

Eighteen

The Spoken Word as Traditional Art

Bob Fulcher
Norris, Tennessee

Plain talk in Tennessee is not meant to be bland. Conversation can be a brawl of jests, proverbs, parables, and vocabulary, endorsed by tradition and powerful enough to overwhelm any rhetorician unarmed with such resources. Good storytellers are expected in our pulpits, our courts, our work places—they are welcomed everywhere. Our self-image insists that we have time for good talk.

Numerous historians and critics have suggested that a preference for the spoken word distinguishes southern culture and has even contributed, in their minds, to a relative dearth of literary genius in the region. In *The Oral Tradition in the South,* Waldo Braden wrote, "The South is truly an oral society. Being more attuned to the spoken word than to the printed page, southerners looked upon their speakers as important sources of information, inspiration, and entertainment, and regarded them along with warriors and hunters as heroes."[1]

Native wit wins respect in almost any circle of Tennessee society. Our public speakers have influenced the way we talk to each other, in public forums and in private, and a few have had a national influence. The great importance of our oral traditions, though, lies in their universality. No folk art is more ingrained in day-to-day life in modern Tennessee.

There is no "Tennessee style" of speaking or storytelling that stands entirely apart, however, as we share these assets with our regional neighbors. Yet we identify ourselves and others through the use of language and stories, sorting out ethnic background, occupational expertise, or the depth of one's wisdom, cleverness, and experience.

The Discovery of Tennessee Speech

Not long after Tennessee statehood, writers began to take notice of the peculiarities of speech on the old Southwest frontier. Published in 1834, *A Narrative of the Life of David Crockett* is "a document of importance in the history of American English, being replete with dialectal usages, proverbial expressions, and spellings representing non-standard pronunciations," according to historians James Shackford and Stanley Folmsbee.[2] Famous in his time as a Tennessee politician who had opposed Andrew Jackson, Crockett had stated in a letter to his publishers that his manuscript "needs no correction of spelling or grammar, as I make no literary pretensions." Shackford and Folmsbee conclusively proved that a ghostwriter serviced the manuscript, and this ghostwriter, they believed, added some grammatical errors for "flavor." Although the ghostwriter may have embellished the speech to reflect common stereotypes of how an uneducated frontiersman would sound, the editors also believed the work accurately reflected interviews with Crockett and portrayed his style of speech, which was rough and direct. Speaking of his courting adventures, for instance, Crockett recounts, "I continued in this down-spirited situation for a good long time, until one day I took my rifle and started a hunting. While out, I made a call at the house of a Dutch widow, who had a daughter that was well enough as to smartness, but she was as ugly as a stone fence."[3]

Crockett's book had been preceded by a few travel books that reported on frontier boasting, by backwoods dispatches that were the specialty of the New York newspaper *The Spirit of the Times,* and by the outrageous speeches of Nimrod Wildlife, the leading figure of James K. Paulding's popular play, *The Lion of the West* (1830, revised 1831 and 1833). The Crockett narrative was so powerful and popular, however, that soon these earlier sources of language and tales were ascribed to Crockett.

Crockett's autobiography was followed by a series of almanacs, published from 1835 to 1856, offering fictional stories in dialect with Crockett as hero. The popularity of such yarn spinning and the quaint and clever qualities of the dialect tempted numerous authors in the nineteenth century. George Washington Harris's *Sut Luvingood: Yarns* (1867) consists of brilliant, rough tales entirely in dialect, set in East Tennessee, while Mary Noailles Murfree wrote romantic novels between 1884 and 1920 that also sought to present the features of East Tennessee speech.

The language of Tennesseans, like the music, food, and architecture of the state, is spiked with anachronisms and relics from England and Africa. The first considerations of Tennessee speech in scholarly publications were concerned with old and unusual words and expressions. Entitled "Waste-Basket of Words," a note in an 1889 edition of the *Journal of American Folklore* may be the first entry on Tennessee words in an academic journal. Submitted by a Washington bureaucrat who had noticed the words on pension claims, the terms, he stated, "may nearly all be set down to Kentucky and Tennessee." The list included "Molly-cotton.—A rabbit," and "Griff.—A certain man is described as having a 'griff complexion.' He belonged to a colored regiment, but the particular shade intended I am unable to say."[4]

In that same year, Calvin S. Brown Jr. of Vanderbilt University published a list of thirty-nine interesting and ancient usages among black and white sources in *Modern Dialect Notes.* Brown, who had worked in Obion County, implied that his Tennessee sources were old or uneducated, though he often cited the character of Uncle Remus found in the stories of Joel Chandler Harris. Among the Tennessee words that also appear in Shakespeare or the King James Version of the Bible, he noted *bully, divel, handkercher, heap, holp, howsomever, ruination,* and *sallet.*

The first detailed linguistic survey in Tennessee began in the summer of 1937, initiated by Joseph S. Hall of Cornell University. Working as a student technician in the newly developed Great Smoky Mountains National Park, Hall gathered linguistic data from former and current residents within and just outside the park boundaries. Rather than ask about words, he solicited bear stories and other family tales, while filling four notebooks with entries regarding pronunciation, morphology, syntax, and vocabulary. The following summer he obtained a Presto recorder, so large as to require a truck for transportation and dependent upon AC power supply, and a more portable aluminum disc recorder. Setting up in Civilian Conservation Corps camps with the cumbersome Presto machine or traveling "up rough roads to remote mountain homes" with the smaller unit, Hall was able to preserve dozens of stories and ballads, "bygone methods of weaving and cooking," traditional remedies, plant lore, and superstitions. His study contended that "most of the Elizabethan forms which survive into the Southern Appalachians continued in standard use into the seventeenth, eighteenth, and (sometimes) the nineteenth centuries." He concluded, differing from many romantic descriptions to the contrary, that "Great Smokies speech is not Elizabethan English transplanted to America. Yet it possesses a rugged, colorful and imaginative character, a pleasant archaic flavor, and deserves to be recorded for the benefit of future students of American civilization."[5]

Word collecting continued in Tennessee in the latter part of the twentieth century. Kelsie B. Harder, a native of Perry County, published numerous collections of occupational and traditional terminology in the 1950s and 1960s, examining marble playing, musseling, and farming. For many years following, he specialized in the study of place names.

Gordon R. Wood of the University of Chattanooga (now the University of Tennessee at Chattanooga) initiated a notable linguistics study that included Tennessee in 1957. Wood undertook a lexical survey of eight southern states as a necessary step in developing a linguistic atlas of the South. His findings brought out a complicated war of words. By comparing the distribution of synonyms, such as *tow sack* and *crocker sack,* he found evidence of the migration of southern words down the east coast and along the southern coastal plain, probably with cotton planters, with some of the vocabulary reaching up to Tennessee. His maps show distinct boundaries in the use of certain words: *snake doctor* is used west of the Eastern Highland Rim and *snake feeder* is used to the east as a synonym for dragon fly. *Mosquito hawk,* another dragonfly synonym, is common on the Gulf Coast and up the Mississippi River Valley and has scattered usage in Middle Tennessee. The southern term for fireplace log supports is *fire dogs,* but that usage is found only along the Mississippi and in Tennessee River counties; throughout the rest of the state they are known as *dog irons.* Wood concluded that the words from northern and midland sources had influenced southern midland or midsouthern dialect, representing most of Tennessee. The influence of south midland vocabulary seems to pour down the Shenandoah Valley, into the interior South, while the gulf southern dialect flows up the Mississippi River valley, following the Ohio, then the Cumberland River, into Middle Tennessee.

In addition to sustaining older words and terms, Tennessee speakers have decorated their talk with proverbial phrases and comparisons that might be old as Adam but handy as a shirt pocket. The first item discussed in the Tennessee Folklore Society's 1935 collecting guide was unusual expressions: "They are not necessarily slang; they may be provincialisms, or entirely correct English." The guide mentioned *hist wood* or *hurry wood* as synonyms for kindling. A person using highbrow language *is beyond the reach of my 'simmon pole. Make hay while the sun shines,* and *he is as green [unlearned] as a goose* are variants of traditional phrases that Shakespeare knew also. Seventy such items were reported from Chester County in 1974 that correspond to Shakespearean proverbs. A Blount County study from 1938 found eighty proverbial items that were established before 1500, citing *fat as a pig* (known from 1485), *the devil take the hindmost* (known from 1470), and *let sleeping dogs lie* (from Chaucer).[6]

Again, David Crockett's autobiography is full of traditional phrases. "My love was so hot as might nigh to burst my boilers," he claimed, and "my heart would begin to flutter like a duck in a puddle; and if I tried to outdo it and speak, it would get right smack up in my throat, and choak me like a cold potato [*sic*]." In charming his future mother-in-law, he was "salting the cow to catch the calf," but the woman turned against Crockett, "and looked at me as savage as a meat axe."[7]

Novelist Harry Harrison Kroll (1888–1967) used everyday speech in his fiction and studied these spoken words. He depended upon the everyday speech he naturally learned "among the share crops on the old Roellen road out of Dyersburg, Tennessee," where "about all the people I knew were poor whites and Negroes." He heard a language that "was a mixture of very simple strong word, earthy metaphor, barnyard vulgarity, and proverbs. Country people like to express their ideas in philosophical proverbs. It saves wear and tear on their scanty vocabularies. When in trouble they 'search the scriptures,' for easily remembered texts which convey their tears and dreams and hopes and fears." Kroll heard genius and eloquence in their wordplay, too, and as a graduate student at the George Peabody College for Teachers compiled a dictionary of backwoods words and phrases that H. L. Mencken regarded as "one of the best studies ever made on folk speech." While accepting the inevitable replacement of his native idiom with new language, Kroll did not like it. "Culture and education have got us 'by the tail with a downhill pull,' and from here on our world will never really be the same," he wrote. "Most of the eloquent proverbial materials have become embalmed in *A Dictionary of Americanisms, The Home Book of Proverbs, Tennessee Folklore Bulletin,* and such other worthy morgues of human speech."[8]

Riddles, Rhymes, Jingles, and Wordplay

Wisdom and poetry exist, also, in the riddles, rhymes, jingles, and recitations that appear as spoken bits of wordplay. In 1936 T. J. Farr, an education professor at Tennessee Polytechnic Institute (now Tennessee Technological University) and an early officer in the Tennessee Folklore Society, published the first collection of riddles gathered exclusively in Tennessee. His collection included true riddles, conundrums, and word puzzles.

The rhyming structure of many riddles enhanced their cleverness, and young children occasionally quoted such riddles on "recitation day" at their rural schools when they were called on to offer a short verse or declamation to their peers. Children borrowed other well-traveled material, too, including bits of song lyrics, popular poetry, or folk rhymes. A turn-of-the-century recitation piece from James Ledbetter of Fentress County resembles the nonsense verses in Mother Goose and the wild pioneer boasts:

I got up one Sunday morning,
Three hours by noon,
Saddled up three quarts of sour milk,
And rode around five miles above the bag of
moonshine,
And there I met old Johnny Whimper,
(You know the old scamp as well as I do.)
I told him to grind me three pecks of fine
meal flour,
Said, no he wouldn't, fer he couldn't.
Picked him up by the seat of his britches
Throwed him through the stitches and hitches,
Broke his neck three feet above the barn door,
Eat a keg of tar and drank a keg of wine,
And slid on down the axle of the world.[9]

More common were simple rhymes chanted or sung in children's games, but sometimes bearing ancient traditional beliefs, such as:

Marry in black, you'll wish yourself back;
Marry in blue, you'll always be true;
Marry in red, you'll wish yourself dead;
Marry in green, you'll be ashamed to be seen;
Marry in brown, you'll live out of town;
Marry in white, you've chosen all right.[10]

Thomas W. Talley had many ideas about the evolution of folk rhymes among African Americans. Talley, a professor of chemistry and science at Fisk University, was born in Shelbyville, Tennessee, just a few years after his parents had been freed from slavery in Mississippi. Sometime before 1920 Talley began to collect traditional verses from rural blacks, other professors, students, former students, family members, and from his own memory. These were first published in 1922 as *Negro Folk Rhymes,* with Talley's essay appended. In the rhythm of almost every verse, Talley heard 2/4 or 4/4 time, "whether the Rhyme is, or is not, sung." He recognized the meter from jubilee songs performed by the famous Fisk University Jubilee Singers, and from shouted calls at old-fashioned dances. "It is of interest to note also," he observed, "that the antebellum Negro while repeating his Rhymes which had no connection with the dance usually accompanied the repeating with the patting of his foot upon the ground." He was "counting off the invisible measures and bars of his Rhymes, things largely unseen by the world but very real to him." "When the Negroes were transported to America and began to sing songs and to chant words in another tongue," Talley supposed, "they still sang strains calling, through inheritance, for the

Thomas W. Talley. Courtesy of Special Collections, Fisk University Library.

accompaniment of their ancestral drum."[11] In each of the 349 songs and rhymes he collected, Talley heard a percussive link to Africa.

The structure of the rhymes had African ancestry as well. Talley corresponded with missionaries and, for comparative purposes, also published verses from destinations of the African diaspora: Liberia, the Congo, Jamaica, Venezuela and Trinidad. He noted that "call and response" was a fundamental form in traditional African communication, and he suspected a development in many pieces "from plain prose to repeated rhyme . . . to sung rhyme," as with one he remembered from childhood:

> "Did yer feed my cow?" "Yes, Mam!"
> "Will yer tell me how?" "Yes Mam!"
> "Oh, w'at did you giv 'er?" "Cawn an' hay."
> "Oh, w'at did you giv'er? "Cawn an' hay."[12]

Talley further theorized that most Negro folk rhymes were created for use within this call and response form, but only the calls remained because they were texts that could be used with any "response" refrain. Eventually the response was forgotten and it disappeared.

Talley knew that the texts had layers of meaning; some, he suspected, had foundations as old as ancient Egypt. He often brought up material that white collectors could not obtain or understand, because it had developed under the extremes of slavery and segregation. "The Negro," he concluded, "has given or probably will give the last crop of Folk Rhymes."[13]

The currency of rhyming among African Americans has not abated, with rap music being the most recent example. It draws upon traditional motifs and models for creative, even spontaneous, invention, with *toasts* deserving credit as a parent form. Toasts are long, narrative poems—often including clever boasts or taunts, ornamented with slang, vulgarity, or street talk—which serve as verbal showpieces, cautionary tales, and pure entertainment. Folklorist Roger Abrahams believes that recitations from the minstrel stage had some kinship with toasts, but that ornate, bawdy toasts delivered at drunken meetings of the secret and semisecret societies of the British Isles established the form, which was somehow assimilated into black culture by the early twentieth century. Toasts recorded from black and white Tennessee informants include a variety of local and the most widely distributed odes: *The Signifying Monkey, The Great Titanic, The Dyin' P.I.* (Player International), and *The Punks of Fort Pillow.* The stylized boasting used in professional wrestling has borrowed from the outrageous brags used in toasts, which, in turn, seems to be directly descended from the frontier boasting attributed to David Crockett.

The Storytelling Tradition

Storytelling has been valued as a state asset since the *Crockett Almanacs* credited uncommon abilities in the art to Col. David Crockett and his frontier kind. Since 1973, the National Storytelling Festival in

Jonesborough has attracted a sizable following to an event that presents a slate of mostly "professional tellers," artists who carefully compose or adapt their material for rehearsed, dramatized presentations. This professionalized art represents a new kind of informal theater, rather than storytelling in a style traditional to Tennessee, but the event and its host organization, Storytelling Foundation International, have promoted storytelling of many kinds. Nearby East Tennessee State University offers a master's degree program in storytelling, which has especially appealed to teachers, librarians, religious teachers and ministers, drama students, and therapists. Through these programs and events, storytelling becomes a structured art form.

Personal experience narratives, which may be considered the last real vernacular storytelling in our modern society, have been and still are the most popular genre of storytelling in everyday life. With traditional form, style, and function, an incident is told and retold until it becomes a polished piece. Tennessee's first historians—John Haywood, J. G. M. Ramsey, A. W. Putnam, and Lyman Draper—documented anecdotes, legends, and lore as they interviewed the state's aging pioneers and military heroes. Hunting stories, war experiences, lost treasure, and scrapes with Indians, animals, criminals, and hard weather provided much family lore. By the 1840s, Tennessee newspapers were publishing nostalgic letters with pioneer reminiscences, contributing to the spread of family and traditional stories. Journalists have continued to popularize local folktales and humorous stories: columnists Bert Vincent and Sam Venable at the *Knoxville News-Sentinel* and Hugh Walker at the *Nashville Tennessean* made good reputations with this interest, and the long-running and current feature, *The Heartland Series* from WBIR television in Knoxville, has managed national cable distribution of its four-minute episodes of East Tennesseans telling their own stories.

Traditional stories, though, exist beside and apart from their static form reported by the news media. Folklorist Lynwood Montell compared oral versions of the alleged crimes and hanging of Calvin Logsdon, in Jamestown in 1872, with newspaper accounts, court records, and diary entries from the period. The event, a gory triple murder of two women and a child, left stories that included the miraculous survival of a second child, the plot by two sisters to commit the murders and pin it on Logsdon, Logsdon's prophecy that a flood would follow his hanging to prove his innocence, and the disturbing difficulty in carrying out the sentence—the hangman's rope broke twice. Here, as in other cases, Montell found that oral histories provided the additional details and the framework features necessary to understand "the entire story."[14]

Supernatural events are another prominent feature in traditional storytelling repertoires. Ghost, or "haint," tales can be collected from most families to this day, including personal accounts of inexplicable events, handed-down stories that draw upon traditional motifs (rattling chains, cold spots, spectral visits), or entirely traditional tales told for entertainment. Witches were rarely innocuous like most haints, however, and witch stories are less likely to be told. Traditionally, witches were in league with Satan, gaining their status through a blasphemous act such as cursing God while shooting at the sun.

Robertson County's Bell Witch is Tennessee's most famous supernatural story. Appearing as a demonic spirit, the Bell Witch allegedly harassed John Bell's family from 1816 to 1820, then returned in 1827. The diary of Richard Bell Williams was ostensibly the basis for *An Authenticated History of the Famous Bell Witch,* published in 1894. This book has been followed by at least eleven studies, which have included modern accounts and a parallel Mississippi version of the legend.

There have not been extensive Tennessee collections of *Marchen* (the "fairy" or wonder tales of Europe) but, undoubtedly, they were scattered about in family traditions, often as "Jack" stories. The Harmon family, of Cades Cove, recorded a handful of Jack stories for a Library of Congress researcher in 1939, but their family roots were in Beech Mountain,

National Storytelling Festival

WHAT BEGAN IN 1973 AS A SMALL GATHERING OF APPALACHIAN STORYTELLERS HAS EVOLVED OVER a generation into one of the nation's premier gatherings of storytellers. The National Storytelling Festival, held every October in Jonesborough, is the most prestigious storytelling festival in the nation. The International Storytelling Center, which is headquartered in Jonesborough, sponsors the annual festival. "We all live in a network of stories. There isn't a stronger connection between people than storytelling," emphasizes Jimmy Neil Smith, the institution's executive director.[1]

The first festival in 1973 attracted about sixty people, but numbers rapidly increased. In 1975 organizers created the institutional predecessor to the current association. By 1980, one thousand people were attending the event and by the mid-1980s, five thousand listeners were convening every October in the Jonesborough historic district. Today, an estimated ten thousand attend the annual gathering. One of the festival's most popular places is the Swappin' Ground, where visitors can take their turns, no more than ten minutes, telling grand tales.

The former National Storytelling Association is now the International Storytelling Center; it has developed into one of Tennessee's key folklife institutions. The center's headquarters, designed by Ken Ross Architects in association with architect Robert A. M. Stern, opened in 2001. Located next to the restored Chester Inn, the center has a library, a story archives, a three-acre park, and an education and interpretation facility. The foundation also has launched a site on the Internet, reaching storytellers who have yet to make the fall trek to the festival.

Carroll Van West, Middle Tennessee State University

Note

1. Bruce Watson, "The Storyteller is the Soybean . . . the Audience Is the Sun," *Smithsonian* 27 (Mar. 1997): 61.

North Carolina, a region especially noted for such material. Thomas Talley's *Negro Traditions* included trickster stories, etiological folktales, and, motifs that Talley believed were derived from historic episodes or observations. He offered a lengthy analysis of the importance and meaning of these stories in another unpublished manuscript, "Origin of Traditions."

TALL TALES AND JOKES

A more universal narrative form, the joke, has received less scholarly study. Tall tales are an early Tennessee joke form based upon straight-faced exaggeration. Nathaniel Jones, born in Maury County in 1820, reported on the fertility of his neighbor's garden: "Potatoes grew to such enormous sizes that one of the vines ran across the creek and was used as a foot log until the following spring. In removing the drift that had lodged against the vine, to prevent an overflow, he killed a score of minks that had wintered in the potato vine. When gathering beans for dinner, the cook carried a torch, as the corn was so tall and the foliage and vines were so thick that she could not see her way without a light."[15] A self-published booklet from 1988, *100 Tennessee Tall Tales and wee whoppers (From All 100 Counties)* by Reed Scarbrough, suggests they have not gone out of fashion.

Irishman stories are another older joke form well known in Tennessee. Ethnic humor regarding Irish,

African American, Polish, and Jewish people has often been based on their perceived or exaggerated naïveté as immigrants to an unfamiliar world. Irishman jokes were widely published in nineteenth-century Tennessee newspapers, but traditional Irishman tales were lengthier accounts of foolish misunderstandings.

Folk idioms have been essential tools in many professional fields. American popular theater was beset with stereotypical dialogue humor and jokes in the form of blackface minstrelsy for almost one hundred years. "With its rapid emergence in the 1840s minstrelsy gained acclaim as America's only distinctive contribution to the theater," noted Robert Cogswell, but now "this once venerated show business tradition stands as a deplorable and embarrassing aspect of the past."[16] Cogswell's exemplary study, the only detailed analysis of commercially recorded blackface routines, found that traditional black humor was often reworked for the comedy recording, which began to appear in 1892.

Flournoy Miller and Aubrey Lyles, both Tennesseans, first joined forces as students at Fisk University in Nashville, and became the "foremost Negro blackface team of the 1920s," according to Cogswell. He considered their work "deriving both from Afro-American sources and from their own theatrical genius, . . . closely interwoven with standard blackface fare." He noted Miller's claim to have "haunted poolrooms, taverns and general stores," seeking 'curious phrases' and malapropisms for his scripts, but attributed the influence of Miller and Lyles to their originality and their success in turning "from nostalgic minstrel visions of slavery to satirical treatments of the independent black community, the problems of urban life, migration, and wage labor, and the controversial issues confronting their twentieth century audience."[17] Their style was carried to greater popularity by a white team, Charles Correll and Freenan Gosden, who reached millions of radio listeners as *Amos 'n' Andy.*

Medicine shows were staged in less formal settings, along a town street or square, but attracted customers through music and humorous routines. Roy Acuff, Bob Douglas, Curly Fox, and Frazier Moss are among the well-known Tennessee musicians whose first jobs were telling jokes and fiddling in a medicine show. As with minstrel and vaudeville shows, performers in blackface were not uncommon, and traditional jokes, from white and black sources, were adapted, recycled, and retold with effect.

Radio, Television, and the Spoken Word

As mass entertainment media developed, record companies and radio stations displaced the theater and medicine show as the primary outlets for jokes and humorous talk. Announcer George D. Hay (1895–1968) went against the grain with his informal, down-to-earth style on the Grand Ole Opry broadcasts. Unlike the stern voices with precise pronunciation typically found on the radio, Hay blended folksy phraseology with entertaining imagery. Playing himself in the 1940 Hollywood movie *The Grand Ole Opry,* he introduced a star performer: "And now, friends, we present Uncle Dave Macon—the Dixie Dewdrop, with his plug hat, gold teeth, chin whiskers, gate's ajar collar, and that million-dollar Tennessee smile—and his son, Dorris. Let 'er go, Uncle Dave!"[18] Hay's impact was enormous. Besides establishing a role for announcers as entertainers, he provided an early precedent for the hundreds of future radio announcers and disc jockeys who chose a more natural, native voice on the airwaves.

WDIA in Memphis was the first to establish an authentic black accent on southern radio, hiring Nat D. Williams in 1948. Already an active emcee for Beale Street shows, a newspaper columnist, and a high school history teacher, Williams had the breadth of experience and popularity to succeed in spite of the anticipated bigoted protests. Williams's appeal, to a great extent, was his artful use of "down-home street language," in contrast to the straightlaced commentators who surrounded him on the dial. His skills as an

George D. Hay. Courtesy of the Grand Ole Opry Archives.

entertainer were solidly founded on African American traditions of verbal sparring, rhyming, invention, and creative slang. His signature phrase, "Whatchubet," provided a formulaic exclamation that could resolve any monologue. Louis Cantor, college professor and former WDIA announcer, recalled Williams's daily opening: "'Arise, Jackson, and peck on the rock; it's six-thirty by this man's clock' was the familiar prologue. From then on it was an oral fusillade. 'That's right, ladies, it's time to jump into those corsets. You too, Jackson, get out of that bed, you know where to head—that's enough said! Now whatchubet?'"[19]

There was some concern in the black community that his unrefined language tarnished Williams's groundbreaking role, but Williams and the station management sensed a tremendous overall popularity and stuck with it. WDIA became the first southern radio station with all-black programming, the first all-black station in the nation to go fifty thousand watts, and the "first in the country to present an open forum to discuss black problems."[20] The hip tone of Williams and other WDIA announcers was a powerful statement of confidence that African American vernacular speech, ingenuous and jaunty, was legitimate public speech.

The national response was a steady growth of imitation of the WDIA style. Claude Tomlinson on WIVK in Knoxville had developed a popular on-air hillbilly personality known as Little Alf. In 1953 he added the persona Claude the Cat, "a whisker-twitchin', fur shakin', and cool talkin' cat," who introduced a new program, *Ebony Rhapsody,* with an awkward emulation:

> No hillbilly tunes for me and you,
> Gonna play some jazz, rhythm and blues.
> We're here to jive, startin' right now,
> So just sit back while the Cat meows.[21]

By the following year, the station hired its first black deejay, A. C. Wilson, whose hip-talking program, *The Acey Boy Show,* immediately won popularity among Knoxville's black audience.

Tennessee entertainers also significantly shaped radio comedy. The national popularity of the WSM's *Grand Ole Opry* owed much to Uncle Dave Macon's fearless style of rustic joking, rhyming, preaching, and music making. Uncle Dave had learned from many vaudeville and blackface comics, perhaps, but he was loved during his tenure on the Opry (1925–52) as a familiar, authentic voice of the country folk. Macon recorded over 175 sides for the early record labels, and a great many were introduced or interrupted by a quick story or recitation. Following this formula to popularity, other banjo-playing rustic comics have been welcomed in Nashville—Grandpa Jones, David "Stringbean" Akeman, and Mike Snider.

Archie Campbell (1914–1987) was born in Bull Gap, in Hawkins County, and joined WNOX in Knoxville in 1936 as a singer. The station's leading announcer, Lowell Blanchard, saw the need to develop the hillbilly comedy style and encouraged Campbell to develop his character known as Grandpappy. As Campbell recalled, "Lowell Blanchard and I wrote our own material, often borrowing old jokes as all comics always have. . . . We did broad, simple comedy, aimed at a listening audience that was made up largely of country people and working people." As an example, Campbell recalled this dialogue:

Grandpappy: "I've got me a new billy goat."
Lowell: "Where do you keep him?"
Grandpappy: "In the house."
Lowell: "What about the smell?"
Grandpappy: "He'll just have to get used to it like the rest of us."[22]

Campbell eventually went to the Grand Ole Opry, following the death of comic Rod Brasfield, the "Hohenwald Flash." The Grand Ole Opry's NBC network portion, its Armed Forces Radio connection, and, in general, its clear channel signal made Nashville the epicenter of rustic jokes as well as country music. The weekly performances of Minnie Pearl, Whitey Ford, Jerry Clower, and the banjo-playing comedians gave the Opry a structural kinship with minstrel, medicine, and vaudeville shows of the past. To portray the memorable character of Minnie Pearl, Sarah Colley Cannon took images and phrases from a mountain family she had once visited in Sand Mountain, Alabama, as well as her own family's roots in Hickman County, Tennessee. Clower's tale telling borrowed from evangelistic preaching dramatics, an exclamatory style also heard in the commercially recorded humor of Cotton Ivy, a political figure from Decatur County.

Archie Campbell. Courtesy of the Grand Ole Opry Archives.

As television stations developed, they also adopted a musical/comedy variety format. *Hee Haw* became one of America's longest-running television programs, drawing upon the most venerable comics in Nashville, including Archie Campbell, Grandpa Jones, and Minnie Pearl, and giving new life to many older, corny, traditional jokes, many of which had been initially made popular by the Duke of Paducah, a veteran Opry comic of the 1940s and 1950s.

Radio and television stations, dependent on advertising sales for their income, quickly learned to script sales pitches aimed at their plain-talking audiences with the same kind of traditional joking, sloganeering, and storytelling used by medicine show hawkers. Occasionally a sponsor stepped forward to do it himself, such as Knoxville's legendary politician and performer Cas Walker. Walker made enough money in the grocery business to sponsor radio and television shows for forty years. He was an unpredictable emcee and spontaneous comedian, and he advertised his products and sales with brash, coarse, hilarious talk. Audiences watched with wonder that a man cut from such common cloth could imperviously flaunt his

Archie James Campbell

Archie James Campbell (1914–1987), a native of Bulls Gap, Tennessee, used the stories and anecdotes of the small town culture he knew as a boy to make a career for himself as a nationally known entertainer and comedian. His artistry at weaving tales and humorous stories helped sustain the storytelling art form in Tennessee and beyond.

Taking his guitar, a high school graduation present, Campbell turned from art studies at Mars Hill College to entertainment. He began his career in the 1930s working at Knoxville radio stations, including WNOX's *Mid-Day Merry-Go-Round.* Here he developed a comic repertoire, established the humorous character of Grandpappy while in his twenties, and created the influential *Tennessee Barn Dance* radio show, which gave many country music performers early public exposure. For a time, he was a member of Roy Acuff's Crazy Tennesseans musical group.

His career, interrupted by service in the United States Navy during World War II, was quickly reestablished when he returned to radio and public appearances. In 1952, Campbell started *Country Capers* on WROL-TV in Knoxville; it gave country music performers early television exposure in much the same way his radio shows had done. He became a member of the Grand Old Opry in 1958, where he revolutionized country comedy when he appeared one night not in "rube garb" but in a tie and sport coat like the more sophisticated comics of his era.

Throughout the rest of his career, he performed on many national radio and television shows, most notably as an original cast member and head writer of *Hee Haw,* a long-running nationally televised country variety program. In 1969, he was named Comedian of the Year by the Country Music Association. At the time of his death, he was host of Nashville Network's *Yesterday in Nashville*.

As a recording artist, he developed a unique brand of verbal comedy through the use of such old techniques as spoonerisms (transposing consonant sounds in different words) and malaprops (using a word in place of another word that sounds similar for humorous effect). His memorable renditions of well-known fairy tales and children's stories such as "Rindercella" (Cinderella) and the "Pee Little Thrigs" (Three Little Pigs) using these techniques proved immensely popular. Other popular recordings included "Trouble in the Amen Corner," "The Cockfight," and "Bedtime Stories for Adults." This last album was the best-selling country comedy recording of its time.

Campbell, the Groucho Marx of country music, was noted for his ready cigar, earthy humor, and the clever wordplay of his storytelling. His success paved the way for later interpreters of southern rural and small town humor like Andy Griffith, Lewis Grizzard, and Jeff Foxworthy. In later years, Campbell returned to his love of painting, with his works becoming collectors' items, as well as devoting much time to charitable causes. He died on August 29, 1987, and was buried at Powell, Tennessee. His hometown's Archie Campbell Museum perpetuates his life and humor.

Ned L. Irwin, East Tennessee State University

Minnie Pearl. Courtesy of the Grand Ole Opry Archives.

Cas Walker. Courtesy of the McClung Historical Collection.

country ways in public. Former listeners have recalled him advertising: "We've got toilet paper for ten cents a roll, and that's a lot of wipes for a dime. We've got eggs for fifty cents a dozen and on Wednesday we've got cracked eggs for twenty-five cents a dozen. Down at the Central Avenue Store we've got panty hose half off."[23] "Say, neighbors" was his formulaic salutation and exclamation. "It caused me to be imitated a lot. I appreciated everyone that imitated me for I came out better than they did," he said.[24] Walker's success, no doubt, encouraged many other plain-speaking folks to take to the airwaves, and it carried Walker through two terms as Knoxville's mayor and twenty-two more years as city councilman or vice mayor.

Political Speech

As often as entertainers have mimicked the politicians, the politicians have imitated entertainers, enlisting traditional jokes, personal anecdotes, and formulaic religious or patriotic testimonials, well salted with local idioms. Waldo Braden's lifelong work in the criticism of political oratory debunked the myth of a "southern oratory," which presumed that all effective southern speakers used a flamboyant, ornate, emotional style, and that such a style was uniquely southern. He eventually came to the opinion, though, that the southern dependence and comfort with oral tradition made oratory the principal medium of political, religious, and legal/judicial expression.

David Crockett presented himself as an agent in undermining the bombastic, elevated orations of his campaign opponents by merely telling better jokes, offering a good drink, and appearing honest and common. He once amused a gathering of voters by telling his opponent:

> When I set out electioneering, I would go prepared to put every man on as good footing when I left him as I found him on. I would therefore have me a large buckskin hunting-shirt made, with a couple of pockets holding about a peck each; and that in one I would

> carry a great big twist of tobacco, and in the other my bottle of liquor: for I knowed when I met a man and offered him a dram, he would throw out his quid of tobacco and take one, and after he had taken his horn, I would out with my twist and give him another chaw. And in this way he would not be worse off than when I found him; and I would be sure to leave him in a first-rate humour.[25]

Then Crockett addressed his relatively meager campaign chest: "I told him I would go on the products of the country; that I had industrious children, and the best of coon dogs, and they would hunt every night till midnight to support my election; and when the coon fur wa'n't good, I would myself go a wolfing, and shoot down a wolf, and skin his head, and his scalp would be good to me for three dollars, in our state treasury money; and in this way I would get along on the big string."[26] In this manner Crockett mixed truth and exaggeration to delight and identify with the voters, while depicting his competitors as aristocrats.

Andrew Jackson's egalitarian presidential campaigning had already created some public acceptance of these tactics. Only fragments of Jackson's oratory have been preserved, but contemporary observers noted "the remarkable directness of Jackson's speech making." A modern critic remarked, "Although reviled as an illiterate, this backwoods 'hickory pole' always managed to have a point to make in public discussion and to make his point memorable to those who heard it." As an example, when Vice President Aaron Burr was charged with treason, Jackson's colorful comments alluded to a deeper conspiracy that was attempting to ruin Burr: "This persecution was hatched in Kentucky. The chicken died and they are trying to bring it to life here."[27]

Other distinguished politicians excelled in Tennessee talk, such as James K. Polk, who "told anecdotes to perfection; and . . . was equal to the best on the stump."[28] In 1843, he logged 2,300 Tennessee miles in four months, speaking an average of five hours a day. A rhetorical critic described Andrew Johnson as "indubitably crude, but he talked with a flailing directness the people liked to hear."[29] While many orators depended on biblical, Shakespearean, or classical references, Andrew Johnson, in 1858, attacked Tennessee senator John Bell's appeasement of northern interests with a bit of folk verse:

> He wires in and wires out,
> Leaving the people all in doubt
> Whether the snake that made the track,
> Is going North or coming back.[30]

Tennessee governor and U.S. senator Robert Love Taylor was described as an "incomparable stump speaker. . . . His perennial humor was only the tinsel draping of his power, like the sun-embroidered shawl of mist that wraps Niagara's mighty shoulders."[31] Taylor's speeches and lectures were thick with Old South sentimentalism and New South idealism. They labored under a burden of poetic metaphors and abundant adjectives. Ethnic jokes and personal anecdotes interrupted waves of noble meditations. Out in the district, he could speak more plainly. In a race against Ben Hooper in 1912, he prepared this stump speech: "I'm loaded now for the scrimmage and my gun is seven feet long. I am weighted down with revolvers and bowie knives aplenty. My blessed Red Necks and the boys from town and the drummers from everywhere are spoiling for the fight, and we can whip an army of wildcats before breakfast. The wolves of Republicanism and the goblins of special privilege must hunt for tall timber, must take to the swamps and marshes, for we are going to have a mighty snake-killing in Tennessee."[32]

Taylor's invocation was tongue-in-cheek. Throughout the South, though, inflammatory rhetoric had come into fashion, characterizing a period of demagoguery that took plain-folk appeals beyond Colonel Crockett's strategy to an era of extremism, racism, and exploitation. Though Tennessee figures such as Taylor could produce their fair share of demagoguery, the state never produced demagogic leaders as legendary as Huey P. Long, Eugene Talmadge, George Wallace, or a host of others in neighboring states.

Still, plain-folk styling contributed some of the more memorable moments featuring Tennessee politicians in the second half of the twentieth century. During the 1948 campaign for the U.S. Senate, the Memphis-based political machine of Ed Crump attacked Estes Kefauver with a political advertisement denouncing him as a darling of the Communists, and suggested he was like a pet coon, a deceptive creature slipping a paw into places it did not belong. Kefauver first responded with a joke, "The only thing Red about me is my redheaded wife." He soon delivered this retort to the raccoon analogy:

> This animal—the most American of all animals—has been defamed. You wouldn't find a coon in Russia. It is one of the cleanest of all animals; it is one of the most courageous. . . . A coon . . . can lick a dog four times its size; he is somewhat of a giant-killer among the animals. Yes, the coon is all American. Davy Crockett, Sam Houston, James Robertson and all of our great men of that era in Tennessee history wore the familiar ring-tailed, coon-skin cap. Mr. Crump defames me—but worse than that he defames the coon, the all American animal. We coons can take care of ourselves. I may be a pet coon, but I ain't Mr. Crump's pet coon.[33]

Thereafter, Kefauver kept a coonskin cap on hand for public appearances.

Frank Clement (1920–1969) held the limelight as keynote speaker of the Democratic National Convention held in Chicago in 1956. After praises for the populist programs of his party and sharp attacks on the Republican ticket and ideology, Clement turned to the biblical idiom that typified his speeches in Tennessee. His biographer, Lee Seifert Greene, gives an account of the closing of Clement's speech:

> Finally he came to the phrase, "how long, O, America, shall these things endure"; the phrase "How long" was repeated again and again, as Clement, carried along by the attention and the enthusiasm of the crowd, ran on beyond the ending that [had been] prepared for him. At the final exhortation to "fight, fight, fight," the speaker seemed to be struggling against the increasing impulse of the crowd to start the cheering, and the closing Clement theme-words "Precious Lord, take my hand, and lead me on"—were drowned out in waves of applause.[34]

In Greene's analysis, "The frank use of religious themes, so familiar in Tennessee, failed to please some listeners outside the region." Both Kefauver and Clement were punished to a degree by national pundits and political forces, who found their images to be undignified and provincial.

Speaking from the Pulpit

Religious expression in Tennessee is filled with King James's language and the parables of Jesus, but also includes folk speech, traditional jokes, and personal experience narratives. Tennessee preachers have emulated the greatest white Protestant evangelists in America—Sam Jones, Billy Sunday, and Billy Graham—for their masterful storytelling and humor, "expressed in the language of the shop and field," rather than formal oratory.[35] Equally important in many southern Protestant churches is public testimony describing personal salvation, often including details of a prior sinful life. Testimony as to the blessings of salvation and answered prayers, and of the comfort afforded by faith, can also be presented in narrative form. After all, it was at an African American Methodist church in rural Alexandria, Tennessee, that W. E. B. Du Bois made the observations about the power of the black preacher in his classic work *The Souls of Black Folk* (1903).

An emotional worship style came to the South in 1738 with Oxford evangelist George Whitefield and the Great Awakening, and swept through the Tennessee countryside during the Revival of 1800 and the ensuing camp-meeting era. Camp meetings

The Hunt, by Adrienne Outlaw, 2000. Courtesy of the artist.

Sterling cup, by Kimerlen Moore. Sterling silver, 6 × 3 inches. Courtesy of the artist.

TAPETA, by Arlyn Ende, 1986. Collection of UnumProvident Corporation, Chattanooga. Courtesy of the artist and UnumProvident Corporation, Chattanooga.

Wickham Cemetery, Montgomery County. Funerary sculpture, concrete, by Enoch Tanner Wickham. Photograph by Carroll Van West.

Vase and jug made by Betty Scoville, c. 1885, at Nashville Art Pottery, Davidson County. Vase has a redware body with a green leaf decoration, edged in gold cobwebs, and yellow interior glaze. Incised "Nashville Art Pottery" on base; 5¾ inches high. Jug has a redware body with a brown glaze. Incised "Nashville Art Pottery" on base; 8 inches high. The Art Museum, Princeton University, Trumbull-Prime Collection (#37-141 & #37-137). Photograph by John Blazejewski. Courtesy of The Art Museum, Princeton University.

Red Garden XIX, by Henry Easterwood, 1987. Courtesy of Memphis Brooks Museum of Art; gift of AutoZone, Inc. 2001.15.12.

Fountain B. Carter cherry sugar chest, c. 1830. Courtesy of Rick Warwick.

Schoolhouse, Sarah Moore, c. 1920.
Courtesy of Quilts of Tennessee.

Gahalet. Courtesy of Ballet Tennessee, Chattanooga.

were most notably served by passionate and impulsive exhorters, roles that could be filled by women, children, new converts, both black and white laymen, or professional ministers. With great fervor, exhorters called upon the unconverted to give themselves to Jesus. Ordained clergymen, however, delivered sermons from written texts, providing clear guidance and instruction to new church members. The fragmentary recollections of sermons from early nineteenth-century Tennessee are consistent with the observations of Fredrika Bremer, a Swedish traveler, who wrote "the preachers avoided exciting the people's feelings too much," and "they themselves appeared without emotion."[36] Camp meetings could also include a love feast, allowing for personal testimonial. By the end of the nineteenth century, the structure of worship evolved so that sermonizing, exhortation, prayer, testimonial, and singing became intermixed to varying degrees and followed ritualized patterns that were less formal than those in earlier Anglican or Congregational services or even in some camp meetings.

The distinctive characteristics of southern preaching have been traced to George Whitefield's captivating traits. Benjamin Franklin noted, "His delivery . . . was so improved by frequent repetition that every accent, as every emphasis, every modulation of the voice, was so perfectly well turned that without being interested in the subject, one could not help being pleased with the discourse; a pleasure of much the same kind with that received from an excellent piece of music."[37]

The extemporaneous "Appalachian Sermon Style" of many contemporary Holiness, Pentecostal, and Baptist groups was described as "intensely emotional, extremely rhythmical, and highly physical," with "furious volleys of rhetoric that build, hold for ten or twelve minutes on high plateaus of exuberance, subside, and then build again, over and over."[38] Building a hypnotic rhythm with a forceful "haah" at the end of each spoken line, and sometimes including staccato hand claps, the preacher and congregation reach a blissful connection with the Holy Spirit.

Similar characteristics in African American sermons are pervasive and accepted in the mainstream of that culture. Black political leaders have often been clergymen, and the distinguishing traits of the "performed" or "chanted" sermon can be heard in the speeches of Martin Luther King Jr., Reverend Fred Shuttlesworth, and Reverend Jesse Jackson. Spontaneous, delivered in a pentatonic scale common to Baptist hymns, and fueled by antiphonal response from the congregation or church leaders, the preacher reaches a rhythmic pulse that leads the audience or congregation to an ecstatic response. Scholars have suggested a derivation from African religious cultures where drumming and chanting prepare one for spiritual possession, and stressed the influence of camp meeting practices, which often included African American participation.

Reverend C. L. Franklin (1915–1979), "the most famous preacher of the modern gospel era," the father of Aretha Franklin, and, according to Jesse Jackson,

Church of God in Christ leaders, *left to right:* S. M. Couch, Charles H. Mason, and L. C. Page, 1959. Photograph by Ernest Withers. Courtesy of University of Memphis Libraries, Special Collections.

"the high priest of soul preaching," eloquently used this form from his early years in northern Mississippi, through a three-year tenure in Memphis while also studying at LeMoyne College and, finally, in Detroit. His radio broadcasts and recording for Chess Records exposed millions of listeners to his style, described by a Chess promoter in 1984: "Reverend Franklin can roar like a prophet, and console like a parent. He can employ a range of vocal devices to confound a Shakespearean actor, and proceed from example to explanation with the improvisatory ease of a jazz musician or a poet."[39]

No one ever fell asleep in Reverend Franklin's pews. Tennessee folks have helped to change the character of American rhetoric by insisting upon being themselves in their speech, both informal and in more formal settings such as the political stump and church pulpit. Our full history has been told, but never written with its telling brushed with gorgeous language and accents.

Notes

1. Waldo W. Braden, *The Oral Tradition in the South* (Baton Rouge: Louisiana State Univ. Press, 1983), ix.
2. James A. Shackford and Stanley J. Folmsbee, eds., *A Narrative of the Life of David Crockett of the State of Tennessee* (Knoxville: Univ. of Tennessee Press, 1973). This facsimile edition includes annotation and introductory notes to a volume published by E. L. Carey and A. Hart, Philadelphia, 1834.
3. Ibid., 57.
4. H. E. Warner, "Waste-Basket of Words," *Journal of American Folk-Lore* 2, no. 6 (1889): 229.
5. Joseph S. Hall, "Recording Speech in the Great Smoky Mountains," U.S. National Park Service, Region One, *Regional Review* 3 (1939): 7–8.
6. J. A. Richard, "Suggestions for Collecting Folklore," Tennessee Folklore Society *Bulletin* 1 (Feb. 1935): 5; Addie Suggs Hilliard, "Shakespearean Proverbs in Chester County, Tennessee," *North Carolina Folklore Journal* 22 (May 1974): 63–74; Marion E. Blair, "The Prevalence of Older English Proverbs in Blount County, Tennessee," Tennessee Folklore Society *Bulletin* 4 (Mar. 1938): 1–24.
7. Shackford and Folmsbee, *David Crockett,* 60–64.
8. Harry Harrison Kroll, "How I Collect Proverbial Materials for My Novels," Tennessee Folklore Society *Bulletin* 22 (Mar. 1957): 1–5.
9. Bob Fulcher, "Come Meet Some Very Special Neighbors," *Tennessee Conservationist* 44 (July/August 1979): 4.
10. Richard, "Suggestions for Collecting Folklore," 6.
11. Charles K. Wolfe, ed., *Thomas W. Talley's Negro Folk Rhymes* (Knoxville: Univ. of Tennessee Press, 1991), 236.
12. Ibid., 68, 252, 254.
13. Ibid., 285.
14. See, for example, Lynwood Montell, *The Saga of Coe Ridge: A Study in Oral History* (Knoxville: Univ. of Tennessee Press, 1970), 14.
15. Nathaniel Willis Jones, *A History of Mount Pleasant* (Columbia: Maury County Historical Society, 1965), 69.
16. Robert Cogswell, "Jokes in Blackface: A Discographic Folklore Study" (Ph.D. diss., Indiana Univ., 1984), 71.
17. Ibid., 222, 231, 248.
18. Uncle Dave Macon's dialogue at the beginning of *The Grand Ole Opry,* Republic Films, 1940.
19. Louis Cantor, *Wheelin' on Beale* (New York: Pharos Books, 1992), 9.
20. Ibid., 1.
21. Claude Tomlinson quoted in *Great Day (in the Morning): The Biography and Tales of Claude "The Cat" Tomlinson and WIVK Radio as Told to Donna J. Gentry,* ed. Susan Morton Leonard (Knoxville [?]: Privately published, 1988), 9.
22. Archie Campbell with Ben Byrd, *Archie Campbell* (Memphis: Memphis State Univ. Press, 1981), 61.
23. These commercial pitches were recalled by Alcoa, Tennessee, fiddler Charlie Acuff during an interview with the author in 1999.
24. Cas Walker, *My Life History: "A Book of True Short Stories"* (Knoxville: Privately published, 1993), 13.

25. Shackford and Folmsbee, *David Crockett,* 170–71.
26. Ibid.
27. Andrew Jackson, cited in Thomas M. Lessl, "Andrew Jackson (1767–1845)," in *American Orators Before 1900: Critical Studies and Sources,* ed. Bernard K. Duffy and Halford R. Ryan (Westport, Conn.: Greenwood Press, 1987), 238.
28. James K. Polk, cited in Jones, *History of Mount Pleasant,* 42.
29. Robert T. Oliver, *History of Public Speaking in America* (Boston: Allyn and Bacon, 1965), 327.
30. Joseph H. Parks, *John Bell of Tennessee* (Baton Rouge: Louisiana State Univ. Press, 1950), 324.
31. DeLong Rice, introduction to *Lectures and Best Literary Productions of Bob Taylor* (Nashville: Bob Taylor Publishing, 1912), 10.
32. Ibid., 301.
33. Kefauver cited in Joseph B. Gorman, *Kefauver: A Political Biography* (New York: Oxford Univ. Press, 1971), 48–49.
34. Lee S. Greene, *Lead Me On: Frank Goad Clement and Tennessee Politics* (Knoxville: Univ. of Tennessee Press, 1982), 233–34.
35. Dickson D. Bruce Jr., *And They All Sang Hallelujah* (Knoxville: Univ. of Tennessee Press, 1974), 88.
36. William H. Pipes, *Say Amen, Brother!* (Detroit: Wayne State Univ. Press, 1992), 61.
37. Howard Dorgan, *Giving Glory to God in Appalachia* (Knoxville: Univ. of Tennessee Press, 1987), 56.
38. Albert J. Raboteau, *A Fire in the Bones* (Boston: Beacon Press, 1995), 150.
39. *Reverend C. L. Franklin's Sermons,* promotional sheet, Chess Records, 1984.

Suggested Readings

Abrahams, Roger D. *Deep Down in the Jungle: Negro Narrative Folklore from the Streets of Philadelphia.* Chicago: Aldine Publishing, 1963.

Blair, Marion E. "The Prevalence of Older English Proverbs in Blount County, Tennessee." Tennessee Folklore Society *Bulletin* 4 (Mar. 1938): 1–24.

Brown, Calvin S., Jr. "Dialectal Survivals in Tennessee," *Modern Language Notes* 4, no. 7 (1889): 410–18.

Davis, Gerald L. "I Got the Word in Me and I Can Sing It, You Know": *A Study of the Performed African-American Sermon.* Philadelphia: Univ. of Pennsylvania Press, 1985.

Hall, Joseph Sargent. *The Phonetics of Great Smoky Mountain Speech.* New York: Morningside Heights King's Crown Press, 1942.

Hilliard, Addie Suggs. "Shakespearean Proverbs in Chester County, Tennessee." *North Carolina Folklore Journal* 22 (May 1974): 63–74.

Rosenberg, Bruce A. *Can These Bones Live? The Art of the American Folk Preacher.* Rev. ed. Urbana: Univ. of Illinois Press, 1988.

Wood, Gordon R. *Vocabulary Change: A Study of Variation in Regional Words in Eight of the Southern States.* Carbondale: Southern Illinois Univ. Press, 1971.

Nineteen

A Hunger for Theatricals

Two Hundred Years of the Stage in Tennessee

Antoinette G. van Zelm
Middle Tennessee State University

In the award-winning film *Shakespeare in Love,* theater owner-manager Philip Henslowe pessimistically sums up the theater business: "The natural condition is one of insurmountable obstacles on the road to imminent disaster." He quickly tempers this bleak assessment, however: "Strangely enough, it all turns out well."[1]

The same could be said about the history of the theater in Tennessee. Insufficient performance space and competition from the motion picture industry are just two of the many challenges faced by those Tennesseans who sought to establish theater as a meaningful cultural institution. Yet ever since theater gained a foothold in the nineteenth century, the presentation of live drama has been a constant in Tennessee. As such, the theater provides a vivid microcosm of Tennessee society over the years, illustrating the significance of urbanization, community development, leisure activity, and social hierarchy.

Early Tennessee Theater, 1807–1860

The gradual development of the theater in early Tennessee reflected the gradual growth of the state's towns and cities. The first recorded theater production in Nashville, for example, took place the year after the young city received its charter, when patrons witnessed the comedy *Child of Nature, or Virtue Rewarded* and the farce *The Purse, or the Benevolent Tar* in 1807. During these years, Tennesseans who attended the theater took in a night of varied entertainments. Most performances consisted of a play, followed by a song or dance, and concluded by a farce. As the nineteenth century progressed, Tennesseans also expected to see stars from the New York stage showcase their talents. Actor William Jones, the first acclaimed professional to perform in Nashville, strode the boards there in 1818. Apparently, he was ahead of his time; one actor-manager later recalled his difficulty in attracting established actors from the East because so many viewed Tennessee and Kentucky as uncivilized territories inhabited by "semi-barbarians."[2]

Four men in particular whetted Tennesseans' appetite for the theater from the 1810s to the 1830s. Actor-managers Samuel Drake, Noah M. Ludlow, James Henry Caldwell, and Solomon Franklin Smith brought traveling companies of performers to the new western states and built some of the first theaters in the region.

Drake, a Briton who had established himself in Albany, New York, first brought his company to Nashville in 1816. During July of the following year, part of Drake's troupe visited Nashville for a three-week stint under Ludlow's management. Ludlow, a New York City native, hired carpenters to convert a former salt house on Market Street into a theater. Despite the crudeness of this "Temple of the Muses," the theater attracted a dedicated following among the city's elite, according to Ludlow.[3] Without complaint, he later recalled, women sat through five acts on wooden benches with no back support. In September 1817, Ludlow returned to Nashville with a larger company for a six-week season. During these early years, Nashvillians told Ludlow that they were "hungry" for "theatricals."[4] The citizens of Knoxville had to wait longer than midstate residents for the arrival of a professional company. Drake's company staged the first recorded theatrical performance in Knoxville, in a temporary playhouse, in May 1823.

During the early 1820s, the Irish-born Caldwell began from New Orleans an influential western circuit that eventually included Nashville, Huntsville, St. Louis, and Natchez. Caldwell's troupe first reached Nashville in the summer of 1824 and performed at a theater that had opened four years earlier on Cherry Street. In 1826, Caldwell established his own Nashville theater, modeled after his Camp Street Theater in New Orleans, at the corner of Union and Sumner Streets. His first night was a smash—about six hundred attended—and Caldwell's theater would continue to serve visiting companies as late as 1850.

Solomon F. Smith, affectionately known as "Old Sol" because he acted in old men's parts while in his twenties, arrived in Nashville in about 1819. Hoping to join an acting company, probably Ludlow's, he shortly discovered that it had just left for St. Louis, leaving behind its makeshift theater. Smith returned to Nashville in the summer of 1827 with his own troupe of actors, and the group joined Caldwell's company of performers for the fall season. Opening with the play *Town and Country*, the troupe was apparently successful enough to draw the attention of future president Andrew Jackson. Smith performed an original, political song for Jackson and the other patrons that evening. As the Nashville season came to a close, Smith and several other performers traveled to Clarksville and the Kentucky towns of Russellville and Hopkinsville. In Clarksville, the group performed *The Stranger*, a popular play credited with introducing American audiences to theatrical romanticism, and at least one member of the audience became quite engaged with the performance. As Smith recalled in his memoirs, during the final scene of the play, this patron appealed to the title character to take back his wife.

Sol Smith, engraving, frontispiece, *Theatrical Management in the West and South*, New York, 1868. Library Collection, Tennessee State Library and Archives. Courtesy of TSLA.

Noah Ludlow discovered similar intensity within a Nashville audience in September 1831, when former Secretary of War John H. Eaton and his beleaguered wife Peggy attended the comedy *Honeymoon*. The Eatons had recently left Washington, D.C., where Peggy Eaton had been shunned by society and maligned in the newspapers because of her questionable romantic past. In the second act of the play, Ludlow's character, Duke Aranza, declared, "The man that lays his hand upon a woman, save in the way of kindness, is a wretch, whom it were gross flattery to call a *coward!*"[5] Great applause followed, as the full house of patrons demonstrated their support for Mrs. Eaton and their opposition to the treatment she had received from politicians and journalists in Washington.

In the fledgling towns of Tennessee, Smith's and Ludlow's companies constantly encountered a lack of

Noah M. Ludlow, frontispiece, *Dramatic Life as I Found It*, Benjamin Blom, 1966. Library Collection, Tennessee State Library and Archives. Courtesy of TSLA.

facilities, and, sometimes a lack of customers. In the "very small river town" of Memphis during the spring of 1829, for example, Smith's company played in the house of a local resident and took in just $319 in eight nights.[6] A week of shows in Memphis the next year was more successful, although Smith's actors still had to settle for performing in a temporary theater. In Jackson, in the spring of 1829, "for the first and last time, we performed in a *log* theatre!" Smith recalled.[7] Not that the town of Jackson had a permanent theater; Smith and his crew simply fitted up an accessible log building as a theater. They did the same with a carpenter's shop in Greeneville in 1833. In Tazewell that same year, Smith's company performed songs and recitations in the dining room of a hotel, since there was no place large enough in town for them to put on a play. Only about twenty people attended, and Smith was so low on cash that he had to borrow money from a horse drover to pay for the troupe's breakfast the next morning.

Yet many rural Tennesseans demonstrated an enthusiasm for the theater that must have cheered the performers who roughed it on the traveling circuit. Residents of small towns sometimes implored troupes that were simply passing through to put on a show. Smith recalled that in Somerville in 1829, "the inhabitants insisted on our giving an entertainment, which was attended by the whole village." In Bolivar, "the people seemed to *come out of the woods.*" Smith's troupe actually brought in $349 over a week and a half there.[8] Smith and company found themselves greeted enthusiastically in Bean's Station, where they stopped after crossing Clinch Mountain in 1833. The locals requested a show, despite the fact that no lighting existed in the neighborhood. "We gave an entertainment, consisting of songs, duetts [*sic*], recitations and instrumental music, in TOTAL DARKNESS!" Smith recalled.[9] A large group of men and women attended the show and gave the troupe three cheers for not charging for admission. The next morning Smith discovered that village leaders had paid his company's hotel expenses.

During this early period in southern history, an often-strained relationship existed between newly established theaters and churches that were multiplying across the countryside as a result of the Second Great Awakening. Some churches forbade their members to attend the theater. In Tuscumbia, just south of the state line in Alabama, Smith drew the attention of a female resident, who published a poem to honor his appearance and comedic talent. Her first verse reflected her support for Smith but indicated that opponents to the theater were outspoken as well:

> Let bigots rail against the Stage,
> In senseless declamation dull;
> They ne'er, with all their rant and rage,
> Could calm a heart, like thee, "*Old SOL!*"[10]

A few of Sol Smith's Tennessee experiences reflect the church-theater tension, albeit in a humorous way.

During the fall of 1830, Smith was in Bolivar, where the year previous his brother Lemuel had filled in for him as theater manager. Lemuel, however, told those who asked after Sol that he had been converted and was a preacher. Thus, Bolivar crowds now wanted Old Sol to preach, and once he realized that, he obligingly pulled together a sermon for them at the local courthouse.

In terms of entertainment and emotional fulfillment, church revivals and camp meetings certainly provided competition for traveling companies of performers. In the fall of 1831, Smith's company found that a "religious excitement" kept attendance down during a six-night stint in Tuscumbia.[11] Two years later, in Greeneville, a camp meeting resulted in just a handful of theater patrons two nights in succession. Once the camp meeting ended, a large crowd flocked to the troupe's performance of *William Tell, the Hero of Switzerland,* which was followed by a farce and a set of comic songs. Unfortunately, Smith still lost money that night: the local man he had hired as doorkeeper took his job quite literally and apparently refrained from charging patrons who entered through the windows.

Not all early theater in Tennessee came from traveling companies; residents of some communities started their own amateur companies. In 1818, Noah Ludlow managed an amateur theatrical troupe, the Dramatic Club of Nashville, which included as members young men who later became politically prominent, such as Samuel Houston, whom Ludlow described as "the *largest,* if not the most gifted with dramatic ability."[12] The company staged just two productions before it dissolved out of indifference. The Thespian Society of Memphis, formed by a group of young men in 1829, set up a stage in a warehouse before moving to a building in one of the town's seedier neighborhoods. In 1830, the amateurs received some assistance from Sol Smith, who reorganized the group as the Garrick Club. Despite the new name, the troupe disbanded the next year. By late 1831, Knoxville had an amateur company that performed in a private house on Gay Street.

When Sol Smith and his traveling company reached Columbia during the 1831–32 season, they discovered that a histrionic association had established a "very neat little theatre."[13] The company's next stop, Pulaski, also sported a theater owned by the local thespian society. Smith attended one of the society's performances, which included *Soldier's Daughter* and *Three Weeks after Marriage.* Not surprisingly, the local troupe left Smith unimpressed; he described the costumes, reading, and acting as "ludicrous in the extreme."[14] Smith also provided insight into how local customs influenced both the performance and content of the play. He noted that in one scene, the Pulaskians had altered the play slightly, changing the card game of whist to poker, "a game better understood in that section of country."[15] What is more, only men belonged to the Pulaski thespian society; large boys played the female roles and "strided about in a very peculiar and unfeminine manner."[16] Perhaps Columbia's amateur group also excluded women, for a sixteen-year-old female resident of that town followed Smith to Pulaski, hoping to join his company. He promptly sent her back to her family.

Smith's action reveals how carefully some managers cultivated a good reputation for their companies. Long before the settlement of Tennessee, charges of immorality had been directed at theaters in England and America, sometimes with validity. Criticisms leveled at the theater by evangelical religious leaders in the nineteenth-century United States reinforced the perception that the theater was disreputable. No doubt the transience and low pay associated with most acting companies contributed as well. So did the reality that, as one historian of the antebellum theater has pointed out, "in an age of hard drinking, theater people were notoriously hard drinkers."[17] Not surprisingly, in 1858 a Memphis theater manager drew the opprobrium of the local press when he installed a saloon for his patrons, and he apparently closed down the bar shortly thereafter.

Even individuals who enjoyed the theater or knew intimately its practitioners held the dramatic life in low regard. In his memoir, Noah Ludlow recalled that neither his family nor his wife's approved of the couple's chosen profession as actors. In 1850, a young Nashvillian who was studying in Philadelphia wrote to his sister about some of the cultural activities he was enjoying. Within the same paragraph, he praised the acting of Charlotte Cushman, whom he had gone to see three times, and criticized a female acquaintance for agreeing to marry an actor. "I suppose that she could do no better," he concluded.[18]

Because theater managers were always working within extremely tight budgets and had very small profit margins, they opened their doors to all comers. Thus the possibility existed for members of different social classes to mingle, and for some observers this added to the potential disruptiveness of the theater. Throughout the antebellum period, both free blacks and slaves attended theater productions in urban areas. Especially as permanent structures were constructed during the antebellum period, however, managers made an effort to maintain social distinctions within their facilities by charging different prices for different sections of the house. The Memphis Theatre, for example, charged three different admission prices in 1854: one dollar for private boxes and the parquette section, fifty cents for the upper gallery, and twenty-five cents for the gallery reserved for black patrons.

While the conduct of nineteenth-century patrons varied from theater to theater, audience behavior was decidedly less polite than it became during the following century. A general rowdiness often prevailed. In Memphis, the Market Street Theatre announced in 1837, "No smoking or disorderly conduct allowed in the Theatre. Front seats reserved for the Ladies."[19] In the Bluff City, theaters and other public places were often at the mercy of unruly flatboatmen, who had their run of the city until the consequences of a wharf riot in May 1842 quieted them. Throughout the antebellum South, such disturbances as fights, riots, stabbings, shootings, and drunkenness took place frequently in theaters. And playhouses were far from quiet establishments during dramatic performances, as theatergoers cracked and ate nuts, chatted with each other, and made vocal commentaries on the entertainment before them.

Supporters of the theater defended it vigorously. In September 1831, the *Knoxville Register* printed a statement issued by the city's newly formed amateur thespian society. The group declared that it would elevate morals, not lower them: "The Society intends to select for performances, no pieces that can injure public or private morals or call the blush of shame to the cheek of modesty and worth. They intend on the contrary, to support the cause of virtue, to give instruction of the human character, to lash the vices of society, and to afford innocent amusement by the drama."[20] As the amateurs' pronouncement suggests, dramatic groups often staged plays that delivered a strong moral message. One of the most popular antebellum melodramas was Edward Bulwer-Lylton's *Lady of Lyons; or, Love and Pride.*[21] The play extolled the virtues of the common man and promoted the institutions of marriage, family, and home. Typically, successful plays were both preachy and entertaining.

To enhance further their already shaky reputations, many managers regularly dedicated the proceeds of a night's performance to a local charity or other good cause. In June 1830, for example, James Caldwell's Nashville theater featured a vocalist and an acrobat for six nights, with the last performance designated as a benefit for the residents of Charlotte and Shelbyville, where a tornado had recently touched down. In January 1831, a traveling troupe gave a benefit for the Knoxville Female Academy. The New Memphis Theatre staged several benefits in 1860, including one in support of a home for the homeless and one to raise money for the St. Mary's Church organ fund.

As the nation's trans-Appalachian theater circuit became better established and additional permanent facilities for dramatic productions were constructed, antebellum Tennessee theaters increasingly promoted themselves by advertising the appearance of "star" performers. These included actors and actresses who had made a name for themselves regionally. In October 1851, for instance, an advertisement in the *Memphis*

Daily Appeal announced that a Mrs. M. Stuart of the New Orleans and Mobile theaters would highlight the reopening of the Memphis Theatre.

Players direct from the New York stage, however, drew the largest crowds. Playing limited engagements with resident companies, these actors received tremendous adulation. In December 1851, actress Julia Dean graced Nashville's Adelphi Theatre, which had opened eighteen months earlier. Dean wrapped up her visit with a Saturday night performance that, according to a reporter, attracted "the largest and most brilliant and fashionable audience which has ever assembled in our city to greet any artiste, except Jenny Lind."[22] Dean later took the stage at Nashville's Gaiety Theatre, opened by Irish-born actor-manager William H. Crisp in the winter of 1857. Crisp also booked Charlotte Cushman and the renowned Shakespearean actor Edwin Booth. Booth strode the boards in Memphis as well, at Crisp's one-thousand-seat Gaiety Theater (soon to be renamed the New Memphis Theatre). James Murdoch, a prominent American actor known for his beautiful voice, played to large crowds in Memphis in September 1859. He opened the season at the New Memphis Theatre, starring in Richard Sheridan's *School for Scandal.*

Most of the stars wanted to perform in at least one Shakespeare play during their run at a theater. During their tenure at the Memphis Theatre in 1854, Eliza Logan and Charles John Barton (also known as "C. B.") Hill starred in *Romeo and Juliet.* The tragedy *Hamlet* was on the play list of Emma and Daniel Waller, who had toured in England, Australia, and California before coming to the Gaiety Theater in Memphis in 1858. Booth's two-week Memphis run in 1859 included *King Lear, Richard III,* and *Hamlet.* During his stint at the New Memphis Theatre in that same year, Murdoch performed in both *Hamlet* and *Macbeth.*

By and large, the plays presented in Tennessee theaters reflected programming that was popular throughout the nation, but companies occasionally performed plays with regional themes.

The tragedy *Fall of the Alamo, or the Death of Crockett* played to large crowds in Memphis during the 1840s. Send-ups of Yankee characters amused theater audiences in Memphis in June 1843 and July 1846. In addition, it appears that the increasing antebellum dissension over slavery proved to be fodder for the playwright. While a play based on Harriet Beecher Stowe's antislavery novel *Uncle Tom's Cabin* never reached as far south as Tennessee, burlesques of the novel, and plays that rebutted its negative portrayal of slavery, did appear in the slaveholding states. Actor George Jamison brought his play *The Old Plantation; or Uncle Tom As He Is* to Memphis in 1855. The play featured a runaway slave who chose to return to slavery after finding it too difficult to make a living in the North. In contrast, Robert Montgomery Bird's play *The Gladiator,* which had an abolitionist undercurrent, was not staged south of St. Louis after 1847.

During the late antebellum period, theaters in Tennessee gained new competitors in traveling circuses, burlesque, and minstrel shows. When Julia Dean captivated audiences at the Adelphi Theatre in Nashville in 1851, for instance, the reporter who covered Dean's appearance noted that the simultaneous performances of Spaulding's Circus were "more congenial with the taste of a larger portion of our citizens than any other amusement which has ever been offered in our city."[23] In Memphis during the same period, Dan Rice's Circus competed with the opening of the Memphis Theatre, and that playhouse opened its dramatic season in 1856 with the Christy Minstrels.

Other competing forms of entertainment included concerts, ventriloquists, panoramas, and dioramas. In addition, showboats with a variety of exhibits on board drew appreciative crowds. Some of these diversions were also instructional: panoramas presented at Odd Fellows' Hall in Memphis in 1859–60 included *Pilgrim's Progress* and *Scenes from the Arctic Regions.*

When patronage slackened, managers of theaters that focused on literary or "legitimate" drama sometimes put on plays that featured special effects or scheduled variety acts. Sol Smith recalled that he had always tried to present legitimate drama but had sometimes been compelled to give in to public will and lower his standards. In March 1855, James S. Charles, manager of the Memphis Theatre, tried to boost lagging attendance by pairing a play featuring actress Annette Ince with a show of Bartholomew's Trained Dogs and Monkeys. The usually supportive *Memphis Appeal* described it as a "most unfortunate" engagement for a respectable theater: "If learned dogs and monkeys are on a par with 'star' actresses, we claim to be no longer a lover of the drama."[24]

Decades of Decline, 1860–1920

The Civil War brought significant changes to Tennessee theater. Many experienced players and managers headed North and less talented amateurs and semiprofessionals replaced them. The star system of visits by New York–based actors did not end, but it became much less prominent. Theater benefits became war-related, as local citizens sought to raise funds to clothe and equip soldiers at the front.

During the first year of the war, within the Confederacy only Nashville, Richmond, and New Orleans held regular theatrical seasons. The former Gaiety Theater, which had closed in 1860, reopened as the Nashville Theatre in September 1861. Its resident troupe, the Southern Star Company, performed well for manager Walter Keeble, who mostly scheduled standard shows. Few productions made reference to the war. The hostilities intruded soon enough, however. Union troops captured Fort Donelson in February 1862, and the Nashville Theatre closed soon afterward. Later in the month, federal troops occupied Nashville itself.

The occupying forces reopened the Nashville Theatre in April 1862. Most of its patrons had some relationship to the federal military; few local residents attended. Many Nashvillians could no longer afford to attend the theater; others shunned it because they associated it with the occupying forces. Union soldiers, serving as musicians and actors, appeared in some of the Nashville Theatre's productions. Other soldiers did the playhouse far less proud: it closed for about six weeks during the fall of 1862 after some drunken soldiers beat up black patrons at a performance.

Once the Nashville Theatre reopened, it thrived throughout the war. Gen. Ulysses S. Grant took in a performance when he was in the city in December 1863. A few months later, actor John Wilkes Booth drew large crowds during a two-week run at the theater. He performed both comedy and tragedy, including *Richard III,* a play and role made famous by John Wilkes's father, the legendary Junius Booth. The younger Booth staged a benefit at the Nashville Theatre on February 12, 1864, then left the city for Cincinnati. Although Booth had been arrested during the war in both Buffalo and St. Louis for anti-Union actions and speeches, he apparently did nothing to attract the attention of Nashville military authorities.

In May 1863, a second theater opened in Nashville at the Odd Fellows' Hall as the New Nashville Theatre, featuring a resident company of performers. Both theaters drew capacity crowds until the end of the war. During the 1863–64 season, equestrian shows were popular at the New Nashville, while ghost plays had a run at the Nashville Theatre.

After the Union army took control of Memphis in June 1862, the New Memphis Stock Company, the resident company at the New Memphis Theatre, disbanded. The army captain in charge of the theater hired new performers but had to do without the stars who once frequented the playhouse. While the theater staged similar plays to those shown before the war, it also presented an increasing number of novelties and spectacles. At the same time, the city saw the establishment of its first concert-saloons, also known as low varieties, which catered to a male audience by featuring shows of singing and dancing girls. During the war, variety theater also became more prominent in Nashville. In the spring of 1865, two variety houses opened in the city, the Nashville Opera House and Poland's Variety Theatre.

After the Civil War, the theatre encountered a new set of challenges. First, difficult economic times placed Tennessee theaters and their resident companies of performers in jeopardy. Three of the four theaters in operation in Nashville in the spring of 1865 had closed by the end of 1866. Not long after the end of the war, the New Memphis Theatre underwent renovations and raised ticket prices to $1.50. The theater's resident stock company came together again, and stage stars signed up for engagements. The theater could not recapture its previous success, however, in part because of its high ticket prices. The 1868–69 season ended with the dissolution of the resident stock company, and new managers incorporated the theater into a circuit that included New Orleans and St. Louis.

Other challenges included the lack of large performance halls to accommodate growing urban populations and the increasingly extravagant productions staged by theater and opera companies. In the late 1860s, for example, newspapers in Knoxville lamented that the city had no large performance space. Businessman Peter Staub changed all that in 1872, when he built a three-story opera house with a seating capacity of fourteen hundred. The Knoxville Histrionic Society performed *William Tell* for the grand opening on October 1, 1872. Similarly, private funds gave rise to the Vendome Theatre in Nashville. The program for opening night in October 1887 read, "For some years the demand for a theatre commensurate with the rising pretensions of Nashville has been patent; of late the necessity a subject of comment."[25] After concluding that the public would not finance a suitable playhouse, eight men had joined together as shareholders to build the theater. The Grand English Opera Company, which was headlined by singer Emma Abbott, opened the theater with a week of performances. In Memphis, the Greenlaw Opera House opened in 1866 with a seating capacity of twenty-five hundred; however, it only hosted two productive theater seasons, in addition to numerous vaudeville acts, some girlie shows, and several temperance rallies, before it burned down in the early 1880s.

After war and reconstruction, star performers returned to Tennessee and attracted large crowds once again. On his grand tour of the South in 1876, Edwin Booth came to Tennessee and attracted a lot of attention, both because of his stature as an actor and his status as the brother of the late John Wilkes Booth, assassin of President Abraham Lincoln. Edwin Booth, who wanted to perform in Nashville in tribute to his father's esteem for Andrew Jackson, found himself received enthusiastically in both Nashville and Chattanooga, where a brass band greeted his train. Chaos and minor violence broke out in Nashville when tickets for Booth's performances went on sale on February 22, 1876. His appearance in *Hamlet* at the Masonic Theatre drew the greatest interest. Five years later, in February 1881, the internationally renowned Sarah Bernhardt performed in *Camille* at Nashville's Grand Opera House. Patrons and critics loved the show. Bernhardt also appeared in Memphis, where wealthy white patrons hired black "watchers" to stand in line and purchase tickets for them. The "Divine Sarah" reprised the role of Camille twenty-five years later at the Ryman Auditorium in Nashville.[26] In 1896, "prima donna" Lillian Russell, who starred in such musicals as *The Grand Duchess* and *Princess Nicotine,* graced the stage in Memphis.[27]

A resident of turn-of-the-century Nashville, Emma Hicks McDonald, recalled in memoirs that her father had taken her to see several stars, including Joseph Jefferson in his famous role as Rip Van Winkle and Kitty Cheatham, a singer/ actress who was the most acclaimed contemporary player to hail from Nashville. Jefferson, who has been described as "one of the greatest character artists the stage has ever known," attracted large, appreciative crowds to his appearances in Nashville throughout the 1880s and early 1890s.[28] Of the outing to see Cheatham, McDonald wrote, "The most exciting night was the one [my father] took my mother and me to hear or see our very own Kitty Cheatham who was playing in the *Black Crook*. . . . It was shocking to the old folks."[29] Although the *Black Crook* included elegant costumes and graceful dance routines, it ushered

Kitty Cheatham, from *The Marie Burroughs Art Portfolio of Stage Celebrities,* 1894.

in the vaudeville era and has been described as "the grandfather of modern musical comedy."[30] Cheatham was not unique among actors of the literary theater in contributing their talents to vaudeville shows during this period.

Drama purists pointed to the *Black Crook* and other variety shows as examples of a decline in the theater after the Civil War. First minstrel shows, then vaudeville acts, and finally motion pictures all competed with "legitimate," or literary, drama for patrons. Audiences thrilled at spectacles presented by the gymnasts, jugglers, acrobats, ventriloquists, magicians, and trapeze performers who took the stage at minstrel and vaudeville shows. In addition, the price was right, with admission to vaudeville shows (and later movies) usually about five or ten cents and never more than fifty cents. This was much cheaper than the cost of literary dramas. In addition, some variety shows attracted patrons by sponsoring give-away programs at the performances; in Memphis during the 1860s and 1870s, audience members won such items as silverware, cash, jewelry, furniture, and even live pigs.

In response to vaudeville, some theaters focusing on literary drama offered plays that incorporated stunning special effects or emphasized the spectacular in other ways. Noah Ludlow, veteran of early theater companies in Tennessee, criticized late-nineteenth-century patrons as being "corrupted with *fast times,* sensational dramas, and easy, cushioned chairs."[31] Some theaters offered variety acts in addition to traditional plays. Yet that strategy could be a double-edged sword; should a theater present too many mass-entertainment attractions, it could lose the patrons who preferred literary drama. This happened to Leubrie's Theater (formerly the Memphis Theater) in the late 1880s and early 1890s, when it began to have difficulty booking top performers and touring companies because they could make significantly more money in larger cities. Leubrie's in turn scheduled shows to attract a mass audience, including an aquatic production entitled *A Dark Secret* in 1890 and "Lily Clay's aggregation of women who are symmetrical and don't care who knows it" in 1891.[32] The latter show attracted a full house of men and women (including more than 150 standees) but turned out not to be as risque as expected.

Despite the popularity of vaudeville, classical plays still found their way to the stage in Tennessee. In Nashville in 1904, the "Classes in Expression" at Belmont College presented Oliver Goldsmith's *She Stoops to Conquer or, The Mistakes of a Night.* The next year Rudolph E. Magnus and his company of players performed *Everyman,* a fifteenth-century morality play, at Nashville's Watkins Hall.

In addition to such traditional dramas, Tennessee theaters sometimes showcased contemporary pieces that reflected turn-of-the-century social concerns. The near-obsession of white southerners with the place of

Kitty Cheatham

WITH HER "SWEET SOPRANO VOICE," NASHVILLE NATIVE CATHERINE "KITTY" CHEATHAM CAPTIVATED audiences around the world as an interpretive performer of children's songs.[1] Cheatham began her career in comic opera and then moved on to dramatic comedy. She found her niche, however, as a writer, translator, and singer of children's songs.

Born in 1866, Cheatham was the daughter of Richard Boone Cheatham, who surrendered Nashville to the Union army, and Frances Bugg Cheatham. After the death of her father, Cheatham and her mother left Nashville for New York City so that seventeen-year-old Kitty might try her luck on the stage. She joined John McCaull's successful Opera Comique Company, first appearing in the *Black Hussar.* Later, as a member of Augustin Daly's famous company, she gained success as Kate in Alfred Tennyson's work *The Foresters* and played understudy to renowned comedienne Ada Rehan.

By the early twentieth century, Cheatham had established herself as a singer of children's songs. Touring the major cities of the United States and Europe, she drew on a repertoire of more than one thousand songs in nine languages. She highlighted the works of American composers and became one of the first white artists to sing Negro spirituals abroad. Cheatham performed children's concerts for the New York Philharmonic and the Philadelphia Symphony, among other orchestras. She led large community sings and conducted several choral groups.

Cheatham's work in the arrangement of original orchestral programs was considered pioneering. She and Walter Prichard Eaton adapted E. T. A. Hoffmann's fairy tales to music. While Cheatham herself wrote several songs and anthems, she regularly performed songs composed for her by others. All but four of the songs in *Kitty Cheatham, Her Book* (1915) were written for her, and she hoped to advance the careers of young American composers through publication of the book. Cheatham's *A Nursery Garland* (1917) included folk songs from several countries, spirituals, lullabies, and dances. A Christian Scientist, she regularly included Christian themes in her songs and other works.

Cheatham traveled, studied, and lectured abroad, and she used her performances and writings to promote the theme of universality. In 1918, she published *Words and Music of "The Star-Spangled Banner" Oppose the Spirit of Democracy Which the Declaration of Independence Embodies*, arguing that the national anthem threatened the wartime alliance between the United States and Great Britain. Despite her broad world view and her residence in the North, Cheatham identified herself as a "loyal loving daughter" of Tennessee.[2] At her death in 1946, she remained one of the state's best-known ambassadors of song.

Antoinette G. van Zelm, Middle Tennessee State University

Notes

1. *The Marie Burroughs Art Portfolio of Stage Celebrities: A Collection of Photographs of the Leaders of Dramatic and Lyric Art* (Chicago: A. N. Marquis, 1894).
2. Inscription by Kitty Cheatham to the Tennessee State Library, Jan. 1, 1935, in *Kitty Cheatham, Her Book* (New York: G. Schirmer, 1915).

black southerners in society was reflected in at least two programs from this period: *The Clansman,* by Thomas Dixon, Jr., a favorable portrayal of the Ku Klux Klan that later became the groundbreaking film *Birth of a Nation,* and *Negro Folk Song . . . and . . . Sketches from Plantation Life,* by Caroline Lewis Gordon, which celebrated the allegedly happy days of slavery. On a more local level, theaters in Middle Tennessee participated in the crusade to honor the memory of President Andrew Jackson and preserve his former home, the Hermitage. "Costume concerts" to raise funds for the Ladies' Hermitage Association featured occasional recitations as well as songs by performers who wore Tennessee-related historic costumes and jewelry. On May 10, 1889, for example, Mason's Opera House in Murfreesboro hosted one of these benefits. Similar costume concerts, including one to benefit the United Daughters of the Confederacy, took place at the Ryman Auditorium in later years. Another show with local historical significance was the "Sam Davis Drama," which lionized the "Boy Hero of the Confederacy" and was presented in Murfreesboro in 1897.[33]

Turn-of-the-century rural audiences enjoyed "rube dramas" presented by traveling companies that performed under canvas tents.[34] These tent-show plays exploited such rural themes as the glorification of home life and the suspicion of urban ways. Geared to families, tent-show performances flourished in particular between 1900 and 1910. They brought theater to small communities throughout the South. In addition to the "rube dramas," tent-show companies presented uncopyrighted melodramas, comedy-dramas written by the performers themselves, and

The Little Foxes, with Steven Hauck as Horace Giddens, Nan Gurley as Birdie Hubbard, and Persephone Felder-Fentress as Addie. Photograph by David Grapes. Courtesy of Tennessee Repertory Theatre.

The Traveling Toby Tent Show

The traveling tent show, found throughout the southern and midwestern United States, was a major theatrical force that was responsible for keeping rural theater alive from before the turn of the twentieth century through the 1930s. The term "Toby show," in its heyday, denoted a traveling vaudeville-type melodramatic tent show featuring a character called Toby. Toby is defined in *The Oxford Companion to the Theatre,* which draws from material by Robert Downing, as "a stock character in the folk theatre of the United States, a bucolic comedy juvenile leading man in provincial repertory companies of the Mississippi Valley and the Great Southwest."[1] Though many scholars thought the last traveling tent company retired from the road in 1963, in fact there were a very few companies that struggled, with the assistance of private and governmental funding, into the 1990s. The last remaining traveling tent show company is the Hard Corn Players currently based in rural Robertson County, Tennessee.

Toby was the star of the tent show. The plays presented in nearly all Toby/tent companies began as popular scripted melodramas with the Toby character added. Later, due to Toby's popularity, tent show troupers began writing plays for him. Toby shows were placed in rural settings and addressed the unique and important qualities of country life and rural values. Toby personified rural values including honesty, integrity, and responsibility. The character description of Toby was standard. He was portrayed as a red-headed, freckled-faced, silly-kid, rube character. His costume and make-up consisted of four basic elements: a red wig, freckles, a blacked-out tooth, and baggy, tattered clothing. Because of these conventions, the audience recognized Toby the minute he appeared on the stage. Though each Toby actor employed these costume and make-up basics, their characters variously reflected their respective conceptions of Toby and regions wherein they performed. In the southern Appalachians, for instance, the Toby character was often a

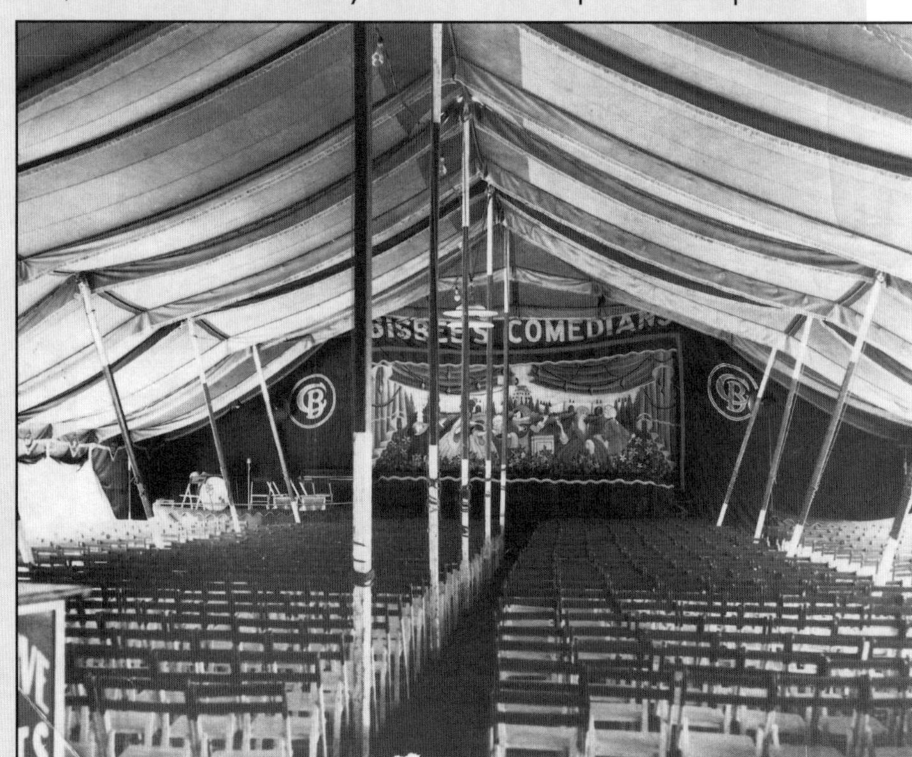

Traveling Toby Tent Show interior for the Bisbee's Comedians. Courtesy of Dawn Larsen and the Theatre Museum of Repertoire Americana.

hillbilly. Toby's comic antics were also a major trait of his character. He was well known for his low comedy. The Toby actor, "with his stock of winks, facial contortions and other tricks acquired through long experience on the boards, always brought the audience to life."[2] Fellow troupers knew Boob Brasfield (sometimes called the "king of Tobys") to be a master of comic facial expression: "He would hitch up his baggy britches, stare stupidly across the footlights and the audience would scream with laughter."[3]

Billy Choate, longtime Toby and manager of Bisbee. Courtesy of Dawn Larsen and the Theatre Museum of Repertoire Americana.

Though tent shows were most popular during the first two decades of the twentieth century, Toby shows peaked somewhat later, in the late 1920s and through the 1930s. The genre began in the late nineteenth century with the rural and small-town Americans' desire for entertainment at their local "opera houses," places where New York touring theatrical companies to smaller opera house repertory companies offered amusements and entertainment. The progression from permanent opera house to temporary canvas theater seems to have occurred for two reasons. First, since opera houses were hot in the summer, they often closed for that season. A tent could provide a well-ventilated performance space and an extended season. Second, and more significant, a tent provided a company a place to perform in towns that boasted no theater or community building, most especially those in the rural South. The most significant increase in the numbers of companies touring came a decade later, due to the agricultural prosperity ignited by World War I and the development of the automobile, which allowed theater companies to expand their circuits to those smaller communities throughout rural America not supported by the railroad.

Though statistics are somewhat contradictory, most scholars cite the Great Depression as the beginning of the end of the tent show. The depression hit the smaller tent companies hard, and many companies folded simply due to lack of funds because rural audiences could no longer afford the luxury of a ticket. Later, movies and automobiles became much more affordable and accessible to individuals in rural communities and so contributed to the tent show's demise. In the late 1950s, television came to the rural community, so it was more convenient and at least initially exciting to sit in your own home and be entertained. The few remaining companies that were on the road in the 1950s were very successful, however, since there was little competition for territory.

One of those remaining companies, Choate's Comedians, later the Bisbee's Comedians, was the largest and best-known tent company to travel rural Tennessee. In show manager Billy Choate's book, *Born in a Trunk,* he described their show's territory and season: "The Bisbee show opened at Lexington, Tennessee the first of April and closed at Collierville, Tennessee the last of October."[4] Various versions of the Choate show, led by Choate's grandfather and father before him, traveled from the spring of 1882 to 1966 through towns in Tennessee including: Lexington, Collierville, Halls, Union City, Obion, Ripley, Russelville, Moscow, Adamsville,

[Continued on next page]

Dyersburg, Parsons, Linden, Hohenwold, Dickson, Waverly, Camden, Bruceton, and McKenzie. Though based in Illinois, they often wintered and rehearsed for the coming season in Memphis. Their show employed many famous tent rep show people including Boob (Lawrence) Brasfield, brother of Grand Ole Opry favorite, Rod Brasfield. Billy Choate presently lives in his hometown of Wayne City, Illinois, performing Toby show benefits yearly for the Wayne City firemen.

The Hard Corn Players have toured and performed in Illinois, Kentucky, and Tennessee since 1991. They are reintroducing this form of theater to rural families by bringing the last of the old-time tent shows to communities in Tennessee.

Dawn Larsen, Volunteer State Community College

Notes

1. Phyllis Hartnoil, ed., *The Oxford Companion to the Theatre* (London: Oxford Univ. Press, 1957), 17.
2. Carol Pennepacker, "A Surviving Toby Show: Bisbee's Comedians," Tennessee Folklore Society *Bulletin* 30 (1964): 50.
3. Jere C. Mickel, "The Genesis of Toby," *Journal of American Folklore* (Oct./Nov. 1967): 155.
4. Billy Choate, *Born in a Trunk* (Kearny, N.J.: Morris, 1994), 2

bootlegged New York stage hits. The companies usually performed vaudeville routines between acts of the featured play.

Eventually motion pictures presented a most difficult challenge to live dramatic performances, but early on the line between the two forms of entertainment was not clearly drawn, and films were not necessarily successful. In March and April 1897, just a year after film's successful debut in New York, actor-manager Oliver Taylor toured films in East Tennessee under the auspices of his short-lived Cineograph Film Company. Taylor did the narration for the films and performed character recitations to keep the audience entertained between the film selections. By the 1910s, however, movie theaters increasingly outnumbered playhouses in Tennessee's cities and towns. In a rather ironic twist, the program for a Kitty Cheatham recital in Nashville in 1915 included an advertisement for The Parthenon, "Nashville's Quality Theater" and site of "The World's Greatest photo PLAYS."[35] The juxtaposition of one of the stage's local stars with a movie palace that claimed to have invested thirty thousand dollars in equipment underscores the transitional nature of the entertainment world in the early twentieth century.

Theater managers who staged live performances tried their best to compete with the new movie palaces. In Knoxville in 1919, residents could see a silent film at any of at least four different theaters and attend such lowbrow musicals as *The Whirly Girly Show* at Staub's Theatre, which desperately tried to stay afloat. Even Knoxville's beautifully designed Bijou Theatre, which opened in 1909 with a seating capacity of sixteen hundred, began to show movies, often in conjunction with vaudeville shows, just six years after opening. In Nashville, the Grand Theatre became the Little Grand Theatre in 1908, with a program of vaudeville and movies, and the Vendome Theatre was turned into a movie hall in 1919. By 1920, there were no theaters left in Nashville dedicated to the production of plays, and nine years later, the last performance by a resident stock company for decades took place in the city. For many years during the middle part of the twentieth century, the Ryman Auditorium was the only venue in the city to stage professional literary theater, and it did so only occasionally. Productions between 1920 and 1955 included *Victoria Regina* and *Mary of Scotland,* both starring Helen Hayes, and *Romeo and Juliet,* with Katharine Cornell and Maurice Evans.

The Theater Revival and the Rise of Community Theater, 1920–2000

From the mid-1920s to the 1960s, the theater experienced a mild renewal through the little theater movement of community-based, amateur drama groups and the growth of academic theater programs at colleges and universities. The University of Tennessee in Knoxville, for example, instituted a theater program as part of its curriculum during this period. The program drew on a long tradition of student dramatic performances, which had been staged by literary societies and dramatic clubs since 1836. The university theater staff joined with local citizens to establish a university-community theater program, based at the Carousel Theater. The Carousel, constructed on the university campus in 1952, was a theater-in-the-round whose walls could be removed for open-air productions during the summer. During the 1950s and 1960s, the theater staged more than two hundred shows, and annual attendance rose to more than seventy thousand. Among the theater's annual offerings was a selection of children's plays. Notably, the Carousel was one of the first theaters in the South to integrate racially, both on stage and within the audience.

In Nashville, twenty little theater groups had been established by 1939, and they had joined to form the Nashville Community Playhouse, Incorporated. Among its fledgling members was the Nashville Children's Theater, created by the local Junior League in 1931. During its early years, the theater presented plays featuring child actors. The city of Nashville acknowledged the group's success in 1960 by building it a permanent playhouse, the first theater in the United States designed specifically for children's programming. Later known as the Nashville Academy Theatre (but presently known again as the Nashville Children's Theatre), it began to employ adult professionals in plays for children. Annual attendance by the mid-1990s reached more than 130,000.

A similar story took place in Chattanooga, where the Little Theatre of Chattanooga began in 1923. The

Carousel Theater. Courtesy of Special Collections, University of Tennessee, Knoxville.

company mounted productions on a regular basis to a small but loyal audience and established a well-respected Youth Theatre aimed at young actors and crews and school audiences. By the end of the century, the company had evolved into one of the largest in the state, the Chattanooga Theatre Center, located in a multi-million-dollar facility along the banks of the Tennessee River in downtown Chattanooga. The center provides classes, workshops, and summer camps as well as a large education outreach program. It mounts more than eighteen productions a year, attracting more than fifty thousand people in 2001.

Another East Tennessee little theater began in Oak Ridge in September 1943. Government workers, who had come to the area as part of the Manhattan Project, organized the Little Theatre of Oak Ridge. For its first performance, the actors put on a talent show/cabaret as a benefit. Next the group staged the play *Arsenic and Old Lace.* All productions group adopted the Oak Ridge Community Playhouse as its new name, and ten years later it bought and renovated an abandoned movie theater as its permanent home. A dramatic group taking over a former movie house certainly suggested that times had improved for playgoers.

By late in the twentieth century, professional theater had returned to many of Tennessee's cities, and amateur theater had become increasingly sophisticated. The amateur Theatre Memphis, which began as the Memphis Little Theatre during the 1920s, became a more permanent and diverse institution during the 1970s and 1980s. After having been housed in various buildings (including a converted swimming pool) for fifty years, the theater opened its season in September 1975 in a building designed specifically for it. The new four-hundred-seat playhouse was located on the border of one of the city's public parks. Beginning in 1984, the theater began to sponsor a triennial new play competition that was so successful that submissions reached five hundred in 1987.

The Oak Ridge Community Playhouse provides another example of a little theater that expanded and excelled late in the twentieth century. In June 1995,

Parallel Lives: The Kathy and Mo Show, first performed in April 2000, followed by two HBO specials. The Memphis version featured Jenny Odle Madden *(left)* and Kim Justis *(right),* who play dozens of roles while looking "very, very pretty." Photograph by Steve Roberts. Courtesy of Theatre Memphis.

the theater group won first place at the American Association of Community Theatre Festival for its production of *Falsettoland,* a Tony Award–winning musical about the lives of seven people and the effect of AIDS on their relationships. Oak Ridge successfully staged the musical in October 1994. Not only did the playhouse organization win critical and popular acclaim, it also evolved into a vital, year-round arts institution. Its season ran from June to May, and it offered a variety of productions through its Mainstage, Junior Playhouse, and Footlight Series. The Oak Ridge company also worked with the local high school to produce two plays each year.

Of more recent vintage but equally notable for its growth toward greater strength as a community institution, the Road Company of Johnson City developed from a two-week project in 1972 to a partnership with the local Parks and Recreation Department twenty years later. With a mission to produce original plays about the history and culture of Northeast Tennessee, the company explored such themes as democracy on the frontier and the moonshine trade.

Another successful community theater venture began in Memphis during the 1960s, when high school student Jackie Nichols and some friends started a dramatic group called the Circuit Players. While at Memphis State University, Nichols continued the troupe, which put on such avant-garde works as a rock music production of *The Fantasticks* and the anti–Vietnam War play *We Bombed New Haven.* In November 1975, Nichols began a professional offshoot of his Circuit, Inc., organization when the Playhouse on the Square opened with a performance of *Godspell.* During the 1980s and 1990s, both Circuit Playhouse (the community theater) and Playhouse on the Square (the professional theater) instituted a range of educational programs, sponsored one of the few theaters of the deaf in the country, and instituted programs to increase accessibility to theatergoers with limited means.

In Tennessee's largest cities, community theaters offered a stunning diversity of drama. In Nashville, for example, the Epiphany Players produced Christian plays, often in area churches. The Actors' Playhouse, meanwhile, staged controversial plays and the more obscure works by modern playwrights. Theatre Parthenos performed outdoor shows at Nashville's replica of the Parthenon. During the summers, the Nashville Shakespeare Festival gave free performances in Centennial Park.

Although professional theater had reached its nadir during the first half of the twentieth century, by the 1970s a resurgence was visible, and the number of professional offerings continued to increase over the next thirty years. A striking variety of professional endeavors originated throughout the state. In Knoxville, the Bijou Theatre Center sponsored a resident company dedicated to staging plays related to literature requirements at regional schools, housed a school of theater arts for teens and children, and offered rental space for visiting performing arts groups. The oldest commercial building in downtown Knoxville, the Bijou had gone from being a vaudeville theater in 1909 to an adult movie theater in the 1970s before being renovated to become the only not-for-profit performing arts center in East Tennessee. Also in Knoxville, the Carpetbag Theatre began as a forum for cultural expression by African Americans. It staged original plays about the black experience and took them on tour nationally and abroad. Works produced by the theater tackled such difficult themes as domestic violence, access to the marketplace for people of color, the effect of the death penalty on African American life, and the influence of black feminism. In West Tennessee, the Blues City Cultural Center carries out a similar cultural mission for bringing the theater to urban and rural African Americans. The Black Repertory Company began in Memphis in 1998 as an offshoot of Playhouse/Circuit theater, with Tony Horne as managing director and Harry Bryce as artistic director. The company's first season as an independent entity came in 2000–2001. It performs African American musicals and drama for adults and children in venues across Memphis.

One of the most successful theatrical experiments in the state took place in rural Crossville with the development of the Cumberland County Playhouse, which opened as a summer theater in 1965. Established by Paul Crabtree, it developed into an extensive performing arts center that included three theaters, as well as production facilities and studios. Called the "miracle on the mountain," the playhouse featured works related to Tennessee history, such as the musical *Tennessee, USA!* and the *Spirit of the Mountains.*[36]

In the Nashville metropolitan area, theatergoers by 1990 could choose from twenty-four theatrical organizations. Among these, the leading professional theater complex was the Tennessee Performing Arts Center, which had opened in 1980. The state-owned center boasted three theaters: Andrew Jackson Hall, which hosted Broadway shows; James K. Polk Theater, which featured the professional Tennessee Repertory Theater; and Andrew Johnson Theater, home of the Circle Players, Nashville's oldest community dramatic group.

Establishing itself as the single most influential company in Nashville, and the largest of the state's professional companies, the Tennessee Repertory Theater, by the beginning of the twenty-first century, was producing a full season of theater, from off-

Broadway comedies and dramas to contemporary musicals. Established in the mid-1980s by artistic director Mac Pirkle and arts patron Martha Rivers Ingram, The Rep (as it is known) was the South's fourth-largest theater company by 2001. Pirkle left the company in 1998 and was replaced by David Grapes, who began to shift The Rep's productions to be more "actor-centered and more literature-centered," as Grapes told an interviewer in the April 2001 issue of *Stage Directions.* In 2001–2002, the company collaborated with the Nashville Symphony on *West Side Story* and mounted productions of *The Miracle Worker, Dinner with Friends,* and *God's Man in Texas.* The Rep also has expanded its educational and community outreach programs.

The capital city is also home to the American Negro Playwright Theater, founded by the influential African American actor and playwright Barry Scott. Scott's company in the late 1990s developed a solid regional reputation for innovative productions and a willingness to delve into meaningful issues. Black Taffeta and Burlap, established by Stella Reed in 1990, is another African American company in Nashville.

In Nashville and throughout the state, the link between the theater and education became stronger in the late twentieth century. Collaborations took place between community theaters and local colleges and universities. Many theaters instituted educational programs for elementary and secondary students. Good examples are the various educational outreach initiatives of Theatre Bristol, which mounts its productions at the historic Paramount Center for the Arts. Training opportunities for individuals planning an acting career also increased. Aspiring actors or players hoping to refine their skills could attend classes at Nashville's Acting Studio, founded in 1980. The studio also offered the Young Adults Professional Program for high school students. By 1986, prospective actors could audition for acceptance at the Acting Studio Conservatory, a full-time program that included participation in Tennessee Repertory Theater productions. The Repertory Theater also managed its Humanities Outreach in Tennessee program, which brought theater to hundreds of thousands of students.

Although the late twentieth century saw a renewal of interest in live theater, it was also a period in which the theater had to compete with an increasingly powerful home entertainment industry. The lure of cable television, videocassettes, and Internet access kept many people on their couches rather than out on the town. In addition, many theaters remained underfunded, with some companies seemingly getting by on devotion and determination alone. Yet, "strangely enough, it all turns out well"; locally produced theater continues to expand statewide. Residents of Clarksville enjoy the Roxy Theater, while in Covington patrons attend productions at the Ruffin Theater, a former movie theater restored to showcase the performing arts in the late 1980s. Now in its second decade, the Cannon County Center for the Arts in Woodbury has won acclaim for its dramatic and musical productions. In Union City, the recently restored Capitol Theater features a variety of performing arts shows. Restoration of the art deco–styled Crockett Theater, formerly a movie house, has brought the stage to life in Lawrenceburg; a similar process began in 2001 with the reopening of the historic Palace Theater in Crossville.

At the start of the twenty-first century, theater in Tennessee also continues to serve as an important microcosm of society. The number and variety of theater offerings reflect the diversity of cultural backgrounds and interests among the citizens of contemporary Tennessee.

NOTES

1. Marc Norman and Tom Stoppard, *Shakespeare in Love,* directed by John Madden, 122 min., Miramax Films, 1998, videocassette.
2. Noah M. Ludlow, *Dramatic Life as I Found It* (St. Louis: 1880; reprint, with introduction and index by Francis Hodge, New York: Benjamin Blom, 1966), 172.
3. Ibid., 113.
4. Ibid., 174.

5. Ibid., 387.
6. *The Theatrical Journey-Work and Anecdotical Recollections of Sol. Smith, Comedian, Attorney at Law, etc., etc.* (Philadelphia: T. B. Peterson & Brothers, 1854), 34.
7. Ibid., 35.
8. Ibid., 34–35.
9. Ibid., 123.
10. Ibid., 60.
11. Ibid., 59.
12. Other participants in the company included John H. Eaton, Wilkins Tannehill, William Fulton, Ephraim H. Foster, and William C. Dunlap. Honorary members included Andrew Jackson and Felix Grundy. Ludlow, *Dramatic Life,* 167.
13. *Theatrical Journey-Work,* 60.
14. Ibid., 61.
15. Ibid., 62.
16. Ibid., 61.
17. James H. Dormon Jr., *Theater in the Ante Bellum South, 1815–1861* (Chapel Hill: Univ. of North Carolina Press, 1967), 246.
18. Alex C. Robertson to Miss L. L. Robertson, Philadelphia, Nov. 14, 1850, Laura (Brown) Robertson Papers, Tennessee State Library and Archives, Nashville (hereafter cited as TSLA).
19. *Memphis Enquirer,* Apr. 15, 1837, in Raymond S. Hill, "Memphis Theatre, 1836–1846," West Tennessee Historical Society *Papers* 9 (1955): 50.
20. *Knoxville Register,* Sept. 21, 1831, in G. Allan Yeomans and Paul L. Soper, "The Theatre," in *Heart of the Valley: A History of Knoxville, Tennessee,* ed. Lucile Deaderick (Knoxville: East Tennessee Historical Society, 1976), 459.
21. Dormon, *Theater in the Ante Bellum South,* 261. *The Lady of Lyons* was staged by a traveling company at Hart's Saloon in Memphis in 1842 and at the Memphis Theatre on November 2, 1854. *American Eagle,* May 6, 1842, in Hill, "Memphis Theatre," 52; *Memphis Daily Appeal,* Nov. 2, 1854, [p. 3].
22. "Miss Julia Dean at Nashville," *Spirit of the Times* 21 (Jan. 3, 1852): 552.
23. Ibid.
24. *Memphis Appeal,* Mar. 4, 1855, in Charles C. Ritter, "'The Drama in Our Midst': The Early History of the Theater in Memphis," West Tennessee Historical Society *Papers* 11 (1957): 25.
25. "Grand Inaugural of the New Theatre Vendome," Invitations, Programs, etc., Tennessee Historical Society Collections, TSLA.
26. Lewis S. Maiden, "Three Theatrical Stars in Nashville, 1876–1906," *Southern Speech Journal* 31 (Summer 1966): 344.
27. [Alexander Erskine] to Mary, Memphis, Nov. 7, 1896, George Washington Gordon and William Tecumsah Avery Papers, TSLA.
28. Maiden, "Three Theatrical Stars," 344.
29. Emma (Hicks) McDonald, "Just Things that Might Be of Interest Past and Present," typescript, [2], TSLA.
30. Albert F. McLean Jr., *American Vaudeville as Ritual* (Lexington: Univ. of Kentucky Press, 1965), 18.
31. Ludlow, *Dramatic Life,* 113.
32. *Memphis Appeal-Avalanche,* Jan. 3, 1891, in Kenneth T. Rainey, "Footlights and Sidelights: The Last Years of the Memphis Theater (Leubrie's Theater)," West Tennessee Historical Society *Papers* 41 (1987): 71–72.
33. *Confederate Veteran* 5 (July 1897): 363.
34. Molly Posey, "The Big Tent: Theatre and Vaudeville Entertainment Thrived in Traveling Canvas Show From 1890 to 1930," *Southern Theatre* 34 (Fall 1992): 12.
35. Recital Program, John Trotwood Moore Papers, TSLA.
36. Clara Hieronymus, "Spotlights: Two Hundred Years of Tennessee Theater," in *The Tennessee Bicentennial Arts and Entertainment Festival Program* (Nashville: Tennessean, 1996), 22.

Suggested Readings

Bristow, Eugene K. "From Temple to Barn: The Greenlaw Opera House in Memphis, 1860–1880." West Tennessee Historical Society *Papers* 21 (1967): 5–23.

Brockett, O. G. "Theatre in Nashville During the Civil War." *Southern Speech Journal* 23 (Winter 1957): 61–72.

Dormon, James H., Jr. *Theater in the Ante Bellum South, 1815–1861.* Chapel Hill: Univ. of North Carolina Press, 1967.

Faulkner, Seldon. "[The New] Memphis Theatre Stock Company." In *American Theatre Companies,*

1749–1887, ed. Weldon B. Durham, 345–51. Westport, Conn.: Greenwood Press, 1986.

Henderson, Jerry. "Nashville in the Decline of Southern Legitimate Theatre During the Beginning of the Twentieth Century." *Southern Speech Journal* 29 (1963): 26–33.

Hieronymus, Clara. "Spotlights: Two Hundred Years of Tennessee Theater." In *The Tennessee Bicentennial Arts and Entertainment Festival Program.* Nashville: Tennessean, 1996.

Hill, Raymond S. "Memphis Theatre, 1836–1846." West Tennessee Historical Society *Papers* 9 (1955): 48–58.

Ludlow, Noah M. *Dramatic Life as I Found It.* St. Louis: 1880; new edition with introduction and index by Francis Hodge, New York: Benjamin Blom, 1966.

Maiden, Lewis S. "Three Theatrical Stars in Nashville, 1876–1906." *Southern Speech Journal* 31 (Summer 1966): 338–47.

Morrow, Sara Sprott. "A Brief History of Theater in Nashville, 1807–1970." *Tennessee Historical Quarterly* 30 (Summer 1971): 178–89.

Rainey, Kenneth T. "Footlights and Sidelights: The Last Years of the Memphis Theater (Leubrie's Theater)." West Tennessee Historical Society *Papers* 41 (1987): 62–73.

Ritter, Charles C. "'The Drama in Our Midst': The Early History of the Theater in Memphis." West Tennessee Historical Society *Papers* 11 (1957): 5–35.

Smith, Sol. *Theatrical Management in the West and South for Thirty Years.* New York, 1868; new edition with introduction and index by Arthur T. Tees, New York: Benjamin Blom, 1968.

Yeomans, G. Allan, and Paul L. Soper. "The Theatre." In *Heart of the Valley: A History of Knoxville, Tennessee,* ed. Lucile Deaderick, 457–81. Knoxville: East Tennessee Historical Society, 1976.

Twenty

Theater Dance in Tennessee
A Twentieth-Century Tradition

Karen Wilson
Chattanooga

Dance is solely present in the moment. Once the performance is over, the art is over. Whatever lingering emotion the audience may experience fades with time and distance until he or she is lucky enough to once again enter the community hall, auditorium, theater, or other performance arena.

The tradition of dance in Tennessee, as in almost every state in the nation, follows two paths: the deep tradition of vernacular dance and the much more recent story of theater dance. Of the two traditions, much more attention has been directed at vernacular dance, especially in the work of folklorists Gail Matthews, Elizabeth Fine, LeeEllen Friedland, and Michael Kline. They have documented a rich traditional dance legacy, beginning with Native Americans who danced for social and ritual occasions. Dance was an assertive, emotional way of defining community, culture, and identity for native peoples as well as the European settlers and their African American slaves who came to share the land of Tennessee.

Many traditional dances survive today. Freestyle clogging was established in the North Carolina mountains in the late 1920s and became very popular in the 1950s and 1960s. This dance is linked to the much earlier traditions of flatfooting, or buckdancing, as is the very popular precision clogging, a dance often performed by groups at the Grand Ole Opry. The Appalachian, or Old Time, Square Dance probably dates to the settlement era when Scots-Irish, English, German, and French Huguenots blended and adapted some form of Old World square dancing to their interests and needs on the southwest frontier. In general, the Old Time Square Dance begins with dancers forming one large circle, then

Dance team at Cumberland Homesteads, Crossville. Photograph by Ben Shahn. Courtesy of the Library of Congress, Prints & Photographs Division, Farm Security Administration—Office of War Information Photograph Collection (reproduction number LC-USF33-006269-M1 DLC).

dividing into two-couple sets (called circle fours) that dance various figures, and finally the caller brings all dancers back into a large circle. A more recent and popular dance form is the Western Square Dance, which was imported to Tennessee in the mid-twentieth century. More complex and structured than Old Time Square Dance, the Western Square Dance also is much more popular across the country. African American stepping (or blocking) can be found across the nation as well. It is a precise, synchronized dance with deep roots in African culture and in African American ring shouts. The traditional dance of the Cherokees harkens to ancient social and sacred expressions, while Cherokee fancy dance is a modern form that developed out of the twentieth-century pow wow movement.

These culturally expressive vernacular dances are the foundation of the Volunteer State's dance tradition, one that has been immeasurably enriched by the emergence of theater dance in the late twentieth century. This chapter focuses on this comparatively neglected aspect of Tennessee's dance history.

Theater Dance Comes to Tennessee, 1900–1950

While dance has been part of human existence since the beginning of time, dance as a theatrical art form is a product of the nineteenth century. Even though ballet traces its roots to the French court of Louis XVI, not until the 1830s and 1840s, when ballerinas Marie Taglioni, Fanny Cerito, Carlotta Grisi, and Lucile Grahn took European audiences by storm, did ballet become an established art form. In the early twentieth century, Russian ballerina Anna Pavlova toured the world and spent the years during World War I in the Americas familiarizing thousands with the ethereal world of ballet. Pavlova performed in Tennessee in 1914, followed by American great Isadora Duncan, who danced at the Ryman Auditorium in 1919.

The first instruction in theater dance in Tennessee took place at a few private academies in Memphis and Nashville. The important dancer and choreographer Hermes Pan (c. 1910–1990) was born Hermes Panagiotopoulus in Memphis. Later acclaimed for his Hollywood musical work with Fred Astaire, Pan studied at Nashville's Miss Georgia's Private School in 1930. Dance instruction became more professional in 1928, when Sarah Jeter and Louise Smith, teachers at the Ward-Belmont School for Young Ladies in Nashville, were named co-directors of the school of dancing at the new Nashville Conservatory of Music. Jeter and Smith conducted dance studios and directed dance productions, training the area's first generation of ballet dancers. Their Dance Department became one of the conservatory's most visible and applauded programs. Then in 1930, Jeter invited her former instructor and dance pioneer Ruth St. Denis to conduct a three-week course at the conservatory for southern dance instructors. St. Denis and her husband Ted Shawn had established the extremely influential Denishawn school of dance in 1915 as the country's first significant school of dance with a standardized curriculum of instruction. St. Denis used her weeks in Nashville to teach dance instructors the basics of the Denishawn principles. Seven years later, Ted Shawn taught a summer-school course at the George Peabody College for Teachers in Nashville.

These Tennessee efforts, however, were minuscule compared to the explosion in theater dance taking place in New York City in those same years. George Balanchine established the American Ballet in 1934; Agnes de Mille introduced ballet to Broadway in the stage production of *Oklahoma* in 1943. Balanchine, Martha Graham, Alvin Ailey and others helped to established a distinctly American style of dance. Suddenly, New York was exploding with dance and dancers. Professional dancers were largely tied to New York City, if they wanted to make a living at their art. Touring companies made occasional forays into other states, but in Tennessee traveling companies were much more common in theater, even opera, than ballet. The first major ballet company to visit Tennessee, the American Ballet Theatre from New York City, did not perform here until 1961.

Ted Shawn and Ruth St. Denis. Courtesy of the Nashville Room, Nashville Public Library.

Establishing Professional Ballet Companies, 1960–2000

Regional ballet companies slowly developed in the South. Dorothy Alexander, the founding director of what was then called the Atlanta Civic Ballet (now Atlanta Ballet), hosted the first Southeastern Regional Ballet Festival in 1956. A dance instructor pioneer in Nashville during that same decade was Albertine Maxwell. One of her many students, Mary McGavock of Nashville, studied ballet under Maxwell until 1961, when she went to continue her studies at the Boston Conservatory of Music; McGavock then danced professionally in the Boston area until returning to Nashville in 1975.

In general, however, it took another generation for the regional movement to take hold throughout the nation. By the 1970s, new degree programs and departments at colleges and universities, new performing halls and venues, new private academies, and dedicated patrons created a stronger institutional infrastructure for theater dance. The Tennessee Association of Dance (TAD), for example, was formed in 1971, and served as the first statewide support agency for the encouragement and development of dance. Both TAD and the Tennessee Arts Commission (TAC) showed interest in and support for Ballet South, a company established in Memphis during the 1970s. George Latimer was one of the company's principals. One of its early dancers, Peggy Burks, who is now a member of the dance faculty at the University of Tennessee, received a TAC grant to be a soloist at Ballet South in 1979 and then began teaching dance at the University of Memphis from 1979 to 1982. Burks next became the founding artistic director of the Nashville City Ballet in 1983—and its principal dancer—before becoming the director of the School of Nashville Ballet in 1987.

Efforts by dance professionals and advocates were reinforced by a larger popular enthusiasm for ballet created by such dance celebrities as Margot Fonteyn, Rudolf Nureyev, and Mikhail Baryishnikov (who even performed in Chattanooga and Nashville in 1991). The popularity of movies such as *The Turning Point, Footloose,* and *Flashdance* reflected this heightened awareness in the popular culture and made ballet and dance virtual household words, encouraging many parents to enroll their children in dance classes.

This Heart. Photograph by Marianne Leach. Courtesy of Marianne Leach and the Nashville Ballet.

New academies and instruction from trained professional dancers further reflected the modern growth of dance in Tennessee. Most major cities began to offer professional dance training by artists who had professional performing experience. Dancers personally trained by Balanchine, Ailey, Graham and other international artists settled in Tennessee and other states where they opened schools and began the development of civic and regional companies which would lead to Tennessee's own professional dance companies and the regular presentation of full length theater dance in the state's four largest cities.

Mars and Venus. Courtesy of Ballet Memphis.

Memphis and Nashville established major companies in the mid-1980s. Ballet Memphis traces its history to 1985, when artistic director and native Memphian Dorothy Gunther Pugh founded Memphis Youth Concert Ballet as a training ground for young dancers. Soon becoming Memphis Concert Ballet with two professional dancers and a corps of trainees, the company operated on a budget of $75,000. In the 1990s, the company's Michael Telvin and Judy Telvin substantially improved the corps and expanded its offerings to the public. At the beginning of the twenty-first century, the company, known as Ballet Memphis, employs a roster of twenty-four professional dancers with a $2.5 million budget and pres-

The Little Mermaid. Courtesy of Ballet Memphis.

ents a full season of home performances at the Orpheum Theater and touring performances throughout West Tennessee, Mississippi, and Arkansas. Assistant artistic director Karl Condon, former principal dancer with Boston Ballet, brings a Balanchine heritage to Memphis. Together, Pugh and Condon produce company repertory that includes classics such as *The Nutcracker, Giselle,* and *The Sleeping Beauty,* along with contemporary works by Shapiro and Smith, Trey McIntyre, Lila York, and Danny Buraczeski. In addition, the company operates various outreach programs while its affiliated Ballet Memphis School trains area dancers.

Nashville Ballet likewise began as a school and civic company. Through the efforts of a dedicated group of enthusiasts, most particularly Nashville native and former managing director, Jane Fabian (another past student of Albertine Maxwell), the small civic company made the transition to a fully professional ballet company in 1986. Dedicated to presenting Nashville and the region with quality professional dance, Nashville Ballet also maintains its own school, which trains potential dancers as well as offers classes to those who wish to pursue dance purely as an avocation. Nashville Ballet presents a yearly home season at the Tennessee Performing Arts Center and tours throughout the Southeast. Past artistic directors include Dane LaFontsee and Eddy Meyer. Currently under the artistic direction of Paul Vasterling, the company presents both classical and original works including the traditional *Nutcracker.* Ballet Mistress Elaine Thomas brings the heritage of Ashton and McMillian from her Royal Ballet background. The company supports a full roster of dancers who are trained in classical ballet. In addition, Nashville Ballet is an integral part of the local community with its outreach program titled Dance Power. Dance Power encompasses a series of original children's works presented free to the community at public libraries throughout the city. In-school programs introduce Middle Tennessee students to the art of dance through residencies, performances and student visits to Nashville Ballet studios. A Girl Scout Dance Badge workshop offers local girl scouts the chance to explore possible careers in dance, take a ballet class, and attend a company performance.

The City Ballet Knoxville developed along a different path. Rather than create from within, the Knoxville Arts Council agreed to a plan that would partner the city with an already established ballet company. The Cincinnati Ballet Company established a sister-city relationship with Knoxville in 1988, creating the Knoxville City Ballet. Each city would

Patrons and the Arts in Tennessee

In our democratic society, public funding for the arts is often inadequate to support a wide range of expressions and traditions. Tennessee patrons of the arts not only made up the difference; they indelibly shaped the state's arts landscape. In nineteenth-century Nashville, for instance, the Tennessee Historical Society commissioned portraitist Washington Cooper to paint Tennessee governors; then the society funded Clark Mills's equestrian statue of Andrew Jackson on Capitol Hill. The Centennial Club of Nashville supported the paintings of Willie Betty Newman, along with other local artists. In Memphis, the Beethoven Club sponsored local performances by international stars in the 1890s and then continued as major support for the twentieth-century development of opera and symphony music in the Bluff City.

Urban women philanthropists expanded Tennessee arts institutions in the early 1900s. In 1916 Bessie Vance Brooks provided funds for Memphis' Brooks Museum of Arts, the state's first major art museum. From the 1910s to the 1930s, Anne T. Thomas supported Chattanooga cultural initiatives. Bertha Potter encouraged both performance and visual arts in Nashville. Bertha Clark's devotion to classical music made the Knoxville Symphony possible. Several major private benefactors supported the influential—but short-lived—Nashville Conservatory of Music in the late 1920s.

The Great Depression closed the conservatory and threatened to curtail many of the state's recent achievements in the arts. Through various New Deal programs, representing the state's first significant era of public funding for the arts, the federal government kept arts alive as it supported painters, sculptors, photographers, architects, musicians, dramatists, and composers, who left a collective legacy of artistic expressions, from the run-of-the-mill to the truly remarkable in a brief span of nine years.

After World War II, the American painter Georgia O'Keefe donated a significant body of modern art to the Fisk University, a collection that now comprises the heart of the university's Van Vechten Museum. Chattanooga capitalist George T. Hunter established the Benwood Foundation, which in 1951–52 provided funds and the donated Hunter mansion to create the Hunter Gallery of American Art. Between 1946 and 1960, Walter Sharp and Huldah Cheek Sharp were instrumental in establishing the Nashville Symphony and the Cheekwood Museum of Art. Fundraisers and community involvement in the Memphis Orchestral Society and the Memphis Art Council led to the establishment of the Memphis Symphony Orchestra by 1960.

Then in 1967 came the creation of the Tennessee Arts Commission, which is an independent agency of the state of Tennessee. As emphasized by authors throughout this book, the Commission has been an important force in expanding the state's artistic horizons through its support for theater, opera, dance, museums, and music, but it also has preserved, recorded, and enhanced the state's craft traditions. The Commission's mission—"that the citizens of Tennessee have access to and participate in the arts"—is amply demonstrated through its support of this book effort, of arts festivals statewide, of arts organizations and museums, and of individual artists. There is no doubt that the arts legacy of Tennessee would be far more meager if not for the leadership and activism of the Tennessee Arts Commission.

Patrons and foundations remain the foundation of many arts endeavors. The Frist Foundation has supported many of the capitol city's arts institutions as well as established its own Frist Center for the Visual Arts, which, in turn, supports any arts initiatives in Nashville area schools and neighborhoods. The Benwood Foundation and Lyndhurst Foundation enhance urban life in Chattanooga through support to places such as the Tivoli Theater and arts groups, large and small. But scores of individuals generous with their money and dedication continue to be important. In the 1970s Margaret Oakes Dixon and Hugo Dixon left their Memphis estate and arts collection to serve as the nucleus of the Dixon Gallery of Art. In the late 1990s, Memphis businessman J. R. Hyde has been a crucial supporter of Ballet Memphis. Rudi and Honey Scheidt of Memphis helped to upgrade major improvements and fund major expansions in the Memphis arts scene, from their support of the Memphis Symphony, Memphis College of Art, Opera Memphis, and Memphis Arts Festival to their donations for the School of Music at the University of Memphis. Happy Booker has devoted her service to the East Tennessee Opera Guild and the founding of the Knoxville Opera while Mary Cortner Ragland, a founder of the Nashville Symphony, also helped to establish the Nashville Opera Association in 1981.

Through her leadership in the creation of the Tennessee Performing Arts Center (TPAC) and the Tennessee Bicentennial Celebration, Martha Rivers Ingram, chair of Ingram Industries since 1995, has shaped the Tennessee arts environment like no other individual. A native of South Carolina, Ingram was instrumental in garnering enough private support to convince the state to fund TPAC in Nashville during the late 1970s. Then Ingram helped to secure quality programming for the center through her board service with the Nashville Ballet, Nashville Symphony, Nashville Opera, and the Tennessee Repertory Theatre. In 1996, she chaired the successful Tennessee Bicentennial Celebration, which brought Tennesseans together to stage a festival of music, dance, and drama to commemorate two hundred years of statehood.

Tennessee's patrons—both public and private—have helped to build a lasting institutional and educational infrastructure for the arts, one that comprises one of the most important trends in the twentieth-century history of Tennessee culture.

Carroll Van West, Middle Tennessee State University

maintain a separate board of directors and management structure while sharing artistic faculty and dancers. In 1996 the City Ballet changed its cultural partner to the Tulsa Ballet. Under the artistic direction of Marcello Angelini at the beginning of the twenty-first century, the City Ballet/Tulsa Ballet Theater's thirty-two professional dancers perform home seasons in both Knoxville and Tulsa, along with various touring engagements, and certain educational efforts.

Chattanooga Ballet, formed as Chattanooga Center for the Dance in 1975, has seen numerous directors yet has chosen to remain essentially a school and a training company. Nancy Lane Wright, Stanley Zompakos, and Alexander Bennett have served as directors. (Nancy Lane Wright went on to establish Chattanooga's Dance Theater Workshop.) In 1984, Barry and Anna Baker-Van Cura of Ruth Page's Chicago Ballet were named artistic directors and remained with the company until 1987. Since then a collaboration of faculty and general director Robert Willie has overseen Chattanooga Ballet. The company employs two professional dancers, one ballet master, and supplements its corps with local dancers. Officially in residence at the University of Tennessee at Chattanooga, Chattanooga Ballet focuses on instruction, dance education, and sponsorship of community and cultural events. The company performs an annual *Nutcracker,* and a spring concert dedicated to original choreography.

Ballet Tennessee, also located in Chattanooga, is under the artistic direction of Barry and Anna Baker-Van Cura. Founded in 1987, the company is a regional training company made up of professional and student dancers. The company presents both classical and contemporary works, offers classes in its affiliated school Baker–Van Cura Ballet Centre, sponsors a summer workshop with internationally recognized guest faculty

The Firebird with Anna Baker-Van Cura and Barry Van Cura. Courtesy of Ballet Tennessee, Chattanooga.

and offers outreach programs in conjunction with the city's Parks and Recreation Department.

As the major professional companies established themselves, other dancers sought to create smaller companies devoted to the instruction and performance of modern dance. Both groups have benefited from grants from the Tennessee Arts Commission and various corporate sponsors. Founders/artistic directors Donna Rizzo and Andrew Krichels in 1986 established the Tennessee Dance Theater (now dormant) to perform works by internationally recognized choreographers such as Doris Humphrey, Bill Evans, and Mark Dendy as well as original works by the directors. The company collaborated with Nashville musical artists such as Chet Atkins, Mark O'Connor, Mike Reid, and David Schnaufer. Nashville's Uhuru Dance Company performs African cultural traditions in the form of dance, music, theater, and storytelling, with a dance emphasis on modern dance and liturgical dance.

Tennessee Children's Dance Ensemble is a unique professional children's modern company, directed by Dr. Dorothy M. Floyd until her death in 2002. Located in Knoxville, the company has performed throughout the United States and abroad. Floyd studied extensively under modern dance pioneer Mary Wigman and returned to Knoxville in the 1960s to open Dancers Studio, considered to be the first school in the South to focus on modern dance. In 1981, she established the Tennessee Children's Dance Ensemble composed entirely of children ages ten to sixteen. The company has performed works by such recognized choreographers as Peter Pucci, Claire Bataille, and Michael Mao. Associate Artistic Director Irena Linn also creates choreography for the company. In addition to a full schedule of touring, the company performs locally in concerts and schools, hosts master-classes, gives lecture demonstrations, and provides in-service training for teachers.

Circle Modern Dance, a relative newcomer to the Knoxville dance scene, was founded in 1990. Under the artistic direction of Kimberly Matibag and Mark Lamb, the company performs original works designed to bring the art form alive, encourage diversity, and promote dance advocacy. This young company performs solo concerts and collaborates locally with the Knoxville Opera Company, Dogwood Arts Festival, and the Knoxville Museum of Art. The company is actively involved with the Knoxville Institute of the Arts in bringing dance to local school children.

In Memphis, Ann Halligan Donahue and Judith Tribo Wombwell in 1987 founded Project: Motion to promote modern dance and modern dance education to a wide Bluff City audience. Donahue and Wombwell left Memphis for new opportunities eight years later, but the core company reorganized in that same year and has since presented yearly programs of challenging, diverse, and innovative dance programs, enlarging its season to four shows annually.

Numerous cities in the state have established civic ballet and modern companies using student and guest professional dancers. These organizations play an essential role in developing both audiences and future dancers. Ballet Arts in Jackson, under the di-

Dr. Dorothy M. Floyd, TCDE founder and artistic director, and Michael Mao of New York in the dance studio with students preparing Mao's *Song of Helena.* Courtesy of Tennessee Children's Dance Ensemble, Knoxville.

rection of Pat Brown; Appalachian Ballet in Maryville, headed by Amy Moore Morton; Mountain Movers, directed by Judith Woodruff in residence at East Tennessee State University in Johnson City; Civic Ballet of Chattanooga, headed by Donna Massari and David Wood; Epiphany in Nashville, directed by Grete Grzyana-Teague; Memphis Dance Group under the direction of Tania Castroverde; Barking Legs Theater, headed by Ann Law in Chattanooga; Oak Ridge Civic Ballet; and the State of Franklin Dance Alliance in Kingsport all illustrate the fact that dance is flourishing in Tennessee. These directors, along with the directors of Tennessee's fully professional companies, are dedicated to training dancers, advocating for dance, and providing quality dance experiences to their communities and beyond.

Along with Tennessee's growing number of professional and civic companies, the state's educational institutions are host to varied and growing dance programs. The University of Memphis offers a Bachelor of Fine Arts in Dance while maintaining a performing company, Voices. Graduates of this program are working in all aspects of the dance field nationwide. Both Moira Logan and Holly Lau of the University of Memphis are familiar and respected faces of dance in Tennessee. The dance program at the University of Tennessee at Knoxville, under the direction of Gene McCutchen, is undergoing a renaissance and currently

Dancers of Tennessee Children's Dance Ensemble. Courtesy of TCDE, Knoxville.

offers a minor in Dance. Dance programs at Vanderbilt University, headed by Michelle Douglas, and the University of the South, directed by Phoebe Pearigen, offer classes and present national and international dance programs to their communities. Middle Tennessee State University is reviving its dance track with the recent hiring of Ann Shea to direct the program along with veteran Tennessee teacher Nancy Ammerman (yet another former student of Albertine Maxwell and former artist-in-residence with the Memphis Ballet Company). The University of Tennessee at Martin offers a bachelor in fine arts with emphasis in dance while the University of Tennessee at Chattanooga is the institutional home of the Chattanooga Ballet. Vanderbilt University regularly presents internationally renowned dancers and companies such as the Martha Graham Dance Company, the Alvin Ailey Repertory Ensemble, and the Paul Taylor Dance Company.

Public elementary and secondary educators in Tennessee also are beginning to recognize the importance of the arts and dance in particular to Tennessee students. Fine and performing arts magnet schools in Knoxville, Nashville, and Chattanooga offer students the chance to follow an intensive arts and academic curriculum (with a dance focus) from elementary through high school. Private schools such as Nashville's Harpeth Hall, under the direction of Leslie Mathews, along with Chattanooga's Baylor School, under the direction of Karen Smith, and Girls Preparatory School (GPS) in Chattanooga offer respected dance programs. For instance, GPS's Terpsichord, founded in 1954 by Peggy Thomas and currently under the direction of Cathie Casch, is one of the oldest student modern dance companies in the state. The Governor's School for the Arts was another important source of support and encouragement for young dancers.

Tennessee's growing dance community further demonstrates the importance of the art form to a significantly large and growing number of Tennesseans. The Tennessee Association of Dance (TAD) underscores this trend. Founded in 1971, the organization's mission is to encourage and support the development of dance in Tennessee. Under the executive direction of Judith Woodruff, TAD provides statewide communication, advocacy, fellowship, scholarships, and recognition to Tennessee dancers through newsletters, a web site, and annual conferences with internationally known master teachers. TAD has been responsible for bringing to Tennessee such artists as Melissa Hayden, Mira Popovich, Daniel Maloney, Daniel McKayle, Jilliana, Joel Hall, Deborah Hadley, Keith Lee, Kevin Martin, and Eleanor D'Antuono, to name but a few, giving Tennessee dancers continued access to the best in dance.

While Tennessee may have been slower than its northern neighbors in developing an ongoing dance presence on the national scene, the state is working on all levels—local, regional, and statewide—to continue its artistic growth in dance, a significant new horizon in Tennessee performing arts.

SUGGESTED READINGS

Cohen, Selma J., ed. *International Encyclopedia of Dance.* New York: Oxford Univ. Press, 1998.

Fine, Elizabeth C., and Jean H. Speer, eds. *Performance, Culture, and Identity.* Westport, Conn.: Praeger, 1992.

Jones, Loyal. *Minstrel of the Appalachians: The Story of Bascom Lamar Lunsford.* Boone, N.C.: Appalachian Consortium Press, 1984.

Nutter, Liz. "Dancing to a Two Steppin' Heritage." *Tennessee Bicentennial Arts and Entertainment Festival Program.* Nashville: *Tennessean,* 1996.

Pearigen, Phoebe. "Dance Companies." In *Tennessee Encyclopedia of History and Culture,* ed. Carroll Van West, Connie L. Lester, Anne-Leslie Owens, and Margaret D. Binnicker, 232. Nashville: Tennessee Historical Society, 1998.

Tennessee Association of Dance. Web site: www.tennesseedance.org.

Archival Sources

Jeter-Smith Collection. Nashville Room, Metropolitan Nashville and Davidson County Public Library, Nashville.

Twenty-one

Tennessee in Film

Leslie Richardson
The University of the South

Since statehood, and perhaps before, Tennesseans have lived with plurality, but citizens of their state have identified with one of the three grand divisions: west, middle, and east, each with a distinct geography, history, and population. The image of Tennessee as three-states-in-one has probably worked to its disadvantage as a location for Hollywood movies, however. The variety of Tennessee's geography and the complexity of its past should provide worthy subject matter for the full Hollywood treatment, but popular filmmakers may have recognized the difficulty of finding in Tennessee's variety the single stereotype that is necessary to trigger audience response. If audiences cannot easily identify Tennessee with the Old South or the frontier, for example, then Hollywood has had no time to put the record straight. Popular movies do not set out to educate their audiences. Instead, they shape the popular version of history by catering to audience expectations. Historical and regional authenticity is rarely necessary for box office success, or even for artistic excellence.

Belmont Theater, Nashville, n.d. Photograph by Wiles Studio. Tennessee Historical Society, Marr-Holman Collection, Manuscripts Division, Tennessee State Library and Archives. Courtesy of TSLA.

Economic pressures and the reliance on special effects in modern Hollywood are among the reasons why few movies have been filmed, either in part or in whole, in Tennessee. Studios have had huge investments in back lots and sound stages; therefore, it was more efficient to build a set and film a movie on the Hollywood backlot than to transport a crew and equipment thousands of miles in the interests of regional authenticity. Even today a location can be created more economically and convincingly inside the studio laboratories than on location. For this reason, American studio films, known the world over for their sleek professionalism, have lacked the grainy "poetry of real life" that Knoxville-born film critic James Agee admired in European and Asian productions.

From the silent movie era to the present day, Hollywood films have explored two myths which continue to shape American identity: the lone hero in conflict with antagonists on the frontier, and the Confederacy as romantic underdog in the Civil War. Many Hollywood directors have found expression for these national myths in the history and geography of Tennessee.

TENNESSEE AS A LOCALE AND THEME IN AMERICAN FILM

Tennessee possesses an impressive catalogue of photogenic features: the Mississippi River on the west, forest-covered mountains in the east, and swamps, plantations, whitewater streams, hardscrabble farms with log cabins, industrial cities with mirrored skyscrapers, handsome courthouse squares, and Victorian villages scattered in between. If a setting did not exist already, a studio could fabricate it out of the raw material of Tennessee's geography, particularly since most vegetation can be made to grow in the state, except perhaps the Spanish moss of Hollywood's Old South imagining. In short, Tennessee's landscape has everything a movie company might need, except an ocean.

The landscape was not a strong enough lure to bring Hollywood to Tennessee in the early days. Neither the silent movie *Sam Davis, the Hero of Tennessee* (1915) nor later large-budget MGM movies such as *The Frontiersman* (1927) and *Morgan's Last Raid* (1929) were filmed on location, and John Huston's *Red Badge of Courage* (1951) recreated the Battle of Shiloh in California. Hollywood's first foray into the state came in 1923, when director Alan Holubar brought a crew to Franklin to make *The Human Mill.* Holubar based his story on a historical novel by John Trotwood Moore, then the state librarian and archivist. Using local, aging Civil War veterans as extras, the movie was filmed on open land near the actual battlefield in order to recreate the scale and ferocity of the Battle of Franklin. When Holubar died before the project was completed, work was suspended, and the footage was later lost.

Two years later Buster Keaton announced plans to film a portion of his new movie *The General* on location in Tennessee. The story is based on a participant's account of a Union foray into Confederate territory in 1862. A group of Union soldiers known as Andrews Raiders hijacked a locomotive, the *General,* in Atlanta and drove it north at sixty miles an hour into Tennessee, destroying track and burning bridges along the way until they were captured and later hanged by the Confederates. To please contemporary audiences who preferred to see southerners as romantic heroes, Keaton turned the story on its head. He made the Yankees the villains and combined the Confederates into one hero, Johnny Gray, a decided underdog even to his short stature. Johnny recaptures the General and wins the girl through a combination of typically Keatonian virtues of modesty, American practical know-how, and dogged refusal to submit to the odds. While taking liberties with history, Keaton, a train enthusiast, was historically accurate about the locomotive itself. He leased a logging railroad in East Tennessee in preparation for shooting and requested permission to borrow the original *General* from its owners, the Louisville and Nashville Railroad. When some Tennessee patriots objected that a heroic enterprise was being turned into a Buster Keaton slapstick comedy, Keaton gave up his Tennessee location and moved the entire production to Cottage Grove, Oregon. (In 1956, Disney took the story of Andrews Raides, made the Union soldiers the heroes, and released it as *The Great Locomotive Chase.*)

In 1929, the year that sound came to the screen, King Vidor, a southerner, directed the musical *Hallelujah* partly in Tennessee. *Hallelujah* was a "race" movie designed for African American audiences. It was one of the first movies ever made with an all-black cast. Although most critics agree that Vidor's treatment of the age-old theme of innocence seduced by the temptations of the city was a serious attempt to depict a family's grief and passion, they do not consider it a valid picture of American folk culture since the performers were directed, costumed, made up and

Taylor-Made Pictures

One of the most unique documentary records of any type in America are the films, recordings, and photographs that the Reverend L. O. Taylor made of African Americans in Memphis during the 1930s and 1940s. A charismatic and emotional Baptist preacher, Taylor consciously set out to record in movies, photographs, and audio tapes the lives, events, and sounds of the Bluff City's African American communities in an era of Jim Crow segregation. As depicted in the 1989 award-winning documentary, *Sermons and Sacred Pictures: The Life and Work of Reverend L. O. Taylor,* the films were about important African American religious and political events (Taylor made movies of his annual trips to the National Baptist Convention, showing his parishioners famous landmarks of the cities he visited, as well as parts of the convention and the legendary ministers who spoke there), weddings and community celebrations, and, perhaps most importantly, commonplace events and average people carrying out their everyday lives. As a documentary filmmaker, Taylor brought a sense of intimacy and casualness to his movies, which were shown on a regular basis at segregated African American theaters and at his church in Memphis. Taylor made his movies and recordings for many reasons. He enjoyed being a filmmaker—as a dynamic minister he possessed a personal charm and an effective theatrical sense, which carried over to his moviemaking. As a community activist, Taylor wanted to nurture a positive self-image and identity for Memphis's blacks, so his work celebrated their very existence in a time when few black faces—except when depicted in often vicious stereotypes—could be found on southern silver screens. The Center for Southern Folklore in Memphis has the state's best collection of Taylor's amazing documentary legacy.

Carroll Van West, Middle Tennessee State University

photographed by whites. The success of *Hallelujah* influenced the film industry in significant ways.

The coming of sound to the movies signaled the end of the small but thriving independent black film industry that lacked the capital to make the technological changes necessary for sound production. Second, as the September 1929 review in *Variety* predicted, perhaps overconfidently, "if the colored race can appeal on the shadowy screen to all, in other than colored comedy, the Negro dramatic and musical comedy actor may find a place in the studios." The success of *Hallelujah* may have opened opportunities in the number of parts available for African Americans in mainstream film and in the "race" film market, but other doors were closed to them by the near demise of the independent industry. One exception was the films about African American community and religious life produced in Memphis by the Reverend L. O. Taylor's company, Taylor-Made Pictures, in the decades of the 1920s and 1930s.

Race was a pervasive factor in shaping the American moviegoing experience. Following the passing of Jim Crow laws in the 1890s, African Americans were segregated and in most cases barred from white places of amusement. Even a Hollywood spectacular like *Hallelujah* would have had limited distribution in the South, where white theater owners hesitated to book films with racial issues or with any but stereotypical black characters. Movie houses for black patrons existed in the larger Tennessee cities, but Nashville, for example, had only one black theater to serve its 42,836 black citizens. All-black theaters in the South were often too small and dilapidated to attract a middle-class audience, and furthermore they exhibited only worn-out prints and never first-run musicals. Middle-class black Tennesseans generally refused to enter white movie theaters by the segregated entrances or to sit, all classes together, in a restricted part of the gallery. In the small towns, the option did not even exist because rural white theaters usually did not have the second floor or balcony required for segregated seating. Fisk University's Charles Johnson, who surveyed consumption patterns among urban blacks in the South in 1929, found that product endorsement ads by famous Hollywood stars had little appeal to African American consumers who refused to attend either segregated white theaters or substandard black ones.

During the Depression decade of the 1930s, themes from Tennessee history attracted a few Hollywood directors. MGM's *The Gorgeous Hussy* (1936), directed by Tennessean Clarence Brown, featured Joan Crawford in the story of the Eaton Affair that almost wrecked President Andrew Jackson's first term in office. Two years later, Cecil B. DeMille's film *The Buccaneer* told the story of Jean Laffite, Andrew Jackson, and the Battle of New Orleans. But the only movies filmed on location in Tennessee in the 1930s were documentaries. The best known is Pare Lorentz's *The River* (1937), sponsored by the New Deal's Resettlement Administration. With an original score by Virgil Thomson and a sonorous script by Lorentz himself, the film documents the evils of sharecropping, unchecked erosion, flooding, and soil exhaustion in land that was subject to regular flooding by the Mississippi River system. Beginning at the river's source and following its course through the Delta to New Orleans, the film was almost complete when the rains began which inaugurated the disastrous flood of 1937. Dissatisfied with the footage he had shot up to that point and confident of continued government support, Lorentz gathered his crew at Memphis and began filming again.

Clarence Brown, charcoal. Courtesy of Special Collections, University of Tennessee, Knoxville.

The River reflects Lorentz's admiration for Soviet cinematic themes and techniques. In the 1920s and 1930s, Soviet filmmakers such as Eisenstein and Pudovkin were proud to be propagandists, using their art for the purpose of social renewal. Though *The River* is often exaggerated and didactic in the manner of Soviet cinema, Lorentz's artistic use of montage creates stylized visual effects that have the elegance of music. Like his Soviet counterparts, Lorentz uses skewed camera angles and sweeping panoramic shots to form an apostrophe to the land and to the dignity of the people who work it. The message of the film is an endorsement of government intervention in flood control because, as the voice-over rhythmically repeats, "poor land makes poor people." After seeing *The River,* President Roosevelt advocated its distribution in chain theaters. Hollywood's opposition to what they believed was unfair government-sponsored competition in the making of *The River* was soon dampened by the universal acclamation that greeted the film after Paramount took over distribution. With this film, Pare Lorentz assumed a place in the pantheon of classic documentary filmmakers, and Tennessee, like other states affected by Mississippi River flooding, participated in

Clarence Brown with actors portraying Andrew and Rachel Jackson in *The Golden Hussy.* Courtesy of Special Collections, University of Tennessee, Knoxville.

the American myth of a long-suffering and enduring heartland.

Tennessee locations figure in a less widely known documentary, *People of the Cumberlands* (1937), a two-reeler made by Frontier Films, a production group which had a reputation in the 1930s for doctrinaire Marxism. Photographer Ralph Steiner, assisted by Elia Kazan, filmed the movie largely at the Highlander Folk School in Monteagle. Highlander was chosen as a location for People of the Cumberlands because it was known as a training center for rank-and-file miners, textile laborers, and farm workers. Frontier's intention was to promote unionization among the people of the Cumberland Mountains. Erskine Caldwell's script portrayed the school as a catalyst for confrontations between management and labor, oppressor and oppressed.

The film's lasting value is due to Steiner's success in showing the people as individuals rather than as illustrations of political rhetoric. As with Walker Evans's photographs in James Agee's chronicle of Alabama sharecroppers, *Let Us Now Praise Famous Men,* Steiner's shots derive their power from the dignity and beauty of the poor. The opening sequence shows a grim-faced miner, a mother holding a child, a girl eating from a tin can, a ruined house.

The evident tension between art and doctrine in *People of the Cumberlands* is reminiscent of those Soviet directors who were officially criticized for "formalist error" because their visual images soared free of the restraints of politics. When Steiner returned to New York with footage of workers enjoying themselves at picnics, participating in three-legged rages and hog callings, the people at Frontier Films accused him of political naïveté and sent him back to the Cumberlands with instructions to put "more Karl Marx into the film." Frontier's purpose was educational, not aesthetic. In order to highlight the oppressive nature of management and inspire the workers to take action, Frontier later inserted a docudrama sequence recreating the murder of union organizer Barney Graham at Wilder, Tennessee. Although some critics deplore such additions to Steiner's original film, others consider the added footage of the labor rally of miners and textile workers at LaFollette on July 4, 1937, and of the TVA footage similar to that in *The River* to be powerful and technically innovative demonstrations of the populist enthusiasm of the thirties. Eleanor Roosevelt, who saw *People of the Cumberlands* at its White House showing in 1938, later defended the Highlander Folk School, as Steiner himself had done, against charges that it was a Communist training ground.

With a close eye on the war in Europe, Hollywood in the forties turned to the Cumberland Plateau to find an American hero. *Sergeant York* (1941), directed by Howard Hawks, is one of the most popular movies ever made about Americans and war. Its protagonist is a Tennessean from the hamlet of Pall Mall in Fentress County who, armed only with a rifle and a pistol, captured a German machine gun battalion at the battle of Meuse-Argonne during the last days of World War I. The authenticity of the Tennessee locations and characters was carefully checked at every point by York himself, his neighbors, members of his family, and a "technical adviser" named Donoho Hall who seemed to the studio executives to be a genuine example of backwoods Tennessee wisdom. York personally prevailed upon thirty-nine-year-old Gary Cooper, despite Cooper's feelings of unworthiness, to play the war hero; he rejected a Hollywood starlet who had been chosen to play the part of his wife, preferring instead a fifteen-year-old unknown. To avoid charges of creating fictional propaganda to encourage America's entry into the war in Europe, the studio's researchers verified and reproduced the smallest details of York's experiences in the war, including the design of his regiment's flag. As a result, the film still wears well because it manages to avoid sensationalism and excessive stereotyping in favor of a low-key sincerity.

The concern with authenticity in *Sergeant York* did not extend to actual location shooting, however. After visiting the community of Pall Mall and making notes about the geography and architecture, the Hollywood crew returned to California and constructed a forty-foot Appalachian mountain out of timber, cloth, plaster, soil, and live trees on the Warner Brothers' back lot. Mounted on a turntable, it had sixteen faces and was equipped with spare peaks and precipices to replace any that might break off during filming.

The release of *Sergeant York* in 1941, coming as it did when Germany's victory in Europe seemed possible, convinced many Americans that isolationism was no longer feasible. The story of a humble Tennessee patriot, a conscientious objector who reluctantly took up arms in a European conflict because the cause was just, appealed to a growing audience at this crucial period in American history. The real-life York's personal conflict between pacifism and duty mirrored America's own debate. In addition, York was appealingly modest. For years he had resisted lucrative offers to publicize his heroism, but needing money for the construction of a Bible school in Fentress County, he agreed to meet producer Jesse Lasky in Crossville and later at the Hermitage Hotel in Nashville where, with the help of a lawyer, he effected an unusually favorable contract that guaranteed a flat fee for himself and a percentage of the gross receipts as well. When York visited the White House along with Gary Cooper and Tennessee Senator Kenneth McKellar, President Roosevelt expressed his approval of the film's themes and the timing of its release. *Sergeant York*'s success owed something to the political situation, but its continued appeal must owe something to its mythic hero: a backwoods superman who expresses the American virtues of decency and rugged individualism.

Frontier heroes and Civil War themes remained popular in films that depicted Tennessee and Tennesseans during the 1950s, even as the lavish costume dramas that romanticized the Old South began to disappear. *The President's Lady*, based on a novel by Irving Stone, starred Susan Hayward and Charlton Heston in a story of the Jacksons' life before the presidency. Heston wore well in the role of Andrew Jackson: when Anthony Quinn decided to remake *The Buccaneer* in 1958, he cast Heston as Old Hickory. Sometime Jackson ally and antagonist, David Crockett, became a television star in the Disney television series of 1955–56. The popular theme song and a successful merchandising campaign made the Tennessee frontiersman a hero to a generation of American children. Disney's largely unhistorical Crockett was a proto-hippie who wore his coonskin cap as a badge of independence, was equally at ease in the woods and in Congress, opposed all injustice and pretension, and defended the oppressed, particularly the Indians whom he understood and admired.

In 1960, two movies about Tennessee contributed to the debate over modernism in American culture. Almost a quarter century after he had worked on *People of the Cumberlands,* Elia Kazan returned to Tennessee to direct his own film, *Wild River,* starring Lee Remick and Montgomery Clift. Filmed on the Hiwassee River in Bradley County, *Wild River* is the story of a diehard landowner who opposes the Tennessee Valley Authority. This time, the government agency is cast in the role not of savior but of monolithic oppressor. In choosing Tennessee as the location for a backward and impoverished community defined by hypocrisy and vigilante violence, Kazan contributed to the enduring Hollywood stereotype. "Under an onionskin thin surface," he said, "is a titantic violence: that is drama. I don't think Northern people, especially Northern intellectuals, know much about it. I didn't until I went to the South and lived there."

Although not filmed in Tennessee, Stanley Kramer's *Inherit the Wind* (1960) dramatized an episode in the state's history that was still controversial, the Scopes Trial held in Dayton in 1925. Clarence Darrow (Spencer Tracy) and William Jennings Bryant (Frederick March) are flawed heroes engaged in an epic courtroom debate played out against the predictable Hollywood scene of local boosterism and southern backwardness.

Hollywood had early on portrayed the South as backward, crude, and violent, a crucible for what Wilbur J. Cash called "the white tribal ethos" defined by racial prejudice, mob mentality, religious fundamentalism, and corrupt politics. Movies such as Tennessean Clarence Brown's *Intruder in the Dust* (1949) and John Ford's *Tobacco Road* (1941) explored the dark side of the South, and both were associated with Tennessee actress Elizabeth Patterson. Born in 1874 in Savannah, Tennessee, Patterson was a character actress who often played devoted mothers or crotchety old women.

In the 1970s, Hollywood produced several films depicting the violence and ignorance of the rural South. *I Walk the Line* (1970), based on a novel by Tennessean Madison Jones and directed by John Frankenheimer, was filmed in the Upper Cumberland region. The image of a law and order South found expression three years later in a low-budget sleeper called *Walking Tall.* Filmed largely in Henderson and Jackson, it is the story of Buford Pusser, a violent and distinctly un-Disney kind of hero who overcame all odds as sheriff of McNairy County. *Walking Tall* is a glamorized version of Pusser's real-life career. It is redeemed from the "hick flick" genre by the presence of a black deputy who helps the sheriff bring fair treatment to citizens of both races who are oppressed by gamblers, pimps, bootleggers, and an inadequate legal system. Though with connotations of right-wing majoritarianism, *Walking Tall* is notable for its portrayal of black characters in a positive light. Pusser himself is portrayed as both avenging angel and frontier superman who defends all citizens, black and white, victimized by the system. The popularity of the original film led to two sequels, the second of which was also filmed in and around Henderson, and in 1981 a short-lived television series of the same name.

Nashville and the country music scene had been a source for Hollywood films since the 1940s, but most were low-budget productions with a thin story line. *Grand Ole Opry* (1940), starring Roy Acuff, *Country Music Holiday* (1958), starring Ferlin Huskey, and *Nashville Rebel* (1966), starring Waylon Jennings, served largely as outlets for Grand Ole Opry stars to play themselves and perform recent hits. Then in 1975, Robert Altman made *Nashville,* still the most significant film made in and about

Actress Jessica Lange portrays country singer Patsy Cline in *Sweet Dreams,* which was filmed in Nashville. 1985, HBO/Silver Screen Partners. Courtesy of Tennessee Film, Entertainment & Music Commission.

Tennessee. A variation on the putting-on-a-show plot familiar in American musicals since *42nd Street,* Altman's *Nashville* is the story of a fictional presidential candidate's visit to Tennessee's capital city to promote his candidacy in the state primary by staging an extravaganza featuring country and western stars from the Nashville music scene. Among traditional musical comedy motifs in the film is that of the established star who becomes incapacitated before the show, thus allowing the new star to emerge. *Nashville* is a bleak but amusing satire on the New South, showing it to be a Noah's ark of empty complacencies. By the use of semidocumentary effects such as live concert footage, overlapping dialogue, improvisation, and narrative ellipsis, Altman exposes America's fantasy of community. Nashville, with its country music industry, becomes a symbol of the entire country's obsession with spectacle and celebrity. The final show is staged at the rebuilt Parthenon, icon of Nashville's created past.

Made on the eve of America's Bicentennial celebration, *Nashville* parodies romantic love, the family, civic responsibility, even Sunday morning churchgoing. Filmed on location as James Agee would have approved, *Nashville* portrays the New South as a region eviscerated by media hype. The southerner, once defined by a strong sense of place, has become the modern Everyman without special attachment to his region.

The success of *Nashville,* however, did little to alter the dominant Hollywood assumption that country music plus Tennessee equaled "hick flick." *W. W. and the Dixie Dance Kings* (1975), filmed partly in Nashville, starred Burt Reynolds who had established himself as a modern southern frontier hero in such movies as *Deliverance* (1972) and *White Lightning* (1973). Country music stars continued to receive Hollywood attention in the 1980s. *Coal Miner's Daughter* (1980), the biography of Loretta Lynn, earned Sissy Spacek the Oscar for Best Actress. *Sweet Dreams* (1985) was the story of Patsy Cline. Both movies included scenes filmed on location in Nashville and Middle Tennessee.

Growing national interest in country music was one reason Hollywood began to produce big budget

Top: Mark Rydell *(left, in jacket)* directs Sissy Spacek and Mel Gibson *(far right)* in a scene from *The River,* which was filmed in Laurel Run and Church Hill in East Tennessee. Copyright 1984, Universal Pictures. Courtesy of Tennessee Film, Entertainment & Music Commission.

Left: Jane Fonda and costar Levon Helm (center) with director Daniel Petrie (right) on the set of *The Dollmaker,* which was filmed in East Tennessee. Copyright 1984, Finnegan Productions/ ABC. Courtesy of Tennessee Film, Entertainment & Music Commission.

films in the state; another reason was that Tennessee itself had begun to court the movie industry. In 1979, Governor Lamar Alexander established a film commission, now called the Tennessee Film, Entertainment, and Music Commission, to market the state to the entertainment industry and to serve as liaison between out-of-state film companies and location scouts, talent agencies, and the legal and technological services that have grown up in Nashville and Memphis around the music industry. The efforts of the film commission, especially its partnership with the Memphis and Shelby County Film and Television Commission (established in 1985), meant that more major Hollywood movies were filmed wholly or in part in Tennessee from 1980 to 2000 than in all of the years before. Although the number of films made in the state has increased, Tennessee locations are still mostly doubles for somewhere else, as in such films as *Star Man* with Jeff Bridges (1984), *The Dollmaker* (1984) with Jane Fonda and Tom Hanks, Disney's *Jungle Book* (1994), *At Close Range* (1985) with Sean Penn, *The Silence of the Lambs* (1990) with Anthony Hopkins and Jodie Foster, *The People vs. Larry Flynt* (1997), *The Rainmaker* (1997), and *The Green Mile* (1999) with Tom Hanks, a prominent feature of which is Tennessee's former state penitentiary, now used exclusively as a movie set.

Hollywood movies that feature Tennessee both as subject and as location are still infrequent. *Marie*

Top: Sydney Pollack, director, takes a break during filming of *The Firm* in Memphis's Court Square. 1993, Paramount Pictures. Courtesy of the Memphis and Shelby County Film and Television Commission and the Tennessee Film, Entertainment & Music Commission.

Right: Jeff Bridges and Karen Allen in *Starman,* which was filmed in several counties between Nashville and Chattanooga. Copyright 1984, Columbia Pictures, Inc. Courtesy of Tennessee Film, Entertainment & Music Commission.

(1986) brought Sissy Spacek back to Tennessee where she played Marie Ragghianti, the whistle blower who helped to bring down the administration of Governor Ray Blanton in the late 1970s. The film, shot in and around Nashville, inaugurated the film career of Fred Thompson who played himself as Ragghianti's attorney. *This Thing Called Love* (1993), directed by Peter Bogdanovich, featured Nashville locations in a story about a young girl who makes it in the country music industry. Memphis locations were highlighted in Sydney Pollack's film *The Firm* (1993), a story of corruption in a Memphis law firm based on the novel by John Grisham.

Rare is the movie where the work of a Tennessee author has been made into a film about Tennessee. One exception is Jim Jarmusch's bizarre *Mystery Train* (1989), the leisurely, poetic journey of two young Japanese lovers on a rock and roll pilgrimage to

Actor Michael Clarke Duncan is interviewed outside the former Tennessee State Penitentiary in Nashville during a break in filming *The Green Mile.* 1999, Castle Rock Entertainment/Warner Bros./Darkwoods Productions. Courtesy of Tennessee Film, Entertainment & Music Commission.

Memphis. Another exception is Stephen John Ross's *Old Forest* (1983), a film adaptation of Peter Taylor's haunting short story set in Memphis.

Television movies based on best-selling books by Tennessee's Alex Haley have all been filmed elsewhere. Haley's historical novel *Roots* was made into an eight-part ABC miniseries, which reached an astounding 70 percent of the American viewing audience when it premiered in 1977. Its 130 million viewers broke the record that had been held, ironically, by the television broadcast of *Gone with the Wind* the year before. The popularity of *Roots* underscores the appeal of the South in all its familiar trappings, but *Roots* reversed the stereotypes. In this film, it is the white characters who are evil and the black characters who are noble. Nevertheless, despite its revisionist view of slavery, fueled by the frustration and anger of the civil rights controversies of the previous ten years, *Roots*' portrayal of the Old South as a land of white-columned plantation houses is finally no less stereotyped than that of *Gone with the Wind* or D. W. Griffith's *Birth of a Nation.* And despite the sensationalist appeal of scenes of beatings, rapes, and miscegenation inflicted by whites on blacks, the ending of *Roots* is in its way as utopian as that of *Birth of a Nation.* Both films conclude with visions of concord, and both endings seem to have been tacked on to the more memorable episodes of brutality and racial hatred that went before. In 1979, thanks to the success of the original miniseries, ABC presented a sequel, *Roots: the Next Generation,* which

Christopher Walken *(left)* and Sean Penn star in *At Close Range* (1986), which was filmed in several Middle Tennessee locations, including Franklin. Hemdale Film Corp./Orion Pictures. Courtesy of Tennessee Film, Entertainment & Music Commission.

took the story from the nineteenth century to Haley's own youth in Henning, Tennessee, and later to his search for his family past. Haley asserts at the end of *Roots* that everyone, black and white, may find their identity in family history.

Roots projects the story of a black family's nightmare in slavery through the lens of that family's survival into modern times, united and contented at last. The story has the enduring power of myth. The widespread criticism about its lack of historical authenticity is an issue as old as Hollywood itself. Since 1915, when President Woodrow Wilson praised *The Birth of a Nation* as "history written with lightning," critics have doubted the suitability of lightning as a reliable writing tool. Creative artists from Griffith to Haley interpret history according to standards of scholarship somewhat different from those of academic historians. Questions inevitably arise about how much artistic license is permissible in dramatizing a historical event when factual evidence is fragmentary or ambiguous or lacking altogether. One critic concludes that in movies and television "truth, accuracy, and a proper respect for history . . . have been routinely subordinated" to the audience's demand for sex, scandal, and depravity.[1] On the other hand, history on film can explore personalities, emotions, and the physical conditions of environments in a way that documentaries, dependent as they are on archival record, cannot. Griffith and Haley created successful fictions, which, from their different perspectives, deepen and complicate the myth of the South in the American imagination.

Documentaries about Tennessee have, to some extent, filled the vacuum that James Agee deplored as the absence of regionally inspired and regionally produced American films. A 1978 video called *Raw Mash: Hamper McBee* celebrates the frontier virtues of hard work and self-reliance in the biography of a Tennessee mountain moonshiner and storyteller. Filmed on location near his birthplace beneath Natural Bridge in the woods of eastern Franklin County, the thirty-minute color documentary by Sol Korine and Blaine Dunlap has McBee telling stories, singing ballads, and demonstrating the disappearing art of making moonshine of sufficient quality to "slap you right back in the creek." Part of the fascination of this award-winning program is the portrayal of McBee as a southern eccentric and wild man living in harmony with the land and in defiance of the law. Equally fascinating is the movie's educational thrust. We follow McBee step by step as he constructs a still, stokes the fire, stirs in the mash, and cools the brew. He frequently reminds us as he carries heavy sacks of corn and chops logs for the fire that this work is hard and dangerous. We respond to his humor as we admire his energy, physical strength, and engineering skill. At the end of the process, our attention and McBee's dedication are rewarded by a crystal clear trickle from the keg. McBee pronounces the whiskey good enough for Christmas. There is a surprise ending: the peaceful autumn woods are rocked by an explosion in which the still is blown to pieces. The end title credits this minor apocalypse to the efforts of the Tennessee Alcoholic Beverage Commission.

Since Agee so strongly endorsed the documentary tradition in American film, it is appropriate that a documentary on the life of Agee himself, filmed as he would have preferred in "actual rather than imitated places," was acclaimed for its original artistry, winning the Blue Ribbon for Literature at the 1980 American Film Festive. *Agee* (1979) was produced by the James Agee Film Project under the direction of Ross Spears, a filmmaker who answered to Agee's own criterion of a "gifted amateur" informed by energy, eye, conviction, and delight. The ninety-minute biography frames significant episodes in Agee's short, passionate, and creative life with interviews with all three of his wives, as well as with such friends as Father Flye, the Episcopal priest who had been his teachers at St. Andrew's School near Sewanee; his Harvard roommate, the poet Robert Fitzgerald; the critic Dwight Macdonald; his colleague, the photographer Walker Evans; and film director John Huston, for whom he wrote the script of *The African Queen.*

Sinking Creek Film Festival

MANY NASHVILLIANS BELIEVE THAT THE NASHVILLE INDEPENDENT FILM FESTIVAL, HELD ANNUALLY for a week in early June, got its start in 1998 at the Belcourt Cinema in Nashville's Hillsboro Village. In fact, the South's longest-running independent film festival, which celebrated its thirty-third year in 2002, was founded on a small farm in East Tennessee. Originated by Mary Jane Coleman in 1969, the festival was named "Sinking Creek" after a small stream on Coleman's Greeneville farm. Since then it has grown exponentially, attracting national attention and corporate sponsorships. A key partnership with Regal Cinemas provides an Oscar-qualifying screening opportunity to the festival winner.

The Sinking Creek Film Festival, which changed its name to the Nashville Independent Film Festival in 1998 and moved from the Vanderbilt University campus, has just begun to be recognized for its enormous contribution to the world of independent film. Nashville Independent Film Festival alumni number in the thousands and include scores of animators and documentary filmmakers who, while well-known in film circles, have only recently gained mass public recognition on a scale once unheard-of for independent film. John Lasseter (*Toy Story*) and Ken Burns (*The Civil War, Baseball, Lewis and Clark, Jazz*) showed early works at Sinking Creek. Joan Gratz (*Mona Lisa Descending a Staircase*), Frank Mouris (*Frank Film*), Jessica Yu (*Sour Death Balls*), Les Blank (*Werner Herzog Eats His Shoe*), Tom Neff (*Sunflower in a Hothouse: Red Grooms*), and Will Vinton (*California Raisins*) earned Academy Awards for shorts and animations that were shown at Sinking Creek. Masterful works of documentary filmmaking—all later aired on PBS—such as *Crumb* (the story of 'keep on truckin' cartoonist R. Crumb), *Guerrillas in Our Midst* (a chronicle of the underground feminist art movement in New York City), *Sherman's March* (a humorous personal retelling of the Civil War), *American Tongues* (the evolution of American English), and *Common Threads* (a history of the AIDS quilt), while not Festival entries, were all premiered in Nashville under the auspices of the festival.

The Nashville Independent Film Festival, for many years one of the very few National Endowment for the Arts grant recipients in Tennessee, has always received major support from the Tennessee Arts Commission, which was a founding sponsor in 1969. In recent years the festival has been recognized as one of Nashville's unique cultural assets by the grantmaking arm of the Metro Nashville Arts Commission. Nashville's Frist Foundation has generously donated both the funds and the technology to allow the festival to follow the leaps and bounds growth of the film industry and the online universe (www.nashvillefilmfestival.org).

In its first fifteen years, the festival attracted a total of ten thousand viewers and averaged around one hundred entries per year. In its thirtieth year (1998), the festival received more than 450 entries and its viewership over a five-day period totaled close to ten thousand. The tremendous growth of the festival reflects the increasing popularity of independent film and the considerable maturation of the Nashville (Sinking Creek) Independent Film Festival, which shone for many years like a tiny beacon of light guiding many a would-be independent filmmaker through the stormy seas of studio moviemaking.

Susan W. Knowles, Former Treasurer, Sinking Creek Film Festival

Spears rhythmically edits these interviews among dramatizations, documentary footage of the Depression, still photographs, and a clip from Huston's film, *The Bride Comes to Yellow Sky* (1952), in which Agee plays a bit part as a jailbird, himself the physical type of the rawboned and lanky frontiersman.

Steven J. Ross, a communications professor at the University of Memphis, made several important documentaries, including the Emmy nominated *By the River I Stand* (1993) about the Memphis Sanitation Workers' strike of 1968; *Oh Freedom After Awhile* (2000), about a sharecroppers' strike in Missouri and which received the Tennessee Independent Film Maker Award; and *Black Diamonds, Blue City,* which tells the story of the Memphis Red Sox, the city's baseball team in the old Negro League. Ross's most recent project is a documentary about the life and work of Winslow Homer.

The tradition of independent filmmaking continues into the twenty-first century in Tennessee. The Nashville Independent Film Festival, formerly known as the Sinking Creek Film Festival, is an annual showcase for film and video. It receives more than five hundred entries a year in its competition. The Memphis Film Forum, established in 1998, has curated a film series for the National Civil Rights Museum and stages the Memphis International Film Festival. The Valleyfest Independent Film Festival has taken place in Knoxville since 1998. Thanks to these incentives, and to filmmaking departments at schools across the state, several hundred feature films, documentaries, and television productions have been made in Tennessee in the last twenty years.

TENNESSEANS AS ACTORS AND DIRECTORS

Tennesseans have made their mark in Hollywood as actors and directors. Clarence Brown grew up in Knoxville, where his parents worked in the Brookside Mills. He received degrees in electrical and mechanical engineering from the University of Tennessee. After serving as a flight instructor in World War I, he went to Hollywood where his engineering experience helped him to master the technical intricacies of filmmaking. His movies are notable, however, for their pictorial style and their emphasis on lighting and composition that he had learned during a long apprenticeship with the director Maurice Tourneur at Universal Studios. Brown was also known as a director with a special flair for getting the best out of his stars, especially female stars like Greta Garbo, Joan Crawford, Norma Shearer, and Rosalind Russell. He is famous for directing Elizabeth Taylor in her first major starring role in *National Velvet* (1944). He received three Oscar nominations as Best Director. The Clarence Brown Theater at the University of Tennessee is located on land that he donated to his alma mater.

A 1952 script conference for *Dusty Portrait. Left to right:* Sumner Locke-Elliot, writer; Fred Coe, producer; Delbert Mann, director. Courtesy of Special Collections, Vanderbilt University.

Other prominent Tennessee directors are Fred Coe and Delbert Mann, the latter having directed more than fifty films and over a hundred television shows. Once a student of Coe's at the Nashville Community Playhouse, Mann first won acclaim for his television production of *Marty* in 1953. After a series of successful films in the 1960s, his peers elected him president of the Directors' Guild of America. His tel-

Frederick H. Coe

FREDERICK H. COE (1914–1979), LEADING PRODUCER AND DIRECTOR DURING THE "GOLDEN AGE OF television" of the 1950s, was born in Mississippi, but raised in Nashville and called Tennessee home. Nurtured in the arts and theater at Nashville's Hume Fogg High School, Coe began his career doing radio dramas for WSM in Nashville. In 1945, the National Broadcasting Company (NBC) hired him as a production manager. He was named head of NBC's *Playhouse* in 1948, from where he would launch a spectacular series of dramas and television programs.

Coe was the primary creative force behind the *Philco-Goodyear Playhouse,* a highly regarded live performance anthology produced in New York City. His work in this and other anthologies, such as *Playhouse 90,* yielded such television classics as *Marty* by Paddy Chayefsky, *The Trip to Bountiful* by Horton Foote, *The Death of Billy the Kid* by Gore Vidal, *Days of Wine and Roses,* and *Peter Pan,* which starred Mary Martin and was the highest-rated program yet on television when it aired in 1955. Coe was famous for nurturing the creative side of television. He supported writers like Chayefsky, Foote, Vidal, Tad Mosel, and J. P. Miller, directors Delbert Mann (also from Nashville) and Arthur Penn, and young actors such as Grace Kelly, Paul Newman, Nancy Marchand, and Rod Steiger.

Coe's success in television led to opportunities both on the stage and movie screen. On Broadway, he produced *The Miracle Worker* and *All the Way Home,* which won a Pulitzer Prize. In 1965, he directed the film classic, *A Thousand Clowns,* following which Coe's period of significance in American drama largely ended. He died in 1979. A member of the Television Hall of Fame, Coe was inducted into the Broadcasting and Cable Hall of Fame in 1994.

Carroll Van West, Middle Tennessee State University

evision production of *All Quiet on the Western Front* (1979) won a Golden Globe Award.

In 1947, Clarence Brown's film, *The Yearling,* made a star of another Tennessean, Nashville-born Claude Jarman Jr., a fifth-grader whom Brown discovered while traveling incognito throughout the South looking for a lead for his film. Jarman's portrayal of the love of a child for a foundling deer won him a special Academy Award. "The only thing I know about directing children," Brown said, "is the performance I got from Claude. Every word, every action, every gesture was manipulated. The boy was smart enough to do just what I told him." Jarman later played a role in Brown's adaptation of the Faulkner novel *Intruder in the Dust* (1947) and was a star in the John Ford–John Wayne western *Rio Grande* (1950), acting in a total of eleven movies between 1946 and 1956. He then retired from film acting (except for a role in the television movie

The Yearling with Gregory Peck and Claude Jarman Jr. Courtesy of Special Collections, University of Tennessee, Knoxville.

Patricia Neal. Photograph by Carl Van Vechten. Courtesy of the Library of Congress, Prints & Photographs Division, Creative Americans: Portraits by Carl Van Vechten, 1932–1964, Collection (reproduction number LC-USZ62-103708 DLC).

Centennial in 1978), becoming director of the San Francisco Film Festival and manager of the San Francisco Opera House.

Many other Tennesseans have had success in Hollywood. Elizabeth Patterson of Savannah and Patricia Neal of Knoxville became major stars. Neal won an Academy Award for her role in *Hud* (1963). Polly Bergen, like Neal a native of Knoxville, starred in *Cape Fear,* and then enjoyed a long career in cinema, television, and Broadway. Cybill Shepherd from Memphis, Sondra Locke from Shelbyville, Oprah Winfrey from Nashville, and Dolly Parton from Sevierville began their Hollywood careers with major successes. Shepherd starred in *The Last Picture Show* (1971), and Locke was nominated for the Academy Award for Best Supporting Actress in *The Heart Is a Lonely Hunter* (1968). Winfrey, who lived as a teenager in Nashville and attended Tennessee State University, was a television celebrity before she surprised many of her fans and Hollywood executives with her sensitive performance in *The Color Purple* (1985). Parton, likewise, confounded skeptics with her ability as both a comic and dramatic actress in her debut in *9 to 5* (1980). Kathy Bates, a graduate of White Station High School in Memphis, won an Oscar for her role as an obsessed fan in *Misery* (1990). Nashville's Reese Witherspoon, a graduate of Harpeth Hall School, received a Golden Globe nomination for her role in *Election* (1999) and starred in the summer 2001 hit *Legally Blonde* and the 2002 hit *Sweet Home Alabama.*

Working-class America found its most enduring icon in Elvis Presley, a Tennessean by choice. After moving to Memphis at the age of thirteen, Elvis

Memphis native Cybill Shepherd stars in Turner Network Television's *Memphis.* Copyright 1991, Turner Pictures, Inc. Photograph by Gene Trindl. Courtesy of the Memphis and Shelby County Film and Television Commission and the Tennessee Film, Entertainment & Music Commission.

Director John Frankenheimer *(center)* prepares to film a scene of *Against the Wall* with Chattanooga native Samuel L. Jackson *(left)* and cast members Steve Harris *(second from right)* and Kyle MacLachlan at the Tennessee State Penitentiary in Nashville. 1994, HBO. Courtesy of Tennessee Film, Entertainment & Music Commission.

worked part time as an usher at a downtown movie theater. Later in Hollywood, Elvis played himself on screen and became one of the top-grossing movie stars of all time. Like Fred Astaire, Elvis is one of the few stars for whom films were created solely to be vehicles for his personality and talent. Debuting in *Love Me Tender* (1956), a Civil War western in which he sings four songs before getting shot, and then returns to sing another in ghostly form, Elvis starred in nearly thirty musicals and two documentaries, *Elvis: That's the Way It Is* (1970) and *Elvis on Tour* (1972), neither of which was set in Tennessee. Though in no way distinguished by acting style, originality, or cinematic technique, Elvis's early films were joyful variations on the standard American musical comedy theme of the individual who opposes pretentiousness and inhuman authority. *In Jailhouse Rock* (1957), for example, he plays an ex-con who becomes a pop star. With an exuberant screen presence reminiscent of Gene Kelly's muscular all-American style, Elvis on screen is at the center of a charmed circle that includes all those people, on the screen and in the audience, who feel the loss of personal liberty. His charisma derives from both white and black styles. His way of speaking and dressing, his body movements, and his songs harmonized elements of honky tonk with white Pentecostal, black rhythm and blues, pop and country. His screen persona might be said to project a new kind of southern stereotype for Hollywood: the country boy as Byronic hero, unique and immediately recognizable.

Two African American actors from Tennessee, Morgan Freeman and Samuel L. Jackson, have become Hollywood stars. Freeman, from Memphis, arose to prominence in *Driving Miss Daisy* (1989) and is now a major leading man. Jackson, who grew up in Chattanooga, moved from supporting to starring roles in a short time. He played the lead in *Shaft* (2000), a movie that was originally scored by another

Top: Tennessee State Prison, administration building. Courtesy of Tennessee Film, Entertainment & Music Commission.

Above: Actor Chuck Norris *(left, in vest)* and cast members take a break on the set of *Delta Force 2: Operation Stranglehold,* which was filmed in several Carter County locations in East Tennessee in 1990. Pathe Communications/MGM. Courtesy of Tennessee Film, Entertainment & Music Commission.

Tennessean, composer and actor Isaac Hayes. One of Hollywood's most acclaimed newcomers, Knoxville-born Quentin Tarantino, directed *Reservoir Dogs* (1993) and *Pulp Fiction* (1994), both of which recall the complex plots and flashbacks of the 1940s.

NOTE

1. Robert Brent Toplin, *History by Hollywood* (Urbana: Univ. of Illinois Press, 1996), 5.

SUGGESTED READINGS

Birdwell, Michael E. *Celluloid Soldiers: Warner Bros.'s Campaign Against Nazism.* New York: New York Univ. Press, 1999.

Campbell, Edward D. C., Jr. *The Celluloid South: Hollywood and the Southern Myth.* Knoxville: Univ. of Tennessee Press, 1981.

Chappell, Fred. "The Image of the South in Film." *Southern Humanities Review* 12 (Fall 1978): 303–11.

Doss, Erika. *Elvis Culture: Fans, Faith and Image.* Lawrence: Univ. Press of Kansas, 1999.

French, Warren, ed. *The South and Film.* Jackson: Univ. Press of Mississippi, 1981.

Kirby, Jack Temple. *Media-Made Dixie: The South in the American Imagination.* Baton Rouge: Louisiana State Univ. Press, 1978.

Krampner, Jon. *The Man in the Shadows: Fred Coe and the Golden Age of Television.* New Brunswick, N.J.: Rutgers Univ. Press, 1997.

Macdonald, Dwight. "Eisenstein, Pudovkin and Others." *The Emergence of Film Art.* 2d ed. Edited by Lewis Jacobs. New York: W. W. Norton, 1979.

Mann, Delbert. *Looking Back . . . at Live Television and Other Matters.* Los Angeles: Directors Guild of America, 1998.

Neal, Patricia. *As I Am: An Autobiography.* New York: Simon and Schuster, 1988.

Stewart, Joel. *Ralph Steiner: Filmmaker and Still Photographer.* Zucker, New York: Arno Press, 1978.

Toplin, Robert Brent. *History by Hollywood.* Urbana: Univ. of Illinois Press, 1996.

Williamson, J. W. *Hillbillyland: What the Movies Did to the Mountains and What the Mountains Did to the Movies.* Chapel Hill: Univ. of North Carolina Press, 1995.

Young, Jeff, ed. *Kazan: The Master Director Discusses His Films.* New York: Newmarket Press, 1999.

Part Five

The Performance Arts

Music

Twenty-two

Symphony and Opera in Tennessee

Perre Magness

Memphis

Cultural life on the Tennessee frontier left something to be desired. As nineteenth-century historian James Dick Davis wrote, "Music had its expression in the banjo and violin, with 'Old Zip Coon' and 'Arkansaw Traveler' representing the height of musical taste."[1] But as wealth increased, churches and schools brought a civilizing influence, and the merchants and planters who built fine houses began to long for the refinements of the cities back east—or at least their wives and daughters did. Their wishes came true periodically through performances by touring artists. But not until the middle of the twentieth century were there permanent local organizations with regularly scheduled performances of symphonic music and opera in Tennessee's cities.

Bertha Walburn-Clark, Elisa Walburn Stong *[sic]*, and Harold Clark. Courtesy of the McClung Historical Collection.

The Knoxville Symphony Orchestra has the distinction of being the oldest continuing orchestra in the Southeast, giving its first public performance in 1925. The founder and first conductor was Bertha Walburn Clark. Born Bertha Roth in Ohio in 1882, her German parents gave her a love of music, and she studied violin and voice at the Cincinnati Conservatory of Music. In 1903, a year after her graduation, her family moved to Knoxville, and she and her sister opened a violin and viola studio. She was frequently asked to play at churches and clubs, and she performed at the opening of the fashionable Atkin Hotel in 1910. Her performances were so well received that she recruited her most advanced students to form an ensemble, which became a regular attraction at the hotel. Guests like the conductor Walter Damrosch and composer Victor Herbert complimented the ensemble's playing.

Finding capable musicians in Knoxville to fill out the sections for a full orchestra was difficult, and the original group was decidedly amateur, with each member paying dues of fifty cents a month to buy their music.

Nineteenth-Century Touring Companies

As life on the Tennessee frontier acquired the patina of civilization, sizable towns in the state began to attract touring artists. Although the quality of some of the performances was probably on a level with the work of the Duke and the Dauphin in *Huckleberry Finn,* at least the visitors brought a touch of the world to the stages of the state. By the 1850s, well-known artists were including Tennessee on their tours. Memphis and Nashville, easily accessible river cities, were the most usual stops. Jenny Lind, the "Swedish Nightingale," toured in 1851, performing in both Nashville and Memphis, and her sponsor, P. T. Barnum, was said to have made seven thousand dollars from one concert.

Touring dramatic companies usually brought their own orchestras, or at least a fiddler or two, and local talent was pressed into service as accompaniment. Arditi's Italian Opera Company performed several operas at the Adelphi Theater in Nashville in 1854, the most eagerly awaited of which was *Lucia di Lammermoor,* as many Nashvillians prided themselves on their Scots heritage. But the audience was bewildered when the kilted cast sang in a foreign tongue, and there was much confusion when singers who were supposed to be dying sang on and on. The *Nashville Gazette* later lectured its readers, "If a man in his death agony is heard to sing the hearer must not become disgusted at the outrage thereby inflicted, but must catch in the mystic flow of song the spirit of the dying man." There were many in town whose religious scruples would not allow them to attend the theater. Rosa DeVries, the star of the company, gave a special concert for them at the Odd Fellows Hall.

Carlo Patti, the brother of famed soprano Adelina Patti, organized an orchestra in Memphis just before the Civil War. Carlo came from a musical family; legend has it that he was born backstage at the Teatro Madrid during the intermission of a performance of *Norma* in which his mother was singing the lead! He left Memphis in a hurry to join the Confederate

Bertha Clark dedicated her life to upgrading performance standards and generating community support. A series of three programs was presented in 1926 under the name "The Walburn Clark Little Symphony." The first, a free concert given by the twenty-five-piece orchestra in the Farragut Hotel, featured a guest soloist, cellist Louisa Knowlton. One week later, the orchestra gave a benefit concert at the same location. Guest soloists and charity concerts became part of the orchestra's tradition from these early days.

When the Tennessee Valley Authority located in Knoxville in 1933, newly arrived employees brought musical and administrative talents as well as support. Bertha Clark managed the whole operation: arranging the programs, hiring and hosting guest artists, obtaining musical scores, designing tickets and programs, renting halls, leading rehearsals, supervising publicity, and soothing ruffled feathers along the way. In 1935, a board of three directors was elected from the members of the orchestra to manage business affairs, leaving Clark as music director. Chartered by the state as a nonprofit institution, the group became the Knoxville Symphony Orchestra, with the first official concert on November 24, 1935. For the first time, the conductor was paid fifty dollars a concert, auditions were held, and members no longer paid dues.

By the 1940s there were fifty musicians playing two or three concerts a season to an annual audience of seven hundred. The Knoxville Symphony Society was formed to provide financial support and business management. The first concert to take place under the sponsorship of the Knoxville Symphony Society was held on December 7, 1941. Just hours before, the news of the bombing of Pearl Harbor had come. By coincidence, the symphony that night played army, supposedly to escape the too-ardent attentions of a local girl, Belle Edmondson (who later gained fame as a Confederate spy). Carlo had the distinction of serving in both the Confederate and Union armies before the war was over.

Groups with exotic names like the Ghioni-Susini Italian Opera Troop, the Patti-Strakosch Italian Opera Company, the Isabell McCullough Opera Troope, the Parodi Company, the Emma Abbott Opera Company, and the Frederica Opera Troupe toured the South in the nineteenth century. A native Memphian, Marie Greenwood Worden, toured with her own company, the Marie Greenwood Opera Company, before settling in Memphis in the 1890s to give music lessons.

Staub's Theater, built in 1872, was the center of Knoxville's cultural life. The Greenlaw Opera House in Memphis was begun before the Civil War and flourished in the 1870s before it was destroyed by fire in 1883. It was home to everything from the Mozart Society to minstrel and vaudeville shows. Despite its impressive name, the sixteen-hundred-seat auditorium hosted as many temperance and political meetings as it did musical events.

The Ryman Auditorium (built as the Union Gospel Tabernacle between 1888 and 1892) in Nashville hosted performances of the Metropolitan Opera of New York and the French Opera Company of New Orleans in the early years of the twentieth century. New York's Metropolitan Opera staged *Carmen* in Memphis and Nashville in 1901.

One of the most popular touring performers was Thomas Wiggins, known as "Blind Tom," an African American musical genius who was said to be able to play the most difficult compositions on the piano after having heard them only once. From Norwegian violinist Ole Bull, touring in the 1850s, to Polish pianist Ignace Paderewski in 1901 and 1902, many international music stars appeared in Tennessee.

Perre Magness, Memphis

Sergei Rachmaninoff, 1925. Knoxville was among the cities included in Rachmaninoff's last concert tour before his death. Courtesy of Special Collections, University of Tennessee, Knoxville.

Roland Hayes

ROLAND HAYES'S LIFE IS A STUDY IN ARTISTRY OVERCOMING PREJUDICE. HAYES USED HIS MUSIC TO TRANscend historical and racial boundaries, paving the way for African Americans in the classical concert music field.

Hayes was born in 1887 in the Flatwoods, a Negro settlement in northern Georgia near the town of Curryville. He was born on the plantation where his mother, Fannie Mann Hayes, had been a slave and became a tenant farmer. His father, William, also a former slave and his first music teacher, died in 1898, when Roland was just eleven.

In 1900 Fannie Hayes moved her family to Chattanooga, and Roland became a member of Monumental Baptist Church and its choir. Here he met and trained with Arthur Calhoun, an organist and choir director who had trained at Oberlin College.

Roland Hayes. Courtesy of the Chattanooga African-American Museum.

In 1905, Hayes went to Nashville, where his voice and musical talent gained him admission to Fisk University despite his lack of formal education. During his years at Fisk, he sang at every possible musical event to earn money for his tuition and room and board. In 1911, he traveled with the Fisk Jubilee Singers to Boston and decided to stay in Boston to undertake serious study. By mid-fall of that year, Hayes was studying music with Arthur Hubbard and working as a page boy at the John Hancock Life Insurance Company.

Hayes financed his earliest public recitals himself in Boston at Symphony Hall in 1916 and 1917. He traveled to London in 1920, giving his first European concert in Aeolian Hall in May. Because he was a man of color, many people came to the concert out of curiosity, but the beauty of his music led to his command performance before King George V and his family on April 23, 1921. This royal recognition opened many doors for Hayes, and he was equally well received in Paris.

Hayes's success in Europe brought a new American response upon his return in 1923. An engagement with the Boston Symphony Orchestra—the first performance by an African American with a major American orchestra—on December 2, 1923, garnered outstanding reviews. Hayes became the first African American to give a recital at Carnegie Hall in 1924. Now able to obtain professional management and promotions, he appeared with the finest symphony orchestras in Europe and America.

In September 1932, Hayes and Helen Alzada Mann married; they had one daughter, Afrika Franzada.

Hayes continued to perform all over the country, even into his sixties and seventies. At all times he encouraged the development of young talent and served as mentor to young artists. During his lifetime Hayes received many honors, and numerous colleges awarded him honorary degrees.

Roland Hayes gave his last concert at age eighty-five at the Longy School of Music in Cambridge, Massachusetts. His last Chattanooga concert was in 1969 at age eighty-two. He died on January 1, 1977.

Vivian P. Greene, Chattanooga African-American Museum

Beethoven's Fifth Symphony, which was to become a symbol of victory during the next four years.

In 1946, Clark retired as conductor but continued as principal violist and served on the board of directors until her death in 1972 at the age of eighty-nine. She was succeeded in the 1946 season by Lamar Stringfield, Pulitzer Prize–winning composer of the symphonic suite *From the Southern Mountains.*

David Van Vactor, a flutist, was in command of the orchestra for twenty-five years, from 1947 to 1972. He was active in the organization of a music department at the University of Tennessee, began a series of concerts for children, and created a competition for young composers and soloists with a scholarship program. The orchestra library was founded in 1949, and the women's auxiliary was organized in 1952. In the 1954–55 season, the opera *Die Fledermaus* was presented. It was so well received that operatic programs were presented throughout the 1960s. The orchestra began its Connoisseur Concerts of contemporary music in 1960–61. Van Vactor was also a composer; his cantata *The New Light* was performed in 1954, his *Christmas Songs for Young People for Chorus and Orchestra* in 1960–61. He is still, in the early twenty-first century, the only person to be named composer laureate of Tennessee.

Hungarian Arpad Joo became conductor in 1973, when he was only twenty-five years old. During his tenure, he expanded the repertoire; professionalized the orchestra (paying all of its members for the first time); and helped form a youth orchestra. He was succeeded in 1977 by another Hungarian, Zoltan Rozsnyai, who founded the Knoxville Chamber Orchestra in 1981 and conducted twelve summer concerts during the Knoxville World's Fair in 1982. Under his leadership, the orchestra increased its number of performances and ensemble appearances as well as its budget.

At the beginning of the twenty-first century, the KSO is made up of eighty professional musicians, led by Kirk Trevor since 1984. Tens of thousands of East Tennesseans hear performances annually at classical, pops, family and educational concerts; each year the orchestra performs for fifty thousand school children.

The symphony's success in presenting operas demonstrated the need for an opera company. The Knoxville Civic Opera Company was created in 1976 and gave its first performance of *La Traviata,* with nationally known Tennessee native soprano Mary Costa, in 1978. Since 1978, the company has mounted over fifty productions. Since 1988, educational programs have reached over sixty thousand people, primarily students, and have introduced opera as an art form using the Knoxville Opera Studio Apprentices.

The first official season of the Chattanooga Symphony was 1933, although a symphony had been organized as a community group in 1909. Melvin Margolin conducted from 1933 until 1936, and Borden Jones took over for the 1936–37 season. In the early years, rehearsals were held in the County Courthouse, and the thirty to thirty-five musicians received no pay other than the pleasure of performing. Civic and financial backing was hard to come by, and audiences seldom exceeded two hundred.

In 1937, the Juilliard Foundation brought Dr. Arthur Plettner, a young composer and conductor, to Chattanooga. In the twelve years of his tenure, he created a professional organization. In 1949, the Chattanooga Jaycees spearheaded a fund-raising campaign that led to the employment of Joseph Hawthorne as full-time conductor. From 1956 to 1965, Julius Hegyl was conductor, succeeded by Charles Gabor for one season, and then by Richard Cormier, who brought needed stability to the orchestra from 1967 to 1983.

The Chattanooga Opera Association was formed in 1943 by Dr. Werner Wolff, a refugee from Nazi Germany. With no money, no trained singers, no orchestra, and no established audience, he and his wife, Emmy Land Wolff, who was stage director under his leadership, began their life in this country with great ambition to produce opera. The first performances were held in high school auditoriums, using singers from the Chattanooga area. In the third season, Ottakar Cadek, a violinist, commuted from Birmingham and acted as concertmaster for both the symphony and the opera orchestra that Wolff conducted.

Players borrowed from the U.S. Army Band at Fort Oglethorpe, Georgia, frequently filled in the orchestra. The opera began performing at the Tivoli Theater in 1963. Robert Carter Austin was artistic director from 1974 to 1983.

To facilitate fund-raising in the community, the symphony merged with the forty-two-year-old Chattanooga Opera Association in 1985. That year Vakhtang Jordania of the Soviet Union was engaged as conductor and musical director for both groups. Over the next six seasons, he rebuilt the symphony into a major force in Chattanooga's arts scene. Jordania established a core orchestra comprised of selected full-time musicians, expanded the orchestra's performances to include contemporary works and world premiers, and welcomed internationally acclaimed soloists such as Jean-Pierre Rampal and Itzhak Perlman as guest artists. In 1992, Robert Bernhardt, a native of Rochester, New York, took the leadership of the organization. Bernhardt continued the orchestra's growth as musicians and expanded its educational programming.

Today the Chattanooga Symphony and Opera Association is the only combined organization of its kind in the United States. It presents over one hundred performances a year, ranging from string quartet programs to fully staged opera. There are symphony concerts, pops concerts, opera produc-

Francis Arthur Robinson

FRANCIS ARTHUR ROBINSON (1910–1980) IS BEST REMEMBERED AS THE LONGTIME SPOKESMAN FOR the Metropolitan Opera in New York. Born in Mount Pleasant, Tennessee, he was educated at Vanderbilt University and served as a lieutenant in the United States Navy during World War II. Before he moved to New York and worked for the Met, Robinson was a reporter and Sunday editor of the *Nashville Banner*; a writer, actor, and producer for WSM Radio; and a theatrical press representative and company manager in association with William Fields and the Playwrights' Company.

Francis Robinson, as assistant manager, Metropolitan Opera, c. 1976. Courtesy of Special Collections, Vanderbilt University.

At various times in his long association with the Metropolitan Opera, Robinson served as assistant manager, director of the Press Department, of Public Relations, and of Box Office and Subscriptions; and tour director. He was popular with opera fans for his "Biographies in Music" and presentations during radio and television broadcasts. To millions of listeners, he was the voice of the Met. He also wrote many articles and sound recording liner notes as well as two books: *Caruso: His Life in Pictures* (1957) and *Celebration: The Metropolitan Opera* (1979). Robinson was a longtime member of the Board of Trust at Vanderbilt University and left his invaluable collection of correspondence, photographs, ephemera, subject files, and artifacts to the Vanderbilt University Library.

Sara Harwell, Vanderbilt University

tions both staged and unstaged, young peoples concerts with the Chattanooga Youth Symphony, and school performances. A new program introduces music to kindergarten classes throughout the year, culminating in a full concert at the end of the year.

One of the state's oldest orchestras was formed in one of Tennessee's newest cities. In 1943, biochemist Waldo Cohn came to the new "atomic city" of Oak Ridge with the Manhattan Project. He spotted a small notice in a mimeographed bulletin asking for musicians to meet at a certain time and place. He took his cello, discovered like-minded musicians, and they formed a quartet. As more scientists and servicemen were assigned to Oak Ridge, the number attending rehearsals grew. The first musical performance was on December 19, 1943, as part of an interdenominational worship service. By June 1944, there were enough musicians for the group, now called the Oak Ridge Symphonette, to present a public concert. Only a few months later, having added brass and woodwind players, the sixty-five-member Oak Ridge Symphony, conducted by Cohn, gave its initial concert in November, presenting Bach's *Suite Number 3,* Schubert's

Dr. Werner Wolff and his wife, Emmy Land-Wolff. Courtesy of Chattanooga-Hamilton County Bicentennial Library.

Nationally and Internationally Known Opera Singers from Tennessee

- Grace Moore
- Mignon Dunn
- Gail Robinson
- Patricia Welting
- Nancy Tatum
- Elizabeth Carter
- Sylvia Stahlman
- Richard Vernon
- Naomi Moody
- Mary Costa
- Marguerite Piazza
- Ruth Welting
- Kallen Esperian
- Vera Little
- Dawn Upshaw
- James Melton
- Donnie Ray Albert
- Roy Cornelius Smith

Grace Moore (and child, identity unknown), December 20, 1937. Courtesy of the McClung Historical Collection.

Unfinished Symphony, and a suite from Berlioz's *Damnation of Faust.*

The army, in its desire to promote good morale, supported the fledgling symphony and provided touring artists like Nathan Milstein. The end of the war, however, meant that the population of Oak Ridge was halved, and many of the musicians left to return to civilian life. Army support ended. "We didn't know whether we'd have a town left, much less a symphony," one musician recalled.[2] A committee was formed to help fill the vacancies. When David Van Vactor came to Knoxville in 1947 to head the Knoxville Symphony and form the University of Tennessee's Music Department, the two orchestras began sharing musicians and rotated performances between Oak Ridge and Knoxville.

Once freed from army support and supervision, Cohn and others organized the Oak Ridge Civic Music Association (ORCMA) in 1947 to sponsor the symphony and chorus concerts and to bring in outside professionals. Concerts were presented on two nights in a six-hundred-seat high school auditorium, and the symphony played to packed houses. "After all, it was the only show in town," Cohn chuckled.[3]

One notable concert featured the premier of Arthur Roberts's *Overture for the Dedication of a Nuclear Reactor* (a work dedicated to the Oak Ridge Symphony, with themes based on the letters A, E, and C (for the now defunct Atomic Energy Commission). Isaac Stern came to perform with the symphony several times beginning in 1948 because he was a friend of Cohn's. Yaltah Menuhin, pianist sister of famed violinist Yehudi Menuhin, lived in Knoxville while her husband was in the army, and, because of her friendship with Cohn, played with the symphony.

Cohn conducted the symphony for eleven years. Since then, there have been several other conductors, including Richard Cormier, who commuted from Chattanooga from 1968 to 1970; Edward Zambara (1970–74); Donald Neuen (1974–79) from the University of Tennessee's Music Department; Robert Lyall (1980–90); and John Welsh (1991–2000). Currently, at the beginning of the twenty-first century, the conductor is Serge Fournier. In the 1999–2000 season, the ORCMA celebrated its fifty-fifth year and honored Waldo Cohn, its founder, with symphony and chorus concerts, a concert series with guest soloists and chamber groups, and a performance of the musical comedy *Funny Girl.*

The Kingsport Symphony Orchestra was formed in 1946. All forty-three members were volunteers, and concerts, held in the middle school auditorium, were free to the public. Contributing members of the organization donated five dollars, and "patrons of means" were encouraged to give ten dollars. Today the orchestra has sixty-five paid musicians and performs seven regular season concerts in the seventeen-hundred-seat Eastman Chemical Company Employee Center Auditorium, in addition to three more concerts in Bristol, Tennessee/Virginia, and Abingdon, Virginia, and performances at such public events as the July Funfest. The Symphony Chorus and the fifty-member audition-only Kingsport Youth Symphony also perform.

Over the years of its existence, the Kingsport Symphony has had nine conductors: Robert W. Barrigar (1947–53), Elbert S. Hurt Jr. (1953–54), Arpad Kurinsky (1955–56), William S. Boyer (1956–64), Willem Bertsch (1964–81), John Gordon Ross (1981–91), Mark Deal (1991–92), David Itkin (1992–96), and Cyrus Ginwala (1996–present). The

Walter Sharp, soprano Helen Jepson, and William Strickland. Courtesy of the Nashville Symphony.

orchestra celebrated its fiftieth anniversary with the premier performance of a work by Tennessee composer Kenton Coe honoring the orchestra. Other premieres have included works by contemporary composers Donald Reid Womack and David See.

Although performances of classical music in Nashville date to the nineteenth century, and an early-twentieth-century effort at creating a symphony produced some memorable performances, the present Nashville Symphony is another post–World War II institution, founded in 1946. Arts patron Walter Sharp came back from service in World War II with the dream of live classical music in Nashville. He brought back something more—a conductor. While stationed in Maryland in the U.S. Army, Sharp met Warrant Officer William Strickland, who had impressed Sharp with his ability to improve an army band into a respectable group. The two men were reunited at Fort Sam Houston in Texas, and after the war Sharp invited Strickland to Nashville to meet with the city's cultural leaders to discuss founding a symphony. Strickland was an Ohio native who had earned a reputation as an organist before turning to conducting.

The Nashville Civic Music Association was chartered in 1946, and a newly organized symphony gave

John Wesley Work III

JOHN WESLEY WORK III (1901–1967) WAS A SIGNIFICANT COMPOSER, STUDENT OF FOLK MUSIC, AND director of the Fisk Jubilee Singers in the mid-twentieth century. Born in Tullahoma, his parents were John W. Work II and Agnes Haynes Work. His father was a former Fisk professor and president of Roger Williams University, and his parents nurtured his musical talent. Work received his undergraduate degree in history at Fisk, but then entered the Institute of Musical Arts (now the Juilliard School of Music) in New York City in the mid-1920s, during the height of the Harlem Renaissance. He later completed his musical education with a master's degree in music education from Columbia University in 1930, and then, after receiving support from the Julius Rosenwald Foundation, he attended Yale University and completed a bachelor's degree in music in 1933.

Work was actively involved in Fisk's musical programs and instruction for almost forty years. He was first named director of Jubilee Music in 1927; twenty years later, he became the Fisk Jubilee Singers' director and reestablished it as a major student-centered performance group. He also developed a reputation as a composer. His cantata, *The Singers*, was first performed in 1941. His *Venvalou* was performed in 1959. Another choral piece of note, *My Lord, What a Morning*, was performed in Boston in 1965 and later at the United Nations. In all, Work authored approximately 115 compositions.

Work is also significant as a scholar of African American folk music. His collection *American Negro Songs and Spirituals* remains an authoritative reference, and he continued to document sacred and secular performers through the 1960s. His papers and some of his field recordings are in the Special Collections of the Fisk University Library. Work died on May 17, 1967.

Carroll Van West, Middle Tennessee State University

Suggested Reading

Roach, Hildred. *Black American Music*. 2d ed. Malabar, Fla.: Krieger, 1992.

its first concert on December 10. At the first concert, the orchestra performed Beethoven's *Seventh Symphony* and *Tennessee Variations,* composed for the occasion by Strickland's friend Cecil Effinger. Strickland made sure there was at least one work by an American composer on each program. Although Nashvillians bought two thousand season tickets for the first six concerts, community support was uncertain in the early years, but the orchestra survived. From the early days, the "women's committees" assisted in fund raising; the Symphony Guild was organized in 1950–51 in response to a fiscal crisis. Volunteers sold tickets at the door, held preview luncheons, and started the Italian Street Fair (now defunct), which became the largest continuous symphony fund-raiser in the nation in the late twentieth century, grossing $600,000 in 1995. The Symphony Guild also provides teaching manuals and educational programs for the schools.

Strickland left the symphony after the 1950–51 season. Guy Taylor, who, like Strickland, programmed American music and contemporary composers, succeeded Strickland and served as conductor to 1959. In the 1950s, a series of eminent composers came to the George Peabody College for Teachers; most were also symphony guest conductors or composers. The Nashville Choral Society, organized in January 1947, was recognized officially as the vocal arm of the Nashville Symphony Orchestra in 1974.

The symphony formed ties with members of Nashville's country and western music community. Minnie Pearl narrated Saint-Saëns's *Carnival of the Animals* in 1952. Tex Ritter sang with the Nashville Youth Orchestra, and Eddy Arnold sang with the symphony while Chet Atkins, the legendary guitarist, also played pops concerts with the symphony. Members of the symphony players also contributed to the unique "Nashville Sound" by playing in the city's recording studios.

Although the audience was racially integrated in the late 1950s, the orchestra was not, and the board balked at hiring an African American violinist. Taylor left Nashville after this dispute. In 1963, the symphony orchestra and chorus were integrated. Taylor's successor, Willis Page, oversaw the Nashville Symphony's first recording, *Themes from the Great Symphonies,* made for Dot Records in 1960. Thor Johnson replaced Page in 1968. Under his leadership, the Nashville Little Symphony, a core group, toured East Coast concert halls as well as giving nearly one hundred school performances. Johnson was diagnosed with a brain tumor in late 1974 and died a few weeks later.

Michael Charry, who had been assistant conductor with the Cleveland Orchestra, served as the conductor from 1976 to 1982. He oversaw pops concerts becoming a part of the regular season subscription, organized the orchestra's move to the Tennessee Performing Arts Center in 1980, and guided a fully staged production of *Madama Butterfly.* This led to other opera productions before the opera company split from the symphony. In 1983, Kenneth Schermerhorn succeeded Charry and continues to be the conductor and music director.

Along with these achievements, the orchestra experienced some difficulties during the decade. In 1981, contract talks with the musicians broke down,

Thor Johnson and the Nashville Symphony in rehearsal. Courtesy of the Nashville Symphony.

and a federal mediator had to be called in. Tensions continued, and in February 1985 the players went on strike. The contract signed the following April made orchestra membership a full-time job with full-time pay for most of its members, and an abbreviated season was performed. But the orchestra's financial problems were overwhelming and in February 1988, the board released the musicians and the staff, closed the office, shut down the symphony, and declared bankruptcy. By October, however, the musicians had renegotiated, a new financial plan was in effect, and the 1988–89 season began late, located in the less expensive War Memorial Auditorium (compared to the symphony's prior home in Jackson Hall of the Tennessee Performing Arts Center). Steven Greil, co-owner of a country and rock concert promotion and management firm, took over as executive director. He stayed for five and a half years, long enough to put the orchestra back on a firm financial footing and to return its performances to Jackson Hall.

Thor Johnson, the former music director of the Nashville Symphony, planted the seed for Nashville Opera, when his will bequeathed a sum of money to the Tennessee Performing Arts Foundation earmarked for operatic efforts involving the symphony. In 1980, his successor, Michael Charry, recruited Mary Ragland, director of the Middle Tennessee Metropolitan Opera Auditions, as producer of the first production, *Madama Butterfly.* She chartered the Nashville Opera Guild as a support group. In 1997, the merger of the Nashville Opera and the Tennessee Opera Theatre (an education division for the training of young talent) created the Nashville Opera Association. Ever since, the company has steadily progressed, with more annual productions, more lavish sets, and constantly improving performances. The company has performed works ranging from *HMS Pinafore* to *Der Rosenkavalier* to *Turandot.* The latter opera was a 2001–2002 coproduction with Opera Memphis.

Outreach programs include Arts Partners in Education and OperaNet, which bring opera to young people. In the fall of 1999, the company moved to the new Nashville Opera Center, a fully contained production center consisting of office space, storage for sets and costumes, and a state-of-the-art rehearsal hall.

There were several short-lived orchestras in Memphis around the turn of the century, but in 1938, Burnet C. Tuthill, a professor of music at Southwestern at Memphis (now Rhodes College), formed the Memphis Symphony. By the 1940s it was playing five or six concerts a season, but it folded in 1947 with a deficit.

In 1952 the Memphis Sinfonietta was organized, under conductor Vincent de Frank, who had studied in Indiana, played with the St. Louis Symphony, and performed as a cellist under Tuthill. The opening concert was held at the Goodwyn Institute on January 25, 1953, with twenty-one players performing

Vincent de Frank with Jane and Judy Nobles, 1957. Courtesy of University of Memphis Libraries, Special Collections.

works by Vivaldi, Schubert, Strauss, and Mozart. The Memphis Orchestral Society was formed as the sinfonietta's sponsoring organization. By 1960, the orchestra had grown and the name was changed to the Memphis Symphony.

After thirty-two years at the podium, Vincent de Frank retired in 1984 and was replaced by Alan Balter, who led the symphony until his retirement at the end of the 1997–98 season. In April 1999, the appointment of David Loebel as the third music director and conductor was announced.

The Memphis Symphony League was organized as a volunteer support group in 1958, the 125-member Symphony Chorus was formed in 1965, and the Memphis Youth Symphony was formed in 1966 and now includes three orchestras. At the beginning of the twenty-first century, the seventy-five-member Memphis Symphony plays more than one hundred concerts each season, including a masterworks series, chamber and pops concert series, family concerts, outdoor concerts, Fourth of July and New Year concerts, and an annual special tribute to Dr. Martin Luther King Jr. The symphony performs with Ballet Memphis, Opera Memphis, and the Memphis Arts Festival. The annual Memphis in May Sunset Symphony brings thousands to the banks of the Mississippi River. According to the American Symphony Orchestra League, the Memphis Symphony is one of the leading providers of free community service concerts in the nation. In November 1996, the symphony left the Vincent de Frank Music Hall at Ellis Auditorium for a temporary home until the completion of Memphis's new downtown performing arts center.

Opera has a long history in Memphis, going back to the days of nineteenth-century touring companies. The Beethoven Club, organized in the 1890s, brought many great opera singers to Memphis, including Enrico Caruso, Amelita Galli-Curci, Emma Eames, Nellie Melba, and Lily Pons. The Beethoven Club was instrumental in many of the city's musical developments, including the beginning of summer opera, the founding of Opera Memphis, the sponsoring of the Metropolitan Opera Regional Auditions, and encouraging hundreds of young musicians with scholarships and performance opportunities.

The Metropolitan Opera of New York first appeared in Memphis in 1901, but the height of its association with the city was from 1940 until 1984, when Memphis was a regular stop on its annual tour. The three days of performances were a grand social season as people came from the surrounding states to dress formally and attend the opera and the parties accompanying the season.

For many, opera in Memphis meant opera under the stars. The Memphis Open Air Theater (MOAT) presented the operettas of Sigmund Romberg, Victor Herbert, and Rudolph Friml in the Overton Park Shell (later named the Raoul Wallenberg Shell) for fourteen seasons beginning in 1938. The Overton Park Shell was built in the 1930s as a WPA project. Audiences enjoyed the cool evening breezes and the moonlight, while the sounds of music drowned out the noises of insects in the trees. Singers remembered the difficulties of competing with the sound of planes approaching the airport and the occasional insect in the mouth, but the audiences loved the atmosphere and the music. Then the growing availability of air conditioning and television spelled the end of MOAT, and its last season was the summer of 1951.

In 1956, the ladies of the Beethoven Club were instrumental in recruiting a group of influential Memphians to found a regional opera company; thus the Memphis Opera Theater was chartered. A performance of *La Traviata* in 1956 was followed by a performance of *Tosca* in 1957, then *Die Fledermaus, Amahl and the Night Visitors,* and *Trial by Jury* in 1958.

At first, local singers were used and volunteers built sets and costumes. As the company grew, regional singers and directors were brought in, sets and costumes were rented from other companies, and the name was changed to Opera Memphis. By the mid-1970s, the company was presenting international stars like Justino Diaz and Donald Gramm in *Don Giovanni,* and Birgit Nilsson in *Turandot* in 1971; Beverly Sills in *Lucia di Lammermoor* in 1973, *The*

Overton Bandshell, Memphis. Courtesy of Memphis/Shelby County Public Library and Information Center–Memphis and Shelby County Room.

Daughter of the Regiment in 1977, and *Die Fledermaus* in 1980; Jerome Hines in *Faust* in 1977, *Attila* in 1979, and *Eugene Onegin* in 1984; Grace Bumbry and Justino Diaz in *Tosca* in 1979; and Joan Sutherland in *La Traviata* in 1981. When the Metropolitan Opera ended its national tours in the early 1980s, Opera Memphis provided the opportunity to hear international singers like these. In the 1980s and 1990s, young American singers were featured in starring roles.

In 1976, Opera Memphis and Memphis State University (now the University of Memphis) established the Southern Opera Theater (SOT) as the educational/outreach division, giving young singers performance experience, touring shows to schools and other venues, and taking grand opera to towns and rural communities where it had never been seen before. SOT evolved into the artists-in-residence program, which tours schools and community groups in three states.

Another division of Opera Memphis, the National Center for the Development of American Opera, commissions and performs new works by American composers. World premieres of operas in Memphis include *Light in August* (based on the novel by William Faulkner), by David Olney, Karen Pell, Tommy Goldsmith, and Tom House; *Riversongs* (a story of the 1927 Mississippi River flood), by Sid Selvidge, which premiered in 1995; *Different Fields* (a football opera by Tennessee resident and former National Football League star Mike Reid and Sarah Schlesinger) in 1996; and *Buoso's Ghost,* by Opera Memphis general/artistic director Michael Ching, performed in 1997.

The Jackson Symphony was founded in 1961. James Petty, a high school music teacher, was the first music director and conductor through the 1986 season, when Jordan Tang, a composer and music director of the Paducah Symphony, took the symphony's reins. Each season the Jackson Symphony presents a seven-concert subscription series, with four classical and three pops concerts. It performs at an annual free outdoor Starlight Symphony and free Christmas concerts.

Since the 1993–94 season, an annual Legend Benefit Concert has introduced a larger segment of the community to the orchestra, bringing nationally known popular artists like Carl Perkins, Charlie Daniels, Ray Charles, and Gladys Knight to perform. The Camerata Youth Orchestra provides performance

Music in Higher Education

MUSIC IN HIGHER EDUCATION IS A TRADITION IN TENNESSEE. THREE PROGRAMS, AT BLAIR SCHOOL of Music in Middle Tennessee, the University of Tennessee in East Tennessee, and the University of Memphis in West Tennessee, are representative of this tradition.

The Blair School of Music in Nashville was named in honor of a patron of the arts. Founded in 1964 as Blair Academy by the Justin and Valere Potter Foundation in honor of Valere Potter's mother, Myra Jackson Blair, the school's mission from the beginning was to teach music, providing the training essential for a performing career or for a creative avocation. First a division of George Peabody College, it became an independent, accredited, non-degree-granting institution in 1977. The school merged with Vanderbilt University in 1981 and now grants the bachelor of arts degree.

The Blair School provides instruction for all ages, offering private, group, and class instructions to pre-college, university, and adult students. Music theory, literature, history, and business courses are also offered. Faculty members, a number of whom have distinguished reputations as artists or composers, perform in a variety of ensembles, including strings, woodwinds, brass, and chamber groups, giving over one thousand performances a year, and students participate in the Vanderbilt Opera Theater, Orchestra, Symphonic Choir, and ensembles.

The Music Department of the University of Tennessee at Knoxville has grown from two teachers in music education in the College of Education into the School of Music within the College of Arts and Sciences, offering bachelor's and master's degrees in all areas of music. The department began as a part of the Summer School of the South, a program initiated in the early 1900s to help public school teachers in the Southeast. In the 1940s, curricular development began under the College of Education; in 1991, the Department of Music and the Department of Music Education merged into a single unit within the College of Liberal Arts.

Faculty and students perform in a variety of ensembles, ranging from the Pride of the Southland Band to the University of Tennessee Opera Theater, which stages two full-scale productions each year, and the Knoxville Opera Studio, a collaboration between the Knoxville Opera Company and the University of Tennessee Opera Theater.

The University of Memphis is the only school in the state to offer the doctoral degree in music. It was first offered in 1977, when the Music Department became part of the College of Communications and Fine Arts. Music was a specialization within the major of education until 1953; master's degrees in music education and applied music became available in 1964. Concentrations are offered in all performance areas in voice and the standard orchestral and concert instruments, composition, musicology, ethnomusicology, sacred music, music education, music business, recording technology, jazz and studio performance, jazz and studio composition and arranging, and Orff Schulwerk and Suzuki pedagogy.

Faculty members have received such coveted awards as the ASCAP and the Prix de Rome and are sought worldwide as performers and lecturers. The department presents over two hundred recitals, concerts, special events, guest lectures, and master classes each year. Faculty and students perform in a variety of ensembles, including the Collegium Musicum, the Ceruti String Quartet, the Southern Comfort Jazz Orchestra, Sound Fuzion, the Gospel Choir, the Double Bass Quartet, and the University of Memphis Brass Ensemble.

Perre Magness, Memphis

opportunities for intermediate and advanced level students. In 1997–98, Saturday Morning Masterclasses were introduced, and in 1999, the Sinfonia Strings was organized to offer beginning string players the chance to gain ensemble experience.

The Bryan Symphony Orchestra at Tennessee Technological University gave its first concert in February 1964, under the name the Tech Community Symphony. The present name of Bryan Symphony was chosen to honor Charles Faulkner Bryan, late Tennessee Tech music faculty member and award winning composer, whose memory is also honored by the Bryan Fine Arts Building. For twenty-seven years, James Wattenbarger served as conductor, conducting over 150 concerts in Cookeville and surrounding communities. In 1990, Wattenbarger passed the baton to Jonathan May for three seasons. Beginning with the 1993–94 season, John Dodson, a Tennessee Tech graduate, became the symphony's third music director.

The orchestra has served as an advocate for a number of contemporary composers. Tennessee Tech's Robert Jager has conducted the premiere of several of his works. The orchestra performs five subscription concerts, free outdoor and indoor education concerts; its recent children's concerts were televised on the university-supported public television station.

In 1969, citizens and music faculty from area colleges and East Tennessee State University joined to create the Johnson City Symphony Orchestra. Gilbert Oxendine, the choir director at Munsey Memorial Methodist Church in Johnson City, served as the initial conductor. In 1974, Dr. James Marable of Oak Ridge succeeded Oxendine as conductor, and during his tenure Marable improved the orchestra's professionalism and expanded its offerings, including guest artists in the performances. Thomas Hinds became the orchestra's conductor in 1982, but he stayed only one year and was replaced in 1983 by Antonia Joy Wilson, the first woman to serve as primary conductor of a symphony orchestra in the state. The present conductor and music director of the orchestra is Lewis Dalvit, who first assumed the orchestra's reins in the 1989–90 season. As only the second resident conductor in the orchestra's history, Dalvit has brought a commitment that has expanded the orchestra's visibility and significance in the community. At beginning of the twenty-first century, the Johnson City Symphony offers a full season of classical and pops music, and presents regular performances for school children from the region.

The Tennessee Philharmonic Symphony in Murfreesboro dates to 1981, when Dr. Laurence Harvin, a professor in the Music Department at Middle Tennessee State University, began conducting the University Community Symphony. Mary Saille Corlew and others established the Middle Tennessee Symphony Guild the following year, and thus a new orchestra, the Middle Tennessee Symphony, began as a partnership between MTSU faculty and students and the wider community. As testimony to its growth and development over two decades, the symphony was renamed the Tennessee Philharmonic Symphony for its 2000–2001 season, with Harvin remaining as music director.

The Nashville Chamber Orchestra (NCO) was established in 1990. It regularly scheduled performances of chamber and symphonic music, as well as its commissions for new compositions, are further indications of the maturation of classical music in the Volunteer State. With Paul Gambill as conductor and music director, the NCO has established an effective Community Partnership Program that has carried the chamber orchestra into many of the region's rural communities.

Although classical music was a part of Tennessee life before the Civil War through touring artists, not until the 1930s and 1940s were there home-grown performing groups. The Second World War broadened the musical horizons of Tennesseans, and the 1950s were a period of growth and stabilization. By the 1960s, there were active symphony seasons in eight Tennessee cities. Each of the orchestras performed works by modern American composers, many of them composed for that orchestra, as well as the standard repertoire.

An important development of the 1970s and 1980s has been the professionalization of orchestras. Although musicians are still underpaid, it is now possible to have a full-time career as a performing classical musician in Tennessee. Despite financial hard times, orchestras have increased the numbers of performances, have increased their community outreach, and have active educational programs aimed at developing new audiences for the future. While nationwide audiences for symphonic music are shrinking, opera audiences are growing—and getting younger. The four opera companies in the state are witnesses to this trend.

The state may be more famous for the Grand Ole Opry than for Grand Opera, and for rock and roll bands than for symphonies, but classical music is alive and well—and growing dynamically—in Tennessee.

Notes

1. James Dick Davis, *History of the City of Memphis, Also the "Old Times Papers"* (Memphis: Hite, Crumpton and Kelly Printers, 1873).
2. June Adamson, "Early History of the Oak Ridge Symphony Orchestra," n.d., and Tom Carlson, "Waldo Cohn—ORCMA's Man of the Century," *Oak Ridger,* June 3, 1999.
3. Ibid.

Suggested Readings

Brewer, Roy C. "Professional Musicians in Memphis (1900–1950): A Tradition of Compromise." Ph.D. diss., Univ. of Memphis, 1996.

Davis, James Dick. *History of the City of Memphis, Also the "Old Times Papers."* Memphis: Hite, Crumpton and Kelly Printers, 1873.

Egerton, John. *Nashville: The Faces of Two Centuries 1780–1980.* Nashville: PlusMedia, 1979.

West, Carroll Van, Connie L. Lester, Anne-Leslie Owens, and Margaret D. Binnicker, eds. *The Tennessee Encyclopedia of History and Culture.* Nashville: Tennessee Historical Society and Rutledge Hill Press, 1998.

Young, J. P. *History of Memphis, Tennessee.* Knoxville: H. W. Crew, 1912.

Other Sources

Information from the individual groups in the form of typescripts, programs, booklets, web sites, and letters to the author.

Twenty-three

Gospel Pearls
Tennesseans and Gospel Music Traditions

Carroll Van West
Middle Tennessee State University

It is odd to read accounts about the rich music heritage of Tennessee and hear only about Nashville and country music, and Memphis and rock 'n' soul music. Our own in-state institutions—the Country Music Hall of Fame and Ryman Auditorium in Nashville and the Smithsonian's Rock-n-Soul Museum, Elvis's Graceland, and the Stax Museum in Memphis—certainly emphasize the same associations, and millions visit these places each year. These museums and sites, in turn, have defined the state as a music mecca: witness the constant media hype about rock icons visiting Graceland or about country and western music stars appearing on the famed stage of the Ryman Auditorium.

It is not odd that Nashville and Memphis possess national and international reputations as popular music centers; they earned that several times over. The oddity is that with all the attention constantly given to the state's musical heritage, the music that serves as the foundation of that tradition—gospel music—is routinely ignored, even though Tennessee is often characterized as (and behind our backs decried as) the buckle of the Bible Belt.

How central are Tennesseans to the history of American gospel music? Consider the significance of the Fisk Jubilee Singers in the development of the Negro spiritual; the contributions to black gospel music from Memphis composers W. Herbert Brewster and Lucie Campbell; the immense popularity of Nashville's The Fairfield Four in the mid-twentieth century; the acknowledged role of Lawrenceburg's James D. Vaughan as the father of southern gospel music; the evolution of Nashville's Amy Grant into the first major star of contemporary Christian music; and the national television presence of Bobby Jones's programs of modern black gospel. Add the fact that the Gospel Music Association—the leading trade association of the genre—maintains its world headquarters in Nashville and hosts the annual induction of new members into the Gospel Music Hall of Fame. Tennesseans may hold a more pivotal role in the history of gospel music than they do in either country and western or rock 'n' soul music.

Songs of Faith: The Nineteenth Century

Gathered around the fireplace of home, the church pulpit, or the potbellied stove of a country store, musicians of nineteenth-century Tennessee sang folk tunes and songs of faith that spoke of their values and beliefs. They adapted and borrowed from much older tunes and texts that mixed all sorts of ethnic and cultural traditions.

Sacred music in early Tennessee—identified by scholars as vernacular religious music—shared several basic characteristics: it typically lacked formal

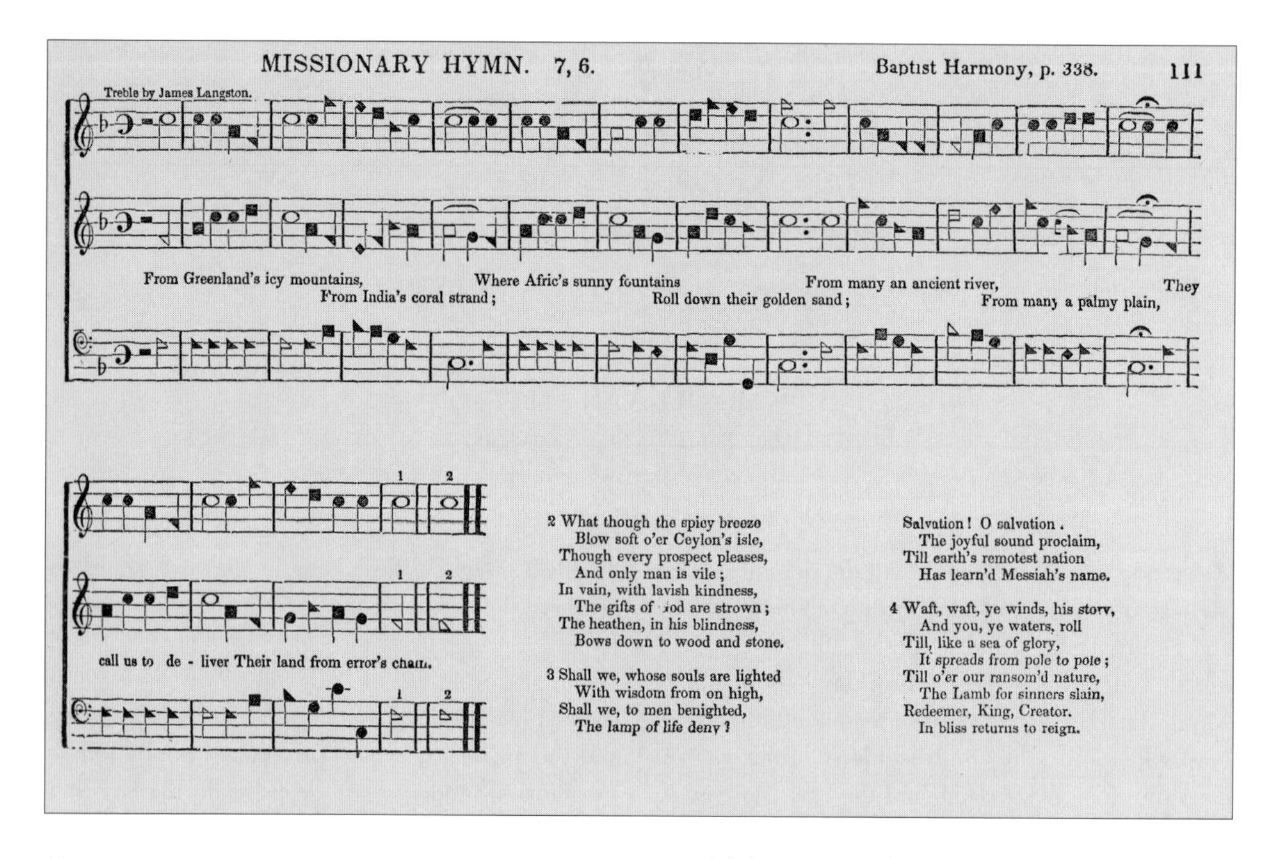

Missionary Hymn from a shape-note songbook of 1847. *The Southern Harmony and Musical Companion*, Philadelphia, 1847. Library Collection, Tennessee State Library and Archives. Courtesy of TSLA.

musical notation, it was performed by groups rather than by individual artists, and it relied on folk songs for tunes. No matter its form, however, sacred music was a constant on the Tennessee frontier. The congregations of Regular Baptists and Separate Baptists—now commonly identified as "Old-Time" Baptists—that filtered into northeastern Tennessee in the late eighteenth century brought along older traditions of lined a cappella singing. The mass singings at the late 1790s and early 1800s camp meetings were emotionally charged, where texts with no music were sung to better-known secular tunes, creating a music that was sacred and secular. Preachers, or sometimes song leaders, led the singings in a call-and-response fashion similar to their sermons.

Of the nineteenth-century music forms, shape-note singing has garnered the most attention. The four-shape-note and later seven-shape-note books consisted of text and various shapes—sometimes called "character notes" or "patent notes"—for musical notation. A leader would voice the notation for a particular song, which the congregation then would sing before beginning the text. The scholarly consensus is that William Little and William Smith's *The Easy Instructor* (1802) served as a guide and songbook for four-shape notation; by approximately the second decade of the nineteenth century, "fa-sola," or four-shape-note, songbooks became available to rural congregations and camp meetings. Shape-note type singing came to Tennessee from the eighteenth-century Singing School Movement of New England, where ministers attempted to improve and expand the role of music within their services by teaching rudimentary musical notation to congregations. This movement, according to scholar Stephen Shearon, "fostered the earliest body of indigenous American musical compositions following the arrival of Europeans."[1]

Within a generation, a few song leaders began training others in shape-note music and sold them copies of popular shape-note songbooks. *The Sacred Harp,* published in 1844, was the most popular songbook for four-shape-note singing, and its songs fall into three major categories: psalm tunes, fuging tunes, and odes or anthems. *The Sacred Harp* was so influential that today many use the terms "Sacred Harp singing" and "four-shape-note singing" interchangeably. Allen D. Carden (1792–1859) of Nashville coauthored and produced two early tunebooks using four-note notation—*The Western Harmony* (1824) and *United States Harmony* (1829)—for use in singing schools. *The Western Harmony* was the first musical publication to come from Nashville, and although Carden remained in the state until his death in 1859, no other songbooks associated with him are known. The Carden books are early, but the most influential Tennessee shape-note books came from William H. Swan and Marcus L. Swan: *Harp of Columbia: A New System of Sacred Music, with Notes for Every Sound, and Shapes for Every Note* (Knoxville, 1848) and *The New Harp of Columbia* (1867).

The shape-note tradition diminished in popularity in the latter decades of the nineteenth century, but it never disappeared. Its many advocates preferred its reliance on the voice, harmonies, and group vocal dynamics. Other liked how shape-note singing reaffirmed community values—as it was a gathering of people who wanted to sing as an ensemble—as well as religious faith. Today, annual singings and even multiple-day singing conventions celebrate the four-shape and seven-shape songs while also commemorating the ways of rural life and sense of community associated with this performance tradition. "Even to those for whom the religious message is not preeminent, a kind of spiritual calm comes from singing these old songs—a sense of historical continuity, a sense of sharing a meaningful tradition with those long dead," observe Ron Petersen and Candra Phillips.[2]

By 1870, a distinctive American music described as "gospel songs" had entered the hymnals of several Protestant denominations. Like their predecessors in shape-note singing, these early published gospel songs borrowed music from folk tunes and contemporary popular music while the emotional lyrics were invariably arranged in a refrain, verse-chorus-verse-chorus pattern. The same characteristics could be found in

The Jubilee Singers, original company, from Fisk University, c. 1882. Merl Eppse Collection. Manuscripts Division, Tennessee State Library and Archives. Courtesy of TSLA.

the late-nineteenth-century spiritual, or jubilee gospel singing, then gaining international recognition through the efforts of the Fisk Jubilee Singers.

The Jubilee Singers began in 1871 as a way for the nascent Fisk University to raise desperately needed funds to continue its ambitious programs of educating the freed people of the South. George White, the university treasurer, enjoyed the students' a cappella singing and had organized informal student groups as early as 1867. However, the American Missionary Association, which sponsored Fisk and underwrote much of its expenses, had no interest in a student group touring the region to raise funds. By 1871, the university faced such an uncertain financial future that its trustees chose to ignore the wishes of the association and decided to let White take a student group, which he eventually named the Jubilee Singers, on the road. The members of the initial nine-member ensemble (double quartets with a pianist) were Isaac Dickerson, Maggie Porter, Minnie Tate, Jennie Jackson, Benjamin Holmes, Thomas Rutling, Eliza Walker, Green Evans, and Ella Sheppard.

In the fall of 1871, the group first toured southern states; next they went to northern cities, where the Jubilee Singers met with an enthusiastic response, especially to their encore of spirituals, then called "slave songs," with their themes of hope, grace, and ultimate redemption sung in a joyful, rhythmic, and animated performance. Slave songs, according to the research of Dena J. Epstein, in part reflected African traditions in their strong rhythms—accomplished with hand-clapping, stomping, and percussion instruments—their improvised texts, and their call-and-response form. Music was an important part of the African religious experience, and slaves often brought music to the forefront of their conversion to Christianity. Slave songs also reflected the music of the camp meeting revivals of the early 1800s, religious and cultural events that African Americans and whites attended together and learned about each other's vernacular music sounds and forms.

As a musical hybrid dependent on West African musical practices, "the unaccompanied folk spiritual served as the most important African American musical tradition up to the Civil War."[3] Slave songs were known in the South in the antebellum era but apparently were unknown in the North until the Civil War. The first important publication of slave songs was *Slave Songs of the United States* (1867), which included 136 examples. Editors William F. Allen, Charles P. Ware, and Lucy M. Garrison wanted to capture the unique songs they had encountered, but formal musical notation could never convey the spontaneity, improvisation, and performance art that characterized slave songs.

The Jubilee Singers's 1871 tour was a considerable financial success, allowing the university to purchase land for a new campus in north Nashville, as well as an artistic success, as the name of the group became commonly used to describe the performance of spirituals as in the terms "jubilee singing" or "jubilee gospel." In 1873, White and the Jubilee Singers sailed to England for a rigorous tour that brought additional acclaim, and even a special concert for Queen Victoria. The group returned with enough money to construct the landmark building, Jubilee Hall, giving the university a firm foundation for the future. And the group brought national notoriety to the school and to the spiritual as a musical form. In 1873 G. D. Pike wrote a fawning account of their accomplishments, *The Jubilee Singers, and Their Campaign for Twenty Thousand Dollars* (1873); four years later, J. B. T. Marsh compiled *The Story of the Jubilee Singers, with Their Songs* (1877). The group continues to tour today.

Fund raising was the primary goal of the Jubilee Singers, but their professional, yet moving and joyous performances also struck at stereotypes held about freedmen by most whites in America and England. The dignified bearing and unquestioned talent of the students also emphasized the potential and worth of African American education.

The Negro spiritual popularized by the Fisk Jubilee Singers was dramatic, even over-orchestrated in its levels of harmony and sound. But for over a generation, the performances of the Fisk Jubilee

Poster announcing a Jubilee Singers performance. Courtesy of Special Collections, Fisk University Library, Nashville.

Singers largely defined the genre as the group not only toured continuously, it also produced and sold songbooks that many African Americans took back to their churches as weekly musical resources. The Jubilee Singers even cut some of the first records by a Tennessee-based group when in 1909 a quartet organized by Fisk professor John Work II and including himself, James Myers, Alfred King, and Noah Rider cut sides for the Victor Talking Machine Company. These early records, concludes music historian Tim Brooks, helped to introduce the Negro spiritual into the mainstream of American music. In his *The Book of American Negro Spirituals,* published by Viking Press in 1925, future Fisk professor James Weldon Johnson compiled and published the first major collection of spirituals since the pioneering work of 1867.

Establishing a Tradition and Building a Business: Twentieth-Century Gospel Music

By the time of the Fisk Jubilee recordings of 1909, a new musical form, later labeled as southern gospel music, was beginning to expand its influence throughout the South. Three Tennesseans—Charles M. Alexander (1867–1920), Homer Rodeheaver (1880–1955), and especially James D. Vaughan (1864–1941)—played pivotal roles in the creation of southern gospel music. Alexander was the first music teacher at Maryville College, but began his career as a gospel song leader after enrolling in the Moody Bible Institute in Chicago in 1892 and spending the following year as the music leader for Dwight L. Moody's efforts to evangelize at the Chicago World's Fair of 1893. Considered the first "Charismatic" evangelistic song leader—able to lead huge crowds in singing gospel songs—Alexander also traveled with notable evangelists R. A. Torrey and J. Wilbur Chapman. Homer Rodeheaver, also of East Tennessee, followed Alexander's lead, serving as song leader of famous evangelist Billy Sunday for twenty years. Music historians credit Rodeheaver as making popular religious songs more lively, personal, and direct than those of the nineteenth century, the type of modern songs of the twentieth century typically labeled as "gospel" music.

Vaughan, however, is the acknowledged "father" of southern gospel music. A native of Giles County, he first studied the seven-shape-note system of sacred music with the influential Reubusch-Kieffer company in Virginia's Shenandoah Valley. An active member of the Church of Nazerene, Vaughan returned to Tennessee at the beginning of the twentieth century and from his home and business in Lawrenceburg, in southern Middle Tennessee, he began to compose and publish his own gospel songbooks, helping to preserve shape-note singing in addition to introducing new forms of sacred music. The first book, *Gospel Chimes,* was so successful that Vaughan was soon publishing a new book every year and by 1911 his books were selling approximately eight hundred thousand copies annually. His books eventually sold in the millions of copies. Known as "convention books," because they were used for Wednesday night singings, homecoming singings, competitions, and other special events, the books remained in demand for the rest of the century and several continue in print today.

James D. Vaughan. Photograph by Carroll Van West. Courtesy of the James D. Vaughan Museum, Lawrenceburg.

In Lawrenceburg, Vaughan published not only books, but an influential magazine, *Vaughan's Family Visitor* (first appeared in 1912 and still in publication in Cleveland, Tennessee), which publicized the songbooks, the later records, and the constant tours of his own teaching quartets. Vaughan's quartets—four men and a pianist—traveled to countless churches to teach congregations and song leaders the new songs and, naturally, to promote the songbooks and records. As many as sixteen quartets traveled throughout the South and Southwest, and some, like the Speer Family, became so individually popular that they left Vaughan and became independent musical groups. Perhaps the most popular Vaughan quartet included Palmer Wheeler, Kieffer Vaughan, John Cook, and Jim Waits, with Dwight Brock on piano. Soon the harmonies of a four-man quartet, accompanied solely by the pounding rhythms of an upright piano, defined the basic sound of southern gospel music.

Once the traveling quartets impressed local song leaders and preachers, many congregations chose to send their leaders, and, in some cases entire choirs, to Lawrenceburg for in-depth training at the Vaughan School of Music, established in 1911. Through the influence of the quartets, the singing school, and the endless supply of songbooks, the evangelical lyrics and driving rhythms of the Vaughan songs could be heard almost everywhere in Tennessee, especially in Pentecostal and other independent churches.

Vaughan adapted modern technology to provide the largest possible audiences for his personal, musical testimonies of faith. Established in 1922, the Vaughan record company (which is considered the first southern-based company to specifically target a southern audience) recorded the quartets and then the Vaughan radio station—WOAN in Lawrenceburg—promoted the new records as one of the state's first commercial broadcast stations. Vaughan managed the various Lawrenceburg enterprises until his death in 1941; Glenn Kieffer Vaughan (1893–1969), a gifted singer and influential teacher at the Vaughan school, became the next president of the Vaughan Music Company.

Title page of *Vaughan's School Songs*. Photograph by Carroll Van West. Courtesy of the James D. Vaughan Museum, Lawrenceburg.

With his interlocking companies of traveling quartets, songbook publishing, records, and radio, James D. Vaughan was a good businessman, but he was foremost an evangelist. The movement he spawned quickly expanded as alumni established their own organizations. In 1926, former Vaughan editor V. O. Stamps teamed with J. R. Baxter Jr. to form the influential Stamps-Baxter Music and Printing Company. Based in Dallas, Texas, Stamps-Baxter aggressively pursued younger composers, sought record deals with mainstream labels, and sponsored radio shows in both large and small markets to sell their products. The company also established its eastern branch office in Chattanooga, giving the Stamps publishing empire and its quartets a very visible presence in Tennessee southern gospel music.

Another important Tennessee southern gospel publisher was R. E. Winsett (1876–1952) of Dayton, who published the popular songbook *Soul Winning Songs* as well as over one thousand gospel songs. His *Pentecostal Power Complete* (1908) sold over one million copies and remains in print today. The Tennessee Music and Printing Company was established in Cleveland during the late 1920s. Now headed by Connor B. Hall (1916–), who also is the editor of the *Vaughan Family Visitor* and editor of the James D. Vaughan Music Company, the company remains an important gospel music publisher. The John T. Benson Publishing Company was the major southern gospel music publisher in Nashville. The company's former vice president and president, and Church of Nazarene leader, Robert Benson Sr. (1930–1987), expanded the company's influence into the late twentieth century, especially through the recordings of the Heartwarming Record Company.

The success of southern gospel music in the early twentieth century paralleled the development of a new urban-based African American sacred music, known as black gospel music. The two different types of gospel had different musical roots, but they were grounded in music forms and performance styles nurtured in Pentecostal and Holiness churches, with the mostly white Church of God (headquartered in Cleveland, Tennessee), and the Church of Nazarene (with its Trevecca Nazarene University located in Nashville) and the mostly African American Church of God in Christ (based in Memphis), being the most important in Tennessee. Historian George R. Rick's description of early-twentieth-century black gospel music—that "Holiness groups . . . began a repertory of religious folk songs characterized by free expression and rhythmic instrumental accompaniment"—likewise was an apt summary of southern gospel music.[4]

Influential early-twentieth-century Tennessee publishers and groups share close associations with the state's major Pentecostal denominations. The relationship between the Church of Nazarene and the publishing houses of James D. Vaughan and John T.

Benson already have been noted. Associated with the Church of God in Christ (headquartered in Memphis) was the significant black gospel harmony quartet known as the Spirit of Memphis (with performances perhaps as early as 1928 by original members Arthur Wright, Luther McGill, James Peoples, and James Darling.) Earl Malone by the Depression decade would become the group's most famous individual and sang at a special 1983 anniversary concert at the Mason Temple of the Church of God in Christ in Memphis. The southern gospel group the LeFevres was closely aligned with the Church of God. Formed in Smithville, Tennessee, as the LeFevre Trio in 1921, the group became known as the BTS (Bible Training School, precursor to the Church of God's Lee University) Quartet from 1929 to 1932. When Eva Mae LeFevre joined the group in 1934, it began a rapid climb to the top of the southern gospel music industry. (The group's Mylon LeFevre would be among the pioneers of contemporary Christian music in the 1970s.)

The influence of Pentecostal and Holiness music and performance traditions on black and white gospel music faded somewhat in the 1930s due to the success of Georgia composer Thomas A. Dorsey, who introduced a more contemporary jazz- and blues-influenced sound to black gospel music, and the impact of radio and its eclectic programs of popular, classical, and sacred music. Dorsey is acknowledged as the father of modern black gospel, and one of his leading interpreters was Willie Mae Ford Smith (1904–1994) of Memphis. Often identified as Mother Smith, she was born in Mississippi but grew up in a family of thirteen brothers and sisters in Memphis and later moved to St. Louis. The Fords established a female family quartet—known as the Ford Sisters—that Willie Mae joined in 1922. Two years later, the Ford Sisters delighted the crowds at the National Baptist Convention, and from that point on, Willie Mae Ford was in demand as a gospel vocal stylist without equal, praised by Mahalia Jackson as a major influence on her own style. Mother Smith herself acknowledged the influence of a Memphis contemporary, Queen C. Anderson (1913–1959), on her singing style. Mother Smith's impassioned southern sound was a perfect vehicle for the improvised, creative compositions of Thomas Dorsey. Mother Smith, along with Mahalia Jackson and Sallie Martin, made Dorsey's tunes widely known and popular across the country.

Dr. W. Herbert Brewster, 1971. Photograph by Hooks Bros. Courtesy of University of Memphis Libraries, Special Collections.

As a prolific composer and promoter, Dorsey is the acknowledged "father" of black gospel music, but three African American Tennesseans—the Reverend Cleavant Derricks (1910–), the Reverend W. Herbert Brewster (1897–1987), and Lucie Campbell (1885–1962)—also are significant composers of black gospel music from the early to the mid-twentieth century. Derricks is a native of Chattanooga who studied at the Cadek Conservatory of Music in Knoxville, Tennessee A&I (now Tennessee State University), and the American Baptist Theological Seminary in Nashville. He wrote over three hundred songs, published several songbooks, and released albums such as the 1975 Canaan release, *Just a Little Talk with Jesus.* Mahalia Jackson and other leading soloists performed and recorded several of Derricks's best-known songs, such as "When He Blessed My Soul."

A native of Fayette County, and the son of sharecroppers, Herbert Brewster received his college degree from Roger Williams University in Nashville. In the late 1920s the Reverend Thomas O. Fuller, a prominent Baptist leader and Brewster's former teacher at Memphis's Howe Institute, asked Brewster to head a new African American seminary in Memphis. Due to intense political pressure from city officials, and from Memphis political boss Ed Crump, the seminary never opened. But Brewster stayed, and during his years as minister of the East Trigg Baptist Church, he began writing gospel songs, influenced by the Bluff City's blues and black gospel music traditions. His first song was "I'm Leaning and Depending on the Lord" (1939), and his most popular songs were "Move on up a Little Higher" (1941), recorded by Mahalia Jackson, and "Surely, God is Able" (1947), recorded by the Ward Singers of Philadelphia. Both recordings sold a million copies by 1950. Brewster later admitted that the midcentury push for civil rights influenced his work. About "Move on Up a Little Higher," he said, "That was a protest idea and inspiration. I was trying to inspire Black people to move up higher. Don't be satisfied with the mediocre."[5] His music, however, found an audience among both whites and blacks. The popular southern gospel groups, the Statesmen Brothers and the Happy Goodman Family, also recorded Brewster songs. Brewster, in addition, composed gospel music dramas, such as *From Auction Block to Glory* and *Sowing in Tears, Reaping in Joy.*

Lucie Campbell graduated from high school in Memphis in 1899, and stayed in the city to shape its musical traditions for the next six decades. A composer of more than one hundred gospel songs, her first song was published in 1919. Two years later, several of her compositions were included in the National Baptist Convention's *Gospel Pearls* (1921), one of the first black gospel songbooks ever published. Music historian Kip Lornell concluded that Campbell's work represented "a cornerstone for black American Protestant singers."[6] Campbell later introduced Marian Anderson to the National Baptist Convention and served as Anderson's accompanist.

The music of Brewster and Campbell, like that of Dorsey and other popular composers of the 1930s and 1940s, gave more prominent roles to soloists and bass singers. Quartets added a lead singer, who often improvised on the melody and added showy vocal techniques. These same changes characterized southern gospel music, especially the increased prominence of the lead singer and the bass singer. Memphis, in particular, became renowned for its many excellent black gospel quartets.

With the rapidly expanding radio market providing mass outlets for gospel music performances, several gospel quartet groups became so popular, in fact, that they found their way onto more mainstream popular music programs or had regular radio programs. In 1942 the John Daniel Quartet, a former Vaughan-group quartet, became the first southern gospel group to perform on the Grand Ole Opry; many more would follow in the years to come.

Lucie E. Campbell (Williams). Courtesy of University of Memphis Libraries, Special Collections.

The Fairfield Four, an African American group that had a regularly scheduled show on Nashville radio powerhouse WLAC, became one of the most popular music groups of any genre in the South. The Swan Silverstone Singers, another black group, performed regularly over Knoxville's WNOX radio in the 1940s. The Spirit of Memphis, the I. C. Hummingbirds, and the Gospel Travelers could be heard on Memphis radio.

The popularity of southern gospel and black gospel quartets reached its peak in the postwar years. One of the more important post–World War II groups was the Oak Ridge Quartet, established by Wally Fowler of Georgia in the town of Oak Ridge, Tennessee, in 1947. The Blackwood Brothers (associated with the V. O. Stamps music empire) were from Mississippi but moved to Memphis in the summer of 1950 and used station WMPS as a base to expand their audience from the Delta into the Upper South and Midwest. Legendary bass singer J. D. Sumner joined the group in 1954, and throughout the 1950s the group had several popular recordings on RCA Victor.

LeFevre Singers. Courtesy of the Gospel Music Association.

Television joined radio as key outlets for both southern gospel and black gospel music in the 1950s and 1960s, and the increased exposure for artists in turn led to more demands for concert appearances. Southern gospel groups like the Speer Family and the Happy Goodman Family performed on regularly scheduled television programs in several southern markets. Radio stations such as WDIA and WMPS in Memphis and KWEM in West Memphis, Arkansas, featured black and white artists, and sponsored major concerts. In East Tennessee the Reverend J. Bazzell Mull (1914–) established southern and mountain gospel music programs at WROL and WNOX in Knoxville during the 1940s, and during the 1950s he became renowned as a gospel concert promoter and radio programmer. By the end of the century, Mull still staged two daily gospel music radio programs and two weekly television shows. He and his wife Elizabeth Brown Mull hosted the traditional Mull Singing Convention on WJBX-FM in Knoxville. Another key East Tennessee promoter was former Oak Ridge Boys's star Herman Harper. As head of the gospel division of Don Light Talent, he booked the Oak Ridge Boys, the Rambos, and other leading groups. In 1986 he formed his own agency, Harper and Associates, which became the most important southern gospel talent agency, convinced officials at Nashville's WSM radio to add the *Gospel Opry* broadcast to its weekend lineup of music, and later served as talent coordinator for the first Opryland Gospel Jubilee.

Southern and black gospel music increasingly influenced midcentury popular music performers. Elvis Presley always acknowledged his love of both southern gospel and black gospel, and he won Grammy Awards for his own gospel recordings, including "There'll Be Peace in the Valley," a Thomas Dorsey song. A devoted fan of the Blackwood Boys, Presley in 1972 convinced J. D. Sumner and his Stamps Quartet to join his sold-out concert tours, adding Sumner's soaring bass vocals to his layered concert sound. Another rock icon, Tina Turner of Nutbush, Tennessee, sang as a teenager at both the Springhill Baptist Church and the Woodlawn Baptist Church near her hometown. WDIA sponsored the first concert, the Goodwill Revue, to be held at Memphis's Mid-South Coliseum in 1964 and the sold-out show began with gospel music from Reverend Cleophus Robinson before it moved into soul music by Brook Benton, Dee Clark, Otis Redding, and Rufus and Clara Thomas.

In bluegrass music, performers devoted a considerable portion of their songbooks and records to southern gospel and mountain gospel music, often singing them a cappella to emphasize the sacred context of the number. Bluegrass gospel music, concluded historian Neil V. Rosenberg, became a "discourse about the sacred within a secular context."[7] Country and western performers, like bluegrass acts, often included at least one sacred song in every concert, typically sung immediately before the show's final number. Johnny Cash, in his famous concerts at San Quentin and Folsom prisons during the late 1960s, included gospel standards, such as "There'll Be Peace in the Valley" and his own composition, "He Turned the Water into Wine." Gospel music songs also became commonly performed numbers on the weekly broadcasts of the Grand Ole Opry while several country and western artists released entire albums devoted to sacred music. The reverse also occurred: in the 1970s the Oak Ridge Boys switched from southern gospel music to modern country music, although the group reserved a section of each concert performance for traditional gospel songs.

By the late twentieth century, gospel music was a well-established business, centered in Nashville, which was home to the Gospel Music Association and most of the major labels specializing in gospel music. Nashville, naturally, was home to the country music industry and the city's music people always had significant associations with pop and rock music as well, especially due to the popularity of Southern Rock in the 1970s. Out of this Nashville cauldron of gospel, country, pop, and rock music would emerge the most influential artist of contemporary Christian music, Amy Grant.

Born in a devout, wealthy Church of Christ family, Grant attended the prestigious Harpeth Hall School and later Vanderbilt University. She burst into the contemporary scene in the late 1970s, and within twenty years she had won five Grammy Awards, twenty-two Dove Awards, and had been named the artist of the year of the Gospel Music Association four times. By 2002, her albums had sold a combined twenty-two million copies. As a contemporary Christian musician, Grant's records emphasized ministry and evangelism within the sound of contemporary pop or even rock music. Its mixture of the sacred and secular was similar to earlier vernacular religious music forms, but contemporary Christian music, born out of the suburbs and a pop-saturated consumer culture, is markedly different than the nineteenth-century blend of sacred and secular and it remains unsettling for many gospel music listeners.

Grant's 1982 album *Age to Age* was the first Christian music album to sell one million copies; she became a national recording and concert star. In 1985, with the album *Unguarded,* Grant began to release her records on both a Christian music label (Myrrh) and a pop label (A&M), thus becoming the first major crossover artist of contemporary Christian music. Her popularity in both the Christian music market and the pop market of adult contemporary radio is more of a reflection of the state of late-twentieth-century popular music and its need for well-crafted, broadly appealing artists and records than the cries of "sellout" heard from various Christian music fans and industry insiders. But the continued evolution of her records of the late 1990s, especially the exceedingly personal (and non-evangelical) *Behind the Eyes* (1997), led to a debate among critics and gospel music fans of whether it was "Christian music" or not. Her recent album, *Legacy: Hymns and Faith* (2002), a combination of ten traditional songs and three new compositions, is an affirmation of her twenty-five years as a contemporary Christian artist.

Grant contributed greatly to the market for contemporary Christian music. By the end of the twentieth century, the Christian music industry had grown into a large market; in the first half of 1999, for example, twenty different albums had sold at least one hundred thousand copies in the previous six months. Bill Hearn, president and CEO of EMI Christian Music Group, told Billboard magazine that the "Christian community [is] doing a much better job of marketing itself to the masses, as opposed to confining ourselves to the subculture Christian community."[8]

That reaching out to broader audiences also characterizes the success of Bill Gaither, with his recordings, concerts, and television specials, in traditional southern gospel music as well as the enduring popularity of Nashville's Bobby Jones and his long-running weekly black gospel television program, *The Bobby Jones Gospel Hour,* shown nationwide on Black Entertainment Television since 1980. Jones's program also shows how black gospel changed from its midcentury reliance on quartets to more of a mass-choir sound by the 1960s and 1970s. Born in Paris, Tennessee, in 1939, Jones received his undergraduate degree from Tennessee State University, and later took a master's degree from that same institution, and earned a doctorate from Vanderbilt University. Jones was a Nashville teacher and then an instructor at Tennessee State University. In 1976, he was one of the organizers of the first Black Expo in Nashville, and that same year, he approached WSMV-TV in Nashville to sponsor a weekly gospel music show. The resulting *Nashville Gospel Show,* with Jones leading the New Life Choir, was an immediate hit. Four years later, he moved the show to the fledgling Black Entertainment Network, where it has become a mainstay of the cable network's Sunday programming. Jones is important not only for his innovative, choreographed choir numbers but also for providing crucial television exposure for a new generation of black gospel singers, like CeCe Winans, Yolanda Adams, Kirk Franklin, and Hezekiah Walker. The recipient of a Grammy Award in 1984, and multiple Dove Awards, Jones still produces his program from his Nashville offices. As Jones told a reporter for the *Chicago Tribune* in a November 7, 1985, interview, "I want to be one of the people to bring gospel music to the real marketplace by educating people about its marvelous and unique features." In the early twenty-first century, there is little doubt that Jones has met, even exceeded, this goal.

Tennesseans such as Bobby Jones, Amy Grant, Herbert Brewster, and James D. Vaughan have made immense contributions to American gospel music. Whether the particular type is southern gospel, black gospel, or contemporary Christian, gospel music comprises the roots of the state's famed music publishing industry; its music recording industry; its radio broadcast industry; and its deep traditions of musical performing. And one only needs to look beneath the surface of rock, soul, and country music, to find the sounds of gospel music as a vital foundation for modern popular music.

NOTES

1. Stephen Shearon, "Shape-Note Singing," in *Tennessee Encyclopedia of History and Culture,* ed. Carroll Van West, Connie L. Lester, Anne-Leslie Owens, and Margaret D. Binnicker (Nashville: Tennessee Historical Society, 1998), 841.
2. M. L. Swan and W. H. Swan, *The New Harp of Columbia: A Facsimile Edition,* with an introduction by Dorothy D. Horn, Ron Petersen, and Candra Phillips (Knoxville: Univ. of Tennessee Press, 2001), xxvi.
3. Joyce Marie Jackson, "The Changing Nature of Gospel Music: A Southern Case Study," *African American Review* 29 (Summer 1995): 188.
4. George R. Ricks, *Some Aspects of the Religious Music of the American Negro* (New York: Arno Press, 1977), 133.
5. Brewster quoted in Kip Lornell, *"Happy in the Service of the Lord": African-American Sacred Vocal Harmony Quartets in Memphis,* 2d ed. (Knoxville: Univ. of Tennessee Press, 1995), 141.
6. Lornell, *"Happy in the Service of the Lord,"* 138.

7. Neil V. Rosenberg, *Bluegrass: A History* (Urbana: Univ. of Illinois Press, 1985), 233.
8. Deborah Evans Price, "Christian Music Enjoys Growth," *Billboard* 111 (July 17, 1999): 8.

Suggested Readings

Brooks, Tim. "'Might Take One Disc of This Trash as a Novelty': Early Recordings by the Fisk Jubilee Singers and the Popularization of 'Negro Folk Music.'" *American Music* 18 (Fall 2001): 278–316.

Cobb, Buell E., Jr. *The Sacred Harp: A Tradition and Its Music.* Athens: Univ. of Georgia Press, 1989.

Epstein, Dena J. *Sinful Tunes and Spirituals: Black Folk Music to the Civil War.* Urbana: Univ. of Illinois Press, 1977.

Fisher, Miles M. *Negro Slave Songs in the United States.* Ithaca: Cornell Univ. Press, 1953.

Jackson, George P. *Spiritual Folk Songs of Early America.* New York: J. J. Augustin, 1937.

———. *White Spirituals in the Southern Uplands.* 1933. Reprint, New York: Dover Publications, 1965.

Lornell, Kip. *Happy in the Service of the Lord: African American Sacred Vocal Harmony Quartets in Memphis.* 2d ed. Knoxville: Univ. of Tennessee Press, 1995.

Reagon, Bernice J., ed., *We'll Understand It Better By and By: Pioneering African American Gospel Composers.* Washington, D.C.: Smithsonian Institution Press, 1992.

Romanowski, William D. "Where's the Gospel? Amy's Grant Latest Album Has Thrown the Contemporary Christian Music Industry into a First-Rate Identity Crisis." *Christianity Today* 41 (Dec. 8, 1997): 44.

Wolfe, Charles K. "Gospel Music, White." In *Encyclopedia of Southern Culture,* edited by William Ferris and Charles R. Wilson, 1013–14. Chapel Hill: Univ. of North Carolina Press, 1989.

West, Carroll Van, Connie L. Lester, Anne-Leslie Owens, and Margaret D. Binnicker, eds. *The Tennessee Encyclopedia of History and Culture.* Nashville: Tennessee Historical Society, 1998.

Twenty-four

Blues, Jazz, and Ragtime in Tennessee

Paul F. Wells

Center for Popular Music, Middle Tennessee State University

One manifestation of the tremendous social and cultural changes brought about by the Civil War and emancipation was the great flowering of African American music in the latter half of the nineteenth century. Although freedom brought new challenges and problems for the former slaves, they were able to enjoy increased mobility, different work situations, and opportunities for education, however limited all these might have been. As living and working conditions changed, so did the contexts in which African Americans performed and listened to music.

On the plantations slave musicians played for white dances in the Big House as well as for frolics in their own quarters. Work songs were a regular accompaniment to field labor, and spirituals provided some food for the soul. With Emancipation, dances moved into noisy saloons, a context in which the old fiddle and banjo combination could easily be drowned out. Guitars, pianos, brass, and woodwinds began to gain favor and contributed to the shaping of new musical styles that merged African rhythmic and improvisatory sensibilities with European harmonic elements. The emergence of sharecropping meant that no longer was most agricultural work done by huge crews of field hands working together, their labors coordinated by song. Field hollers, a form of solo musical expression, took the place of the old call-and-response work songs in many farm fields.

Formal training in the principles of European art music could be gained at Fisk University and other colleges. The Fisk Jubilee Singers introduced African American religious music to the world via the Negro spirituals they performed on their concert tours.

Some African Americans pursued careers as professional songwriters or musicians, working within the prevailing conventions of mainstream American popular music. Gussie L. Davis, for example, was a successful songwriter whose works "We Sat beneath the Maple on the Hill," "Fatal Wedding," and "In the Baggage Coach Ahead" became staples of American sentimental song. White hillbilly artists frequently recorded Davis's songs in the early days of the country music industry. James A. Bland was the writer of "Oh, Dem Golden Slippers" and "Carry Me Back to Old Virginny"; he was a professional minstrel entertainer, touring with Callendar's Original Georgia Minstrels, Haverly's Genuine Colored Minstrels, and other companies.

Ultimately of more importance, however, were those who forged their way ahead to find their own voices and bring new forms of black vernacular music into the mainstream. The new genres of ragtime, jazz, and blues forever changed the fundamental nature of American popular music, completing the shift from the dominance of European musical elements to African ones that had begun with the rise of blackface minstrelsy in the 1840s. Tennessee and Tennesseans played varying roles in the development and dissemination of these new musical genres, most notably in blues. The three styles were not always totally discrete.

Ragtime

Ragtime emerged from African American musical tradition to flourish in the mainstream of American popular music from roughly 1898 to 1918. Although most commonly known as a form of solo piano music, "ragtime" broadly refers to a musical style that was also played on other instruments, such as guitar, and by string bands and other small ensembles. There were also many ragtime songs. The roots of ragtime lie in earlier forms of black vernacular dance music; dances (that is, the dance event, not a particular set of steps) were sometimes referred to as "rags." It has been suggested that the piano took over the roles played by the fiddle and banjo in earlier times, with the left hand providing the chordal accompaniment previously supplied by the banjo and the right hand carrying the melody as the fiddler would. In any event, ragtime is characterized by syncopated rhythm in which the musical accents often fall off the beat—"ragged time."

Of all the new forms of black music, ragtime had the closest ties to European musical conventions in terms of harmonic language, formal structures, and the fact that rags typically were fixed in print. The ragtime tradition was strongest in the Midwest, in cities such as St. Louis, Kansas City, and Chicago, perhaps because there were more opportunities for African Americans to receive formal musical training in these urban areas than there were in the Jim Crow South. Tennessee arguably had the strongest ragtime tradition in the South, with numerous published rags emanating from both Nashville and Memphis.

One of the key figures in the history of ragtime in Tennessee was Jesse French, who founded a piano company in Nashville in 1872. By 1887 French had incorporated his business and had expanded it to include selling and publishing sheet music. His son, Henry A. French, eventually took over the business, which by this time included branches in Memphis, St. Louis, Little Rock, and Birmingham.

The first rag published in Nashville was "Mandy's Broadway Stroll," composed by Thomas A. Broady and published by Henry A. French in 1898. Little is known about Broady, not even whether he lived in Tennessee. French published two other rags by Broady, "Tennessee Jubilee" in 1899 and "Whittling Remus" in 1900.

Charles A. Hunter was a more prolific Nashville-based ragtime composer. Hunter, a blind white man, was born in Columbia, Tennessee, in 1876. His earliest rag, "Tickled to Death," was published in Nashville by Frank G. Fite in 1899. Later rags included "Possum and Taters" (1900), "Tennessee Tantalizer" (1900), and "Queen of Love" (1901), all published by French; "Cotton Bolls" (1901), published by O. K. Houck; and "Just Ask Me" (1902) and "Why We Smile" (1903), published by Fite. Hunter was transferred to French's St. Louis store in 1902 and died in St. Louis in 1906.

Other Nashville rags included Roland C. Flick's "Snowball Babe," A. E. Henrich's "Queen Raglin," Wade Harrison's "Bran Dance Shuffle," several works written and published by Lew Roberts, and W. H. Petway's "When You Dance that Loving Rag." Surprisingly, there was even a bit of ragtime from the Cumberland Plateau. Severino Giovannali wrote and published two rags that carry a Cookeville imprint, but nothing further is known of him or his activities.

Jesse French had a Memphis counterpart in John C. Houck, a Nashvillian who moved to the Bluff City in 1881 and opened a music store there. His son, O. K. Houck, was an early associate of Jesse French but ultimately took over his family's musical enterprises in Nashville, Chattanooga, St. Louis, Little Rock, Birmingham, Shreveport, and New Orleans. In Memphis, Houck published the work of several ragtime writers, including "Gallery Gods Delight" by Joseph H. Denck, "Possum Rag" and "Bulldog Rag" by Geraldine Dobbins, and "Encore Rag" by Tad Fischer. Other Memphis publishers who contributed to the published record of ragtime included the Bluestein brothers and Phil Hacker.

Scholars disagree about whether or not the Tennessee ragtime tradition was sufficiently distinctive to warrant being regarded as a separate school or substyle. Some use the term "folk ragtime" to describe the published Tennessee piano rags, especially those from the midstate, and assert that they incorporate elements and motifs of white as well as black country dance music.[1] Others question the existence of evidence that would support such pronouncements. Musically, the Nashville ragtime composers showed a predilection for the use of pentatonic scales, while the Memphis writers employed more chromaticism, sometimes approaching the character of the lowered thirds and sevenths that are a feature of the blues scale. The Memphis composers also used structures that hinted at the twelve-bar blues form.

A more accurate usage of the term "folk ragtime" might be to describe the music of the instrumental ensembles and soloists who provided music for dances and entertainments, both in rural areas and in large cities such as Memphis and Knoxville. String bands or jug bands comprised of no set number of musicians playing guitars, mandolins, fiddles, banjos, harmonicas, and often with a jug and/or washtub bass, played music that drew on many different sources and styles, including ragtime, blues, and pop music. Many solo guitarists played a style akin to ragtime, in which the bass line was played by the thumb of the right hand, while the melody was played by one or two fingers.

Blues and Related Musics

The first published rags predated the first published blues by more than a decade, and the ragtime craze in the mainstream of popular music was nearly played out by the time blues began its initial run in the commercial arena. However, there is insufficient evidence to assess which form—ragtime or blues—actually came first. The first known use of the term "rag" in connection with a piece of published music occurred in 1896 with Ernest Hogan's song "All Coons Look Alike to Me," in describing an optional "Choice Chorus, with Negro 'Rag' Accompaniment." "The Mississippi Rag" from 1897 was the first piece to carry the word "rag" as part of the title. In contrast, what is regarded as the earliest connection of the concept of having "the blues," that is, to feel sad or depressed, with the three-phrase musical structure now known as the blues, came in 1908 with Antonio Maggio's song "I Got the Blues," published in New Orleans. A year later, "I'm Alabama Bound," also published in New Orleans, carried the notation that it was "also known as the Alabama blues." By 1912, at least four songs with the word "blues" as part of their titles were copyrighted or published, including W. C. Handy's first composition in the genre, "The Memphis Blues."

In spite of his sobriquet, "Father of the Blues," Handy by no means invented the form. Like many

W. C. Handy, 1955. Courtesy of University of Memphis Libraries, Special Collections.

W. C. Handy

William Christopher Handy, born in Florence, Alabama, on November 16, 1873, the son and grandson of Methodist ministers, graduated from Florence District School for Negroes in 1891. Having learned to read music and teaching himself guitar and cornet, Handy determined to pursue a career in music, against his father's wishes. He worked in various musical settings: leading a vocal quartette in Birmingham that traveled as far as St. Louis; performing in bands in Evansville, Indiana, and Henderson, Kentucky; performing in and leading the band of W. A. Mahara's Minstrels in tours throughout the United States, Canada, Mexico, and Cuba; and teaching music at Alabama A&M College. Handy performed the popular music of the day while making mental notes of the folk music that he encountered. From 1903 to 1905 he led the Knights of Pythias band in Clarksdale, Mississippi. In the Delta he became aware of the power and commercial potential of blues music, itself just beginning to emerge into public consciousness. In the right place at the right time, Handy exploited this folk music by arranging it for his band of trained musicians.

Handy, recruited to lead Thornton's Knights of Pythias Band in Memphis, may have commuted between Clarksdale and Memphis, but by 1907 he was residing in the larger city. In 1909 the mayoral campaign of reformist Edward H. Crump engaged Handy's band. Handy picked a folk song (whose lyrics were actually critical of the candidate) to arrange and call "Mister Crump." The tune contained ragtime and blues musical elements, and his band's instrumental-only performances of it helped Crump win the election. In 1912, with blues tunes appearing in sheet music, Handy published this piece as "The Memphis Blues." Modest initial sales led him to sell his copyright. Republished with new lyrics by George A. Norton the following year, the song became a hit. The lyrics mentioned Handy's band prominently and gave him a national reputation, although he collected no royalties from the tune.

In 1913, Handy formed Pace and Handy Music Company with partner Harry Pace and published "The Jogo Blues." His "St. Louis Blues" in 1914 had great success; it was one of the biggest hit songs of the twentieth century. Handy capably supervised several bands operating under his name and employed over sixty musicians. He had additional successful compositions in "Yellow Dog Blues" (1914), "Joe Turner Blues" (1915), "The Hesitating Blues" (1915), "Ole Miss" (1916), and "Beale Street Blues" (1916). His company also published the blues compositions of other songwriters and became known as "The Home of the Blues," a title that would later be transferred to the city of Memphis. Handy's band recorded for Columbia Records in 1917, and in the following year he moved his business and resettled in New York City. Gaining the reputation of being "Father of the Blues," Handy used that title for his autobiography (1941). He continued to publish blues and arrangements of spirituals as well as the important book *Blues: An Anthology* (1926), the first book that tried to explain this music.

Handy received many honors before his death on March 28, 1958. His most creative years as a composer were those he spent in Memphis, and on this work his fame largely rests. Handy Park was dedicated in his honor on Beale Street in Memphis in 1931 and a statue erected there in 1960. His was the first African American portrait to hang in the Tennessee state capitol (1973). The Handy Awards are given annually by the Memphis-based Blues Foundation for excellence in blues music.

David Evans, The University of Memphis

people who are popularly given credit for inventing something, Handy's role was more that of codifier and popularizer than innovator. In a famous and oft-quoted anecdote, Handy, who had received formal training in music theory and performance, described how he himself first became aware of what he described as "the weirdest music I had ever heard." While waiting for a train in Tutwiler, Mississippi, in 1903, Handy heard a "ragged, lean Negro guitarist" playing his instrument by sliding a knife along the strings and repeating a line about "Goin' where the Southern cross the Dog" three times.[2] This description makes it clear that what Handy heard was a type of music that already was in common circulation at the turn of the century, at least among blacks in the Mississippi Delta region.

By his early twenties Handy was touring with Mahara's Minstrels, playing cornet. He eventually led his own band and moved to Memphis, the city with which he is most strongly associated, around 1907. Unfortunate experiences surrounding the publication of his composition "Memphis Blues" in 1912 (including getting turned down by O. K. Houck) led Handy to form his own music publishing company, the Pace and Handy Music Company, in partnership with Harry Pace. This was one of the first music publishing companies to be owned and operated by African Americans. Many of Handy's compositions from this time have become standards in the repertories of professional jazz and blues musicians. These include "Yellow Dog Rag" (1914; later to be retitled "Yellow Dog Blues" when blues became more popular than ragtime), "St. Louis Blues" (1914), "The Hesitating Blues" (1915), "Joe Turner Blues" (1915), and "Beale Street Blues" (1916). Handy continued to enjoy an active performing career, both in Memphis and touring from there. In 1917 he left Memphis, relocating first in Chicago and later in New York, which remained his base of operations for the rest of his life.

"The Memphis Blues, a Southern Rag," by W. C. Handy. Courtesy of the Rare Book, Manuscript, & Special Collections Library, Duke University.

A new era in the dissemination and commercialization of the blues began in 1920 when Mamie Smith, an African American vaudeville singer, recorded "You Can't Keep a Good Man Down," a composition by Perry Bradford, a black Chicago music entrepreneur, for the General Phonograph Company. Smith was not the first African American performer to make phonograph records, but this marked the first time the record industry made a deliberate effort to reach the black audience by marketing music by black performers. The success of her first release warranted a follow-up session, and in August 1920, Smith recorded "Crazy Blues," the first blues song committed to wax. Other companies were quick to tap into this new market and soon were issuing "race" records that appealed to the intended audience as well as a sizable white audience.

Mamie Smith was more of a pop singer than a true blues artist. The first real star of blues recording was Chattanooga native Bessie Smith (no relation to Mamie). Born April 15, 1894, Bessie Smith was singing professionally by the time she was eighteen years old. She toured the South in various shows,

Bessie Smith

Got the world in a jug, the stopper in my hand.

Bessie Smith, "Down-Hearted Blues"

BESSIE SMITH WAS BORN IN CHATTANOOGA ON APRIL 15, 1894. ORPHANED BY AGE NINE, HER EARLY life was one of unremitting poverty. She did have a gift for music, however, and in 1912 she joined a traveling vaudeville show, becoming a star on the southern vaudeville circuit by the late 1910s. As more and more African Americans moved North, so too did Smith, and by the early 1920s she received top billing in theaters throughout the North and South.

Smith made her first documented recording on February 16, 1923, for Columbia Records, "'Tain't Nobody's Bizzness If I Do" on the A side with "Down-Hearted Blues" on the flip side. It was an immediate hit, selling more than 780,000 copies by year's end and leading to a career that included almost two hundred recordings. By the mid-1920s, Bessie Smith was, simply, the most successful black performing artist of her time.

Those who knew her best remembered a high-spirited, generous, and even tender woman who could also be rough, coarse, and crude. The many sides of her personality were reflected in her singing, for she could be passionate, playful, sad, joyful, and more. The main impression of a Bessie Smith performance was of sheer presence. Clarinetist Mezz Mezzrow remembered, "When she was in a room her vitality flowed out like a cloud and stuffed the air till the walls bulged. . . . She just stood there and sang, letting the love and the laughter run out of her, and the heaving sadness, too; she felt everything, and swayed just a little with the glory of being alive."[1] Her fabled force-of-character was reinforced by one of the most expressive voices of the twentieth century. She is one of the first singers to explore and exploit the "blues notes," those pitches that lie between the notes of the conventional scale. She could make one feel pain by hanging just under the note and joy by sliding subtly up to the pitch. No singer of her time, and few since or before, could match the range of her expression.

To Smith's most loyal fans—the African Americans who had moved north with her—she was a voice from back home. But in the 1930s, the world changed; those fans no longer wanted to remember the hurt of their southern roots. African American music became sophisticated and polished; the music of pain—the blues—was out. The new music and the audience passed Smith by, and her popularity plummeted. Her addiction to alcohol did not help matters. And beyond that was a deep-seated anger and frustration that sometimes alienated those who could help her the most. "She had this trouble in her, this thing that wouldn't let her rest sometimes, a meanness that came and took her over," jazz musician Sidney Bechet remembered.[2] In "Long Old Road," one of her last recordings, Bessie sang, "You can't trust nobody; you might as well be alone."

Smith died young, on September 26, 1937, in an automobile accident on Route 61 in the heart of the Mississippi Delta, the birthplace of the blues. She was buried in Philadelphia. A headstone finally placed on her grave in 1970 was paid for in part by Janis Joplin, one of the thousands of blues singers who learned their music from the "Empress of the Blues."

Dale Cockrell, Vanderbilt University

Notes

1. Mezz Mezzrow, *Really the Blues* (New York: Random House, 1946), 114.
2. Sidney Bechet, *Treat it Gentle* (London: Cassel, 1960), 139.

Bessie Smith, February 3, 1936. Photograph by Carl Van Vechten. Courtesy of the Library of Congress, Prints & Photographs Division, Creative Americans: Portraits by Carl Van Vechten, 1932–1964, Collection (reproduction number LC-USZ62-94954 DLC).

sometimes with Gertrude "Ma" Rainey, an older vocalist from Georgia who was a pioneer in vaudeville blues. Bessie made her first record in New York in 1923, and for the next five years she was one of the top-selling blues artists on record. By the end of the decade her career had fallen victim to the twin hazards of alcoholism and the Great Depression. She began to make a comeback in the 1930s but lost her life in an automobile accident in Clarksdale, Mississippi, in 1937.

Bessie Smith was often accompanied on her recordings by leading jazz players such as Louis Armstrong, James P. Johnson, and Clarence Williams. She helped define the so-called "Classic Blues" idiom of strong-voiced women who dominated the early years of the "race" record business. The Classic Blues singers were touring professional entertainers who performed in an urbane, sophisticated style that often displayed much kinship with jazz.

Another Classic Blues singer with Tennessee ties was Ida Cox. Although historians once thought Cox had been born in Knoxville, she actually was from Toccoa, in northeast Georgia. Born Ida Prather in 1896, she began her professional career around 1911 by running away from home to join a traveling minstrel show she heard in her hometown. Like many of her peers, she toured extensively throughout the South. In 1923 she became the first blues artist to record for the Paramount label, a company based in Chicago that became one of the leading early blues labels. She recorded extensively throughout the 1920s and continued touring even after the Depression temporarily disrupted the record industry. Cox retired to her daughter's home in Knoxville in the early 1950s and died in 1967.

A third Classic Blues singer, Alberta Hunter, was born in Memphis in 1895 but established herself professionally first in Chicago and later in New York. She is noted for having been co-writer, with Chattanooga-born Lovie Austin, of "Downhearted Blues," Bessie Smith's first hit.

The contributions to blues history by Handy and the Classic Blues singers notwithstanding, it is in the area of country or down-home blues (and related music) that Tennessee figures most strongly. Blues activity was particularly strong in West Tennessee, especially in Memphis and environs, but the Middle and East regions of the state were also home to some noteworthy artists.

With its proximity to the blues-rich area of the Mississippi Delta, its location on a major waterway, and its role as a trading hub, it is hardly surprising that Memphis became the center of music and entertainment in the region. Like W. C. Handy earlier, many musicians who made their names in the city during the period between the two world wars were born elsewhere. Many, such as Gus Cannon, Will Batts, Walter "Furry" Lewis, Memphis Minnie (Lizzie Douglas), Robert Wilkins, Dan Sane, Jack Kelly, and

Booker T. "Bukka" White, came from Mississippi. Others, such as Sleepy John Estes, Noah Lewis, Hammie Nixon, Frank Stokes, and Yank Rachell came from surrounding communities in West Tennessee. All of these, and many others, had their music captured for posterity by the phonograph companies that were eagerly exploiting the newly discovered market for African American music in the 1920s.

There was a great deal of variety in the music of the Memphis musicians of the era. Although blues figured strongly in their repertoires, and many of these players are commonly regarded as "blues musicians," few, if any, restricted themselves to playing blues exclusively. A respected and influential figure such as Furry Lewis, for example, was an excellent blues player but had a repertoire that also was rich in folk ballads such as "Billy Lyons and Stack O' Lee," "John Henry," and "Kassie Jones." Memphis was also famous for its jug bands, particularly the Memphis Jug Band and Cannon's Jug Stompers. Although both bands recorded many blues numbers, they also played a mix of ragtime-influenced pieces and popular songs, the type of material often referred to as "hokum." In general Memphis music of this era exhibits a strong ragtime influence. There is also somewhat less emotional intensity in the Memphis blues musicians than was found in the music of some of their contemporaries from the Delta.

The most important African American musician of this era to emerge from Middle Tennessee was DeFord Bailey. Because of his unique association with the Grand Ole Opry, Bailey's work is usually considered as part of country music history. However, his music places him squarely within the larger picture of African American rural music or, more properly, within the shared musical traditions common to both white and black rural musicians in Middle Tennessee in the early part of the twentieth century. Bailey recorded a handful of sides in 1927 and 1928, all of which featured the harmonica playing for which he was famous on the Opry. Recordings made later in his life showed Bailey also to have been a fine guitar and banjo player.

DeFord Bailey. Courtesy of the Grand Ole Opry Archives.

The older African American string band tradition of dance music seems to have persisted longer in Middle Tennessee than it did in many other areas of the South. Because the commercial recording companies largely overlooked black fiddlers and banjo players, our knowledge of what was once a rich and flourishing tradition is today quite limited and based on rather scattered documentation.

In 1942, Fisk University professor John Work III recorded the fiddle and banjo team of Frank Patterson of Walter Hill and Nathan Frazier of Nashville. Their music had much more in common with white string bands than it did with that of Memphis jug bands. Another black string band, led by fiddler John Lusk and banjo player Murphy "Murph" Gribble, was active in Warren County, playing for dances and on the streets of McMinnville. Folklorist Stu Jamieson recorded them in 1946. Their repertoire also consisted of old-time fiddle tunes rather than blues or ragtime, but Gribble's finger-style banjo playing gave the band a distinctive character.

The music of white folk musicians in Middle Tennessee suggests that a great deal of interaction occurred between white and black rural musicians. Grand Ole Opry star Uncle Dave Macon, who was born in Smartt Station in Warren County and lived much of his life near Murfreesboro in Rutherford County, knew many songs that were also common in African American tradition. For example, in July 1928 he recorded "Over the Road I'm Bound to Go," which is the same song as "Feather Bed" as recorded by Cannon's Jug Stompers from Memphis in September of that same year. Williamson County's Sam McGee, a frequent musical companion of Macon, was a superb finger-style guitarist and banjo player. His playing owed much to African American styles, having learned directly from black musician Jim Sapp, and his repertoire included many blues or blues-influenced numbers.

Earlier in the century, black folklorist Thomas W. Talley, a professor at Fisk, collected extensively in the rural communities of Middle Tennessee. His work resulted in the publication of *Negro Folk Rhymes* in 1922. Charles Wolfe, in editing a modern reprint of Talley's book, noted more than eighty-five songs collected by Talley that were also known to be in the repertoires of white country musicians of the era.[3]

In addition to Ida Cox, East Tennessee was home to other notable blues artists. The region's cultural and geographic links with Appalachia and the Piedmont areas of Virginia and the Carolinas places its African American musical traditions within what has been called the Southeast blues tradition, as opposed to the Memphis area's ties to the music of the Mississippi Delta.

Perhaps the best-known country bluesman with East Tennessee roots was guitarist and singer Walter Brown "Brownie" McGhee, who was born in Knoxville in 1914. His family soon moved to Kingsport, where his younger brother, Glenville, who also had a career as a musician (as "Stick" McGhee), was born. The brothers played music together in their youth, sometimes joined by their friend Lesley Riddle, who is best known for teaching songs and guitar techniques to the Carter Family, hillbilly singers from southwestern Virginia. Brownie played throughout the region and eventually formed a partnership with North Carolina mouth harp player Sonny Terry.

Knoxville was also the home base of a trio of musicians who were as eclectic as they were talented. Carl Martin, Ted Bogan, and Howard Armstrong performed and recorded in various combinations for over sixty years. Their combined repertoires included everything from straight-ahead blues, to old-time fiddle tunes, to ragtime-influenced pieces, to popular songs.

Although many blues artists traveled to the big northern cities of Chicago and New York to record, some companies took their recording operations on the road in the South to record black artists for their "race" series and white musicians for their "hillbilly" series. Victor was particularly active in making trips to Tennessee and did much to exploit the wealth of African American talent that was to be found in and around Memphis. Beginning in early 1927, Victor personnel made at least one recording trip to the city each year throughout the remainder of the decade. Columbia, Okeh, and Brunswick also ventured to Memphis. In addition, African American performers were recorded by various companies that set up temporary recording operations in Nashville, Knoxville, Bristol, and Johnson City.

In the period following World War II, Memphis continued its role as the center of blues activity in the state. The clubs on Beale Street provided work for many musicians, and in 1948 WDIA became the first radio station in the nation to feature all-black programming. Recording studios and record labels began operating in the city as well. White radio engineer Sam Phillips opened his Memphis Recording Service in January 1950 and began to record the city's black musicians. In the early days of his operation he leased masters to other labels, such as Chess in Chicago, but in March 1952, Phillips launched his own Sun label, soon to become famous as Elvis Presley's first label.

John Lee "Sonny Boy" Williamson

JOHN LEE WILLIAMSON WAS BORN OUTSIDE JACKSON, TENNESSEE, ON MARCH 30, 1914. HE LEARNED blues harmonica from older players in the region, such as Noah Lewis of Henning and Hammie Nixon of Brownsville. After a move to St. Louis, Williamson began making commercial records for RCA Victor's Bluebird subsidiary in 1937 in Aurora, Illinois, and recording in Chicago first in 1939. He settled in Chicago but returned frequently to Jackson. Until his death in Chicago at the hands of muggers on June 1, 1948, he recorded 120 blues songs for RCA and played on further recordings by Robert Lee McCoy, Yank Rachell, Speckled Red, and Big Joe Williams, among others. Some of Williamson's best known pieces, often performed by other artists since his death, are "Blue Bird Blues," "Sugar Mama Blues," "Decoration Blues," "I Been Dealing with the Devil," "My Little Machine," "My Black Name Blues," "Shake the Boogie," "Mellow Chick Swing," and "Good Morning, Little School Girl." A number of his blues memorialized Jackson, including "Jackson Blues," "Blue Bird Blues," "Project Highway," and "Shannon Street Blues."

John Lee "Sonny Boy" Williamson. Courtesy of the T. W. Utley Family and Jackson/Madison County Library.

Williamson was influential not only as a songwriter but as a vocalist and harmonica player. His slightly lisping singing and phrasing both behind and ahead of the beat were widely imitated. Previous singing harmonica players had mostly used the instrument to play instrumental choruses between stanzas. Williamson's innovative use of it to provide fills between his vocal phrases created a seamless sound between his voice and the instrument. His playing was full of blue notes, wails, bends, and varied textures. More than any other player, he made the harmonica a lead instrument in a blues band. At the time of his death he was leading a five-piece band and generating tremendous swing. Had he lived longer, he would undoubtedly have been a leader of modern electric blues in Chicago. As it was, he influenced almost every harmonica player in the blues who came after him, including Forrest City Joe (Pugh), Little Walter (Jacobs), Billy Boy Arnold, and Junior Wells. Another great harmonica player from Mississippi, Aleck Miller, took the name "Sonny Boy Williamson" and had an equally successful career until his death in 1965. John Lee Williamson is buried south of Jackson near his birthplace. The city's annual Shannon Street Blues Festival was established in his honor.

David Evans, The University of Memphis

John Adams "Sleepy John" Estes

JOHN ADAMS "SLEEPY JOHN" ESTES USED VOCALS AND GUITAR TO INTRODUCE HIS STYLE OF TENNESSEE country blues to audiences around the world. Through numerous recordings, concert appearances, spots on television and radio shows, and documentaries, he influenced and taught the folk music he knew. Its melodic sounds derived from European American country music of early Tennessee settlers and the African American slave of his region. An acclaimed songwriter, Estes based his ballads on his experiences living amid racial discrimination and poverty. His extensive musical career spanned more than sixty-five years.

John Adams "Sleepy John" Estes. Courtesy of Sharon Norris.

Estes, born to Millie Thornton and Daniel Estes on January 25, 1899, in Nutbush, Tennessee, lived much of his life in the Brownsville area. Influenced by his father, a farmer and guitar player, and traveling and local musicians from Ripley, Nutbush, and Brownsville, Estes taught himself guitar on a homemade instrument. By 1916 he had teamed with Yank Rachell and Hammie Nixon, both of Brownsville, to do local, Memphis, and out-of-state supper clubs, picnics, fairs, fish fries, minstrel shows, medicine shows, dances, and parties. He recorded with Victor Records in 1929 and then moved to Chicago and recorded with Champion, Decca, and Bluebird Records during the 1930s. Returning to Brownsville in 1941, Estes recorded with Sun, Delmark, Adelphi, and Albatross Records.

Estes made many concert appearances through the 1960s and 1970s, including the First Floor Club in Toronto, Canada, the American Folk Blues Festival tour in Europe, and the Blues Festival tour in Japan. Partially blinded in childhood, he was by 1950 totally blind. Estes died in 1977 after suffering a stroke while preparing for another European concert tour engagement. He is buried in the Elam Baptist Church Cemetery of the Nutbush/Durhamville community, east of Ripley, Tennessee.

Sharon Norris, Nutbush Heritage Productions, Brownsville

Memphis attracted talent the caliber of Rufus Thomas, "Little Milton" Campbell, Bobby Bland, Howlin' Wolf (Chester Burnett), and Riley "B. B." King. Other blues musicians with West Tennessee roots found fame by moving north to Chicago. These included mouth harp players John Lee "Sonny Boy" Williamson and Amos "Junior" Wells, pianist Memphis Slim (Peter Chatman), and vocalist Koko Taylor.

The Popular Bands of Francis Craig and Jimmie Lunceford

CLOSE IN AGE AND GROUNDED IN TENNESSEE, THESE TWO MEN AND THEIR BANDS REPRESENTED THE best of dance music and gained national reputations in the midcentury. Francis Jackson Craig (1900–1966) was a natural pianist. Born in Dickson, Tennessee, this minister's son attended Vanderbilt University, where he founded his first dance band. Craig's was the most popular Nashville society orchestra for three decades. The group played on the first broadcast of Nashville's WSM in 1925 and had a weekly nationwide broadcast over NBC. Craig's tenure at the Hermitage Hotel has been called the longest house orchestra engagement in history. Illustrious performers in his orchestras included Phil Harris, James Melton, Dinah Shore, Snooky Lanson, and Kitty Kallen.

Jimmie Lunceford. Courtesy of Special Collections, Fisk University Library, Nashville.

Craig composed numerous tunes, including "Beg Your Pardon," "Dynamite," Vanderbilt's fight song, and "Red Rose," his theme song. The 1947 composition "Near You" brought him national fame. His recording of it was number one on *Billboard*'s Honor Roll of Hits seventeen consecutive weeks, longer than any other song in history. For "Near You," Craig won the Cleff Award for the outstanding song of 1947.

Though born in Fulton, Missouri, James Melvin (Jimmie) Lunceford (1902–1947) spent his youth in Denver, Colorado, learning to play multiple instruments. By the time he graduated from Fisk University in 1926, he was an experienced orchestra leader. While teaching at (Memphis) Manassas High School from 1926 to 1929, he formed a student jazz band. He later instructed some of these men at Fisk and incorporated them into his band after they graduated.

After several years of playing, recording, and broadcasting (WREC) in Memphis, Lunceford's band appeared at New York City's Cotton Club in 1933. His group featured arrangements by trumpeter Sy Oliver that emphasized two beats in a measure. This "Lunceford two beat" was delivered with panache and precision. Lunceford's orchestra solidified its reputation as one of the great swing bands in November 1940, when it won a famous "battle of the bands" in New York. Among the opponents that night were orchestras led by Benny Goodman, Glenn Miller, and Count Basie.

Lunceford's most popular songs were "Organ Grinder's Swing," "For Dancers Only," and "Uptown Blues." Lunceford toured continually until his untimely death while on the road in Seaside, Oregon.

Robert W. Ikard, Nashville

Suggested Readings

Fernett, Gene. *Swing Out: Great Negro Dance Bands*. New York: Da Capo Press, 1993.

Ikard, Robert W. *Near You: Francis Craig, Dean of Southern Maestros*. Franklin, Tenn.: Hillsboro Press, 1999.

Following on the success of WDIA in Memphis, WLAC in Nashville brought the sounds of black music to the airwaves. Its fifty-thousand-watt signal reached much of the eastern United States. Whereas WDIA featured all-black air talent, especially Nat D. Williams, WLAC's leading personality was John Richbourg ("John R"), who was white. In addition to its programming, the station was instrumental in promoting mail-order sales of recordings of blues and rhythm and blues artists. Local Nashville retailers Ernie's Record Mart and Randy's Record Shop advertised heavily on the station. This served also to promote the Nashboro and Excello record labels, owned by Ernie Young of Ernie's Record Mart, and Dot Records, owned by Randy Wood of Randy's Record Shop. The Bullet and J-B labels, owned by Nashville entrepreneur Jim Bulleit, also played a role in recording and promoting the music of regional black artists.

Jazz

Jazz has occupied only a modest place in the history of music in Tennessee. Nevertheless, a healthy current of interest in jazz always has existed in most large cities in Tennessee, and several musicians with Tennessee roots have made important contributions on the national jazz scene.

Clarinetist Buster Bailey was born in Memphis in 1902. He played with W. C. Handy before moving in 1919 to Chicago, where he played with Erskine Tate and King Oliver. His next move was to New York, where he began a long association with Fletcher Henderson and was featured soloist on many of Henderson's recordings.

Pianist Lil Hardin followed a similar path. Born in Memphis in 1908, she attended Fisk University, where she received training in music. She moved to Chicago two years before Bailey and, like him, joined King Oliver's Creole Jazz Band. In 1924 Hardin married Louis Armstrong, who was also a member of Oliver's band. In addition to leading her own bands, she played an important role in the development of Armstrong's career, encouraging him to strike out on his own, playing piano in his early Hot Five and Hot Seven groups and writing many songs for these bands. She later continued her own career as soloist and bandleader, both before and after her split with Armstrong in 1931.

Bandleader and Missouri native Jimmie Lunceford spent some time in Memphis early in his career. Lunceford, like Hardin, received his early musical training at Fisk, as did future Lunceford band members Eddie Wilcox (piano), Paul Webster (trumpet), Willie Smith (alto saxophone), and Jock Carruthers (baritone saxophone).

Brothers Phineas and Calvin Newborn, pianist and guitarist respectively, were West Tennessee natives who began their professional careers in Memphis. Phineas later played with Lionel Hampton and with Charles Mingus, among others. Calvin worked with Earl Hines and played on recordings by Lionel Hampton and others.

Nashville's African American community supported a modest jazz scene, with Chick Chavis and Don Q. Pullen leading bands that were locally popular. Pullen made a few recordings, including some on the Nashville-based World label. The most prominent jazz musician to come out of Nashville was trumpeter Adolphus Anthony "Doc" Cheatham, who was born in 1905. Cheatham toured and recorded extensively as a sideman and benefited from an early association with Lil Armstrong. His credits include playing on some sides by blues singer Ma Rainey and working with Cab Calloway, McKinney's Cotton Pickers, and Benny Goodman. Cheatham died in 1997.

Trombonist Jimmy Cleveland was born in the tiny town of Wartrace in Bedford County. He attended Tennessee State University before embarking on a professional career in which he has played with Lionel Hampton, Gerry Mulligan, and Quincy Jones, among others. He has also played on countless recordings, including those by Dizzy Gillespie, Miles Davis, Gil Evans, Wes Montgomery, and Kenny Burrell.

Many of Nashville's country musicians flirted with playing jazz in addition to country music. Guitarist Hank "Sugarfoot" Garland, for example, earned great respect among mainline jazz players. In 1960 Garland was invited to bring a group of Nashville musicians to the prestigious Newport Jazz Festival, but riots forced an early closure of the festival before the group had the chance to perform. A 1961 album, *Jazz Winds from a New Direction,* featured Garland playing in the company of drummer Joe Morello, bassist Joe Benjamin, and vibes player Gary Burton.

In East Tennessee, Maynard Baird led a dance band in Knoxville for many years. He recorded a few sides for Vocalion in 1929 and 1930, but his life and work have garnered little attention from jazz critics and historians. Chattanooga produced a few musicians who made their mark outside Tennessee. Pianist Lovie Austin (born Cora Calhoun) recorded with many of the Classic Blues singers including Ida Cox and Alberta Hunter. Bassist Jimmy Blanton played locally and attended Tennessee A&I (now Tennessee State University) before moving to St. Louis. In 1939 he began a long association with Duke Ellington. Blanton's innovative work with Ellington set new standards for jazz bass playing. Yusef Lateef (born William Evans) was an innovative reed player who worked with such top figures as Dizzy Gillespie, Charles Mingus, and Cannonball Adderly.

NOTES

1. David A. Jasen and Trebor Jay Tichenor, *Rags and Ragtime: A Musical History* (New York: Dover Publications, 1978), 21–27.
2. W. C. Handy, *Father of the Blues: An Autobiography* (New York: Macmillan, 1941), 74.
3. Charles K. Wolfe, ed., *Thomas W. Talley's Negro Folk Rhymes* (Knoxville: Univ. of Tennessee Press, 1991), xxv.

SUGGESTED READINGS

Abbott, Lynn and Doug Seroff. "'They Cert'ly Sound Good to Me': Sheet Music, Southern Vaudeville, and the Commercial Ascendancy of the Blues." *American Music* 14 (Winter 1996): 402–54.

Albertson, Chris. *Bessie.* New York: Stein and Day, 1982.

Bastin, Bruce. *Red River Blues: The Blues Tradition in the Southeast.* Urbana: Univ. of Illinois Press, 1986.

Berlin, Edward A. *Ragtime: A Musical and Cultural History.* Berkeley and Los Angeles: Univ. of California Press, 1980.

Booth, Stanley. *Rhythm Oil: A Journey Through the Music of the American South.* New York: Pantheon Books, 1991.

Broome, P. J. (Paul), and Clay Tucker. *The Other Music City.* Nashville, 1990.

Cantor, Louis. *Wheelin' on Beale: How WDIA-Memphis Became the Nation's First All-Black Radio Station and Created the Sound That Changed America.* New York: Pharos Books, 1992.

Dixon, Robert M. W., John Godrich, and Howard W. Rye. *Blues and Gospel Records, 1890–1943.* 4th ed. Oxford and New York: Clarendon Press of Oxford Univ. Press, 1997.

Dixon, Robert, and John Godrich. *Recording the Blues.* New York: Stein and Day, 1970.

Garon, Paul, and Beth Garon. *Woman with Guitar: Memphis Minnie's Blues.* New York: Da Capo Press, 1992.

Gordon, Robert. *It Came from Memphis.* Boston: Faber and Faber, 1995.

Handy, W. C. *Father of the Blues: An Autobiography.* New York: Macmillan, 1941.

Jasen, David A., and Trebor Jay Tichenor. *Rags and Ragtime: A Musical History.* New York: Dover Publications, 1978.

Joyner, David Lee. "Southern Ragtime and Its Transition to Published Blues" (Ph.D. diss., Memphis State Univ., 1986).

McKee, Margaret, and Fred Chisenhall. *Beale Black and Blue: Life and Music on Black America's Main Street.* Baton Rouge: Louisiana State Univ. Press, 1981.

Oliver, Paul. *The Story of the Blues.* Philadelphia: Chilton Book Company, 1969.

Olsson, Bengt. *Memphis Blues and Jug Bands.* London: Studio Vista, 1970.

Seroff, Doug, and Lynn Abbott. "The Origins of Ragtime." *78 Quarterly* 1, no. 10 (1999): 121–43.

Twenty-five

The Music Can Set You Free

Tennessee Rock 'n' Soul, 1948–1968

Michael Bertrand

Tennessee State University

> Why do all of the good artists come from Tennessee? Is it real rhythm crazy down there? Are people really happy for the music? I mean, that's what it sounds like on record.
>
> Reporter to Elvis Presley, 1957

Tennessee. The name, presumably derived from a Cherokee village and having no known meaning, automatically conjures images and sounds that are instantly recognized and comprehended. Pastoral scenes of hills and rural landscapes join with the resonance of guitars, mandolins, fiddles, banjos, and steel guitars to form the mental picture that many have of the nation's sixteenth state. Home to the Grand Ole Opry and a multi-million-dollar music publishing and recording industry, Tennessee has indeed become synonymous with commercial country music.

Yet it is often forgotten that Tennessee also played a central role in the development of the modern grass-roots musical forms of rock and roll and soul music. In fact, in the two decades or so following World War II, numerous performers, producers, songwriters, and radio personalities within the state created and directed the trends that would dominate American popular music. Elvis Presley, Al Green, Carl Perkins, Ike Turner, Jerry Lee Lewis, Rufus Thomas, Tina Turner, Randy Wood, David Porter, Charlie Rich, Willie Mitchell, Sam Phillips, B. B. King, Bill Black, Carla Thomas, Paul Burlison, O. V. Wright, Ann Peebles, Buddy Killan, Mavis Staples, Dorsey Burnette, Christine Kittrell, Steve Cropper, Al Jackson, Duck Dunn, Booker T. Jones, Jim Stewart, Isaac Hayes, Johnny Burnette, Larry Birdsong, Roy Orbison, Cordell Jackson, Arthur Gunter, Hoss Allen, Gene Allison, John Richbourg, Eddie Floyd, Pat Boone, Johnny Ace, Charlie Feathers, Elmore James, Scotty Moore, O. B. McClinton, Gene Nobles, Roscoe Shelton, Jack Clement, Little Junior Parker, the Everly Brothers, Johnny Taylor, Estelle Axton, Chips Moman, Bobby "Blue" Bland, and Dewey Phillips are only some of the native and adopted Tennesseans who introduced much of the world to rock and roll and soul music. Their individual and collective efforts would provide anthems of insurgence for at least two generations of young Americans coming of age in the turbulent postwar era.

The revolutionary sounds emanating from Tennessee both reflected and anticipated the social transformations that shook the late twentieth century. "If all that seems to be a bit much to lay at the door of popular music," two commentators have noted, "just try to imagine those changes taking place without the pulsating undercurrent of that powerful music."[1] From Memphis alone came such Sam Phillips–produced classics as "Rocket 88" by Ike Turner, "Good Rockin' Tonight" by Elvis Presley, "Blue Suede Shoes" by Carl Perkins, and "Whole Lotta Shakin' Goin' On" by Jerry Lee Lewis during

Rufus Thomas, WDIA, 1967. Courtesy of University of Memphis Libraries, Special Collections.

the 1950s, such anthems as Carla Thomas's "Gee Whiz," Booker T. and the M. G.'s "Green Onions," Sam and Dave's "Soul Man," and Otis Redding's "Sittin' on the Dock of the Bay" from Stax Records during the 1960s, and Tina Turner's salute to her hometown, "Nutbush City Limits" and the Issac Hayes anthem "Shaft" from the early 1970s. Tennessee's rock 'n' soul music sustained the people who lived during one of the most tumultuous epochs in the nation's history.

The genesis of rock and roll and soul, of course, did not occur completely in any one place; popular music generally does not work in such a uniform or synchronized manner. Yet Tennessee represented in microcosm the entire American South, a region whose staple exports included music as well as cotton and tobacco. In the land of Dixie, where custom, law, and a rigid hierarchical social structure usually limited the options available for African Americans, women, and the poor to achieve dignity and distinction, music provided, as historian Bill Malone so aptly recognized, "a means of release and a form of self-expression that required neither power, status, nor affluence."[2] For a people who traditionally enjoyed few gratifications associated with material success or political prerogative, music furnished a significant source of personal satisfaction and creative sustenance.

Although it would be an exaggeration to say that Tennessee produced all of the most well-known rock and roll and soul artists, there is little doubt that an inordinate number of those responsible for rendering the music did have connections to the Volunteer state. So the question thrown at Elvis in 1957 persists: why Tennessee?

Economic changes are part of the answer. Historian C. Vann Woodward referred to the transformations that rocked the South in the 1940s and 1950s as the "Bulldozer Revolution," a period when industrialization and urbanization proceeded at a rate three times greater than the country as a whole.[3] By the middle to late 1940s, demographic shifts and the relative financial affluence wrought by modernization and a cold war–driven economy led to greater consumer spending. Exorcizing the wants and deprivations that had accompanied Depression-era poverty and wartime scarcity, postwar Tennesseans sought to enter the material mainstream. In addition to purchasing the labor-saving appliances, innovative gadgets, and newfangled and tail-finned automobiles characteristic of the faddish fifties, they were also buying commercial music.

New patterns of consumption and materialism also shaped the first generation of rock and rollers. Whether black or white, they emerged in the late 1940s and early 1950s, almost without exception, from southern working-class traditions. Although many had recently moved to urban areas, most were not far removed from the land or the shared folk culture that the land for so long had preserved. The social register of rock and roll would include former truck drivers, mechanics, construction laborers, shipyard workmen, tenant farmers, dishwashers, and factory workers who were bound together by their region's distinctive past. Through an attachment to rhythm and blues and performing styles that owed much to African American sources (as well as through clothes, hairstyles, slang, and leisure activities), they were seeking to establish an identity within an unfamiliar and impersonal world. In their own way, through the conspicuous consumption of material goods, they were striving to experience what had always been out of their reach: the accepted middle-class American dream of abundance and all of the benefits that such status bestowed. The well-known story of Elvis Presley—son of a tenant farmer who moved from the country to city, where he found work driving a truck and invigorated his musical tastes and performances with acknowledged quotations from blues singers, country acts, and gospel performers who passed through Memphis—is just one example of what many rock 'n' soul performers experienced in Tennessee.

Cultural dynamics are another part of the answer. Cultural and musical exchange between the races had long characterized Tennessee's musical traditions. The transactions were so thorough and extensive that it is often difficult to untangle a particular music's genealogical legacy. Rural musicians of both races generally shared a common versatility, eclecticism, and repertoire necessary to perform at various community functions. It was not unusual, therefore, for early-twentieth-century black and white performers to render music customarily identified with one race or the other. For example, African American artists who came to prominence before and after World War II often declared that as adolescents they had listened to and enjoyed country music and the Grand Ole Opry on the radio (widespread black radio programming generally did not exist in the South prior to the war, thus leaving listeners with little choice). Smith County's DeFord Bailey, a virtuoso harmonica player, influenced both country and blues artists through his personal performances and stints on the Grand Ole Opry in the late 1920s and 1930s. Likewise, country performers often attributed their success to an African American mentor, although the segregated environment in which they later performed as adults usually precluded open association with their black contemporaries.

The musical exchange did not end there. Blues and jazz introduced innovative techniques and stylings that later performers would adopt, despite the fact that the most prominent jazz entertainers left the South and refused to perform in a segregated Dixie. Bebop musicians contributed vernacular, demeanor, and style (although not necessarily ideology), while gospel vocalists added a musical fervor and their improvised style that had traditionally been confined to the spiritual realm. The rhythm and blues genre that emerged after World War II also influenced performers as it contained elements and themes stressing both the past and the present as a means to acclimate older African American migrants recently relocated to the city. (Honky-tonk, an electrified variant of country music, would do the same for older, displaced whites; country music would also find its way into rock and roll and soul.) Soul would evolve later from the same sources, particularly after the popular music establishment, in focusing exclusively on youth, absolved rock and roll of its regional, working-class, and racial character and its rhythm and blues, gospel, and country roots. Given the latitude, soul music would explore even further than rock and roll the influence of African American forms upon mainstream popular music and culture.

Tennessee also had the advantage of a local recording industry and well-established music publishing businesses. Although hardly on the scale of New York City or Hollywood, Nashville and Memphis had places where independent producers and labels (the "indies") could make their mark. Entrepreneurs with modest means formed small independent record companies that recruited and recorded relatively unknown, yet modern-sounding black artists. (The major recording companies, such as RCA, Columbia, MGM, Mercury, and Capitol, had eliminated most of their commercial ties to grass-roots black music during the Great Depression and World War II when economic collapse and the shortage of shellac forced industry retrenchment.) Technological advances made during and after the Second World War, such as the modern tape recorder and magnetic recording tape (two innovations developed in Hitler's Germany for Nazi propaganda purposes), allowed enterprising record producers to establish relatively inexpensive recording studios in Tennessee. The new Memphis independent record producers, such as Sam Phillips of Sun Records and Jim Stewart and Chips Moman of Stax Records, often contradicted that widely accepted (though often illusive and elusive) version of adult white, middle-class values and concerns by offering recordings that tended to embody the working-class and racial outlooks of their particular customers. Attracting a mixed audience was not a problem for independents like Jim Stewart, but a plus. Audience response and reaction were very important to the smaller, undercapitalized indies, for the public's buying habits determined whether or not the companies would survive. The businessmen and women who owned the independent record companies were generally white, and they had entered the field with the hopes of achieving financial success. They wanted to fill a market niche and become prosperous while doing so.

Sam Phillips. Courtesy of University of Memphis Libraries, Special Collections.

Independent record entrepreneurs depended upon many sources to discover what the public wanted to hear. To stay abreast of the latest trends. they closely monitored local jukebox activity and record sales. Several, such as Phillips, regularly visited record stores that catered to an African American clientele, such as Pop Tunes and Home of the Blues in Memphis. Others, like Ernie Young, entered the recording business after having sold records through his own retail outlet, Ernie's Record Mart. Similarly, Joe Cuoghi, the owner of Pop Tunes, would go on to establish the successful Hi Records, while Don Cherry would launch Home of the Blues Records. Estelle Axton, a coproprietor of Stax Records, opened up a record store at the front of the recording studio, a revamped movie theater on McLemore Avenue in Memphis, in order to gain inside information concerning the music that appealed to record buyers. On many occasions, musicians in the studio would wander into what had once been the theater concession area, listen to the records that were selling, and then incorporate similar sounds and hooks into their own compositions.

Randy Wood, a prospective record retailer who owned an appliance store in Gallatin, was likewise perceptive to the music that appealed to young record buyers. Not having much success selling records (appliance and furniture stores were traditional outlets for recordings that usually helped sell the needed phonograph player), he decided to advertise them on radio station WLAC. A fifty-thousand-watt, clear channel station that garnered listeners throughout the South and much of the nation, WLAC proved to be the perfect promotional vehicle for Wood's record store. A sponsored program (and service), "Randy's Record Shop" would become the largest mail-order record store in the world. White disk jockey Gene Nobles hosted the show, and he became one of the first southern disk jockeys to direct his show to a racially mixed audience. By 1951, from the requests and sales of records, Wood was well aware of popular music trends. Taking advantage of his position as a retailer to know what music appealed to young consumers, Wood opened a recording studio and established his own label. Like other Tennessee record entrepreneurs, he had gotten close enough to feel the pulse of a generation. In the end, independent record labels from Tennessee like Sun, Excello, Hi, Goldwax, and Bullet supplied an important void. They would help provide the publishing infrastructure responsible for the emergence of rock and roll and soul.

The increasing radio exposure for rock and soul music, creating a modern audience for modern music, was crucial for the final part of the answer to the question "why Tennessee?" During the postwar era, radio stations throughout the South—with WDIA in Memphis leading the way—instituted extensive black programming for the first time. As national broadcasting companies abandoned radio for the larger profits available in television, regional radio stations took advantage of the void to localize their playlists. From the Palace Theater on Beale Street in Memphis, for example, WNBR broadcast a weekly "amateur night" show that mixed blues, jazz, pop, and rhythm and blues performers. As a consequence of the desire to snare commercial sponsors and suddenly affluent audiences (African Americans represented a multi-billion-dollar market), major cities in Tennessee and other southern states included at least one radio station that aimed its programming exclusively toward black listeners. Such white-owned stations in turn hired personality disk jockeys, black and white dynamic and magnetic figures such as Dewey Phillips at WHBQ and Nat D. Williams at WDIA in Memphis, whose often frenetic spiels attracted large followings who then purchased the products advertised over the air. To urban blacks the deejay, however, was a cultural hero whose influence transcended his role as record spinner or product plugger; he was an individual who held a very prominent position in the African American community. Like the preacher, the disk jockey furnished listeners with news, advice, and a general world outlook that coincided with the needs and demeanor of his audience. In conjunction with independent record proprietors, disk jockeys also introduced rhythm and blues, rock and roll, and soul to a teen audience, both black and white, eager to consume the new music.

In the Jim Crow South, radio was especially important in introducing whites and blacks to their different musical traditions. Because of segregation, there were not many places where the races could come together on an equal footing. Thriving black club scenes existed in both Memphis (Beale Street)

Nat D. Williams, 1975. Courtesy of University of Memphis Libraries, Special Collections.

Sun Records

AMERICA ENTERED THE 1950S AFFLUENT AND MOBILE WITH A YOUNG GENERATION READY TO MAKE changes, especially in their music. At the end of World War II, broadcasts and hit recordings featured dance orchestras or smooth vocalists like Bing Crosby and the Mills Brothers. A decade later the charts would be topped by the jangling rhythms of "(You ain't nothing but a) Hound Dog." Elvis Presley was introduced to the world by a former farm boy from northern Alabama named Sam Phillips, and popular music would never be the same. How did a poorly funded, independent record label, run by an inexperienced newcomer based in a secondary city of the still-segregated South become a catalyst for sweeping change to the music industry?

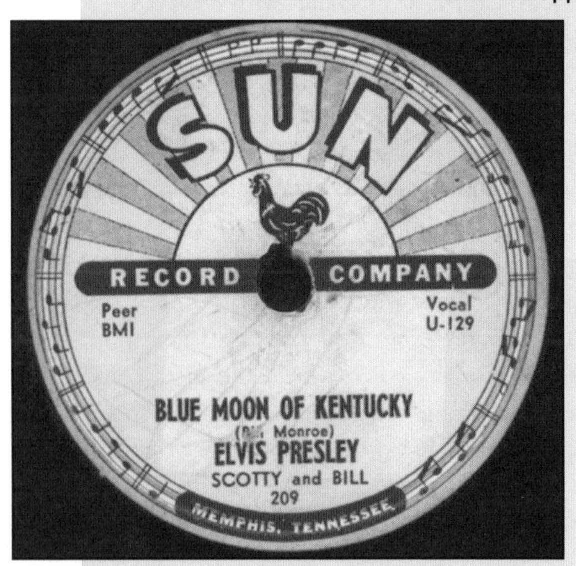

Sun Record Company label of "Blue Moon of Kentucky" by Elvis Presley. From the collections of the Center for Popular Music, MTSU.

When Sam Phillips arrived in Memphis in 1945, just twenty-two years old, he brought a keen ear for the two prevailing musical forms of his region, black blues and white hillbilly music. He also brought engineering skills gained in early radio jobs that would help him create the famous Sun Records sound. Phillips's first job in Memphis was with WREC as an announcer and transcription engineer. He soon opened the Memphis Recording Service to do custom recording on the side. His first ventures into commercial music were recordings of local blues musicians for release by the Modern and RPM labels in Los Angeles and the Chess label in Chicago. Among the artists released to those labels were B. B. King, James Cotton, Rosco Gordon, Joe Hill Louis, and Phillips's own favorite, Howlin' Wolf. Then in 1951 piano player Ike Turner came to town with his cousin Jackie Brentson to record "Rocket 88." This number topped the rhythm and blues charts on Chess, but it also crossed an undefined line to become arguably the first rock and roll record. Phillips credits it with broadening his musical base, which had rested primarily on raw country blues to that point.

By 1952, frustrated by conflicts with the Bihari Brothers (of Modern and RPM) and the Chess brothers, Phillips determined to open his own label. An earlier attempt, the Phillips label, lasted a scant two months in 1950. It had been jointly owned with Dewey Phillips (unrelated), a deejay for WHBQ and one of the first to program black music on a white-owned station. Phillips opened Sun Records in 1952 on his own, with the help of his brother Judd and, later, the partnership of Jim Bulleit of Nashville. Sun debuted with issue number 175 (Johnny London) in April 1952 but did not have a commercial success until March 1953, with Rufus Thomas singing "Bearcat" (number 181). Phillips was prolific and efficient. Biographer Colin Escott has noted that for one hundred dollars Phillips could record, cut, press, and promote a record. He did his own promotion out of the trunk of his car, logging seventy thousand miles or more each year.

With the freedom of his own label, Phillips was able to pursue his interest in country music. In its first years Sun released an alternating pattern of black blues artists (Memphis Ma Rainey, Junior Parker, Little Milton, The Prisonaires, and Billy "The Kid" Emerson) and white country artists (Ripley Cotton Choppers, Earl Peterson, Slim Rhodes, and The Starlite Wranglers). None of the early country releases met with much success, but from the last group were drawn Bill Black and Scotty Moore, who would back Elvis on his first hits.

Elvis Presley had just finished high school when, in the summer of 1953, he paid $3.98 to make a custom record at the studio of Sun Records, 706 Union Avenue. Nearly a year later he was called back to audition for the label and then to record "That's All Right/Blue Moon of Kentucky," released as Sun 209 in July 1954. That record attracted immediate attention, and in the coming year four other singles would be released, ending with "Mystery Train" (number 223) in August 1955. In the fall, Phillips sold Presley's contract to RCA for thirty-five thousand dollars plus five thousand dollars for Presley's back royalties, a huge sum at the time and enough to ease financial woes at Sun. Colonel Tom Parker brokered the deal. Presley's RCA recording of "Hound Dog/Don't Be Cruel" was the best-selling record of 1956.

The success of Elvis Presley attracted an important group of young singers to Phillips and Sun. First in the door was Johnny Cash, followed by Carl Perkins, Jerry Lee Lewis, Roy Orbison, Billy Riley, Charlie Rich, Sonny Burgess, Jack Clement, and many lesser known artists. Cash released material in a straight country vein, but Perkins, Lewis, and others helped define rockabilly and rock. The black artists that Phillips had first recorded gradually faded from the Memphis scene. Most moved to cities outside the South, some to gain their fame with other labels.

The enduring reputation of Sam Phillips and his label rests on his work in the 1950s. His combined talents for recognizing vital new artists and for recording their work produced records that would not be equaled by the later Sun output. Phillips remained the head of Sun Records until 1969, when Nashville producer Shelby Singleton bought the company. Phillips moved on to successful ventures apart from music while his sons, Jerry and Knox, stayed in the business in various roles.

Mayo Taylor, Middle Tennessee State University

and Nashville (Jefferson Street) but few whites ever visited these venues. Some whites, like Elvis, did attend African American churches as spectators watching and listening to the rhythmic motions and sounds of the choirs, but they were comparatively few in number. There were periodic rhythm and blues concerts where separate shows were provided, one for a white audience and another for African Americans. Situations also existed where whites were allowed into balconies of auditoriums to watch black rhythm and blues performances. On many occasions, the music led to pandemonium, and blacks and whites rushed together to create a common dance floor. Daring white teenagers also made their way to nightclubs, such as the Plantation Inn in West Memphis, where African American groups performed for strictly white audiences (no examples are known of the reverse, where African Americans entered white establishments).

But listening to the radio linked urban black teens and white suburban teens to a mixed teen culture that stood outside the boundaries of segregated southern culture. As Peter Guralnick emphasized about the postwar music scene, "the only true integrating factor was radio."[4] While southern youth in the 1950s enjoyed the fruits of the era's exceptional economic growth and prosperity, they also inherited situations and issues that would require substantial psychological and emotional adjustments. Born into a languid rural world that had reached its pinnacle, their generation entered adolescence within an unfamiliar and indifferent urban world that moved rapidly and seemingly without concern for its inhabitants. Estranged, impressionable, and exposed to a greater variety of experiences than any other age group in the South's history, southern teenagers were indeed set to see themselves and the world around them in ways that previous generations would have had difficulty recognizing or understanding. Permanence, a feature so long associated with the South, was no longer as permanent as it had once been.

Accordingly, when the American mainstream beckoned, its greatest allure often rested with southern youth, an uprooted and ostensibly invisible group in search of a salient identity. Forming a community of like-disaffected adolescents, they, unlike their parents, grandparents, and older brothers and sisters, were generally less concerned with what they had left behind than they were about not falling behind. As a consequence, they sought acceptance and status through a modern media that emphasized innovation, particularly in introducing new trends in fashion, hairstyles, vocabulary, heroes, and music. A sense of optimism long absent from the region abruptly materialized, and a younger generation of southerners seized the opportunity to make the postwar American dreams of upward mobility and material acquisition a reality. Braced with a hopeful and flexible perspective uncommon to inhabitants habitually attached to local customs and provincial mores, young people who reached adolescence in the late 1940s and early 1950s became one of the first groups in the South's annals to aspire and succeed in terms that the nation had defined.

Steve Cropper, 1981. Courtesy of University of Memphis Libraries, Special Collections.

For parents and older siblings, individuals who only knew the old outlooks and habits, the perception of order lay in ruins. They often blamed rock and roll and sought to ban the music from the airways and concert stages. When the Beatles played Memphis's Mid-South Coliseum in 1966, for example, the KKK demonstrated outside the arena while church groups and civic leaders sponsored an alternative teen event, attracting thousands, at Ellis Auditorium. Some would never waver in their allegiance to the past; others would acquiesce to or develop various forms of uneasy accommodation. Others embraced the new music as a valuable marketing tool aimed at the teen audience. In a story in the *Memphis Commercial Appeal* of August 21, 1966, a reporter noted that "a survey of several Memphis merchants shows a close partnership today between merchandising and loud music. The louder the music the better because it's aimed at the buying power of the youngsters."

The modern sounds of rock and soul unnerved and invigorated white suburban teens. For black youth, however, radio (especially those stations that incorporated African American personnel and formats) conveyed a message of racial self-affirmation that challenged older and outworn stereotypes. In order to secure audience loyalty, black deejays discussed practical matters, like where blacks could shop without the fear of being embarrassed or harassed by overzealous segregationists. More importantly, deejays and programmers often selected records that advocated topics and themes appealing to their listeners. Themes of respect (the classic song "Respect" was penned by Stax artist Otis Redding), racial progress and achievements, and personal pride were pervasive in the "Memphis soul" recordings released by Stax and Hi Records, contrasting vividly with the more mainstream, white radio focus of the competing "Motown Sound" from Detroit. Radio programmers and deejays who preferred the sounds and messages of Memphis soul thus enjoyed a pervasive influence, not only as a form of entertainment, but also as a means of educating listeners in the language, aspirations, and tastes of African Americans, who had been heretofore generally perceived by whites as an "invisible" segment of southern society.

For younger black southerners who came of age with "Negro-Appeal" radio after World War II, the period signaled a promise that earlier generations had rarely known. Due to tremendous changes within the regional socioeconomic system and the federal government's intervention on behalf of African American civil rights, blacks in the South began to envision an improved future. This optimism revealed itself in the music that many of them produced and consumed. Following the *Brown v. Board of Education* (1954) decision, the popularity of rhythm and blues began to expand beyond its traditional African American base. Integrationist aspirations pushed the music toward the mainstream; more than simply the machinations of an imperialistic music industry set to sell more records, this trend also reflected the continued hope of African Americans for racial progress through assimilation into the mainstream.

The evolution of soul can likewise be traced to developments occurring outside the realm of popular music. By the end of the 1950s, a new wave of young people who had grown up with rock and roll in a generally middle-class environment helped create and popularize what was soon recognized as soul. Just as likely to have lived in settled neighborhoods and suburbs as in government housing projects, such soul-stirrers tended to follow the examples of Clyde McPhatter, Ray Charles, and Sam Cooke, artists who had infused rhythm and blues and pop music with the power of black gospel.

As the civil rights struggle continued into the early 1960s, African Americans began to expect the creation of a pluralist society where inclusion into the mainstream did not necessarily demand the negation or subjugation of one's culture. There was a strong belief that blacks and whites could live together while mutually respecting and appreciating the other. Soul, at least as it was produced in Tennessee recording studios such as Stax and Hi Records, deviated from rock and roll in that it was aimed primarily at African Americans. "Blacker" sounding than the product emerging from Detroit's Motown, the music reiterated the notion that assimilation into the dominant culture did not entail abandoning that which was considered distinctive. The artistic and financial success of Memphis Soul suggested that the concept of racial pride could exist within the reality of desegregation. Paradoxically, soul music would go on to represent the epitome of interracial camaraderie while simultaneously displaying a degree of racial distinctiveness rarely found in rock and roll.

By the mid- to late 1960s, the persistence of institutionalized discrimination as well as the failure of many whites to abandon racism, however, forced many African Americans to adopt a separatist ideology. The music of the period, too, took on characteristics that illustrated the despair associated with the collapse of the civil rights movement. Denied a legitimate political and economic place in the mainstream, African Americans created and consumed a rhythm and blues that became overtly misogynist, male-centered, and self-destructive. Even the music that held the promise to reunite black and white, funkadelic, was couched in a bizarre language and persona that insinuated the impossibility of racial rapproachment in the real world. What was left by

Stax Records

THE OLD ADAGE "TRUTH IS STRANGER THAN FICTION" HAS PERHAPS NEVER BEEN MORE APT THAN IN the case of Stax Records. Started in the late 1950s by Jim Stewart, a white country fiddler who by his own admission knew virtually nothing about black music, by mid-decade Stax had developed a readily identifiable sound that came to define the very essence of black soul music. The influence of the "Stax sound" was such that late 1960s soul recordings by non-Stax artists such as Aretha Franklin and Clarence Carter are, in essence, the sound of Stax being filtered through non-Stax hands.

While undeniably involved in the production and distribution of black culture, from its inception Stax was an integrated company in the studio, in the front office, and, by the late sixties, at the level of ownership. The company manifested Dr. Martin Luther King's dream where blacks and whites came together, not because they were forced to do so, but organically to achieve a collective goal. Paradoxically, all of this occurred in Memphis, Tennessee, a city deeply segregated throughout the 1960s.

The sound of Stax resulted from a number of factors. First and foremost, from 1962 through 1969 virtually every record issued by the company on Stax or its subsidiary label, Volt, featured the same set of musicians—Booker T. and the MG's, often augmented by second keyboardist Isaac Hayes and the Mar-Key horns. Whether the featured artist was Otis Redding, Sam and Dave, Rufus Thomas, Carla Thomas, William Bell, Eddie Floyd, or Johnnie Taylor, the basic sound of the record was a product of the aesthetics and proclivities of the same handful of integrated musicians.

The Stax studio itself, housed in a former movie theater, played a significant role in the company's patented sound. Due to economic considerations, Stewart elected not to level the floor, thereby creating a unique recording environment that was cavernous (at its highest point the ceiling was upwards of forty feet high) and had absolutely no parallel surfaces where sound waves would cancel themselves out. Consequently, Stax recordings tend to have a large reverberant sound that can be readily detected by a discerning ear within a few bars. Finally, virtually all of the sessions held at the company in the 1960s were engineered by either Jim Stewart or guitarist Steve Cropper. Both men shared an aesthetic that emphasized a strong bass sound, prominent horns, and a vocal that was positioned quite a ways back in the mix.

In the late 1960s everything changed at Stax, including its sound. In December 1967, Otis Redding died in a plane crash. In many respects Redding had been the heart and soul of the company in the 1960s. Five months later Stax severed its distribution agreement with the New York–based Atlantic Records. To its horror Stax found that its contractual agreements with Atlantic meant the New York company retained Stax's second most important artist, Sam and Dave, as well as the entire Stax catalogue released up to this point.

For all intents and purposes, Stax Records was forced to start once again from scratch. At this point black promotion man Al Bell acquired a piece of the company. A year later, Bell's share was 50 percent, and by October 1972 Bell owned the company outright. Bell wrought large-scale changes at Stax, bringing in non-Memphis producers, engineers, and artists in an attempt to broaden the company's sales potential beyond the South and Midwest. New artists he signed included Chicago's Staple Singers, the Emotions, and, from Detroit, the Dramatics. He also allowed Stax songwriter Isaac Hayes to record solo records in a hybrid style that fused elements of soul, rock, classical, and jazz. The resulting albums, *Hot Buttered Soul, The Isaac Hayes*

Movement, and *To Be Continued* demonstrated unequivocally that, despite industry wisdom, black artists could generate massive album sales. Up to this point virtually all energy and money within the black music industry was centered around the seven-inch 45 single, the logic being that black consumers could not afford to buy significant numbers of LPs. Hayes's work at Stax paved the way for full-length album works by Stevie Wonder, Marvin Gaye, Curtis Mayfield, and Funkadelic. When Hayes wrote and recorded the soundtrack for the movie *Shaft* in 1971; his hit once again broke barriers, effectively creating the phenomenon of the black movie soundtrack.

Isaac Hayes *(center)* with Ed Cramer *(left)*, president of BMI, and David Porter, 1971. Courtesy of University of Memphis Libraries, Special Collections.

Bell's vision for Stax seemingly had no limits. He expanded the company's recording activities to include pop, rock, jazz, country, gospel, and comedy. With the Staple Singers he produced what are probably the first soul promotion videos, and in 1972 he staged the Wattstax festival and created Stax Films to produce the subsequent Wattstax documentary. In the process Bell expanded the company from a mom-and-pop organization to a two hundred-employee soul powerhouse in the early 1970s.

Although Stax went bankrupt in December 1975, its legacy lives on via numerous pop and rhythm-and-blues covers and rap samples of the company's innumerable hits. In 2003 this legacy was further honored with the opening of the Stax Museum of American Soul located on the very same site on McLemore Avenue that once proudly housed the company's fabled studio.

Rob Bowman, York University

the middle of the 1970s was the vacuous, mechanized, and corporate controlled sound of disco.

To understand the development of Tennessee's version of rock and roll and soul, of course, is to lament over roads not taken and paths left untraveled. Yet it is also to see the possibilities that did exist and to envision that past examples can inform present and future generations. For the post–World War II physical relocations that altered the South so suddenly brought southerners, black and white, into closer contact with one another within the confines of the city. Black radio programming, concerts that featured rhythm and blues performers, and interracial dances exposed white youth to uncommon and positive impressions of their African American counterparts. Such examples countered the mystery that had for too long clouded and tragically distorted the relationship between the region's two largest racial groups. Simplified and standardized caricatures had functioned effortlessly to inform inhabitants about each other without the actual need to come face to face as fellow human beings. Psychological obstacles had always been as prohibitive as legal ones.

The post–World War II era brought new possibilities. As one component in a mix of factors that fed into civil rights advances, rock and roll helped

Elvis Presley, 1975. Courtesy of MTSU.

redefine (or at least scramble) conventional attitudes. The process of rapid urbanization dramatically altered the daily lives and expectations of southern individuals, particularly impressionable young people. The physical relocations also brought southerners, black and white, into closer contact with one another inside the confines of the city. Historically successful at creating spaces for themselves within hostile and adverse surroundings, African Americans could inform through example. Once in touch, white adolescents consequently recognized their black counterparts to be somewhat more sophisticated in coping with a frightening urban environment. Estranged from a fast-paced and more cosmopolitan mainstream society, exiled southern white teenagers conceivably could relate to an alienated black culture on similar terms. However paradoxical this may seem, suddenly subaltern white southerners found security and dignity in various forms of African American style, fashion, dialect, and music. As Ray Pratt has suggested, engaging in such endeavors did the same for whites as it did for blacks: it allowed them to say and demonstrate, "I am somebody."[5]

Yet was the recognition of shared difficulties and emotions enough? Did the music bring about understanding? Unfortunately, the answer is probably not. No language was developed that could cross the racial divide into serious issues involving class, status, occupation, housing, education, and health care. Although soul music did capture the attention of many whites, it also hovered dangerously into areas of stereotype

Southern Rock

THE MUSIC WIDELY KNOWN AS SOUTHERN ROCK HAD ITS POPULAR HEYDAY IN THE 1970S. TENNESSEE served as the home of Southern Rock's largest gathering, the Volunteer Jamboree, which fiddler and songwriter Charlie Daniels and his friends started in 1974 and continued for years.

Southern Rock music, dominated by antiestablishment lyrics and long guitar solos, developed at a great time to challenge authority in America. The Charlie Daniels Band asserted its challenges from the perspective of two beloved images. The yeoman was one image. In the apparently autobiographical song "Long Haired Country Boy," Daniels sneered at anyone who told him what to do, said material comforts were less important than a life of leisure, and above all wanted people to "leave this long haired country boy alone." Other songs, such as "High Lonesome," idealized a life close to nature and away from the worries of city life. The other image was the cowboy. Horses, saddles, pistols, and, especially, cowboy hats marked Daniels and other Southern Rock musicians as heirs to an American tradition that depicted the manly ability to move on as central to the meaning of freedom.

Other Southern Rock musicians had roots in Tennessee. Duane and Gregg Allman were born in Tennessee before moving on to Florida and Georgia, and the band Barefoot Jerry consisted of Nashville musicians drawn to the image and sound of Appalachia. But it was Charlie Daniels who gave Southern Rock a sound and image distinctive to Tennessee.

The state's main contributions to Southern Rock were its connections to country music and the model of the Grand Ole Opry. From his home in Mount Juliet, Charlie Daniels started the Volunteer Jamboree in Nashville in 1974 and moved to Murfreesboro in 1975. Relocating to Nashville in 1977, the Jamboree ran yearly until 1987. Every year, Daniels invited friends in the Southern Rock movement to join him and an eclectic series of surprise guests ranging from Bill Monroe to Papa John Creech to Ted Nugent. With a tradition of playing country music, Daniels was older than most Southern Rock musicians and kept up interests in various musical traditions. Most obviously, his trademark song, "The South's Gonna Do It Again," listed the various Southern Rock groups in a song that combined rock music, Texas swing, bluegrass, jazz, and the blues. In this sense he was true to Nashville music, because the stage of the Volunteer Jamboree often looked a bit like the stage of the Opry, with old friends and strangers meeting through music. Daniels loved family metaphors, both in his songs and at the Jamboree, and he portrayed the event as a big family reunion.

It seems fair to say that Daniels, a North Carolina native, indulged in a kind of Tennessee Overkill. Not only did a huge Tennessee flag dominate the stage at the Volunteer Jamboree, and not only did the annual affair end with the singing of "The Tennessee Waltz." But Daniels also loved to ask, "Ain't it good to be alive and to be in Tennessee?" He had songs called "Tennessee" and "Right Now Tennessee Blues" and sang that "Tennessee Bootleg Moonshine Whiskey / Sure do make a man feel mighty frisky."

Since the 1980s, Daniels's lyrics have taken a turn to the right, as he directed his antiestablishment populism against foreign dictators, drug dealers, and what he understands as a secular liberalism that treats with disdain hard-working, decent country folks like him.

Ted Ownby, University of Mississippi

Cow Punk and Western Beat Music

Rock music critics coined the term "cow punk" to describe a distinctive new music, combining the ragged edginess of punk rock with the earthy directness and honesty of honky-tonk, that arose in southern clubs during the early 1980s. Of the Tennessee bands that embraced cow punk in the 1980s, the most successful was Jason and the Scorchers, who even scored a minor hit on the fledgling MTV Network in 1984. The band's mainstays were singer Jason Rigenberg, who wrote most of the group's original material, guitarist Warren Hodges, bassist Jeff Johnson, and drummer Perry Baggs. Local fans loved the band's creative, energetic concerts. A critic for the *Tennessean* wrote on December 30, 1999, "Rigenberg, especially, pushed himself to the limit every show, climbing on speaker cabinets, billboards, rafters, anything he could find and taking his frenzied delivery straight to the audience." According to local rock musician and songwriter Tommy Womack, in the Nashville punk rock scene in the 1980s "one band stood knees, hips, and shoulders above the rest of them: Jason and the Nashville Scorchers. Before them, rock bands had been unapproachable icons that appeared before us in great barns and sped away before their humanity was unveiled." The Scorchers were different, emphasizes Womack, because they made "it all look somehow realistic to want to do this sort of thing."[1]

Jason and the Scorchers, are, in the early twenty-first century, viewed as pioneers in the Alternative Country or Western Beat Movement. Two of the more notorious and popular of the new Western Beat acts are Bare Jr., fronted by Bobby Bare Jr., the son of country songwriter Bobby Bare, and Hank III, the son of country music star Hank Williams Jr. and grandson of music legend Hank Williams. The most popular Western Beat group is BR-549 (the name refers to the fictional phone number of comedian Junior Samples in his appearances on the *Hee Haw* television show). The band cut its teeth on the college club circuit in Murfreesboro before staking a place out in the honky-tonk scene on lower Broadway in Nashville. BR-549's music reflects the influence of a strong sense of pop culture humor, a reverence for classic country music, and a willingness to stake its own middle ground between country and western and alternative music.

Carroll Van West, Middle Tennessee State University

Note

1. Womack quoted in Michael Gray, "Scorching New Morning," *Nashville Banner*, Sept. 25, 1996.

and caricature. For many white, middle-class and lower-middle-class enthusiasts, soul music, unlike rock and roll, was their only means of contact with African Americans. The promise that rock and roll had contained concerning a true desegregated society, where "an equal amount of white movement toward the black world," seemed to have melted away.[6] By the time soul reached its greatest heights of popularity in the mid-1960s, race continued to divide southerners and other Americans.

For many, however, a mid-1950s editorial in *Cashbox* concerning the significance of musical

Tina Turner in concert. Photograph by Jack Ross, 1987. Courtesy of MTSU.

choices made by southern adolescents still applies: "The whole movement has broken down barriers which in the ordinary course of events might have taken untold amounts of time to do. How better to understand what is unknown to you than by appreciation of the emotional experiences of other people? And how better are these emotions portrayed than by music?" The promise of such a perspective was ironically articulated by a Tennessean who had done much musically to bridge the gap between black and white. As Memphian Elvis Presley implored of a television audience in the year that Martin Luther King was gunned down, "If I can dream of a better land where all my brothers walk hand in hand, tell me why can't my dreams come true?"[7]

They just might. The jury has not yet returned its verdict.

Notes

1. Asheley and Kerria Griffith, "Elvis Presley: A Brief Musical History Lesson," *Stereo Review* 37 (July 1976): 80.
2. Bill Malone, *Southern Music/American Music: New Perspectives on the South* (Lexington: Univ. Press of Kentucky, 1979), 3.
3. C. Vann Woodward, "The Search for Southern Identity," in *The Burden of Southern History,* rev. ed. (New York: Mentor Books, 1969), 19.
4. Peter Guralnick, *Sweet Soul Music: Rhythm and Blues and the Southern Dream of Freedom* (New York: Harper and Row, 1986), 111.
5. Ray Pratt, "The Politics of Authenticity in Popular Blues: The Case of the Blues," *Popular Music and Society* 10 (1986): 74.
6. Craig Werner, *A Change Is Gonna Come: Music, Race, and the Soul of America* (New York: Plume, 1998), 41.
7. Michael T. Bertrand, *Race, Rock, and Elvis* (Urbana: Univ. of Illinois Press, 2000), 226–27, citing Presley's remarks that came at the end of his 1968 televised special on NBC-TV.

Suggested Readings

Bertrand, Michael T. *Race, Rock, and Elvis.* Urbana: Univ. of Illinois Press, 2000.

Bowman, Rob. *Soulsville U.S.A.: The Story of Stax Records.* New York: Schirmer Books, 1997.

Escott, Colin, and Martin Hawkins. *Good Rockin' Tonight: Sun Records and the Birth of Rock in' Roll.* New York: St. Martin's Press, 1991.

Guralink, Peter. *Last Train to Memphis: The Rise of Elvis Presley.* Boston: Little, Brown, 1994.

———. *Sweet Soul Music: Rhythm and Blues and the Southern Dream of Freedom.* New York: Harper and Row, 1986.

McKee, Margaret, and Fred Chisenhall. *Beale Black and Blue: Life and Music on Black America's Main Street.* Baton Rouge: Louisiana State Univ. Press, 1981.

Perkins, Carl, with Dave McGee. *Go, Cat, Go! The Life and Times of Carl Perkins.* New York: Hyperion, 1996.

Turner, Tina, with Kurt Loder. *I, Tina.* New York: Morrow, 1986.

Ward, Brian. *Just My Soul Responding: Rhythm and Blues, Black Consciousness and Race Relations.* Berkeley and Los Angeles: Univ. of California Press, 1998.

Werner, Craig. *A Change Is Gonna Come: Music, Race, and the Soul of America.* New York: Plume, 1998.

Twenty-six

Heartbreakers and Moneymakers
Tennessee's Country Music Industry

John W. Rumble
Country Music Hall of Fame and Museum

"Country music is an authentic part of Tennessee heritage," wrote then-governor Frank G. Clement in a 1963 article for *Billboard* magazine's annual country music review. Praising the music's impressive contributions to Tennessee's economy he proclaimed, "I think its creation and preservation are one of my State's cultural obligations."[1] Over the past eighty years, thousands of Tennesseans have shared Clement's vision. Navigating currents of social and economic change within the nation's evolving popular music industry, they have woven country music into the fabric of Tennessee culture so tightly that country and the Volunteer State are now virtually synonymous. In part, the state's contribution to country music lies in the music Tennesseans have played, sung, performed, and recorded, though they have incorporated a variety of musical styles emerging from Tennessee and other states as well. More important, Tennessee performers and business leaders have played powerful roles in marketing country music, refining its evolving image, shaping the image of the state in the eyes of world, and determining the meanings that the words country music convey not only to Americans, but to people around the globe.

The Call of Professional Show Business

The story of Tennessee's country music industry properly begins with the advent of commercial radio and recording in the 1920s. The professionals who emerged in that decade drew upon many sources, including a rich heritage of Anglo-American fiddle tunes and folk songs, African American folk music, and well-established traditions of secular string band numbers and gospel hymns shared by both races. Tennesseans also learned professionally written music from touring tent shows, medicine shows, minstrel troupes, and vaudeville companies that gave early country stars important show business experience while popularizing Tin Pan Alley songs and music taken from blues, ragtime, and jazz—folk-based commercial styles growing mainly from African American communities.

The rise of radio broadcasting in the 1920s helped many Tennessee country performers gain professional status. By 1930, Bristol (WOPI), Chattanooga (WDOD), Knoxville (WNOX, WROL), Nashville (WSM, WLAC), Lawrenceburg (WOAN), Jackson (WJTS), and Memphis (WMC, WREC) all had radio outlets that let country or gospel singers advertise personal appearances and sell song books. In those days of variety broadcasting, local country musicians filled early morning, noonday, and Saturday-night slots aimed at urban listeners and the state's vast rural and small-town audience.

Radio executives invited a wide variety of entertainers under the country music tent, proving that country has always been as much a marketing category as it has been a style or group of styles. In the 1930s, WMC and WREC featured the western swing numbers of the Swift Jewel Cowboys, and WNOX carried the jazz stylings of the String Dusters. Founded by WSM manager George D. Hay in 1925, the early Grand Ole Opry showcased old-time fiddler Uncle Jimmy Thompson; the rollicking, banjo-whacking Uncle Dave Macon; African American harmonica star DeFord Bailey; several traditional string bands; Pee Wee King's pop-western band; the smooth harmonies of the Delmore Brothers and the Vagabonds—made viable by improved radio microphones—and Roy Acuff, a spellbinding singer of folk tunes and heart songs who first came to prominence in Knoxville radio. For his own Solemn Old Judge persona, Hay called upon his experience as a court reporter for the *Memphis Commercial Appeal* and as announcer for its radio station, WMC. From the outset, Tennessee country radio was never a pure expression of the state's Anglo-American, Appalachian heritage.

Even so, early Tennessee artists and radio programmers deliberately pushed country as southern folk music with a mountain accent, following a pattern in which southerners have borrowed from national cultural forms to create new, hybrid products invested with an aura of nostalgia and regional authenticity. Although many of the Opry cast came from Middle Tennessee and worked in occupations ranging from physician to factory hand, Hay told the press that "every one of the 'talent' is from the back country," and that Opry music was "the unique entertainment that only the Tennessee mountaineers can afford."[2] Outfitting Opry string bands with overalls and floppy hats, he dubbed them Possum Hunters, Gully Jumpers, and Fruit Jar Drinkers. On tour, Macon and Possum Hunters founder Humphrey Bate billed themselves as "moonshiners," and even the Vagabonds—city slickers who had worked pop radio in Chicago—donned rustic stagewear and touted their material as songs "originated by the Pioneer Settlers in the mountains of the Southland."[3]

Applying southern imagery to Pee Wee King's Golden West Cowboys was a stretch, and Appalachian images hardly fit the Swift Jewel Cowboys, emigrants from Texas. Nor would mountain rhapsodies fit Knoxville's "Mid-Day Merry-Go-Round," a comedy-packed country variety show launched by WNOX executive Lowell Blanchard in 1936. Mountain themes also obscured black components of Tennessee country, including DeFord Bailey's harmonica numbers and the black music played by white Opry members Sam McGee, Uncle Dave Macon, and Bill Monroe. Indeed, the blackface minstrelsy of the Opry's 'Lasses and Honey treated African Americans in demeaning caricature.

At the time, however, a southern marketing strategy made sense. In terms of radio shows and record buyers, the South was country music's strongest turf. Most Tennessee country radio acts were southerners, as were most early country recording artists. Northern-based record companies were selling country music as "mountain ballads" or "songs of Dixie," and one early Brunswick Records catalogue even claimed that "Tennessee Mountaineers Give Birth to [the] Only True American Folk Songs."[4] Moreover, the South was then heavily rural, and "country music" meant music from the country. As Americans adjusted to city life and mass media, nostalgia for simpler times offered the comfort of an idealized rural past. Regional folk imagery also countered critics who lambasted the "hillbilly" music lover as "a North Carolina or Tennessee and adjacent mountaineer type of illiterate . . . ignorant, with the intelligence of morons."[5] So, when Roy Acuff joined the Opry cast in 1938, WSM officials shrewdly changed the name of his band from the Crazy Tennesseans to the Smoky Mountain Boys.

In addition, Hay's marketing pitch reinforced the hit-star system that WSM manager Harry Stone, replacing Hay in 1932, his brother David Stone, then head of the station's booking department, and, to a lesser extent, Hay, who still announced the Opry, were creating at WSM. There and at other stations, radio brass wanted new country singers whose appeal lay in their humble origins and their closeness to their fans, as well as in their musicianship. In 1927, when Hay rechristened the WSM Barn Dance as the Grand Ole Opry in a deliberate parody of grand opera, he knew that for every devotee of European classics there were a thousand working-class listeners who took pride in American country music.

Along with the Stones brothers' star-building tactics, Hay's marketing efforts worked, attracting sponsors, helping the Opry compete with rival shows, and above all, selling policies for WSM's parent firm, Nashville's National Life and Accident Insurance Company. The Opry drew most of WSM's fan mail, and for insurance agents nationwide the program was an irresistible door-opener. In the hands of National Life/WSM promoters, country music and life insurance were carefully crafted, complementary products that emphasized friendliness, inclusiveness, and close kinship ties. To be sure, presenting country music as family entertainment smoothed its rough edges. ("By 'closer to the ground,'" Hay wrote of the Opry, "we do not mean dirty.")[6] Helping fill National Life's coffers assured the show's place in the WSM lineup.

National Life's success reflected a pattern of growth and regional assertion then emerging in a long-depressed southern economy. In the popular music industry, however, ingrained patterns of dependency remained. Although WSM began feeding regular original programs to the NBC radio network in 1935, most southern radio stations couldn't match WSM's resources, and even the fifty-thousand-watt, clear-channel Nashville giant relied heavily on network fare produced mostly in New York.

The picture was largely the same in recording and music publishing. During the late 1920s and early 1930s, major labels including Brunswick, Vocalion, and Victor sent producers armed with portable equipment to Knoxville and Johnson City to record East Tennessee musicians such as Clarence "Tom" Ashley and Hugh Cross. In 1927, Victor's Ralph Peer held historic sessions in Bristol that included not only native Tennesseans but also the Virginia-based Carter Family and Mississippian Jimmie Rodgers, soon to become huge national stars. In 1928, Victor came to Nashville to capture Opry string bands and DeFord Bailey on disc. On the lively Memphis scene, Victor recorded the blues-influenced Reece Fleming–Respers Townsend act and the Memphis Sheiks (Memphis Jug Band), a black outfit that shared songs and sounds with white country bands. Still, Tennessee artists such as Uncle Dave Macon and the Allen Brothers (popular around Chattanooga) often trekked to Atlanta, New York, or Charlotte to record, and, with the principal exception of Lawrenceburg's James D. Vaughan Company, the state had no recording industry of note. Likewise, except for a handful of small pop publishing firms and gospel publishers like Vaughn, Nashville's John T. Benson Company (established in 1902), and Dayton's R. E. Winsett Company, Tennessee lacked a solid music publishing base. As a result, songwriters like Memphis-born Bob Miller gravitated to New York, then the music industry's primary crossroads.

Both National Life and Nashville's Life and Casualty Insurance Company, which owned WLAC, might have ventured into recording and publishing. To these firms, however, music was a means to sell insurance, not to develop copyrights and recording stars. Like their colleagues in other Tennessee cities, Nashville businessmen clung to a high-culture concept glorifying classical music. While Nashville insurance moguls tolerated country as one component of marketing, they preferred using radio to burnish the city's image as the Athens of the South, a shrine of higher education with its own symphony orchestra and replica of the Parthenon.

Yet devotion to elitist arts dulled the Athens image as a tool for city boosters in an age of mass media and popular culture. Elitist ideals simply could not inspire the sort of broad allegiance commanded by country music stars. Packaging insurance with country music lifted insurance investors into the South's rising urban commercial class, but neither insurance executives nor their conservative counterparts in other industries would guide Tennessee's music industry in the years ahead. That role would belong to an even newer group of entrepreneurs who rose largely outside traditional business channels. These leaders would promote Nashville's Music City image as an alternative vision that ultimately outshone the Athens ideal and made the Tennessee capital the worldwide capital of country music.

Boom Years

Between 1940 and 1953, Tennesseans harnessed powerful forces in turning country music into a full-fledged industry, living out the American dream of creating wealth through risk taking and hard work. The national recovery engendered by World War II spending, the increasing urbanization that concentrated music markets nationwide, the migration of southerners to defense plants of the Midwest and West Coast, and the intermingling of persons from various regions in military service all stimulated demand for recordings, song books, radio programs, and personal appearances spotlighting Tennessee country performers.

During these years, Tennessee country broadcasting prospered as never before. Memphis stations WMPS and WMC provided temporary homes for the Louvin Brothers and Eddie Hill; in Bristol, WCYB showcased Flatt and Scruggs and the Stanley Brothers. Knoxville grocer Cas Walker continued to sponsor acts on WROL, while WNOX added the "Tennessee Barn Dance," sometimes featured on CBS-Radio's "Saturday Night Country Style" series in the early 1950s.

In Nashville aggressive WSM officials were making the Opry America's leading radio barn dance. In 1939 Harry Stone and New York's William Esty agency (WSM's advertising firm) persuaded the R. J. Reynolds Company to sponsor a half-hour NBC Opry segment, *The Prince Albert Show,* named after Prince Albert Smoking Tobacco. The number of NBC affiliates airing the program rose from twenty-six in 1939 to more than 170 in 1953, reaching a national audience of some ten million. Combined with WSM's far-reaching signal, this helped Stone and WSM program director Jack Stapp attract new, charismatic artists like Ernest Tubb, Eddy Arnold, Red Foley—who replaced Roy Acuff as Prince Albert Show headliner in 1946—and Hank Williams. With only ten thousand watts and no weekly network exposure, WNOX eventually lost much of its country talent to the Grand Ole Opry, including Carl Smith, Bill Carlisle, and Martha Carson. Other country musicians apprenticed with Big Jeff Bess at WLAC before graduating to WSM.

Although WSM continued to produce a variety of national news, children's shows, and pop music programs, it was on Red Foley's daytime NBC show that announcer David Cobb coined the phrase "Music City, USA" in 1950. Within three years, the music trade press was applying these words to Nashville's burgeoning recording industry, also best known for its country stars. The Opry's large talent pool made Nashville a logical recording center. After WSM engineers Aaron Shelton, Carl Jenkins, and George Reynolds formed the Castle Recording Laboratory (c. 1946), artists and producers had a local recording service run by men willing to cut records with the "hot" sound needed for the all-important jukebox trade. By 1947, producers from major labels Decca and Columbia began making regular trips to Castle, and MGM was holding most of its country sessions there. Chicago's Mercury Records (which opened a Nashville office in 1951, four years after Decca did) was a frequent Castle client, as was Hollywood's Capitol Records. The studio also assisted new, locally based labels including Bullet, Dot, Hickory, Tennessee/Republic, Nashboro, and Excello. Nashville musicians such as Grady Martin and Harold

Bradley supplied distinctive back-up work for featured artists, and by the early 1950s Nashville was cranking out hits like Hank Williams's "Cold Cold Heart," Carl Smith's "Hey Joe," and Kitty Wells's "It Wasn't God Who Made Honky Tonk Angels." Red Foley's number-one crossover smash "Chattanoogie Shoe Shine Boy" publicized the state, as did his top-selling "Tennessee Border."

Certainly Nashville didn't have a lock on country recording. Late in the 1940s, Johnson City businessman Jim Stanton organized the Rich-R-Tone label and used area radio studios to record James and Martha Carson, Wilma Lee and Stoney Cooper, and bluegrass legends the Stanley Brothers. From 1948 to 1951, Knoxville's Murray Nash led the country division of Chicago's Mercury label, signing and recording Tennessee-based acts such as Flatt and Scruggs and Bill Carlisle. In the big picture, though, Nashville was Tennessee's chief recording center, a rising player on the national music stage.

Capitalizing on Nashville's central location, WSM's booking department (run by Jim Denny from 1946 until he formed his own agency ten years later) scheduled personal appearances with a vengeance. Opry stars crisscrossed the continent, playing some seventeen hundred road shows a year by 1954. Meanwhile, independent Nashville promoter J. L. Frank helped singers graduate from rural schoolhouses to big-city auditoriums. With his assistance, WSM country and pop talent toured military bases in the United States and Panama in 1941–42 as the R. J. Reynolds–sponsored Camel Caravan. In 1949 an Opry troupe made a ground-breaking trip to United States military bases in Europe.

In music publishing, a national revolution in performance rights licensing fostered the growth of music centers such as Knoxville, Memphis, and Nashville. Under United States copyright law, publishers and songwriters are entitled to compensation for the use of their copyrights in paid public performance. But before 1940, the highly exclusive American Society of Composers, Authors, and Publishers (ASCAP) controlled the collection of fees from radio and other music users, distributing monies largely on the basis of songs' exposure on live, prime-time, network radio shows originating mainly in New York or Hollywood. With the opening of Broadcast Music, Incorporated (BMI) in that year, any songwriter or publisher wishing to join BMI could do so—and collect performance earnings based on live or recorded shows aired not only on the networks, but also on hundreds of independent stations across the land.

One of the first to benefit from BMI's new policies was Nashville's Acuff-Rose Publications, established in 1942 by Roy Acuff and veteran pop songwriter Fred Rose, who had moved to Nashville from Chicago in 1933. A twenty-five-hundred-dollar BMI advance against future earnings helped the infant firm get off the ground, and by 1950 the company was climbing the country and pop charts with hits written by the team of Pee Wee King–Redd Stewart, who composed pop singer Patti Page's classic "Tennessee Waltz," Hank Williams, and Rose himself. New publishers in Knoxville (Valley) and Memphis (Hi-Lo) also prospered under BMI's wing.

Nashville's emergence as a country music stronghold heightened country's southern folk image. Opry stars sang gospel songs steeped in southern, Protestant, fundamentalist traditions, and Acuff carried the banner for traditional southeastern string band music. In 1942, *Billboard* began reviewing country discs as "American Folk Records."[7] The folksy, informal feeling and comic storytelling of Tennessee's country radio shows justified the name, and so did Acuff-Rose song books advertising "Home Folks Favorites."[8] And as country gained widespread economic clout in a patriotic era, it tapped into reservoirs of national pride and respect for material success.

All the while, however, the continuing interplay of smooth and hard-edged sounds changed the kinds of country music Tennesseans were promoting. Even as Eddy Arnold's pop-flavored love songs made him a national sensation, the gravel-voiced Ernest Tubb helped bring honky-tonk's heavy beat and electric guitars from the working class dance halls of Texas to the Grand Ole Opry. From 1949 to 1952, Hank

Williams made the show his platform for honky-tonk classics like "Your Cheating Heart" and "Honky Tonk Blues," better labeled "country and western"—the term *Billboard* adopted in 1949—than folk music.[9] Frankly confronting drinking and divorce, honky-tonk reflected the realistic attitudes of a war-torn world and the difficulties rural Americans faced in the big city.

From Rockabillies to Outlaws

During the postwar decade, Williams's bluesy numbers and boogies such as Red Foley's "Tennessee Saturday Night" bespoke country's ongoing fascination with black musical styles. Then, in the mid-1950s, Tennesseans helped create a potent blend of country and rhythm and blues that gave birth to rock and roll, a hurricane that shook the country music industry to its foundations. This time Memphis took the lead. There the visionary Sam Phillips opened the Memphis Recording Service in 1950, at first recording black bluesmen like B. B. King for Chicago's Chess Records, among other labels. In 1952, Phillips formed Sun Records and soon signed a crop of young rockabillies—white country boys who soaked up blues, country, and gospel like a sponge. First to hit was Elvis Presley, whose initial release paired the blues song "That's All Right, Mama" with a rocked-up version of Bill Monroe's "Blue Moon of Kentucky." With a boost from white Memphis disc jockey Dewey Phillips, then courting young listeners by spinning blues records over WHBQ, the Hillbilly Cat was on his way. Sun artists Carl Perkins, Jerry Lee Lewis, and Johnny Cash followed hard on Presley's heels, carrying rockabilly's interracial sound from its southern roots to a vast American market, white and black.

In the decades since, country singers have often drunk deeply from rock music's well, but in the beginning the new sound set mainstream country on its heels. Enthralled with rock and roll's infectious beat, wild energy, and rebellious attitude, a massive wave of baby boomers now entered the music market. For many country artists, who were historically focused on adult buyers, this meant falling record sales and road-show receipts. As formatted radio took hold, a host of new stations broadcast rock and roll, and some dropped country altogether.

Undaunted, country recording executives responded with three basic strategies. First, they signed acts who reached out to young rock and rollers. RCA's Steve Sholes, based in New York, bought Presley's contract from Sun in 1955 and began recording him in Nashville with assistance from local RCA producer Chet Atkins. (A decade later, Memphis producer Chips Moman would help Elvis out of a slump by supervising sessions at Moman's famous American Recording studio.) Owen Bradley, Decca's Nashville producer, cut rockabilly hits with the versatile Brenda Lee, whose slower love ballads also tugged at teenaged heartstrings.

Second, record labels wooed adult listeners with the pop-flavored Nashville Sound, framing the smooth vocals of Patsy Cline, Jim Reeves, and Eddy Arnold with string and horn arrangements and the background vocals of the Anita Kerr Singers and the Jordanaires. Supporting them were crack studio professionals including guitarists Harold Bradley, Grady Martin, and Ray Edenton; drummer Buddy Harman; bassist Bob Moore; and pianist Floyd Cramer. Guided by Atkins, Bradley, and other producers, artists and background players created seamless hits like Jim Reeves's "He'll Have to Go," Patsy Cline's "I Fall to Pieces," and Eddy Arnold's "Make the World Go Away," which won kudos for Nashville while widening country music's appeal.

Third, Nashville singers and producers retooled mainstream country sounds. Along with innovative licks provided by studio sidemen, multitrack recording consoles gave new life to recordings by Carl Smith, Kitty Wells, and Porter Wagoner. For example, Columbia/Epic producer Billy Sherrill successfully backed the hardcore vocals of George Jones and Tammy Wynette with string sections; by contrast, Owen Bradley gained results by keeping former pop star Conway Twitty's recordings relatively simple. In

Chet Atkins

CHESTER BURTON "CHET" ATKINS (1924–2001), ONE OF COUNTRY MUSIC'S GREATEST INSTRUMENTalists, producers, and promoters of the Nashville Sound, was born the son of a fiddler in Luttrell, Union County, Tennessee. He took up guitar at an early age but first performed on Knoxville's WNOX as a fiddler, a sideman for Johnnie Wright and Jack Anglin, and Kitty Wells. Atkins moved on to Cincinnati's WLW, Nashville's WSM, and Springfield, Missouri's KWTO, backing artists such as the Carter Sisters and Red Foley during the 1940s.

Chet Atkins. Courtesy of the Grand Ole Opry Archives.

In 1950, Steve Sholes of RCA offered the guitarist his first contract. Atkins returned to Nashville and immediately became a prominent studio artist. His musical talents and friendship with Sholes led to his appointment as Sholes's Nashville assistant in 1952. When RCA built its own studio in 1957, Atkins managed it. Before long, Sholes turned over RCA's country operations to his protégé and by 1968, Atkins was a RCA vice president.

Atkins supervised other producers, produced many of his own recordings, and signed such artists as Waylon Jennings, Willie Nelson, Dolly Parton, Jerry Reed, and Charley Pride. As an instrumentalist and producer, Atkins broadened the country music sound to compete with the growing popularity of rock music. By shaping the Nashville Sound, he strengthened the city's position as a recording center and helped establish its fame as Music City.

Throughout his career, Atkins legitimized the role of the country guitar soloist with dozens of albums showcasing his unique "galloping guitar" picking style. Known by many as "Mr. Guitar," the Gretsch and Gibson guitar companies even brought out guitar models built to Atkins's specifications.

In 1973, Atkins was elected to the Country Music Hall of Fame, at that time the youngest individual to be so honored. He resigned as an RCA executive in 1981 and left the label as an artist in 1982 but continued to perform and record until his death on June 30, 2001.

Anne-Leslie Owens, Middle Tennessee State University

Note

This revised entry was initially published in the *Tennessee Encyclopedia of History and Culture* (Nashville: Tennessee Historical Society, 1998) and is used with the permission of the Tennessee Historical Society.

Opry performance with Eddy Arnold. Courtesy of the Grand Ole Opry Archives.

The making of the Nashville Sound. *Left to right:* Gordon Stoker, Anita Kerr, Hank Locklin, Chet Atkins, and Floyd Cramer preparing for a recording session. Courtesy of the Grand Ole Opry Archives.

these ways, Nashville met the challenge raised by Merle Haggard and Buck Owens, hard country headliners of the rising country music center of Bakersfield, California.

By the mid-1960s, Nashville country recording had a solid institutional base. In 1955, Owen Bradley and his brother Harold opened a studio on 16th Avenue South, thus initiating Music Row. RCA followed in 1957 with a Seventeenth Avenue South facility, and together these studios fostered many more. The Bradleys sold their complex to Columbia Records in 1962 and built Bradley's Barn in nearby Mount Juliet, Tennessee, in 1965. Independent labels Starday and Monument moved to Nashville in the late 1950s and soon built studios, and by 1965 Capitol and other majors had joined Columbia in opening local offices.

In the 1970s, Nashville continued to grapple with country's fluid stylistic dynamics. Although Conway Twitty, Loretta Lynn, George Jones, and Tammy Wynette were joined by Moe Bandy and John Conlee, most artists and producers sought the riches that country-pop crossover hits could bring. Barbara Mandrell and Ronnie Milsap embodied the trend, as did Dolly Parton, who left Porter Wagoner's show for multimarket stardom with help from Los Angeles management.

Meanwhile, folk-rock guru Bob Dylan cut three historic albums in Music City. *Blonde on Blonde* (1966), *John Wesley Harding* (1967) and the landmark *Nashville Skyline* (1969)—the latter featuring Johnny Cash on the duet "Girl from the North

Owen Bradley

Owen Bradley (1915–1998), musician and producer, was one of the pioneers of the Nashville recording industry and a developer of the Nashville Sound. Born in Westmoreland, Sumner County, Bradley began his musical career early by assembling musical groups to play at private parties. The Owen Bradley Orchestra, once considered the premier Nashville dance band, played from 1940 to 1964.

Owen Bradley. Courtesy of the Grand Ole Opry Archives.

Beginning in 1935, Bradley worked for WSM radio, first as a spot man and later as pianist and organist. By 1948 he was serving as musical director, coordinating personnel, planning arrangements, and leading the orchestra. Meanwhile, Owen started working with Paul Cohen, head of the country division of Decca Records. While serving as his apprentice, Bradley learned to produce records.

In 1958, Bradley left WSM to open the Nashville Division of Decca Records, serving as vice president. When Decca and MCA merged their companies in the mid-1960s, Bradley continued in this position. Before retiring from MCA in 1976, he produced such country artists as Loretta Lynn, Conway Twitty, Kitty Wells, and Patsy Cline. Like his chief rival, Chet Atkins of RCA, Bradley sought to broaden the sound of country music to appeal to larger audiences. He utilized the traditional country sound in artists like Loretta Lynn, while in other artists like Patsy Cline, he expanded the sound to incorporate nontraditional accompaniments such as piano and soft strings.

In the early 1950s, Owen and his brother Harold formed Bradley's Film Studio, first occupying a building near downtown and later a rented building in Hillsboro Village. In 1954 the brothers purchased a house on Sixteenth Avenue South, the area that would become Music Row. In an attached Quonset hut, they opened a recording studio. In it they recorded such megahits as Patsy Cline's "I Fall to Pieces" and Marty Robbins's "El Paso." The Bradleys sold the studio to Columbia Records in 1962 and constructed a new studio, Bradley's Barn, in Wilson County, where they continued to turn out the hits.

Bradley was inducted into the Country Music Hall of Fame in 1974 and continued working as an MCA producer until retiring in the early 1980s. As his health permitted, he completed freelance studio projects, such as k. d. lang's *Shadowland* album (1988).

Anne-Leslie Owens, Middle Tennessee State University

Country"—showcased studio professionals like steel guitarist Pete Drake, pianist Hargus "Pig" Robbins, harmonica player Charlie McCoy, guitarists Jerry Kennedy and Charlie Daniels, bassist Henry Strzelecki, and drummer Kenny Buttrey. These projects paved the way for country-rock queen Linda Ronstadt and her Nashville-recorded album *Silk Purse* (1970). In 1972, folk-rockers the Nitty Gritty

Dirt Band teamed with Maybelle Carter, Earl Scruggs, Roy Acuff, Doc Watson, and other country legends to make the popular *Will the Circle Be Unbroken,* which also introduced country standards to the college crowd.

Inspired by Johnny Cash, whose magnetic presence and topical songs made him a hero to young listeners, other artists built new bridges to the youth market in an age of social and political upheaval. Chafing at the pop excesses and formulaic methods of the Nashville sound, Willie Nelson, Waylon Jennings, and Bobby Bare bucked the staff producer system by using producers and studios of their own choosing. Their stripped-down stylistic approach, independent spirit, and long-haired look won droves of college-age fans, especially in the fertile musical crossroads of Austin, Texas, where Nelson moved in 1970. In a triumph of packaging and marketing, RCA Nashville's Jerry Bradley (who took over from Chet Atkins) assembled an album of recordings by Jennings, Nelson, Jennings's wife Jessi Colter, and Jennings's sometime-producer Tompall Glaser—its western-styled cover portraying the foursome as fugitives from justice. The first country album with certified sales of more than one million copies, *Wanted! The Outlaws* (1976) opened up vast commercial horizons for country music. As the decade progressed, Hank Williams Jr. and the Charlie Daniels Band won more young fans to country's cause with "Long Haired Country Boy," "A Country Boy Can Survive," and other Southern Rock hits.

The rock and roll onslaught of the mid-1950s also sparked bold action by others whose livelihood depended on country music. Country disc jockeys, publishers, bookers, artists, and songwriters joined recording officials to form the Country Music Association (CMA) in Nashville in 1958. Through demographic research and creative sales presentations, executive director Jo Walker-Meador and her allies introduced advertisers and broadcasters to the selling sounds of country. Exploiting a national trend toward formatted radio, CMA helped boost the number of full-time country stations from eighty-one in 1961 to 1,150 in 1979. Tennessee soon had many full-time country radio outlets, including Clarksville's WDXN; Nashville's WENO, WSIX, and WKDA; Knoxville's WIVK and WROL; Chattanooga's WDOD; Murfreesboro's WMTS; and KWAM in Memphis, though WNOX's switch to a rock format in 1962 took this country warhorse out of the picture. Additionally, CMA promoted WSM's annual Grand Ole Opry Birthday Celebration (begun 1952) as part of Country Music Week, an event attended by country disc jockeys and other personnel; organized seminars on industry issues; opened the Country Music Hall of Fame and Museum in 1967; and worked with WSM in 1972 to create Fan Fair, an annual Nashville gathering where thousands of country fans meet their favorite artists.

As in country radio, Nashville set the pace in country television programming, especially after 1954, when the Federal Communications Commission refused to grant Knoxville's WNOX a television license. Early on, National Life feared that television might hurt the Opry radio broadcast; besides, the Opry spanned the continent, and WSM-TV's reach was tiny in comparison. In 1954–55, as performers clamored for TV exposure and ABC-TV began airing Springfield, Missouri's *Ozark Jubilee* as *Jubilee USA,* WSM allowed independent producer Al Gannaway to film a series of syndicated shows called *Stars of the Grand Ole Opry,* but not to film the Opry itself. In 1955–56 Purina sponsored a series of ABC-TV specials using Opry talent. After 1960, when the Opry lost its NBC-Radio network slot, National Life showed more interest in television. In addition to syndicating recorded Opry shows on radio, the company briefly financed the syndicated TV series *National Life Grand Ole Opry,* again featuring Opry stars but not the show per se.

Beginning with *The Porter Wagoner Show* in 1960, Nashville's Show Biz made Music City the national hub of syndicated country television, at first with single-artist programs. On the network front, Jack Stapp (by now president of Tree Publishing) and WSM president Irving Waugh convinced NBC-TV to carry the first televised *CMA Awards Show,* taped in 1968 at the Ryman Auditorium, the Opry's home from 1943 to 1974. *The Johnny Cash Show,* also staged there, enjoyed brief runs on ABC-TV in 1969, 1971, and 1976. *Hee-Haw,* initially produced at WLAC-TV by the station's 21st Century Productions arm, spent two years on CBS-TV (1969–71) before continuing in syndication into 1994. Two years after the Opryland theme park opened in 1972, newly formed Opryland Productions began offering expert technical support, a new studio, and the new Opry House stage to Los Angeles' Yongestreet Productions (creators of *Hee-Haw*) and to local executives like Show Biz founders Bill Graham and Jane Dowden Grams, who now focused on *Pop! Goes the Country* and other slick multi-artist programs.

The infrastructure of country music in Nashville was now stronger than ever. By the mid-1970s the city had some 250 music publishers, including giants Tree and Cedarwood; nine hundred songwriters, including standouts such as Boudleaux and Felice Bryant ("Rocky Top"), Hank Cochran ("Make the World Go Away"), and Harlan Howard ("Busted"); thirty recording studios; ten pressing plants; BMI and ASCAP offices (opened in 1958 and 1963, respectively); and a host of booking agencies, musicians,

Left: Dolly Parton and Porter Wagoner on stage. Courtesy of the Grand Ole Opry Archives.

Below: Opry performance on the Ryman Auditorium stage. Courtesy of the Grand Ole Opry Archives.

and record company employees, whose combined efforts were pumping an estimated $100 million a year into the city's economy. Noncountry acts broadened Music's City's image, though country stars still drew most of the limelight.

Thanks largely to Tennesseans, country music's image had also evolved with changing times. By promoting the uptown Nashville Sound; heralding country's increasingly urban, prosperous audience; and defining "country" as "American," CMA sought to rid the music of its hayseed trappings. At the same time, *Hee-Haw,* in its campy way, parlayed these same trappings into a twenty-five-year run on television. Even as Dolly Parton, Barbara Mandrell, and others brought the look and sound of country pop to national television, Porter Wagoner kept the rhinestone suits and hard country sound that made his TV show a hit for twenty years. His commercials for the Chattanooga Medicine Company, makers of Black Draught laxative, gave his program a medicine-show quality decidedly at odds with the tuxedos worn by Jim Reeves and Eddy Arnold. An electrified, rock-drenched counterculture—openly opposed to the family values and conservative political views long associated with country music—warmed not only to the Outlaws, but also to Maybelle Carter, cofounder of country's most famous family act, and to bluegrass great Bill Monroe, staunch defender of traditional acoustic music. Along with a variety of male stars, country music now offered outspoken, independent heroines like Loretta Lynn, and after RCA Nashville signed black hitmaker Charley Pride in 1965, African Americans such as Linda Martell and Ruby Falls tried their fortunes in the city. O. B. McClinton, another black country singer, began his recording career on Enterprise (a subsidiary of the Memphis-based Stax label) in 1971 before working in Nashville television.

Amid these swirling currents, country music managed to retain something of its regional folk aura. Publicists seized upon the Nashville Sound's mystique, flowing from the home-grown talents and laid-back ways of the good ol' boys and girls who made hit records. In the late 1950s and early 1960s, Johnny Cash and Flatt and Scruggs successfully rode the folk music wave, and after 1972, Fan Fair strengthened the kinlike bonds between country stars and their followers. Many emerging artists either came from the South or quickly adopted southern customs. Southern rockers preached a gospel of regional pride and independence and hailed the virtues of rural life, though to some ears, songs like Hank Williams Jr.'s "If the South Woulda Won" conjured visions of violent rednecks. Through it all, Nashville music leaders folded these themes into the Music City concept, promoting the city as a magical place where many types of country music could flourish, along with pop, jazz, gospel, and soul music.

Perils of Success

Undergirding the mystique, of course, was the power of cold, hard cash, and as the heydays of Bakersfield and Austin receded, Nashville solidified its role as country music's nerve center. Fueled by the Outlaws, country-pop hits that crossed over to adult contemporary radio, and the buzz surrounding the 1980 film *Urban Cowboy,* country record sales climbed from $150 million in 1973 to $539 million in 1982, a jump from 10 percent of U.S. record sales to 14.7 percent. Many of country music's new converts proved fickle, though, and the pop or rock radio veterans who now staffed country music's growing number of radio stations often shortchanged fans of harder-edged sounds. Sales of country music slid to $393 million in 1984, with market share dipping below 10 percent for several years.

Nashville was partly to blame, but it also led the way to new glory. Beginning with George Strait, Ricky Skaggs, and John Anderson early in the 1980s, Nashville label heads rebuilt their rosters with the likes of the Judds and Randy Travis, who collectively reinjected country with healthy doses of rockabilly, folk, bluegrass, and honky-tonk. These so-called New Traditionalists sparked the country explosion of the early 1990s, in which record sales topped the

$2 billion mark in 1995 and grabbed 16.7 percent of the U.S. market. Assisted by high-quality digital recording and expert producers such as Tony Brown, Jimmy Bowen, Tim DuBois, Harold Shedd, and Jim Ed Norman, artists like Garth Brooks, Clint Black, and Alan Jackson routinely sold albums in the millions, as did Reba McEntire, Trisha Yearwood, and Shania Twain.

The 1990s boom owed much to country broadcasters: 2,427 stations played country music full time in 1994, representing nearly 21 percent of all U.S. radio outlets. Thanks to executives Tom Griscom, Elmer Alley, and E. W. "Bud" Wendell, WSM debuted The Nashville Network (TNN) cable TV channel early in 1983, and after Dallas-based Gaylord Broadcasting bought WSM's radio and cable operations, the Grand Ole Opry, and Opryland later that year, the new network mushroomed. By 1994 TNN reached sixty-four million households with a variety of musical shows—including a weekly Opry segment after 1985—sports coverage, talk shows, news, game shows, and other life-style programming. (At the beginning of the twenty-first century, however, TNN ended its close relationship with country music as a new owner ended the network reliance on "country" shows and in 2001 the weekly broadcast of the Grand Ole Opry switched to Country Music Television.) In 1991 Gaylord bought locally based CMT, which airs country videos; under Wendell's leadership CMT expanded into Europe, Asia, Latin America, and Australia, giving country artists massive worldwide exposure.

Deaton-Flanigen, Scene Three, and other Nashville production firms strengthened the local entertainment industry, which included 250 studios, two dozen booking agencies, 150 management firms, and 30 public relations firms by 1996. Most major record labels based their country divisions in Nashville, and entertainment-related enterprises employed twenty-five thousand persons, raking in $3.2 billion annually. After decades of reluctance, the Nashville Chamber of Commerce now embraced the Music City moniker as a globally recognized logo.

By 1996, though, country's bloom was fading again, and with it the fortunes of many Tennessee music makers. Country radio slid to 2,105 stations by the year 2000, and while the Opry had survived radio's transition from live to recorded broadcasts, the program had largely become a financially marginal showcase for older talent, in part because newer members made few appearances, refusing to give up lucrative weekend road work. Gaylord sold TNN and CMT's domestic operation to CBS in 1997; two years later, CBS dropped many of TNN's country music shows. Fan Fair attendance declined, and by 2000, country record sales had fallen to just over $1.5 billion dollars, with market share down to 10.7 percent. A handful of label groups, most of them subsidiaries of international conglomerates, dominated recording in Nashville. By itself, consolidation was not necessarily a problem, for Nashville label heads now had far more control over packaging and marketing than they did in the 1960s. But combined with escalating recording and video costs, reporting to higher corporate levels increased the pressure to drop artists who could not meet rising sales expectations.

Critics faulted Nashville record executives for signing too many sound-alike acts, promoting too many passionless songs and recordings, sanctioning videos that emphasized surface appeal over real substance, and generally kowtowing to country radio instead of leveraging the control over songs and artists that Nashville label offices had built up over a half-century. Labels did angle for young buyers with youthful new singers, yet much of what they turned out was ear candy. In turn, labels bemoaned the power of huge radio station groups serviced by consultants who often seemed remote from local markets. Essentially a delivery system for commercials, radio had never been in the business of selling records; still, shorter play lists and a growing reliance on upbeat, inoffensive songs was draining country of its grit, thereby alienating much of its fan base.

To some observers, country's quest for commercial success had compromised its very identity. "Severed from its working-class origins," wrote Tony

Scherman in 1994, "country music is becoming a refuge for culturally homeless Americans everywhere." Less "the expression of a living culture," he claimed, it had become "a set of symbols" that listeners could adopt or reject as they chose.[10] Clearly, the music was no longer rural but suburban, far from the rural, small-town, and often impoverished South that gave it birth.

Others have seen things differently. Curtis W. Ellison has argued that country music's traditions and rituals do make it "a distinctive, self-conscious, entertainment community" that embraces modernity while providing "an imaginative means for transcending the negative effects of modernity."[11] Richard A. Peterson and James C. Cobb have stressed that country's stylistic and social origins were never set in stone, and its evolution has always reflected a dialectic of "hard core" and "soft shell" sounds.[12] Country music does celebrate working-class Americans, as Brentwood resident Alan Jackson's 1999 hit "Little Man" attests. Displaying country's persistent ability to explore life's darker side, Mount Juliet's Tracy Lawrence hit with "Time Marches On" (1996); crafted by Nashville songwriter Bobby Braddock, this number explores infidelity and death with straightforward honesty. And whatever the style of the moment, Tennessee country performers help define the music by their informal, self-taught singing and playing; their down-to-earth attitudes; and their special audience rapport.

Popular western stagewear aside, country music still retains a southern connection, and its regional symbols—however consciously crafted—are not wholly devoid of authenticity. Songs such as "How Can I Help You Say Goodbye," penned by Nashvillians Karen Taylor-Good and Burton Collins, uphold country's storytelling tradition, deeply embedded in southern culture. Others, including "Maybe It Was Memphis," invoke the regional climate and its "southern summer nights," or celebrate down-home, rural fun, as in numbers like "Watermelon Crawl." As the music of the Nashville Bluegrass Band and Hendersonville's Ricky Skaggs reveals, southern gospel music still affects country singers, though less so now than fifty years ago. Black singer-songwriters like Texas-born Dobie Gray continue to make Nashville their home. With 1999's "He Didn't Have to Be," transplanted West Virginian Brad Paisley salutes a stepfather and the value of strong family ties, another regional characteristic. Musical refugees from the coasts praise Tennessee's southern hospitality. In spite of its troubles, many still find country music "essentially southern," and comfortingly so.[13]

Announcing country music's demise also seems premature. In its eighty-year commercial history, critics have often foretold its doom only to see it flourish once more. In fact, Tennessee country in the early twenty-first century shows many signs of good health. As of 2000, Tennessee had some 135 country radio stations, some of them airing bluegrass or country classics from the 1950s to the 1970s. Country music thrives in venues ranging from Nashville's Gaylord Entertainment Center and the tiny Station Inn to Knoxville's Tennessee Theater, Bristol's Paramount Theater, Chattanooga's Governor's Lounge and Rockin' Country Club, Denim and Diamonds in Memphis, and Jackson's Casey Jones Village, as well as in hundreds of other clubs and community centers statewide. Bluegrass festivals and fiddle contests abound, revealing durable audiences for various country styles.

Country music also remains an effective instrument for city boosterism and Tennessee tourism. Although Gaylord closed Opryland in 1997, the corporation has restored the Ryman Auditorium and opened Nashville's Wildhorse Saloon. In 2001 a spectacular new Country Music Hall of Fame and Museum opened in downtown Nashville, and tourists—most of them drawn by country music—contribute more than $2 billion annually to the city's economy. In Sevier County, Dolly Parton has made her Dollywood entertainment park a major tourist destination, just as thousands flock to Graceland, Elvis Presley's Memphis mansion. The Bristol Country Music Association sponsors a museum and musical events drawing many visitors each year, and in 1998 Knoxville launched its popular Cradle of Country

Fiddle and Old-Time Music Contests

TENNESSEE TOWNS HOST OVER THIRTY FIDDLE AND OLD-TIME MUSIC CONTESTS EVERY YEAR. WHILE most current contests date only to the 1970s, fiddle contests have a long history in the state. Local competitions often took place on an informal basis on courthouse squares on Saturdays or during annual county agricultural fairs. Community musicians—meaning artists recognized by the local residents as being good, quality musicians—took center stage here, sometimes challenged by traveling musicians who stopped by to size up the competition, and make some money. By the late nineteenth and early twentieth centuries, local chapters of the Daughters of the Confederacy or the Daughters of the American Revolution sponsored more formal competitions in order to perpetuate and honor the "good old times" of the antebellum era. A Fiddlers' Carnival, like that held in Gallatin in October 1899, was an effective way to attract rural people to town.

In the mid-1920s, the Ford Motor Company sponsored national fiddle contests, where competitors first won at the local level, then with the sponsorship of a local Ford Dealer, moved into larger regional and national championships. During the mid-twentieth century, champion fiddlers traveled from town to town, challenging locals to prove who was best. Uncle Jimmy Thompson of the Grand Ole Opry, Arthur Smith from Dickson County, Paul Warren of Hickman County, Curly Fox of Rhea County, and G. B. Grayson of Johnson County were among the most acclaimed fiddlers of this era.

In 1967 a group of musicians and admirers of old-time music created the Tennessee Valley Old Time Fiddlers' Association, which soon sponsored some of the first fiddle and old music contests in the region. Within a decade, the state's best-known music festivals were in operation, including the state of Tennessee Old-Time Fiddlers' Championships (1974) in Clarksville; the Fiddler's Jamboree (1972) at Smithville; and the Uncle Dave Macon Days (1978) in Murfreesboro. These festivals not only highlighted fiddlers, but included competitions in old-time music and bluegrass music, banjo, mandolin, guitar, dobro, clogging, and buckdancing. Like their nineteenth-century counterparts, the modern competitions also provided a forum for community musicians to show off their skills, learn new tunes and performance tricks, and gather to extend their friendships and associations to the next generation of performers.

Other competitions in Tennessee that date at least to 1980 are the Holladay Fiddlers Jamboree (1956); Sewanee Bluegrass Convention (1971); Opryland's Grand Masters Fiddling Championship (1972); Minor Hill Fiddling Convention (1977); Elizabethton Fiddlers Convention (1972); Adams's Bell Witch Festival (1978); Mountain City Fiddlers Contest (1976); Crossville Fiddlers Contest (1976); and the Chattanooga Fall Color Cruise and Folk Festival (1974).

Carroll Van West, Middle Tennessee State University

Music downtown walking tour. Institutions like MTSU's Center for Popular Music, the Murfreesboro-based Tennessee Folklore Society, Nashville's internationally renowned Country Music Foundation—which operates the Hall of Fame and its related publications, library, and educational pro- grams—and the Center for Southern Folklore in Memphis preserve country's past and cultivate its future.

Finally, Tennessee continues to supply outstanding contributors to country music, including performers (Lorrie Morgan, Mike Snider), songwriters (Matraca Berg, Dean Dillon), producers (Allen Butler,

Tennesseans in the Country Music Hall of Fame to 2001

Roy Acuff (1962)
Eddy Arnold (1966)
James R. Denny (1966)
Uncle Dave Macon (1966)
Chet Atkins (1973)
Owen Bradley (1974)
Minnie Pearl (1975)
Kitty Wells (1976)
Lester Flatt (1985)
Rod Brasfield (1987)
Jack Stapp (1989)
Tennessee Ernie Ford (1990)
Frances Preston (1992)
Jo Walker-Meador (1995)
George Morgan (1998)
Dolly Parton (1999)
Homer and Jethro (2001)

John W. Rumble, Historian, Country Music Hall of Fame and Museum

Randy Scruggs), and executives (CMA executive director Ed Benson). If the past is any indication, individuals like these will cope with the thorny problems of country radio and recording, partly by entering new promotional venues via the Internet. Over many decades, Tennesseans have helped transform country music from a scorned minority music into a respected international industry, vastly improving the standing of both state and region within American culture. Considering the creativity and business savvy these leaders have shown, the future of country music in the Volunteer State should prove fascinating to see and hear.

NOTES

1. Frank G. Clement, "Country Music: A Tennessee Heritage," *Billboard,* Nov. 2, 1963, 22.
2. Charles K. Wolfe, *A Good-Natured Riot: The Birth of the Grand Ole Opry* (Nashville: Country Music Foundation Press and Vanderbilt Univ. Press, 1999), 15.
3. Unidentified newspaper clipping in Alcyone Bate Beasley Scrapbook, Country Music Foundation Library and Media Center. The Vagabonds, comp., *Old Cabin Songs of the Fiddle and the Bow* (Nashville: Old Cabin Company, 1932), 5.
4. Ronnie Pugh, "Country Music Is Here to Stay?" *Journal of Country Music* 19, no. 1 (1997): 32–38; *Brunswick Record Edition of American Folk Songs, Volume I, Number 1* (Chicago: Brunswick-Balke-Collender, [c. 1928]).
5. Tony Scherman, "Country," *American Heritage* 45 (Nov. 1994): 42.
6. George D. Hay, "Strictly Personal," *Rural Radio,* Mar. 1939, 30.
7. *Billboard,* Feb. 28, 1942, 61.
8. *Bob Atcher's Home Folks Favorites* (Nashville: Acuff-Rose Publications, 1943).
9. *Billboard,* June 25, 1949, 117.
10. Scherman, "Country," 55.
11. Curtis W. Ellison, *Country Music Culture: From Hard Times to Heaven* (Jackson: Univ. of Mississippi Press, 1995), xvi–xvii.
12. Richard A. Peterson, *Creating Country Music: Fabricating Authenticity* (Chicago: Univ. of Chicago Press, 1997); James C. Cobb, "Rednecks, White Socks, and Piña Coladas?: Country Music Ain't What It Used to Be . . . And It Really Never Was," *Southern Cultures* 5 (Winter 1999): 40–41.
13. Peter Applebome, *Dixie Rising: How the South Is Shaping American Politics, Values, and Culture* (New York: Times Books, 1996), 243.

Suggested Readings

The Country Music Foundation. *Country on Compact Disc: The Essential Guide to the Music.* Edited by Paul Kingsbury. New York: Grove Press, 1993.

———. *Country: The Music and the Musicians.* Edited by Paul Kingsbury, Alan Axelrod, and Susan Costello. Rev. ed. New York: Abbeville Press, 1994.

Ellison, Curtis W. *Country Music Culture: From Hard Times to Heaven.* Jackson: Univ. of Mississippi Press, 1995.

Jensen, Joli. *The Nashville Sound: Authenticity, Commercialization, and Country Music.* Nashville: Country Music Foundation Press and Vanderbilt Univ. Press. 1998.

Lomax, John III. *Nashville: Music City U.S.A.* New York: Harry N. Abrams, 1985.

Malone, Bill C. *Country Music U.S.A.: A Fifty-Year History.* Rev. ed. Austin: Univ. of Texas Press, 1985.

———. *Southern Music, American Music.* Lexington: Univ. Press of Kentucky, 1979.

Nager, Larry. *Memphis Beat: The Lives and Times of America's Musical Crossroads.* With a foreword by Sam Phillips. New York: St. Martin's Press, 1998.

Oermann, Robert K. *A Century of Country: An Illustrated History of Country Music.* With a foreword by Chet Flippo. New York: TV Books, 1999.

Peterson, Richard A. *Creating Country Music: Fabricating Authenticity.* Chicago: Univ. of Chicago Press, 1997.

The Staff of the Country Music Hall of Fame and Museum, comp. *The Encyclopedia of Country Music: The Ultimate Guide to the Music.* Edited by Paul Kingsbury, with the assistance of Laura Garrard, Daniel Cooper, and John Rumble. New York: Oxford Univ. Press, 1998.

Wolfe, Charles K. *A Good-Natured Riot: The Birth of the Grand Ole Opry.* Nashville: Country Music Foundation Press and Vanderbilt Univ. Press, 1999.

———. *Tennessee Strings: The Story of Country Music in Tennessee.* Knoxville: Univ. of Tennessee Press, 1977.

Index

Page numbers in **bold** refer to illustrations